Encyclopedia of Human Emotions

Editors

David Levinson
Berkshire Reference Works, Great Barrington, Mass.

James J. Ponzetti, Jr.
Warner Pacific College

Peter F. Jorgensen
Western Illinois University

Editorial and Production Staff

Brian Kinsey
Project Editor

William Kavanah
Copy Editor

Greg Teague
Proofreader

Carol Donley
Hiram College
Literature Consultant

Cynthia Crippen
AEIOU, Inc.
Indexer

Richard Hollick
Production Manager

Impressions Book and Journal Services, Inc.
Compositor

MACMILLAN REFERENCE USA
Elly Dickason, *Publisher*
Toni Scaramuzzo, *Managing Editor*

ENCYCLOPEDIA OF
HUMAN EMOTIONS

Edited by

DAVID LEVINSON
JAMES J. PONZETTI, JR.
PETER F. JORGENSEN

Volume 2

MACMILLAN REFERENCE USA
New York

Macmillan Library Reference USA
1633 Broadway
New York, NY 10019

Printed in the United States of America

Printing Number
1 2 3 4 5 6 7 8 9 10

Library of Congress Cataloging-in-Publication Data

Encyclopedia of Human Emotions
    edited by David Levinson, James J. Ponzetti, Jr., Peter F. Jorgensen
        p.   cm.
    Includes bibliographical references and index.
    ISBN 0-02-864766-1 (set) — ISBN 0-02-864768-8 (v. 1) —
        ISBN 0-02-864767-X (v. 2)
    1. Emotions—Encyclopedias.   2. Affect (Psychology)—Encyclopedias.
        3. Mood (Psychology) — Encyclopedias.
    I. Levinson, David.   II. Ponzetti, James J.   III. Jorgensen, Peter F.
    BF531.E55   1999
    152.4′03 — dc21
                                                    99-31198
                                                    CIP

This paper meets the requirements of ANSI-NISO Z39.48-1992 (Permanence of Paper).

I

ILLNESS

See Health and Illness

INFANTS AND EMOTIONS

See Human Development: Infancy

INFATUATION

The phenomenon of infatuated love, commonly known by such colloquialisms as love at first sight, love struck, or a crush, is a dominant recurring theme in literature and song—it is something that almost everyone experiences at some time in life. This passionate kind of love is also something that has captured, in relatively recent times, the attention of social scientists.

Theories of Infatuated Love

Scientific interest has resulted in several theories or models of love, each of which addresses some phenomenon akin to infatuation. The most recent of the theories, and perhaps the most useful, was developed by Robert Sternberg (1986). He suggested that the general concept of love can be broken down into several different kinds of love, where each is understood in terms of the combination of three components—passion, intimacy, and decision/commitment. Passion refers to the arousal that leads to the experience of physical attraction and sexual activity. Intimacy refers to those feelings in a relationship that promote a sense of connectedness or bondedness between partners. The decision/commitment component refers to a realization that one genuinely loves the other and that one is committed to maintaining that love in the future. The relative importance of each component is dependent upon the stage of the relationship. In the early stages of a relationship, passion is more important, while intimacy may be of only moderate importance and decision/commitment is of hardly any importance. Since infatuation is often experienced at the initial stages of many romantic relationships, passion would be the primary component associated with infatuation. In fact, Sternberg defines infatuated love as the experience of passionate arousal without the experience of either the intimacy or decision/commitment component. Furthermore, Sternberg suggests that infatuated love can be experienced almost instantaneously upon meeting someone to whom one is attracted. He also states that it can dissipate with equal swiftness.

Other theories also have addressed phenomena akin to infatuation. Ellen Berscheid and Elaine Walster (1974) developed a theory of love that distinguished between what they called companionate love and passionate love. Passionate love for Berscheid and Walster is characterized by strong physiological arousal accompanied by the conviction that the person one is attracted to is the cause of the arousal. This conception is very similar to Sternberg's infatuated love, particularly the emphasis on the experience of intense physiological arousal (his passion compo-

A valentine from around 1909 illustrates the fact that although an infatuation may exist between two people, it cannot develop further without the establishment of intimacy, which in this case is subtly being encouraged by Cupid whispering in the man's ear. (Corbis/Lake County Museum)

nent). Additionally, like Sternberg, Berscheid and Walster also maintain that the experience of passionate love is relatively rapid in its development.

A phenomenon similar to infatuated love is also addressed in the theoretical approach to love proposed by John Lee (1977) and expanded upon by Clyde Hendrick and Susan Hendrick (1986). They suggest that people have preferences for different styles of love. One style, eros, named for the Greek god of love, is characterized as a passionate or physical style of love, typified by early attraction and intense emotion. This description is clearly similar to what is commonly referred to as infatuation.

Infatuation Versus Liking

While it might seem that infatuation is nothing more than an intense liking for another, there are important differences between infatuation and liking. While both might be perceived as initial responses to an attractive other, they are, in fact, quite different. First, there is a distinction in terms of the time period in which infatuation and liking develop. According to Sternberg's model, intimacy is the sole component

contributing to the experience of liking. This implies that liking would most likely develop over a period of time, since time would be required to establish some basis for feeling a sense of intimacy or connectedness with the other. In contrast, as stated previously, infatuated love can be experienced almost instantaneously upon meeting someone to whom one is attracted. Berscheid (1983) argues that the development of emotions associated with simple liking (as in a friendship) tend to develop gradually over time and, further, do not appear to progress into passionate love. A second and perhaps more important distinction is that infatuated love is dependent on the experience of physiological arousal, while simple liking is not. While liking involves only the component of intimacy, infatuation involves only the component of passion. It is this component of infatuation, with its attendant physiological arousal, that is the crucial element of infatuated love.

Infatuated Love and Arousal

While the experience of infatuation always involves arousal, there are a variety of other experiences that also involve states characterized by arousal. The specific emotion that one feels is dependent upon the appropriate cognitive label given to the arousal that occurs within the particular situation. For instance, situations involving obvious physical threat, such as being involved in a holdup, would be accompanied by arousal, and the emotional label given to the arousal would be "fear." Thus, any emotional state, including infatuation, is the result of arousal plus a cognitive label given to the arousal.

As is often the case with emotional experiences, the source of the arousal being experienced also provides cues for the labeling of that same arousal. In the case of infatuated love, the other to whom one is attracted is usually the source of the arousal that generates the cues for the labeling of the emotional experience as "passionate love." While one might be aroused by the physical appearance and verbal or nonverbal behavior of another, it is a past experience with those behaviors in the social setting in which they occur that might also serve as the basis for subsequent labeling of that arousal. In other words, simply being aroused by the presence of an attractive other would not lead to the cognitive label of "infatuation" if the cues available did not define this as infatuation. For instance, an encounter with a prostitute might be arousing, but it would not be labeled "infatuation." If one's knowledge of infatuated love, based on either direct experience or indirect observation from the past, suggests that the current interaction with another (and its accompanying arousal) is typical of infatuation, then it is more likely that a cognitive label of "infatuated love" will be applied. The likelihood of interpreting a given situation as infatuation is encouraged by the (Western) cultural notion that most people will experience passionate love at some time in life. Thus, an individual is likely to interpret at least one interaction with an attractive other as infatuated love. As Zick Rubin (1974) notes, such cultural notions of love are ingrained from a very early age with repeated exposure to fairy tales (e.g., *Cinderella, Sleeping Beauty*), comic books (e.g., *Young Romance*), and movies (e.g., *Titanic, Love Story*). In short, many people grow up believing that every young boy will someday fall in love with a beautiful princess and every young girl will someday fall in love with a handsome prince (not a toad!). Consequently, virtually all individuals are bound to experience some interaction with an attractive other that, accompanied by the perception of physiological arousal, will be interpreted as infatuated love.

Evidence for the role of arousal and the appropriate label applied to that arousal comes from a variety of different studies. In one of the earliest, and perhaps most classic studies, Donald Dutton and Arthur Aron (1974) showed that the arousal created by crossing a high and unstable bridge resulted in increased sexual attraction to an attractive female. Male participants who crossed a safe and stable bridge were not aroused and did not show increased sexual attraction to the same female. Thus, when individuals who were aroused by a nonromantic source (the unstable bridge) were presented with an attractive female, they attributed their arousal not to the bridge but to the attractive female. These individuals viewed the arousal they were experiencing as attraction to the attractive individual, a romantic source for the arousal. Another important study, conducted by Gregory White, Sanford Fishbein, and Jeffrey Rutstein (1981), demonstrated that even arousal generated by exercising contributed to increased sexual or romantic attraction (compared to individuals who did not exercise). In these cases, the true source of the arousal (the bridge and the exercise) was misattributed to an attractive individual, a romantic source. These types of studies show that arousal is a necessary component in infatuation, even when that arousal is generated from a source other than the attractive individual. As long as the arousal is attributed to the romantic source and thus seen as attraction to that source, infatuation will occur.

In most cases of infatuation, the other person, and not some external source such as exercise or a precarious bridge, is a strong enough stimulus to create arousal. If this is the case, then it should be possible to show the role of the arousal in the infatuation process by demonstrating what happens if that arousal is attributed to something other than the person who generated the arousal. In other words, just as infatuation was enhanced by creating arousal in a nonromantic situation and then attributing it to a romantic situation, infatuation would be diminished if arousal naturally occurring through a romantic source was attributed to a nonromantic source.

In fact, research has demonstrated this phenomenon in studies investigating the role of arousal in infatuation. Kimberly McClanahan, Joel Gold, Ellen Lenney, Richard Ryckman, and Gordon Kulberg (1990) had participants interact with an attractive per-

> *The teenage narrator of James Joyce's "Araby" (1914) is infatuated with the sister of one of his friends. His turbulent emotions drive him to watch her from windows and to follow her to school. His adoration of her becomes religious, as he murmurs prayers and praises in her honor. But when he tries to buy her something at the fair, he arrives too late; as the fair closes for the night, he feels frustrated and chagrined and foolish.*

son who either showed strong interest in them (the romance inducing situation) or paid little attention to them (the nonromantic or control situation). Within each of these groups, half of the individuals were given the opportunity to misattribute any arousal they were experiencing to a vitamin mixture that they were told produced side effects described as pleasant excitement (arousal). The remaining participants were told that the vitamin mixture had no side effects. The vitamin mixture actually was a placebo, with no effects whatsoever. The participants in the romance inducing situation who were not given the opportunity to misattribute their arousal showed strong attraction to the attractive individual. In other words, they attributed their arousal to the attractive person, the source that produced the arousal. In comparison, participants in the romance inducing situation who were given the opportunity to misattribute their arousal to the vitamin, were no more attracted to the attractive individual than those participants in the nonromantic situation. In other words, they attributed their arousal to the vitamin, rather than to the attractive person, the source that actually produced the arousal. Scott Thompson and Gold (1998) have replicated this misattribution finding using a methodology that induced infatuation through a video format that participants were lead to believe was interactive television. Collectively, these studies demonstrate that arousal plays a crucial role in the infatuation process. If arousal is missing or is attributed to something nonromantic, then infatuation does not occur.

All of the studies described above demonstrate that physiological arousal plays an important role in one's experience of initial romantic or sexual attraction toward another—the infatuation process. More specifically, the work of Gold and his colleagues provides empirical support for the notion that infatuation, in particular, is dependent upon the experience of physiological arousal, as posited by the theories of infatuated (passionate) love proposed by Sternberg and Berscheid and Walster.

Cognitive Aspects of Infatuation

Infatuated love is a state characterized not only by an emotional component that includes physiological arousal and sexual attraction to the other, but by a cognitive component of mental arousal as well. This cognitive component includes intrusive thinking and preoccupation with the other, an intense longing for union with the other, and what Elaine Hatfield (1988) has termed *idealization* of the other. The saying that "love is blind" is a reflection of this idealization process.

There is some empirical evidence for this cognitive aspect of infatuation. For instance, Alan Kerckhoff and Keith Davis (1962) found that couples in short-term relationships were much less likely to attribute negative qualities to their partners. Thus, idealization was more marked in the early stages of a relationship, where infatuation would occur. More recent evidence for cognitive distortions reflecting idealization were found in a study by Gold, Ryckman, and Norman Mosely (1984), as well as the studies by McClanahan and her colleagues (1990) and Thompson and Gold (1995). In all of those investigations, participants were led to believe that the attractive individual who was the stimulus for infatuation held attitudes that were very dissimilar to their own. In spite of this obvious dissimilarity between themselves and the attractive individual, participants were still strongly attracted to the individual. Additionally, in each of these studies, the infatuated participants accurately recalled the dissimilar attitudes of the attractive other, indicating that they were aware of the obvious dissimilarity between those attitudes and their own. One explanation for the attraction despite the dissimilarity is found in the fact that the infatuated participants evaluated the attractive individuals dissimilar attitudes more positively than noninfatuated participants. It seems that the adage "love is blind" is only partially correct. The idealization here occurred not by the infatuated participants distorting the beliefs of the attractive individual but by seeing those attitudes as less foolish, more mature, and more rational than would be the case if they were not infatuated. These repeated findings show strong evidence that infatuation is characterized both by physiological arousal and by mental arousal resulting in processes such as idealization.

While some work has begun in the area of infatuated love, much more needs to be learned about this widespread phenomenon.

See also: DESIRE; INTIMACY; LOVE; LUST

Bibliography

Berscheid, Ellen. (1983). "Emotion." In *Close Relationships,* ed. Harold H. Kelley, Ellen Berscheid, Andrew Christensen, John H. Harvey, Ted L. Huston, George Levinger, Evie McClintock, Letitia Anne Peplau, and Donald R. Peterson. New York: W. H. Freeman.

Berscheid, Ellen, and Walster, Elaine. (1974). "A Little Bit About Love." In *Foundations of Interpersonal Attraction,* ed. Ted L. Huston. New York: Academic Press.

Dutton, Donald G., and Aron, Arthur P. (1974). "Some Evidence for Heightened Sexual Attraction under Conditions of High Anxiety." *Journal of Personality and Social Psychology* 30:510–517.

Gold, Joel A.; Ryckman, Richard M.; and Mosley, Norman R. (1984). "Romantic Mood Induction and Attraction to a Dissimilar Other: Is Love Blind?" *Personality and Social Psychology Bulletin* 10:358–368.

Gold, Joel A., and Thompson, Scott A. (1997). "Infatuation Induction: Evidence for Arousal." Paper presented at the annual meeting of the Eastern Psychological Association, Washington, DC.

Hatfield, Elaine. (1988). "Passionate and Companionate Love." In *The Psychology of Love*, ed. Robert J. Sternberg and Michael L. Barnes. New Haven, CT: Yale University Press.

Hendrick, Clyde, and Hendrick, Susan. (1986). "A Theory and Method of Love." *Journal of Personality and Social Psychology* 50:392–402.

Kerckhoff, Alan C., and Davis, Keith E. (1962). "Value Consensus and Need Complementarity in Mate Selection." *American Sociological Review* 27:295–301.

Lee, John A. (1977). "A Typology of Styles of Loving." *Personality and Social Psychology Bulletin* 3:173–182.

McClanahan, Kimberley K.; Gold, Joel A.; Lenney, Ellen; Ryckman, Richard M.; and Kulberg, Gordon E. (1990). "Infatuation and Attraction to a Dissimilar Other: Why is Love Blind?" *Journal of Social Psychology* 130:433–445.

Rubin, Zick. (1974). "From Liking to Loving: Patterns of Attraction in Dating Relationships." In *Foundations of Interpersonal Attraction*, ed. Ted L. Huston. New York: Academic Press.

Sternberg, Robert J. (1986). "A Triangular Theory of Love." *Psychological Review* 93:119–135.

Thompson, Scott A., and Gold, Joel A. (1995). "Infatuation with Dissimilar Others: Idealization, Dissonance Reduction, or Crystallization?" Paper presented at the annual meeting of the Eastern Psychological Association, Boston.

Thompson, Scott A., and Gold, Joel A. (1998). "Infatuation: Viewing the World through Rose-Colored Glasses?" Paper presented at the annual meeting of the Eastern Psychological Association, Boston.

Walster, Elaine. (1970). "Passionate Love." In *Theories of Attraction and Love*, ed. Bernard I. Murstein. New York: Springer.

White, Gregory L.; Fishbein, Sanford; and Rutstein, Jeffrey. (1981). "Passionate Love and the Misattribution of Arousal." *Journal of Personality and Social Psychology* 41:56–62.

Scott A. Thompson
Joel A. Gold

INTIMACY

Intimacy is a powerful, complex phenomenon. Most people feel a strong need to be close to others, yet sometimes such intimacy can be scary. When people get extremely close to others, they allow themselves to be vulnerable—their intimate partners know their deepest and darkest secrets. By revealing such secrets, people open themselves up to potential judgment and rejection. However, intimate relationships can also be a safe haven where people express their innermost feelings and feel loved and accepted for who they really are. Moreover, people sometimes release their negative emotions, such as fears, doubts, and insecurities, in intimate interactions with close friends, family members, and romantic partners.

Defining Intimacy

Most contemporary social scientists view intimacy as more than a single emotion. Rather, they see intimacy as a broad concept that refers to feelings, behaviors, and relationships. Karen Prager (1995, p. 18), a social psychologist, gave the following examples to show that intimacy is multifaceted:

- When Jorge looks at Mariano, he feels a rush of warmth and love (intimacy seems to be an emotion).
- Jerry holds his infant close and strokes his skin (intimacy seems to describe tender physical contact).
- Yan Chang tells Alice a secret, and Alice promises not to reveal it to anyone (intimacy seems to involve sharing private information).
- Kareem is married to Aretha (intimacy seems to describe a kind of relationship).
- Marta knows that when Dwight purses his lips and looks away, he's feeling nervous (intimacy describes how well two people know each other).
- Wilma and Betty reminisce about their many shared experiences (intimacy seems to describe a kind of interaction).
- Felicia caresses Alex (intimacy seems to describe sexual contact).
- Mark feels close to Greg while they are fishing in silence (intimacy requires no communication).
- Marion stands close enough to Edward for him to feel her breath on his face (intimacy describes how two people occupy space together).

These examples show that intimacy is incorporated into people's emotions, behaviors, and relationships. At the core of intimacy is a feeling of closeness and the sharing of one's innermost self.

Intimate Feelings

Intimacy is related to both positive and negative emotions. On the positive side, intimacy is related to emotions such as love, warmth, joy, and passion. On the negative side, some people fear intimacy.

Love

Feelings of intimacy are a key component of love. Robert Sternberg (1988), a psychologist, proposed the triangular theory of love. According to this theory, love is made up of three components: intimacy, passion, and commitment. Intimacy is the warm, emotional component that consists of feelings that promote closeness, bondedness, and connectedness. Passion is the hot, motivational component that includes physical involvement. Commitment is the cool, cognitive component that involves deciding to love someone and committing to maintain that love. Of these three components, intimacy is theorized to be the most foundational or basic to the experience of love. Thus, although intimacy is only one component of loving relationships, it is a key component.

Warmth

Intimacy is also closely associated with feelings of warmth and caring. Communication researchers Peter Andersen and Laura Guerrero (1998) described interpersonal warmth as a feeling of closeness or emotional connectedness that is pleasant and comfortable. When people feel interpersonal warmth, they feel in sync with their environment and experience a sense of interconnectedness and comfort with other people. Most often, these feelings of warmth occur in the context of close relationships and intimate interactions. For example, a person might feel interpersonal warmth when he or she is in a crowded room and locks eyes with a best friend or romantic partner who is across the room. Even in the midst of a crowd, the person feels connected to the friend or partner. People often associate special places with the warm, cozy, and safe feeling that comes from experiencing intimacy in the company of loved ones. As Dorothy Gale's famous line from *The Wizard of Oz* (1939) proclaims, there is often "no place like home." These feelings of interpersonal warmth that are characteristic of intimate interactions and relationships make people feel comfortable enough to reveal their innermost selves. Warmth is just one of many emotions related to intimacy, but it may be the most central.

Joy

Joy or happiness is also related to intimacy. Carol Magai and Susan McFadden (1995) summarized more than a century of research on what causes infants to display joy. Their summary showed that babies tend to look happiest when they see a parent's face, when their limbs are lightly and playfully shaken, when they are tickled or hear someone singing, and when someone opens a curtain around their cradle. These findings show that infants experience joy when interacting with others. Research by psychologist Phillip Shaver and his colleagues (1987) found similar results for adults, who reported that they experienced the most happiness when they felt loved and accepted and when they received affection and praise from others. Thus, both children and adults tend to feel happiness in the context of intimate interactions with others. Research has also shown that having close, intimate relationships is an essential ingredient in the recipe for a happy life. Thus, happiness can be viewed as a by-product of intimate interactions and close relationships. In other words, experiencing intimacy makes people feel happy.

Passion

When most people are asked to think about an intimate relationship or an intimate encounter, they think of a romantic relationship or a sexual situation. However, the presence of sexual passion is not necessary for intimacy to be experienced. People have intimate relationships with close friends and family members without experiencing sexual attraction or sexual intimacy. In romantic relationships, however, passion and intimacy are often closely connected. Sternberg's triangular theory of love, for example, includes both passion and intimacy as part of romantic love and consummate love. Romantic love often characterizes the beginning of romantic relationships; people are getting to know one another and are not yet fully committed. In these early stages of romantic relationships, couples are often drawn together by feelings of intimacy and passion. Consummate love occurs in relationships that are highly intimate, passionate, and committed. This is the type of love that is often depicted in the happy endings of movies. In American society, most people strive for this type of love. Another type of love, infatuation, includes passion but not intimacy or commitment. Here, people feel sexually attracted to someone but have not yet developed a truly intimate relationship with that prospective partner. Thus, passion and intimacy coexist in some interactions and relationships but not in others.

Fear of Intimacy

Although intimacy is related to various positive emotions, some people fear intimacy. Elaine Hatfield (1984), a social psychologist, noted that when people come to her for therapy, one of the biggest issues she deals with is their fear of intimacy. According to Hatfield, people report fearing intimacy for at least six different reasons: fear of exposure, fear of abandon-

---

A grandchild narrates Alice Walker's "Medicine" (1968). As the child goes to wake her grandparents up in the morning, she finds them sleeping snuggled up to each other. The grandmother sleeps with the sick grandfather because of the comfort she brings him. Her long unbraided hair is better medicine for him than any prescription. The poem is physically shaped like a long, curly lock of hair.

ment, fear of angry attacks, fear of loss of control, fear of one's destructive impulses, and fear of losing one's individuality. The first three of these fears stem from worry about self-image, while the last three stem from worry about the loss of individual control and freedom.

People who fear exposure worry about making themselves vulnerable. When people expose their inner selves, they are revealing their deepest hopes, dreams, fears, and idiosyncrasies to other people. In doing this, people risk having someone they care deeply about discover all of their faults and sources of shame. Ultimately, the fear of such discoveries can lead to the second fear—the fear of abandonment.

People who fear abandonment worry that if someone gets to know them too well they will be rejected or abandoned. Hatfield (1984, p. 210) provided the following example for fear of abandonment:

One of my favorite graduate students was a beautiful Swedish woman. At one time, three sociologists at the University of Wisconsin were in love with her. Her problem? She pretended to be totally self-confident, bright, charming. In intimate affairs, each time she tried to admit how uncertain she was, to be herself, the men lost interest. They wanted to be in love with a *Star*, not a mere mortal like themselves.

People also worry about their partners using what they say against them. This is the fear of angry attacks. For example, people might worry that if they admit to a coworker that they do not know how to do something, the coworker will tell others that they are incompetent. Even in close relationships this can be a fear. A person might be afraid to reveal past sexual experiences to a partner because he or she thinks that the partner might get angry. There is also the possibility that partners in a close relationship will use private information as ammunition during arguments. For these reasons, it is clear that entrusting innermost thoughts and feelings to others can be a risky venture.

People who fear losing control worry that if they become too close to someone, they will not be able to control their thoughts and feelings—someone else will have too big of an effect on them. Hatfield argued that this is more of a problem for men than women because men are traditionally supposed to be "in control" of themselves, other people, and the situation.

People might also fear their own destructive impulses. If they keep a lot of negative emotion inside, they might fear that letting it all out could be dangerous. For example, a man might not tell a woman that he loves her because he fears that if she rejects him he will be so distraught that he might hurt himself or her. Similarly, a woman might not want to know that her husband is having an affair because she is afraid

of flying into a jealous rage. In these cases, it is the feeling of intimacy (and the violation of that intimacy) that could lead people to engage in destructive behaviors.

Other people fear losing their own individuality or personal identity. As Hatfield (1984, p. 212) put it, one of the "most primitive fears of intimacy" is "the feeling that one would be engulfed by another, the fear that one would literally disappear as he or she lost himself in another." This fear represents the push and pull that many people feel between the competing forces of wanting to be closely connected to others and wanting to be independent and self-sufficient. Leslie Baxter (1988, 1990), a communication researcher, developed dialectics theory to help explain this push and pull. According to this theory, people have seemingly contradictory needs, such as wanting connection with others and at the same time wanting autonomy. Baxter calls this the autonomy-connection dialectic. People also have the need to share private information with others and to keep some information private. This is the openness-closedness dialectic. The trick is for people to balance these needs so that they can be close to someone without feeling smothered by the relationship. It is interesting to note that many people complain that their relational partners either do not give them enough affection (too little connection, too much autonomy) or do not give them enough freedom (too much connection, too little autonomy). Achieving the right balance between these forces appears to be an important part of maintaining happy intimate relationships.

Intimate Communication

Communication is essential to maintaining happy relationships. Research on intimacy has generally found three groups of behaviors that are related to intimacy and closeness: nonverbal immediacy cues, self-disclosure and other verbal messages, and relational maintenance behaviors.

Nonverbal Immediacy

Nonverbal immediacy cues, according to Andersen (1985), are behaviors that signal interpersonal warmth, increase physical or psychological closeness, increase sensory input (in the form of being better able to see, touch, and smell the other person), and indicate availability to communicate. Andersen and Guerrero (1998, p. 313) described six general classes of nonverbal immediacy behaviors that are related to intimacy and interpersonal warmth:

- spatial behaviors, including close conversational distances, direct body orientations, forward leans, and communicating at the same level or in the same physical plane,

- tactile behaviors, including pats, squeezes, hugs, kisses, soothing contact, massages, sexual contact, and face touches,
- eye behavior, including increased gaze, mutual eye contact, and pupil dilation,
- body and face behaviors, including smiling, general facial pleasantness, affirmative head nods, expressive gestures, head tilts, bodily relaxation, and open body positions,
- vocal behaviors, including more variation in pitch and tempo, reinforcing interjections such as "uh-huh," greater vocal fluency, warmth, pleasantness, and expressiveness, and soft voices that draw people close, and
- time-related behaviors, such as spending time with people, being on time, being patient, and focusing solely on the partner and the conversation (rather than on multiple tasks at one time).

While all of these behaviors are undoubtedly important in sending messages of intimacy and in creating intimate emotions, such as love, warmth, and happiness, messages that include touch may be particularly important. As Stephen Thayer (1986, p. 8) stated, "Touch is the signal in the communication process that, above all other communication channels, most directly and immediately escalates the balance of intimacy. . . . To let another touch us is to drop that final and most formidable barrier to intimacy." Touch is also essential for healthy physical development. Judee Burgoon and her colleagues (1996), who are experts in nonverbal communication, summarized research showing that infants who are deprived of touch sometimes have physical and emotional problems both as children and as adults. Burgoon and her colleagues also noted that petting an animal can reduce blood pressure in some nursing home patients. Similarly, hugs can reduce stress in both adults and children. Taken together, these findings suggest that touch has therapeutic effects in addition to conveying intimacy.

A special type of touch, sexual contact, is also highly associated with intimacy. In fact, Prager's (1995) work on intimacy discusses both touch and sexual contact as primary forces shaping the intimacy level of interactions and relationships. Of course, not all intimate relationships involve sexual contact. In romantic relationships, however, behaviors such as kissing and having sexual intercourse can undoubtedly send powerful messages of intimacy, and they can help two people feel interconnected both psychologically and physically. In *The Diary of a Young Girl* (published in 1952),

A pair of lovers in Asolo, Italy, demonstrates their intimacy publicly with both an embrace and a kiss. (Corbis/Annie Griffiths Belt)

Anne Frank wrote of the following encounter on April 28, 1944:

> He came toward me, I flung my arms around his neck and gave him a kiss on his left cheek, and was about to kiss the other cheek, when my lips met his and we pressed them together. In a whirl we were clasped in each other's arms, again and again, never to leave off. Oh, Peter does so need tenderness. . . . For the first time in his life he has given of himself . . . shown his real self.

This passage vividly describes how a simple kiss can lead to strong feelings of intimacy and the revelation of one's inner self.

Verbal Intimacy

Verbal communication is also important in signaling intimacy and creating feelings of warmth and interconnectedness. In fact, self-disclosure has long been regarded as the primary way that people create intimate relationships. The process of self-disclosure is perhaps best described in Irwin Altman and Dalmas Taylor's (1973) classic work on social penetration theory. According to this theory, relationships become increasingly intimate as people self-disclose information. The term *self-disclosure* refers to revealing private information about oneself to others. Altman and Taylor likened the process of self-disclosure to the peeling of an onion. The outer layer of an onion is soft and easy to penetrate, while the inner core of an onion is harder to penetrate. Also, there are many layers in an onion. Similarly, Altman and Taylor described how people reveal themselves to others in layers, with the most superficial information revealed readily and the most private information revealed only to highly trusted people. When people first meet someone, they will usually only reveal superficial information, such as where they were born and what they do for a living. As they get to know the person better, they will probably touch upon different topics but not reveal any information that is highly private. Altman and Taylor suggested that once they have established a close relationship, people feel freer to disclose private information.

According to social penetration theory, there are three levels of self disclosure: depth, breadth, and frequency. The term *depth* refers to how intimate or private information is. Information that makes up the "core" of who one is, including hopes, dreams, and fears, is the most private. The term *breadth* refers to the range of topics that people talk about with someone. For example, one might restrict conversation to work-related topics with a coworker but talk about a large variety of topics with a best friend. The term *frequency* deals with the amount of time that is spent disclosing information to someone. People in close relationships usually disclose to one another on a regular basis. People also disclose to strangers who they will probably never see again. For example, people often disclose to strangers on an airplane. The more depth, breadth, and frequency that is involved in the self-disclosure, the more intimate the communication and the closer one is likely to feel toward the other person.

Although self-disclosure is the most important form of verbal intimacy, it is not the only way in which people express intimacy using verbal communication. Andersen and Guerrero (1998) suggested that verbal immediacy, forms of address, and personal idioms all function to communicate intimacy. Verbal immediacy includes saying "we" instead of "I" and talking in present tense rather than past tense. This form of language shows that two people are connected to one another. Forms of address that are informal rather than formal are also more intimate. For example, calling someone "Tim" is more informal than calling him "Timothy," but calling him "Timothy" is more informal than calling him "Mr. Green," "Mr. Timothy Green" or "Vice President Green." Personal idioms include the private nicknames that are used for others. Calling someone "Honey" or "Babe" is obviously an intimate form of expression. Teasing insults, such as affectionately calling a younger sibling "squirt" can also function as intimate forms of verbal communication.

Relational Maintenance Behaviors

Intimacy is often expressed during daily activities with others. Steve Duck and his colleagues (1991) have shown that routine, mundane behaviors, such as talking to one another when getting home after work or doing the dishes together, are essential to maintaining intimate relationships. These types of behaviors show that people want to spend time with someone, and that they are active participants in the relationship. Communication researchers Daniel Canary and Laura Stafford (1994) described several types of behavior that help people maintain intimate relationships. Included among these behaviors are positivity, openness, assurances and supportiveness, social networking, and sharing activities and tasks. Positivity includes behaviors such as complimenting someone. Openness involves sharing private information with someone and listening to their problems and concerns. Assurances and supportiveness involve letting people know that one is committed or loyal to them, and being there to help them in times of crisis. Social networking involves accepting and dealing with one another's family and friends. Sharing activities and tasks includes doing things together and sharing responsibility for tasks such as household chores.

An excerpt from Louisa May Alcott's classic novel, *Little Women* (1868), helps illustrate how sharing tasks and activities are associated with intimacy. In this passage, Laurie proposes marriage to Amy as they share a boat ride in Switzerland:

> Amy . . . accepted an oar. She rowed as well as she did many other things; and, though she used both hands, and Laurie but one, the oars kept time, and the boat went smoothly through the water.
> "How well we pull together, don't we?" said Amy, who objected to silence just then.
> "So well that I wish we might always pull in the same boat. Will you, Amy?" very tenderly.
> "Yes, Laurie," very low.
> Then they both stopped rowing, and unconsciously added a pretty little tableau of human love and happiness to the dissolving views reflected in the lake.

As this passage shows, behaviors such as sharing tasks combine with nonverbal (voice tone) and verbal (the proposal and acceptance) messages to create highly intimate interaction.

The Importance of Intimacy

Intimacy is important throughout the life span. The child development literature includes several theories that illustrate the key role that intimacy plays in the lives of children and young adults. Erik Erikson's (1963, 1980) psychosexual stages and John Bowlby's (1969, 1973, 1980) attachment theory are especially informative.

According to Erikson's theory, trust and intimacy are two crucial stepping stones in the process of developing a positive self-identity. Erikson believed that during the first year of a child's life, he or she learns to trust or mistrust others based on interaction with caregivers. If the child emerges from this stage with a healthy sense of trust, he or she will be better able to develop intimate relationships later in life. Of course, a small dose of mistrust is also healthy so that children can discriminate between dangerous and safe situations. In young adulthood, Erikson theorized that people feel a strong need to develop close, intimate relationships that move beyond adolescent love. According to his theory, young adults (between nineteen and twenty-five years of age) who do not develop intimate bonds will feel isolated and lonely.

Bowlby's attachment theory makes similar predictions. A basic principle behind attachment theory is that people are predisposed to form close, intimate bonds with others. For children, such bonds are especially important because children depend on others to take care of them. Children who develop secure, healthy attachments with parents learn to regard themselves and others positively, and they feel free to explore their environments and try new things. According to this theory, children who are securely attached to their parents develop a capacity for intimacy that extends into their adult relationships.

Intimacy is also crucial for adults. In *Intimate Relationships* (1992), Sharon Brehm reported that 90 to 95 percent of the American population marries at least once in their lifetime. She also reported that married people tend to be happier and less lonely than single, divorced, separated, or widowed people. Robert Weiss

(1973) has shown that both the quality and quantity of relationships affect loneliness. People who have a low quantity of relationships often feel socially isolated. People who do not have at least one high-quality intimate relationship report feeling emotional isolation. In other words, they feel that they have no one with whom to share their innermost thoughts and feelings. This type of loneliness can lead to feelings of alienation and depression. As Mother Teresa has been quoted as saying, "Loneliness is the most terrible poverty."

Some people have trouble developing and maintaining healthy intimate relationships and combating loneliness. Work on attachment in adult relationships, for example, shows that some people are either fearful of intimacy or crave excessive intimacy. Kim Bartholomew (1990, 1993), a social psychologist, described four attachment styles: secure, dismissive, fearful avoidant, and preoccupied. A secure individual is comfortable with intimacy, values close relationships, and has a positive self-concept. A dismissive individual is highly self-sufficient, has trouble trusting others, and sees relationships as relatively unimportant. A fearful avoidant individual has been hurt in past relationships and is hesitant to become intimate with others for fear of being rejected or abandoned. A preoccupied individual craves excessive intimacy and interconnectedness. In many cases, this need for excessive intimacy ends up driving potential partners away, leaving the preoccupied person feeling lonely and rejected.

Obviously, intimacy is an important part of people's lives. Individuals who feel connected to others tend to feel better about themselves as well as their relationships. They also tend to feel less lonely and isolated. For lonely individuals, intimacy can be elusive. Yet intimacy can be found in simple actions, such as sharing a smile or sitting in front of a cozy fire with someone. Intimacy also characterizes some of the most memorable moments in people's lives, such as hearing someone special say "I love you" for the first time. Intimate moments such as these help make life richer and happier for everyone.

See also: ACCEPTANCE AND REJECTION; ATTACHMENT; ATTRACTIVENESS; BOWLBY, JOHN; COMMUNICATION; ERIKSON, ERIK HOMBURGER; FRIENDSHIP; HAPPINESS; INFATUATION; LONELINESS; LOVE; RELATIONSHIPS; TRUST

Michael Ondaatje, in The English Patient *(1993), portrays several forms of intimacy. One is the intimacy between a nurse and her dying patient as she devotes herself to caring for him, changing dressings and sheets, keeping him clean, easing his pain, listening to his stories, and reading to him. Another form of intimacy in the novel is sexual intimacy between lovers.*

Bibliography

Altman, Irwin, and Taylor, Dalmas. (1973). *Social Penetration: The Development of Interpersonal Relationships.* New York: Holt, Rinehart & Winston.

Andersen, Peter A. (1985). "Nonverbal Immediacy in Interpersonal Communication." In *Multichannel Integrations of Non-*

verbal Behavior, ed. Aron W. Siegman and Stanley Feldstein. Hillsdale, NJ: Lawrence Erlbaum.

Andersen, Peter A., and Guerrero, Laura K. (1998). "The Bright Side of Relational Communication: Interpersonal Warmth as a Social Emotion." In *Handbook of Communication and Emotion: Theory, Research, Applications, and Contexts,* ed. Peter A. Andersen and Laura K. Guerrero. San Diego, CA: Academic Press.

Bartholomew, Kim. (1990). "Avoidance of Intimacy: An Attachment Perspective." *Journal of Social and Personal Relationships* 7:147–178.

Bartholomew, Kim. (1993). "From Childhood to Adult Relationships: Attachment Theory and Research." In *Learning about Relationships,* ed. Steve Duck. Newbury Park, CA: Sage Publications.

Baxter, Leslie A. (1988). "A Dialectical Perspective on Communication Strategies in Relationship Development." In *Handbook of Personal Relationships,* ed. Steve Duck. New York: Wiley.

Baxter, Leslie A. (1990). "Dialectical Contradictions in Relationship Development." *Journal of Social and Personal Relationships* 7:69–88.

Bowlby, John. (1969). *Attachment and Loss, Vol. 1: Attachment.* New York: Basic Books.

Bowlby, John. (1973). *Attachment and Loss, Vol. 2: Separation.* New York: Basic Books.

Bowlby, John. (1980). *Attachment and Loss, Vol. 3: Loss.* New York: Basic Books.

Brehm, Sharon S. (1992). *Intimate Relationships,* 2nd ed. New York: McGraw-Hill.

Burgoon, Judee K.; Buller, David B.; and Woodall, W. Gill. (1996). *Nonverbal Communication: The Unspoken Dialogue,* 2nd ed. New York: McGraw-Hill.

Canary, Daniel J., and Stafford, Laura. (1994). "Maintaining Relationships through Strategic and Routine Interaction." In *Communication and Relational Maintenance,* ed. Daniel J. Canary and Laura Stafford. San Diego, CA: Academic Press.

Duck, Steve W.; Rutt, Deborah J.; Hurst, Margaret H.; and Strejc, Heather. (1991). "Some Evident Truths about Conversations in Everyday Relationships: All Communications are Not Created Equal." *Human Communication Research* 18:228–267.

Erikson, Erik H. ([1950] 1963). *Childhood and Society.* New York: W. W. Norton.

Erikson, Erik H. ([1959] 1980). *Identity and the Life Cycle.* New York: W. W. Norton.

Hatfield, Elaine. (1984). "The Dangers of Intimacy." In *Communication, Intimacy, and Close Relationships,* ed. Valerian J. Derlega. New York: Academic Press.

Magai, Carol, and McFadden, Susan H. (1995). *The Role of Emotion in Social and Personality Development: History, Theory, and Research.* New York: Wiley.

Prager, Karen J. (1995). *The Psychology of Intimacy.* New York: Guilford.

Shaver, Phillip; Schwartz, Judith; Kirson, Donald; and O'Connor, Cary. (1987). "Emotion Knowledge: Further Exploration of a Prototype Approach." *Journal of Personality and Social Psychology* 52:1061–1086.

Sternberg, Robert J. (1988). "Triangulating Love." In *The Psychology of Love,* ed. Robert J. Sternberg and Michael L. Barnes. New Haven, CT: Yale University Press.

Thayer, Stephen. (1986). "Touch: Frontier of Intimacy." *Journal of Nonverbal Behavior* 10:7–11.

Weiss, Robert S. (1973). *Loneliness.* Cambridge, MA: Massachusetts Institute of Technology Press.

Laura K. Guerrero

J

JAMES, WILLIAM

b. New York, New York, January 11, 1842; *d.* Chocorua, New Hampshire, August 26, 1910; *psychology, philosophy, education, religion.*

William James is considered by many experts to be the leading American psychologist of the first half of the twentieth century. This evaluation is also viewed by many to be somewhat ironic since few of James's ideas have had a long-term effect on psychology and they have been largely eclipsed by the works of others. It is most likely that James's reputation is based not so much on any specific contributions to psychology or philosophy but rather to his general influence as a brilliant theorist, creative thinker, dynamic personality, exciting teacher, and inspiring writer. In short, it is his strength of character and mind that have produced his reputation.

William James, the son of Henry James, Sr., and Mary (Walsh) James, was born into an upper-class New York family in 1842. His grandfather, also named William James, had become wealthy buying and selling land, and Henry James, Sr., used the money to support his own career as an armchair theologian and philosopher. As a result, the family was part of an elite intellectual circle that included the philosopher and poet Ralph Waldo Emerson. Henry James, Sr., also made use of the family fortune to ensure that his five children received the best possible education. William James, his brother Henry (who later became popular as a novelist), and their siblings were all educated in Europe, where they were exposed to all forms of art

and literature. James initially choose to be a painter but later switched to medicine, which his father suggested would be a more lucrative and stable pursuit. He entered Harvard in 1861 and graduated with a medical degree in 1869, although he never practiced medicine. Instead, James taught anatomy and physiology before teaching Harvard's first course in psychology in 1875. He was initially interested in experimental psychology and founded a psychology laboratory at Harvard in the 1870s. In 1878, James began writing his classic work, the two-volume *Principles of Psychology,* which did not appear until twelve years later, five years after he had achieved the rank of full professor. This publication, along with a later one-volume version, became the standard work in psychology and the basic reading in psychology courses around the nation for the following several decades. However, by 1890, James had moved away from experimental psychology and saw himself more as a philosopher with interests in religion, hypnosis, and spirituality. His disillusionment with laboratory psychology and his basic reason for moving away from psychology were set forth at the close of his *Principles:* "The more sincerely one seeks to trace the actual course of psychogenesis, the steps by which as a race we have come by the mental attributes we possess, the more clearly one perceives 'the slowly gathering twilight close in utter night.'" Despite his pessimism about the explanatory power of psychology, his book established psychology as a legitimate scholarly discipline in American higher education and directed the field toward a scientific rather than humanistic approach. James's work introduced such basic concepts of psychology as self, stream of consciousness, habit, and will.

James also set forth his theory of emotion, later commonly referred to as the James-Lange theory of emotion (to reflect that the basic ideas were arrived at independently by James in 1884 and the Swedish physiologist Carl Lange in 1885). The theory states that bodily sensations are the cause of emotional states. For example, laughing makes a person feel happy, crying makes a person feel sad, and running away makes a person feel scared. Although the theory has subsequently been rejected as either simply wrong or overly deterministic and simplistic, it was an important formulation in its time for three reasons. First, it was an attempt to study and explain the relationship between bodily sensations and emotional states or feelings, a topic that had been largely ignored up to that point. Second, it represented a shift to a more scientific approach to psychology in which the focus was on behavior that could be observed and measured. And, third, it was one of the first attempts to address the issue of exactly what an emotional response is and how can it be measured (an issue that remained unsolved through the twentieth century). Thus, while James did not produce the right answers, he did ask the right questions in terms of the subsequent study of emotion within scientific psychology.

In 1902, in accord with his new interests and with his view of himself as a philosopher, James published *The Varieties of Religious Experience,* in which he rejected the theological, structural approach to religion and replaced it with a functional perspective in which he addressed the role religion plays for the individual and society. James had moved from being a scientist to being a humanist and saw religion as an institution that made life easier and better for many people. He focused on religion as an inner experience (what later in the century came to be called spirituality) that could make the world a richer and better place. He also viewed science and religion not as opposite forms of explanation but as compatible forms that each supplied important answers about the nature of the universe and human existence. James's philosophical works on topics such as truth and the nature of the universe have not been widely admired by other philosophers, who tend to view him as a psychologist and see more value in his ideas of psychology that were set forth in *Principles.*

From his childhood, James was troubled by various physical maladies, including poor eyesight and a bad back. He also suffered from emotional distress that at times left him deeply depressed and troubled. It has been suggested by some people that his emotional problems might today be diagnosed as a bipolar (manic-depressive) disorder and that they may have contributed to his general outlook on life, to his shift in interest from psychology to philosophy, and to his interest in emotional states and their links with behavior. James was married in 1878 to Alice Howe Gibbons, and they had four children who lived to adulthood and one who died in childhood. Alice was a source of support for him throughout his life, and it is likely that the stable home life she provided aided in his coping with his physical and emotional problems. James died at his home in Chocorua, New Hampshire, with his reputation as one of the most important people in America intact.

See also: EMERSON, RALPH WALDO; PHILOSOPHY; PSYCHOLOGY OF EMOTIONS

William James. (Corbis/Bettmann)

Bibliography

James, William. (1890). *Principles of Psychology,* 2 vols. New York: Holt.

James, William. (1902). *The Varieties of Religious Experience.* New York: Longmans, Green.

James, William. (1909). *The Meaning of Truth.* New York: Longmans, Green.

James, William. (1987). *Essays, Comments, and Reviews,* ed. Ignas K. Skrupskelis and Frederick Burkhardt. Cambridge, MA: Harvard University Press.

Myers, Gerald E. (1986). *William James: His Life and Thought.* New Haven: Yale University Press.

Wilshire, Bruce W. (1984). *William James: The Essential Writings.* Albany: State University of New York Press.

David Levinson

JEALOUSY

Jealousy is typically defined as the thoughts, feelings, and behaviors that follow the perception of a threat to one's romantic relationship (or ability to maintain it) from a rival. In other words, whatever one does, feels, and thinks in the course of addressing that threat is jealousy.

What is that experience like? When asked to describe their jealousy experiences, people commonly mention the sorts of thoughts, feelings, and behaviors that are also involved in episodes of anger, sadness, and fear. People feel hurt, angry at the other man or woman, angry at the partner, fearful of losing the partner, and sad at the loss of trust. They demean or physically attack the rival or the partner, monitor the partner's behavior, and withdraw from interactions with others. They blame the rival or partner for what has happened, see themselves as inadequate, and blame themselves for what has happened. Because of this, jealousy is sometimes characterized as a "blend" of these other, presumably more basic, emotions.

It is, of course, not at all surprising that these emotions would occur in response to a partner's infidelity (or supposed infidelity). If the infidelity is interpreted as a betrayal, one would be expected to feel angry; if it is seen as a reminder of one's inadequacies or of the fragility of the relationship, one might be expected to be fearful at the prospect of losing the partner; and if one focuses on the loss of the partner or of trust, sadness would be expected. Because of this, some have argued that jealousy is not an emotion at all but merely a label for the situation in which these other emotions occur.

Is Jealousy Really an Emotion?

Jealousy-provoking situations can be interpreted in a variety of ways, each of which could produce some other emotion. An infidelity could, for example, be construed in terms of the obstruction of one's goals, a lack of certainty about a desired outcome, or the loss of something one values. These sorts of appraisals are linked to anger, fear, and sadness, respectively.

Some researchers and theorists take the position that the word *jealousy* is used to convey the circumstances in which anger, sadness, or fear were evoked. When a person says he or she is jealous, it conveys to the audience that the individual has one or more of those emotions and that they arose in the context of concerns about a partner being attracted to someone else. The audience, then, calls up a "mental model" of what romantic jealousy is typically like—what jealousy feels like, what people do and think when they are jealous, what sorts of things trigger jealousy and end it. That is, they make the inference that the individual's emotional experience is similar to the idealized representation of jealousy episodes that they carry around in their heads, one they have distilled from years of hearing about, witnessing, and experiencing jealousy. Indeed, research shows that this mental representation includes many features of anger, sadness, and fear.

But research also shows that there are elements of jealousy episodes that are associated more or less uniquely with jealousy rather than with anger, sadness, or fear. In one study by Don Sharpsteen and Lee Kirkpatrick (1997), for example, subjects were asked to sort cards, each with one of eighty-six commonly mentioned features of jealousy on it, into piles that represented the emotions involved in jealousy episodes. Through a statistical procedure called "cluster analysis," the researchers determined which features had tended to get sorted together. In essence, there were four large clusters of features, one that clearly represented anger (e.g., "want to hurt someone," "arguing with my partner," and "act grouchy"), another that represented fear (e.g., "feel insecure," "feel overwhelmed," and "feel confused"), a third that represented sadness (e.g., "feel hopeless," "have no energy," and "feel rejected"), and a fourth cluster that the researchers described as "idealized jealousy." This fourth cluster included all of the elements that cognitive-motivational models of emotion typically posit as ingredients of emotion episodes: antecedent events and appraisals of them (e.g., "someone has invaded what is yours"); affective, behavioral, and cognitive responses (e.g., "feel threatened," "keep track of the partner," and "think about the situation"); and coping strategies (e.g., "pretend you don't care"). The authors of that study argued that these were the features

---

Eudora Welty's narrator in "Why I Live at the P.O." (1941) is so jealous of her sister, Stella-Rhondo, and of all the attention she seems to get, that the narrator grabs as many possessions as she can, piles them in a wagon, and moves into the local post office where she works. This spiteful action does not seem to bother the rest of the family much at all, as if they were used to it.

that defined jealousy in their subjects' minds and that these subjects did, indeed, make distinctions among anger, fear, sadness, and jealousy.

Furthermore, in another study, Sharpsteen (1995b) found that subjects' ratings of the intensity of a fictitious person's jealousy varied with the applicability of these idealized-jealousy features to that person's emotional state but not with the applicability of the anger, sadness, or fear features. This happened despite the fact that all four sets of features had been generated originally by people who had been asked to describe their jealousy experiences. It seems, then, that people see jealousy as comprising thoughts, feelings, and behaviors that, collectively, distinguish jealousy episodes from episodes of other emotions, although they recognize that anger, fear, and sadness also occur during jealousy episodes. In terms of people's mental representations of these emotions, they clearly do differ, and the differences probably matter. People may, for example, be more forgiving of someone's offensive behavior if they think it stems from jealousy than if they think it stems from, say, anger. Or perhaps the coping strategies that work for anger, fear, or sadness do not work for jealousy. At any rate, people have apparently found it worthwhile to distinguish among these emotions.

But what makes jealousy episodes distinctly different from episodes of these other emotions? Why say one is jealous rather than saying one is angry, sad, or fearful? The answers to these questions lie both in the meaning that the romantic relationship (and its loss) has for the jealous individual and in the strategies he or she uses to cope with the situation and its fallout.

Why Are Romantic Rivals Threatening?

One reason a rival for one's partner's affections may be problematic is that he or she threatens to disrupt the routines, plans, and goals that the jealous person shares with the partner. Each member of a couple typically has at least some goals that require the collaboration of the other member for their fulfillment, such as having children or achieving economic security. A partner's infidelity (or the prospect of infidelity) raises the possibility that those goals will not be realized.

There are, however, deeper explanations, ones that spell out why a partner's philandering should make a person jealous (with or without a disruption of plans) as opposed to, say, angry. Each hinges on the supposition of a particular kind of relationship between the jealous person and his or her partner.

The emotional bond between romantic partners can be characterized as an attachment, much as infants' bonds with their caregivers are attachments. According to attachment theory, infants are built to form close emotional bonds (i.e., attachments) with their caregivers. The predisposition to form these attachments continues throughout life, although the object of the attachments changes with age. Infants and children typically form attachments with mothers and fathers, older siblings, and others on whom they may come to rely for nurturance and support. Adults, on the other hand, typically form attachments with other adults. That is the essence of healthy romantic relationships—a reciprocal attachment (and caregiving) bond.

Infants also appear to be built to maintain close physical proximity to their attachment figures. This proximity eventually comes to be represented psychologically as a sense of security. When proximity is disrupted by separation, most infants make attempts to get the attachment figure back. Jealousy may be seen as the adult equivalent of this sort of behavior. Jealousy-provoking situations threaten to disrupt one partner's attachment to the other, so they stimulate adult versions of infant attachment behavior. Infants cry and scream in fear (if not terror) when separated from their attachment figures; they express anger toward the attachment figure when he or she returns (perhaps in an attempt to punish him or her and prevent future separations); and they withdraw from social interactions following extended separations. To the extent that jealousy reflects the operation of this "attachment system" (i.e., feelings and behaviors aimed at achieving physical or psychological closeness to the attachment figure), adults, as well, would be expected to fear the loss of their attachment figure, punish him or her for attempts to leave, and be sad at the loss of the partner (if it came to that). Notice, though, that according to this conceptualization of jealousy there need be no disruption of plans and routines, per se, in order for jealousy to be triggered. Rather, it is the disruption of a sense of security that triggers jealousy. From an attachment perspective, then, jealousy is a manifestation of attachment behaviors that are geared toward maintaining physical proximity or psychological proximity (e.g., a sense of shared commitment to the relationship) to the partner.

But romantic partners are also often sexual partners, and the internal wiring that stimulates attempts to maintain an attachment relationship may not be the same wiring that stimulates attempts to maintain a mating relationship. In fact, people's use of the terms *romantic jealousy* and *sexual jealousy* may reflect their implicit understanding that jealousy could arise from two different motives.

According to those who use evolutionary psychology as an explanatory framework for understanding jealousy, jealousy evolved as a way for humans to protect investments in their offspring. By being motivated emotions that generally accompany it, in that jealousy would be directed specifically toward redirecting the partner's and the rival's behavior in an effort to ensure paternity, for a man, and in an effort to maintain the flow of resources, for a woman (though these need not be conscious goals). Sexual jealousy, for example, might be likely to involve attempts at bringing back a wandering partner (which is the goal of attachment behaviors as well), but sexual jealousy might also involve attempts at separating the partner from the rival (which would not be the primary function of attachment behavior). Knowing how people will behave in jealousy-provoking situations, then, might depend on knowing the extent to which the relationship has been maintained by attachment concerns or sexual ones.

Variability in Jealousy Behavior

Although jealousy episodes are apparently similar enough to each other to allow people to form a mental category for them, they are also likely to differ from person to person. From an attachment perspective, reactions to jealousy-provoking situations would be mediated by the individual's expectations of his or her effectiveness at restoring security and of the partner's responsiveness to attempts to do so. Because people's expectations differ, their jealous behavior differs. From an evolutionary perspective, jealousy would be mediated by threats to genetic investments. Because the threats facing ancestral men were different from the ones facing ancestral women, contemporary men and women become jealous in different situations. Variability in the onset and character of jealousy experiences, then, can be explained in terms of both attachment and evolution.

Attachment Styles

People (both infants and adults) can be attached to a caregiver or partner in several different ways. In other words, there are different ways of interacting with an attachment figure in times of stress (such as separation or potential separation from the attachment figure). These different ways of interacting are referred to as *attachment styles* and are presumably learned through actual experiences with attachment figures.

Those who are securely attached behave as if they are confident in their attachment figure's sensitivity and responsiveness to their needs, and as if they believe they are competent to influence the attachment figure's behavior ("I'm o.k., and so are you"). When jealous, those who are securely attached are more likely than others to express anger toward their partners and to report being brought closer to their partners as a consequence of the jealousy episode.

In a fit of jealousy, William Shakespeare's Othello (played by Jack Good) strangles his innocent wife, Desdemona (played by Sharon Gurney). (Corbis/Hulton-Deutsch Collection)

by "jealous" feelings and thoughts and by behaving in a "jealous" manner, early humans would have increased the odds of their genes being passed on to future generations. For a man, jealous behavior would have involved efforts at ensuring that the partner's offspring were also his own. If they were not, he stood to invest his resources (e.g., time, energy, and provisions) in another man's genes. Obviously, this would have left fewer resources available for offspring that did carry his genes, making it less likely that they would survive to reproduce and pass his genes further down the evolutionary pipeline. For a woman, a partner who left with her rival may have taken his resources with him, leaving the woman to fend for their offspring on her own. In both cases, those who got jealous would have been more likely to pass on their genes than would have others. If their jealousy had a genetic basis, a tendency toward becoming jealous would, with successive generations, have spread throughout the population. From this point of view, jealousy is distinct from the

Those who are anxiously attached behave as if they see their attachment figures as potentially responsive but doubt they are deserving of, or capable of eliciting, timely help or cooperation ("You're o.k., but there's something wrong with me"). Thus they are especially likely to monitor the partner's behavior, behave in a clingy fashion, and avoid overt displays of anger that might drive the partner away. In addition, anxious people are especially likely to become jealous. Owing to their lack of self-confidence and their extreme vigilance in monitoring the partner's behavior, the anxiously attached tend to jump to conclusions when the partner's intentions may be ambiguous. Notice that this sort of behavior is likely to annoy the partner and create the emotional distance the anxious person fears, perpetuating the mental models of relationships that underlie his or her attachment style.

The avoidantly attached behave as if they expect rejection, indifference, or smothering interference from the attachment figure and are capable of, indeed prefer, dealing with stressful situations on their own ("I'm o.k., but there's something wrong with you"). They therefore are especially likely to withdraw from the partner when jealous, terminate the relationship, and, perhaps as a consequence, feel sad. This behavior is likely to reinforce the avoidant person's beliefs about relationships, either by prompting attachment behavior (e.g., overwhelming attempts to achieve closeness) from the partner or creating an impenetrable barrier to intimacy. In fact, the average length of avoidant and anxious persons' most important love relationship is just barely half that of secure persons', suggesting that the insecurely attached do have trouble maintaining relationships.

Although early research on jealousy was not based on attachment theory, many of the findings of that research are easily conceptualized in attachment terms. For example, those who report the most frequent and intense jealousy experiences tend to be those who see themselves as inadequate in relationships and see their partners as less involved in the relationship than themselves. In attachment terms, these sorts of perceptions are characteristic of the anxious-ambivalent attachment style, and it is indeed this group that reports the most frequent jealousy episodes.

Sex Differences

Although sex differences in the frequency and intensity of romantic jealousy do not appear to be strong or consistent (i.e., in some studies men report more jealousy, in other studies women do), with the introduction of evolutionary theorizing to the study of jealousy, the issue of differences between men and women became something of a hot topic. Support for evolu-

tionary arguments would generally hinge on finding that men and women respond to jealousy-provoking situations in predictably different ways or that they respond with jealousy to different types of situations, not necessarily that they differ in how often they become jealous.

One such evolutionary argument is that because ancestral men and women faced different challenges in passing on their genes, contemporary men and women are provoked to jealousy in different situations. Ancestral women ought to have been especially concerned about emotional infidelities, whereas ancestral men ought to have been especially concerned about sexual infidelities. Emotional infidelities threatened a woman's hold on her partner's resources: His attachment to another woman would have been a signal that he might devote those resources to her. He could, however, have had sex with as many other women as he wanted (which, if the theory is true, would probably have been a lot) and sacrifice only a minimal amount of resources. A man's partner has relatively little to lose, in terms of her own reproductive success, by his purely sexual affairs. On the other hand, women's sexual infidelities would have threatened men's confidence in paternity. In principle, a man's partner could have formed attachments with whomever else she chose, but as long as she did not have sex with those men he could have been sure that her offspring carried his genes.

David Buss and his colleagues (1992) conducted the first research based on this argument, and they did indeed find that men were more psychologically and physiologically distressed by sexual infidelities than by emotional ones and that women were more distressed by emotional infidelities than sexual ones. These findings have been replicated in several countries, lending some support to the idea that these differences between men and women are universal.

In another study based on evolutionary principles, Sharpsteen (1995c) asked men and women to imagine themselves in a romantic relationship with someone who would be either a good parent or a bad one. They then imagined that that partner had an affair and rated the likelihood that they would become jealous. Because jealousy is geared toward maintaining relationships, and because people probably like someone who is described as a good parent better than someone who is described as a bad parent, at least in the abstract, it may seem intuitively obvious that people would become more jealous over the good parent's affair than the bad one's. But evolutionary principles suggest this would be true for only one of the sexes. In this study, and as predicted, men judged themselves more likely to become jealous when their partner would be a good mother than a bad one. Men lose more if a good mother for their offspring leaves than if a bad one does—a bad mother, by definition, would jeopardize his investment in their offspring, whereas a good mother would behave in ways that enhance the odds of their offspring surviving to reproduce. Counterintuitively, but also as predicted from evolutionary principles, women saw themselves as more likely to become jealous when their partner would be a bad father than when he would be a good one. If a bad father leaves, he takes his resources with him. A good father, though, would continue to contribute resources to his (and her) offspring even after he left. Thus, a woman has more to lose, genetically speaking, when a bad father moves on than when a good one does, and thus more to gain by becoming jealous.

As one might expect, the evolutionary approach is not without its critics. Several researchers have argued that, although men and women may truly differ in the situations that are most likely to evoke jealousy, it is due to their different beliefs about what will happen in each situation rather than because they are wired differently. For example, the "double-shot hypothesis" states that some people believe that the two types of infidelities (emotional and sexual) tend to co-occur. When asked to imagine an emotional infidelity, these people would infer that a sexual infidelity was also taking place, thus giving them a "double shot" of provocation for jealousy. This hypothesis is supported by the finding of David DeSteno and Peter Salovey (1996a) that subjects name as the most distressing type of infidelity the one that they believe most strongly implies the other. Furthermore, women are especially likely to believe that emotional infidelities imply sexual ones, accounting for their fairly substantial bias toward greater distress over emotional rather than sexual infidelities.

Naturally, the double-shot hypothesis has been criticized, as well. Perhaps the most damaging criticism is that it posits sex differences in beliefs about the implications of jealousy-provoking situations but it does not say where those beliefs originate. The evolutionary approach, however, can account for them: The beliefs accurately reflect evolved differences in the extent to which one type of infidelity actually does imply the other. Because the minimum investment in parenting is so much less for a man than a woman (e.g., one act of intercourse versus one act of intercourse plus nine months of gestation and several years of caring for one's offspring), it would have been beneficial to ancestral men to mate often with many women and without emotional involvement or commitment. Women, on the other hand, being the more heavily investing sex, would have benefited from requiring commitment (one sign of which is emotional involvement) along with sex. In fact, many studies show that men find it easier to have sex without emotional involvement than do women.

Type of Threat

Jealous behavior is an attempt to maintain a relationship in the face of threats from a romantic rival. Losing one's partner to a rival is more likely to produce jealousy than is losing the partner because of rejection, destiny, or fate. Broadly speaking, there are two types of threats that might trigger jealousy. One is a threat to the relationship directly from a rival, and the other is a threat to self-esteem stemming from comparisons with a potential rival. Threats to self-esteem challenge one's sense of adequacy as a partner, stimulating concerns that the other partner might leave. In one study, Sharpsteen (1995a) asked subjects to imagine themselves in four types of jealousy-provoking situations that embodied both threats to the relationship and threats to self-esteem. Subjects' judgments of how likely they would be to become jealous reflected their judgments of the overall level of threat. Thus, people do seem to weigh both types of threat when appraising jealousy-provoking situations.

These findings can be explained in terms of both attachment theory and evolutionary principles. From the attachment perspective, either type of threat would undermine one's sense of security about the relationship. From the evolutionary perspective, a rival undermines the emotional bond shared by the partners, and a threat to one's self-esteem undermines one's sense of adequacy as a mate. Indeed, jealous women are relatively more likely than jealous men to take steps to protect their relationship, whereas jealous men are more likely to take steps to protect their self-esteem. In evolutionary terms, this preserves the flow of resources (for women) and maintains self-confidence (for men).

Conclusion

Although previously depicted as a sort of personal weakness, current conceptualizations of jealousy describe it as a protective reaction, one geared toward maintaining intimate relationships. Certainly, jealousy can, at relatively low levels of intensity, stimulate communication about the boundaries of a relationship, revive passion, and bring two partners closer together. At higher levels, however, jealousy has the potential to become dangerous. Male jealousy, for example, contributes substantially to homicide and wife battering across a wide variety of cultures.

Both the attachment perspective and the evolutionary perspective suggest that jealousy is deeply ingrained in humans. To that extent, it is irrational. But humans also come equipped with the ability to reason.

Knowing the origins of jealous reactions can allow people to distinguish their impulses from their interests and to think rationally about how to deal constructively with jealousy-provoking situations.

See also: ANGER; ATTACHMENT; ATTRIBUTION; COMMITMENT; CONFLICT; ENVY; HATE; LOVE; RELATIONSHIPS; TRUST

Bibliography

Bringle, Robert G., and Buunk, Braam P. (1985). "Jealousy and Social Behavior: A Review of Personal, Relationship, and Situational Determinants." In *Review of Personality and Social Psychology, Vol. 2: Self, Situations, and Social Behavior,* ed. Phillip Shaver. Beverly Hills, CA: Sage Publications.

Buss, David M. (1994). *The Evolution of Desire: Strategies of Human Mating.* New York: Basic Books.

Buss, David M.; Larsen, Randy J.; and Westen, Drew. (1996). "Sex Differences in Jealousy: Not Gone, Not Forgotten, and Not Explained by Alternative Hypotheses." *Psychological Science* 7:373–375.

Buss, David M.; Larsen, Randy J.; Westen, Drew; and Semmelroth, Jennifer. (1992). "Sex Differences in Jealousy: Evolution, Physiology, and Psychology." *Psychological Science* 3:251–255.

Buunk, Braam P.; Angleitner, Alois; Oubaid, Viktor; and Buss, David M. (1996). "Sex Differences in Jealousy in Evolutionary and Cultural Perspective: Tests from the Netherlands, Germany, and the United States." *Psychological Science* 7:359–363.

DeSteno, David A., and Salovey, Peter. (1996a). "Evolutionary Origins of Sex Differences in Jealousy? Questioning the 'Fitness' of the Model." *Psychological Science* 7:367–372.

DeSteno, David A., and Salovey, Peter. (1996b). "Genes, Jealousy, and the Replication of Misspecified Models." *Psychological Science* 7:376–377.

Kirkpatrick, Lee A., and Hazan, Cindy. (1994). "Attachment Styles and Close Relationships." *Personal Relationships* 1:123–142.

Salovey, Peter, ed. (1991). *The Psychology of Jealousy and Envy.* New York: Guilford.

Sharpsteen, Don J. (1993). "Romantic Jealousy As an Emotion Concept: A Prototype Analysis." *Journal of Social and Personal Relationships* 10:69–82.

Sharpsteen, Don J. (1995a). "The Effects of Self-Esteem Threats and Relationship Threats on the Likelihood of Romantic Jealousy." *Journal of Social and Personal Relationships* 12:89–101.

Sharpsteen, Don J. (1995b). "The Mental Representation of Romantic Jealousy: A Blended Emotion (and More)." Paper presented at the June meeting of the International Network on Personal Relationships, Williamsburg, VA.

Sharpsteen, Don J. (1995c). "Sex, Attachment, and Infidelity: The Context of Jealousy." Paper presented at the April meeting of the Southwestern Psychological Association, Austin, TX.

Sharpsteen, Don J., and Kirkpatrick, Lee A. (1997). "Romantic Jealousy and Adult Romantic Attachment." *Journal of Personality and Social Psychology* 72:627–640.

White, Gregory L., and Mullen, Paul E. (1989). *Jealousy: Theory, Research, and Clinical Strategies.* New York: Guilford.

Don J. Sharpsteen

JOY

See Happiness

K

KANT, IMMANUEL

b. Königsberg, East Prussia, April 22, 1724; *d.* Königsberg, East Prussia, February 12, 1804; *philosophy.*

The German philosopher Immanuel Kant is considered by many scholars to be the most influential philosopher of the modern era. He is also one whose works were and continue to be widely and intensively studied—partly because they are difficult to understand and partly because they are complex and bring a new, critical perspective to philosophy. His work influenced all of philosophy that followed him, especially the schools of Kantianism and Idealism.

Kant was the fourth of nine children born to Johann Georg Kant, a harness maker, and Anna Regina (Reuter). Johann and Anna were adherents of the Pietist movement and raised their children in accord with its rigid moral and religious code. It has been suggested by some biographers that this upbringing was behind Kant's later attacks on religion. His mother, to whom he was especially close, died when Kant was thirteen years of age. After completing religious school, he enrolled the University of Königsberg in 1740 and studied under the philosopher Martin Knutzen. In 1746, Kant's father died, and after graduating with a master's degree later that year, Kant turned to private tutoring in order to support himself. For the next nine years, he tutored the children of wealthy families, and then in 1755, he returned to the University of Königsberg and earned a doctoral degree in the natural sciences. The degree enabled Kant to take the lowly position of private lecturer at the university, a position he held for the next fifteen years.

At first, Kant remained attracted to the natural sciences, but at the same time, he read the works of philosophers carefully, being especially drawn to the ideas of the Scottish philosopher David Hume and the French writers Voltaire, Charles-Louis de Secondat de Montesquieu, and Jean-Jacques Rousseau. Kant later moved into the field of philosophy and in 1763 wrote *The Only Possible Ground of Demonstration for the Existence of God,* which questioned the philosophical proofs that were being offered at the time for the existence of God. Kant wrote several other treatises that criticized contemporary ideas in philosophy and religion although they brought him little attention at the university and he continued to remain a lecturer rather than a professor. Kant declined several offers of professorships elsewhere as he preferred to remain in his native city and, in fact, remained there his entire life. Kant devoted his life to reading, thought, and teaching and organized his daily life to accommodate these interests. He never married, was devoted to his students (who were, in turn, devoted to him), and was often in poor health. In 1770, at forty-six years of age, Kant was finally promoted to the position of professor of logic and metaphysics, with his latest book, *On the Form and Principles of the Sensible and Intelligible Worlds,* drawing some attention.

With his promotion to the position of professor, Kant entered the third and most productive stage of his philosophical career. Over the next twenty years he would produce the works that would make him one of the leading philosophers of all time. In 1781, he pub-

Immanuel Kant. (Corbis/Bettmann)

lished his major work, *Critique of Pure Reason.* This was followed by *Prolegomena to Any Future Metaphysics* (1783), the revised edition of *Critique of Pure Reason* (1787), *Critique of Practical Reason* (1788), *Critique of Judgment* (1788), and other works. Scholars in later years came to see *Critique of Pure Reason* as one of the two (the other being Plato's *Republic*) most important books in Western philosophy.

Kant studied and wrote about ethics, aesthetics, religion, politics, morality, and law. In doing so, he became the best-known and most influential philosopher of the last third of the eighteenth century, with his works being translated and taught in Great Britain, The Netherlands, and Germany. His ideas and writing were complex and controversial and produced much discussion in the European philosophical community. The most serious controversy of Kant's career came in the 1790s when his series on religion, *Religion within the Bounds of Pure Reason,* was banned by the Prussian government, partly because it attacked religion and partly because of Kant's support of freedom and the French Revolution. Kant arranged for publication outside of Prussia, and his difficulties with the government continued. Already sick and weak, he retired from the university in 1799 and died five years later. Kant received no honors during his lifetime, and the final five years were marked by illness and senility.

Because his writing style is heavy and difficult to read and because his ideas are complex, it is difficult to summarize Kant's ideas. Basically, in his critical approach to reason, he sought to save what he found useful in the thought of the rational and empiricist philosophers and combine the two approaches to produce a more powerful system of thought and explanation. Kant believed that in experiencing the world, humans use both their senses and their minds, with the senses bringing the matter of experience and the mind bringing the form of experience. Kant also distinguished between two "worlds": (1) the phenomenal world, which humans can experience through the senses and mind, and (2) the noumenal world, which is the world of things in and of themselves, which humans cannot experience. As regards ethics, Kant suggested that ethnical behavior is guided by rationality and that acting in a moral manner is rational behavior. His approach to ethics was not especially unique and actually reflected Christian teachings of the eighteenth century. Finally, as regards religion, he rejected all arguments for the existence of God as being logically flawed, although he did not himself reject the idea of God.

Kant had little use for emotion in his thought and writings and clearly differentiated between reason and "the inclinations," which included feelings, moods, and desires. Although Kant did not view reason as being the only vehicle for the explanation, he saw no role for emotion in the process. Thus, he continued the tradition of excluding emotion from serious philosophical study. However, some experts suggest that Kant had a role in the reconsideration of emotion in the human experience as some of his writings suggest that he knew and understood the importance of feelings in appreciating life and saw emotion as an important component of religion. In addition, it was Kant who argued that "nothing great is ever done without passion," although it is his critic, the German philosopher Georg Hegel, who is credited with the quote.

See also: HUME, DAVID; PHILOSOPHY; PLATO

Bibliography

Cassirer, Ernst. (1981). *Kant's Life and Thought.* New Haven, CT: Yale University Press.

Guyer, Paul, ed. (1992). *The Cambridge Companion to Kant.* Cambridge, Eng.: Cambridge University Press.

Kant, Immanuel. ([1781] 1990). *Critique of Pure Reason,* tr. J. M. D. Meiklejohn. New York: Prometheus Books.

Kant, Immanuel. ([1788] 1997). *Critique of Judgement,* tr. James Creed Meredith. New York: Oxford University Press.

Kant, Immanuel. ([1788] 1997). *Critique of Practical Reason,* ed. Mary Gregor. New York: Cambridge University Press.

Kerszberg, Pierre. (1997). *Critique and Totality.* Albany: State University of New York Press.

David Levinson
Ben Manning

L

LAW

See Hate Crimes

LITERATURE

The Bible, a shopping list, a love letter, an essay, a novel, the newspaper, even e-mail, are all examples of "literature" that invades people's lives and shapes their emotions—forever renewing and changing the individuals. Literature and the self share a peculiar complicity because, as John O'Neill (1982) points out, stories are self-made while they make the self. In other words, the stories that literature tells affect the emotions of the reader, and the emotions of the reader in turn affect how well the literature conveys its lessons.

Is literature capable of stirring something more in people than mere emotion? Yes, because what literature tells are the lessons of truth and falsehood, which involve passions. Although contemporary popular language makes little or no distinction between the terms *passion* and *emotion*, literature generally refers to emotion as the moods and states of "being," such as fear, envy, and rage, while passion is related to suffering, or how one's spirit bears its own suffering in the process of "becoming." Literature preserves these differences in its grand narratives of self-discovery.

Literature charts the fragile experiences and lessons through which insight is gained tragically or otherwise reluctantly. While emotions may be instructive, and in some sense blind, passions restore vision and destiny and ultimately offer a "strategy of accommo-dation" for mapping emotional outbursts into productive activities. Passions are everything that people become, yet they are regulated by life's first and last narratives—birth and death. The writer has a privileged position because he or she sees the end from the beginning and places the hero and the reader between life and death. Because of this, literature is an instrument through which people can explore the fears and anxieties of death and life as the writer plays with emotions from both ends—acting as both the inexperienced "child" of invention and the tormented broker of death.

Classical Works

Literature is obsessed with stories that chart how passions are either fulfilled or thwarted. Plato's *Symposium* narrates a philosophical feast where the desire between bodies is both prolonged by the eating ritual and exacerbated by its indulgence. The feast adds beauty, sacrifice, worship, service, glory, and despair to the reader's understanding of love. But the reader must also see that love always loses—one must love and lose before one can go on to love again. This is best illustrated by Socrates's rejection of Alcibiades, thereby pursuing the passion for beauty and truth over the emotions of seduction. Love's grief brings on the sacred emotions of sorrow, terror, anguish, and despair—all of which are an approximation to the highest good of wisdom and temperance.

In *The Essays* (1588), Michel de Montaigne extended the classical passion for balance not only in weighing oneself between the visceral and intellectual delights but in observing the relations between force and tenderness, which he described in a poem where Mars forcefully embraced Venus. The technique of essaying is an opportunity for the writer to invent the self through a continuous interaction of intellect with emotion. Montaigne used the technique of writing *The Essays* to explore the grammar of the passions that are situated in stability, being, judgment, and plentitude.

In contrast, Marquis de Sade's *Philosophy in the Bedroom* (1782) suggests that only the most extreme versions of gratification matter in the process of making oneself. Thus he trades classical scholarly desire for impassioned inquiry for a porno-erotic version of impassivity toward the subject. The true "libertine" is one whose narrative lies in the immediacy of perverse sexual gratification. If the libertine scenes of sadomasochism are to reflect the accuracy of one's desires, then Sade has condemned the human soul to the level of the primitive instincts that are found in nature. However, Sade's literature can be raised beyond the immediacy of this sexual perversity and viewed as a passionate commentary about power and self-regulation, love and revolution, preservation and sacrifice. As a writer, Sade is surely asking the reader to ponder the limits of passion while pondering its possibilities.

Don Juan (1665), by Jean-Baptiste Molière, is another example of this struggle between the quest for emotional fulfillment and an obligation toward reasonable moral conduct. Don Juan's own seduction is lodged in the fragile balance between total sexual exploit and the fear of losing a love object. Molière's message is that seduction ends when the single passion of commitment begins—"the whole pleasure of love lies in change." Any fixed narrative spells the end of "love" for Don Juan: "[Once] we are the master, there's nothing more to say and nothing more to wish for; all the beauty of the passion is finished, and in the tranquillity of such a love we fall asleep."

Johann Wolfgang von Goethe's *The Sorrows of Young Werther* (1774) again suggests that sorrow and pain are inseparable from happiness and pleasure. Werther treats this complicity between love and loss as the dreadful reality that underwrites all happiness. The pain of unrequited love, fueled by the passion of obsessive worship, takes over and finally destroys Werther. These narratives insist that people are never so much ruled by their emotions as they are ruled by their passions.

The works of William Shakespeare show that emotions are historical, political, and familial narrative events. Consider Shakespeare's moments of human emotion represented by Richard II's melancholy, Hamlet's anxiety, and King Lear's prophetic madness. Each maps onto the larger stages in the human lifecycle—Richard's melancholy becomes anyone's melancholy, associated with any lost "kingdom" or object; Hamlet's anxiety becomes anyone's anxiety over death and its ghosts; and Lear's madness becomes anyone's elderly return to babble, tears, and drool. Shakespearean emotions often refuse any rational-moral limitation and thus move beyond the pleasure principle to achieve an expression of human universality represented by the building and destroying of families. Shakespeare's stories are never so much about achieving emotional "closure" as they are about contemplating the paths that are opened by the extreme emotions. Harold Bloom (1998) observes that Shakespeare canonized the passions in Western secular consciousness.

Modern Works

Mary Shelley's *Frankenstein* (1816) brings the passion for "self-making" into the modern period. Not unlike a writer's passion for creating life, Dr. Frankenstein finds life and death to be the ideal sites on which to begin a study of the structure of "being human." Frankenstein is both the emotional alchemist who conjoins spirit with dead matter and the melancholic who is propelled by a fire that consumes his own heart. His world empties out as he pursues his own furies—reflected in the nameless monster.

Jane Eyre (1847), by Charlotte Brontë, is a puzzling story regarding how women's passion might be achieved. It is impossible for Jane, a governess, to gain any understanding of herself in the face of an emotionless Rochester, the father of her charge. While Jane has a passion for emotion, Rochester is emotionless in his passion. This creates the central puzzle in the story: How shall the emotionless and the emotional reconcile? A peculiar reversal takes place, and possibly accounts for the final union of opposites; Jane, the ingénue, becomes worldly, while Rochester becomes a man emotionally wracked with loss. This is consistent with the fact that in most literature, the male figure is routinely exposed as being far less capable of coping with loss than is the female figure.

In Jane Austen's *Sense and Sensibility* (1811), it is the passion for emotional completeness that drives the Dashwood sisters' search for love against the social and moral constrictions of property and parsonage. Thus, Elinor's baroque *ascetic* gauges the tempo of her emotions so as never to be overextended, while Marianne's sensual *aesthetic* bursts with emotion alongside the rational-moral framework of male countenance and propriety. The sense and sensibility in the story are clearly female in nature and offer greater insights and answers to the predicaments of love than do the male grammars of sport and ownership. Austen's narrative gives the reader the idea that to know one's passions

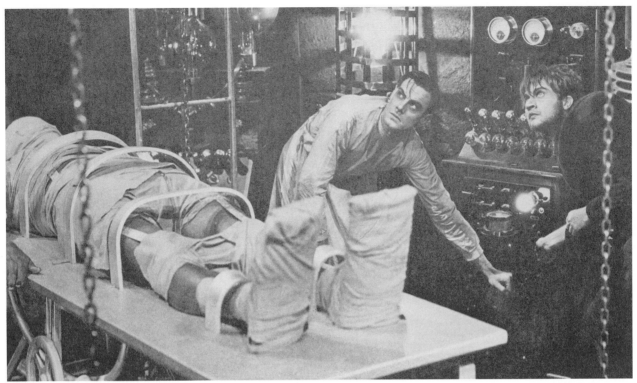

Dr. Frankenstein (played by Colin Clive, center) prepares to bring his monster to life in a scene from the 1931 movie version of Mary Shelley's Frankenstein. (Corbis/Bettmann)

is to solve the riddle from the beginning—nothing falls outside the passions that will eventually solve everything, not wealth, not property, not prestige.

The cathartic function of literature, described in Aristotle's *Poetics*, relies upon the expression of the emotions in order to cleanse the self of them. Part of the enjoyment of recognition in the emotions, even when pain, destruction, and loss are involved, is that the reader can exclaim, "Ah, yes, that is me." The function of catharsis is key to Sigmund Freud's psychoanalytic invention for soul searching. Freud saw the individual to be at once torn between the urge to satisfy the biological drives (i.e., to satiate hunger and sexual desire at all costs—his "constancy principle") and the activities of culture that protect against the violent drives of nature. Much like literature, the psychoanalytic narrative presented by Freud in "Introductory Lectures on Psychoanalysis" (1916), puts forth a method for assembling meaning beyond the emotions and locates the passions as the exceptional roots for life's reason. Freud's case histories are really his own literary "novellas" as seen in the case of "Dora" (1905), "Little Hans" (1909), and "Leonardo da Vinci and a Memory of His Childhood" (1910). The literary method used by Freud in reporting the case histories shows that he was not simply analyzing the destructive emotions of each patient; his writing doubles as a structure for sublimating his own passions, which he relocates in the stories of art, literature, and drama.

Postmodern Works

The postmodern writer deals with the godless future of all things. Events and their predictability provide the irony at the core of all that one can know. Humans are caught on a planet that is abandoned not only by love but by God, who has left out of frustration. Thus, Martin Amis's *Money* (1984) reinvents the modern artist as the high priest of urban melancholy. Beyond the recognition that man is making himself at the risk of losing himself, Amis vows that the loss of identity, power, success, and reason, *is* the reason for being. The making is in the losing! This is not inconsistent with other postmodernist writers who displace the process of self-making onto contextual objects, such as technology, cities, cyborgs, and space.

Toni Morrison's *Jazz* (1992) also questions whether passion has gone elsewhere. Could passion have been absorbed by the concrete cities and structures? For Morrison, the so-called human condition becomes less passionate the less and less it remembers. But literature can help to reengage people with these passions and raise them to the levels of the story, legend, or myth. Cityscapes, according to Morrison, function like cultural memory devices because they produce all of the mourning associated with remembering the lost ties and broken hopes that have filled their inner streets and alleyways. Cities are living, organic systems for cultural remembering. Cities' souls suffer too as they exude the new culture of ambiguity and ambivalence.

Conclusion

People enter into relationships with literature much as they enter into relationships with other individuals. However, the emotions that people feel while reading a literary work are often of "epic" proportions. Because literature is capable of such strong influence with regard to emotions, it would be fair to consider it comparable to a living, breathing entity. After all, it is no less capable of instructing one's passions than are those living, breathing bodies with whom one interacts on a daily basis.

See also: ARISTOTLE; DRAMA AND THEATER; FREUD, SIGMUND; PLATO; POETRY

Bibliography

Bloom, Harold. (1998). *Shakespeare: The Invention of the Human.* New York: Penguin Putnam.
Freud, Sigmund. (1961). *Civilization and Its Discontents,* tr. James Strachey, New York: W. W. Norton.
Freud, Sigmund. (1988). *Art and Literature,* tr. James Strachey, New York: Penguin.
Freud, Sigmund. (1990). *Case Histories, Vol. I,* tr. James Strachey, New York: Penguin.
Frye, Northrop. (1982). *The Great Code: The Bible and Literature.* London: Penguin.
Frye, Northrop. (1990). *Myth and Metaphor,* ed. Robert D. Denham. Charlottesville: University Press of Virginia.
O'Neill, John. (1982). *Essaying Montaigne.* London: Routledge & Kegan Paul.
O'Neill, John. (1992). *Critical Conventions: Interpretation in the Literary Arts and Sciences.* Norman: University of Oklahoma Press.
Solomon, Robert C. (1980). "Emotions and Choice." In *Explaining Emotions,* ed. Amélie Oskenberg Rorty. Berkeley: University of California Press.

Douglas Arrowsmith

LONELINESS

Loneliness is an unpleasant, distressing emotional state that arises out of dissatisfaction with the quality of one's social relationships. Lonely people feel a sense of agony, abandonment, emptiness, and anguish, and they feel misunderstood by others. Scientists define loneliness as a discrepancy between a person's *actual* and *desired* levels of social contact. When people want more quantity and quality in their social relationships than what they currently feel they have, they experience loneliness. This definition of loneliness has two important implications. First, not all people who lack social contact are lonely. Many people confuse "aloneness" with "loneliness." Some people are very comfortable being alone frequently and are therefore not lonely. Second, not all people with very large social networks are non-lonely. Some people may have a lot of friends but still be dissatisfied with the quality of these relationships and feel a profound sense of loneliness. For these people, feeling lonely can be particularly devastating since they may feel that there is no real reason for feeling lonely.

Loneliness is a social emotion. Social emotions are those emotions, such as guilt, embarrassment, and shyness, that humans experience in relation to other people. Inherently social animals, humans are predisposed to seek out companionship and form emotional connections with others. When they fail to achieve social bonding or when they find those bonds unsatisfying, they feel lonely.

Social scientists generally recognize two dimensions of loneliness: emotional loneliness and social loneliness. Emotional loneliness results from the lack of a close attachment figure, such as a romantic partner. Social loneliness results from a lack of ties to a cohesive social group, such as a group of friends or a social organization. These needs are complementary. Consequently, achieving one of these social goals will not prevent loneliness if the other is not equally satisfied. This may explain why some people with many friends (but no romantic partner) may still feel lonely and why a married person (without many other friends) may feel lonely.

Unlike related problems such as depression or social phobia, there are no recognized criteria for determining whether someone is "lonely" or not. However, many different research studies suggest that loneliness is a very common experience no matter who one is, and popular culture provides evidence of this. References to loneliness abound in the titles and lyrics of popular songs, from Roy Orbison's 1960 classic "Only the Lonely" to John Cougar Mellencamp's "Lonely Ol' Night," to more recent examples such as Anita Baker's "Lonely" and "4 Seasons of Loneliness" by Boys II Men. It is ironic that rock musician Sting often spoke of being lonely yet sang one of his band's more popular songs, "So Lonely," to thousands of adoring fans.

Demographic Features

Loneliness appears to be a universal phenomenon—status, success, and popularity do not guarantee that one will not be lonely. Although experiences may differ, people of all ages and cultures suffer from loneliness.

Sex

Research results documenting the effect of sex on loneliness are mixed. Carol Marangoni and William Ickes (1989) suggest that the mixed research results may be a reflection of willingness to report feelings of loneliness. Females will often report greater levels of loneliness when the measures explicitly refer to being lonely, whereas males tend to report higher levels of loneliness in measures that refrain from using these terms. S. Lau and Gerald Gruen (1992) suggest a stronger social stigma exists for lonely males than for lonely females.

Sex may be a moderating factor with regard to different types of loneliness. Alfons Marcoen and Mia Brumagne (1985) measured parent-related and peer-related loneliness in children and young adolescents. While no sex differences were found with respect to peer-related loneliness, boys reported more parent-related loneliness.

There is evidence that both sexes share some commonalities with respect to loneliness. John Berg and Ronald McQuinn (1989), in a study of college students, found loneliness to be significantly related to self-disclosure and network density for both men and women. However, women's loneliness was strongly related to self-disclosure, while men's loneliness was more strongly related to network size.

Age

Across the life span, people often suffer loneliness as a result of causes that reflect the different life stages. Several large-scale national surveys indicate that anywhere between 10 percent and 25 percent of the population have felt lonely during the few weeks prior to the administration of the surveys. While one might assume these figures only apply to adolescents and adults, research demonstrates that children are also afflicted. In fact, Daniel Perlman (1988) believes that transmission of loneliness from parent to child as well as problems or obstacles related to initial attachment contribute to the experience of loneliness during childhood.

Data reporting exactly which specific age groups suffer the most during childhood and adolescence are inconsistent. However, there is little dispute that adolescents report a high level of loneliness rarely achieved by other age groups in the same survey. In a survey of more than sixteen hundred adolescents, Bruce Roscoe and Grant Skomski (1989) classified approximately 20 percent of the respondents as being "lonely."

Upon reaching adulthood, factors such as marital status, marital satisfaction, and size and density of social networks appear to be related to reports of loneliness. However, again, the data are inconsistent with respect to particular age groups. In a study by Diane Barretta and her colleagues (1995) adults between thirty-one and sixty-five years of age were lonelier than those between eighteen and thirty years of age.

An examination by Tracey Revenson and Jeffrey Johnson (1984) demonstrated a significant decrease in loneliness across the life span. It is interesting to note that college students have been found to report levels of loneliness that are not significantly different from those reported by retirees. Stereotypes of lonely senior citizens apparently flourish, while research on loneliness and the elderly does not strongly support this widely held conception. Elizabeth Dugan and Vira Kivett (1994) note that the older rural adults in their sample reported experiences of loneliness that were very similar to those of the general population. Also, in addition to the studies that find a decrease in loneliness over the life span, results from numerous studies attest to the non-age-related character of loneliness. Perlman (1988) argues that many of the "causes" of loneliness in the elderly are not necessarily age-specific, supporting the theory that the pairing of old age and loneliness is illusory.

Culture

Scientific studies of loneliness have been conducted in countries such as England, Fiji, Japan, New Zealand, Puerto Rico, Sweden, and the United States among others. These studies suggest not only that loneliness is common in many cultures but that members of some cultures experience more loneliness than do Americans. For example, Warren Jones and his colleagues (1985) administered a loneliness survey to a large sample of college students in Puerto Rico and the United States. The results indicated that the Puerto Rican students were more lonely than the American students.

Although loneliness is fairly common in most cultures, what may differ from culture to culture are the features that are associated with loneliness. Jones and

---

Edwin Arlington Robinson's poem "Mr. Flood's Party" (1921) pictures Old Eben Flood walking home alone, a little tipsy but in a good mood. He has outlived all of his friends and family, so he parties by himself, drinking from his jug and talking to himself to keep himself company. Underneath the surface, though, Old Eben is radically alone.

his colleagues (1985) found that loneliness was negatively associated with self-disclosures among Americans but not among Puerto Ricans. Similarly, Earl Ginter and his colleagues (1994) found that loneliness was more strongly associated with anxiety in an Asian culture of Pacific Islanders, whereas it was largely unrelated to anxiety among a group of Caucasian or East Indian Pacific Islanders.

Linda Wood (1986) determined that different cultures sometimes use different linguistic devices to communicate about loneliness, reflecting a different cultural "construction" of the loneliness experience. For example, Germans use different words for the process (*Vereinsaman*, "to become lonely") and the state (*Einsamkeit*, "loneliness"). These different linguistic practices may reflect a more differentiated view of loneliness among Germans that English speakers lack.

Causes of Loneliness

Various factors may cause loneliness. These causes include situational factors as well as individual characteristics.

Events and Situational Factors

Events or situations that take people away from those with whom they have a close relationship are obvious causes of loneliness. Many events, such as moving to a new city or school, the death of a spouse or friend, the break-up of a romantic relationship, or starting a new job, can be detrimental to the quality of people's social relationships, resulting in loneliness.

Jones and his colleagues (1990) argue that such events trigger loneliness because of four major reasons. First, they are simultaneously unpleasant and difficult to control. Second, they occur infrequently, making it difficult to develop and practice effective coping skills. Third, they often prompt coping strategies, such as watching television, that do not involve other people. Fourth, they increase feelings of dissimilarity with others. These factors work together to intensify feelings of loneliness when such events threaten close relationships.

How much and for how long people experience loneliness in response to specific events depends in large part on their coping skills. Some people respond to such events by increasing their sociability and seeking out other people. Other people cope with emotional distress by withdrawing from society and watching television, listening to the radio, or consuming alcohol or drugs. These coping mechanisms may bring temporary relief and distraction from the anguish of loneliness, but they do little to reduce the problem in the long run. Coping methods that involve seeking out others and spending time in places where there will be opportunities to interact with others seem to be the most effective at reducing loneliness caused by environmental and situational stresses.

Social Skills Deficits

Social skills involve the ability and motivation to communicate with others in a way that is appropriate and effective. Poor social skills are a problem for many people who are lonely. Jones, Steven Hobbs, and Don Hockenbury (1982) were among the first to develop and test the hypothesis that lonely people exhibit deficits in social skills. They found that lonely people, compared to non-lonely people, made fewer partner references, asked fewer questions, and emitted fewer statements indicating partner attention. Jones and his colleagues concluded that one area of social skills in which lonely people experience particular difficulty is partner attention. Lonely people fail to send messages of involvement or concern to their interaction partners. This lack of partner attention may be symptomatic of an inhibited sociability.

Ami Rokach and Heather Brock (1998) note that instead of feeling motivated to initiate interactions with others, many lonely people actually shrink inside themselves as a means of self-preservation against further pain caused by failed attempts to connect with others. Lau and Gruen (1992) found that lonely people are condemned on numerous psychological and interpersonal measures, which would naturally decrease their chances of escaping loneliness. In addition, Elaine Hatfield and her colleagues (1994) claim that loneliness may actually breed a kind of "emotional contagion" between lonely people and those they interact with, causing others to retreat from the lonely individuals.

Numerous studies indicate that lonely people consistently describe their social skills more negatively than non-lonely people. Furthermore, observers appear to agree with these negative assessments, whether they are third-party observers to lonely people's conversations, conversational partners of lonely people, or even teachers of lonely students.

Behaviorally, lonely people talk less in conversations with strangers and roommates, engage in less self-disclosure with opposite-sex partners, and emit fewer back-channels (e.g., "mm-hmm," "yeah," "I see") and interruptions in conversations. In laboratory conversations, lonely subjects typically rate themselves and are rated by others to be less involved in the conversation than non-lonely subjects. Research by Mark Leary and his colleagues (1986) suggests that it is precisely these behaviors that handicap the lonely person because these behaviors elicit boredom, and typically rejection, from fellow subjects. This general lack of involvement in conversations illustrates an interesting

Observing other individuals who have obviously established close relationships and are involved in shared activities can lead to feelings of social isolation and loneliness. (Corbis/Todd Gipstein)

paradox—lonely people, by definition, desire more intimate and meaningful contact with others, but they send messages of disinterest and noninvolvement. Presumably, these messages express exactly the opposite of what the lonely person wants.

Maladaptive Cognitions

Considerable attention has been given to problematic cognitions that are strongly linked to loneliness. Two dominant themes in this area of research have been negative attributional styles and negative expectations and evaluations of others.

Attributions are explanations about why things happen. People may share these attributions with others or keep them to themselves. It is clear that most lonely people try to understand *why* they are lonely and generate attributions for their lonely state. For example, Letitia Peplau and her colleagues (1979) asked lonely students to explain the causes of their loneliness. Their generated attributions included explanations such as "My not trying hard enough to meet someone," "My being too shy," "My not knowing what to do to start a relationship," "Other people don't try to make friends," and "My personality." Many of these attributions have a self-blaming quality. Lonely students who made self-blaming attributions were more likely to be depressed than those who attributed their feelings of loneliness to more temporary, situational factors.

One incongruity associated with loneliness is the tendency to blame the self for being lonely (e.g., "I am no fun to be with.") while considering the external events that contribute to loneliness (e.g., "There are no opportunities to meet people my age.") to be outside of one's control. Lonely people tend to attribute the events that they feel caused their loneliness to uncontrollable and unpredictable factors. This attributional tendency further fuels feelings of hopelessness and helplessness.

An explanation for lonely people's diminished sociability and social interest, despite the longing for more intimate contact, may come from their negative expectations and evaluations of other people. Numerous studies reveal that lonely people often hold negative views of other people. Lonely people make negative ratings of strangers, whom they have just interacted with, as well as their well-known friends. Lonely subjects also make more negative attributions about the motives of others in interpersonal situations and exhibit very little trust in other people, even their closest peers. Some people have hypothesized that the lack of trust in others serves to rationalize the lonely person's failure to develop rewarding relationships.

Counterbalancing their negative evaluations of others, lonely people also expect others to hold negative opinions about them. When lonely people are asked to predict how others will react to them, they often assume that others will dislike them. This feeling, along with their generally negative view of others, may partially explain why lonely people send a message of detachment and noninvolvement during social interactions with others. If one holds a negative view toward others and expects others to hold a negative view toward the self, it stands to reason that such a person would be avoidant, detached, and somewhat withdrawn in social interactions. Moreover, James Check and his colleagues (1985) provide evidence that lonely people may actually express more hostility and engage in more aggressive behavior toward others than nonlonely people.

It is unfortunately the case that lonely people are trapped in an emotional and cognitive dilemma—they want more intimacy and more meaningful relationships, but they continue to hold negative views of themselves and expect others to do the same. In conversations, lonely people behave in a way, perhaps as a result of deficient social skills, that virtually ensures negative social outcomes.

Dysfunctional Family Relations

Many people would think that family interactions and relationships help prevent loneliness. That is, those who have close, satisfying relationships with parents or those who are married with a spouse to turn to for social support should experience less loneliness. However, this does not appear to be the case.

Quality relationships with family members do little to prevent or alleviate the experience of loneliness. In fact, Jones and Teri Moore (1990) found that the more social support students had from their family, the *more* lonely they were. While a person's loneliness may cause family social support to increase, it is clear that these types of relationships do little to help the situation. An intriguing study of elderly women further explains why seemingly warm and positive family relationships can actually be associated with *increased* loneliness as an adult. Lars Andersson and his colleagues (1990) obtained retrospective reports of parent-child relationships from a large sample of elderly women who were between seventy and ninety years of age. Children who had an excessively close, warm, nurturing relationship with at least one parent were significantly *more* lonely as elderly adults than those who were in a control group. Andersson and his colleagues concluded that the effects of overinvolvement from parents can be as harmful as underinvolvement or neglect when it comes to producing lonely children. This is due in part to the fact that parental overinvolvement can create a sense of narcissism in the child.

Another reason that family relationships and involvement may fail to buffer against loneliness is that they are relationships of obligation. Consequently, lonely people may find little solace in social support from people whom they feel are obligated to offer it. By the time people reach adolescence, they are specifically looking for close social contacts with individuals who are not family members, such as a romantic partner or a best friend.

Some scientific evidence indicates that loneliness may run in the family. Patricia Henwood and Cecilia Solano (1994) surveyed a sample of first-grade children and their parents and found that children's loneliness was significantly correlated with that of their mothers. In other words, the more lonely the mother was, the more lonely the child was. The exact cause for this correlation is unknown.

In contrast to the evidence on parent-child relationships, relationships with siblings may be more helpful in preventing loneliness. Interactions with siblings are typically negatively associated with the experience of loneliness among young people. James Ponzetti and Camilla James (1997) have found that the closer young people are to their siblings, the less loneliness they experience. However, when these sibling relationships turn sour and conflict ensues, loneliness becomes worse. Sibling relationships can often provide the kind of companionship with an age-matched peer that many young people (and even some older people) find desirable. This may explain why good sibling relationships are more effective at preventing loneliness than parent-child relationships.

While it is the case that unmarried people report higher levels of loneliness than do married people, some individuals feel very lonely despite being married. A study conducted by Alton Barbour (1993) indicated that 20 percent of the wives and 24 percent of the husbands studied were significantly lonely. Lars Tornstam's (1992) study in Denmark revealed that 40 percent of the married participants felt lonely often or sometimes. People commonly think that marriage protects people from feeling lonely because there is always a potential companion around. Obviously, for some married people this is not the case.

Many people enter into marriage with unrealistic expectations for happiness, sociability, and intimacy. People often stay in unsatisfying marriages because of external barriers to marital dissolution (e.g., children, religious beliefs, and finances). This experience of dissatisfaction fuels a cascade of negative emotions that include loneliness and alienation. Feeling loneliness within the context of a marriage is particularly devastating. Rokach and Brock (1997, p. 294) point out that "being lonely is painful, but being married and lonely can be excruciating. Being part of a union that is exalted and revered . . . as perhaps the most intimate of human connections engenders almost impossible expectations of closeness and intimacy that become searingly poignant when unfulfilled."

Related Problems

Correlations between depression and loneliness are very strong, indicating that many people who are lonely are also depressed and vice versa. A number of studies have attempted to explore the precise nature of the relationship between depression and loneliness. At least two such studies, conducted by Diane Brage and William Meredith (1994) and Alexander Rich and Martha Scovel (1987), indicate that loneliness is a causal factor in depression. There is reason to believe that the strong associations between depression and loneliness may be due to the two problems sharing a common origin. The events in life that often make people depressed (e.g., the death of a spouse or close friend, the loss of a job) often make people lonely as well. Evidence, however, indicates that these two emotional states are still distinct problems—one can be depressed and not lonely, or one can be lonely but not depressed.

Another problem that is strongly associated with loneliness is social anxiety. Unlike its relationship with depression, loneliness is commonly thought to be the result, not the cause, of the experience of social anxiety. People who experience social anxiety are concerned that the image they present to the public falls below the image that they would like to convey. As a result, many people with social anxiety simply avoid contact with other people. In so doing, they believe they are avoiding creating the negative impression in others that they fear. As a result, they fail to make the kind of close social contacts that most humans desire, leading to loneliness. This phenomenon creates a trap for many socially anxious people. The social isolation and withdrawal that they employ to avoid public embarrassment simultaneously fuels their loneliness. Although there are many lonely people who are not socially anxious, many who are socially anxious suffer from loneliness.

Loneliness is frequently associated with feelings of low self-esteem. There are several reasons why these two feelings may go hand in hand. First, people with low self-esteem may deem themselves unworthy of the attention and affection of others. Consequently, they may be less willing to put themselves in situations in which they can interact with others and less willing to invest in the effort of trying to develop rewarding relationships with others. Second, people who are lonely, particularly for a long duration, may begin to question their self-worth. Many lonely people tend to blame themselves for things that do not go well in their lives. It is easy to see how this style of thinking about the self could deteriorate one's self-esteem.

See also: ABANDONMENT; ANXIETY; ATTACHMENT; ATTRIBUTION; BOREDOM; GENDER AND EMOTIONS; GRIEF; HOPELESSNESS; HUMAN DEVELOPMENT; PAIN; RELATIONSHIPS; SADNESS; SELF-ESTEEM

Bibliography

Andersson, Lars; Mullins, Larry C.; and Johnson, D. Paul. (1990). "Parental Intrusion Versus Social Isolation: A Dichotomous View of the Sources of Loneliness." In *Loneliness: Theory, Research, and Applications*, ed. Mohammadreza Hojat and Rick Crandall. Newbury Park, CA: Sage Publications.

Barbour, Alton. (1993). "Research Report: Dyadic Loneliness in Marriage." *Journal of Group Psychotherapy, Psychodrama, and Sociometry* 46:70–72.

Barretta, Diane; Dantzler, Debbie; and Kayson, Wesley. (1995). "Factors Related to Loneliness." *Psychological Reports* 76:827–830.

Berg, John H., and McQuinn, Ronald D. (1989). "Loneliness and Aspects of Social Support Networks." *Journal of Social and Personal Relationships* 6:359–372.

Brage, Diane, and Meredith, William. (1994). "A Causal Model of Adolescent Depression." *Journal of Psychology* 128:455–468.

Check, James V. P.; Perlman, Daniel; and Malamuth, Neil M. (1985). "Loneliness and Aggressive Behaviour." *Journal of Social and Personal Relationships* 2:243–252.

Dugan, Elizabeth, and Kivett, Vira R. (1994). "The Importance of Emotional and Social Isolation to Loneliness among Very Old Rural Adults." *Gerontologist* 34:340–346.

Ginter, Earl J.; Glauder, Ann; and Richmond, Bert O. (1994). "Loneliness, Social Support, and Anxiety among Two South Pacific Cultures." *Psychological Reports* 74:875–879.

Hatfield, Elaine; Cacioppo, John T.; and Rapson, Richard L. (1994). *Emotional Contagion*. New York: Cambridge University Press.

Henwood, Patricia G., and Solano, Cecilia H. (1994). "Loneliness in Young Children and Their Parents." *Journal of Genetic Psychology* 155:35–45.

Jones, Warren H.; Carpenter, Bruce N.; and Quintana, Diana. (1985). "Personality and Interpersonal Predictors of Loneliness in Two Cultures." *Journal of Personality and Social Psychology* 48:1503–1511.

Jones, Warren H.; Hobbs, Steven A.; and Hockenbury, Don. (1982). "Loneliness and Social Skill Deficits." *Journal of Personality and Social Psychology* 42:682–689.

Jones, Warren H., and Moore, Teri L. (1990). "Loneliness and Social Support." In *Loneliness: Theory, Research, and Applications*, ed. Mohammadreza Hojat and Rick Crandall. Newbury Park, CA: Sage Publications.

> *T. S. Eliot's "Lovesong of J. Alfred Prufrock" (1917) finds the lonely and timid Prufrock wondering if he dare talk to the women who "come and go"—apparently confident in their conversation about Michaelangelo. Prufrock notices the lonely men in shirtsleeves who lean out of windows, and when he walks on the beach and imagines mermaids are singing to each other, he assumes they do not sing to him. He feels afraid and foolish, unable to overcome his shyness.*

Jones, Warren H.; Rose, Jayne; and Russell, Daniel W. (1990). "Loneliness and Social Anxiety." In *Handbook of Social and Evaluation Anxiety*, ed. Harold Leitenberg. New York: Plenum.

Lau, S., and Gruen, Gerald E. (1992). "The Social Stigma of Loneliness: Effect of Target Person's and Perceiver's Sex." *Personality and Social Psychology Bulletin* 18:182–189.

Leary, Mark R.; Rogers, Patricia A.; Canfield, Robert W.; and Coe, Celine. (1986). "Boredom in Interpersonal Encounters: Antecedents, and Social Implications." *Journal of Personality and Social Psychology* 51:968–975.

Marcoen, Alfons, and Brumagne, Mia. (1985). "Loneliness among Children and Young Adolescents." *Developmental Psychology* 21:1025–1031.

Marangoni, Carol, and Ickes, William. (1989). "Loneliness: A Theoretical Review with Implications for Measurement." *Journal of Social and Personal Relationships* 6:93–128.

Pearl, Tracy; Klopf, Donald W.; and Ishii, Satoshi. (1990). "Loneliness among Japanese and American College Students." *Psychological Reports* 67:49–50.

Peplau, Letitia Anne; Russell, Dan; and Heim, Margaret. (1979). "The Experience of Loneliness." In *New Approaches to Social Problems*, ed. Irene Hanson Frieze, Daniel Bar-Tal, and John S. Caroll. San Francisco: Josey-Bass.

Perlman, Daniel. (1988). "Loneliness: A Life-Span, Family Perspective." In *Families and Social Networks*, ed. Robert M. Milardo. Beverly Hills, CA: Sage Publications.

Ponzetti, James J., and James, Camilla M. (1997). "Loneliness and Sibling Relationships." *Journal of Social Behavior and Personality* 12:103–112.

Revenson, Tracey A., and Johnson, Jeffrey L. (1984). "Social and Demographic Correlates of Loneliness in Late Life." *American Journal of Community Psychology* 12:71–85.

Rich, Alexander R., and Scovel, Martha. (1987). "Causes of Depression in College Students: A Cross-Lagged Panel Correlation Analysis." *Psychological Reports* 60:27–30.

Rokach, Ami, and Brock, Heather. (1997). "Loneliness and the Effects of Life Changes." *Journal of Psychology* 131:284–298.

Rokach, Ami, and Brock, Heather. (1998). "Coping with Loneliness." *Journal of Psychology* 132:107–127.

Roscoe, Bruce, and Skomski, Grant G. (1989). "Loneliness among Late Adolescents." *Adolescence* 96:947–955.

Segrin, Chris. (1993). "Social Skills Deficits and Psychosocial Problems: Antecedent, Concomitant, or Consequent?" *Journal of Social and Clinical Psychology* 12:336–353.

Segrin, Chris, and Kinney, Terry. (1995). "Social Skills Deficits among the Socially Anxious: Loneliness and Rejection from Others." *Motivation and Emotion* 19:1–24.

Tornstam, Lars. (1992). "Loneliness in Marriage." *Journal of Social and Personal Relationships* 9:197–217.

Weiss, Robert S. (1973). *Loneliness: The Experience of Emotional and Social Isolation*. Cambridge, MA: Massachusetts Institute of Technology Press.

Wood, Linda. (1986). "Loneliness." In *The Social Construction of Emotions*, ed. Rom Harre. New York: Basil Blackwell.

Chris Segrin
Lisa E. Allspach

LOVE

The term *love* is defined in the third edition of *Webster's New World College Dictionary* (1997, p. 801) as "a deep and tender feeling of affection for or attachment or devotion to a person or persons . . . a strong, usually passionate, affection of one person for another, based in part on sexual attraction . . . sexual passion . . . sexual intercourse." This definition can serve as a start for a psychological theory of love but not as an end because psychologists seek an understanding that goes beyond a simple dictionary definition. But there is one contrast in this dictionary definition that will express itself in psychologists' conceptualizations as well: the contrast between the tender and affectionate aspects of love on the one hand and the passionate and explosive aspects of love on the other.

Clinical Theories of Love

Psychologists have proposed a number of different clinical theories of love. The fact that there are a number of such theories attests to the importance psychologists place on love, and the diversity of the definitions attests to the range of views psychologists hold about this most fundamental of human emotions. Most clinical theories of love are based on experience of therapists with patients. For this reason, there is more of a tendency for clinicians to view love as an overcoming of some failure or obstacle.

Psychodynamic Viewpoints

Most familiar to the general reader, perhaps, are the psychodynamic views, including the views of Sigmund Freud and the neo-Freudians who followed him. Freud proposed in 1922 that love could be viewed in terms of sublimated sexuality. Because people cannot express love physically whenever and to whomever they want, individuals must devise ways of compensating. Love is one such way. It is a societally acceptable way of channeling sexual impulses. Theodore Reik suggested in 1944 that love arises out of dissatisfaction with oneself and one's lot in life. People fall in love because they feel inadequate and somewhat hopeless. Love offers them a hope of salvation. Melanie Klein in 1953 proposed a related view, according to which love arises from one's dependency on others and for the satisfaction of one's needs.

The psychoanalytic definitions of love seem to deal more with its passionate, fiery, and explosive side, as expressed in the above dictionary definition. More recently, in 1979, Dorothy Tennov introduced the concept of *limerence*, a passionate kind of love characterized by intrusive cognitive activity, acute longing for another, and intense dependency on that other. This is the kind of love that Stanton Peele and Archie Brodsky suggested in 1976 is addictive and that Denis de Rougemont described in 1940 as seeming to require obstacles and impediments for its survival. Indeed, Kenneth Livingston suggested in 1980 that love is a process of uncertainty reduction: Once the uncertainties are removed and there are no obstacles to the consummation of love, love seems to depart.

The idea of love's being explosive and full of fire is not limited to psychological theorizing. In the Persian story of Layla and Manjun, a chieftain's son goes mad with love for Layla, his schoolmate, earning himself the name Manjun, meaning "madman." He runs away from civilization, goes naked, and eats only grass. He explains his strange behavior by saying that love is his fire and his essence. Manjun's description of love as fire is not uncommon in love stories. In Indian mythology, the god of love, Kama, is often identified with the god of fire, Agni. Fire is an appropriate metaphor for love because both of them spread quickly and are potentially destructive, as is illustrated in the West African story of "The Fire of Life," in which a girl walks into a forbidden sacred bush and subsequently falls in love with a young man. Her punishment is to be thrown into a fire. Obstacles play a major role in literature as well. In the myth of Pyramus and Thisbe, continued in *Romeo and Juliet* and *West Side Story*, the lovers are forbidden by their parents and by society in general even to see each other. Their love survives despite—or perhaps because of—these obstacles. Edith Hamilton (1942) notes in the case of Pyramus and Thisbe that love cannot be forbidden. Or as she puts it in another way, the more the flame is covered up, the hotter it burns.

Humanistic Viewpoints

Humanistic psychologists attempted to put a more positive face on love. Abraham Maslow suggested in 1954 that the psychoanalytic characterization applies only to what he termed *deficiency love* (d-love), which arises from needs for security and belongingness. Indeed, the term *deficiency* provides an apt characterization of most of these theories, in that they view love as arising from some lack or a feeling of something missing within the person who is experiencing love. But Maslow also proposed the concept of *being love* (b-love), which arises out of a person's higher level emotional needs, especially the desire for self-actualization and actualization of another. Similarly, Eric Fromm suggested in 1955 that love could be viewed as arising out of care, responsibility, respect, and knowledge of another.

The more spiritual notion of love that derives from the humanistic standpoint can be found in literature as well, as discussed by Robert J. Sternberg in *Cupid's Arrow* (1998). True love is typically viewed in the great love stories as being spiritual, which puts it beyond the realm of the mundane and that which can be bought. The body is unimportant: True lovers may never even have touched, as in the story of Layla and Manjun. In the Chinese story of "The Student Lovers," Yingtai dis-

Pyramus and Thisbe, as represented in this painting by Jan Gossaert (also known as Jan Mabuse), were an ill-fated pair of Babylonian lovers. Thisbe was supposed to meet Pyramus by the mulberry tree near the tomb of Ninus, but before they could meet, she was scared away by a lion. When Pyramus arrived, he found a veil that had been dropped by Thisbe and stained with blood by the lion. Assuming that the lion had eaten Thisbe, Pyramus committed suicide. When Thisbe returned and found her lover dead, she stabbed herself. (Corbis/Francis G. Mayer)

guises herself as a boy in order to be able to go to school. She meets a boy named Shanbo, and they become close friends and study partners. Yingtai falls in love with Shanbo but cannot reveal her disguise. Her parents summon her home and inform her that she is betrothed to someone else. Meanwhile, Shanbo learns that Yingtai is a girl and dies of grief when he realizes that he cannot marry her. She visits the grave on her wedding day and it opens to receive her. According to the legend, one can still see two butterflies on the tomb, even today. The spiritual union of lovers can make separation and even death bearable. In the Indian play *Shakuntala*, Shakuntala's lover, King Dushyanta, says upon leaving her that it is his body that leaves, not he. His body moves away, but not his mind.

Cognitive Viewpoints

Cognitive viewpoints within the clinical tradition stress the role of the mind (cognition) in love. For example, Scott Peck suggested in 1978 that love should be viewed largely as a kind of decision and then a commitment to that decision. After the initial strong physical attraction of a romance, a couple must settle down to the day-to-day living that makes them a team. When hard times come, it is the commitment to the decision to love that gets the couple through.

Ellen Berscheid and Elaine Walster (now Hatfield) also emphasized the role of cognition in a theory of love they proposed in 1974. However, their theory differed from Peck's and drew on a theory of emotion earlier proposed by Stanley Schachter and Jerome Singer (1962). According to Walster and Berscheid's two-component theory of love, people should be vulnerable to experiencing love whenever they are intensely aroused physiologically. People may then label this arousal in a number of ways. One of the possible ways of labeling it is as love. Thus, according to this theory, love is the cognitive labeling of arousal as love.

Social-Psychological Theories of Love

The theory of Walster and Berscheid is intermediate between clinical and social-psychological theories of love. Social-psychological theories of love differ from clinical theories roughly in three ways. First, their theoretical base is in social rather than clinical psychology. Second, they tend to have been derived from typical everyday populations rather than from clinical populations. Third, they generally have been subjected to somewhat more stringent empirical tests than is the case for clinical theories.

The Triangular Theory of Love

When the three traditions in clinical psychology described above are compared, each seems to emphasize a somewhat different aspect of love. The psychodynamic tradition emphasizes the passionate aspect of love, the humanistic tradition emphasizes the intimate aspect of love, and the cognitive tradition (at least in Peck's theory) emphasizes the commitment aspect of love. A theory that combines these three aspects of love into a single theory is the triangular theory of love proposed by Sternberg in 1986.

The triangular theory of love holds that love can be understood in terms of three components that can be viewed as the vertices of a triangle: intimacy, passion, and commitment. To better understand the triangle of love, one must know something of each vertex. The intimacy component refers to those feelings in a relationship that promote closeness, bondedness, and connectedness. The passion component of love consists of those motivational and other sources of arousal that lead to the experience of passion. It includes what Elaine and William Walster referred to in 1981 as a state of intense longing for union with the other individual. In a passionate loving relationship, sexual and related motivational needs may well predominate in one's subjective experience. The decision/commitment component of love consists of two aspects, a short-term one, which is the decision to love another person, and a long-term one, which is the commitment to maintain that love over time.

Although one can speak of the three components of love separately, they interact, and in practice, it may be quite difficult to separate them. These components of love and their interrelations can be better understood by considering the kinds of love to which they may give rise when in different combinations. There are eight subsets of components of love: nonlove, liking, infatuated love, empty love, romantic love, companionate love, fatuous love, and consummate love. Each subset differs in the kind of loving experience to which it gives rise. Consider the limiting cases.

Nonlove refers to the absence of all three components of love. Nonlove characterizes the large majority of personal relationships, which are simply casual interactions that do not involve love at all.

Liking results when one experiences the intimacy component of love without the passion and decision/commitment ones. In liking, one feels closeness, bondedness, and warmth toward another without feeling intense passion or long-term commitment.

Infatuated love is love at first sight. Infatuated love, or simply, infatuation, results from experiencing passionate arousal in the absence of the intimacy and decision/commitment components of love. Infatuations can arise almost instantaneously and dissipate as quickly under the right circumstances.

In Love in the Time of Cholera *(1988), by Gabriel Garcia Marquez, the love of Florentino Ariza and Fermina Daza lasts for more than fifty years even though she is married to Dr. Juvenal Urbino for almost all of that time. After Juvenal dies, Florentino and Fermina, both now in their seventies, resume the passionate love affair that they had left off half a century before.*

Empty love emanates from the decision that one loves another and is committed to that love in the absence of both the intimacy and passion components of love. It is the kind of love that one sometimes finds in stagnant relationships that have been going on for years but that have lost the mutual emotional involvement and physical attraction that once characterized them. In societies with matchmakers, empty love may precede rather than follow other kinds of love.

Romantic love derives from a combination of the intimacy and passion components of love. In essence, it is liking with an added element, namely, the arousal brought about by physical attraction and its concomitants. According to this view, then, romantic lovers are bonded emotionally as well as being drawn physically to each other.

Companionate love evolves from a combination of the intimacy and decision/commitment components of love. It is essentially a long-term, committed friendship, the kind that frequently occurs in marriages in which the physical attraction (a major source of passion) has died down.

Fatuous love results from the combination of the passion and decision/commitment components in the absence of the intimacy component. It is the kind of love sometimes associated with Hollywood and with whirlwind courtships. It is fatuous in the sense that a commitment is made on the basis of passion without the stabilizing element of intimate involvement. Although the passion component can develop almost instantaneously, the intimacy component cannot; hence, relationships based on fatuous love are at risk for termination and, in the case of shotgun marriages, for divorce.

Consummate, or complete, love results from the combination of the three components. It is the kind of love that many people strive for, especially in romantic relationships. Attaining consummate love can be analogous to meeting one's target in a weight-reduction program: Reaching the goal is often easier than maintaining it. The attainment of consummate love is no guarantee that it will last.

The triangular theory predicts that (a) intimacy, passion, and commitment can be measured somewhat distinctly, (b) that the presence of each of these components should be associated with happiness in close relationships, and (c) that couples will be more satisfied with their close relationships to the extent that their triangles are congruent—that is, they have the same amounts (sizes of triangles) and balance (shapes of triangles) in their loving relationship.

The theory published by Walster and Walster in 1981 contained two of the seven kinds of love proposed by the triangular theory. Their theory distinguishes between passionate and companionate love, the former ignited more by what the triangular theory refers to as passion and the latter fueled more by what the triangular theory refers to as intimacy. Therefore, this theory and the triangular one are largely compatible.

Colors of Love

John Alan Lee proposed a theory of "colors of love" in 1977. According to this theory, which has been rather extensively tested by Clyde and Susan Hendrick (1986), love can be characterized by the following six major styles:

1. eros, characterized by physicality as well as a possible sense of the exotic, where the lover finds a beloved whose physical presentation of self embodies an image already held in the mind of the lover,
2. ludus, referring to play-like or game-like love (based on the use of the term by Ovid),
3. storge, characterized by slowly developing affection and companionship,
4. mania, characterized by obsession, jealousy, and great emotional intensity,
5. agape, a form of altruistic love found when the lover views it as his or her duty to love without expectation of reciprocation, and
6. pragma, a practical style of love involving conscious consideration of the demographic and other objective characteristics of the loved one.

The social-psychological theories of love address many questions about the structure of love, but they seem to have less to say about how love develops.

Learning Theories of Love

Strictly speaking, learning theories have been applied primarily to interpersonal attraction (i.e., an individual's tendency or predisposition to evaluate another person or symbol of that person in a positive way) rather than to love. However, because they have had an important effect on the field of love (even though they do not deal directly with it) and because they can easily be extended to loving relationships, these theories do merit at least a brief consideration.

Bernice and Albert Lott were among the first to apply such a framework, first in 1968 and then again in 1974. They suggested that people are more attracted to those who reward (reinforce) them more. Individuals tend to be less attracted to people who punish them. Attraction will result when one experiences reward in the presence of a person. Thus, an individual can come to be attracted to someone not just because that person directly reinforces him or her, but because the individual has experienced reinforcement in the presence of that other person. An extrapolation of this theory would be that individuals come to love those who reinforce them.

Several other versions of learning-type theories have been applied to understanding attraction. For example, equity theory, which shares elements of both learning and social-psychological theories, is associated primarily with Hatfield, Walster, and Berscheid. It posits, first, that people try to maximize their outcomes (i.e., the rewards minus the punishments received). Second, when one finds oneself in an inequitable relationship (i.e., one is receiving rewards and punishments incommensurable with those received by the partner), one becomes distressed, the amount of distress being proportional to the inequity experienced. Finally, one will attempt to eliminate that distress by restoring equity to the relationship—the greater the experienced inequity, the greater the effort to restore equity.

Developmental Theories of Love

Developmental theories of love provide a way of understanding how love develops over time. Development can refer either to how love has evolved over evolutionary time or to how love evolves over the course of a single lifetime. These theories differ from the theories considered so far in their greater emphasis on development as an ongoing process, whether over the time course of evolution or of the life span of a single individual.

Evolutionary Theories of Love

Evolutionary theories of love have been proposed by David Buss, Glenn Wilson, and others. Most of these theories, which are from the 1980s and 1990s, correspond to the formation of a new field of psychology sometimes referred to as evolutionary psychology.

According to the theory proposed by Wilson, adult love is an outgrowth of at least three main instincts. The first instinct is the need of the infant to seek protection through its parents or substitutes for its parents. The evolutionary function of attachment is primarily protection from predators. People thus tend to seek attachments most when they are somehow threatened from the outside. The second basic instinct is in some respects the flip side of the coin, the parental protection instinct. People seek not only to be protected by their lovers but to protect them as well. Thus, Wilson argued, men often are attracted to women who in certain ways resemble infants, such as having big eyes and soft skin. They describe their lovers as cute and cuddly, use diminutive nicknames, and often indulge in baby talk when becoming affectionate.

Women often enjoy the little-boy aspects of their boyfriends and husbands and use diminutive nicknames as well. The evolutionary function is the protection that one gives to the other and, thereby, to the child of any pair relationship, who will need the other as a parent. The third kind of instinct is sexual. Wilson suggested that sexual imprinting develops around the age of three or four years of age and that sexual orientation arises at that time.

Wilson and Buss believe that men tend to form short-term sexual liaisons more readily than women because they can afford to be less selective in their choice of sexual partners. In particular, men can rather easily spread their genes through frequent sexual liaisons and can continue to do so throughout much of their adult life. Women tend to be more selective because they have more limited opportunities to spread their genes. They ovulate once a month (and only prior to menopause) and can be impregnated only once every year or so, whereas there is almost no limit to the number of women that a man can impregnate, even within a short time span. For women, given their more limited opportunities, their best bet in terms of having the best possible children—genetically—is to be careful about their choice of men to mate with and about when to mate. Women thus tend to be selective and to seek men who have more resources and who tend to be older.

Buss has suggested eight evolutionary-based goals of acts of love, all leading to increased reproductive success. They include resource display, exclusivity, mutual support and protection, commitment and marriage, sexual feelings, reproduction, resource sharing, and parental investment. Although Buss's and Wilson's evolutionary theories might seem untestable, in fact, they are not. In 1994, Buss reported data from a multitude of cultures suggesting similar patterns in relationships across cultures, all of which are predicted by evolutionary theory (such as the preference of men for younger women and of women for older men).

Attachment Theory

Evolutionary theorists link love to attachment, and attachment theorists do so as well, although usually concentrating on the development of love over the span of the lifetime rather than over the span of evolutionary time. Since the mid-1980s, Phillip Shaver and Cindy Hazan (1993) have elaborated upon an attachment view of love that borrows concepts of attachment from the work of developmental psychologists such as John Bowlby (1988) and Mary Ainsworth (1989).

Ainsworth observed that infants, when separated from their mothers and placed in a strange situation with someone unknown to them, tended to react in one of three ways. Secure infants could tolerate brief separations and then would be happy when the mother came back; they seemed to have confidence that their mother would in fact come back. Avoidant infants seemed to be relatively detached upon their mother's return; they seemed more distant from their mothers and less trusting of them. Anxious-ambivalent or resistant infants had great difficulty tolerating the separation and would cling to the mother upon her return, at the same time that they would show ambivalence toward her. Attachment styles are powerful not only within a lifetime but across generations. Research has suggested that attachment styles tend to cross over three generations—from grandmothers to infants—and that they tend to be stable through the life span.

According to the attachment theory of love, lovers in close relationships (and other relationships as well) tend to have one of three different styles in a relationship: secure, avoidant, or anxious-ambivalent. A person's style is a matter of individual differences and derives in part from the kind of attachment one has had to one's mother when young.

Secure lovers find it relatively easy to get close to and achieve intimacy with others. These people can be comfortable in depending on others and in having others depend on them. They do not worry about being abandoned or about someone's getting too close to them. Intimacy is easy for these lovers.

Avoidant lovers are uncomfortable being close to or intimate with others. They find it difficult to trust others completely and to allow themselves to depend on others. They get uncomfortable when anyone gets too close and often find that their partners in love want to become more intimate than they find comfortable. Intimacy is difficult for these lovers. It now appears that there are actually two kinds of avoidant lovers. One kind is fearful, afraid of getting close to and feeling intimacy toward others. The other kind is dismissive, simply preferring to keep an arm's length from others. These lovers reject intimacy.

Anxious-ambivalent (resistant) lovers find that others are reluctant to get as close as the lovers would like. They often worry that their partners do not really love them or want to stay with them. They want to merge completely with another person—a desire that sometimes scares others away. The level of intimacy they have never seems to be enough.

Attachment theory is probably the most widely researched topic in the study of love today. There is extensive evidence for the validity of the theory and for its applicability in a variety of kinds of relationships. At the same time, attachment is currently being viewed by many in the field not so much as a trait but as a person-situation interaction. One may have a tendency toward more than one attachment style, depending upon the person one is with and the circumstances under which the relationship occurs. This more flexible form of the theory seems to hold more promise than a rigid form in which people have to be classified as falling strictly into one category or another.

Love As a Story

A more recent developmental view was proposed by Sternberg in 1998. According to this point of view, love is a story and individuals are the authors. Love stories have a beginning, a middle, and often, an ending. The ending is sometimes predicted at the beginning of the relationship, although the two partners may not predict the same ending because they are viewing the relationship in terms of different stories. Thus, partners' stories may or may not coincide. These stories are constantly being written, revised, and rewritten, even after the fact. As a result, the story one hears about a failed relationship after it has ended may be quite different from the story one heard at the time the relationship was ongoing. All perceptions of a relationship are filtered through stories. An individual cannot know anything about a relationship except through his or her story of it, and this knowledge may change if the story changes.

Stories are socialized throughout a lifetime via the interactions between the person and his or her environment. People can and usually do have multiple stories simultaneously. These multiple stories are arranged hierarchically with the more desirable stories being located toward the top of the hierarchy. The stories are not right or wrong, per se, but are compatible or incompatible and adaptive or maladaptive. People often create self-fulfilling prophecies as they try to make their stories come true. In other words, the relationship that represents their idealized story is brought into being, for better or worse. Efforts to bring about change must involve changing the stories or else one ends up treating symptoms rather than causes. Thus, effecting behavioral change will not be adequate to make an unsatisfactory relationship satisfactory because the story motivating the behavior is at least as important as the behavior. Behavior that might be intolerable under one story (such as intimate touching) might be eagerly accepted under another.

Each story has two complementary roles. The roles may or may not be symmetrical. That is, in some stories, two people each act the same way toward each other; in other stories, people act different toward each other. There is no exhaustive list of the stories people can have, and indeed, the number of potential stories is infinite. But in the present form of the theory, twenty-four stories and variants of them constitute a working list. The stories are as follows:

People sometimes enter into a love relationship with an idealized fantasy in mind about finding the perfect mate to share their romantic "happily ever after" sunset ending. (Corbis/Douglas Peebles)

addiction: strong anxious attachment, clinging behavior, anxiety at the thought of losing the partner,

art: love of partner for physical attractiveness, importance to person of partner's always looking good,

business: relationships as business propositions, money is power, partners in close relationships as business partners,

collectibles: partner viewed as "fitting in" to some overall scheme, partner viewed in a detached way,

cookbook: doing things a certain way (recipe) results in a relationship being more likely to work out, departure from recipe for success leads to increased likelihood of failure,

fantasy: often expects to be saved by a knight in shining armor or to marry a princess and to live happily ever after,

game: love as a game or sport,

gardening: relationship needs to be continually nurtured and tended to,

government: either one partner dominates or even controls the other (autocratic) or the two partners equally share power (democratic),

history: events of relationship form an indelible record, keep a lot of records—mental or physical,

horror: relationships become interesting when one terrorizes or is terrorized by a partner,

humor: love is strange and funny,

mystery: love is a mystery and one should not let too much of the self be known,

police: one has to keep a close tab on a partner to make sure he or she toes the line, or one needs to be under surveillance by a partner to make sure one behaves,

pornography: love is dirty, to love is to degrade or be degraded,

recovery: survivor mentality, view that after a past trauma a person can get through practically anything,

religion: either conceptualizes love as a religion or as a set of feelings and activities dictated by religion,

sacrifice: to love is to give of oneself or for a partner to give of him or herself, science: love can be understood, analyzed, and dissected, just like any other natural phenomenon,

science fiction: views the partner as an alien—incomprehensible and very strange,

sewing: love is whatever you make it,

theater: love is scripted, with predictable acts, scenes, and lines,

travel: love is a journey, and

war: love is a series of battles in a devastating but continuing war.

Sternberg and his colleagues have tested the theory of love as a story on two groups of participants. The investigators found certain higher-order themes that seemed to integrate clusters of stories, such as whether partners are equal or unequal in power in the relationship. They also found that certain stories tended to predict unhappiness in relationships and that couples with more similar stories tended to be happier in their relationships than did couples with less similar stories.

Conclusion

There is no one right approach to love. Each approach addresses somewhat different questions and thus provides somewhat different answers. Clinical theories seem most to deal with motivational aspects of love, particularly in people with problematic relationships. Social-psychological theories deal with the structure of love in normal individuals. Learning theories deal with aspects of how interpersonal attraction, and perhaps love, develop, but in a less satisfying way than do developmental theories. Ultimately, perhaps a theory will be developed that encompasses all of these different approaches to love. In the meantime, these diverse theories provide somewhat specialized insights into love in its diverse aspects.

See also: ACCEPTANCE AND REJECTION; ATTACHMENT; BOWLBY, JOHN; DESIRE; EMPATHY; FRIENDSHIP; INFATUATION; INTIMACY; LUST; RELATIONSHIPS; SYMPATHY

Bibliography

Ackerman, Diane. (1994). *A Natural History of Love.* New York: Random House.

Ainsworth, Mary D. S. (1989). "Attachments beyond Infancy." *American Psychologist* 44:709–716.

Berscheid, Ellen. (1988). "Some Comments on Love's Anatomy: Or, Whatever Happened to Old-Fashioned Lust?" In *The Psychology of Love*, ed. Robert J. Sternberg and Michael L. Barnes. New Haven, CT: Yale University Press.

Berscheid, Ellen, and Walster [Hatfield], Elaine. (1974). "A Little Bit About Love." In *Foundations of Interpersonal Attraction*, ed. Ted L. Huston. New York: Academic Press.

Bowlby, John. (1988). *A Secure Base: Clinical Applications of Attachment Theory.* London: Routledge.

Buss, David M. (1994). *The Evolution of Desire: Strategies for Human Mating.* New York: Basic Books.

De Rougement, Denis. (1940). *Love in the Western World*, tr. Montgomery Belgion. New York: Pantheon.

Freud, Sigmund. ([1922] 1955). "Certain Neurotic Mechanisms in Jealousy, Paranoia, and Homosexuality." In *The Standard Edition of the Complete Psychological Works of Sigmund Freud, Vol. 2*, ed. James Strachey. London: Hogarth Press.

Fromm, Erich. (1955). *The Sane Society.* Greenwich, CT: Fawcett.

Hamilton, Edith. (1942). *Mythology.* Boston: Little, Brown.

Hendrick, Clyde, and Hendrick, Susan. (1986). "A Theory and Method of Love." *Journal of Personality and Social Psychology* 50:392–402.

Klein, Melanie K. (1953). "The Oedipus Complex in the Light of Early Anxieties." *Revista de Psicoanalisis* 10:439–496.

Lee, John Alan. (1977). "A Typology of Styles of Loving." *Personality and Social Psychology Bulletin* 3:173–182.

Livingston, Kenneth R. (1980). "Love As a Process of Reducing Uncertainty." In *On Love and Loving*, ed. Kenneth S. Pope. San Francisco: Josey-Bass.

Lott, Albert J., and Lott, Bernice E. (1968). "A Learning Theory Approach to Interpersonal Attitudes." In *Psychological Foundations of Attitudes*, ed. Anthony G. Greenwald, Timothy C. Brock, and Thomas M. Ostrom. New York: Academic.

Lott, Albert J., and Lott, Bernice E. (1974). "The Role of Reward in the Formation of Positive Interpersonal Attitudes." In *Foundations of Interpersonal Attraction*, ed. Ted L. Huston. New York: Academic.

Maslow, Abraham H. (1954). *Motivation and Personality.* New York: Harper & Row.

Peck, M. Scott. (1978). *The Road Less Traveled: A New Psychology of Love, Traditional Values, and Spiritual Growth.* New York: Simon & Schuster.

Peele, Stanton, and Brodsky, Archie. (1976). *Love and Addiction.* New York: New American Library.

Reik, Theodore. (1944). *A Psychologist Looks at Love.* New York: Farrar & Rinehart.

Schachter, Stanley, and Singer, Jerome. (1962). "Cognitive, Social, and Physiological Determinants of Emotional State." *Psychological Review* 69:379–399.

Small, Melinda F. (1995). *What's Love Got to Do with It?* New York: Anchor Books.

Shaver, Phillip R., and Hazan, Cindy. (1993). "Adult Romantic Attachment: Theory and Evidence." In *Advances in Personal Relationships, Vol. 4*, ed. Daniel Perlman and Warren H. Jones. London: Kingsley.

Sternberg, Robert J. (1986). "A Triangular Theory of Love." *Psychological Review* 93:119–135.

Sternberg, Robert J. (1998a). *Cupid's Arrow: The Course of Love through Time.* New York: Cambridge University Press.

Sternberg, Robert J. (1998b). *Love Is a Story.* New York: Oxford University Press.

Sternberg, Robert J., and Barnes, Michael L., eds. (1988). *The Psychology of Love.* New Haven, CT: Yale University Press.

Tennov, Dorothy. (1979). *Love and Limerance.* New York: Stein & Day.

Walster [Hatfield], Elaine, and Walster, G. William. (1981). *A New Look at Love.* Reading, MA: Addison-Wesley.

Wilson, Glenn. (1981). *The Coolidge Effect: An Evolutionary Account of Human Sexuality.* New York: Morrow.

Wolkstein, Diane. (1991). *The First Love Stories: From Isis and Osiris to Tristan and Iseult.* New York: HarperCollins.

Robert J. Sternberg

LUST

In 1976, presidential candidate Jimmy Carter did an interview for *Playboy* magazine. He surprised many conservative elements in the American public by revealing that he had, indeed, experienced "lust in his heart." Aside from revealing that he was a rather normal adult male, Carter had intended to communicate that his moral code inhibited him *from acting on* this lust. Many scholars of human sexuality and emotion noted with wry humor, however, that regardless of his intention to act or not, Carter had assigned his lust to the wrong body part.

Among other things, this anecdote illustrates that lust is an evocative word; it brings to mind a host of other terms associated with the larger "taboo topic" of sex. For example, talking about lust might lead one to think about sexual fantasies, eroticism, sexual desire, sexual arousal, sexual intercourse, large breasts, muscular chests, erections, ejaculation, and orgasm. Individual sexual experiences and preferences, gender, and the context determine what associations people make and whether they verbalize them or not. But in general, lust is an emotion closely tied to other features of human sexuality in fairly systematic ways.

Furthermore, because sexuality in many cultures is linked to the romantic love complex, lust is often associated with real or imagined intimate relationships —though in very complicated ways. Some people view lust as dehumanizing or objectifying, as focused on physical features of another person; for these people, lust seems inappropriate to feel toward someone whom they love. Other people would say that lust is a very strong element of their romantic relationships. Some people would say they feel lust for a classmate, coworker, neighbor, or movie star with no sense that it threatens their primary relationship, not only because they would not act on it, but because the other components of attraction (e.g., shared interests, respect, caring, support) simply are not present.

Lust and Related Terms

Although the distinctions among lust, sexual desire, sexual arousal, and sexual activity are not usually necessary for most people, such distinctions are important for sex therapists and marriage counselors. If an individual or a couple is receiving professional help for sexual problems, finely drawn distinctions can help

professionals isolate the nature of the problem and provide more focused therapy.

Charles Moser (1992), a professor of sexology at the Institute for Advanced Study of Human Sexuality in San Francisco, California, offers the following definition of lust: "a strong clearly sexual response to an individualized specific set of real or imagined sensory cues (visual, auditory, olfactory, tactile, and/or gustatory)" (p. 66). Moser further specifies that some of the cues that stimulate lust are what might be called "core" cues and some are what might be called secondary or "eroticized" cues.

Core lust cues are set early in life. They are integral to a person's sexual identity, and consequently, they are very resistant to change. For most people, in most cultures, core lust cues are fairly closely tied to their evolutionary history. That is, because human survival depends upon reproduction, humans tend to be aroused by attributes of adult members of the opposite sex. For example, because fertility in women declines with age and eventually ceases, evolution has encouraged men to become aroused by youthful features and signs of reproductive potential such as healthy bodies, large breasts, and wide hips. When individuals have core lust cues that are different from these, cultures typically mark these differences as deviant. For example, people use the labels *pedophile* for individuals whose core cues are associated with children and *homosexual* for individuals whose core cues are associated with members of the same sex. It is important to emphasize that core cues and the sexual response they elicit are not, in Moser's view, under the conscious control of individuals because they are not "learned" in the classic sense that other aspects of sexuality are learned. However, the actions that an individual might chose to perform or not perform based on his or her lust cues are controllable.

Secondary or eroticized lust cues are the array of cues that people come to associate with arousal through experience. Sometimes this experience is indirectly gained, as when people respond sexually to cues in movies, on television, or in magazines such as *Playboy* and *Glamour*. Anyone who has eaten raw oysters knows that there is a silky (some would say slimy) surface texture that facilitates their smooth movement through the mouth and down the throat when they are swallowed whole. This oral-tactile sensation has been eroticized by scenes in films such as *Tom Jones,* where Tom's dinner companion fixes her eyes upon his and exaggerates the sensuality of the scene. The folk belief that oysters are an aphrodisiac further contributes to the overall eroticism of the otherwise common act of having dinner. Sometimes the experience is more direct and personal. Maybe a person's sexual partner wears a certain perfume or aftershave. That

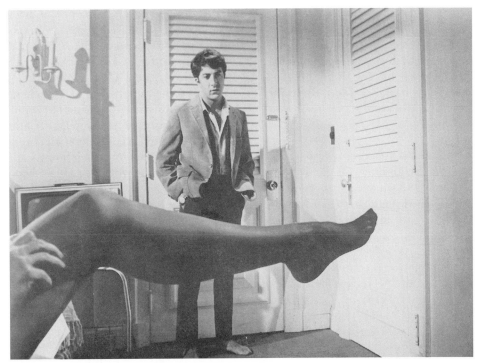

In the 1967 film The Graduate, *Dustin Hoffman played a college graduate who was receiving strong eroticized lust cues from Anne Bancroft, who played the wife of his father's friend. Hoffman's character struggled to reconcile these cues with the fact that Bancroft's character was an older woman and that personal relationships were at stake.* (Corbis/Bettmann)

scent becomes so strongly associated with the individual's sexual arousal that it stimulates a sexual response even when worn by another person. This is not to say, of course, that lust cues can be randomly or infinitely eroticized, nor can they replace the early cues tied to sexual identity. As Moser (1992) specifies, "The eroticized object or behavior must be presented in the context of an appropriate partner. For example, if a heterosexual man eroticizes certain types of lingerie, he may not have a sexual response by seeing it in a store or if worn by a male" (p. 67).

Moser (1992) also defines sexual desire in order to distinguish it from lust. He says that desire does not need to be triggered by outside stimuli but is a more conscious, "probably hormonally mediated perception of an interest in sex" (p. 67). Unlike lust, sexual desire is an urge or need to have sex that can be satisfied, at least for a time, through masturbation or sexual intercourse. Lust, by comparison, is not an urge or need and therefore not satisfiable, in a physical sense, through sexual release.

Stephen Levine (1984, 1987) offers a definition of sexual desire that is compatible with Moser's but somewhat broader. He refers to sexual desire as a "propensity to behave sexually" resulting from the interaction among three factors: biological *drive* or need (which as Moser suggests is at least partly hormonal, though not entirely); cognitions that generate the *wish* to behave sexually (consistent with Moser's notion of being a "conscious perception"), and psychological processes that yield a *willingness* or motivation to behave sexually. Influence on any one of these factors can affect whether sexual desire is experienced and/or whether sexual desire, if experienced, is accompanied by sexual activity. For example, consider these possible variations:

1. Biological drive can be diminished by age, fatigue, or illness, but a person can still feel sexual desire for a partner because a strong attachment or love is emotionally arousing.
2. A person might wish to behave sexually, even when drive is low or absent, to feel loved, to feel masculine or feminine, or to please a partner.
3. A person might wish *not* to behave sexually (even when sexual drive is present) because of fear of pregnancy or disease or because moral codes prohibit sexual involvement.

4. The willingness to behave sexually is more likely if drive and motivation are high; however, sexual behavior does not automatically follow, nor are drive and motivation necessary for sexual behavior to occur. The willingness to engage in sexual behavior depends upon the situation, the behaviors of the partner, and prior experience.

Levine's description of sexual desire points to a key difference between desire and lust. Of the two, sexual desire is more dynamic and situationally responsive. It can be prompted by physiological arousal, but it can also stimulate physiological arousal. It can precede, accompany, or even follow sexual activity. In addition, of the two concepts, sexual desire is more likely to be influenced by the interpersonal context in which it is embedded. In a review of the reciprocal influences between sexual desire and relationship factors, Sandra Metts, Susan Sprecher, and Pamela Regan (1998) note that sexual desire and sexual frequency tend to be high in early stages of relationship development, with a characteristic decline in later stages. For most couples, this decline can be attributed to decreased arousal from habituation, increased stress from work, money, and child rearing. For couples who are in love and satisfied with their relationship in general, good communication helps in processing these changes. For couples who do not understand these changes, cannot communicate about their sexual needs or concerns, and/or are unhappy in other areas of the relationship, changes in sexual desire are viewed as symptomatic of a failing relationship and, consequently, contribute to problems in other areas.

However, to say that sexual desire is the more explicitly relational construct does not mean that lust plays no role in sexual relationships. For good or ill, lust plays an important role in many relationships. Imagine the scenario in which two people meet who happen to have many of the lust cues desired by the other. This stimulates sexual arousal and, because the other person is the proximate cause, the arousal is interpreted as sexual attraction. These partners will experience a great deal of passion in their relationship and probably have strong "sexual chemistry" if they have sex. This scenario is not inherently problematic. However, if the lust cues are physical attributes that change over time and no other basis of attraction emerges, the attraction is likely to dissipate when the lust cues change. More unfortunate are the cases where the relationship is not in the best interest of either or both of the individuals (e.g., an affair that could destroy a primary relationship) but the sexual attraction is too reinforcing or addictive to terminate the relationship.

Another type of problem can arise when persons have aesthetic ideals different from their sexual ideals. According to Moser (1992, p. 67), "a sexual ideal displays the individual's lust cues, even if they are not recognized as such by the individual. An aesthetic ideal is someone who fits a beauty stereotype." If these ideals are difficult to find in the same person, a man or woman may feel frustrated in relationships because they "seek out" the aesthetic ideal (e.g., someone tall and blonde) but find their most satisfying sexual relationships to be with the sexual ideal (e.g., short and dark).

Empirical Research

The empirical research on lust tends to be subsumed under the broader concept of sexual desire. Many scholars believe that, although lust can be technically distinguished from sexual desire, the sexual sensations are similar and individuals make pragmatic distinctions based on their subjective interpretations of the context. Thus, a common approach in the empirical research is to integrate the two terms into a single definition as reflected in the following quote from a study by Helen Kaplan and Trude Owett (1993, p. 4):

On the level of subjective experience, sexual desire or lust is an urge that impels men and women to seek out, initiate, and/or respond to sexual stimulation. Moreover, a state of aroused desire or passion lends emotional color and pleasure to genital functioning.

In a similar vein, Peter Bertocci (1988) coined the term *lust-sex* to capture the emotional quality of this subjective experience. He defines lust-sex as an emotion experienced toward another person who is considered "attractive in ways that facilitate sexual advances and intercourse" (p. 222).

This brief discussion is important to remind readers that when this entry talks about the research on sexual desire, one can assume that most of the findings apply also to lust because the researchers are interested in the more general notion of sexual interest broadly conceived. However, one should not forget that clinical sex therapists often need to make very fine distinctions between these two concepts. This caveat aside, what conclusions can be drawn about sexual desire and lust based on empirical research?

First, medical research has shown that hormones play a role in both sexual desire and lust. As testosterone levels rise in young men at puberty, their sexual interest increases and they develop physical attributes that signal their maturity and serve as potential lust cues. Correspondingly, increased estrogen levels in young women stimulate the development of physical attributes that signal their maturity and serve as potential lust cues. It is important to note, however, that testosterone in women is also essential to activate the sex centers in the brain and make women sexually responsive. Hormonal changes and their slightly different effects in men and women explain in part why men reach their sexual peaks in their twenties and then experience a decrease over the life span whereas women reach their sexual peaks in their thirties and experience very little decline over the life span.

Second, psychological research has shown that the brain is not merely a biochemical environment. Rather it is a complex web of connections among arousal patterns, emotions, learned responses, knowledge structures, and so forth. Hormones influence only part of the total sexual syndrome. People with perfectly normal hormone profiles differ markedly in their levels of sexual desire, their frequency of sexual activity, and their satisfaction with sexual activity. This is due in part to unique individual associations. For example, in most people, sexual arousal is pleasurable and activates the emotions, such as joy, that are associated with pleasure. If, however, sexual arousal has been repeatedly associated with aversive stimuli (e.g., ridicule or criticism), it might be felt as unpleasurable and activate emotions, such as fear or anger, that are associated with pain. This negative association can lead to suppression of sexual arousal, avoidance of sexual activity, or demeaning (even violent) treatment of a sexual partner when sexual activity does occur.

Third, sociological research has shown that the associations among sexual arousal, sexual desire/lust, and sexual activity are influenced by a shared evolutionary history but are also shaped and reformulated by particular cultures and religious communities in particular historical circumstances. As mentioned previously, core lust cues typically facilitate mating between members of the opposite sex. David Buss (1989, 1994) has found evidence to support the notion that evolutionary selection has given rise to mate selection practices and differences in the sexual scripts of males and females across a variety of cultures. For example, because parental investment in raising offspring is much greater for women as compared to men, natural selection favored women who were attracted to and pair-bonded with men who displayed strength, social status, and qualities that would assure protection and nurturance of themselves and their offspring. Alternatively, because men have much less parental investment in raising offspring, natural selection favored a wider range of partners who were assessed on physical attributes of fertility and receptivity to sexual intercourse. Of course, as Robert Hinde (1984) noted, social structures such as the institution of marriage and cultural mandates against infidelity have moderated some of the direct effects of these differences. Nonetheless, scholars present compelling evidence that in societies where men and women are free to select their mates and engage in sexual activity outside of marriage, observed differences between men and women in modern times are consistent with an evolutionary perspective. These differences include more frequent sexual arousal for men, heightened arousal to visual cues for men, and greater affective linkage between sexual desire and relationship qualities for women. For example, Karen Donahey and Richard Carroll (1993) found that while married women who had low sexual desire were also likely to report that they were dissatisfied with their relationship, married men with low sexual desire did not link it to relationship quality. John Townsend (1995) found for a sample of college students that women who engaged in "low-investment" sexual intercourse (i.e., casual sex) experienced negative emotions of vulnerability, anxiety, and distress, even when they described themselves as sexually liberal. If they were not able to induce their sexual partners to express commitment to them and the relationship, they terminated the relationship. For males, no comparable pattern emerged. This suggests that the biological and psychological aspects of sexual desire and lust are influenced in important ways by human evolutionary history and the sex role expectations of contemporary social norms.

See also: ATTRACTIVENESS; DESIRE; GENDER AND EMOTIONS; LOVE; RELATIONSHIPS

Bibliography

Beck, J. Gayle; Bozman, Alan W.; and Qualtrough, Tina. (1991). "The Experience of Sexual Desire: Psychological Correlates in a College Sample." *Journal of Sex Research* 28:443–456.
Bertocci, Peter A. (1988). *The Person and Primary Emotions.* New York: Springer-Verlag.
Buss, David. (1989). "Sex Differences in Human Mate Preferences: Evolutionary Hypotheses Tested in 37 Cultures." *Behavior and Brain Science* 12:1–49.
Buss, David. (1994). *The Evolution of Desire: Strategies in Dating Relationships.* New York: Basic Books.
Donahey, Karen M., and Carroll, Richard A. (1993). "Gender Differences in Factors Associated with Hypoactive Sexual Desire." *Journal of Sex and Marital Therapy* 19:25–40.
Hinde, Robert A. (1984). "Why Do the Sexes Behave Differently in Close Relationships?" *Journal of Social and Personal Relationships* 1:471–501.
Kaplan, Helen Singer. (1979). *Disorders of Sexual Desire.* New York: Simon & Schuster.
Kaplan, Helen Singer, and Owett, Trude. (1993). "The Female Androgen Deficiency Syndrome." *Journal of Sex and Marital Therapy* 19:3–24.
Levine, Stephen B. (1984). "An Essay on the Nature of Sexual Desire." *Journal of Sex and Marital Therapy* 10:83–96.
Levine, Stephen B. (1987). "More on the Nature of Sexual Desire." *Journal of Sex and Marital Therapy* 13:35–44.

Metts, Sandra; Sprecher, Susan; and Regan, Pamela C. (1998). "Communication and Sexual Desire." In *Handbook of Communication and Emotion,* ed. Peter A. Anderson and Laura K. Guerrero. San Diego, CA: Academic Press.

Moser, Charles. (1992). "Lust, Lack of Desire, and Paraphilias: Some Thoughts and Possible Connections." *Journal of Sex and Marital Therapy* 18:65–69.

Singer, Barry, and Toates, Frederick M. (1987). "Sexual Motivation." *Journal of Sex Research* 23:481–501.

Townsend, John Marshall. (1995). "Sex Without Emotional Involvement: An Evolutionary Interpretation of Sex Differences." *Archives of Sexual Behavior* 24:173–206.

Sandra Metts

M

MASS MEDIA

See Advertising; Attitudes; Persuasion; Propaganda

MEN AND EMOTIONAL ABUSE

See Emotional Abuse: Men

MIND-BODY DICHOTOMY

Despite amazing advances in knowledge about the interactions between the mind and the body, scientists continue to treat the mind and the body as though they were unrelated. This dichotomization has its roots in Platonic theory. Plato taught that because breath (psyche or spiritus) ceased with death, the spirit, and by extension the mind, was independent of the body. Plato was the first to say that the spirit (later changed to soul) was immortal and separate from the mortal body. Since soul and body were different entities, they followed different rules. As a result, "divine madnesses" such as prophetic, religious, poetic, and erotic madness should be understood separately from physical illness. Because diseases of the soul, which were of course diseases of the mind, were given by the gods, they could never be understood or cured by methods of the body.

Plato's concept of the soul was at odds with the Hebrew Scriptures, which used the term *soul* to refer to a living being (not just a human). Eventually, Christian doctrine incorporated the Platonic concept of the soul as the defining human quality that transcended the body. The reinterpreted belief was that people had an immortal soul and a mortal body and that the body was resurrected while the soul lived on after death.

Although many people today think that science inhibits religion, the reverse has been true for much of Western history, when Christianity has been the dominant social and political force. When early Christian philosophers taught that the human body was made in God's image, the study of the body, even after death, was a defilement that warranted severe punishment. During this time, medicine was grounded in mystical theories—based on inference without objective study. Scientific understanding could not develop until it became possible to open the earthly vessel that housed the soul. Only when the body and the soul were formally separated did it become possible to obtain permission to experiment on the body. Once the soul became immortal, the body became not much more than a complicated system of nuts and bolts. The mechanical body could be relegated to profane science when it was freed from its connection with the spiritual soul.

Included in the soul were all those intangibles that are now equated with the mind—will, action, passion, conflict, conscience, pleasure, agony—split off from the physical realm. Like closeness to God, goodness, and the meaning of life, emotional experience became immaterial, to be understood only by those who knew the spirit. While medicine and physiology concerned themselves with a mechanistic body, the soul remained the province of the clergy. In modern times, psychology grew out of philosophy, which was concerned primarily with the nature of experience and consciousness rather than with clinical or theoretical matters.

As the specialties of the body flourished, they were divorced from the specialties of the mind. Since the mind was an entirely different domain from the body, its study required an entirely different method. When new technologies were developed to measure biological reality, there was little thought of applying them to mental events. Many scientists thought it was just as well to ignore the complex and confusing interactions with the mind, which there were no techniques to study anyway.

Attempts to Integrate Mind and Body in Psychiatry

The term *psychiatry* ("mind healing" in Greek) was coined in 1808 by a German anatomist named Johann Reil. While psychology was a branch of philosophy, psychiatry was originally an offshoot of neurology. In fact, one of the first psychiatric textbooks was *A Treatise on Diseases of the Forebrain,* written in 1884 by neuropathologist Theodur Meynert. Early psychiatrists, who were concerned mainly with the major psychoses, believed that these disorders would ultimately be linked to specific anomalies in the brain, as were paralysis, aphasia, and other neurological disorders.

As it turned out, many of the severe, irreversible mental illnesses of the nineteenth century were caused by clear-cut structural damage to the brain. About 50 percent of chronic mental hospital patients suffered from mental manifestations of diseases such as tertiary syphilis, hypothyroidism, and mental retardation. However, each time a pathological cause for an illness was identified, it related back to neurology. In order not to lose its attachment to the empirical, neurology abandoned mental syndromes such as schizophrenia and mania for which there seemed little chance that demonstrable pathology would be found. Neurology held on a while longer to hysteria, which produced neurological symptoms, but this was dropped from the ranks of neurological illness when it was found not to be associated with structural lesions of the nervous system. As neurology became progressively more identified with known neuropathology, everything distinctly mental became relegated to psychiatry, which became by default the specialty of the unknown.

Throughout the first half of the twentieth century, the same sequence was repeated many times. Instead of learning about possible mind-body interactions in psychiatric illness, mental specialists lost contact with any problem for which they were successful in finding a physical source. The only reason why psychiatry did not disappear was that it was impossible to demonstrate any bodily changes for most mental illnesses. These conditions remained psychiatric only because they could not be proven to be physical.

Within the specialty of the mind, a parallel split developed between the empirical and the non-empirical. One group of psychiatrists continued to believe that a neuropathological cause of mental disorders existed but could not yet be identified. Retaining its allegiance to the observable, this group continued to study those severe mental illnesses that, like neurological syndromes, lent themselves to objective classification and the implication of a physiologic cause. The other camp detached itself from biological science as it was then conceived to concern itself with a side of the mind to which science as yet had no access. This move began a divergence between the objective and the subjective in the study of mental disorders that has more recently undergone a kind of renaissance that flies in the face of data that demonstrate mind-body interactions in psychiatric illness.

Descriptive Psychiatry

The most influential leader of the empirical branch of the new psychiatry was Emil Kraepelin. Kraepelin, who was trained in neuropathology as well as psychiatry, had two important mentors. One was Wilhelm Wundt, a physiologist and psychologist who helped to move psychology out of the realm of philosophy by making it an experimental science. The other was Wilhem Griesenger, an early nineteenth-century neuropsychiatrist who held that "psychological diseases are brain diseases." Kraepelin, Eugen Bleuler, and the other descriptive psychiatrists devoted most of their professional lives to describing the major mental illnesses systematically. Lacking any treatments, they had to content themselves with meticulous observations of signs and symptoms that they hoped might one day lead to the identification of discrete syndromes for which causes and therapies might eventually be found. Their descriptions are the cornerstone of such modern diagnoses as bipolar disorder and schizophrenia (as detailed in the American Psychiatric Association's *Diagnostic and Statistical Manual,* 4th edition).

Although he created detailed descriptions, Kraepelin acknowledged that even for the psychoses it was impossible to know their etiology. Nevertheless, he continued to believe that persistent application of the scientific method eventually would uncover the neurological basis of these illnesses, which would make it possible to develop specific treatments. Demonstrating that mental illnesses had a physical substrate would then reestablish psychiatry's connection to other medical specialties and reinforce its identity as a scientific discipline.

Psychoanalysis and Descriptive Psychiatry

While the descriptive psychiatrists continued the search for biological underpinnings of mental disorders, another group of psychiatrists believed that the best way to understand mental phenomena was with mental techniques. The new subspecialty of psychoanalysis, abandoning biomedical technology and identifying with the mental side of the mind-body split, used as its main investigative and therapeutic trial emotions and memories that emerge in a transference relationship.

As with descriptive psychiatry, psychoanalysis had its roots in neurology. The neurologists Jean Charcot and Pierre Janet (who was also a psychologist) had come to suspect that conversion symptoms such as paralysis, deafness, and blindness were expressions in the language of the body of neurotic conflicts. Their theory was proven correct when purely psychological techniques—first hypnosis and suggestion, and later Sigmund Freud's "talking cure"—proved effective in treating conversion.

Having begun his career as a neuropathologist, Freud never stopped believing that, to a large extent, mental phenomena are dependent on physiologic phenomena. In 1895, he attempted to develop an ambitious theory of the biology of the mind in his "Project for a Scientific Psychology." The "project" was an attempt to extrapolate directly from contemporary concepts of how neurons functioned to a theory of how the mind functioned. This attempt proved futile because the neurophysiology of the time was based on a hydraulic model in which neurons discharged stored energy when too much energy built up, a model that does not correspond to the ways in which neurons actually function. When it became clear to Freud that his attempt to link neurology directly to psychology did not work, he ordered that the "project" be destroyed.

Realizing that it was impossible to draw direct correlations between the way the brain worked and the way the mind worked, Freud made a tactical decision to ignore the biological and examine only the psychological. In restricting himself to a purely psychological frame of reference, Freud was able to maximize the information that he could obtain from the psychoanalytic method, just as researchers who were biologically oriented were able to gather data more efficiently by ignoring the psychological. However, in severing his intellectual and emotional ties with neurology and its careful observations, Freud also drew away from descriptive psychiatry, which had remained on the somatic side of the mind-body dichotomy. The benefit of abandoning the empirical was that it was possible to identify more completely with the emotional world of the patient. The price was greater vulnerability to loss of objectivity in the face of immersion in the unconscious.

Because of widespread hostility toward psychoanalysis in European society around the beginning of the twentieth century, there was increasing pressure for practitioners of this new field to band together for support. Finding open communication with the medical community increasingly difficult, psychoanalysts became more concerned with banding together with like-minded professionals for the emotional survival of their discipline. In analytic societies, discussion groups, and journals, it became more important to protect the field from attacks from without than to integrate the purely psychological approach with descriptive psychiatry. Refusing to "alloy" what Freud called "the pure gold of analysis" with the "copper" of other techniques, psychoanalysis began to evolve in analyst Robert Knight's words, from "a science of the mind" to "the doctrine of a founder."

There was one attempt to keep psychoanalysis and descriptive psychiatry from following completely divergent paths when Bleuler expressed an interest in psychoanalysis, which he felt added the depth that descriptive psychiatry lacked. Because Bleuler was one of the most influential figures in organized psychiatry, Freud wanted him not only to believe in the analytic model but to fight wholeheartedly for a worldwide psychoanalytic movement. However, Bleuler did not wish to dedicate himself completely to psychoanalysis. Freud attributed Bleuler's lack of total commitment to unanalyzed resistance and withdrew from the collaboration. Freud then decided that because psychiatry tried to identify the bodily causes of mental disorders so they could be treated like other causes of illness, it had nothing to do with psychoanalysis, which was interested in the "purely mental." It was not a great leap for Freud from this stance to the position that, unlike psychiatry, psychoanalysis was not a medical subspecialty.

Psychosomatic Medicine

The term *psychosomatic* was coined in 1818 by Johann Heinroth when he proposed that insomnia was a mental disturbance as well as a physical disturbance. Modern "psychosomatic illnesses" were first described in the 1920s by psychoanalyst Felix Deutch, but the term did not catch on until it was popularized in the early 1950s by another psychoanalyst, Flanders Dunbar. An organized effort to study psychosomatic disorders was announced in the inaugural issue of the *Journal of Psychosomatic Medicine* (now called *Psychosomatic Medicine*), which sought to show how "psychic and somatic phenomena take place in the same bio-

French neurologist Jean Charcot uses a female subject as he conducts a clinical lecture at Salpetriere in Paris in 1887. (Corbis/Leonard de Selva)

logical system and are probably two aspects of the same process."

Psychosomatic theory held that physical symptoms, like mental symptoms, can be used to express repressed emotions and drives. Patients who have blind spots for certain conflicts but are able to recognize other mental states develop mental symptoms such as anxiety or obsessions. Patients who are unable to recognize or tolerate emotions at all (i.e., who are alexithymic) shift emotional conflict to the physical realm in the form of behavioral symptoms such as acting out, somatic symptoms in the absence of actual bodily dysfunction (e.g., conversion symptoms, somatization disorder), or psychosomatic illnesses.

Because of the many bi-directional connections between the mind and the body, there is an intimate relationship between bodily perception and bodily function. Hunger, for example, activates digestive mechanisms that include release of hormones such as cholecytokinin and vasoactive intestinal peptide. In turn, these hormones act as neurotransmitters in brain regions that mediate hunger, anxiety, and as-

pects of emotional arousal. Through activation of the sympathetic nervous system, release of neurotransmitters of arousal such as norepinephrine, and stimulation of the hypothalamic-pituitary-adrenocortical axis, anger and fear prepare the body for action by increasing heart rate and blood pressure, mobilizing energy stores, and suppressing the immune response. At the same time, activation of these arms of the stress response feeds back to the brain to create anxiety.

When an emotion is expressed openly, it promotes mental or physical activity that leads to resolution of the physiologic changes that are evoked by the emotion. If feelings are kept out of awareness, however, they cannot be dissipated through action. As a result, their correlates in physiology continue unabated. The physical result of unmetabolized emotion (e.g., tachycardia, muscle tension, or an upset stomach) does not have any particular symbolic meaning and will continue for as long as the emotion remains unresolved.

If the body is basically intact, the chronic physiologic stimulation of unresolved emotional conflict might be uncomfortable, but it is not particularly dangerous. However, an organ that is vulnerable to continued excitation may begin to break down. For example, a chronically angry person whose heart was vulnerable to overstimulation by adrenal stress hormones such as epinephrine might be prone to develop life-threatening arrhythmias, while someone with the same emotional problem but a normal heart might just have sinus tachycardia or an occasional premature beat. In someone else with the same unresolved emotion whose blood vessels were the weak link in the biological chain, unrelenting over-responsiveness to the stimulus for vascular contraction might lead to high blood pressure.

At first, these physical effects related to emotional mobilization can be reversed when the emotion that stimulates them is resolved. However, a vulnerable organ that is subjected to enough ongoing mental stress may be permanently changed. Once the heart gets used to beating at an excessive rate or the blood vessels remain in spasm long enough, the affected system may reset itself to a new and pathological level of functioning that is independent of the mental state that occasioned it and that persists after the emotions that provoked it are gone. The resulting disease might make the sufferer feel weak, helpless, dependent, anxious, guilty, ashamed, or angry. The disease might have symbolic meaning, and it might provide secondary gains such as attention and relief from responsibility or money. However, the bodily symptoms do not directly symbolize the original conflict.

Psychosomatic theory goes beyond this kind of one-way psychogenic view to propose a bi-directional relationship between psychological vulnerabilities to unrestrained emotion and physical vulnerabilities to the biological effects of those conflicts. For example, at the same time that inherent dysregulation of noradrenergic components of the sympathetic nervous system and the cardiac conduction system create a liability toward instability of cardiac rhythm under stress, a tendency to dysregulation of noradrenergic arousal systems in the brain may create innate tendencies to excesses of emotions such as fear and anger that activate the heart. Ongoing emotional arousal creates a sense of psychological or physical danger that is too intense to handle with ordinary defenses, and one never gains a sense of mastery over emotional conflict. The same physical process, therefore, is the cause and the result of personality traits that convey vulnerability to both cardiac disease and anxiety.

Psychosomatic theory originally held that specific mind-body links existed for specific psychosomatic illnesses. For example, a peptic ulcer was supposed to begin with congenitally high levels of the gastrointestinal hormone pepsinogen, which stimulated chronic hunger that could only be soothed by the frequent presence of food in the stomach. Since feeding occurs in the context of parent-child interactions that are the prototype of the dependent relationship, if a parent is unable to respond effectively to the increased neediness that is associated with the excessive distress that is associated with eating, the child will develop conflicts about dependency. Later in life, threats to dependent relationships result in excessive emotional arousal, which is diverted through the weak link of an increase in the physiology of hunger. The greater release of pepsinogen then would result in increased abdominal distress, even more dependency, and ultimately a peptic ulcer. This hypothesis was supported by one large prospective study conducted by gastroenterologist I. Arthur Mirsky in the 1950s, but the study was never replicated.

More detailed studies of the stress response have tended to refute the idea that there are specific psychological constellations that set the stage for specific diseases. Instead, it appears that certain global emotional states such as anxiety, hopelessness, and grief lead to global alterations in bodily functioning that interact with whatever vulnerabilities in bodily systems result from heredity or early experience. The major significance of the personality in physical disease may be in determining vulnerabilities to stresses that have specific meanings to people who cannot handle them. The nature of the stress may be less important than the degree to which it overwhelms mental defenses, subjecting vulnerable regions in the body to excessive pressures that cause mental or bodily breakdown.

Clinical Applications of Mind-Body Interactions

Beginning with the development of physical therapies for mental disorders that now include medications, electroconvulsive therapy, bright light, repetitive transcranial magnetic stimulation, and a high-density negative ion generator and extending to imaging and neurochemical studies of mood and other psychiatric disorders, the demonstration of a physical dimension of disorders of mood finally made it possible to begin to renegotiate the centuries-old deal that had removed the mind from the area of biological investigations. Science had so permeated popular culture by this time that even the Church could acknowledged the legitimacy of the mind as an object of scientific study—the result of which could contribute to rather than compete with spiritual health. This change was noted in a 1958 address that Pope Pius XII gave to the First International Congress of Neuropsychopharmacology:

> We have, gentlemen, the most sincere esteem for your work, for the aims of your labor, and for the results already shown. In examining the articles and works pub-

lished on the subjects which interest you, it is easy to see that you render valuable service to science and to humanity. You have already been able to come to the assistance of many sufferers for whom, previously, medical science admitted it had no help. You are now able to bring back mental health to sick people who were formerly considered lost and we sincerely share the joy that his knowledge brings you.

In the present state of scientific research, rapid progress can be obtained only by means of wide cooperation on an international scale. . . . It is to be hoped that it will extend not only to all specialists in psychopharmacology, but also to psychologists, psychiatrists, and psychotherapists—to all those, in short, who have anything to do with mental sickness [Ayd, 1991, p. 80].

Not everyone in the mental health professions had as much foresight as Pope Pius. Instead, many individuals continued to adhere to the outmoded belief that treatments of the body have nothing to do with treatments of the mind. Even after more than fifty years of experience with the modern era of psychopharmacology, clinicians who adhere to a strict psychological model continue to believe that relieving symptoms with medications will rob the patient of the motivation to continue psychotherapy. Some therapists who do not want to cross the mind-body barrier suggest that new adaptations learned while a patient is taking a medication may not persist in the mental state that develops when the patient stops taking the medication.

A scientific approach to the development of new medications has not prevented practitioners in the psychopharmacologic camp from adhering to equally unsupported assumptions. Some individuals view mental disorders purely as biological entities, as if emotional distress had nothing to do with the mind. These practitioners assert that any problem with mood worth treating can be cured by medications. As with psychotherapists who do not "believe in" medications, some psychopharmacologists ignore evidence of the effectiveness of psychotherapy and continue to view it as at best inferior to medications.

Practitioners whose emotional attachment to outmoded dichotomizations are not altered by the facts can hardly lay claim to a scientific grounding of their practice. The least interaction between mind and body that has been demonstrated is the finding in a few studies that combinations of psychotherapy and antidepressants are no more effective than either one alone for some mildly to moderately depressed patients. However, for more severely or chronically depressed people, psychotherapy and pharmacotherapy are additive. Far from undermining the motivation for psychotherapy, medications reduce the overwhelming distress, paralyzing despair, and inability to muster motivation that make it impossible to confront and overcome conflict psychologically.

As much as biological methods of assessment and treatment have enriched the therapy of the mind, the necessity of integrating the two points of view continues to cause anxiety among professionals that is reduced by clinging to old-fashioned deceptions that keep mind and body separate. Rather than truly understand how to use physical interventions in the mental realm, clinicians who wish to cling to a purely psychological orientation dismiss them as ineffective, only for those who are really sick, or just for temporary symptom suppression, or they unrealistically idealize them as being beyond their competence to master or as being means of totalitarian mind control. Rather than learn how to talk to their patients, clinicians who wish to see only the bodily side of the equation rely totally on medications to change every intricacy of the mind. On both sides of the mind-body gap, clinicians do not feel obliged to learn new approaches because the approaches are viewed as passing fads or fancy versions of the methods that are already being used.

At the very moment when scientific data support a better integration than ever of mental and physical approaches to mood disorders, economic forces are returning mental health care to the pre-scientific era. Under the unproven assumption that it is cheaper to treat mood disorders first with medications, and then if psychotherapy is needed to have a presumably cheaper nonmedical therapist provide it, managed care organizations increasingly refuse to pay for treatment of the mind and body by the same practitioner. These attempts to save money by authorizing the minimal amount of treatment that will restore a modicum of functioning direct the attention of patients and practitioners away from data that shows that more vigorous early interventions and appropriate maintenance treatment can save money by preventing later deterioration and disability.

Only when reimbursing agencies, as the new representatives of spiritual belief in Western society, begin to appreciate mind-body interactions will practitioners be encouraged to provide the appropriate balance between mental and physical interventions, allowing aggressive early treatment to prevent later complications that are more difficult to reverse.

See also: ANGER; ANXIETY; ANXIETY DISORDERS; CONSCIOUSNESS; FEAR AND PHOBIAS; FREUD, SIGMUND; GRIEF; HOPELESSNESS; MOOD DISORDERS; NEUROBIOLOGY OF EMOTIONS; PHILOSOPHY; PLATO; PSYCHOANALYTIC PERSPECTIVE; STRESS

Bibliography

Akiskal, Hagop S. (1996). "The Prevalent Clinical Spectrum of Bipolar Disorders: Beyond DSM-IV." *Journal of Clinical Psychopharmacology* 16(2, suppl. 1):4S–14S.

Alexander, Franz, and French, Thomas M. (1948). *Studies in Psychosomatic Medicine*. New York: Ronald Press.

Altshuler, Lori L.; Post, Robert M.; Leverich, Gabriele S.; Mikalauskas, Kirstin; Rosoff, Ann; and Ackerman, Laura. (1995). "Antidepressant-Induced Mania and Cycle Acceleration: A Controversy Revisited." *American Journal of Psychiatry* 152:1130–1138.

Avissar, Sofia, and Schreiber, Gabriel. (1992). "The Involvement of Guanine Nucleotide Binding Proteins in the Pathogenesis and Treatment of Affective Disorders." *Biological Psychiatry* 31:435–459.

Ayd, Frank J. (1991). "The Early History of Modern Psychopharmacology." *Neuropsychopharmacology* 5:71–83.

Barefoot, John C., and Schroll, Mark. (1996). "Symptoms of Depression, Acute Myocardial Infarction, and Total Mortality in a Community Sample." *Circulation* 93:1976–1980.

Consensus Development Panel. (1985). "NIMH/NIH Consensus Development Conference Statement, Mood Disorders: Pharmacologic Prevention of Recurrences." *American Journal of Psychiatry* 142:469–476.

Dubovsky, Steven L. (1994). "Beyond the Serotonin Reuptake Inhibitors: Rationales for the Development of New Serotonergic Agents." *Comprehensive Psychiatry* 55(2, suppl.):34–44.

Dubovsky, Steven L. (1997). *Mind-Body Deceptions*. New York: W. W. Norton.

Dubovsky, Steven L.; Thomas, Marshall; Hijazi, Amal; and Murphy, James. (1994). "Intracellular Calcium Signaling in Peripheral Cells of Patients with Bipolar Affective Disorder." *European Archives of Psychiatry and Clinical Neuroscience* 243:229–234.

Gershon, Elliot S. (1990). "Genetics." In *Manic-Depressive Illness*, ed. Frederick K. Goodwin and Kay Redfield Jamison. New York: Oxford University Press.

Kupfer, David J.; Frank, Ellen; and Perel, James M. (1992). "Five-Year Outcome for Maintenance Therapies in Recurrent Depression." *Archives of General Psychiatry* 49:769–773.

Linnoila, Markku, and Virkkunen, Matti. (1992). "Biologic Correlates of Suicidal Risk and Aggressive Behavioral Traits." *Journal of Clinical Psychopharmacology* 12:19S–20S.

McBride, Patricia A.; Brown, Richard P.; and DeMeo, Michael. (1994). "The Relationship of Platelet 5-HT2 Receptor Indices to Major Depressive Disorder, Personality Traits, and Suicidal Behavior." *Biological Psychiatry* 35:295–308.

Mirsky, I. Arthur. (1957). "The Psychosomatic Approach to the Etiology of Clinical Disorders." *Psychosomatic Medicine* 5:424–430.

Mirsky, I. Arthur. (1958). "Physiologic, Psychologic, and Social Determinants in the Etiology of Duodenal Ulcer." *American Journal of Digestive Disease* 3:285–311.

Post, Robert M. (1992). "Transduction of Psychosocial Stress into the Neurobiology of Recurrent Affective Disorder." *American Journal of Psychiatry* 149:999–1010.

Siever, Larry J., and Davis, Kenneth L. (1985). "Overview: Toward a Dysregulation Hypothesis of Depression." *American Journal of Psychiatry* 142:1017–1025.

Soares, Jair C., and Mann, J. John. (1997). "The Anatomy of Mood Disorders: Review of Structural Neuroimaging Studies." *Biological Psychiatry* 41:86–106.

Stein, Marvin. (1986). "A Reconsideration of Specificity in Psychosomatic Medicine: From Olfaction to the Lymphocyte." *Psychosomatic Medicine* 48:3–22.

Thase, Michael E. (1992). "Long-Term Treatments of Recurrent Depressive Disorders." *Comprehensive Psychiatry* 53(9, suppl.):32–44.

Wortis, Joseph. (1988). "The History of Psychiatry." *Biological Psychiatry* 23:107–108.

Steven L. Dubovsky

MOOD

Although everyone knows from firsthand experience what being in a happy or sad mood feels like, researchers have often found it difficult to define moods and to distinguish them from emotions. Hence, any discussion of mood requires that the key differences between moods and emotions be addressed first.

What Is a Mood?

Numerous attempts have been made to distinguish moods from emotions. As William Morris (1989) highlights, the emerging consensus emphasizes four aspects. First, and most important, emotions have a specific referent (they are "about" something), whereas moods do not. This distinction is apparent in ordinary language when people say that they are afraid "of" something or angry "about" something but that they are "in" a bad mood. Thus, the term *mood* generally refers to the feeling state itself, whereas the term *emotion* refers both to the feelings and what the feelings are about. Second, emotions typically have a sharp rise time in response to a specific event, whereas moods may come about more gradually and their causes may be more obscure. Third, moods tend to endure for some time, whereas emotions are more temporary. In many cases, a positive or negative emotional experience may leave one "in" a good or bad mood after the emotion dissipates. Finally, moods are thought to be less intense than specific emotions and less likely to attract an individual's attention. As a consequence, moods may function in the background of other activities, influencing a wide range of cognitive processes and overt behaviors. In contrast, emotions and the events that cause them are often the focus of attention, as a comparison between being angry about something and being in a bad mood may illustrate: While anger focuses people on what they are angry about, being in a bad (or a happy) mood may color all of the diverse experiences of the day. It is this diffuse and unfocused nature of moods that is at the heart of their pervasive effect.

The Experience and Influence of Mood

Mood states are characterized by a variety of changes, including feelings, thoughts, bodily states, and action tendencies. The feelings that make up moods have so many shades that some researchers ask participants to describe their feelings using as many as 132 adjectives. A positive mood may include happiness, cheerfulness, or serenity, while a negative mood may include sadness, hostility, or anxiety. Still, most studies treat moods broadly as being positive and negative.

But mood is much more than feeling. Many descriptions of mood highlight its power to transform the way people see and think about the world. This is the experience reported by William Shakespeare's Hamlet (Act II, Scene ii), who, having "lost all mirth," no longer perceives mankind as the noble "paragon of animals"—but as the "quintessence of dust." The once "excellent canopy, the air," has become to him a "pestilent congregation of vapors." Philosophers, such as Martin Heidegger, concurred, stating that moods "change what can matter to one."

Memory and Judgment

Psychological research confirmed these observations. In numerous studies reviewed by Norbert Schwarz and Gerald Clore (1996), people have been found to evaluate nearly everything more positively when they are in a good rather than bad mood. This has been true for topics ranging from consumer goods and the state of the economy to the quality of their lives. In these studies, moods have been experimentally induced—either by minor events (e.g., finding a dime or receiving a cookie), exposure to valenced material (e.g., watching a sad video or recalling a happy event from one's past), or natural circumstances (e.g., sunny or rainy weather or the outcome of sporting events)—with similar results across different manipulations. While it is interesting in its own right that finding a dime or watching one's favorite sports team win a game can improve one's life-satisfaction or optimism about the future, the crucial question is how moods can have these effects. Two different explanations have been offered. One focuses on the effect of moods on what people recall from memory, and the other highlights the use of one's feelings as a source of information.

Research into the effect of moods on memory shows that individuals are more likely to recall positive material from memory when they are in a happy rather than sad mood. Following initial suggestions by Alice Isen and her colleagues (1978), Gordon Bower (1981) conceptualized these effects in an associative network model of memory. Moods are thought to function as central nodes in an associative network, which are linked to related ideas, events of corresponding valence, autonomic activity, and muscular and expressive patterns. When new material is learned, it is associated with the nodes that are active at learning. Accordingly, material acquired while in a particular mood is linked to the respective mood node. When the person is in the same mood later on, activation spreads from the mood node along the pathways, increasing the activation of other nodes, which represent the related material. When the activation exceeds a certain threshold, the represented material comes into consciousness. This model makes two key predictions. First, memory is enhanced when the feeling at the time of encoding matches the feelings at the time of retrieval (state-dependent learning). Thus, people are more likely to recall material acquired in a particular mood when they are in the same, rather than a different, mood at the time of recall. Second, any given material is more likely to be retrieved when its affective tone matches the individual's mood at the time of recall (mood-congruent memory). Thus, information of a positive valence is more likely to come to mind when people are in a happy rather than sad mood.

Although both predictions received considerable support in experimental and clinical research, this research also revealed a number of complications. In general, mood-congruent recall is most likely to be obtained for self-referenced material, such as autobiographical events. For example, when in a happy mood, people are more likely to recall happy rather than sad events from their kindergarten days. It is important to note, however, that autobiographical material meets the conditions of both of the above hypotheses: When something good (bad) happens to people, it puts them in a positive (negative) affective state, and its subsequent recall is facilitated when they are again in a similar affective state. This situation simultaneously provides for matching mood states at learning and recall (thus satisfying the conditions of state-dependent learning) and for matches between the valence of the material and the mood at recall (thus satisfying the conditions of mood-congruent memory).

From this perspective, mood effects on judgment are mediated by mood-congruent recall from memory. When asked how satisfied people are with their life, for example, they presumably recall relevant information from memory. However, positive material is more likely to come to mind when people are in a happy mood, whereas negative material is more likely to come to mind when people are in a sad mood. Thus, what people recall is biased by the mood they are in and any judgment based on the recalled information will also show a mood-congruent bias.

As an alternative approach, Schwarz and Clore (1983, 1996) suggested that feelings themselves may serve as a source of information in making a judgment. Specifically, individuals may simplify the judgmental task by asking themselves "How do I feel about it?" Some evaluative judgments refer, by definition, to one's affective reaction to the target (e.g., feelings of liking) and one's current feelings may indeed be elicited by the target of judgment. However, the undifferentiated and unfocused nature of moods makes it difficult to distinguish between one's affective reaction to the object of judgment and one's preexisting mood state. Accordingly, individuals may misread their preexisting feelings as a reaction to the target, resulting in more positive evaluations under happy rather than sad moods.

Weather and environment, such as this desolate foggy street in Pienza, Italy, have been shown to have the potential to affect individuals' judgments. (Corbis/ Hubert Stadler)

If so, mood effects should be eliminated when the informational value of one's current feelings for the judgment at hand is called into question. Empirically, this is the case. For example, Schwarz and Clore (1983) called people on sunny or rainy days and asked them to report their general life-satisfaction and their current mood. It was not surprising that respondents reported lower life-satisfaction, and being in a worse mood, when called on rainy rather than sunny days. In one condition of this experiment, however, the interviewer pretended to call from out of town and first inquired about the weather, apparently as a private aside. Under this condition, respondents' moods no longer influenced their general life-satisfaction judgments, presumably because drawing their attention to the weather made them aware that their current feelings are due to a temporary and extraneous source and do not reflect the overall state of their life. Such a discounting effect would not be expected if the effect of mood were mediated by mood-congruent recall. Attributing one's sad mood to the rainy weather only discredits the informational value of the sad mood as a reflection of one's life in general; it does not discredit the implications of actually experienced negative life-events that may come to mind.

These and related findings indicate that moods, emotions, bodily states, and phenomenal experiences may themselves serve as sources of information. When individuals ask themselves, "How do I feel about this?," they may use their apparent reaction to the object of judgment as "data" in forming a judgment. This results in more positive judgments when they are in a good rather than bad mood, unless they are aware that their current mood may not bear on the judgment at hand. Accordingly, feelings may influence judgments either directly, by serving as sources of information, or indirectly, by influencing what comes to mind. In both cases, individuals arrive at more positive judgments when in a good rather than bad mood.

Moods and Reasoning Strategies

In addition to influencing memory and evaluative judgment, moods have been found to influence reasoning strategies in social contexts. In general, individuals in a sad mood are more likely to use a systematic, data-driven reasoning strategy, with considerable attention to detail. In contrast, individuals in a happy mood are more likely to rely on preexisting general knowledge structures and problem-solving shortcuts, with less attention to detail.

These differences can again be traced to the informative functions of moods, as discussed by Schwarz and Clore (1996). People usually feel bad when they encounter a threat of negative outcomes or a lack of positive outcomes, and feel good when they obtain positive outcomes and are not threatened by negative ones. Hence, moods reflect the nature of the psychological situation. Because thought processes are usually tuned to meet the requirements of the situation, feelings that signal different requirements may result in the use of different reasoning strategies. When a negative mood signals a problematic situation, the individual is likely to attend to the details at hand, investing the effort necessary for a careful analysis. In contrast, when a positive mood signals a benign situation, the individual may see little need to engage in cognitive effort, unless this is required by other current goals. Hence, the individual may rely on preexisting knowledge structures, which have worked well in the past, and may prefer simple problem-solving actions over more effortful, detail-oriented judgmental strategies.

Mood effects on processing style are eliminated when the informational value of the mood is undermined. This parallels the findings in the judgment domain discussed above. This finding supports the informative functions logic and is incompatible with competing approaches that attempted to trace mood effects on processing style to differential influences of happy and sad moods on individuals' cognitive capacity. Pervasive influences of moods on individuals' processing style have been most consistently observed in the domain of person perception and persuasion.

In forming an impression of others, people can rely on detailed information about the specific person, such as the person's behaviors, or they can simplify the task by drawing on preexisting knowledge structures, such as stereotypes pertaining to the person's social group. Consistent with the above perspective, being in a good mood has consistently been found to increase stereotyping. When in a good mood, people are more likely to rely on general information about "this type" of person and less likely to consider the specific person's individual behaviors and idiosyncrasies. In contrast, being in a sad mood reliably decreases stereotyping and increases the use of information about the specific person. Across many person-perception tasks, individuals in a chronic or temporary sad mood have been found to make more use of detailed individuating information, to be less influenced by the order of information presentation, and to be more accurate in performance appraisals than individuals in a happy mood, with individuals in a neutral mood falling in between. Similar findings have been obtained for individuals' reliance on scripts pertaining to typical situations (such as having dinner in a restaurant) versus their reliance on what actually transpired in the situation. Throughout, individuals in a good mood are more likely to rely on preexisting general knowledge structures, proceeding on a "business-as-usual" routine, whereas individuals in a sad mood are more likely to pay close attention to the specifics at hand, much as one would expect when negative moods provide the individual with a problem signal.

Research into mood and persuasion parallels these findings. In general, a message that presents strong arguments is more persuasive than a message that presents weak arguments, provided that recipients are able and motivated to process the content of the message and to think about the arguments. If recipients do not think carefully about the arguments (e.g., because they are distracted or not motivated to do so), the advantage of strong over weak arguments is eliminated. Numerous studies have demonstrated that sad individuals are more likely to engage spontaneously in detailed message processing than happy individuals, with individuals in a neutral mood falling in between. As a result, sad individuals are strongly influenced by compelling arguments and not influenced by weak arguments, whereas happy individuals are moderately, but equally, influenced by both. Hence, a strong message fares better with a sad than with a happy audience, but if communicators have nothing compelling to say, they better put recipients into a good mood before they say it.

Happy individuals' spontaneous tendency not to think about the arguments in much detail can be overridden by other goals or explicit task instructions. What characterizes the information processing of happy individuals is not a general cognitive or motivational impairment but a tendency to rely spontaneously on simple problem-solving methods and general knowledge structures in the absence of goals that require otherwise. As a result, happy individuals' style of reasoning may be described as highly flexible. When required by relevant goals, they engage in detail-oriented, effortful reasoning strategies, but in the absence of such goals, they rely on general knowledge structures that have served them well in the past. In pursuing relevant goals, happy individuals have also been found, by Isen (1987), to engage in more playful and creative thinking, much as may be expected when happy moods signal a benign situation that allows people to take some risk and to try out novel solutions. In contrast, sad individuals' detail-oriented style of reasoning is less flexible, presumably because ignoring the problem signal provided by a bad mood may often have negative consequences.

Behavioral Influences

Moods manifest themselves in bodily responses and overt actions in addition to feelings and thoughts. Jean-Paul Sartre (1948, p. 64) described the effects of sadness in the following way: "There's a muscular resolution, pallor, coldness at the extremities; one turns toward a corner and remains seated, motionless, offering the least possible surface to the world. One prefers the shade to broad daylight, silence to noise, the solitude of a room to crowds in public places or the streets." Again, research has confirmed the pervasive effect of moods.

In one of the more surprising real world examples, detailed analyses of the Dow Jones Industrial Index over several decades has shown that the stock market is more likely to go up when Wall Street experiences a sunny rather than a rainy day, presumably reflecting increased optimism on sunny days. Similarly, individuals in a happy mood are more likely to leave big tips and to initiate conversations with others, presumably reflecting their more positive assessments of the social situation. Moreover, happy individuals are consistently more likely to help others, at least when the helping situation itself is not aversive. When the situation itself is aversive, happy individuals may avoid the situation altogether in an effort to protect their own good mood. Thus, the diverse experimental findings are consistent with the everyday knowledge that happy individuals are more optimistic, outgoing, generous, and helpful than sad individuals, although they may hesitate to expose themselves to situations that threaten their pleasant feelings.

In contrast, the effect of negative moods is more complex. On the one hand, individuals in a sad mood are more pessimistic and more likely to arrive at negative assessments of their social situation. Yet, this tendency is often counteracted by an attempt to improve one's mood through engagement in positive and enjoyable behaviors. Sad individuals have been found to help others when they were led to assume that this would be a pleasant experience that may improve their mood; yet, they were unlikely to help when they were led to believe that it would not alleviate their negative feelings. Moreover, individuals are likely to analyze their negative more than their positive feelings—and when this analysis results in the identification of an unrelated source of one's mood, the mood's effect is lessened, as reviewed earlier. For these reasons, the effect of negative moods on behavior is likely to be more transitory than the effect of positive moods, and numerous studies are consistent with this conclusion.

Finally, moods may influence not only how individuals react to the world but how others react to the individuals. For example, Stephen Strack and James Coyne (1983) had research participants talk for fifteen minutes with another person who was in a depressed or nondepressed mood. Following the conversation with the depressed partner, participants reported being in a more depressed, anxious, and hostile mood themselves and were less willing to engage in future interactions with their partner. Similar effects were ob-

tained in a more naturalistic setting. Hence, moods may often set up a self-fulfilling prophecy. While moods influence how people experience the world and react to it, mood-colored behavior may induce others to treat an individual in a way that apparently confirms that the world is the dreadful, or wonderful, place that he or she expects it to be.

Measurement and Individual Differences

For research purposes, moods have been induced through experimental manipulations that allow researchers to isolate the causal effect of a mood state. As an alternative strategy, one may measure the moods people happen to be in. While this approach allows for the capture of the natural variation in moods, it is difficult to infer if any observed differences in thoughts or behavior are due to the mood itself or to some other characteristic of the person. Accordingly, experimental procedures and measurement procedures provide different information and complement one another. To measure an individual's mood, researchers can draw on different strategies.

Mood Measures

Most researchers are interested in the subjective experience of mood. Self-report measures ask participants to rate how they are feeling "right now" or how often or intensely they felt a particular affect during some time period (e.g., the past week). Self-report measures include checklists, scales, rating dials, and diaries. A widely used instrument, the Multiple Affect Adjective Checklist, provides participants with 132 adjectives to characterize their current feelings. Participants' responses can be analyzed as reflecting a single pleasant-unpleasant dimension, or they can be grouped into three, highly intercorrelated, scores for depression, anxiety, and hostility. Another popular measure is the Positive and Negative Affect Schedule (PANAS, which presents twenty adjectives—ten for measuring positive affect and ten for measuring negative affect. Participants rate the extent to which they experience each feeling on a five-point scale ranging from "not at all or slight" to "very much." One valuable aspect of PANAS is its ability to capture changes in positive affect independently from changes in negative affect. This is important as findings by David Watson and Lee Clark (1997) suggest a relative independence of positive and negative affect; an increase in positive affect may not be accompanied by a simultaneous decrease in negative affect and vice versa. Measures of this type can be used with the experience sampling technique, where participants repeatedly report on their moods at randomly determined times for several weeks. Using this technique, researchers can discover dynamic properties of mood, such as variability over time, and their link to important variables, such as daily events and physical symptoms.

Although they are very popular, self-report measures have their drawbacks. Participants may not be willing to report moods that create an unfavorable impression of them. Moreover, affective changes may not be reported if they are too weak to be consciously experienced or if they occur in the background of ongoing activity and participants do not notice them. One solution to these problems is to measure moods indirectly by assessing changes in thought and perception, as discussed above. Participants can be asked to recognize as quickly as possibly whether stimuli presented on a computer screen constitute words or nonwords. Participants in a good mood are faster to recognize positive words, while participants in a bad mood are faster to recognize negative words. Some researchers avoid relying on participants' reports altogether and use observer ratings. Observers such as peers (friends or family) or psychological experts can rate participants' behavior on verbal content, voice tone, facial expression, gestures, or body movement and classify the degree to which these features express positive and negative affect.

Given that the changes associated with moods are quite subtle, many of the psychophysiological techniques available for the study of emotions are less useful when dealing with moods. An exception is a technique called facial electromyography, which allows for the detection of microexpressions that are invisible to the naked eye. Electrical signals given off by contracting muscles are recorded using miniature sensors placed on the face. Muscles responsible for furrowing of the brow (frowning) are active in unpleasant states, while muscles responsible for pulling the corner of the mouth back and up (smiling) are involved in positive states. As John Cacioppo and his colleagues (1993) have noted, these physiological measures tend to be more appropriate for the assessment of strong emotions than for the assessment of subtle moods.

Individual Differences

Research based on self-reports suggests important individual differences in the experience of moods. First, there are stable differences in people's propensity to experience good or bad moods, which are related to classic dimensions of personality, such as extraversion-introversion and neuroticism. Extraverts are cheerful and enthusiastic, while people high on neuroticism report various negative affects. Advances in the fields of neuroscience and psychopharmacology suggest that these differences may be related to the relative activation of the approach or withdrawal system and to individual differences in the level of serotonin. Moreover, Christopher Peterson (1991) has

found that people who habitually blame negative events on causes that are internal ("It is not the situation, it is me"), stable ("It is going to last forever"), and global ("It is going to undermine everything I do") experience more negative moods than people who explain negative events by external, unstable, and local causes.

Second, individuals also vary in terms of the intensity with which they react to emotional events, a trait referred to as "emotional reactivity" by Randy Larsen and Ed Diener (1987). Related to this trait, individuals differ in their affective variability. Whereas some people experience pronounced mood cycles, others' moods show less fluctuation.

Third, a large body of literature suggests that women are more likely to experience sad and depressed moods than are men. However, the observed gender differences may to some extent reflect that women are more willing to report sad moods than are men, which is consistent with traditional sex roles. Nevertheless, the observation that women are also more likely to experience clinical depression confirms likely gender differences in the experience of mood. Overall, however, researchers know much less about the demographic correlates of everyday moods than about the correlates of affective disorders, mostly because detailed mood measures have rarely been used with representative samples.

See also: GENDER AND EMOTIONS; HAPPINESS; MOOD DISORDERS; PERSUASION; SADNESS; SARTRE, JEAN-PAUL

Bibliography

Bower, Gordon H. (1981). "Mood and Memory." *American Psychologist* 36:129–148.

Cacioppo, John T.; Klein, David J.; Berntson, Gary G.; and Hatfield, Elaine. (1993). "The Psychophysiology of Emotion." In *Handbook of Emotions,* ed. Michael Lewis and Jeannette M. Haviland. New York: Guilford.

Forgas, Joseph P. (1992). "Affect in Social Judgments and Decisions: A Multi-Process Model." In *Advances in Experimental Social Psychology, Vol. 25,* ed. Mark P. Zanna. San Diego, CA: Academic Press.

Isen, Alice M. (1987). "Positive Affect, Cognitive Processes, and Social Behavior." In *Advances in Experimental Social Psychology, Vol. 20,* ed. Leonard Berkowitz. New York: Academic Press.

Isen, Alice M.; Shalker, Thomas E.; Clark, Margaret S.; and Karp, Lynn. (1978). "Affect, Accessibility of Material in Memory, and Behavior: A Cognitive Loop?" *Journal of Personality and Social Psychology* 36:1–12.

Larsen, Randy, and Diener, Ed. (1987). "Affect Intensity As an Individual Difference Characteristic: A Review." *Journal of Research in Personality* 21:1–39.

Larsen, Randy, and Fredrickson, Barbara. (1999). "Measurement Issues in Emotion Research." In *Well-Being: The Foundations of Hedonic Psychology,* ed. Daniel Kahneman, Ed Diener, and Norbert Schwarz. New York: Russell Sage Foundation.

Morris, William N. (1989). *Mood: The Frame of Mind.* New York: Springer-Verlag.

Nolen-Hoeksema, Susan, and Rusting, Cheryl. (1999). "Gender and Well-Being." In *Well-Being: The Foundations of Hedonic Psychology*, ed. Daniel Kahneman, Ed Diener, and Norbert Schwarz. New York: Russell Sage Foundation.

Panksepp, Jaak. (1993). "Neurochemical Control of Moods and Emotion: Amino Acids to Neuropeptides." In *Handbook of Emotions*, ed. Michael Lewis and Jeannette M. Haviland. New York: Guilford.

Pervin, Lawrence A. (1993). "Affect and Personality." In *Handbook of Emotions*, ed. Michael Lewis and Jeannette M. Haviland. New York: Guilford.

Peterson, Christopher. (1991). "The Meaning and Measurement of Explanatory Style." *Psychological Inquiry* 2:1–10.

Sartre, Jean-Paul. (1948). *The Emotions: Outline of a Theory*. New York: Philosophical Library.

Schaller, Mark, and Cialdini, Robert B. (1990). "Happiness, Sadness, and Helping: A Motivational Integration." In *Handbook of Motivation and Cognition: Foundations of Social Behavior, Vol. 2*, ed. Richard Sorrentino and E. Tory Higgins. New York: Guilford.

Schwarz, Norbert; Bless, Herbert; and Bohner, Gerd. (1991). "Mood and Persuasion: Affective States Influence the Processing of Persuasive Communications." In *Advances in Experimental Social Psychology, Vol. 24*, ed. Mark P. Zanna. San Diego, CA: Academic Press.

Schwarz, Norbert, and Clore, Gerald L. (1983). "Mood, Misattribution, and Judgments of Well-Being: Informative and Directive Functions of Affective States." *Journal of Personality and Social Psychology* 45:513–523.

Schwarz, Norbert, and Clore, Gerald L. (1996). "Feelings and Phenomenal Experiences." In *Social Psychology: Handbook of Basic Principles*, ed. E. Tory Higgins and Arie Kruglanski. New York: Guilford.

Strack, Stephen, and Coyne, James C. (1983). "Social Confirmation of Dysphoria: Shared and Private Reactions to Depression." *Journal of Personality and Social Psychology* 44:798–806.

Thayer, Robert E. (1996). *The Origin of Everyday Moods*. Oxford, Eng.: Oxford University Press.

Watson, David, and Clark, Lee A. (1984). "Negative Affectivity: The Disposition to Experience Aversive Emotional States." *Psychological Bulletin* 96:465–490.

Watson, David, and Clark, Lee A. (1997). "Measurement and Mismeasurement of Mood: Recurrent and Emergent Issues." *Journal of Personality Assessment* 68:267–296.

Weary, Gifford; Marsh, Kerry L.; Gleicher, Faith; and Edwards, John A. (1993). "Social-Cognitive Consequences of Depression." In *Control Motivation and Social Cognition*, ed. Gifford Weary, Faith Gleicher, and Kerry L. Marsh. New York: Springer-Verlag.

Norbert Schwarz
Piotr Winkielman

MOOD DISORDERS

Mood is the unique, subjective emotional manner by which a person experiences the world. This includes the individual's experiences of the past, the present, and the future. Mood may be normal, depressed, or elevated. Mood can be affected by external events such as disappointments, losses, successes, and achievements. It can be affected by thoughts, memories, and internal experiences. Individuals normally experience a wide range of moods and feel more or less in control of their moods. They can generally attribute their mood to their current psychological state—when reading a tragic novel, the reader might feel sad and distraught, and when viewing a film about a great victory, the viewer might feel jubilant and triumphant. These moods would be transient in nature, and the person would feel more or less in control. Affect, on the other hand, is the observed outward expression of emotion. Affect may be consistent or inconsistent with the individual's subjective description of emotions.

Mood disorders (referred to officially as affect disorders until 1987) are a group of clinical conditions in which there is a sense of loss of control over one's mood. Individuals with mood disorders frequently report a quality to their mood that is difficult to describe—words such as *depressed* or *elated mood* do not adequately explain the person's experience. Martha Manning (1995, pp. 112, 114), a clinical psychologist who has written extensively about her own experience of depression, describes the loss of control and the qualitatively distinct mood: "I'm getting less good at faking it. People in my family are noticing and asking what's wrong. My friends give me invitations to talk, to cry. I love them for their caring, but I want to run away. I have lost their language, their facility with words. I am in new territory and feel like a foreigner in theirs. . . . My world is filled with underwater voices, people, lists of things to do. But they are so fast and slippery that I can never keep up. Every inch of me aches. I can't believe that a person can hurt this bad and still breath."

History

Descriptions of mood disturbances can be found in the Old Testament as well as in the classics. As early as 400 B.C.E., Hippocrates suggested the theory that mental illness is a disease of the brain. Anlus Corneluis Celsus, in *De Re Medicina* (30 C.E.), described melancholia as being a depression caused by black bile. In 1854, Jules Fabret and Jules Baillarger, two French psychiatrists, individually recognized alternating episodes of mania and depression as a single disorder.

In 1899, Emil Kraepelin divided the psychotic disorders into manic-depressive psychosis and dementia praecox (i.e., schizophrenia). Manic-depressive psychosis included circular insanity, mania, and melancholia. These disorders had episodic courses and a better prognosis. Dementia praecox was considered to be a chronic deteriorating illness. European psychiatry has been dominated by descriptive biological psychiatry, following the approach of Kraepelin and focusing on describing and categorizing mental illnesses.

In the United States, psychiatry in the first half of the twentieth century was dominated by the theories of psychoanalysis and Adolph Meyer's psychobiology approach. Meyer viewed psychiatric disorders as reactions to life's stressors. The American Psychiatric Association's first *Diagnostic and Statistic Manual* (DSM-I), published in 1952, was strongly influenced by Meyer's theories, and mental disorders were described as reactions to psychosocial stressors. The second edition (DSM-II), which was published in 1968 and eliminated Meyer's ideas of a mental disorder stemming from a person's reactions to stressful events, represented a shift in American psychiatry to a more descriptive biological model. Psychoanalysis was still very influential in American psychiatry and the terms *neuroses* and *personalities* were still used (i.e., depressive neuroses and cyclothymic personality). In the third edition (DSM-III), published in 1980, the official psychiatric methodology turned to a purely descriptive categorization of disorders, and American psychiatry adopted a standardized research-oriented medical model. The revision of the third edition (DSM-III-R) and the fourth edition (DSM-IV) refined the descriptive, standardized criteria for diagnosis. The phenomenon of American psychiatry becoming more descriptive and biologically oriented, referred to as the re-medicalization of psychiatry, has led to debates about the nature of psychiatry, which has been transformed from the study of the psyche to the diagnosis and treatment of distinct mental disorders.

Mood disorders in the DSM-IV are organized in the following sections: mood episodes, depressive disorders, bipolar disorders, and other mood disorders. Each section begins with diagnostic features, followed by a discussion of epidemiology, associated features, and specific gender, age, and cultural features.

Mood Episodes

The four mood episodes are major depressive episode, manic episode, mixed episode, and hypomanic episode. These are the building blocks upon which a diagnosis of a mood disorder is made; they are not diagnoses in their own right.

A major depressive episode consists of a period of depressed mood or anhedonia (i.e., the loss of pleasure in nearly all activities). These symptoms must persist for most of the day, nearly every day, for at least two consecutive weeks. In addition, the individual must experience at least four of the seven following symptoms: weight loss, insomnia or hypersomnia, psychomotor agitation, fatigue or loss of energy, feelings of worthlessness or excessive guilt, difficulty concen-

trating or indecisiveness, or recurrent thoughts of death or suicide. The symptoms must cause clinically significant distress or impairment in social, occupational, or other important areas of functioning. The symptoms cannot be due to a general medical condition, a substance (drug of abuse or medication), or bereavement.

A manic episode is characterized by a distinct period of persistently elevated, expansive, or irritable mood lasting at least one week (or less if hospitalization is required). In addition, the individual must have three of the following seven symptoms: inflated self-esteem, decreased need for sleep, more talkative, racing thoughts, distractibility, increase in goal directed activity, or excessive involvement in pleasurable activities that have a high potential for painful consequences (e.g., excessive spending, sexual indiscretions, or foolish business investments). The mood disturbance must be sufficiently severe to cause marked impairment in functioning (occupational or social) or to necessitate hospitalization, or there must be psychotic features—the presence of delusions (i.e., false beliefs) or hallucinations (i.e., unrealistic perceptions). The symptoms must not be caused by a general medical condition or the effects of a substance (i.e., drugs of abuse or medication).

A mixed episode is present if an individual meets criteria for both a manic episode and a major depressive episode nearly every day for a period of one week. The mood disturbance must be sufficiently severe to cause marked impairment in functioning or to necessitate hospitalization, or there must be psychotic features. The symptoms must not be caused by a general medical condition or the effects of a substance.

A hypomanic episode is an attenuated manic episode and is defined as a distinct period of manic symptoms that lasts for at least four days but is not severe enough to cause marked impairment in functioning or to necessitate hospitalization. There are no psychotic features. The hypomanic symptoms are not caused by a general medical condition or the effects of a substance.

Depressive Disorders

Depressive disorder classifications include major depressive disorder, dysthymic disorder, and depressive disorder not otherwise specified.

The essential feature of major depressive disorder is a clinical course that is characteristic of one or more major depressive episodes without a history of a manic episode, mixed episode, hypomanic episode, and is not due to a general medical condition or substance abuse. If the individual is suffering a first episode, then the diagnosis is major depressive disorder-single episode. If the person has been symptom free for a period of at least two months and suffers another depressive episode, then the diagnosis is major depressive disorder-recurrent. If a manic, mixed, or hypomanic episode develops at some future point, then the diagnosis is changed to bipolar disorder.

Major depressive disorder is one of the more common psychiatric disorders. The lifetime prevalence rate has been estimated at about 15 percent, perhaps as high as 25 percent for women. The DSM-IV reports the lifetime risk for major depressive disorder in community samples to be between 10 to 25 percent for women and 5 to 12 percent for men. The disorder is consistently reported to be twice as common in adolescent and adult females as in adolescent and adult males. The rates in women and men are highest for individuals between twenty-five to forty-four years of age, whereas rates are lower for both women and men who are over sixty-five years of age. The Epidemiological Catchment Area study reported by Myrna Weissman and her colleagues (1988) found the average age of onset was twenty-seven years for both males and female. In more recent years, however, epidemiological studies by the Cross-National Collaborative Group (1992) have shown that individuals appear to have an earlier age of onset. Major depressive disorder is 1.5 to 3 times more common among first-degree biological relatives of individuals with this disorder than among the general population, indicating that there is a hereditary component to this disorder.

A major depressive disorder, by definition, must last at least two weeks. It is estimated that an average untreated episode will last six months or longer, and the termination may be gradual or abrupt. Recovery, either spontaneously or with treatment, is the usual outcome, but a chronic course is not rare. The DSM-IV reports that one year after the diagnosis of a major depressive disorder, about 40 percent of the patients have no symptoms, 20 percent have some symptoms but do not meet criteria for a major depressive episode, and 40 percent still meet criteria for a major depressive episode. Some long-term studies have found that 12 percent of individuals are still ill five years after the onset of a major depressive episode. Risk factors for a more chronic course include the severity of symptoms initially, a long duration of illness prior to treatment, history of alcoholism, a concurrent chronic medical condition, and other psychiatric disorders.

Major depressive disorder is usually a recurrent disorder, and the number of prior episodes predicts the likelihood of developing a subsequent episode. About 50 to 60 percent of individuals who have had an episode of major depressive disorder can be expected to have a second. Those who have had two episodes have a 70 percent chance of having a third, and those who have had three episodes have a 90 percent chance of having a fourth. About 5 to 10 percent of individuals who have been diagnosed with a major depressive disorder-single episode will eventually have a manic episode and will eventually be diagnosed with a bipolar disorder. A long-standing clinical observation is that stressful life events frequently precede the first or second episode of a major depressive disorder. This correlation appears to diminish with subsequent episodes. One theory proposed to explain this is that the first or second episode causes changes in the biology of the brain, leaving the individual at higher risk for subsequent episodes following less stressful events, or even in the absence of any stressors. There is a lifetime risk of suicide in about 15 percent of individuals suffering from major depressive disorder.

Individuals experiencing bereavement due to the death of a loved one may have symptoms similar to those that are characteristic of a major depressive episode. Symptoms associated with bereavement include feelings of sadness, insomnia, decreased appetite, and, in some cases, loss of weight. Bereavement is not considered a mental disorder in the DSM-IV. It is a category that could be considered the focus of clinical attention if a person were to seek help from a practitioner. Individuals experiencing bereavement may meet criteria for a major depressive episode if the symptoms of bereavement persist longer than two months after the loss. If the symptoms are more severe within two months of the loss and are considered beyond the range of normal grieving, then a diagnosis of major depressive disorder is warranted. Symptoms that are not characteristic of bereavement and indicate a major depressive disorder include: guilt related to issues beyond those surrounding the death of a loved one, preoccupation with death other than thoughts of being dead to be with the deceased person, morbid preoccupation with worthlessness, marked psychomotor retardation, prolonged and marked functional impairment, and hallucinating experiences other than thinking that he or she hears the voice of, or transiently sees the image of, the deceased person.

Once diagnosis of a major depressive disorder, single episode or recurrent, has been made, the clinician can also specify other features. For example, the presence of psychotic symptoms such as delusions or hallucinations can be included in the diagnosis. Other features could include a postpartum onset (within four weeks of the birth of a child) or a seasonal pattern in which depressive episodes occur in relation to a particular season. The seasonal pattern usually involves winter depressive episodes. The prevalence of this pattern is much higher in women, who account for 60 to

90 percent of the people with a seasonal pattern. Age is also a factor as a seasonal pattern is associated with younger individuals.

Dysthymic disorder is another diagnosis of a mood disorder of the depressive type. Individuals with dysthymic disorder have chronic, low-grade depression that does not meet criteria for a major depressive episode. The chronically depressed mood occurs most of the day, more days than not, for at least two years. In children and adolescents, the mood may be irritable, and the duration must be for at least one year. In addition to the depressed mood, the individual must experience two of the following six symptoms: poor appetite or overeating, insomnia or hypersomnia, low energy, low self-esteem, poor concentration or difficulty making decisions, and feelings of hopelessness. These symptoms must not be caused by a general medical condition or substance abuse.

Dysthymic disorder frequently begins in childhood, adolescence, or early adult life. The onset is often subtle. The lifetime prevalence of dysthymic disorder is about 6 percent. Women are 2 to 3 times more likely to develop the disorder than are men. An important point in diagnosing dysthymic disorder is that during the two-year duration of symptoms, there cannot be a major depressive episode diagnosed. After two years have elapsed and a major depressive episode occurs, there can be a superimposed major depressive disorder in addition to dysthymic disorder. This is referred to as double depression. About 20 to 25 percent of individuals with major depressive disorder have the disorder superimposed on a dysthymic disorder. These individuals generally have a poorer prognosis. Persons with dysthymic disorder have high rates of other psychiatric conditions. Some estimates are that as many as 75 percent of individuals with dysthymic disorder have other disorders, including major depressive disorder, anxiety disorders, substance abuse, and personality disorders.

Depressive disorder not otherwise specified is a category for disorders with prominent depressive features that do not meet criteria for diagnosis as a major depressive disorder or dysthymic disorder. This is often the case with the elderly, in whom depressive symptoms are frequently found. The symptoms commonly do not meet criteria for a major depressive disorder or dysthymic disorder but cause distress and impairments. The diagnosis of depressive disorder not otherwise specified would be used if the depressive symptoms were superimposed on a psychotic disorder or during the residual phase of schizophrenia. Included here is premenstrual dysphoric disorder, which is characterized by symptoms of depression, anxiety, irritability, and lability, regularly occurring during the last week of the menstrual cycle and remitting within a few days of the onset of menses. Also included in this classification are minor depressive episodes that last two weeks or recurrent brief depressive episodes. This category can also be used in situations in which the clinician has concluded that a depressive disorder is present but is unable to determine whether it is primary, due to a general medical condition, or related to the use of a substance.

Bipolar Disorders

Bipolar disorders include bipolar I disorder, bipolar II disorder, cyclothymic disorder, and bipolar disorder not otherwise specified. The essential feature of these disorders is that they all involve a clinical course that is characteristic of a manic, hypomanic, or mixed episode. Manic mood disturbance makes up one pole of a mood instability disorder. The other pole is the depressive pole. It is possible to have a diagnosis of a bipolar disorder and only have manic symptoms, either a single episode or recurrent episodes. The majority of patients, however, will have mood episodes with characteristics of both poles—mania and depression.

Bipolar I disorder is characterized by at least one manic episode and may also involve depressive episodes. A manic episode, by definition, must last for one week and usually begins suddenly over days or sometimes over hours. A manic episode usually lasts a few weeks to a few months if not treated and is frequently either preceded or followed by a major depressive episode. The lifetime prevalence of bipolar I disorder is about 1 percent. The DSM-IV gives the prevalence of bipolar I disorder in community samples at between 0.4 to 1.6 percent. Bipolar I disorder occurs equally in men and women. Males are more likely to have first episodes of mania, while women are more likely to have first episodes of depression. The average age of onset for the first manic episode is in the early twenties, but it can occur anywhere from early adolescence to age fifty. The Epidemiological Catchment Area study reported by Kimberly Burke and her colleagues (1990) found the median age of onset to be eighteen years in men and twenty years in women. About 10 to 15 percent of adolescents with recurrent major depressive episodes go on to develop bipolar disorder. Mixed episodes tend to be more frequent in adolescents. There appears to be, in the early 1990s, a tendency toward an earlier age of onset of bipolar disorder. First-degree biological relatives of individuals with bipolar I disorder have elevated rates of bipolar I disorder (4 to 24 percent), bipolar II disorder (1 to 5 percent), and major depressive disorder (4 to 24 percent), suggesting strong evidence of a genetic influence in the development of bipolar I disorder. Bipolar I disorder is a recurrent illness, and the DSM-IV estimates that more than 90 percent of individuals who have a single manic episode go on to have other episodes of mania or depression. About 7 percent of bipolar I disorder patients do not have further episodes, and 40 percent have a chronic disorder. Approximately one-third of all bipolar I disorder patients have evidence of significant social decline. On long-term follow-up, about 40 percent of bipolar patients have more than ten episodes. As the disorder progresses, the time between episodes often decreases. Another feature of bipolar I disorder is a high incidence of alcohol and substance abuse. Lifetime suicide risk is 10 to 15 percent in bipolar I disorder.

Bipolar II disorder, which was a new diagnostic category presented in the DSM-IV, is characterized by recurrent major depressive episodes and hypomanic episodes. The DSM-IV estimates that the lifetime prevalence of bipolar II disorder is about 0.5 percent. Roughly 60 to 70 percent of hypomanic episodes in bipolar II disorder occur immediately before or after a major depressive episode. Hypomanic episodes usually precede or follow major depressive episodes in a characteristic manner for individuals. The number of episodes of bipolar II disorder tends to be higher than for recurrent depressive disorders. Between 5 and 15 percent of bipolar II disorder patients have more than four episodes per year and qualify as rapid-cycling types. If an individual develops an episode that meets criteria for a manic episode, the diagnosis is changed to bipolar I disorder. The lifetime risk of suicide is 10 to 15 percent for bipolar II disorder. The DSM-IV has taken the position that any manic or hypomanic episode that is induced by a psychotropic drug does not qualify as a manic or hypomanic episode. The DSM-IV specifies that the diagnosis is a substance-induced mood disorder.

Cyclothymic disorder is a chronic, fluctuating mood disturbance disorder. Mood fluctuates between episodes of hypomania and depressive episodes that do not meet full criteria for a major depressive episode. This condition must exist for a period of two years in adults or one year in children and adolescents. If there is a major depressive episode before two years, then the diagnosis is changed to bipolar II disorder. If there is a major depressive episode after two years, then there is a diagnosis of bipolar II disorder superimposed on cyclothymic disorder. Cyclothymic disorder often begins early in life. In the general population, the prevalence of cyclothymic disorder is estimated at 1 percent. The incidence is much higher in psychiatric outpatients and may account for 3 to 10 percent of all psychiatric outpatients. About one-third of individuals with cyclothymic disorder subsequently develop a bipolar I or bipolar II disorder. There is also a high incidence of personality disorders in individuals with cyclothymic disorder. An estimated 10 percent of outpatients with borderline personality disorder also have a diagnosis of cyclothymic disorder. The male-to-female ratio is equal in community samples but higher in women in clinical settings (at about 3 to 1). The age of onset of cyclothymic disorder is about fifteen to twenty-five years of age.

Bipolar disorder not otherwise specified is the diagnosis for individuals who suffer with bipolar symptoms that do not meet full criteria for bipolar I or bipolar II disorders. An example of this might be manic symptoms and depressive symptoms that do not meet minimal duration criteria for a manic episode or a major depressive episode. This diagnosis could also be used if there is a bipolar disorder but the clinician cannot determine if it is primary, the result of a general medical condition, or substance induced.

Mood Disorders Due to a General Medical Condition

A mood disorder due to a general medical condition is diagnosed if an individual has a prominent and persistent disturbance of mood that is judged to be caused by the direct physiological affects of a general medical condition. There must be evidence from the medical history, examination, or laboratory tests that there is an etiological connection between the medical condition and the mood disturbance. This may involve clinical judgment in some cases.

There are certain medical illnesses that are highly correlated with mood disturbances. These include degenerative neurological conditions (Parkinson's Disease, strokes), metabolic conditions (vitamin B-12 deficiency), endocrine conditions (thyroid disorders), autoimmune disorders (systemic lupus erythematosos), infections (HIV), and certain cancers (pancreatic). The pattern of onset and the pattern of prevalence reflect the medical etiology of the mood disturbance. The diagnosis of other medical conditions is considered more variable as a causative factor. Some psychiatrists, called biopsychiatrists, strongly advocate that many mood disturbances are caused by an underlying medical condition.

The mood disturbances do not need to meet full criteria for an episode, but the predominant symptom type is indicated—the diagnosis could be mood disorder due to a general medical condition with depressive features or manic features. If dementia is diagnosed, this has a separate subtype included in the diagnosis itself—dementia of the Alzheimer's type with depression has its own diagnosis in the DSM-IV.

Substance-Induced Mood Disorders

The essential feature of a substance-induced mood disorder is that there is evidence from medical history, examination, or laboratory tests that the mood disturbance occurs in association with drug use (intoxication) or withdrawal states, which includes up to four weeks after the cessation of substance use. There are signs that indicate the temporal onset of symptoms either during intoxication or during withdrawal.

The prevalence of this disorder is not known. The widespread use of alcohol, recreational drugs, the number of toxic chemicals in the environment and workplace, and the number of prescription drugs that could cause mood disorders indicate that the prevalence of this disorder is probably high. Substance-induced disorders must always be considered when evaluating a person with mood disorder symptoms.

Treatment

Once the diagnosis of a mood disorder has been made, a treatment plan is developed. This plan, obviously, depends on the type of disorder that has been diagnosed.

Depressive Disorders

The first intervention for depressive disorders involves safety. If there is evidence of a suicide risk, the person is usually hospitalized for protection and safety. After the person's safety has been established, treatment is begun and involves psychotherapy and/or psychopharmacology. It is commonly believed that a combination of psychotherapy and pharmacotherapy is the most effective treatment for depressive disorders. This is the position taken by the American Psychiatric Association (1993). The U.S. Department of Health and Human Services (1993) has taken a different position on this issue, stating in their guidelines that pharmacotherapy is the best first-line treatment for moderately to severely depressed patients. These guidelines recommend psychotherapy as an option for patients (with mild to moderate depression) who prefer that treatment option.

Prior to 1987, there were only a few antidepressant medications available. One group of medications was called tricyclics, and the other was called monoamine oxidase inhibitors (MAOI). These drugs were shown to be effective in treating the symptoms of depression when compared to a placebo. In more severe depression, the difference between medication effect and placebo effect was the highest. In less severe depression, the difference between medication effect and placebo was diminished. Both the tricyclics and the MAOIs were difficult medications to use. They caused many side effects and could cause serious adverse reactions in many individuals. Since 1987, many new antidepressants have been introduced. These include Prozac (fluoxetine), Paxil (paroxetine), Zoloft (sertralene), Luvox (fluvoxamine), Wellbutrin (bupropion), Effexor (venlafaxine), Serzone (nefazodone), and Remeron (mirtazapine). These drugs are much safer to use and generally cause less side effects than the older antidepressants.

The mechanism of action of all antidepressant medications appears to involve their effects on neurotransmitters in the brain. All of the antidepressants have an effect on the serotonin or neurepinepherine in the brain. Most effect the absorption or activity of serotonin and neurepinepherine. The exact manner by which this helps improve a depressed mood remains uncertain. Outcome studies have usually found that antidepressant medications are effective in 60 to 80 percent of individuals, compared to a placebo response of 30 to 40 percent. There is generally a two- to three-week delay between the start of medication and a response. Some antidepressants, such as the tricyclics and MAOIs, because of side effect potential, are started at low doses and increased gradually until and antidepressant effect is achieved. The newer antidepressants are much better tolerated and can be started at what will usually be an effective dose; slow, gradual increases are not usually necessary.

If there is no response or if there is an inadequate response to a single drug, there are options. Another medication (such as lithium, thyroid hormone, buspirone, or another antidepressant) can be added to enhance or augment the first antidepressant, or another antidepressant can replace the one previously given. Once a person has had a positive response to a medication, it should be continued for about one year, since premature discontinuation has been correlated with a higher incidence of the reemergence of depressive symptoms. If depressive episodes are recurrent, then maintenance medication may be necessary for several years.

If psychotic symptoms are present, then a combination of antidepressant medication and antipsychotic medication is used. The presence of psychotic symptoms is also one indication for the need of electroconvulsive therapy (ECT). Other indications for the need of ECT include high suicide risk, treatment resistance, and a previous good response to ECT.

Light therapy, which involves exposure to bright light, is used to treat depression with a seasonal pattern. In particular, light therapy appears to have beneficial effects in dealing with winter depression.

In addition to pharmacotherapy, ECT, and light therapy, psychotherapies are used to treat depressive disorders. Research on cognitive therapy and interpersonal therapy has demonstrated that both of these therapies are effective in the treatment of depression. Other types of therapy, such as long-term psychoanalytic therapy and supportive psychotherapy, are widely used to treat depressive disorders. However, there

In one form of light therapy, a victim of seasonal affective disorder wears a pith helmet fitted with a battery-powered full-spectrum fluorescent light to provide the equivalent effect of being exposed to natural sunlight. (Corbis/Jim Sugar Photography)

have not been randomized controlled trials demonstrating the effectiveness of these therapies.

Cognitive therapy, which was developed by Arron Beck (1979), is based on the theory that distorted cognitions or beliefs cause depression. Cognitive therapy attempts to correct these distorted cognitions or beliefs. The goals are to relieve depression and to prevent recurrence by identifying negative thoughts and replacing them with more realistic and positive ways of thinking. Cognitive therapy also focuses on rehearsing these new cognitive responses and changing behavioral responses.

Interpersonal therapy (IPT), which was developed by Gerald Klerman and his colleagues (1984), focuses on one or two of an individual's current interpersonal problems. The assumption is that current interpersonal problems are likely to be involved in precipitating or perpetuating depressive symptoms. The goal of therapy is to help the person become more effective in dealing with current interpersonal problems that are associated with the onset of symptoms. Four problem areas often associated with depression are unresolved grief, difficulty with role transitions, interpersonal disputes, and interpersonal deficits. Research studies have demonstrated that IPT is superior to no treatment and equal to pharmacotherapy for mild to moderate depression.

The effectiveness of brief psychodynamic psychotherapy has been studied but not as extensively as cognitive therapy or IPT. The goal of brief psychodynamic psychotherapy is to resolve core personality conflicts that are assumed to give rise to depression. Long-term psychoanalytic psychotherapy and supportive psychotherapy have not been studied in randomized controlled trials. These therapies are used extensively in clinical practice. It has been pointed out that it is not accurate to say they are ineffective. One can, however, say they have not been shown to be effective in randomized controlled trials.

Bipolar Disorders

Bipolar disorders are viewed as chronic, recurrent illnesses. Treatment is focused on resolution of acute symptoms and prevention of future episodes. If a person suffers from acute mania, hospitalization is often indicated. Individuals may require involuntary commitment if they are using very poor judgment and are at risk of harming themselves or others.

The main intervention after safety has been assured is to resolve the manic episode. Lithium had been the treatment of choice for mania. Major tranquilizers have frequently been used in combination with lithium. Other medications, mostly anticonvulsants, have more recently been shown to be effective in controlling mania. These medications include Depakote (valproic acid), Tegretol (carbamazepine), and Neurontin (gabapentin). Combinations of lithium and anticonvulsants are also frequently used.

Once mania has been controlled, maintenance therapy is necessary. Lithium has been shown to be effective in reducing the frequency, severity, and duration of both manic and depressive episodes with somewhat better effectiveness for mania. Depakote and Tegretol have not been studied for long-term maintenance but are frequently used alone or in conjunction with lithium. Once stabilized, discontinuation of maintenance medication is associated with a high relapse rate. Any decision to discontinue successful maintenance therapy should be carefully considered.

Psychotherapy also plays a role in the treatment of bipolar disorder. No particular psychotherapy has been shown to be uniquely effective. Psychotherapy focused on helping the individual deal with the effect of a chronic, recurrent illness and the importance of maintenance medication is crucial.

Depressive episodes, in the course of bipolar disorder, are often effectively treated with lithium. Antidepressant medication could be used, but caution must be used since antidepressant medication could precipitate a manic episode. Using lithium in combination with antidepressant medications would reduce this risk. ECT is often necessary to treat a severe depressive episode in the course of a bipolar disorder.

Other Mood Disorders

If a mood disorder due a general medical condition is diagnosed, then treatment needs to be directed toward the most effective management of the general medical condition. If a mood disorder persists, then medication and psychotherapy for the mood disorder should be added. The medical illness and the psychiatric disorder should be treated simultaneously.

The treatment of substance-induced mood disorders also involves an integrated approach. An individual who is abusing substances needs detoxification and substance abuse treatment. If the person is no longer using the substance and a mood disorder persists or is severe, then simultaneous treatment of the substance abuse and the mood disorder is the plan of choice.

See also: ANXIETY DISORDERS; FEAR AND PHOBIAS; GRIEF; MOOD; PSYCHOANALYTIC PERSPECTIVE; PSYCHOPHYSIOLOGY OF EMOTIONS; PSYCHOTHERAPY; SEASONAL AFFECTIVE DISORDER

Bibliography

American Psychiatric Association. (1993). "Practice Guideline for Major Depressive Disorder in Adults." *American Journal of Psychiatry* 150(suppl.):1–26.

American Psychiatric Association. (1994). *Diagnostic and Statistical Manual of Mental Disorders*, 4th ed. Washington, DC: American Psychiatric Association.

Beck, Aaron T. (1979). *Cognitive Therapy and the Emotional Disorders*. New York: Penguin.

Burke, Kimberly C.; Burke, Jack D., Jr.; Regier Darrel A.; and Rae, Donald S. (1990). "Age of Onset of Selected Mental Disorders in Five Community Populations." *Archives of General Psychiatry* 47:511–518.

Cross-National Collaborative Group. (1992). "The Changing Rate of Major Depression: Cross National Comparisons." *Journal of the American Medical Association* 268:3098–3105.

Feighner, John P.; Robins, Eli; Guze, Samuel B.; Woodruff, Robert A., Jr.; Winokur, George; and Munoz, Rodrigo. (1972). "Diagnostic Criteria for Use in Psychiatric Research." *Archives of General Psychiatry* 26:57–63.

Gabbard, Glen O. (1994). *Psychodynamic Psychiatry in Clinical Practice*. Washington, DC: American Psychiatric Press.

Gold, Mark S. (1987). *The Good News About Depression: Cures and Treatments in the New Age of Psychiatry*. New York: Villard Books.

Jamison, Kay Redfield. (1995). *An Unquiet Mind: A Memoir of Moods and Madness*. New York: Knopf.

Jefferson, James W., and Greist, John H. (1994). "Mood Disorders." In *The American Psychiatric Press Textbook of Psychiatry*, 2nd ed., ed. Robert E. Hales, Stuart C. Yudofsky, and John A. Talbot. Washington, DC: American Psychiatric Press.

Kaplan, Harold I.; Sadock, Benjamin J.; and Grebb, Jack A. (1994). *Kaplan and Sadock's Synopsis of Psychiatry*, 7th ed. Baltimore, MD: Williams & Wilkins.

Klerman, Gerald L.; Weissman, Myrna M.; and Rounsaville, Bruce J. (1984). *Interpersonal Psychotherapy for Depression*. New York: Basic Books.

Kocsis, James H., and Klein, Daniel N., eds. (1995). *Diagnosis and Treatment of Chronic Depression*. New York: Guilford.

LaBruzza, Anthony L. (1994). *Using the DSM-IV: A Clinician's Guide to Psychiatric Diagnosis*. Northvale, NJ: Jason Aronson.

Manning, Martha. (1995). "New Hope for Depression: The Fact, the Fiction, and the Light at the End of the Tunnel." *New Woman*, November, pp. 112–140.

Morrison, James. (1995). *DSM-IV Made Easy*. New York: Guilford.

Persons, Jacqueline B. (1998). "Indications for Psychotherapy in the Treatment of Depression." *Psychiatric Annals* 28(2): 80–83.

Rosenthal, Norman E. (1989). *Seasons of the Mind*. New York: Bantam.

U.S. Department of Health and Human Services. (1993). *Depression in Primary Care: Detection, Diagnosis, and Treatment*. Rockville, MD: Agency for Health Care Policy and Research.

Volkan, Vamik, ed. (1985). *Depressive States and Their Treatment*. Northvale, NJ: Jason Aronson.

Weissman, Myrna M.; Leaf, Philip J.; Tischler, Gary L.; Blazer, Dang; Karno, Marvin; Bruce, Martha L.; and Florio, Louis P. (1988). "Affective Disorders in Five United States Communities." *Psychological Medicine* 18:141–153.

Lawrence N. Rossi

MOTIVATION

Conventionally, motivation is defined in terms of the control of behavior—specifically, the process by which behavior is activated and directed toward some definable goal. The mechanisms of control range from relatively simple reflexes to such complex motives as those for achievement, affiliation, and power. All motivational mechanisms are genetically based at some level, but the degrees of freedom of behavior from direct genetic control vary from relatively inflexible, "hardwired" unconditioned responses that have been evolved to perform specific functions (i.e., special-purpose processing systems) to responses that are intimately attuned to learned situational influences (i.e., general-purpose processing systems). The essential function that is served by the evolution from special- to general-purpose processing systems is increased flexibility of response. If the notion of "evolutionary progress" has any useful meaning, it arguably involves the increasing of flexibility of behavior.

Like motivation, emotion is conventionally defined in terms of goal-directed behaviors, such as fighting, fleeing, and attraction. In contrast to motivation, emotion is typically associated with subjectively experienced feelings that accompany such actions, such as anger, fear, and love. Also in contrast to motivation, emotion is often associated with accompanying expressive displays (e.g., facial expression, gesture, vocal quality) and peripheral physiological arousal responses (e.g., skin conductance, heart rate, respiration). Subjective, display, and arousal responses do not always agree with one another; people who are facially expressive often show fewer autonomic responses (e.g., skin conductance deflections) than do less expressive people.

All emotional responses involve manifestations of activated and directed motivational potential—subjective experiences, expressive displays, and physiological arousal responses are all manifestations of motivational dispositions. The relationship between motivation and emotion is analogous to the relationship between energy and matter in physics. One never sees energy directly, for energy exists as a potential in matter (e.g., in an object held at a height, in a coiled spring, in the molecules of an explosive). When the potential energy is released by an effective stimulus (e.g., dropping the object, releasing the spring, lighting the explosive), one sees the manifestation of potential energy in matter (e.g., in light, heat, and force). Similarly, one never sees motivation directly, but when motivational potential is released by an effective stimulus, one sees the manifestation of motivational potential in behavior, including emotional behavior. According to this view, motivation and emotion are two sides of the same coin, and emotional responses can be considered to be readouts of motivational potential.

Fundamental Types of Motivational Systems

The least flexible of motivational mechanisms can be observed in the simplest of creatures, such as the single-celled prokaryotic bacteria (which, unlike eukaryotes, lack a nucleus to hold their genetic material). These presumably cannot involve the subjective, display, and arousal responses that are typically associated with "emotion." Nevertheless, such simple creatures can exhibit remarkably complex behaviors, in-

Highly emotional reactions to particular social issues, such as abortion, can motivate individuals (on both sides of the issue) to take action and make their opinions known. (Corbis/Joseph Sohm; ChromoSohm Inc.)

cluding coming together in multicelled forms. Such behaviors are controlled by reflexes that are relatively simple in themselves but are organized into complex systems that are regulated by communicative signals—both internal and external to the organism.

Virtually all creatures can be demonstrated to exhibit four general sorts of motivated behavior: arousal, approach-avoidance, agonistic, and prosocial behaviors. Arousal, approach-avoidance, and agonistic behaviors are generally "selfish," in that they function to maintain the survival of the individual organism. Arousal involves a dimension of behavior from quiescence to vigorous activity; approach-avoidance involves tendencies to advance versus retreat; agonistic behaviors involve competitive responses. The fourth class of behavior functions to maintain the species, sometimes at the expense of the individual. These prosocial behaviors include primitive aggregative and sexual behaviors and always involve automatic or spontaneous communication between individual organisms. Such communication involves specific displays in the sending individuals and preattunements to, or intrinsic abilities to respond appropriately to, those displays in receivers.

Motivational mechanisms that involve arousal, approach-avoidance, agonistic, and prosocial behaviors can be traced in virtually all living things, from prokaryotes to humans. In humans and presumably most other mammals, these four types of behavior all involve the subjective, display, and arousal responses that are associated with "emotion." One conceptualization, then, is that emotion involves the readouts of motivational systems in relatively advanced creatures that have the capability for subjective experience, display, and peripheral physiological arousal (e.g., the more advanced mammals). A more general conceptualization is that emotion involves the readout of motivational systems at any level. Thus, Ross Buck (1985) defined motivation to be "the potential built into systems of behavior control" and emotion to be "the actualization or readout of motivational potential." In the latter view, even simple creatures are capable of "emotion," although they may not be capable of subjective experience, display, and peripheral physiological responding.

Levels of Motivational Systems

Biologically-based motivational systems are organized hierarchically, with the more recently evolved, or phylogenetically newer, systems being progressively farther up the hierarchy and progressively more open to influence from the organism's experience with regard to classical conditioning, instrumental learning, higher-level cognitive processing, and, in humans, language. This hierarchy is expressed anatomically as well as functionally; in effect, form and function are linked. In the brain, phylogenetically older functions are associated with subcortical mechanisms, such as the brainstem, midbrain, hypothalamus, and basal ganglia, while phylogenetically newer and more complex functions are associated with cortical (layered) brain tissue. Paul MacLean's (1990, 1993) triune theory suggests that the human brain embodies three successive stages of the evolution of brain and behavior, with the phylogenetically newer structures superimposed over the older ones. The "reptilian brain" involves subcortical mechanisms that organize individual and social behavior in reptiles, the "old mammalian brain" involves three- to five-layered cortical tissue that is involved in the control of behavior in mammals, and the "new mammalian brain" involves the phylogenetically newer six-layered cortical tissues that are involved in advanced cognitive processing and language. The reptilian brain is associated with the brainstem, midbrain, and basal ganglia, and the old mammalian brain is associated with the limbic system.

Reflexes: Kineses, Taxes, and Tropisms

Reflexes involve the simplest level of motivational mechanism, with direct (i.e., unconditioned) stimulus-response associations—actions "released" by highly specific internal or external stimuli such as the release of saliva by the presence of food. Thus, with reflexes, the behavior is activated by specific stimuli and directed by the simple structure of the reflex mechanism (i.e., it is structured biologically). Spinal reflexes such as the knee-jerk reaction involve the arrangement of sensory and motor neurons between the knee and the spinal cord. In effect, this arrangement embodies the motivational potential, which is read-out (actualized) by the neurologist's tap on the knee. Kineses include all body movements, while taxes involve locomotor and/or orienting responses that are controlled by some stimulus. Tropisms are organized taxes that can make up complex self-organizing systems that result in such behaviors as an organism moving toward the light. Human orienting, motor, and vegetative behaviors (including movement and balance, digestion, immune system responses) are modulated and "smoothed" by innumerable reflexes, all working automatically and without volitional input (i.e., unconsciously).

Associative learning (i.e., classical conditioning) may modify reflexes; the immune system may, for example, organize an allergic reaction to a plastic flower. Such learning can involve internal bodily processes serving as conditioned or unconditioned stimuli—interoceptive conditioning. Gregory Razran (1961) suggested that each person undergoes a unique history of interoceptive classical conditioning, which results in what he called an "observable unconscious." For example, if one's parents fight at the dinner table, internal responses that are associated with eating and digestion could come to elicit fearful reactions. Such conditioned emotional responses are capable of having significant and extensive effects on the individual (e.g., influencing immune system responding and therefore physical health).

Instincts or Fixed-Action Patterns

Like reflexes, instincts involve behaviors that are relatively innate or fixed by inheritance and can be involved in complex systems organized and regulated by communicative signals. Unlike reflexes, instincts involve sequences of overt behaviors (which may be quite complex) that are performed in the external environment, such as the migratory behavior of birds or fish. Also, instincts are typically releaser by events (releasers) in the external environment, such as the day/night cycle, and the instinctive behavior sequences typically are associated with a specifiable function, similar to a desirable end-state or goal, such as moving to a warmer climate. Thus, with instincts, the behavior is activated by releasers and directed by a relatively fixed sequence of behavior that has been structured by evolution (i.e., structured phylogenetically). Behavior sequences that are governed by instincts are relatively fixed; if the external environment changes (e.g., salmon runs are blocked), the species cannot easily change and may face danger of extinction.

Instinctive behavior sequences may require environmental priming during a sensitive period (i.e., the critical period) to become effective. In imprinting, abilities to respond appropriately to other members of the species are fixed during early experience. Konrad Lorenz (1965) demonstrated that a newborn gosling that was isolated from its mother would readily follow a person, an adult goose, or a moving box and that it could not then be induced later to follow its mother. Harry Harlow (1971) demonstrated that early and prolonged isolation from other individuals of the same species could produce disastrous deficits in later social and emotional competence. In humans, attachment, or the capacity to bond, may involve instincts. As with the monkeys studied by Harlow, human experience in early affectionate relationships with adults and peers appears to be necessary and perhaps sufficient to establish the capacity for bonding. Early abuse may disrupt such learning, contributing to the inability to bond, which is characteristic of sociopathy.

Drives

Drives differ from instincts in that the organism has the flexibility to alter its behavior in response to changing characteristics of the environment. Drives involve natural tissue needs, such as needs for air, food, water, sex, temperature regulation, and pain avoidance. The satisfaction of these needs constitutes a natural desirable end-state or goal that is associated with the drive. Unlike reflexes and/or instincts, internal cognitive representations or "subjective experiences" of the need signal drives that involve desires such as hunger, thirst, sexual desire, or pain. Desires represent the nature of needs within the brain in such a way that the organism can attend to needs before they become critical. In doing so, desires contribute a new order of flexibility to behavior.

To satisfy a drive, the organism must alter or adapt its behavior to fit the external environment, by learning where to find and how to exploit resources such as food, water, and sexual partners—while escaping/avoiding pain. Generally, a drive will first activate the organism, as when a sleeping mouse awakens hungry. The drive then directs behavior; the animal begins to search the environment for food, ignoring other stimuli. When food is found and consumed, tissue needs are satisfied and the drive is satiated. The arousal, direction, and satiation of behavior are associated with neurochemical systems that involve dopamine, norepinephrine, and endorphins, respectively. Studies of place preferences in animals suggest that each of these neurochemicals may be associated with subjective experiences that involve reward, and these neurochemical systems are associated with potential drugs of abuse in humans, including cocaine, amphetamine, morphine, benzene (alcohol), and nicotine.

The chain of behavior that leads to satiation is reinforced, so that it is more likely to recur when the need is aroused in that environment in the future. Stimuli that are associated with the satiation of needs become "positive incentives," while stimuli that are associated with nonreward or punishment become "negative incentives." In either case, the stimuli that are associated with reward or punishment become themselves capable of eliciting "acquired drives." In this way, environmental stimuli come to be associated with positive or negative experiences of the individual animal, allowing the individual animal to respond flexibly to changes in the environment. In the terms of Robert White (1959), the animal becomes competent and effective in dealing with environmental contingencies. Thus, with drives, the behavior is activated by bodily needs that are associated with subjectively experienced desires and is directed by the structure of the positive or negative features of the environment as experienced by the individual (i.e., it is structured ontogenetically).

In humans, acquired drives can be associated with virtually any stimulus. Money, for example, is a powerful positive incentive that does not satisfy any needs or desires in itself, but it is strongly associated with the satisfaction of desires. Acquired drives that are associated with goals of personal achievement (e.g., having power, influence, and affiliation with others) are common motives in humans. Researchers such as David McClelland (1965) have found that there are strong individual differences in the strength of achievement, power, and affiliation motives, which appear to be associated with socialization practices. There are also gender differences in such motives, and much controversy exists about the extent to which these differences are due to socialization, biologically-based sex differences, or a combination of the two.

Affects

Like reflexes, instincts, and drives, affects are based upon specific "hard-wired" neurochemical systems in the brain; however, affects do not serve highly specific functions. Instead, affects involve general response tendencies in relation to the environment—to be aroused or quiescent, fight or flee, to approach or avoid, to love or hate, to hide or explore. Like drives, affects involve subjective experiences, but affects differ from drives in that a specific bodily need is not involved. Instead of the desires that are associated with specific needs, affects involve more general feelings. The primary affects analyzed by Silvan Tomkins (1962–1963) include happiness, sadness, fear, and anger. Each of these affects are associated with specific neurochemical systems and expressive displays. Social affects, such as pride, guilt, and shame, are associated with general tendencies to be attached to and cooperate with other individuals. Cognitive affects, such as curiosity and surprise, are associated with exploring the environment.

The capacity to experience the affects is innate and unlearned; however, the circumstances under which affects are experienced and the ways in which they are expressed require learning. Thus, with affects, the behavior is activated by stimuli that evokes subjectively experienced feelings and directed according to socially learned situational conditions. Learning about the affects (i.e., emotional education) is unlike other sorts of social learning in that the affects are "private events" that are experienced subjectively; others do not have direct access to the affects that are experienced by the individual. Other aspects of emotional responding are also distinguished by their degree of accessibility—expressive displays are more accessible to others than to the responder, and most peripheral physiological arousal responses are not accessible to anyone without special equipment.

Individual Differences in Motivation

Although motivational systems are genetically based, experience is usually necessary to actualize motivational potential. For this reason, motivation is an arena where the interaction between biology and experience is particularly important; both influences must be taken into account. For example, as noted, early affectionate relationships are necessary to actualize attachment potential. Moreover, the degrees of freedom between motivation and behavior increase at higher levels of complexity. Indeed, at higher levels, motivational systems are designed to be flexible; they are, in a sense, "hard-wired to be flexible."

Individual differences in motivation thus may reflect both genetically based differences in "temperament" as well as differences in experience and social learning. The influences of genes versus environment are notoriously difficult to pry apart. Studies that show similarities between monozygotic twins (i.e., "identical twins") have been touted as evidence of the importance of genetic determination, but most monozygotic twins are also monochorionic, sharing the same choriod plexus. Therefore, the prenatal chemical environment is shared as well. Studies of monozygotic twins who are dichorionic—who are genetically identical but experienced different prenatal environments—show less commonality. For example, research reported by Jeanne Phelps, James Davis, and Kevin Schartz (1997) has shown that monochorionic monozygotic twins show a concordance for schizophrenia of 60 percent, so that if one twin is schizophrenic there is a high likelihood that the other is schizophrenic as well. For dichorionic monozygotic twins, the concordance rate is much lower at 10.7 percent, which is similar to the concordance rate of dizygotic twins (i.e., "fraternal twins"). Most studies of monozygotic twins do not investigate whether they are monochorionic or dichorionic. Therefore, the results might reflect similarities in the prenatal environment rather than genetic similarities.

Attachment

Attachment bonds and associated affiliative behaviors are shared to some extent by all mammals and are demonstrated by social systems that are characterized by recognition, preference, and negative responses to separation. Separation produces distress vocalizations in many species of birds and mammals; nestling birds, chicks, kittens, puppies, monkeys, apes, and human infants all show separation-induced distress vocalizations. Jaak Panksepp and his colleagues (1997) found that the brain regions that are associated with these distress calls are rich in the brain's endogenous opiates, and they suggested that the brain opiate systems constitute, in effect, a physiological substrate for attachment and social cohesion. Sally Mendoza and William Mason (1997) showed that species that are characterized by attachment systems often show socially-mediated buffering of stress, with the physiological signs of stress being lowered by the presence of others. Studies by Solomon Asch (1952) and Stanley Milgram (1965) of conformity and obedience confirmed that tendencies to be swayed by and to follow social influence are among the strongest of human motives. Such tendencies to be influenced arguably are based biologically upon attachment.

John Bowlby (1969, 1973, 1980) described the infant's emotional attachment with the caregiver, with consequent emotional distress upon separation and joy/elation with bonding and reunion. When a primate infant (human or nonhuman) is separated from its caregiver, the first response is typically protest, including crying and active searching. This gives way to despair, which involves passivity and sadness. If the caregiver continues to be apart from the infant, detachment may occur in which expressions of distress cease and there is disregard and avoidance if the caregiver returns. Many naturalistic and laboratory studies have supported Bowlby's theory. Studies using the "strange situation" such as those by Mary Ainsworth (1978), where the mother briefly leaves the child and then returns, have established three attachment styles: secure, anxious/ambivalent, and avoidant. Secure attachments, according to Bowlby (1973, p. 235), grow out of consistent expressions of love by the caregiver, which give the infant "confidence in the availability of attachment figures," with less tendency toward the "intense or chronic fear" that is experienced by those who lack such confidence. Inconsistency on the part of the caregiver tends to produce an anxious/ambivalent attachment, along with signs of protest; the child tends to cry more and to explore the physical and social environment less than the secure child and shows signs of anxiety and anger that are mixed with attachment behaviors. Consistent rejection of the infant can lead to the infant's learning to avoid the caregiver, resulting in an avoidant detachment.

Security of attachment is critical to self-esteem and social relationships. Phillip Shaver and Cindy Hazan (1993) found that people who have a secure attachment are relatively confident about being loved, in comparison to people who have an anxious/ambivalent or avoidant attachment. Shaver and Hazan found that subjects with a secure attachment described their most important love relationships as happy, friendly, and trusting; subjects with an anxious/ambivalent attachment described love as involving more obsession, desire for reciprocation, extreme sexual attraction, and jealousy; and subjects with an avoidant attachment described a fear of intimacy, jealousy, and relatively few positive love experiences. Only subjects with a secure attachment reported that in some relationships, romantic love never fades. Subjects with an anxious ambivalent attachment reported that it is easy to fall in love, but both they and subjects with an avoidant attachment reported that it is rare to find true love.

Sex Differences

The degree to which sex differences in motivation in humans are based upon innate factors or differences in socialization is exceedingly difficult to determine. Both temperamental differences and socialization pressures tend to act in the same direction, with males tending to be more active and aggressive and females being more passive and nurturing. The conclusion that at least some portion of sex differences are due to differences in temperament comes from several sources. First, the male sex hormone testosterone is associated with aggressive behavior in many species, including humans. Moreover, among virtually all vertebrates and particularly among primates, males are more aggressive than females. In species such as the whiptail lizard and sea bass, an individual may actually change gender, going from male to female and back again depending upon the social environment. In such species, the same individual tends to be more active and aggressive when it is male and more passive and nurturing when it is female.

On the other hand, sex-role learning in humans begins early and is pervasive, with boys encouraged to enact "macho" roles and girls encouraged to enact feminine roles, regardless of their individual proclivities. In both sexes, the range of choices that are open to the individual tends to be restricted by sexual stereotypes. Moreover, both sexes have a range of individual differences, with some females being aggressive and some males being passive. Such people tend to be particularly victimized by the inflexible adherence to stereotypes.

See also: ACHIEVEMENT MOTIVATION; ATTACHMENT; BOWLBY, JOHN; DESIRE; GENDER AND EMOTIONS; GENETICS; SATISFACTION; SELF-ESTEEM; TEMPERAMENT

Bibliography

Ainsworth, Mary D. Salter. (1978). *Patterns of Attachment: A Psychological Study of the Strange Situation.* Hillsdale, NJ: Lawrence Erlbaum.

Asch, Solomon. (1952). *Social Psychology.* Englewood Cliffs, NJ: Prentice-Hall.

Bowlby, John. (1969). *Attachment and Loss, Vol. 1: Attachment.* New York: Basic Books.

Bowlby, John. (1973). *Attachment and Loss, Vol. 2: Separation.* New York: Basic Books.

Bowlby, John. (1980). *Attachment and Loss, Vol. 3: Loss.* New York: Basic Books.

Buck, Ross. (1976). *Human Motivation and Emotion.* New York: Wiley.

Buck, Ross. (1984). *The Communication of Emotion.* New York: Guilford.

Buck, Ross. (1985). "Prime Theory: An Integrated View of Motivation and Emotion." *Psychological Review* 92:389–413.

Buck, Ross. (1994). "Social and Emotional Functions in Facial Expression and Communication: The Readout Hypothesis." *Biological Psychology* 38:95–115.

Buck, Ross, and Ginsburg, Benson. (1991). "Emotional Communication and Altruism: The Communicative Gene Hypothesis." In *Altruism: Review of Personality and Social Psychology, Vol. 12,* ed. Margaret Clark. Newbury Park, CA: Sage Publications.

Cofer, Charles N., and Appley, Mortimer H. (1964). *Motivation: Theory and Research.* New York: Wiley.

Harlow, Harry F. (1971). *Learning to Love.* San Francisco: Albion.

Kleinginna, Paul R., and Kleinginna, Anne M. (1981a). "A Categorized List of Motivation Definitions, with Suggestions for a Consensual Definition." *Motivation and Emotion* 5:263–291.

Kleinginna, Paul R., and Kleinginna, Anne M. (1981b). "A Categorized List of Emotion Definitions, with Suggestions for a Consensual Definition." *Motivation and Emotion* 5:348–379.

Lorenz, Konrad. (1965). *Evolution and Modification of Behavior.* Chicago: University of Chicago Press.

MacLean, Paul D. (1990). *The Triune Brain in Evolution: Role in Paleocerebral Functions.* New York: Plenum.

MacLean, Paul D. (1993). "Cerebral Evolution of Emotion." In *Handbook of Emotions,* ed. Michael Lewis and Jeannette M. Haviland. New York: Guilford.

McClelland, David C. (1965). "Toward a Theory of Motive Acquisition." *American Psychologist* 20:321–333.

Mendoza, Sally P., and Mason, William A. (1997). "Attachment Relationships in New World Primates." In *Annals of the New York Academy of Sciences, Vol. 807: The Integrative Neurobiology of Affiliation,* ed. C. Sue Carter, I. Izja Lederhendler, and Brian Kirkpatrick. New York: New York Academy of Sciences.

Milgram, Stanley. (1965). "Some Conditions of Obedience and Disobedience to Authority." In *Current Studies in Social Psychology,* ed. Ivan D. Steiner and Martin Fishbein. New York: Holt, Rinehart, and Winston.

Panksepp, Jaak; Nelson, Eric; and Bekkedal, Marni. (1997). "Brain Systems for the Mediation of Social Separation-Distress and Social-Reward: Evolutionary Antecedents and Neuropeptide Intermediaries." In *Annals of the New York Academy of Sciences, Vol. 807: The Integrative Neurobiology of Affiliation,* ed. C. Sue Carter, I. Izja Lederhendler, and Brian Kirkpatrick. New York: New York Academy of Sciences.

Phelps, Jeanne A.; Davis, James O.; and Schartz, Kevin M. (1997). "Nature, Nurture, and Twin Research Strategies." *Current Directions in Psychological Science* 6:117–121.

Razran, Gregory. (1961). "The Observable Unconscious and the Inferable Conscious in Current Soviet Psychophysiology." *Psychological Review* 68:81–147.

Scott, John Paul. (1992). "The Phenomenon of Attachment in Human-Nonhuman Relationships." In *The Inevitable Bond: Examining Scientist-Animal Interactions,* ed. Hank Davis and Dianne Balfour. New York, Cambridge University Press.

Shaver, Phillip R., and Hazan, Cindy. (1993). "Adult Romantic Attachment: Theory and Evidence." In *Advances in Personal Relationships, Vol. 4,* ed. Daniel Perlman and Warren Jones. London: Kingsley.

Tomkins, Silvan S. (1962–1963). *Affect, Imagery, Consciousness,* 2 vols. New York: Springer.

White, Robert W. (1959). "Motivation Reconsidered: The Concept of Competence." *Psychological Review* 66:297–333.

Ross Buck

MOURNING

See Grief; Sympathy

MOVEMENT

See Body Movement, Gesture, and Display; Emotion Experience and Expression; Facial Expression; Universality of Emotional Expression

MUSIC

The old saying has it that music has charms to sooth the savage breast. However true that adage may be, music also has the power to excite, calm, disturb, or cause a range of emotions. Although people may be immune to the power of one type of music or other, few people are immune to all types of music. In fact, the music that excites one person may leave another cold or produce hostile reactions. For what is generally considered an abstract art form, music produces rather concrete reactions.

Philosophy of Music and Emotion

The study of emotional response to art and beauty in general is part of the philosophical field of aesthetics. Music is a form of artistic expression, and as with other forms of artistic expression (such as dance and literature), human beings react to music in emotional ways. Most experts agree that the reaction to music is both intellectual and emotional and that the two sets of reactions are related to one another. The philosopher Blaise Pascal's statement that "the heart has reasons that reason does not know" sums up this view.

Another view of the relationship between music and emotion is self-expression theory. As articulated by philosopher Susanne Langer, self-expression theory holds that the artist is pouring out real feeling when practicing his or her art. What is heard are the true feelings of the artist. Langer argues that music is the logical expression of emotions, not merely the cause of that expression. She also seems to argue that there is a vocabulary of emotions that can be expressed in music but not articulated in words. The composer or composer-performer somehow draws on this vocabulary and expresses the meanings within them.

Other philosophers, including John Dewey and Robin Collingwood, disagree with this view. They maintain that art has a direct expression and an indirect expression. The indirect expression takes one into the realm of art. It is an idea that views art as being the expression of emotion recollected in tranquility. Art is, therefore, seen to be an autobiographical expression of the performer's (or the composer's) emotions.

The philosopher Arthur Schopenhauer believed that music is a language that is capable of expressing all types of emotions. It goes beyond the mere expression of personal feelings—it takes one to the essence of feeling itself. Music, he felt, is not like other arts. It is not merely a copy of the ideas. Rather, it is a copy of the will. This copying of the will makes music extremely powerful, enabling it to penetrate to a person's very core. Schopenhauer believed that other arts dealt with shadows but that music cut directly to the essence, for example, of joy or grief. He believed that music's consequences are "stronger, quicker, more necessary and infallible" because people have been musicians everywhere and at all times without being able to account for how they communicate and express their ideas. This view of music as a language has been a quite popular one with modern linguists and those people who are interested in symbol systems.

The German philosopher Friedrich Nietzsche built on this idea of the relationship between music and language when he posed an Apollonian-Dionysian dichotomy in art. In contrast to the Apollonian type of art, representing form and rationality, music is a Dionysian form, representing drunkenness and ecstasy. His book *The Birth of Tragedy from the Spirit of Music* (1872) anticipates many twentieth-century trends in understanding the role of symbol making in human culture. He coined the term *symbolical analogue* to express the manner in which artists order and heighten the components of the real world. His expression of the Apollonian-Dionysian conflict in art influenced Igor Stravinsky, who felt that music had the ability to generate potent myths. Stravinsky hated programmatic music because it weakened the true power of music through mere imitation.

The terms *language* of music and *grammar* of music are used because of the wide variety of emotions that music can express and evoke for the listener. Moreover, various musical forms and structures are associated with particular emotions. Only verbal language has the same power to generate expressions of such range and exactness. Early philosophers, following in the footsteps of the great mathematician Pythagoras, tended to hold to the belief that music reflected planetary movements. The French philosopher René Descartes agreed that music was indeed mathematical, and he concurred with Plato that music could lead to immorality. He asserted that if there had to be music, it should be temperate in rhythm and simple in melody. However, the German philosopher Georg Wilhelm Friedrich Hegel believed that music was able to convey numerous emotions in all of their subtleties. He favored vocal music above instrumental music because vocal music was less subjective and able to express ideas more clearly. Hegel argued that music of any kind is largely subjective and is experienced within the listener because its essence is rhythm. Each of these philosophers was primarily interested in the manner in which music stirs emotion in the listeners. They noted the easy manner in which music blends with all of the other arts and religion—and in so doing heightens the emotion of each. Additionally, many philosophers of art see music primarily in terms of expressing emotion.

There is general agreement that emotions have sociological and physiological components as well as psychological ones. Lovers of music are well aware of the physiological response that music can produce. Moreover, they are often also aware of the need to place the music in some sort of cultural context in order to elicit its meaning. The individual, or psychological, dimension of emotion is also important in assessing one's response to music. In spite of what others may do, the individual may not like what he or she is supposed to like or may respond favorably to music that is disliked by others.

Psychology of Music and Emotion

Psychologists are aware that culture affects the structure of music as it affects the structure of other languages. It provides rules that create a framework of expectations. However, the psychologist Julian Thayer notes certain universal elements in musical sounds that convey similar emotions to people no matter what their backgrounds may be. High-pitched music, for example, is generally viewed to be happy, while low-pitched music is not. Similar universal responses to fast, slow, and moderate tempos have been noted. Moderate rhythms are those that correspond to the human heartbeat at around eighty beats per minute. Anthropologists are aware of the use of chanting and insistent rhythms to induce altered states. Maurice Ravel's *Bolero*, through its use of insistent rhythms, arouses sexual feeling, for example. Anthropologists and psychologists have examined the manner in which drumming may change neurological patterns to bring about psychological changes.

Avram Goldstein, a pharmacologist, conducted a study to determine what gives people an emotional thrill when they listen to music. He played large sections of individuals' favorite music to them and then analyzed their self-reports. He discovered that people describe listening to their favorite music as giving them a chill or goose bumps or causing tears. Goldstein argues that these thrills are caused by the production of endorphins in music listeners, tying the physiological response of music to the limbic system.

But music is more complicated than a mere automatic response. Goldstein indicates that different people perceive the emotional content differently. In commenting on that fact, Anne H. Rosenfeld (1985, p. 49) notes that a person might "describe a certain bright and lively merry-go-round tune as 'happy music,' knowing that [people] usually say such tunes are happy. But the music may actually be strangely depressing because it's a reminder of a painful childhood event at an amusement park or an evocation of a childhood now lost and mourned."

According to psychologists, then, an emotional response to music is the result of a complex mix of factors, including physiological structures, associations with past experiences, cultural determinants, musical training or lack thereof, and expectations resulting from all of these factors.

Music across Cultures

The study of the history and ethnography of music shows quite clearly that music is a cultural universal. That is, all cultures have music of some form, although there is much variation across cultures and over time in exactly how music is manifested and in what meanings composers, performers, and listeners assign to music.

Asian Indian culture recognizes the importance of the ecstatic experience associated with music. In India, there has long been a strong connection between music and religion. Vedic hymns are among the earliest forms of ancient Indian music. Melody and rhythm work together to support a religious story line. In Indian music, the narrator-singer is as important to the music as the instrumentalists are. There is very little concept of vocal or instrumental idiom in the Western sense. Indian music has little reliance on chords, and its reliance on microtones, minute divisions of the octave, fosters the importance of the vocalist. Improvisation also serves to increase excitement in performance. This improvisation takes place against the strong rules of the raga musical form and the interplay between vocalist and instrumentalist.

Chinese music similarly relies heavily on vocal narrative and religion for its effect. The tradition goes at least as far back as Confucius, who held that music was essential to a harmonious universe. For Confucius, music and government form an integral whole. No one without a knowledge of music should be trusted to govern, for music reveals character. Confucius taught that there are six emotions associated with it: sorrow, satisfaction, joy, anger, piety, and love. Moreover, music and the universe are in harmony—they work together to bring order to the world and make lying impossible. On the Chinese stage, standard songs that could be used in any opera were used to express specific emotions in specific situations. This use of stock songs associated with particular emotions made it easy to tell a story to people who spoke many different dialects. Music was also associated in China with dancing and acrobatics.

Korean music has its own grammar that must be mastered to understand its emotional effect. Although Korea is geographically located near China and Japan, its musical system and interpretation is significantly different from both of those cultures. The three musical systems have influenced each other, but they have each remained unique and tied to their respective cultures. There are two major categories of Korean traditional music: music for the elite ruling class (*chongak*) and music for the commoners (*sokak*). These broad divisions, of course, have a number of major subcategories. Each type of music has its own particular instrumentation and purpose. Some music, for example, is reserved for court performances or weddings or religious rituals. These restrictions are determined by the particular feeling or emotion that is attached to each type of music.

Haitian music also has religious connotations and connections. Combined with dance and language, music is instrumental in expressing meaning and communicating sacred secrets. It also enables people to receive sacred messages as well as express them.

Gypsy music is often considered to be among the most powerful of musical forms. Flamenco music, a type of gypsy vocal music, is related to dance and is accompanied by guitar music. There are three types of gypsy music and dance: grand, intermediate, and light. Grand music is intensely sad and deals with themes of death, anguish, despair, or religion. Light music deals with love and happy themes. Each form of music has its own characteristic rhythm and associated style of dancing.

Music is often associated with erotic feelings. Islamic music is no exception to the rule. When fashionable secular music emerged in Islamic areas, usually associated with erotic dance and drinking, it led to religious opposition. Arguments against this music came from the Koran. There were Islamic supporters of secular music, and both supporters and adversaries of secular music found arguments for their stand in sacred Islamic writings. One strong source of support for music, seeing little difference between sacred or secular music, came from the important mystical brotherhoods, for which music and dance were a means toward unity with God.

Javanese music in Indonesia is capable of expressing many different types of emotion. These run the full gamut from passion to meditation. In quiet meditative pieces, a bamboo flute and a two-stringed lute that is played with a bow accompany the female singer. The performance features a great deal of improvisation and density of tone to promote the meditative nature of the composition. Xylophones, a large zither, and the sitar aid this density, which comments on the overall melody.

Music and Emotion in the Western World

Although many critics may scoff at the open show of emotions in music as being too "corny" or "overly sentimental," listeners thoroughly enjoy "letting it all hang out," as attendance at rock, jazz, and New Age concerts demonstrates. Classical music also has a long tradition of sentimental performance. After all, Liberace copied his candelabra setting from Frédéric-François Chopin himself. In the nineteenth century, women wept profusely over the performance of Louis Moreau Gottschalk's piano composition *The Dying Poet.* These open displays of sentiment demonstrate both active listening and a bonding with the music and other fans. Elvis Presley was neither the first nor the last performing artist to have fan clubs and screaming fans. In fact, nineteenth-century classical pianists had their own weeping and screaming entourages.

Classical music, which includes the works of Wolfgang Amadeus Mozart, is filled with emotion, in contrast to the usual stereotype of restrained and controlled music of reason. Mozart himself was in love with the Italian style from the early days when he was taken on tour by his father to display his precocious talent. He eventually wrote operas in Italy after satisfying the music masters of his great dramatic musical ability. Mozart was a master of evoking and manipulating emotions. His works are filled with humor, passion, and deep, brooding emotion (as the case demands). Although all classical music expresses emotion, opera, the marriage of music and drama, is perhaps the most emotional of all Western music forms. Opera takes place in a complex performance setting. It requires the talents of many performers, the hall, the settings, instrumentalists, stage designers, dancers, and other artists and production specialists. The over-

A gypsy woman dances flamenco in Madrid, Spain. Flamenco is a dance style that was developed by the Andalusian gypsies and is usually performed to music of the Spanish guitar. (Corbis/Paul Almasy)

all effect of these combined elements can be emotionally overpowering.

Country music in the United States is also noted for its emotional content. Certainly, it has made a conscious effort to wear its heart on its sleeve. Many titles of hit songs openly refer to lost love, cheating partners, and other heart-breaking events. The "tear in my beer" approach is openly embraced without embarrassment by the country music fans.

Similarly, rap music is a means for expressing the deep emotions found among inner-city black youths. Its defenders often argue that no other musical form captures their innermost ideas and feelings in quite the same manner. It is both a means for expressing and shaping ideas and feelings within a subcultural framework and a means of expressing those ideas and feelings in a broader context. The rhythm and rhyme of the genre is embraced as a boundary mechanism that keeps out the uncool while expressing and reflecting the emotions of the cool, who see themselves as disenfranchised by the wider society. Certainly, there are few people who are neutral about "gangsta rap."

It elicits strong emotions in its listeners—white and black.

An emotional response can also be created by the music of a military band. The big military band draws on a relatively unchanging program. The big sound of the band itself draws a physical response that is related to emotions. Moreover, the big band reflects common emotions: patriotism, nostalgia, and agreed-upon truths. It does so in a no-nonsense tone of certainty.

The therapeutic role of music is well established. Dentists, who are generally feared, have long played soothing music to relax patients. Operating rooms now use soothing music to help reduce the use of anesthesia. Additionally, research has demonstrated the healing value of music. Music helps the body heal itself through stimulating the release of endorphins. Speech and language pathologists use music to help restore lost speech abilities. Many stroke victims find that speaking is impossible but singing is not. Through singing a phrase, the ability to speak may be restored. Music can also help prevent problems by reducing stress. Since most music stimulates people, the choice of music must be carefully made if it is supposed to relax the individual.

Music and Emotion in Film

Filmmakers have long known that music is important to their overall product. The psychologist Roger Brown (1989, p. 113) asked, "Why, when I first saw the Grand Canyon and the Piazza San Marco and the Alps, did I feel that these things had all been more moving in Cinerama? Why? Because both God and man forgot to put in the music." For Brown and other psychologists, music clearly adds emotional dimensions to life. They have no doubt that it packs an emotional punch. They have used music to heighten the emotional content of that which is visually presented. Techniques have ranged from using the works of classical composers, to taking bits and pieces from popular tunes, to having completely original scores written for the films. Hans Eisler, a German composer, and Sergey Prokofiev, a Russian, both adhered to the theory of conforming their film compositions to the pace and emotions of the cinematic compositions. A number of other luminaries, including Aaron Copland, Marc Blitzstein, and Virgil Thomson, Ralph Vaughan Williams, Benjamin Britten, Sir William Walton, Alan Rawsthorne, and Richard Rodney Bennett, have also contributed to film music.

Music and Humor

Many musicians use humor to loosen up the audience and their fellow-performers. Louis Armstrong was one of the masters, if not the greatest master, of using humor to heighten the overall emotional effect of his music, poking fun at pretension and hypocrisy. Dizzy Gillespie stated that he used humor to loosen up his musicians so they would perform in a relaxed manner, thereby concentrating on the music rather than worrying about the audience. Gillespie was not the only musician to appreciate the use of humor, as even a cursory glimpse of music history reveals. Leonard Bernstein, for example, regularly lectured on the role of humor in music. Mozart, Joseph Haydn, Charles Ives, and many other "serious" composers regularly employed humor in their works.

A primary element of all humor is surprise. Moreover, the closer humor approaches the sacred or set aside, the greater the potential for surprise and the richer the possibility of humor. It is not surprising then that the most polished musicians have the potential for juxtaposing the ridiculous and the sublime in order to reveal, through humor, something about the nature of reality. The best of musical humor reveals something serious. The taunting humor of Haydn's *Surprise Symphony* parallels the mocking of the bourgeoisie and other pretenders to culture found in the best plays of Jean-Baptiste Molière. Similarly, the best works of Mozart mock pretension while revealing the depths of true feeling, as in *La Nozze di Figaro*. Even the "serious" *Don Giovanni* is filled with sly asides and musical wit. Gillespie, a master of the triage-comic, as well as satire, would use the bridge of "Manteca" to chant "I'll never go back to Georgia!" at the height of the civil rights movement. He also used the sacred Yoruba melody that became "Swing Low, Sweet Chariot" for his parody, "Swing Low, Sweet Cadillac." The serious message came through more deeply in the midst of the sacred melody, rich with its associations of escape from slavery for African Americans.

It is, therefore, wrong to conceive of humor in music as being something that is confined to comic opera, musical comedy, operettas, or obvious parodies. Similarly, while children's music is filled with humor, it should not be dismissed as meaningless or "light" simply because of its humor. That humor is, in fact, an essential part of the music and is critical for teaching children to appreciate great music of any genre. Moreover, while humor in music may be used, as humor was used in Williams Shakespeare's great tragedies, to provide comic relief, relief is not its only use. Humor often is essential to the composer's or performer's artistic purpose of revealing the "essential reality behind the merely superficial reality of everyday life." The innate joy of discovering the "cosmic joke" of life itself bubbles over into the humor of great music as it does with the language of magnificent poetry and prose, enriching and deepening the listeners' lives. Mozart's comic operas show the heights to which humor and music can be blended. Operatic comedy blends both music and words to exaggerate the comic. Moreover, operatic comedy can display the dilemmas of different characters all at one time, through intercutting music. Music can overcome the confusion that results when three or four characters talk at once. The music, moreover, carries much of the humor. Music provides a device to order the confusion of comedy and lay it out in a formal manner. Comic composers use the interplay of plot and music to great effect, probing great psychological depths in their characters and using music to add to the analysis and fill in that which words cannot quite capture.

The Role of Emotion in Music Appreciation

No one has yet fully explained the role of emotion in aesthetic appreciation. Indeed, the formalists deny that emotion is relevant to understanding art. Art, including music, they argue, is about colors. Music, then, is about tone colors. It is not about evoking emotions or even expressing them. It is about form and the relationship of one form to another. It does not convey any emotion at all. Its meaning is within itself. The formalists truly argue an "art for art's sake" position.

This position is in complete opposition to that of many other views of music. The doctrine of affects, for example, put forward by the German aestheticians, is a theory of musical aesthetics that was accepted by the late baroque theorists and composers. It held the proposition that "music is capable of arousing a variety of specific emotions within the listener." The theory held that the composer could arouse a number of emotions through resorting to an appropriate musical procedure or device. Use of these procedures would invoke an involuntary response in the listener because there is an inborn connection between the musical stimulus and the listener's response.

Some philosophers of art argue that music can be said to express particular emotions when its structure is similar to that of the humans undergoing those emotions. Music is said to convey a particular emotion when it has A, B, C, and D rather than when it has E, F, G, or H. For example, music is joyous when it is light, quick, and somewhat simple rather than heavy and somewhat ponderous. Although these qualities are said to be in the music rather than in the composer

or the listener, the composer and listener must interpret the music to understand the emotions in the music.

See also: DANCE; DESCARTES, RENÉ; DRAMA AND THEATER; NIETZSCHE, FRIEDRICH WILHELM

Bibliography
Barzun, Jacques. (1996). "Is Music Unspeakable?" *American Scholar* 65(2):193–202.
Brown, Roger. (1989). "Three Principles of Explanation." *Journal of Personality and Social Psychology* 19(Oct.):109–125.
Celletti, Rodolfo. (1994). "The Poetics of the Marvelous." *Opera News* 59(1):10–14.
d'Azevedo, Warren L. (1958). "A Structural Approach to Aesthetics: Toward a Definition of Art in Anthropology." *American Anthropologist* 60:702–714.
d'Azevedo, Warren L. (1960). *The Artist Archetype in Gola Culture.* Reno: Desert Research Institute, University of Nevada.
Egan, Ronald. (1997). "The Controversy over Music and 'Sadness' and Changing Conception of the 'Qin' in Middle Period China." *Harvard Journal of Asiatic Studies* 57:62–66.
Gard, Carolyn. (1997). "Music 'n' Moods." *Current Health* 23(8):24–26.
Han, Kuo-huang, and Mark, Lindy Li. (1983). "Evolution and Revolution in Chinese Music." In *Musics of Many Cultures: An Introduction,* ed. Elizabeth May. Berkeley: University of California Press.
Hernandez, Deborah Pacini. (1995). *Bachata.* Philadelphia: Temple University Press.
Heins, Ernst. (1970). "Cueing the Gamelan in Javanese Wayang Performance." *Indonesia* 9:101–127.
Karl, Gregory, and Robinson, Jenefer. (1995). "Shostakovich's Tenth Symphony and the Musical Expression of Cognitively Complex Emotions." *Journal of Aesthetics and Art Criticism* 53(4):401–415.
Lee, Kang-sook. (1983). "Certain Experiences in Korean Music." In *Musics of Many Cultures: An Introduction,* ed. Elizabeth May. Berkeley: University of California Press.
Madell, Geoffrey. (1995). "What Music Teaches about Emotions." *Philosophy* 71(275):63–82.
Martin, Robert L. (1996). "Musical 'Topics' and Expression in Music." *Journal of Aesthetics and Art Criticism* 53(4):417–424.
May, Elizabeth, ed. (1983). *Musics of Many Cultures: An Introduction.* Berkeley: University of California Press.
Motluk, Alison. (1997). "The Big Chill." *New Scientist* 150(2027):817–819.
Rosenfeld, Anne H. (1985). "Music, the Beautiful Disturber." *Psychology Today* 19(Dec.):48–51.
Wade, Bonnie C. (1983). "Some Principles of Indian Classical Music." In *Musics of Many Cultures: An Introduction,* ed. Elizabeth May. Berkeley: University of California Press.
Wilder, Sander Call. (1996). "I Believe in Music." *Vital Speeches* 62(15):479–480.

Frank A. Salamone

N

NATIONAL CHARACTER AND CULTURE

See Culture; Culture-Bound Syndromes; Universality of Emotional Expression

NEURAL SYSTEMS: FROM ANIMALS TO HUMANS

Most of the neural systems that generate emotionality in animals are situated in ancient brain areas that are deep below the massive surrounding canopy of the neocortex. Human brain imaging studies, using modern techniques such as positron emission tomography and functional magnetic resonance imaging, affirm such a conclusion. Unfortunately, those techniques are not optimal for visualizing the deepest brain stem areas where animal studies indicate that various executive circuits for coordinating emotional arousal are closely intertwined. The precise number and nature of the systems that govern basic human emotions is still debatable, but substantial clarity is emerging from cross-species brain studies. In animals, distinct brain systems that mediate emotions have been identified with electrical and chemical stimulation of specific brain areas, yielding evidence for a variety of executive brain systems for basic emotions: SEEKING, RAGE, FEAR, LUST, CARE, PANIC, and PLAY. Some congruent human data is also available.

Since these evolutionarily-derived emotional circuits are only necessary—rather than sufficient—bases for the various human emotions, capitalized labels will be used here to highlight that specific brain systems are being designated rather than all of the many attributes that go into every type of real-life emotional experiences. Many conceptual distinctions must be made in order to understand the full complexity of the various interacting brain systems that constitute each integrated emotional response. Diverse behavioral, autonomic, and psychological responses and feelings characterize each affective state. Many elements are shared among several emotions (e.g., general arousal), while others are unique to a specific emotional state. Mood states probably reflect modest arousal of the same brain systems that mediate full-blown emotions. However, there is still little certainty about such issues since most neuroanatomical, neurophysiological, neurochemical, and neuropsychological attributes of these systems remain to be scientifically studied, especially in humans.

Although a neuroscientific understanding of the these systems is only beginning to be formulated, researchers will always need to distinguish the brain's broad state control functions, such as general arousal and attentional processes that modulate every affective and cognitive function (e.g., via the actions of norepinephrine, serotonin, and acetylcholine). The most prolific amino-acid transmitters, glutamate and gamma-aminobutyric acid (GABA), provide detailed resolution to each and every emotional and cognitive response, and functional specificity is achieved only through their actions in specific networks of the brain, which establishes global, dynamic states of brain organization. While all of the above chemistries help construct many emotional details, they do not appear to constitute emotionally specific codes within the brain. On the other hand, neurochemical systems, such as the neuropeptides (which are very small protein-like chains of amino acids), do arouse discrete types of emotional and motivational tendencies. Thus, the mood or emotion programs that prevail at any one time probably emerge partly from the ability of specific neuropeptides to select among the many evolutionarily prepared emotional dispositions that exist in the action-readiness repertoire of each animal.

Although many of the specific emotional systems of the brain appear to be organized around distinct neuropeptide circuits that can sustain arousal of different integrated emotional and motivational tendencies, some emotions may also be characterized by specific biogenic amine systems, such as the mesolimbic and mesocortical dopamine circuits (e.g., the SEEKING arousal system). It is through an understanding of such specific neurochemical systems in animals that the greatest insight concerning the neural bases of the basic human emotions is being achieved.

The Seven Basic Systems

The SEEKING system is an emotional system that allows organisms to acquire a variety of rewards in their environment—from food to sex. Animals readily self-stimulate (i.e., voluntarily apply electrical stimulation) along the trajectory of this system, if they are allowed to do so, through appropriately implanted electrodes. When this system is active, animals eagerly approach or search for any of a variety of items that are needed for survival. As has already been mentioned, this system consists of specific neurochemical circuits, especially the mesolimbic and mesocortical dopamine circuits arising from the ventral tegmental area of the midbrain (the so-called A-10 neuronal group). Many neuropeptide systems that carry specific information converge on this system (e.g., Substance P, opioids, neurotensin, and cholecystokinin). It is now clear that this circuitry is much more responsive to the anticipation of rewards than the consumption thereof. It also mediates the desire for artificial drug rewards, including psychostimulants (e.g., cocaine and amphetamine) and opioids (e.g., morphine and heroin), as well as the cravings that humans commonly develop for alcohol, nicotine, and a variety of other addictions.

A RAGE system that can arouse angry attack behaviors runs from the corticomedial amygdaloid areas through the anterior lateral hypothalamus to the periaqueductal gray. The RAGE system is based on a cascading network of neuronal communications, as is every other emotional system. Substance P is a key component of the amygdala-to-hypothalamus part of the circuit, and excitatory influences descend from there to the periaqueductal gray via excitatory amino acids such as glutamate. Opioids are powerful inhibitory influences in this emotional system. Presumably the cognitive processes that normally arouse this network are those that detect reward presence and absence in the frontal cortex, yielding a frustrative-anger response when expected rewards are not forthcoming, or when other irritations such as physical restraint and various threats assail an organism.

A distinct FEAR system interlocks with the RAGE system at all levels of the brain, although there is some major divergence in the higher reaches of these systems, such as the amygdala, where FEAR is situated in the more lateral and central zones. Certain learned fears emerge from sensory inputs into the FEAR system arising from surrounding cortical areas, and they are neurochemically solidified through the facilitation of glutamatergic inputs into the FEAR system. A large number of neuropeptide modulators exist within the FEAR system, but the different components of the integrated responses that arise from each of these influences remains to be worked out. Also, it is not known whether the feeling of fear emerges more from higher or lower components of this system, although there are some important lines of evidence to suggest that the lower components are more critical and essential. The higher components, of course, are more important for mediating fear learning and the development of phobias.

Among the various prosocial systems of the brain, sexual LUST provides a foundation for several others, such as those for maternal CARE and social bonding. The distinct modes of male and female sexuality are substantially organized around vasopressinergic and oxytocinergic influences respectively, and these circuits find their epicenters in preoptic and ventromedial hypothalamic areas. Sexual urges are sensitized by widely distributed hormone and various neurotransmitter receptors along the trajectory of these systems, with testosterone activating vasopressinergic systems and estrogen activating oxytocinergic systems. The urges for sexual contact are mediated by the higher reaches of these systems (centered in the corticomedial amygdala and the bed nucleus of the stria terminalis). All of these higher systems converge on the periaqueductal gray of the midbrain, which controls specific motor and autonomic outputs and permits sexual urges to interact intensely with many other emotional systems. The orgasmic/reward component of sex appears to have a strong oxytocinergic influence in both males and females, whereas the jealous/aggressive aspects of male-typical sexuality are more strongly linked to vasopressinergic arousal in the brain. Many other neuropeptides, including luteinizing hormone-releasing hormone and cholecystokinin, are also important for mediating integrated sexual as well as maternal urges.

Nurturant CARE systems that mediate maternal devotion revolve around the prolactin and oxytocinergic systems of the brain. This makes a nice evolutionary story since these same hormones mediate the birth of babies (by increased uterine contractions), reflecting an important principle of brain emotional organization. Molecules that have been devoted to certain peripheral physiological functions participate in the related psychological functions within the brain. Oxytocin circuits arouse maternal intent partly by activating dopaminergic SEEKING systems, while the pleasure of opioid release from mother-infant touching may provide feedback to each concerning the adequacy and emotional satisfactions of ongoing nurturant behaviors. Social attachments are mediated by all three of the neuropeptides that are implicated in maternal behavior—with abundant evidence for oxytocin and opioids and some evidence for prolactin.

All young birds and mammals that develop social bonds with caregivers exhibit separation distress responses when the bonds are disrupted, the most prominent response being vocal protest. These separation calls have been used to determine the location of separation distress—the behavioral indices of the so-called PANIC system of the brain. The relevant pathways course between anterior basal forebrain areas, such as the bed nucleus of the stria terminalis, dorsal preoptic, and ventral septal areas, descending via the dorsomedial thalamic zones to the periaqueductal gray. It remains likely that the highest functional components of the system, which may regulate many aspects of social emotions, emerge from anterior cingulate zones. The core of this system, as with most other emotional systems, appears to be glutamatergic, and the neuropeptide that most clearly promotes arousal of this emotional response is corticotropin releasing factor (CRF). The neuropeptides that strongly suppress arousal of this system, perhaps not surprisingly, are the same as those that regulate nurturant CARE, namely oxytocin, opioids and prolactin.

A basic neural system for rough-and-tumble PLAY exists in the mammalian brain, but relatively little is known about its neuroanatomy, except for the fact that touch inputs are important for the activation of play and an epicenter for playful impulses does exist in the parafascicular and nearby midline areas of the thalamus and brain stem. Many neurochemical systems modulate arousal of playfulness, but no "command" influence has yet been definitively demonstrated. A simplified approach to studying play/joy circuitry in rats has been revealed by the existence of a "laughter" type of response (i.e., 50 KHz chirping)

to tickling that predicts playfulness. Among the intriguing links of these findings to human psychopathology are the possible relationships to attention deficit hyperactivity disorders (ADHD), which may reflect, in part, excessive playfulness that is not easily tolerated in classroom situations. All of the drugs used to treat ADHD are powerful inhibitors of playful activities in animals, and apparently in humans.

Implications for Further Emotion Research

The study of these seven basic circuits provides the best strategy for understanding the brain organization of emotionality. Of course, each of these systems is very complex with widespread influences throughout the brain. Researchers have started to visualize the neural activation in rat brains during brief episodes fear and other emotions using c-fos immunocytochemistry (which can highlight all the nerve cells that are active in animal brains during specific psychobehavioral states). These results of these studies indicate that there are a number of brain areas (from the giant cells of the brain stem to practically all areas of the cortex) that are aroused by emotional arousal. Obviously, an enormous number of brain areas are recruited by all emotional states, perhaps indirectly through massive ascending neural systems from the brain stem that control waking, such as acetylcholine and norepinephrine circuits.

Although it is certain that the mammalian brain does contain basic emotional systems (i.e., affect programs), that evolutionary fact should in no way be taken to detract from the fact that many emotional constructs and nuances are surely socially learned. The sophisticated learning and language mechanisms of the human brain, in conjunction with various higher brain influences, allow each of the emotional networks to generate many variations and elaborations on the basic themes. Thus, the amplification of SEEKING urges by frontal cortex, FEAR and RAGE by the temporal areas, and PANIC and other social emotions by anterior cingulate zones provides ample neuronal space for the generation of many socially constructed emotions in human brains. It is noteworthy that all of these emotion rich areas are situated anteriorly in the cortical mantle. In other words, emotions are more related to frontal executive/motor functions than to posterior sensory/perceptual functions of the cerebral hemispheres. The fact that the non-speaking right hemisphere tends to be more emotional than the left suggests several other interesting aspects of emotionality that may be unique to humans, such as a refined ability to exhibit emotional regulation and deception.

One of the key remaining issues of emotion research, largely unstudied, is how the brain actually constructs emotional feelings. Three general possibilities have been proposed: (1) that feelings are created by "somatic markers" that reflect the bodily changes that accompany emotions, (2) that feelings arise from various subcortical systems interacting with higher "working memory" systems, and (3) that feelings emerge from the intrinsic neurodynamics of emotional command systems interacting with a primordial neurosymbolic representation of "the self," which may be instantiated presumably through the neuronal construction of a primordial "virtual body." An attractive aspect of the last view is that it permits emotional values to interact with the extended reticular-thalamic activating system at its very base. This view also helps one to better understand how emotions are global state functions of both body and brain, not simple reflections of information processing functions that can be simulated easily on digital computers.

Conclusion

It is becoming increasingly evident that affective states are more integrally related to the lower than the higher reaches of emotional systems. Such primitive, internally experienced affective states may permit organisms to implement various global and archetypal psychological and behavioral attitudes effectively in the world, promoting certain sustained action tendencies and congruent modes of higher brain information processing.

In a sense, emotional systems are the brain's fundamental and archetypal intentional systems that provide a solid neurobiological grounding for a primary-process form of consciousness. It is easy to conceptualize how more complex aspects of consciousness may have been built on this solid foundation of values. Since the extended reticular-thalamic activating system is believed to govern awareness of external events and to provide a workshop of consciousness, one can envision how emotional values govern most other brain activities.

All of these hierarchically organized brain operating systems exhibit considerable plasticity. Not only do they come under the control of neutral environmental events through learning, but every experience can probably modify the vigor of each of these genetically constructed emotional systems. Through the interactions of these systems with environmental events, an epigenetic landscape of mental development is established that has profound lifetime consequences for each organism.

See also: BIOCHEMISTRY OF EMOTIONS; GENETICS; MOOD; NEUROBIOLOGY OF EMOTIONS; PSYCHOPHYSIOLOGY OF EMOTIONS

Bibliography

Baars, Bernard J. (1996). "Understanding Subjectivity: Global Workspace Theory and the Resurection of the Observing Self." *Journal of Consciousness Studies* 3:211–216.

Berridge, Kent C., and Robinson, Terry E. (1998). "What Is the Role of Dopamine in Reward: Hedonic Impact, Reward Learning, or Incentive Salience." *Brain Research Reviews* 22:347–354.

Carter, C. Sue; Lederhendler, Izja; and Kirkpatrick, Brian, eds. (1997). *The Integrative Neurobiology of Affiliation.* New York: New York Academy of Sciences.

Crenshaw, Theresa L., and Goldberg, James P. (1996). *Sexual Pharmacology: Drugs That Affect Sexual Functioning.* New York: W. W. Norton.

Damasio, Antonio R. (1994). *Descartes' Error: Emotion, Reason, and the Human Brain.* New York: G. P. Putnam.

Krasnegor, Norman A., and Bridges, Robert S., eds. (1990). *Mammalian Parenting.* New York: Oxford University Press.

LeDoux, Joseph E. (1996). *The Emotional Brain: The Mysterious Underpinnings of Emotional.* New York: Simon & Schuster.

Nelson, Eric, and Panksepp, Jaak. (1998). "Brain Substrates of Infant-Mother Attachment: Contributions of Opioids, Oxytocin, and Norepinephrine." *Neuroscience and Biobehavioral Reviews* 22:437–452.

Newman, James. (1997). "Putting the Puzzle Together, Part I: Towards a General Theory of the Neural Correlates of Consciousness." *Journal of Consciousness Studies* 4:47–66.

Panksepp, Jaak. (1982). "Toward a General Psychobiological Theory of Emotions." *Behavioral and Brain Sciences* 5:407–467.

Panksepp, Jaak. (1993a). "Neurochemical Control of Moods and Emotions: Amino Acids to Neuropeptides." In *Handbook of Emotions,* ed. Michael Lewis and Jeannette M. Haviland. New York: Guilford.

Panksepp, Jaak. (1993b). "Rough-and-Tumble Play: A Fundamental Brain Process." In *Parent-Child Play: Descriptions and Implications,* ed. Kevin MacDonald. Albany: State University of New York Press.

Panksepp, Jaak. (1998a). *Affective Neuroscience: The Foundations of Human and Animal Emotions.* New York: Oxford University Press.

Panksepp, Jaak. (1998b). "Attention Deficit Hyperactivity Disorders, Psychostimulants, and Intolerance of Childhood Playfulness: A Tragedy in the Making." *Current Directions in Psychological Sciences* 7:91–98.

Panksepp, Jaak. (1998c). "The Periconscious Substrates of Consciousness: Affective States and the Evolutionary Origins of the Self." *Journal of Consciousness Studies* 5:566–582.

Panksepp, Jaak; Siviy, Steve; and Normansell, Larry. (1984). "The Psychobiology of Play: Theoretical and Methdological Perspectives." *Neuroscience and Biobehavioral Reviews* 8:465–492.

Rosen, Jeffrey B., and Schulkin, Jay. (1998). "From Normal Fear to Pathological Anxiety." *Psychological Review* 105:325–350.

Schultz, Wolfram. (1998). "Predictive Reward Signal of Dopamine Neurons." *Journal of Neurophysiology* 80:1–27.

Siegel, Allan; Roeling, Thomas A. P.; Gregg, Thomas R.; and Kruk, Menno R. (1999). "Neuropharmacology of Brain-Stimulation-Evoked Aggression." *Neuroscience and Biobehavioral Reviews* 23:359–389.

Jaak Panksepp

NEUROBIOLOGY OF EMOTIONS

Neurobiologists have long sought to understand the brain circuitry that mediates emotion. This effort reflects the general aim of neurobiologists to identify biological mechanisms that underlie human experience. In addition, in the case of emotion the neurobiological approach is also seen as one way to gain insights into the basic dimensions and properties of emotional experience. The hope is that neurobiological investigations will show how emotion can be dissected into fundamental information processing functions and then brought together within a circuitry that supports the fullness of emotional experience and expression.

Emotion and memory influence each other at multiple levels. Some aspects of the emotional expression of memories involve a dedicated circuit in the brain that operates in parallel with other memory systems. This memory system mediates the learning and expression of emotional responses to stimuli of learned significance even in the absence of conscious memory for the same experiences. Thus, sometimes individuals can feel nervous, happy, or scared at an image that evokes memory, even before or in the absence of the ability to declare the source of such feelings. In addition, emotional experiences are arousing, thereby increasing attention paid to particular events. Consequently, emotional activation affects memory in a general way, both indirectly by influencing a broad range of perceptual and motivational systems that provide the contents of new memories and directly by influencing the memory storage process itself.

Early Research Efforts

The first theoretical proposal of a brain system for emotion was provided by the neuroanatomist James Papez in 1937. Within his larger scheme for dividing psychological processes into anatomical pathways, Papez postulated that sensory experiences took distinct pathways for "thought" and "feelings." The stream of thought, he proposed, involved channeling the sensory inputs from the thalamus to the wide expanse of the cerebral cortex on the outer (lateral) surface of the brain. The stream of feeling, he argued, followed a different path from the thalamus to the particular cortical area known as the limbic lobe plus the neighboring hypothalamus. Conversely, Papez speculated on the existence of a specific brain circuit for emotion that involved a complementary system of structures that was hidden on the rim of the cortex and inside the brain. His proposed circuitry had a circular scheme that involved divisions of the hidden cortex on the midline (cingulate cortex) projecting into cortical areas in the temporal lobe (the parahippocampal cortex and hippocampus), and from there to subcortical nuclei in the mammilary bodies of the hypothalamus, and then finally to anterior nuclei of the thalamus, and thence back to the midline cingulate cortex. Papez suggested that the circular interactions between cortical and hypothalamic structures might mediate integration between cortical and subcortical processing of emotions. Outputs of this circuit then might be sent from the midline and temporal cortical areas into other cortical areas involved in the stream of thought, to mediate conscious experience of emotion, and from the hypothalamus to lower brainstem pathways to mediate bodily (autonomic) emotional responses.

At around the same time, other evidence indicated a critical role for additional temporal lobe areas in emotion. In 1939, Heinrich Kluver and Paul Bucy described a syndrome of affective disorder that followed removal of the temporal lobe in monkeys. This disorder was characterized by "psychic blindness," which was reflected mainly as a blunting of the emotional reactions usually associated with fear to novel objects. Part of this disorder involved an impairment in object recognition, a disorder known as agnosia. This aspect

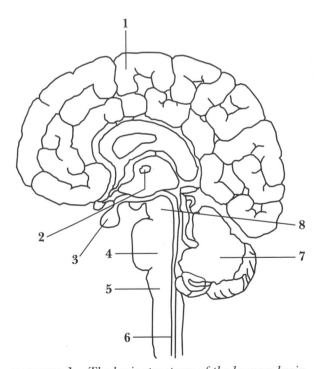

FIGURE 1 *The basic structures of the human brain include (1) the cerebral cortex, (2) the thalamus, (3) the pituitary gland, (4) the pons, (5) the medulla oblongata, (6) the spinal cord, (7) the cerebellum, and (8) the midbrain.*

of the disorder is now associated with damage to the cerebral cortex within the temporal lobe. Another part of the disorder was the "taming" of these normally aggressive animals, as well as other abnormalities of social behavior. This aspect of the disorder has been attributed to the amygdala, a hidden subcortical area within the temporal lobe.

These distinct components of an emotional system in the brain were integrated into a more elaborate theoretical structure by Paul MacLean in 1949. He combined the observations of Papez and Kluver and Bucy with clinical observations on emotional disorders and electrophysiological evidence of visceral sensory inputs to the hippocampus and other parts of the Papez circuit, arguing for the existence of a distinct "visceral brain." Using the full breadth of evidence from these various sources, MacLean expanded further on Papez's notion of distinct informational processing streams and on the anatomical components of the emotional system. He introduced the term *limbic system* as the anatomical designation of the emotional circuit and included within it the full Papez circuit plus the amygdala, septum, and prefrontal cortex. MacLean distinguished the functional domain of this system (mediating emotional experience) from the lower brainstem structures (mediating instinctive behavioral stereotypes) and the higher cortical areas (mediating cognitive functions).

There have subsequently been many modifications to the notion of the limbic system. The evidence expanded the critical connectional pathways both forward toward the frontal lobe and backward toward the midbrain, such that the neuroanatomist Walle Nauta proposed in 1958 that the system should be viewed as a continuum of structures throughout the brain. The strong connections of classic limbic structures have become so intertwined with other brain systems that the term itself has become somewhat outmoded. This and other evidence has brought into question whether the specific components of the limbic system were correctly identified, and indeed whether one can outline a distinct system for emotion. Nevertheless, newer research has identified specific pathways associated with the old limbic system that are critical elements in emotional output.

Modern Research

The focus on emotion and emotional memory has shifted to a key brain structure located in the temporal lobe: the amygdala. This is justly deserved because the amygdala lies in a central position between cortical information processing elements, limbic circuitry, and hypothalamic output mechanisms. The amygdala involves a complex collection of interconnected nuclei,

usually separated into a lateral and basolateral group and a central and medial group. As it turns out, this division roughly corresponds to the major input and outputs of amygdala processing. Thus, sensory inputs from the thalamus and cortex project mainly to the lateral and basolateral nuclei, whereas cortical and subcortical amygdala outputs originate mainly in the central and medial nuclei.

Several studies have shown that the amygdala receives widespread sensory inputs from the thalamus and cerebral cortex. These are derived largely from taste nuclei, gut (vagus nerve inputs), and auditory thalamic nuclei; they are not derived from the main somatosensory or visual thalamic nuclei. Cortical inputs are derived through the olfactory bulb and olfactory cortex, plus higher order sensory inputs from all forms by way of the cortex surrounding the rhinal sulcus (insular and perirhinal cortex). In addition, parts of the prefrontal cortex and hippocampal region send substantial inputs to the lateral amygdala nucleus. The internal connectivity of amygdaloid nuclei is complex, and it is characterized mainly by a distribution of connections from the lateral nucleus to the basal nucleus and central nucleus, which are also interconnected. Thus, inputs that may have been segregated at the input stage are likely to converge within the amygdala.

There are two main output targets of the amygdala. One set of outputs from the amygdala is to the cerebral cortex. Most of this output is mediated by components of the thalamus and direct connections to cortical areas (including the perirhinal, entorhinal, and prefrontal areas) that project to a broad variety of cortical areas. In addition, the amygdala projects heavily to multiple areas at the base of the brain, including the bed nucleus of the stria terminalis, substantia innominata, horizontal limb of the diagonal band, and basal nucleus of Meynert. These projections then secondarily influence widespread cortical areas. Also, the basal amygdaloid nuclei project to components of motor systems and to the lateral hypothalamus and several brainstem motor, autonomic (vagus nerve), and endocrine effector areas. These multiple connections support a broad array of responses that are generated by direct stimulation of the amygdala and are observed in the complex syndrome of behaviors associated with emotional output, including motor responses (such as freezing) and autonomic modulation (such as changes in heart rate and blood pressure).

Emotional Expression

Following on Kluver and Bucy's initial findings of the "blunting" of affect in monkeys with damage to the temporal lobe (including the amygdala), several studies have shown that selective amygdala damage results in a syndrome characterized by decreases in responsivity to affective stimuli, failure to show normal orienting responses (including changes in heart rate and respiration), and diminished discrimination of galvanic skin response (the change in skin resistance associated with sweating). Monkeys and rats with amygdala damage also demonstrate diminished selectivity in feeding, diminished sensitivity to food deprivation, and depressed shifts in behavior normally associated with changes in food reward magnitude or type of food rewards.

A study by Nancy Hebben and her colleagues (1985) of a human patient with damage to the amygdala confirmed the blunting of affective responsiveness and offered some further insights into the nature of this disorder. In the clinical setting, the patient was known to endure without complaint painful conditions including hemorrhoids and did not produce a normal galvanic skin response to electrical stimulation. He rarely mentioned being hungry, even when meals were delayed, and he ate in a normal manner when given a meal. These observations were followed up in a systematic study that showed failure to identify stimuli as being "painful" no matter how intense they were. In addition, the patient showed a diminished capacity to appreciate his own state of hunger, such that even after substantial overeating at a dinner meal the patient would only say he was "finished"; he would not characterize himself as "full." These findings suggested that the major effect of amygdala damage was a diminished accessibility of information about internal states.

Other studies of the role of the human amygdala in the perception of affective stimuli have focused on responses to faces. Ralph Adolphs and his colleagues (1994) and Hans Breiter and his colleagues (1996) have shown that damage to the amygdala results in impaired ability to recognize emotion in human faces. The diminished capacity for the appreciation and labeling of facial expressions, was not accompanied by any general deficits in language, memory, or perception (including normal ability for recognition of familiar faces). One patient did perceive fearful faces as expressing emotion but refused to characterize the expression as fearful, leading the investigators to conclude that she could perceive the facial expression but that it did not activate responses associated with fear.

Emotional Memory System

Is emotional experience just a part of the everyday memories that people bring to conscious recollection? Or is there a memory system for emotional memories that is independent from the one for conscious mem-ories? Or does emotion just enhance memory processing? Certainly, individuals do consciously recall emotional experiences, so these clearly can be a part of declarative memory. There is also substantial emerging evidence that some aspects or some types of emotional memory are accomplished by a distinct system, parallel to that for conscious memory. In addition, emotion can indeed enhance all kinds of memory.

In a classic case study performed in 1911, the neurologist Edouard Cleparede pricked the hand of an unsuspecting female patient who had amnesia. Subsequently, the patient refused to shake Cleparede's hand, although she could not recall the painful incident. In 1989, the neurologist Antonio Damasio and his colleagues described intact affective learning in their amnesic patient known as Boswell. Even though he could not learn to recognize the hospital staff, he consistently claimed he liked those with whom he had repeated positive encounters over those with whom he had negative encounters. These and other case studies show that memory for emotional aspects of experiences can indeed be dissociated from conscious memory for the same experiences.

What neural system mediates the capacity to form emotional memories? Perhaps the best studied example of emotional memory involves the brain system that mediates simple forms of fear conditioning. In particular, the work of Joseph LeDoux (1996) and Michael Davis (1992) has focused on the specific elements of the pathways through the amygdala that support learning to fear a simple auditory or visual stimulus. The critical elements of the relevant pathway include auditory sensory inputs to two different circuits through the thalamus. One of these circuits involves auditory inputs to areas of the thalamus that project directly to the lateral amygdaloid nucleus. The other circuit involves inputs to the thalamus that project to the primary auditory area of temporal cortex, which in turn projects to secondary temporal areas and the perirhinal cortex. These secondary auditory cortical areas are the source of cortical input to the amygdala, particularly the lateral and basolateral nuclei of this structure. Those areas of the amygdala then project into the central nucleus, which is the source of outputs to subcortical areas controlling a broad range of fear-related behaviors, including autonomic and motor responses.

LeDoux and his colleagues have focused on the input side of these circuits. Their studies have examined the psychology and neurophysiological responses of these structures in animals during the course of a simple tone-cued fear-conditioning task. Rats are initially habituated to a testing chamber, and then they are presented with multiple pairings of a tone and a brief electric shock through the floor of the cage. Subsequently, conditioned fear was assessed by measuring the autonomic response to the tone as reflected only in changes in arterial pressure and motor responses as reflected in a stereotypic crouching or freezing behavior. Unconditioned responses to the tone were evaluated by presenting other animals with unpaired tones and shocks.

Initial experiments were aimed at identifying the critical input pathway to the amygdala. Animals with selective damage in the lateral amygdala showed dramatically reduced conditioned responses to the tone, in the measures of both autonomic and motor responses. Unconditioned responses to the tone or shock were not affected by this damage. In addition, broad destruction of all auditory areas of the thalamus eliminated conditioned responses. However, selective removal of either of the prominent direct inputs to the lateral amygdala were individually ineffective. Thus, damage to the thalamic area that projects directly to the lateral amygdala or of the entire auditory cortex that projects directly to the amygdala did not reduce either the autonomic or freezing response. However, elimination of both of these inputs produced the full effect seen after lateral amygdala damage. Thus, for this simple type of conditioning, either the direct thalamic or the thalamo-cortical input pathway is sufficient to mediate conditioning.

Additional studies were aimed at an additional component of fear conditioning observed in these studies. After conditioning, when rats were replaced in the conditioning chamber they began to freeze even before the tone conditioning stimulus was presented. Thus, they appeared to condition both to the tone and to the environmental context in which tones and shock had been paired. This contextual fear conditioning was selective to the environment in which the conditioning occurred. Furthermore, contextual fear conditioning could be dissociated from conditioning to the tone by presenting conditioned tones in a different environment. Trained animals did not freeze prior to tone presentation in the different environment, but they did freeze when the tone was presented. Moreover, contextual fear conditioning was mediated by a different pathway than tone-cued fear conditioning. The researchers trained the animals on the standard version of the task and then assessed freezing both immediately after the rats were placed in the conditioning chamber and then in response to the tone. Amygdala damage blocked conditioned freezing to both the context and the tone. In contrast, damage to the hippocampus selectively blocked contextual fear conditioning, sparing the conditioned response to the tone. Thus, combining these data with the known anatomy of these brain structures, it can

be deduced that the full set of circuits mediating fear conditioning in this task involve a set of parallel and serial pathways to the amygdala. The most direct pathway is from the areas within the auditory thalamus. A secondary path through the auditory thalamo-cortical circuit can also mediate tone-cued conditioning. Contextual fear conditioning involves an even more indirect pathway by which multimodal information arrives in the hippocampus and is sent to the amygdala by way of the subiculum.

Davis and his colleagues investigated a different form of fear conditioning known as fear potentiated startle. In this task, animals were initially exposed to pairings of a light or a tone with foot shock. Subsequently, their reflexive startle response to a loud noise was considerably augmented in the presence of the conditioned light or tone. Potentiated acoustic startle did not occur after unpaired presentations of the light or tone and shock, so it was as valid a measure of fear conditioning as those employed in the previously described studies. The brain pathway for fear potentiated startle contains many of the same elements of the amygdala circuit studied by LeDoux and his colleagues, as they intersect with the acoustic reflex pathway. These studies have confirmed the essential role of the amygdala in fear conditioning, showing that damage to the lateral or basal amygdala or the central amygdala nucleus prevents conditioning and abolishes expression of previously learned acoustic startle responses. Correspondingly, electrical stimulation of the amygdala enhances acoustic startle. Other studies by this group have focused on identifying the critical output circuitry for fear potentiated startle. These studies have shown that the pathway from the amygdala to the brainstem regions constitutes the critical circuit for expression of potentiated startle.

The notion that the amygdala is central to associating rewards (and fear) with stimuli has been traced to the psychologist Larry Weiskrantz who studied the effects of removal of the amygdala in monkeys. In these studies, Weiskrantz (1956, p. 390) concluded that "the effect of amygdalectomy, it is suggested, is to make it difficult for reinforcing stimuli, whether positive or negative, to become established and recognized as such." Neurophysiological data showing strongly held reward-related responses, and their relation to unlearned reinforcing stimuli, has supported the view that the amygdala maintains neural representations of stimulus-reward associations. Thus, the notion that the amygdala plays a critical role in mediating stimulus-reward associations is widely held.

Yet, in studies on learning after damage to the amygdala, this notion has proven difficult to establish unambiguously. Thus, the findings across a broad variety of learning tasks has indicated that amygdala damage sometimes results in impairments in simple stimulus-reward learning tasks and sometimes does not. The psychologists Robert McDonald and Norman White (1993) have suggested that the mixture of results may be explained by distinguishing cases where learning can be mediated by the establishment of stimulus-response associations even in the absence of normal stimulus-reward associations. Thus, in most simple conditioning and discrimination tasks, animals are rewarded for producing a specific behavior, for example, a choice and approach toward a particular stimulus. In such cases, they argue that the reinforcer increases the likelihood of that response mediated by brain systems that do not involve the amygdala. In particular, in their study of different forms of radial maze learning, animals with amygdala damage normally acquired consistent approach responses to illuminated maze arms when specifically rewarded for such approach behaviors. In contrast, when the training involved simply feeding animals in an illuminated maze arm, with no requirement for an approach behavior, amygdala damage blocked a subsequent conditioned place preference. This distinction was made particularly compelling by the demonstration that damage to the extrapyramidal motor system had the opposite pattern of effects, blocking the learning of approach responses but not affecting the conditioned place preference.

Arousal and Attention

In addition to its functions within a specific brain system for emotional learning, it has become increasingly clear that the amygdala is also a nodal structure in the modulation of memory processes by diverse pathways. One proposal is that the amygdala, and particularly the central nucleus, plays a critical role in arousal and attention. This influence may be mediated by a collection of ascending systems in the brainstem and base of the forebrain that receive inputs from the central amygdala nucleus. These areas project to the brain areas involved in orienting behaviors and widespread areas of the cerebral cortex in a pathway that is associated with increased vigilance and attention. The psychologist Bruce Kapp and his colleagues (1992) have provided substantial data showing that rapid differential conditioning of neurons in the central amygdala nucleus are associated with fear conditioning and, correspondingly, that damage to this area blocks a particular form of conditioned heart rate response. In addition to its influence over unconditioned and conditioned reflexive responses, Kapp and colleagues have argued that amygdala activation results in a generalized arousal of cortical processing mechanisms. They have shown that stimulation of the

central nucleus elicits low-voltage fast activity associated with an aroused state in the cortex, and that activity in the central nucleus during heart rate conditioning naturally precedes episodes of neocortical fast activity.

Consistent with these observations, the psychologists Michela Gallagher and Peter Holland (1994) found that rats with central nucleus damage were deficient in acquiring conditioned orienting responses. They initially trained rats to approach a food cup in response to a light stimulus and then paired the light stimulus with a tone stimulus. They found that rats with central nucleus damage were unaffected in learning conditioned approach responses to visual and auditory stimuli and even acquired a second-order conditioned approach response to the tone at the normal rate. In this study, the investigators also observed orienting responses the animals made to the conditioning stimuli, responses that consisted of rearing on the hind legs and orientation to the light source. In striking contrast to the fact that amygdala damage had no effect on conditioned approach responses, they found that the conditioned orienting responses that normal animals made to the visual conditioned stimulus were abolished. Combining their findings with the results of other studies, Gallagher and Holland have argued that a major influence of the amygdala in learning is to increase attention to predictive stimuli.

Emotional Experience and Hormonal Influences

An additional line of research implicates the amygdala as being a critical nodal point in the modulation of all types of memory through emotional arousal. This work indicates that affectively charged experiences that activate stress hormone production begin a cascade of neurochemical and neural events that influence the amount of memory consolidation within the brain's memory systems. According to this view of emotional influences on memory, the amygdala is a main target of stress hormone activation. Its activation is modulated by other neurohormonal systems, and its targets of influence include other memory systems.

Stressful events that activate the sympathetic nervous system and pituitary-adrenal axis result in the release of epinephrine and glucocorticoids by the adrenal glands. These hormones have a variety of effects associated with the "fight-or-flight" response, including increased heart rate and blood pressure, diversion of blood flow to the brain and muscles, and mobilization of energy stores. There is a wealth of evidence that this activation also improves memory storage for experiences surrounding the activation and that the amygdala is critical to this influence on memory.

Investigations on the facilitation of memory by adrenal hormone activation in animals has largely focused on experiments that involve the systemic injection or brain infusion of drugs after the initial learning, with the common result that subsequent memory performance is altered. These effects typically depend on administration of the drug within minutes after training. There is generally no effect if administration of the drug is postponed for an hour or more. The post-training administration procedure eliminates the possibility that the drugs are altering perception, arousal, or motor performance during the learning experience. Conversely, this methodology, combined with the importance of the timing of the drug administration, provides strong evidence that the neurochemical events that are involved influence the after-learning consolidation of memories. These studies have provided extensive evidence that administration of epinephrine or adrenal glucocorticoids improve memory for inhibitory avoidance and that these effects are mediated by the amygdala.

In an elegant systematic series of studies, the psychologists Larry Cahill and James McGaugh (1998) have provided a framework for the pathway by which these effects are exerted. According to their scheme, glucocorticoids released during stressful events, or administered by injection, can enter the blood brain barrier and directly influence steroid receptors in the brain. Epinephrine does not enter the blood brain barrier easily, however, so it is likely that its effects are exerted by way of peripheral stimulation. In addition, other evidence shows that stress results in the release of norepinephrine within the amygdala, which stimulates the functions of this structure in mediating arousal and memory.

Evidence that emotional arousal can affect different forms of memory, and that this effect is mediated by the amygdala, comes from studies in both animals and in humans. In a series of experiments, Cahill, McGaugh, and their colleagues examined the influence of emotional content on conscious memory in humans. Their tests involved presentation of a series of slides and a narrative that told either a story about a mother and son involved in a traumatic accident or a control story with neutral emotional content. The story had three parts. In the beginning and end parts, the emotional and neutral stories are quite similar and are low in emotional content. In the middle section of the emotional story, the boy is critically injured, and the events are depicted graphically; in the neutral story, no accident occurs. In subsequent delayed memory testing, normal subjects show enhanced recall for the emotional component of the story, as compared to the parallel section of the neutral story. In contrast, subjects who were given a drug that blocks norepinephrine (i.e., an antagonist) showed no facilitation of declarative memory of the emotional component of the story, even though they rated that component of the story as being strongly emotional and their memory performance on other parts of the story was fully normal. Furthermore, control studies showed these effects were not due to direct effects in retrieving memories—the norepinephrine blocker given just before the retention test did not retard the normal memory enhancement of memory for emotional events. A subsequent study has now shown that a drug that increases the effectiveness of norepinephrine (i.e., an agonist) further enhances memory for the emotional component of the story.

The amygdala has also been strongly implicated in the enhancement of memory for emotional events in humans. A patient with Urbach-Wiethe disease, a disorder that results in selective bilateral amygdala damage, was tested in the emotional story experiment. Compared to control subjects, this patient failed to show enhancement of memory for the emotional part of the story. The patient performed as well as the control subjects on the initial neutral segment of the story and rated the emotional material as affectively strong. In a complementary brain imaging study on normal human subjects, the amygdala was activated during the viewing of emotional material, and this activation was related to enhanced memory for that material. In different brain scanning sessions, subjects viewed film clips that were strong or neutral in emotional content. The amount of activation in the right amygdala was greater for the emotional stories than for the neutral stories, and memory for the emotional stories was greater than that for the neutral stories. Furthermore, the amount of amygdala activation was related to performance in a delayed test of memory for the material in the emotional films but not in the neutral films.

Conclusion

Early research identified several interconnected brain structures on the inner rim of the cerebral hemispheres that were involved in receiving and interpreting emotional information. Modern research has focused on the amygdala, a small almond-shaped nucleus that lies deep in the temporal lobe and is critically involved in at least three emotional "systems" that play different roles in emotion and memory. These systems (which attach emotional significance to otherwise neutral stimuli, enhance learning and memory performance in a general way, and enhance memory processing) usually work together to promote rapid acquisition of emotional responses to important stimuli and to strengthen people's memories for the circumstances that surround emotional learning.

See also: BIOCHEMISTRY OF EMOTIONS; MIND-BODY DICHOTOMY; PSYCHOPHYSIOLOGY OF EMOTIONS

Bibliography

Adolphs, Ralph; Tranel, Daniel; Damasio, Hanna; and Damasio, Antonio R. (1994). "Impaired Recognition of Emotion in Facial Expressions Following Damage to the Human Amygdala." *Nature* 372:669–672.

Aggleton John P., ed. (1992). *The Amygdala: Neurobiological Aspects of Emotion, Memory, and Mental Dysfunction.* New York: Wiley.

Breiter, Hans C.; Etcoff, Nancy L.; Whalen, Paul J.; Kennedy, William A.; Rauch, Scott L.; Buckner, Randy L.; Strauss, Monica L.; Hyman, Steven E.; and Rosen, Bruce R. (1996). "Response and Habituation of the Human Amygdala During Visual Processing of Facial Expression." *Neuron* 17:875–887.

Cahill, Larry, and Mcgaugh, James L. (1998). "Mechanisms of Emotional Arousal and Lasting Declarative Memory." *Trends in Neuroscience* 21:294–298.

Cleparede, Edouard. (1911). "Recognition and 'Me-ness.'" *Archives de Psychologie* 11:79–90.

Damasio, Antonio R.; Tranel, Daniel; and Damasio, Hanna. (1989). "Amnesia Caused by Herpes Simples Encephalitis, Infarctions of the Basal Forebrain, Alzheimer's Disease, and Anoxia/Ischemia." In *Handbook of Neuropsychology, Vol. 3,* ed. Francois Boller and Jordan Grafman. Amsterdam: Elsevier.

Davis, Michael. (1992). "The Role of the Amygdala in Fear and Anxiety." *Annual Review of Neuroscience* 15:353–375.

Gallagher, Michela, and Holland Peter C. (1994). "The Amygdala Complex: Multiple Roles in Associated Learning and Attention." *Proceedings of the National Academy of Sciences USA* 9:11771–11776.

Hebben, Nancy; Corkin, Suzanne; Eichenbaum, Howard; and Shedlack, Karen. (1985). "Diminished Ability to Interpret and Report Internal States after Bilateral Medial Temporal Resection: Case H. M." *Behavioral Neuroscience* 99:1031–1039.

Kapp, Bruce S.; Whalen, Paul J.; Supple, William F.; and Pascoe, Jeffrey P. (1992). "Amygdaloid Contributions to Conditioned Arousal and Sensory Information Processing." In *The Amygdala: Neurobiological Aspects of Emotion, Memory, and Mental Dysfunction,* ed. John P. Aggleton. New York: Wiley.

Kluver, Heinrich, and Bucy, Paul. (1939). "Preliminary Analysis of Functions of the Temporal Lobes in Monkeys." *Archives of Neurology and Psychiatry* 42:979–997.

LeDoux, Joseph E. (1996). *The Emotional Brain.* New York: Simon & Schuster.

MacLean, Paul D. (1949). "Psychosomatic Disease and the 'Visceral Brain.' Recent Developments Bearing on the Papez Theory of Emotion." *Psychosomatic Medicine* 11:338–353.

McDonald, Robert J., and White, Norman. (1993). "A Triple Dissociation of Memory Systems: Hippocampus, Amygdala, and Dorsal Striatum." *Behavioral Neuroscience* 107:3–22.

Nauta, Walle J. H. (1958). "Hippocampal Projections and Related Neural Pathways to the Midbrain in the Cat." *Brain* 81:319–341.

Papez, James. (1937). "A Proposed Mechanism of Emotion." *Archives of Neurology and Psychiatry* 38:725–743.

Weiskrantz, Larry. (1956). "Behavioral Changes Associated with Ablation of the Amygdaloid Complex in Monkeys." *Journal of Comparative and Physiological Psychology* 49:381–391.

Howard Eichenbaum

NIETZSCHE, FRIEDRICH WILHELM

b. Röcken, Prussia, October 15, 1844; *d.* Weimar, Germany, August 25, 1900; *philosophy, psychology, theology.*

Friedrich Nietzsche was a nineteenth-century German philosopher and writer whose work drew considerable interest in the last half of the twentieth century. Although ignored during his lifetime and for decades after his death, Nietzsche is now considered to be one of the more significant philosophers of the modern world. He used an open and free style of thought and writing in an attempt to understand and explain the basis of modern Western society, thought, morality, and ethics. Although he made no systematic attempt to explain emotion, Nietzsche, unlike other philosophers of his time, did view the emotions and passion as important elements of the human experience.

Nietzsche was born in Prussian Saxony and raised in a devout Lutheran home. His father, Ludwig, and his mother's father were both pastors, and his father wrote several books in support of Protestantism. After his father died when Nietzsche was five years old, Nietzsche was raised in a household of women—his mother, Franziska; his younger sister, Elisabeth; his maternal grandmother; and two maiden aunts. The family moved to Naumburg in 1850, and Nietzsche attended a private school before receiving a scholarship in 1858 to Schulpforta, the most prestigious Protestant boarding school in Germany. Nietzsche was a fine student, and after graduating in 1864, he moved on to the University of Bonn. He later transferred to the University of Leipzig to continue to study theology and philology with Friedrich Wilhelm Ritschl, who had been a former professor at Bonn. Nietzsche became Ritschl's prize student, and after military service in 1867 and another year at the University of Leipzig in 1868, Nietzsche was appointed, on Ritschl's recommendation, to a provisional professorship at the University of Basel in 1869. The appointment was unusual in that Nietzsche was not a Swiss citizen, nor had he yet earned a doctoral degree. The situation was quickly remedied; the University of Leipzig awarded Nietzsche a doctorate based on his published work and he was made a Swiss citizen in 1870, at which point Nietzsche received his professorship appointment.

The decade at Basel was one of scholarly growth that was marked by periods of serious illness. Nietzsche became close with the German composer Richard Wagner, but by 1878, the friendship ended over Nietzsche's rejection of Wagner's fierce German nationalism and anti-Semitism. In 1872, Nietzsche published his first book, *The Birth of Tragedy from the Spirit of Music,* an attempt to explain Greek tragedy that was widely ignored or misinterpreted by other philosophers who mistook it for a work of classical scholarship. In the book, Nietzsche introduced the Apollonian-Dionysian dichotomy and employed it as an explanatory model. He suggested that nations or cultures could be described as either Dionysian (open, passionate, ecstatic, close to nature) or Apollonian (rigid, serene, controlled). Clearly, he considered the former to be superior and blamed the end of classical Greek civilization on the ultimate dominance of Apollonianism. Nietzsche also criticized nineteenth-century Germany as being Apollonian in nature. The Apollonian-Dionysian dichotomy was employed by social scientists in the middle decades of the twentieth century to explain cross-cultural differences in emotional expression, but it was ultimately rejected after research showed that universals and variations in emotional expression across cultures are far more complex that can be explained by such a simple model. In 1879, Nietzsche found himself too ill to continue teaching and resigned his professorship.

The final years of Nietzsche's short life have been called the decade of isolation and creativity, and they lasted from his retirement in 1879 until he was incapacitated by serious deterioration of his mental functioning in 1889. The exact cause or causes of Nietzsche's illnesses are not fully known, but it is likely that many of his problems and ultimately his death were the results of tertiary syphilis. For these ten years, Nietzsche lived mostly alone, half blind, on a small Swiss pension in boarding houses in Switzerland, Italy, and southern France. He had minimal contact with other people, and nearly all of his significant friendships came to an end. In spite of everything, it was the most intellectually productive period of his life and the period when he wrote the works that were to make him a world-renowned philosopher some five decades after his death: *The Gay Science* (1882), *Thus Spoke Zarathustra* (1883–1885), *Beyond Good and Evil* (1886), and *On the Genealogy of Morals* (1887).

By January 1889, Nietzsche's physical and mental condition had deteriorated to the point where he could no longer care for himself. Friends and family in Germany took him to Basel, where he was placed in the city mental hospital. Nietzsche was subsequently released to the care of his mother, with whom he lived until she died in 1897. His sister then looked after him until his death in 1900. Nietzsche's work, in spite of its later influence, drew little attention during his lifetime. It did, however, influence early psychoanalysts, such as Sigmund Freud, Alfred Adler, and Karl Jung, who praised Nietzsche's consideration and use of the emotions and his willingness to explore and reveal his

Friedrich Nietzsche. (Corbis/Bettmann)

own emotions. Freud went so far as to say that Nietzsche had a deeper understanding of himself than any man who had ever lived or was ever likely to live.

For the first half of the twentieth century, Nietzsche's reputation was damaged, and his was work ignored because of its association with fascism and Nazism in Germany. Nietzsche's sister and her husband (who committed suicide in 1889) were strong nationalists and anti-Semites, and through her control of Nietzsche's writings, she selectively released, forged, altered, and destroyed documents to support national socialism in Germany. It is not surprising, therefore, that Nietzsche had few champions outside of Germany during these years. The sad irony was that Nietzsche himself was strongly opposed to German nationalism and anti-Semitism, a fact that became generally known only after World War II. Since then, the study of Nietzsche's work has become and remains a major activity in the fields of religion, theology, literature, and psychology.

Nietzsche's early writings are seen as being fairly conventional and falling within the categories of romanticism, reason and science, and literature. The works created by Nietzsche after 1882 are considered by experts to constitute his "mature" ideas, and they contain the core of his ideas that are considered to be significant today. With regard to the study of human emotion, Nietzsche believed strongly that emotion, and especially passion, plays a major role in the human experience. Nietzsche lived a passionate life, wrote passionately, sought to understand his own feelings, and argued that emotion must be considered along with reason in attempt to understand and explain the world and the place of humans in it. Nietzsche clearly distinguished between positive and negative emotions (i.e., resentment), and he paid considerable attention to the negative, instinctual emotions that underlie human behavior. Nietzsche's passion did not sit well with other philosophers, who preferred to focus on rationality and reason. Because he was neither a logical writer nor an organized writer, Nietzsche did not produce any general guidelines for the study of emotion within philosophy.

In addition to his ideas about emotion and passion (which are actually not the key elements of his work), Nietzsche contributed numerous new ideas to philosophy, theology, and psychology, including his criticism of the destructive role of self-deception, the concept of the "will to power," the idea of struggle in human existence, and his criticism of Christian culture as being destructive of human creativity. These ideas had an enormous influence on intellectual life in the twentieth century and have played a role in shaping the work of major philosophers such as Albert Camus, Michel Foucault, Karl Jaspers, and Martin Heidegger; theologians such as Paul Tillich and Martin Buber; and literary figures such as Thomas Mann, Hermann Hesse, André Malraux, André Gide, George Bernard Shaw, and William Butler Yeats. Nietzsche was a tragic figure who gained little recognition and even less praise during his lifetime, but, as he himself wrote, some men are born after their death.

See also: FREUD, SIGMUND; MUSIC; PHILOSOPHY

Bibliography

Clark, Maudemarie. (1990). *Nietzsche on Truth and Philosophy.* Cambridge, Eng.: Cambridge University Press.

Hayman, Ronald. (1980). *Nietzsche: A Critical Life.* New York: Oxford University Press.

Kaufmann, Walter. (1974). *Nietzsche: Philosopher, Psychologist, Antichrist,* 4th ed. Princeton, NJ: Princeton University Press.

Solomon, Robert C., ed. (1973). *Nietzsche: A Collection of Critical Essays.* Garden City, NY: Anchor Press.

David Levinson
Ben Manning

NUTRITION

See Food and Eating

OLD AGE AND EMOTIONS

See Human Development: Old Age

ORATORY

Appeals to emotions have long been a method used by orators to persuade their audiences to act or perform in a certain way. Such appeals have often been controversial, as it has been thought that decisions based on emotions are decisions based on weaknesses or desires. For example, Plato compared the use of rhetoric (which includes the use of emotional appeals) to the art of a pastry chef—both rhetoric and baking appeal to a person's senses and appetites but neither are nourishing. Sweets will eliminate hunger, but they will not provide health. Plato would have even banned most poets from his ideal state because of their appeal, through their poetry, to the passions of their audience, enslaving them to their emotions and preventing the audience from making reasoned decisions that would lead them to virtue and happiness. Contemporary thinkers also express deep concern about the use of emotional appeals by speakers and in politics and advertising. Are there rules or guidelines that can help a speaker in deciding how ethically to use appeals to the emotions? Is an audience capable of resisting such appeals? Is the use of emotional appeal ethical?

The Classical Period

In the time of Plato and Aristotle, the governments of the world consisted largely of kings who made all of the decisions for their people. But in Athens, and some of the other Greek city-states, a new form of government was developing called democracy. In a democratic state the focus is on the individual and the individual's place in society. Citizens (though not all inhabitants, since slaves and women did not have rights) had to be educated in order for the democratic process to work. They attended the popular assemblies and courts of law wherein many of the decisions of government were made. The study of rhetoric became important because citizens needed to be able to persuade others or say things in a convincing manner.

Aristotle said that things that are true and things that are just have a natural tendency to prevail over their opposites and if they do not it is the fault of the speakers themselves. Therefore, he placed a great deal of responsibility on public speakers to educate themselves and to develop the skills necessary to express effectively that which is "true" and that which is "just." Aristotle's teacher, Plato, believed that truth was eternal and unchangeable and that one comes to know truth by looking at one's inner self and by engaging in the dialectic. The dialectic is a method of inquiry, a type of discussion wherein participants formulate precise definitions, reason carefully and rigorously, and maintain an open mind as they search for the truth. An example of this method would be a jury, wherein members, with an open mind and based on the facts and their own inner wisdom, must arrive at consensus as to whether a charge against an individual is true or false beyond a reasonable doubt. Aristotle believed that the platonic method of arriving at truth, while useful in some situations, provided little practical help in arriving at decisions with regard to everyday affairs. He believed in taking a rhetorical approach to decision making wherein the goal was not so much in finding an absolute truth but rather in convincing an audience to make the best possible decision. He thought that truth in the extreme was easy to find but most questions fell between the extremes, in the gray areas, so one needed a more practical method to employ when making decisions and in motivating others to act. He did not believe that truth naturally manifested itself on its own through discussion but rather an individual had to form an argument conscientiously and overtly wherein truth would come out through the use of the various "means" of persuasion. These means of persuasion are appeals to the logic (logos), ethics (ethos), and emotions (pathos) of an audience.

Logos refers to an appeal to reason. Aristotle believed that all people were reasonable and so if a reasoned and logical argument could be formed by a speaker then his or her audience would agree with the point being made. The syllogism was the backbone of this kind of appeal. A syllogism occurs when a relationship defined in the first premise sets up a reasoning sequence that leads to a claim. For example,

> Students who study hard get good grades.
> Mary and John study hard.
> Therefore, Mary and John get good grades.

A relationship between studying hard and good grades is established in the first premise and leads to the subsequent conclusion. When using logos, or in developing a reasoned argument, one should try to use evidence to back up the premises and conclusion. Types of evidence would include facts and figures, general and specific examples, and testimony or quotes from experts in the topic area. If the evidence is strong and cited properly, it will provide a firm foundation for the argument being made.

Aristotle believed that appeals to ethos, or character, were the most effective means of persuasion. It was believed that if an audience trusts the speaker then that alone may allow the speaker to prevail—regardless of the logic and evidence used. The three elements of ethos are good will, good sense, and good character. (Modern theorists like to refer to four elements: competence, good will, moral character, and dynamism.) It was believed that by leading a good and moral life and by referring to various virtues such as

courage, wisdom, generosity, self-control, and justice a speaker could inspire and, thereby, persuade an audience. It was believed that happiness was directly tied to the living of a virtuous life, so if a speaker refers to virtues and is virtuous in his or her own conduct a linkage occurs between the speaker's reference to virtue and the audience's view of their own virtue. If the audience sees itself as virtuous, they are happy.

Pathos, or an appeal to the emotions, was viewed by Aristotle as more problematic. He was concerned that an audience could be manipulated by emotional appeals, and, since many are controlled by their passions and emotions, an audience would be persuaded by a speaker not because of the strength of the argument or because it was good for society but because of an audience member's own individual weaknesses or selfish need to satisfy a passion. It was believed that emotional appeals should never be made without also using logic and ethics. Aristotle believed that appeals to pathos were ethical if they appealed to one's "mean" (i.e., a point between the extremes) and not to one's excesses or deficiencies. For example, if a speaker wants to make an appeal dealing with the emotion of confidence, he or she should not refer to recklessness (excess) or cowardice (deficiency) but rather to courage (the mean). Or, if one appeals to anger he or she should not refer to apathy (deficiency) or being short tempered (excess) but rather to gentleness (the mean). Therefore, according to Aristotle, it is ethical to use emotional appeals if logos and ethos are also used and if the appeals are made to the audience's mean.

Contemporary Thought on the Use of Emotions

Contemporary theorists accept many of the ideas of the Classical thinkers but take a different perspective on oratory and the emotions. Unlike Aristotle, they do not believe that people are essentially rational; they believe that decisions are based on a whole range of other criteria. Contemporary theorists believe that a speaker does not really persuade anyone—rather the speaker provides the listeners with the elements needed for the audience to "self-persuade." People self-persuade to a degree because of reasoning but primarily because they "identify" with one or more of the following:

1. the speaker as an individual—one who shares common demographic or psychological characteristics,
2. the speaker's experiences or references that ignite a memory for the audience,
3. a symbol, code, or form that the speaker employs, verbally or nonverbally, and is recognized

by the audience member and awakens his or her interest, or

4. the speaker's passion or emotional intensity that then causes the audience member to be swayed by his or her own emotional reaction to the speaker

A speaker expresses his or her passion and emotional intensity through an effective use of vivid sense imagery and various literary devices as well as an effective style of delivery. The use of literary devices such as metaphor, simile, personification, and apostrophe and imagery such as visual, auditory, tactual (touch), gustatory (taste), and olfactory (smell) serve as means by which a speaker can appeal to the emotions of his or her audience. These literary devices and images ground a speaker's message in the experience of the audience and guide the audience into an engagement of the message on an emotional level. Being told that murder is bad by a credible person is one level. Using

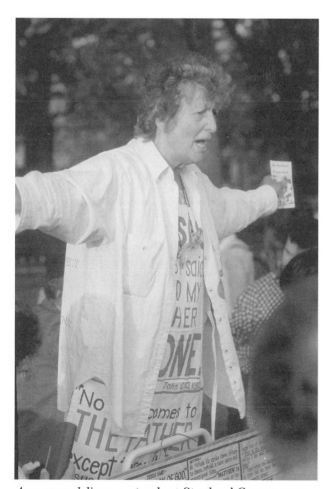

A woman delivers a speech at Speakers' Corner, a section of London's Hyde Park that is used as a forum for public oratory and debate. (Corbis/Sean Aidan; Eye Ubiquitous)

evidence and reasoning that shows the harm murder does to individuals and society is another level. But presenting an incident of murder by using vivid sense imagery and descriptive language moves the message to yet another level—one far more sublime and emotionally charged.

Delivery of Emotional Appeals

Emotional appeals will have little effect if they are not delivered well so it is necessary for orators to develop effective verbal and nonverbal public speaking skills. The elocutionist movement, which began in the mid-eighteenth century and grew in popularity throughout the first part of the twentieth century, emphasized the need for dynamic use of one's voice, gestures, and facial expression. It was thought that each internal emotion had an external manifestation. In fact, elocutionist John Walker, in his *Elements of Elocution* (1810), listed seventy-one emotions (including such emotions as fear, tranquility, joy, sadness, cheerfulness, and pity), and provided a detailed description of how the speaker should use his or her voice, gestures, and facial expressions to convey convincingly each of the emotions. For example, Walker described the emotion of fear as follows:

> Fear is a mixture of aversion and sorrow, discomposing and debilitating the mind upon the approach or anticipation of evil. When this is attended with surprise and much discomposure, it grows into terror and consternation. Fear, violent and sudden, opens wide the eyes and mouth, shortens the nose, gives the countenance an air of wildness, covers it with deadly paleness, draws [up the hands] with the fingers spread, to the height of the breast, at some distance before it so as to shield it from the dreadful object. One foot is drawn back behind the other, so that the body seems shrinking from the danger, and putting itself in a posture for flight. The heart beats violently, the breath is quick and short, and the whole body is thrown into a general tremour. The voice is weak and trembling, the sentences are short, and the meaning confused and incoherent.

Such a performance, as described above, presented exactly as described with sincerity and great intensity, could most certainly touch the emotions of many audience members. The problem, however, is that people do not all experience each individual emotion in the same way. Also, following a script for the display of emotion often results in melodrama and a lack of sincerity. The *mechanics* of effective delivery can be practiced and learned and are a valuable contribution by the elocutionists. However, in modern times, students of public speaking are taught that the *motivations* of effective delivery must come from within themselves—not from a script or book.

The Question of Ethics

Many organizations have developed codes or guidelines that stress the importance of always using emotional appeals in a responsible manner. Such appeals should be backed by sound evidence and reasoning and presented by speakers who have established their credibility on a given topic. Emotional appeals should never degrade another person or their ideas. Nor should they be used to cloud over an issue or divert attention away from the issue. The intent of the emotional appeal should be an attempt to bring about a greater good without using misleading information. The audience should come away from the persuasive event better informed, perhaps even more empathetic, but with their choice-making capacity left intact.

Not all persuaders, however, use emotional appeals ethically. Is the audience capable of resisting these appeals? Research has shown that if the audience is well educated, with high self-esteem, they tend to be able to resist emotional appeals. However, audience members who are not well educated and who have lower self-esteem tend more easily to follow charismatic leaders who use strong emotional appeals. So, generally speaking, if one wants to resist emotional appeals, one should strive for a good education and seek out the life experiences that would help develop high self-esteem or a positive self-concept.

Is the use of an emotional appeal ethical? As explained above, an emotional appeal is ethical if it is backed by the proper use of logos and ethos. The three should work hand in hand, providing an audience with a comprehensive understanding of the idea or topic being raised.

Emotional appeals can serve a very positive function in oratory, since through such appeals the speaker can help his or her audience better empathize and understand an idea or event. Through the use of vivid sense imagery and powerful language devices an orator can re-create an emotion-laden event, transporting an audience through space and time and enabling the audience to relive the event on not only a factual plane but on a emotional plane as well. In a well-crafted speech, the emotional appeals are the "spice in the sauce" that gives the speech its flavor and punch. Emotional appeals can contribute greatly to an audience's understanding of a message, so speakers should incorporate such appeals whenever ethically appropriate.

See also: ARISTOTLE; COMMUNICATION; DRAMA AND THEATER; PERSUASION; PLATO; POETRY

Bibliography

Aristotle. (1954). *The Rhetoric and Poetics of Aristotle.* New York: Random House.

Cooper, Martha D., and Nothstine, William L. (1996). *Power Persuasion: Moving an Ancient Art into the Media Age,* 2nd ed. Greenwood, IN: Educational Video Group.

Golden, James L.; Berquist, Goodwin F.; and Coleman, William E. (1976). *The Rhetoric of Western Thought.* Dubuque, IA: Kendall/Hunt Publishing.

Ken Hawkinson

P-Q

PAIN

For most people, pain is simply a response to potential or actual injury. It is a passing warning signal that disappears with the danger. Under many circumstances, pain is a useful response for preventing people from sustaining extensive burns, bruises, and lacerations during everyday behaviors. The experience of minor pain or discomfort will cause a shift in position, a roll during sleep, and the avoidance of certain postures that would otherwise result in damage to the joints. For many clinical conditions, however, pain has long ceased to be a useful warning sign. It is not easy, for example, to imagine the severe pain of a burn, particularly when a large portion of the body surface has received third-degree burns, destroying all layers of the skin. The pain suffered by such patients is extremely high and continues for several months. The injury occurred long ago, but the "warning" continues. Like a burglar alarm that sounds accidentally, this type of pain is continuous, irritating, and useless. To help patients suffering from such pain, the many mysteries that lie beyond the apparent simplicity of the pain experience must be solved.

A constant puzzle for pain researchers is the variability between a given injury and the experience of pain—the size of the injury is not always directly related to the amount of resulting pain. For example, one of the most painful experiences by far is induced by the seemingly trivial process of passing a kidney stone. Under certain conditions, the kidney concentrates some components in the urine and creates small kidney stones. Small pieces of the stones occasionally break off and pass into the ureter that leads from the kidney to the bladder. The pieces are rarely more than twice the diameter of the ureter and can be driven by the pressure of urine building up behind. As the pushing ensues, the ureter wall goes into waves of localized contraction. During the contraction, agonizing spasms of pain sweep over the patient and he or she usually collapses. Pale and rigid, with a racing pulse and knees drawn up, the patient remains motionless until the stone passes into the bladder, at which point there is immediate and complete relief. The actual mechanical changes that take place are trivial but the experience is phenomenal.

Variability can also be observed with chronically painful conditions such as arthritis. While pain is a major complaint of patients suffering arthritis, there seems to be no clear correlation between the advance of the disease and the amount of pain suffered. Even during the advanced stages, when joint inflammation indicates the presence of chemical irritants that excite pain receptors in the bone and the joint capsule, some patients continue to report no pain.

In spite of these examples of variability, there is certainly an important relationship between the experience of pain and the biology of injury. Still, pain is so much more than a simple response to injury, and it is this fact that makes treatment, and even definition, of pain controversial and difficult.

Defining Pain

Defining pain usually involves a combination of cognition (thinking), sensation, and affective (emotional) processes. This biopsychosocial model of pain, rather than understanding pain as merely a physical reaction to a stimulus, sees it as a conscious experience that may be modulated by mental, emotional, and sensory mechanisms.

Pain was first described as a multidimensional phenomenon by Ronald Melzack and Kenneth Casey in 1968, and this understanding continues to be reflected in the definition of pain used by the International Association for the Study of Pain: an unpleasant sensory and emotional experience associated with actual or potential tissue damage, or described in terms of such damage. The definition is not perfect, most notably because it ignores the cognitive processes, but it does avoid the problem of defining pain as the response to painful stimulation. This definition also serves as a useful reminder that pain is an experience that does not, so to speak, automatically spring forth from the depths of the person's mind fully formed and without modulation.

Howard Leventhal (1984) has proposed a model of pain processing that is unique in that it proposes parallel processing of the informational and emotional aspects of the sensory experience and provides the beginning of an explanation about how pain evolves. According to Leventhal, once stimulus information passes through the spinal gate (i.e., a hypothesized system for the regulation of information within the spinal cord), it is organized and elaborated by three hierarchical mechanisms in the central nervous system.

The first level in the hierarchy of the central nervous system is perceptual-motor processing, and the second level is schematic processing. Both of these levels are considered to be preconscious (i.e., they are not available to insight or reflection). Perceptual-motor processing involves the activation of an inborn set of expressive motor reactions to environmental stimuli. Schematic processing involves the automatic encoding of the experience in relation to the general informational, emotional, and sensory aspects of pain experiences that are already stored in the memory.

Emily Dickinson has several poems that capture the insistence and apparent endlessness of pain. In "Pain has an element of Blank" (1890), she speaks of not remembering when the pain started, as if it has always been there, and "has no future but itself." In "After great pain, a formal feeling comes" (1929), Dickinson emphasizes the loss of feeling. One feels wooden, stiff, leaden, like a stone after the great pain finally goes away. One remembers the pain "as Freezing persons recollect the Snow."

At the third, higher level, it has been proposed that a set of abstract rules about emotional episodes and the associated voluntary responses arise over time because of self observation and voluntary efforts to cope with emotion provoking situations. These rules are highly variable with experience. Following Leventhal, Stuart Derbyshire (1999) has suggested mechanisms for incorporating pain into developing conscious awareness. The development of conscious awareness leads to a specific structure of pain experience that maintains a relationship with biological processes on the one hand and the higher psychological functions (of sociocultural origin) on the other. In this way, people can use their understanding of the experience of pain to inform their understanding of the central biology of pain.

The Neurobiology of Pain

Specificity theory and the hypothesis of a centralized pain center dominated early research into the central mechanisms of pain. This traditional theory of pain was first proposed by René Descartes in 1664. Descartes suggested that a painful stimulus transferred energy to "threads" running through the body that opened pores in the head and signaled pain. Thus, pain was produced just as pulling at one end of a rope causes a bell connected to the other end to strike. More than three hundred years later, many textbooks on neurology, neurophysiology, and medicine still describe the essence of Descartes's theory as the basis for understanding pain. In the modern interpretation, stimulation of so-called pain fibers relays information to a hypothesized pain center somewhere in the brain. A painful stimulus, therefore, becomes that which activates the pain fibers and center, and pain becomes activity in the pain center. Although specificity theory was a considerable advance on previous thinking and is not without merit, it ultimately collapses because it fails to account for the variable relationship between injury and pain. In addition, it fails to capture adequately the underlying neurology of pain.

A series of experiments to uncover the location of the pain center, initially believed to be seated in the cerebral cortex, were carried out during the twentieth century. Wilder Penfield and Edwin Boldrey (1937) stimulated eight hundred areas of the somatosensory cortex (part of the rippled gray matter that envelops the brain and sits just beneath the scalp—it is the parietal region of the cortex sitting posterior to the primary sulcus), which is known to be involved in certain sensory processes, but they found that only eleven of the areas elicited pain. Despite this finding, special effort was made to place the pain center in the somatosensory cortex and to eliminate pain by surgery in this area. During neurosurgical operations, the stimulation of many other areas of the cortex generally failed to produce pain. Such infrequent reports of pain led to the belief that the pain center was not located in the cortex but was instead a thalamic function. Hence, thalamic neurons were also destroyed in an attempt to abolish pain. This procedure may produce pain relief, but often it does not—in some cases, it can even make the pain worse. Many other medical procedures have drawn on the logic of a specific pain system, destroying selected nerves or pathways in the central nervous system in an attempt to control pain. Central lesions (i.e., tissue being surgically removed, burnt away, or destroyed in some other way) have been placed in the cingulum bundle, frontal white matter (i.e., spinal cord), pulvinar, amygdala, frontothalamic tracts, pituitary, and hypothalamus in an attempt to produce pain relief. Lesions of these sites are sometimes effective in controlling the unpleasantness of chronic pain, but they are ineffective with regard to acute pain. The basic failure of medical techniques based on specificity theory has led to the abandonment of ideas based on a specific pain center. They have been replaced with the suggestion that there is a widespread pain system involving many different neural structures.

Figure 1 illustrates, in schematic form, some of the regions of the brain currently believed to be involved in pain processes. Two major pain systems can be distinguished: the phylogenetically old pathways that course medially through the brainstem, and the newer pathways that maintain a lateral course in the brainstem. The medial pathways, which ascend in the ventrolateral spinal cord, have multiple synaptic connections along their route, and they relay widely in the brain stem before projecting to the amygdala and other limbic structures. Most fibers of the medial system pass all the way to the medial and intralaminar nuclei of the thalamus. The medial system transmits impulses to the brain slowly and exhibits poor localization (i.e., the medial system is poor at recognizing where on the body incoming information originates). The lateral pathways pass upward to the brain through the anterolateral white matter with no synaptic connections. The lateral system terminates predominantly in the ventrobasal complex of the thalamus before projecting to the somatosensory cortex. In contrast to the medial system, the lateral system transmits impulses rapidly along highly organized pathways.

Studies of brain processes during painful experiences have provided varying results (as was the case with neurosurgery studies). In response to acute and chronic noxious experiences, changes in brain activity have been demonstrated in the anterior cingulate cortex (100% of the time), the insula cortex (75% of the

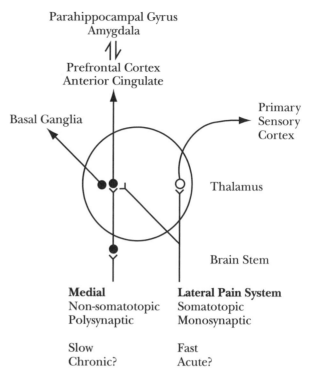

FIGURE 1   *A schematic representation of the medial and lateral pain systems. The medial system is a slow system with poor ability to localize. The projections of the medial system are to areas that are associated with emotional cognitive processes. In contrast, the lateral system is a very fast system with somatotopic organization at each level—meaning it is well organized for localizing incoming stimulation. The lateral system projects predominantly to the somatosensory cortex.*

time), the thalamus (50% of the time), the prefrontal cortex (47% of the time), the primary somatosensory cortex (47% of the time), the lentiform nucleus (42% of the time), and the secondary somatosensory cortex (31% of the time). Occasional findings have also been reported in the inferior parietal cortex, brain stem, and amygdala. The basis for the variability in the results among groups who are supposed to be experiencing the similar sensation of pain is far from understood. The concept of a "neuromatrix" that is made up of the various regions of the brain (each with its own function) and is responsible for processing pain-related information is consistent with the concept that pain is a combination of cognitive, affective, and sensory processes. In short, the regions related to the medial pain system are thought to be responsible for the affective and cognitive components of pain, while the regions related to the lateral system are thought to process the location and intensity of the pain. With this in mind, researchers are moving toward an understanding of pain that involves change and development at both the psychological and the physiological levels.

The Development of Pain

A number of articles in both medical and bioethical journals have discussed the question of whether a fetus can feel pain. Trying to solve this question, which involves assessing an experience without an explicit verbal report, is fraught with difficulty, and it is not surprising that the debate has generated controversy. On the one hand, there is the tendency to "err on the safe side" and assume that pain exists until it is proven otherwise. On the other hand, there is the important scientific need to answer this important question. The main shortcoming of the fetal pain literature is that it tends to equate physiological responses, such as an increase in neurotransmitter response, with the experience of pain itself. Such a view fails to adequately explain the mediating links between physiology and experience. It also fails to account for the changeable psychological and physiological nature of pain. Ultimately, adopting the position that assumes a fetus experiences pain can lead to implausible conclusion.

Obstetrician Frederick Leboyer (1975, p. 10) gives the following harrowing description of birth:

> The child? Oh, dear God, it can't be true! The mask of agony, of horror; and above all the hands, raised to the head in the classic gesture of despair. This is the gesture of the mortally wounded, the moment before they collapse. Can birth hold so much suffering, so much pain?

Leboyer is convinced that babies suffer overwhelming trauma and agony during birth and that this may lead to considerable psychological problems during later life. Despite the development of a comprehensive system of "primal therapy" that aims to resolve the continuing repercussions of birth, there is little to commend such counseling. There is, for example, no evidence that babies born by cesarean section suffer any less psychological problems than babies who are born naturally. Leboyer's mistake is a common one. Outward reflexive behavior in the presence of noxious stimulation, what Leventhal refers to as expressive motor reactions, is interpreted as the manifestation of pain and suffering—the "silent scream." This notion is a moral blunder that draws a false equivalence between observer and observed. The inborn tendency toward expressive actions and gestures, along with the organized reflexes of the newborn, may form the prerequisites for emotional development and the unfolding of human experience. However, saying that those behaviors are indicative of pain is the same as assuming that the process of development is already completed. Figure 2 shows a comparison between the development of conscious awareness in children and the experience of pain. The three levels of Leventhal's hierarchy and the added dimension of self-awareness form the substance of the four "pain dimmer switches."

The dimmer framework shown in Figure 2 borrows heavily from the work of Susan Greenfield (1995), but there are considerable differences in emphasis and interpretation. The aim of this framework is not to say that there cannot be any rudimentary awareness of pain by a fetus or newborn but to make apparent the basic stages of the cognitive and conscious development of a human being. This approach requires a definition of what is *different* about the fetal or newborn experience—if there is any experience at all. For example, Greenfield highlights that because children live in the present they tend not to dwell on pain. Although they usually overreact to a relatively trivial mishap, the tears are frequently banished by some distraction. As soon as a new event in the external world arises, consciousness of the original pain vanishes. Children's memories gradually improve with age and linguistic skill until, by the time they are five or six years of age, personal anecdotes and projections into the future become common. Between two and five years of age, therefore, pain shifts from being a temporary interruption of ongoing activity (i.e., a distraction) to being a more threatening disruption of existence (i.e., a source of suffering).

This understanding of the relationship between the experience of pain and the basic development processes renders the variability of the pain experience across culture, gender, and age less mysterious.

Understanding the Variability

One of the most striking examples of the effect of culture on pain is the South Asian Indian hook-swinging ritual described by David Kosambi (1967). The ritual derives from an ancient practice involving the selection of one individual to represent the power of the gods. The role of the chosen "celebrant" is to bless the children and crops in neighboring villages. During this blessing process, steel hooks, attached by strong ropes to the top of a special cart, are pushed under the skin and muscles on both sides of the celebrant's back. Hanging from the ropes, the celebrant is moved from village to village. At the climax of the ceremony in each village, he swings free (hanging only from the hooks embedded in his back) and blesses the children and the crops. Thinking about this procedure induces a feeling of discomfort that is manifestly lacking in the celebrant, who, far from displaying evidence of pain, appears to be in a state of exaltation.

There is no reason to think that these people are, in general, physiologically different from anyone else. It is the interaction of their understanding, beliefs, and physiology at that time that seems to give rise to their apparent lack of pain experience. Figure 3 shows a proposed relationship between stress, tension, negative mood changes, and biological adaptation that leads to increased, rather than decreased, responsiveness to stimulation.

It is now generally believed that there are important differences between the male pain response and the female pain response that have important implications for health research. Women make greater use of the health-care system, and this has led to the proposition that women are therefore more sensitive "pain detectors" than are men. While this disproportionate use of the health-care system by women is well documented, the evidence regarding responses to experimental pain is more conflicting—sometimes greater sensitivity for women is reported and sometimes no difference is reported. The discrepancy between the clear evidence that women use the health-care system more than men and the inconclusive results with regard to experimentally induced pain is puzzling. It is

possible that the experimental investigation of male and female responses to pain often fails to produce conclusive results because the differences between individuals (male or female) make the response variability too great for the detection of specific gender differences.

Differences in psychological factors such as anxiety and depression between men and women could account for some of the reported sex differences in response to pain. This suggestion has received empirical support. Over the three-day period of their experiment, Stefan Lautenbacher and Gary Rollman (1993) observed that as women became less anxious about induced heat pain their pain tolerance approached that of the male group. This is consistent with the fact that focusing on the less bothersome characteristics of pain reduces the perceived magnitude of the pain, while "anxious monitoring" of sensations increases the likelihood of perceiving pain and can predict the magnitude of chronic pain. Georg Adler and Wagner Gattaz (1993) have even suggested that anxiety and impaired stress coping lower pain perception thresholds in depressive patients. The question then arises as to why these factors should differ from men to women.

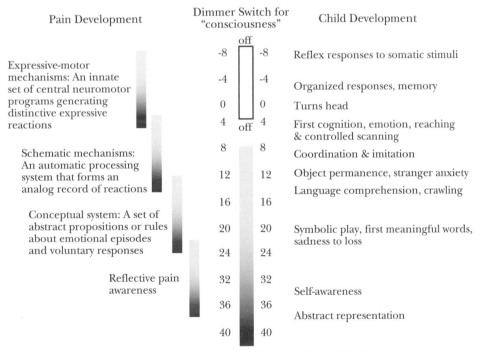

FIGURE 2   *The dimmer switch. On the left is the hierarchical development of pain as described by Howard Leventhal. Expressive-motor and schematic mechanisms are both considered preconscious. Activation of the main consciousness switch occurs around four months of age. The corresponding cognitive development necessary for the increasing complexity of Leventhal's pain hierarchy is shown on the right. The numbers represent age in months: "-8" is one month after conception, and "0" is birth.*

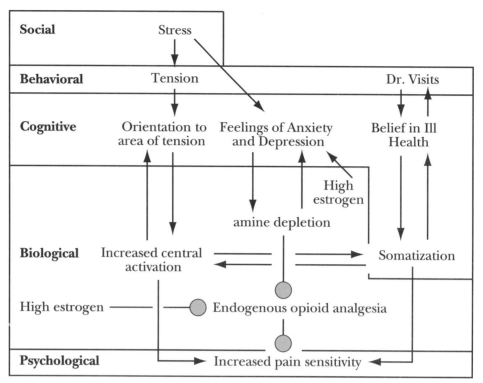

FIGURE 3   *A schematic representation of the multiple factors that are involved in pain. Arrows indicate possible causal links, and filled circles indicate attenuation. Stress in the social space affects the behavioral and cognitive areas, producing changes in the biological space. The cascade finally leads to change in pain sensitivity.*

The work of George Brown and Tirril Harris (1978) and Charlotte Feinmann and Malcolm Harris (1984) has demonstrated the importance of life events as a cause of psychological distress. The latter authors emphasize that stress from life events is a fundamental factor in the development of facial pain. Peter Croft and Andrew Rigby (1994) report a similar relationship for lower back pain. Thus, social stress can be a source of variability in the development of ill health.

The life events themselves, which vary in character but often evolve around the family, include parental neglect or abuse before a child is eleven years of age, having three or more children under five years of age in the family, chronic ill health in the family, and divorce. Because women still carry most of the domestic

W. H. Auden, in "Surgical Ward" (1971), describes the isolation that is experienced by those suffering pain, so overwhelming that their whole world is pain. "They are and they suffer, that is all they do," says the narrator at the opening of the poem.

responsibilities within the family, they are more likely to experience more of the stresses that lead to ill health and painful disorders. The expectation that women should take on the bulk of domestic responsibility is not just an "ideological" issue. Demographic patterns of employment indicate that only 11 percent of women with children under four years of age work full time, and women cite looking after the family as their main reason for not seeking work in 26 percent of the cases, compared with only 2 percent for men. Even when women continue to work, they experience increased feelings of conflict and take on a substantially greater share of the total household workload than do men. In families with three or more children, Ulf Lundberg and his colleagues (1994) have found that the difference between women's and men's total workload increases to about twenty hours per week. This increased responsibility for the family crosses cultural barriers, as do the associated increases in stress and fatigue.

It is not clear how life stress can lead to the development or worsening of a pain disorder. However, once a person perceives life to be beyond control, he or she is at risk for depression and other detrimental mood changes. These mood changes, particularly anxiety, can predict a drop in pain threshold. Examination by Mark Stein and his colleagues (1995) of the factor structure of the Wender Utah Rating Scale revealed that women have more anxiety and depression with physical complaints such as headaches and stomach aches, and experimental studies by both Richard Hudiburg and his colleagues (1993) and Rand Conger and his colleagues (1993) have shown that women respond more readily to both home and work "hassles" with increased physical complaints. Figure 3 confirms that stress and tension can change a previously nonnoxious bodily sensation into a sensation that is more intense and noxious. Increases in central (brain) activity and decreases in amines (neurotransmitters) mediate this change. Amine depletion in turn inhibits endogenous descending analgesia, and this may exacerbate, in females, the already hormonal (estrogen) inhibited endogenous opioid analgesia. Heightened physiological arousal is associated with heightened attentional focus on bodily sensation, which is inadvertently encouraged by visits to the doctor.

Conclusion

There are universal patterns of behavior that are exhibited in response to noxious stimulation. In addition, verbal descriptions of pain identify recognizable signals concerning the presence, nature, intensity, duration, location, reference, and temporal course of the pain experience. A general similarity in pain experience across age, gender, and culture is, therefore, to be expected. However, it is wrong to conclude from this general experience that there is a direct relationship between stimulus and pain. Such a view leads to an oversimplified view of both the neurophysiology and psychology of pain. To understand the essence of pain is to understand the mediation between physiological response to stimulation and the conscious expression of pain that is shaped by individual and social experience.

See also: DESCARTES, RENÉ; HEALTH AND ILLNESS; MINDBODY DICHOTOMY; NEUROBIOLOGY OF EMOTIONS

Bibliography

Adler, Georg, and Gattaz, Wagner F. (1993). "Pain Perception Threshold in Major Depression." *Biological Psychiatry* 34:687–689.

Apkarian, A. Vania, and Hodge, Chris J. (1989). "Primate Spinothalamic Pathways: 1. A Quantitative Study of the Cells of Origin of the Spinothalamic Pathway." *Journal of Comparative Neurology* 288:447–473.

Berkeley, Karen. (1997). "Sex Differences in Pain." *Behavioral and Brain Sciences* 20:371–380.

Bouckoms, Anthony J. (1989). "Psychosurgery." In *The Textbook of Pain,* ed. Patrick D. Wall and Ronald Melzack. Edinburgh: Churchill Livingstone.

Brown, George W., and Harris, Tirril. (1978). *Social Origins of Depression.* London: Tavistock.

Burgess, John A., and Tawia, S. A. (1996). "When Did You First Begin to Feel It? Locating the Beginning of Human Consciousness." *Bioethics* 10:1–26.

Conger, Rand D.; Lorenz, Frederick O.; Elder, Glen H.; Simons, Ronald L.; and Ge, Xiaojia. (1993). "Husband and Wife Differences in Response to Undesireable Life Events." *Journal of Health and Social Behaviour* 34:71–88.

Croft, Peter R., and Rigby, Andrew S. (1994). "Socioeconomic Influences on Back Problems in the Community in Britain." *Journal of Epidemiology and Community Health* 48:166–170.

Derbyshire, Stuart W. G. (1997). "Sources of Variation in Assessing Male and Female Responses to Pain." *New Ideas in Psychology* 15:83–95.

Derbyshire, Stuart W. G. (1999). "Locating the Beginnings of Pain." *Bioethics* 13:1–31.

Derbyshire, Stuart W. G.; Jones, Anthony K. P.; Gyulai, Ferenc; Clark, Stuart; Townsend, David; and Firestone, Leonard. (1997). "Pain Processing during Three Levels of Noxious Stimulation Produces Differential Patterns of Central Activity." *Pain* 73:431–445.

Donaldson, Margaret. (1992). *Human Minds: An Exploration.* London: Penguin.

Feinmann, Charlotte, and Harris, Malcolm. (1984). "Psychogenic Facial Pain." *British Dental Journal* 156:165–168.

Glover, Vivette, and Fisk, Nicholas. (1996). "We Don't Know; Better to Err on the Safe Side From Mid-Gestation." *British Medical Journal* 313:796.

Graham, Jennifer. (1998). "Primal Therapy: A Stillborn Theory." In *Controversies in Psychotherapy and Counselling,* ed. Colin Feltham. London: Sage Publications.

Greenfield, Susan A. (1996). *Toward a Science of Consciousness: Journey to the Centers of the Mind.* New York: W. H. Freeman.

Hudiburg, Richard A.; Brown, Sara A.; and Jones, Morris T. (1993). "Psychology of Computer Use: XXIX. Measuring Computer Users' Stress: The Computer Hassles Scale." *Psychological Reports* 73:923–929.

Kosambi, David D. (1967). "Living Prehistory in India." *Scientific American* 216:105–114.

Lai, Gina. (1995). "Work and Family Roles and Psychological Well-Being in Urban China." *Journal of Health and Social Behaviour* 36:11–37.

Lautenbacher, Stefan, and Rollman, Gary B. (1993). "Sex Differences in Responsiveness to Painful and Non-Painful Stimuli Are Dependent upon the Stimulation Method." *Pain* 53:255–264.

Lautenbacher, Stefan, and Strian, Friedrich. (1991). "Sex Differences in Pain and Thermal Sensitivity: The Role of Body Size." *Perception and Psychophysics* 50:179–183.

Leboyer, Frederick. (1975). *Birth without Violence.* London: Wildwood House.

Leventhal, Howard. (1984). "A Perceptual-Motor Theory of Emotion." *Advances in Experimental Social Psychology* 17:117–175.

Lundberg, Ulf; Mardberg, Bertil; and Frankenhauser, Marianne. (1994). "The Total Workload of Male and Female White-Collar Workers As Related to Age, Occupational Level, and Number of Children." *Scandinavian Journal of Psychology* 35:315–327.

Melzack, Ronald, and Casey, Kenneth L. (1968). "Sensory, Motivational and Central Control Determinants of Pain." In *The Skin Senses,* ed. Dan Kenshalo. Springfield, IL: C.C. Thomas.

Melzack, Ronald, and Wall, Patrick D. (1988). *The Challenge of Pain.* London: Penguin.

Merskey, Harold. (1991). "The Definition of Pain." *European Journal of Psychiatry* 6:153–159.

Penfield, Wilder, and Boldrey, Edwin. (1937). "Somatic Motor and Sensory Representation in the Cerebral Cortex of Man As Studied by Electrical Stimulation." *Brain* 60:389–443.

Stein, Mark A.; Sandoval, Ron; Szumowski, Emily; Roizen, Nancy; Reinecke, Mark A.; Blondis, Thomas A.; and Klein, Zanvel. (1995). "Psychometric Characteristics of the Wender Utah Rating Scale (WURS)." *Psychopharmacology Bulletin* 31:425–433.

Unruh, Anita M. (1996). "Gender Variations in Clinical Pain Experience." *Pain* 65:123–167.

U.S. Public Health Service. (1990). *Hanes II Epidemiological Survey.* Washington, DC: U.S. Government Printing Office.

Waddell, Gordon. (1987). "A New Clinical Model for the Treatment of Low-Back Pain." *Spine* 12:632–644.

Wade, James B.; Price, Donald D.; Hamer, Robert H.; Scwartz, Steven M.; and Hart, Robert P. (1990). "An Emotional Component Analysis of Chronic Pain." *Pain* 40:303–310.

Wall, Patrick D. (1989). "Why the Definition of Pain Is Crucial." In *The Textbook of Pain,* ed. Patrick D. Wall and Ronald Melzack. Edinburgh: Churchill Livingstone.

Stuart W. G. Derbyshire

PASSION

See Desire; Infatuation; Intimacy; Love; Lust

PERSONALITY

Emotions, which form an important part of everyday experience and functioning and constitute a significant aspect of what patients talk about in psychotherapy, are of considerable interest to personality psychologists. This interest focuses on the nature of specific emotions and emotion in general, on individual differences in the experience and expression of emotions, and the relation of specific emotions to other aspects of personality functioning, such as thinking, motivation, and health.

Emotion and the Major Approaches to Personality

Historically there have been four major approaches to personality theory: psychoanalysis, phenomenology, trait psychology, and social cognitive theory. The importance of emotions in personality functioning is recognized in each of these theories, although the importance attached to emotion, how emotional experiences are understood, and the degree of interest in specific emotions varies among them. All four of these approaches give attention to the emotion of anxiety, and the majority give attention to the emotion of depression.

Emotion clearly plays a central role in psychoanalytic theory, perhaps a more central role than in any of the other theoretical approaches. This is true in terms of both the range of emotions considered as well as the role of emotion in total personality functioning. Of central importance is the emotion of anxiety and the ways in which the person attempts to defend against this painful emotion (i.e., the mechanisms of defense). In psychoanalytic theory, anxiety is viewed as a signal to alert the person to impending danger, with the signal being based on the experience of a past trauma. As such it has functional or adaptive value, although more extreme efforts to defend against anxiety are associated with the development of psychopathology. Particular attention is given to anxiety associated with the expression of sexual and aggressive instincts or drives. There have been many different interpretations of the cause of depression. Early psychoanalytic views focused on the turning inward of aggressive drives that otherwise would be expressed toward others. Later views emphasized the importance of early experiences of loss and the sense of helplessness in situations involving the loss of self-esteem. In addition to attention given to the clinically important emotions of anxiety and depression, other emotions such as mistrust, shame, and guilt are viewed as being associated with conflicts experienced during the first five years of development. Thus, individual differences in anxiety and in the experiencing of other emotions are viewed as the outcome of problems experienced during the early stages of development, with the importance of specific emotions being associated with developmental fixations or arrests at specific time points or stages of development. More recent developments in psychoanalysis, known as object relations theory, focus on the association of specific emotions with earlier important persons (objects), giving less attention to the importance of drives and conflicts associated with specific stages of development.

Phenomenological theory emphasizes the ways in which people experience themselves and the world about them. The leading figure in the development of this approach in relation to personality theory was Carl Rogers. Although Rogers emphasized the importance of emotion generally in relation to the phenomenal world of the individual, he did not give much attention to specific emotions. An exception to this was the attention given to the emotion of anxiety. Originally Rogers viewed anxiety as the result of a discrepancy or incongruity between the way a person

How an individual responds to emotion-producing situations is closely related to that person's personality, whether the response be frustrated crying (in this case, by a child) or calmly coping with the situation (in this case, by the father). (Corbis/ Annie Griffiths Belt)

views the self and emotions that are experienced. Thus, if the person views the self as caring and experiences uncaring feelings, there is an incongruity between self and experience that results in anxiety. Similarly, if a person views the self as hostile and experiences tenderness, anxiety is experienced as the result of this incongruity between self and experience. Although never totally rejecting this view, Rogers later emphasized the importance of experiences of loss of positive regard from others in the development of anxiety. According to this view, based on earlier experiences, individuals associate certain feelings with the loss of positive regard from important others, which results in the association of anxiety with these feelings. In other words, it is the potential for loss of positive regard from important others that leads to the association of anxiety with particular feelings. Whereas early experiences of unconditional positive regard from others lead to an openness to experience and acceptance of a wide range of feelings, experiences of conditional positive regard are associated with anxiety and lead the developing child to protect the self from experiences that might lead to the loss of positive regard. Protection can take the form of distorting experience or denying (pushing out of awareness) experience. In his emphasis on anxiety as an emotion associated with threat and the efforts of the person to defend against anxiety, Rogers's view is simi-

lar to that of Sigmund Freud, although he rejected Freud's emphasis on drives, the unconscious, and stages of development.

Trait theory represents one of the oldest approaches to personality. According to this approach, individuals can be characterized by broad dispositions, called traits, to think, feel, and behave in particular ways. Raymond B. Cattell and Hans J. Eysenck were two important early trait theorists. Cattell distinguished among ability traits, temperament traits, and dynamic (motive) traits. Temperament traits relate to the emotional life of the person and Cattell emphasized the importance of individual differences in emotional traits such as reserved versus outgoing, emotionally unstable versus emotionally stable, and trusting versus suspicious. For the most part, attention was not directed toward factors leading to the development of individual differences in these traits, although the importance of hereditary and biological factors was recognized. Eysenck emphasized three broad trait dimensions along which individuals differ: neuroticism, introversion-extraversion, and psychoticism (i.e., sensitivity to others and social custom as opposed to insensitivity to others, impulsivity, and rejection of social custom). He also emphasized the importance of hereditary and biological factors in the development of individual differences in these major dimensions of personality. Trait theory has since come to focus on five major dimensions of personality: neuroticism, extraversion, openness to experience, agreeableness, and conscientiousness. Although all five can be viewed as having emotional components to them, the first two, which are similar to dimensions emphasized by Cattell and Eysenck, are of particular significance in this regard. Anxiety and depression are both viewed as components of neuroticism, and individual differences with regard to these trait dimensions are associated with hereditary and biological factors.

Social cognitive approaches to personality emphasize the importance of information processing for all aspects of individual functioning; that is, how the person takes in, stores, and retrieves information is viewed as fundamental. Many different theorists are associated with such a view, but what they hold in common is an emphasis on cognitive processes; they are interested in the association of specific cognitions and cognitive processes with specific emotions. In other words, these theorists view emotions as the consequence of cognition (i.e., what a person feels is a result of what and how that individual thinks). Within this general approach, differences occur in the nature of the essential cognitive factors involved in specific emotions. For example, George Kelly, an early proponent of the importance of cognition in personality, suggested that anxiety occurs when a person confronts events that he or she does not know how to interpret or understand. Threat, an even more painful emotion, occurs when an individual's way of interpreting or understanding the world is in danger of requiring comprehensive change because it no longer seems able to account for and predict events. Social cognitive psychologist Albert Bandura emphasizes the importance of self-efficacy beliefs. Self-efficacy beliefs involve individual assessments of their ability to cope with specific situations. According to Bandura, low self-efficacy beliefs in the face of dangers is the cause of anxiety, whereas low self-efficacy beliefs in relation to attaining rewards is the cause of depression. Other cognitive personality psychologists emphasize the role of specific thoughts and beliefs as well as more general ways of thinking in their study of emotion. For example, the tendency to have negative thoughts, to explain negative events as being due to the self (as opposed to others or chance), and to view negative conditions as global and stable (as opposed to specific events with the potential for change) is seen as being implicated in depression. In this regard, the work of Aaron T. Beck is of particular importance in the area of psychotherapy because he emphasizes in his study of depression the role of negative thoughts concerning the self, the world, and the future. The task of cognitive therapy, then, is to facilitate change in cognitions so that changes in emotion will occur. In sum, cognitive personality psychologists share an emphasis on the content of thought and general thought processes in emotion although the specific thoughts and thought processes emphasized vary from theorist to theorist.

Research on Emotion and Individual Differences in Emotion

With the cognitive revolution in psychology, dating roughly to the early 1960s, there was greater emphasis placed on how people think, to the relative neglect of how people feel. Where cognition and emotion were related to one another, the emphasis was placed on the influence of thoughts on feelings and behavior. Since that time, however, there has been greater interest in emotion and the influence of feelings on thinking or cognition. Influential in this regard has been the work on what is known as basic emotions theory or differential emotions theory, which derived principally from the efforts of Silvan Tomkins, Paul Ekman, and Carroll Izard. According to this view, there are basic, fundamental, or primary emotions that are universal. The exact number of basic emotions varies somewhat from theorist to theorist, generally ranging from eight to fourteen (e.g., interest-excitement, enjoyment-joy, distress-anguish, disgust-revulsion-contempt, anger-rage, shame, fear). These emotions, or affects as they often are called, are innate and part of humans' evolutionary heritage. In other words, people do not learn to be afraid, angry, or disgusted, although they do learn when, where, and in response to which stimuli to respond with these emotions. For example, although there appear to be universal stimuli for disgust, namely those having contamination properties, what is considered to be disgusting by some individuals or cultures can be considered a source of joy by others (e.g., eating ants can be considered disgusting or a delicacy). In addition, the emotion or affect system is viewed as central to motivation; that is, emotions have an energizing or motivational effect. Due to the central importance of emotion, many thoughts and memories are organized in terms of their association with the same emotion. In other words, important experiences are linked in the mind in terms of their common emotional qualities rather than because of purely cognitive similarities. Also, a person's emotional or mood state influences that individual's thoughts about the past, present, and future. Thus, a depressed mood state causes a person to remember past negative events and to focus on negative aspects of the present and future. Finally, since emotions are motivational and organize cognition and action, they are central to an individual's personality. In other words, as a result of constitutional factors as well as experience, individuals differ in the frequency and intensity with which particular emotions are experienced. Thus, the defining aspect of each person's personality is the organization of his or her emotional life (i.e., the emotions that tend to be experienced, the patterns of relations among emotions, and the events or situations related to the experiencing of these emotions).

It should be noted that other personality psychologists, such as Richard Lazarus, give greater attention to cognitive considerations in their analysis of emotion. According to Lazarus, emotions involve appraisal processes and beliefs about the self and the world. Specific emotions result from the person's appraisal or assessment of the relation between an event and personal goals, in particular whether the event is perceived to facilitate or thwart goal attainment. This relation between goals and appraisal of potential benefit or harm is called a core relational theme. For example, the emotion of anger results from the belief that a demeaning offense has been committed against the person or someone valued by the person, the emotion of anxiety results from the appraisal of uncertain threat, and the emotion of sadness results from the appraisal that an irrevocable loss has been sustained. In other words, rather than emphasizing universal emotions that are based in evolutionary heritage, the emphasis is on how each emotion expresses a belief about the relation between an event and personal goals. In addition, there is an emphasis on how people attempt to cope with stress, or the appraisal that events threaten harm rather than benefit to the individual's goals. In particular a distinction is made between problem-focused forms of coping (e.g., efforts to alter the situation) and emotion-focused forms of coping (e.g., emotional distancing, escape-avoidance, seeking social support). Individuals differ in their tendencies to favor particular coping methods, although most individuals also vary their coping method from context to context. An important part of personality, then, is the core relational themes emphasized by the person and the methods used to cope with emotions associated with stress.

In terms of individual differences in emotion, the broadest distinction made by personality psychologists is with regard to positive and negative emotion. Rather than viewing positive and negative emotion as opposites, personality psychologists view them as distinct categories of emotion such that individuals can be high or low on each. In other words, individuals can tend to be high or low on both positive and negative affect or high on one and low on the other. A disposition to be high on negative affect is strongly associated with the trait of neuroticism and increased risk of health difficulties (e.g., coronary difficulties and poorer immunological system functioning).

Distinct from the tendency to experience positive or negative emotions is the mood associated tendency toward optimism or pessimism. The optimism-pessimism dimension involves the tendency to believe that good, as opposed to bad, things will generally occur in one's life. Research suggests that individuals differ in their general tendencies to be optimistic or pessimistic and that these tendencies are fairly stable over time. In addition, there is evidence that individuals scoring high on optimism tend to be higher on positive affect, to be better at handling stress, to have better physical well-being, and to recover better from injury and illness than individuals scoring high on pessimism. Optimistic individuals also tend to take more direct action and to be more planful in their adaptive efforts than pessimistic individuals. In sum, individual differences on the optimism-pessimism mood dimension have been found to be associated with broad areas of psychological and physical well-being.

A number of other emotion-related variables on which individuals differ have been studied by personality psychologists. For example, individuals differ not only in their general levels of positive and negative affect but in the intensity of these affective experiences and the variability with which they experience positive and negative emotions. In terms of the latter, two individuals can have the same average level of positive or negative affect but, whereas one experiences the same level fairly constantly, the other experiences wide swings on one, the other, or both. Another important individual difference variable is how emotion is regulated, the extent to which emotion is expressed or suppressed. Although impulsive expressions of emotion can have detrimental consequences for the person, so too can the generalized tendency to suppress or inhibit emotion. For example, there is evidence of a link between the tendency toward suppression of emotions and the development of psychosomatic disorders. Other personality research is involved with the study of differences in the extent to which individuals avoid emotional situations as opposed to seeking them out, the extent to which individuals are able to regulate emotion through attention deployment measures as opposed to being obsessed with affect-laden thoughts, and the extent to which individuals use measures such as social support and substance abuse to modulate emotion. Considerable research points to a relation between substance abuse and the effort to avoid negative emotion and increase positive emotion.

Conclusion

Many theories of personality are derived from experiences with patients in therapy, and psychoanalytic theory is a prime example. As such, since individuals tend to focus on the feelings involved in the difficulties they bring to the attention of therapists, it is not surprising that such theories have devoted attention to the importance of emotion in personality functioning. Particularly noteworthy in this regard is the attention given to the emotion of anxiety. Beyond this, comprehensive personality theories differ in the importance attached to emotion in personality functioning, in the attention given to specific emotions as opposed to emotion in general, and in the interpretations given for the occurrence of specific emotions. In addition to the efforts of some personality psychologists to include emotion as part of a comprehensive personality theory, other personality psychologists have focused their theoretical and research efforts on emotion and attempted to extend these efforts to include other aspects of personality functioning. Regardless of differences in the extent to which such personality psychologists emphasize universal emotions and the role of cognition in emotion, there is agreement that a basic aspect of personality is the organization of emotions within the person. The organization of emotions is viewed as including the tendency to experience specific emotions, the relations among emotions, the situations in which emotions tend to be experienced, and the ways in which individuals regulate their emotions. Finally, some personality psychologists focus their efforts on particular emotions or aspects of the emotion regulation process on which individuals differ. There is clear evidence of a number of important individual difference dimensions in this regard and research indicates that such differences have important implications for virtually all other aspects of human functioning.

See also: ANXIETY; ATTACHMENT; CATTELL, RAYMOND BERNARD; COGNITIVE PERSPECTIVE; DEFENSE MECHANISMS; EYSENCK, HANS JURGEN; FREUD, SIGMUND; GENDER AND EMOTIONS; HUMAN DEVELOPMENT; MOTIVATION; PSYCHOANALYTIC PERSPECTIVE; PSYCHOLOGICAL ASSESSMENT; PSYCHOTHERAPY; ROGERS, CARL RANSOM; SELF-ESTEEM; TEMPERAMENT

Bibliography

Bandura, Albert. (1986). *Social Foundations of Thought and Action.* Englewood Cliffs, NJ: Prentice-Hall.

Beck, Aaron T. (1976). *Cognitive Therapy and the Emotional Disorders.* New York: International Universities Press.

Cattell, Raymond B. (1965). *The Scientific Analysis of Personality.* Baltimore, MD: Penguin.

Ekman, Paul. (1993). "Facial Expression and Emotion." *American Psychologist* 48:384–392.

Eysenck, Hans J. (1990). "Biological Dimensions of Personality." In *Handbook of Personality: Theory and Research,* ed. Lawrence A. Pervin. New York: Guilford.

Izard, Carroll E.; Libero, Deborah A.; Putnam, Priscilla; and Haynes, O. Maurice. (1993). "Stability of Emotion Experi-

ences and Their Relations to Traits of Personality." *Journal of Personality and Social Psychology* 64:847–860.

Kelly, George A. (1955). *The Psychology of Personal Constructs.* New York: W. W. Norton.

Lazarus, Richard S. (1993). "From Psychological Stress to the Emotions: A History of Changing Outlooks." *Annual Review of Psychology* 44:343–357.

Pervin, Lawrence A. (1993). "Personality and Affect." In *Handbook of Emotion,* ed. Michael Lewis and Jeannette Haviland. New York: Guilford.

Pervin, Lawrence A. (1996). *The Science of Personality.* New York: Wiley.

Rogers, Carl R. (1961). *On Becoming A Person.* Boston: Houghton Mifflin.

Tomkins, Silvan S. (1963). *Affect, Imagery, and Consciousness.* New York: Springer.

Lawrence A. Pervin

PERSPECTIVES ON EMOTION

See Anthropology of Emotions; Biochemistry of Emotions; Cognitive Perspective; Folk Theories of Emotion; Historical Study of Emotions; Neurobiology of Emotions; Psychoanalytic Perspective; Psychology of Emotions; Psychophysiology of Emotions; Sociology of Emotions

PERSUASION

Emotions play a central role in the persuasion process. Attitudes are often established and then changed by repeated associations between an attitude object and a state of emotional arousal. Emotional appeals are common in advertising and in political rhetoric, and such appeals can produce changes both in one's feelings that are associated with an attitude object and in one's beliefs about it. The emotional component of attitude can be changed even by persuasive communication that depends primarily on logical or rational argumentation. And a person's mood during exposure to a persuasive communication can influence that person's ability or motivation to scrutinize the information.

Emotion in Models of the Persuasion Process

Research on the persuasion process is dominated by two similar theoretical models. One is the elaboration likelihood model developed by Richard Petty and John Cacioppo. The other is the heuristic-systematic model developed by Shelly Chaiken and Alice Eagly. Both models share the fundamental assumption that people want to hold correct, valid, and accurate attitudes. When the recipient of a persuasive communication is motivated to scrutinize the message, and when the situation or setting permits issue-relevant thinking and elaboration, attitude change is achieved through a change in cognitive structure. Because attitude change in this context is achieved through a process of cognitive elaboration, it is referred to as "systematic processing" in the heuristic-systematic model and as "central-route persuasion" in the elaboration likelihood model. Under these conditions, factors such as argument quality chiefly determine the amount and direction of attitude change.

It is often the case that message recipients are not strongly motivated to scrutinize or engage in deep elaboration of the arguments in a persuasive communication; the issue may be perceived as being unimportant, or the message recipient may not want to expend the necessary cognitive effort. The situation or setting can also interfere with message-relevant thought, as often happens when the message recipient is distracted or occupied with other tasks. Nevertheless, features of the persuasion setting may provide a basis for attitude change. For example, message recipients can rely on simple inferential rules or heuristic devices to make attitudinal judgments without having to engage in deep processing of message content. Thus, by applying the simple rule that "experts can be trusted," a message recipient can decide to accept arguments that are attributed to experts and to reject arguments that are attributed to non-experts. Because attitude change in this context is achieved in the absence of deep cognitive elaboration, it is referred to as "heuristic processing" in the heuristic-systematic model and as "peripheral-route persuasion" in the elaboration likelihood model.

The elaboration likelihood model identifies some additional mechanisms through which peripheral-route persuasion can be achieved, such as the repeated pairing of an attitude object with an emotionally-arousing stimulus. In these cases, attitude change may occur in the absence of issue-relevant thought and without the use of judgmental heuristics.

Classical Conditioning

Attitudes are frequently established and changed by repeated pairings of the attitude object with an emotionally arousing stimulus or event. Mass media advertising offers numerous illustrations—consumer products are often and consistently paired with pleasant scenes, uplifting music, and desirable social images. It is hoped that, over time, the presentation of an initially neutral or even disliked product will begin to elicit a favorable emotional response as a result of its previous association with an emotionally arousing event.

Research conducted primarily during the 1950s and 1960s demonstrated classical conditioning of attitudes. In the typical experiment, target objects (such

as personal names) were paired repeatedly with evaluative words (such as positive or negative adjectives). When people were later asked to rate the pleasantness of the target objects, the objects were rated as being more pleasant when they had been paired with favorable rather than with unfavorable words. In the language of classical conditioning, the target object is a conditioned stimulus, and the evaluative words are the unconditioned stimuli. The unconditioned stimuli have the property of spontaneously eliciting a positive or negative unconditioned response. Through repeated pairing of a conditioned stimulus with an unconditioned stimulus, the conditioned stimulus eventually elicits a positive or negative conditioned response, even in the absence of the original unconditioned stimulus.

Throughout the 1960s and 1970s, some controversy developed concerning the classical conditioning of attitudes. Some researchers suggested that the previously observed effects were not due to classical conditioning but rather to artifacts of the experimental procedures. Most of the argument came down to whether or not the classical conditioning effects depended on people being aware of the contingency between a conditioned stimulus and an unconditioned stimulus. By the early 1990s, the consensus was that such effects can be obtained even when people are not aware of the conditioned stimulus/unconditioned stimulus contingency. It therefore appears that attitudes can be classically conditioned. Additional results have shown that the classical conditioning process depends on relatively simple emotional mechanisms. From this perspective, classical conditioning procedures appear to cause a change in attitudes that is best described as peripheral-route persuasion.

Fear and Threat Appeals

Persuasive communications are often designed to scare people into compliance with an advocated course of action. This approach is commonly used to promote healthful behaviors—if one exercises regularly, eats a balanced diet, and does not smoke then the chances of developing heart disease, obesity, and lung cancer are greatly reduced. Public safety communications warn about the undesirable consequences of failing to wear seatbelts, insurance companies relate the tragic stories of parents who compromised their own children's welfare by failing to purchase life insurance, and manufacturers of home alarm systems dramatize the horror and sense of violation that occurs when one's home has been burglarized.

Theory and research on fear appeals began in the 1950s and were based on the idea that people are motivated to avoid or reduce unpleasant emotions that

Come to where the Cancer is.

Smoking kills more Americans each year than alcohol, cocaine, crack, heroin, homicide, suicide, car accidents, fires, and AIDS combined.

An antismoking poster created by a twelve-year-old student in New York City uses fear appeal in a parody of a popular cigarette advertising campaign. (Corbis/Bettmann)

are aroused by threatening communications. This may lead people to accept the conclusion of a persuasive message if such acceptance helps to lessen the aversive emotional state. The advocated position may be rejected, however, if its acceptance does not sufficiently diminish or remove the perceived threat, if the level of arousal is so intense that it interferes with message comprehension, or if the threat is so great that it elicits some kind of defensive or avoidance response.

This theoretical view was elaborated and refined throughout the 1970s. By that time, the emerging view was that the effectiveness of a fear appeal depends on several factors. One important factor is that recipients of a fear appeal must be convinced that the advocated coping response is an effective way to reduce or avoid the perceived threat. This is generally known as response efficacy. Another important factor is that message recipients must be convinced that they are capable of performing the recommended action. This is generally known as self-efficacy. In terms of the elaboration-likelihood and heuristic-systematic models of persuasion, fear arousal may influence a person's ability or motivation to scrutinize message content and may therefore be a significant determinant of systematic or central-route processing versus heuristic or peripheral-route processing. Despite the theoretical controversy in this area, the major effect is regularly obtained—increasing fear is associated with greater attitude change.

Research on fear appeals represents the largest concentrated effort to understand the persuasive effect of emotion-arousing communications. Clearly, persuasive communications are often designed to arouse emotions other than fear. It is not unusual for appeals to elicit excitement, joy, anger, or disgust. Mass media advertising often makes use of appeals based on sex, humor, or sympathy. Nevertheless, research on emotion-arousing communications has focused primarily on fear, to the exclusion of other discrete or fundamental emotions. A general exception is research on advertising, but even there the focus is at the level of "feeling effects" or "warmth" engendered by advertising rather than on a discrete emotional response. Additional research is needed to understand how appeals based on other forms of emotional arousal (such as sex or humor) facilitate (or hinder) the achievement of persuasive goals.

Emotional Versus Rational Appeals

It is important to ask whether appeals that are based on emotion are any more or less effective than appeals that are based on well-reasoned and coherent arguments. Instances of both approaches are easily found in consumer product advertising. Image-based advertisements associate desirable personal, social, and emotional images with a product, even though the image may have nothing to do with the product itself. In contrast, quality-based advertisements establish the utility of a product by emphasizing its features and attributes. Of course, the two approaches are not mutually exclusive, and it is common for a single product to be advertised using both approaches (either separately or in combination). In general, image-based advertising can be viewed as being emotional appeals, and quality-based advertising can be viewed as being rational appeals.

Surprisingly little research has examined the relative effectiveness of emotional versus rational appeals. Some studies indicate that emotional appeals encourage heuristic processing of persuasive messages, whereas rational appeals encourage systematic processing. These results complicate the comparison of emotional versus rational appeals. The focus in such studies is an interaction between the form of the appeal (emotional versus rational) and the kind of processing that is elicited (heuristic versus systematic). Thus, for emotional appeals, the presence of peripheral or heuristic cues will enhance persuasion regardless of the quality of the argument. In contrast, for rational appeals, persuasion will primarily be the result of argument strength.

Other studies emphasize the role of individual differences as mediators of the effects of emotional versus rational appeals. For example, Mark Snyder and Kenneth DeBono identified self-monitoring as a personality characteristic that could potentially determine the relative effect of image-oriented versus quality-oriented appeals. The high self-monitor is a person who is especially sensitive to situational cues in interpersonal settings and who uses those cues as a guide to behavior; the low self-monitor is a person who uses internal cues and personal attributes (attitudes, feelings, values) as a guide to behavior. Snyder and DeBono found that high self-monitors were more responsive to appeals that were based on image (emotional appeals), whereas low self-monitors were more responsive to appeals that emphasized quality (rational appeals).

The relative effectiveness of emotional versus rational appeals is an understudied problem. Research results through the 1980s indicate that the problem is a complicated one. The form of an appeal (emotional versus rational) interacts with the nature of processing and with individual differences among people.

Mood and Persuasion

It is common for people to be experiencing a good or bad mood during exposure to a persuasive communication. Television advertising may be embedded within a stream of programming that engenders either a negative mood (such as reports on the evening news about violent crimes) or a positive mood (such as a situation comedy). Exposure to magazine advertising or newspaper editorials may be surrounded by stories and headlines that arouse mild positive or negative affective states. Radio advertising is typically preceded by music that may make the listener feel good, relaxed, or energetic. And exposure to messages on billboards or subway placards often occurs when the message recipient is experiencing some tension or nervousness because of especially heavy traffic or a noisy and polluted environment.

These situations differ from cases of classical conditioning in two important ways. First, although mood is aroused in the persuasion setting, the source of that arousal is independent of the communication itself. Second, the particular mood that happens to accompany a persuasive communication may not be reliably associated with that message on repeated exposure or in different contexts. Indeed, very different moods may be experienced during receipt of the same message on separate occasions. Thus, if coincidentally experienced mood influences the persuasive effect of a

communication, it is likely to do so through mechanisms other than classical conditioning.

The elaboration likelihood model helps to identify a potentially important way in which a person's experienced emotion may influence the persuasion process. A good mood (compared to a neutral mood) appears to increase one's reliance on judgmental heuristics and to reduce systematic processing of complex information. Thus, being in a good mood should reduce the likelihood of message elaboration or central-route persuasion, and it should increase the likelihood of heuristic processing or peripheral-route persuasion. Several studies support this hypothesis. In the typical study, people are placed into either a positive, a negative, or a neutral mood. They are then exposed to one of several persuasive communications that vary in terms of central processing cues (such as argument strength) and in terms of peripheral processing cues (such as source expertise). People who are placed into a good mood are generally more responsive to the peripheral cues than they are to the central cues.

Two distinct explanations can be offered for the result that positive mood reduces the likelihood of elaboration. One possibility is that a good mood reduces a person's ability to engage in systematic processing of complex information. Positive affect has been shown to increase the accessibility of positive information from memory, to increase the complexity of cognitive content, and to promote a broader and more integrated organization of knowledge. All of this presumably consumes cognitive capacity, leaving the message recipient less able to devote the cognitive resources that are needed to elaborate on a persuasive communication. Another possibility is that a good mood reduces one's motivation to engage in systematic processing. People may avoid cognitive effort that threatens their good feelings, or they may interpret positive affect as indicating that systematic processing is not necessary to deal effectively with the demands of the current setting.

It is not yet clear whether positive emotions reduce systematic processing because of a reduction in ability, a reduction in motivation, or both. By the early 1990s, some studies supported the reduction-in-motivation hypothesis, and other studies supported the reduction-in-ability hypothesis.

Dissonance Arousal and Attitude Change

People sometimes do or say things that are inconsistent with their own attitudes. They may take a so-called counterattitudinal position for the sake of argument (playing the devil's advocate) because someone has asked or instructed them to do so (a debate), or for purposes of self-presentation or self-gain

Isaac Bashevis Singer's "Gimpel the Fool" (1953) has a protagonist who is so gullible that he makes most readers a little angry. People can persuade him that the children his wife bears are his, though he has not had sexual relations with her. People enjoy persuading him to believe impossible things, but Gimpel chooses to believe, and he becomes a kind of holy fool, expecting truth and decency from people.

(a political campaign). Counterattitudinal behavior often produces a phenomenon known as cognitive dissonance. Specifically, cognitive dissonance occurs when an actor must assume personal responsibility for the counterattitudinal action, perceives the attitude and behavior to be personally important and relevant, and anticipates negative and irrevocable consequences as a result of the action. Cognitive dissonance is assumed to be an aversive experience, and people are generally motivated to reduce or eliminate it. One way to reduce cognitive dissonance is to change one or more of the dissonant elements. Thus, the experience of cognitive dissonance often causes a change in one's attitude.

Two important observations are that cognitive dissonance is accompanied by heightened physiological arousal and that the phenomenal experience is aversive. Substantial indirect evidence also suggests that cognitive dissonance produces effects on performance that are similar to those that are produced by other sources of arousal (such as drugs or exercise).

An influential line of research in the 1970s examined the question of why people are motivated to reduce cognitive dissonance. One possibility is that people change their attitudes in an effort to reduce the arousal (regardless of its hedonic value). Another possibility is that cognitive dissonance produces attitude change because people are motivated to reduce the negative affect (regardless of degree of arousal). Several studies indicate that dissonance-induced attitude change occurs because people are motivated to reduce negative affect rather than to reduce nonspecific arousal.

Affective and Cognitive Responses to Persuasive Communications

The outcome measure in most persuasion experiments is a single-item self-rating of agreement with an attitudinal position. The implied unidimensionality stands in contrast to the theoretical and scientific distinction between the affective and cognitive components of attitude. It is reasonable to expect that a single persuasive communication can have unique effects on affect and cognition, especially when the message includes elements of both rational and emotional appeals. Research conducted throughout the 1990s found that persuasive communications can have distinct and independent effects on self-report measures of the affective and cognitive components of attitude. For example, a person's thoughts in response to a persuasive communication may be more heavily influenced by the affective than by the cognitive component of the person's attitude.

Measurement problems have created a significant obstacle to studying emotion-related functioning in attitude research. Indeed, the methods that are most commonly used to assess attitudes are better-suited for measuring the cognitive than the affective component (e.g., semantic differential scales, equal-appearing interval scales, and cognitive response protocols). Although attitude researchers have occasionally used nonverbal measures, such efforts have not been generally successful.

One notable exception has been the application of facial electromyographic measurement in the study of affective and cognitive responses to persuasive communications. Specific patterns of facial expression appear to be associated with each of the primary emotions. Even activity in the face that is too small to be visibly detected may be associated with emotional episodes. Electromyography provides a method for measuring and quantifying such covert changes in the facial musculature, and these measures can reveal both the direction and the intensity of affective responses. Patterns of facial electromyographic activity indicate that affective responses are more positive during receipt of a proattitudinal or neutral message than during receipt of a counterattitudinal message. In addition, facial electromyographic measures tend to be only weakly correlated with the favorability of listed thoughts. Thus, persuasive communications may have unique and distinct effects on the affective and cognitive components of attitude as indicated by the pattern of facial electromyographic measures.

Conclusion

Models of attitude change allow for multiple roles of emotion in persuasion. Future research may benefit by considering how the characteristics of persuasive appeals interact with different fundamental or discrete emotions. Additional insight might also be gained by using attitude measures that capture or preserve more information about affective and emotional responses. In addition to facial electromyography, measures based on voice quality or central-neural processes may be especially fruitful.

See also: ADVERTISING; ATTITUDES; PROPAGANDA

Bibliography

Breckler, Steven J. (1993). "Emotion and Attitude Change." In *Handbook of Emotions*, ed. Michael Lewis and Jeannette M. Haviland. New York: Guilford.

Cacioppo, John T., and Petty, Richard E. (1979). "Attitudes and Cognitive Response: An Electrophysiological Approach." *Journal of Personality and Social Psychology* 37:2181–2199.

Chaiken, Shelly; Liberman, Akiva; and Eagly, Alice H. (1989). "Heuristic and Systematic Information Processing Within and Beyond the Persuasion Context." In *Unintended Thought*, ed. James S. Uleman and John A. Bargh. New York: Guilford.

Eagly, Alice H., and Chaiken, Shelly. (1993). *The Psychology of Attitudes*. Fort Worth, TX: Harcourt, Brace, Jovanovich.

Isen, Alice M. (1987). "Positive Affect, Cognitive Processes, and Social Behavior." In *Advances in Experimental Social Psychology, Vol. 20*, ed. Leonard Berkowitz. San Diego, CA: Academic Press.

Jorgensen, Peter F. (1998). "Affect, Persuasion, and Communication Processes." In *Handbook of Communication and Emotion*, ed. Peter A. Andersen and Laura K. Guerrero. San Diego, CA: Academic Press.

Mackie, Diane M., and Worth, Leila T. (1991). "Feeling Good, But Not Thinking Straight: The Impact of Positive Mood on Persuasion." In *Emotion and Social Judgments*, ed. Joseph P. Forgas. Oxford, Eng.: Pergamon Press.

Petty, Richard E., and Cacioppo, John T. (1981). *Attitudes and Persuasion: Classic and Contemporary Approaches*. Dubuque, IA: Wm. C. Brown.

Petty, Richard E., and Cacioppo, John T. (1986). "The Elaboration Likelihood Model of Persuasion." In *Advances in Experimental Social Psychology, Vol. 19*, ed. Leonard Berkowitz. San Diego, CA: Academic Press.

Petty, Richard E.; Gleicher, Faith; and Baker, Sara M. (1991). "Multiple Roles for Affect in Persuasion." In *Emotion and Social Judgments*, ed. Joseph P. Forgas. Oxford, Eng.: Pergamon Press.

Rogers, Ronald W. (1983). "Cognitive and Physiological Processes in Fear Appeals and Attitude Change: A Revised Theory of Protection Motivation." In *Social Psychophysiology: A Sourcebook*, ed. John T. Cacioppo and Richard E. Petty. New York: Guilford.

Schwarz, Norbert; Bless, Herbert; and Bohner, Gerd. (1991). "Mood and Persuasion: Affective States Influence the Processing of Persuasive Communications." In *Advances in Experimental Social Psychology, Vol. 24*, ed. Mark P. Zanna. San Diego, CA: Academic Press.

Snyder, Mark, and DeBono, Kenneth G. (1985). "Appeals to Image and Claims About Quality: Understanding the Psychology of Advertising." *Journal of Personality and Social Psychology* 49:586–597.

Sutton, Stephen R. (1982). "Fear-Arousing Communications: A Critical Examination of Theory And Research." In *Social Psychology and Behavioral Medicine*, ed. J. Richard Eiser. Chichester, Eng.: Wiley.

Steven J. Breckler

PHILOSOPHY

Philosophers have worried about emotions for more than two thousand years, trying to understand how they fit into an adequate picture of humans and their place in the world. In philosophy, the emotions are first of all a concern of ethics, the art of living well. Only secondarily are they a matter for scientific inquiry.

Emotions in the History of Philosophy

The emotions have a troubled history in philosophy. Two and a half thousand years ago (in the fifth century B.C.E), the great Greek philosopher Socrates warned his students against the danger of the passions, which, he said, make people behave irrationally. For much of the history of philosophy, the search for wisdom has begun with the principle "Reason must be the master." The emotions must be subdued, controlled, and, where possible, eliminated. Philosophy itself has long been characterized as the work of reason and rationality attempting to rise above and beyond the irrational power of the passions.

But, of course, virtually every philosopher has also recognized that there are extremely valuable emotions—the passion of love; a passion for justice, for beauty, for truth; religious faith; and the love of wisdom, philosophy (literally, *philein*, meaning love, and *sophia*, meaning wisdom). The history of philosophy might thus be portrayed as a struggle between two competing conceptions of emotion, one negative (where emotions are considered to be misleading, distorting, and irrational) and the other positive (where emotions are considered to be inspiring and motivational). These two views have always had an uncomfortable coexistence.

One solution to this divergence in views is to divide the emotions into two different groups: a group of positive emotions that are, in the words of German philosopher Friedrich Nietzsche, "life-enhancing," and another group of negative emotions that are destructive, or "life-stultifying." It is only the negative emotions, in other words, that are irrational, antagonistic to good sense and wise decision making. The positive emotions are among the most important features of the good life. Thus, Socrates praised the love of wisdom and Jesus praised the love of God, but both warned their disciples not to get carried away with such negative emotions as anger, hatred, and jealousy. In Asia, Buddhists also warned against those emotions that are "agitations" and cause frustration and suffering.

In the Middle Ages, Christian philosophers like Saint Thomas Aquinas carefully separated emotional virtues (love, faith, hope, and charity) from emotional vices (anger, envy, pride, and greed). In the eighteenth century, David Hume and his friend Adam Smith defended what they called "the moral sentiments," including sympathy, the ability to "feel with" other people. Sympathy, they argued, was a universal feature of human nature. Soon after, the great German moral philosopher Immanuel Kant sharply separated the emotions and other "inclinations" from morality, but he held up for admiration such sentiments as compassion, respect, and a love of duty.

Of particular interest in this history are the ancient Stoics, who taught in both Greece and Rome for almost six hundred years (300 B.C.E to 300 C.E.). While most philosophers separated reason from the emotions (or "passions"), the Stoics suspected that these were not so different after all. Emotions, they suggested, are a kind of judgment, different ways of construing the world. Unfortunately, however, most emotions are mistaken judgments, self-destructive and frustrating ways of understanding the world. Anger, for example, includes the mistaken belief that the world is to blame for personal misfortunes, that life should be without suffering, without loss. The project of the Stoics, accordingly, was to help individuals get over their emotions through philosophy, by making the right kinds of judgments. But their very important insight was that emotions and reason are not so different in kind. They are both ways of understanding the world, even if emotions, unlike the insights of reason, are conceptual errors (ways of misunderstanding the world) and conducive to misery.

Baruch (Benedict) Spinoza was a seventeenth-century Stoic, and like the ancient Stoics he saw the emotions as misguided judgments about life and humans' place in the world. He also saw the emotions as forms of "thought" that, for the most part, misunderstand the world and, consequently, make individuals miserable and frustrated. But unlike the Stoics, Spinoza did not aspire to "psychic indifference." He had a clear view of the positive emotions as well, in particular the love of God that would allow people to attain a certain sort of "bliss."

Among twentieth-century philosophers, the French existentialist Jean-Paul Sartre deserves special mention, for he suggested a challenging new way of thinking about emotions. Sartre described the emotions as "magical transformations of the world," willful stratagems for coping with a difficult world. An emotion, in other words, does not just happen to an individual. People choose their emotions for a purpose, to help them save face or to help them to fight or flee from danger. But even Sartre remained a rationalist when it came to emotions. Emotions are degraded forms of behavior, he insisted, even including such positive emotions as love and joy. With rational reflection people can free themselves from their own emotions, which for him, are traps people set for themselves.

Emotions and Method

Modern philosophers have also grappled with a different kind of problem. In the seventeenth century, the French scientist-mathematician-philosopher René Descartes tried to understand the peculiar place of the emotions in the perplexing interplay between the mind and the body. It was Descartes, more than any other philosopher, who introduced this troublesome problem—the mind-body problem—into the core of philosophical concerns. The problem, simply stated, is that mind and body seem to be two entirely different kinds of phenomena. The body is physical, in space, publicly observable and available for scientific study. The mind, by contrast, has no physical properties and cannot be located in space (except for some hard to pin down connection with a particular person and his or her brain). Each person's mind can be observed by only that person (making it, in that sense, the most "private" thing in the world). And, because it can be observed by one and only one person, the mind is not available for scientific study. Many philosophers, in the interest of modern science, have tried to do away with the mind as such altogether. They have suggested, for example, that the mind is nothing but the brain, or, perhaps, it is like a program in a computer—nothing

René Descartes, the French mathematician and philosopher, is sometimes referred to as the father of modern philosophy. (Corbis/Bettmann)

but a function of extremely complicated neurological processes.

The emotions have an awkward place in this picture for reasons that Descartes understood particularly well. The emotions, unlike many mental phenomena, are distinctively bodily. Anger, for example, almost always includes muscular tension, a quickening of the heart, a flushing of the face, and what the American philosopher-psychologist William James called "the urge to vigorous action." On the other hand, anger also includes—necessarily includes—certain feelings, desires, and thoughts, what might be called the mental "content" of emotions. Philosophers who deal with the emotions have traditionally been more concerned with the nature of this content rather than the mechanisms and processes that tend to be the focus of biological and psychological studies. The question of content can best be approached through two basic but interrelated avenues—through phenomenology, the direct description of experience, and through an examination of the language used to ascribe and describe emotions.

The first approach, although it has been adopted by some psychologists, tends to violate the scientific method, which insists on public, verifiable, factual claims. The study of the language used to ascribe and describe emotion suffers from the same sort of suspicion because it too depends upon the first person case and reference to "private" experience. Some philosophers, accordingly, have objected to the idea of a "private language" of emotions that by its very nature refers to experiences that can be "had" and confirmed by only one person. They have joined the ranks of the more behaviorally-inclined psychologists and insist that emotion language ultimately refers—must refer —only to that which is public, verifiable, and teachable, namely behavior. This would include linguistic behavior. Some philosophers have rejected the use of first person descriptions and ordinary language altogether, appealing to biology and cognitive science for elimination of emotion talk altogether.

How then should individuals think about emotion? Which of the most evident aspects of emotion—that is, the various sensory, behavioral, cognitive, and social phenomena that are typically associated with an emotion—should people take to be most essential? Philosophers do not doubt that all emotions ultimately have their causes in the brain, but few philosophers take this to be definitive of emotion. It is also true that virtually all emotions get expressed (however minimally) in behavior. But should behavioral tendencies or sequences of actions or certain basic gestures be taken as essential? A great deal of detailed work in psychology has shown the enormous subtlety and the seemingly "hard-wired" nature of basic patterns of fa-

cial expression. Philosophers remain skeptical. What is in question is not the data but the implied shift in conception from the emotion to the symptom of emotion. What is it that causes the twitch or gesture? The emotion would seem to be the perception, the awareness, the realization that is expressed, not the expression itself.

There are philosophers of a somewhat behaviorist bent who have suggested that an emotion is nothing but its behavioral expression, though certainly not a single gesture but an open-ended sequence of actions. An emotion is not a "ghostly inner event," according to Gilbert Ryle, but a "multi-track disposition" to behave in any number of recognizable ways. So, too, philosophers have tried to understand emotion not as an inner feeling but as a value-laden description of a social situation. For example, the significant difference between shame and embarrassment does not seem to be a difference between internal feelings but rather a difference between descriptions of the external situation. Nevertheless, most philosophers would insist that without some sort of distinctive internal feelings, the behavior in question could not be the expression of an emotion. But what are these "distinctive internal feelings"? And are they really feelings?

Emotions As Feelings

Many philosophers hold onto the old Cartesian view that an emotion is a kind of feeling. An emotion must have a "subjective" or "introspective" aspect, although what this means is (in light of Sigmund Freud's work) a matter of considerable dispute. This is often summarized in the idea that an emotion is a kind of feeling, but what sort of feeling? William James argued that an emotion is a set of sensations caused by visceral responses. This seems plausible, but, unfortunately, the Jamesian theory is wrong—at least in its details. Some of the feelings found in emotions are of this kind (e.g., the feeling of queasiness in the stomach, feeling flushed in the face), but others are not. Feeling ashamed, for example, involves a complex set of feelings of failure and rejection (or potential rejection) by other people. Some theorists have tried to save the idea that emotions are feelings by employing the vague notion of "affect," but such terms do little more than cover up the problem. What is the nature of feeling in emotion, and are feelings all that there is to emotion?

The answer to the latter question is no. A person who claims to love another on the basis of his or her strong feelings but who is inconsiderate and uncaring, who does nothing whatever to help the other person in need, does not love. This is not to say that love is nothing but behavior. But it is to say that feelings are not enough. The right actions must be there too.

The nature of feelings in emotion turns out not to be a single or a simple question. Some feelings, as has been noted, are of a straightforward physiological variety. Psychoneurologists suggest that some basic emotions (anger, fear, disgust, and surprise, for example) are really "hard-wired" in the brain. They are "affect programs" that have evolved as autonomic systems for quick emergency responses and give rise to both the characteristic physical feelings and the characteristic and usually involuntary facial expressions that are associated with such emotions. (People can learn or teach themselves to make these expressions in the absence of any such emotions, but such skills, though useful both in acting and feigning emotion, are clearly secondary to the "natural" expressions that can be perceive even in very young children.)

But there are also feelings of a much more sophisticated kind that are characteristic of most if not all emotions. These are feelings that are defined not in terms of bodily changes but by the fact that they are about the world. Philosophers describe this important feature of emotions, that they are about the world, as intentionality. Thus, love is not just a set of feelings (such as nausea, a sense of warmth, feeling giddy, or light-headedness). Love necessarily involves feelings for another person. So, too, anger consists of much more than the familiar feelings of rage (such as a feverish feeling, muscle tension all over one's body, especially in the face and arms, the feeling that one is "about to explode"). It encompasses much more intelligent and learned feelings that have to do with a sense of fairness, a sense of purpose (and the frustration of purposes), and a sense of having been offended. But, then, although people might agree that such ways of comprehending the world are necessarily subjective (i.e., bound to one's personal perspective and experience), they might well balk at calling these complex responses to the world "feelings." Indeed, they are in many ways more like beliefs about the world.

Emotions As Belief

Beliefs, like emotions, are intentional. They are about the world. Furthermore, emotions, like beliefs, involve information, knowledge, and values. It is only in exceptional cases, cases that require explaining, that one can be afraid without believing that there is anything about which to be afraid. (Phobias are aberrant and sometimes pathological for this reason.) For a person to be angry is for them to believe that someone or something has offended or frustrated them. And they can be wrong about this. (The person may not have said what the angry person believed was said, or the person may have said it but did not intend it as an offense.) This has led many authors, some following the ancient Stoics, to argue that the emotions are just beliefs, judgments, or thoughts.

Whether or not this is so (and whether or not an emotion requires some kind of feeling along with belief) depends on the emotion. James suggested that anger is unthinkable without an "urge to vigorous action" and other feelings besides. But long-term love, while it will almost certainly be punctuated by various feelings, does not seem to consist primarily of such feelings. What does endure, throughout many ups and downs, are such beliefs as "this person is very important to me" and such desires as "I want what is best for this person." Without those, one could argue that so-called love is not love, or, in the words of William Shakespeare, "love is not love which alters when it alteration finds." Jealousy includes the belief that something valuable is about to be lost or taken away. Sadness includes the belief that something has already been lost. Indignation includes the recognition that there has been some serious violation. Virtually all emotions presuppose or have as their preconditions certain sorts of beliefs, judgments, or thoughts.

One plausible exception to this theory are those very general ways of being in the world that are known as moods. Moods are like emotions except that they do not have a determinate object. One might say that they are about everything rather than something in particular. (Thus, an individual can be in an angry mood and thus become angry about almost anything.) Some philosophers have been particularly interested in moods. The German philosopher Martin Heidegger, for example, suggested that moods are humans' way of constantly "being tuned" to the world. In this sense, individuals are always in a mood. Some moods may be negative (generally referred to as a "bad mood"), but others are positive, and Heidegger, like the Stoics, thought that philosophy—how people learn to think about the world—could have a powerful effect on moods.

Philosophers and the "Why?" of Emotions

Philosophers try to explain emotions, although their explanations are usually different from the sorts of explanations offered by scientists. They are interested primarily in a person's reasons for having an emotion and the justifiability of those reasons. Particular instances of emotion seem to be subject to two sorts of explanation. First, emotions seem to require an explanation that invokes a person's belief and attitudes toward the world. A man is angry because he believes that so-and-so wronged him, or a woman is saddened because she has found out that she has just lost a loved one, and so on. But this cannot be a complete account of emotional explanation. Emotions are also explained by citing the fact that a person has been sleepless all week, is ill, or has been given some medication. In other words, explanation of emotion may cite an underlying cause that may or may not make mention of the object of emotion. The cause may be physiological, for example, an underlying state of irritability, an ingested drug or a direct surgical stimulation of the brain. The cause may be some state of affairs or an incident that "triggered" the person's emotion, but this may not be the intentional object of the person's emotion nor need he or she have any memory or awareness of it. (Subliminal messages presumably work this way.)

How are causal explanations to be reconciled with explanations in terms of beliefs and attitudes? Many philosophers have tended to emphasize the importance of one form of explanation over the other or to reduce all explanations to causal explanations or to belief-and-desire "reason"-type explanations. The latter provides a fuller account of the intentionality of an emotion by describing not only its object (e.g., "She's angry because she's been offended.") but the specific details of the situation, the person's beliefs and various attitudes. The former provides an explanation in terms of an underlying cause that may or may not make mention of the object of emotion. Very often, however, the citation of a cause of emotion (its initiating stimulus or "trigger") and the account of the object of the emotion will be nominally the same (e.g., "He got mad because she stepped on his toe."). The problem that has been addressed by many philosophers (and the subject of several weighty studies) has been the relation between these two types of explanation and the various problems in understanding them together.

The fact that emotions involve beliefs and these beliefs in turn imply reasons means that the relationship between emotions and rationality, as the Stoics suggested, needs to be reconsidered. Many philosophers and psychologists have written as if the emotions were not only irrational but also non-rational (i.e., merely feelings or physiological processes that are not related to intelligence). Aristotle, one of the great ancient philosophical analysts of emotion, argued that an emotion could be appropriate or inappropriate, foolish or prudent, not just on the basis of whether or not it was acceptable in the circumstance in question (though that social dimension was certainly essential) but on the basis of the perceptions, beliefs, and desires of the individual.

The fact that emotions consist, at least in part, of beliefs means that they can be evaluated in terms of rational standards: Are they appropriate to the context? Do they consider the facts of the matter? Are their perceptions fair and their evaluations reason-

able? Indeed the argument is now prevalent and persuasive that emotions cannot be understood without grasping their reasons, and these reasons in turn provide a basis for the evaluation of the emotions. Sometimes, an emotion enhances a person's life, or it provides exactly the right motivation and direction for getting out of a dangerous or difficult situation. Other emotions, however, may be plainly self-defeating and self-destructive, not to mention disruptive and antisocial. The question is not, then, whether emotions (in general) are rational or irrational, but whether emotions, in given circumstances, are rational or not, whether the reasons for the emotions are good reasons, and whether the emotions are appropriate and functional for the occasion.

As this notion of the rationality of emotions moves to center stage, the relevance of emotions to ethics becomes more obvious. Mere feelings tend not to be matters of morality. Having a headache or feeling nauseous is not a moral issue. But issues about whether one feels sympathy or sadness and whether it is love or hate that motivates behavior cut right to the heart of ethics. So, too, behavior is not, all by itself, the basis on which people praise and blame others. Praise and blame are given because of intentions and motivations, even when the actions themselves misfire. (Thus, a person who tries to help someone because of compassion may be praised, even if the rescue effort is a failure. But a person who tries to kill someone because of hatred and unwittingly saves that individual's life instead is not thereby praised.)

Insofar as emotions have reasons and are therefore justifiable or not, along with the related behaviors, the question arises about whether the same reasons are valid for everyone or whether both the emotions and their reasons vary from culture to culture and perhaps even from individual to individual. To be sure, the contexts vary. A person who gets jealous because a romantic partner has coffee with someone else would be justified in some cultures but not in others. But could one say that a person has a right to get jealous whenever someone threatens to take away something precious (even though what suggests that threat may be very different in different cultures or situations)? Philosophers cannot answer the empirical questions of the universality or relativity of emotions (and should not try), but they can and should clear away the dogmatic assumptions and mistaken conceptions of the past. There is nothing in the nature of emotion that assures universality, but neither is it so obvious that emotions differ so much from place to place. There is such a thing as the general "human condition"—the fact that individuals are born as helpless infants and take a long time to grow, the fact that they need food, drink, shelter, and sleep, the fact that they get sick and know that they are going to die—and on the basis of these general similarities in human lives, one may well suppose that certain emotions and reasons for emotion will be general too.

Conclusion

Scientists, however driven and curious in their work, are supposed to remain "objective," dispassionate. Philosophers, however, are not scientists, and the greatest philosophers have always been passionate about their work, passionate about their beliefs, and engaged in the business of trying to change the world. Accordingly, the emotions are not just something to be studied; they are to be lived. But the relation moves in two directions, and if philosophers should be passionate, the emotions also have a good deal to learn from philosophy. If a person sees the world as nothing but a competitive jungle in which each person would be wise only to look out for him- or herself, it is almost certain that his or her emotions will be very defensive, often frustrated and hostile, and largely negative with only a few fleeting moments of positive emotion. On the other hand, if one sees one's life as a gift and looks at one's good fortune with gratitude, the most enduring emotions will be positive, despite inevitable losses and setbacks. A life of love is a life well-lived, a theory about which most of the great philosophers have agreed.

See also: ANGER; ARISTOTLE; ATTRIBUTION; CONSCIOUSNESS; DESCARTES, RENÉ; EMERSON, RALPH WALDO; ENVY; FOLK THEORIES OF EMOTION; HATE; HISTORICAL STUDY OF EMOTIONS; HOPE; HUME, DAVID; JAMES, WILLIAM; JEALOUSY; KANT, IMMANUEL; LOVE; MIND-BODY DICHOTOMY; MOOD; NIETZSCHE, FRIEDRICH WILHELM; ORATORY; PLATO; PSYCHOPHYSIOLOGY OF EMOTIONS; SARTRE, JEAN-PAUL; SIN; SPINOZA, BARUCH; SYMPATHY

Bibliography

Bruge, G. M. A., ed. (1974). *Plato's Republic.* Indianapolis, IN: Hackett.
Calhoun, Cheshire, and Solomon, Robert C., eds. (1984). *What Is an Emotion? Classic Readings in Philosophical Psychology.* New York: Oxford University Press.
Descartes, René. ([1649] 1989). *Passions of the Soul,* tr. Stephen Voss. Indianapolis, IN: Hackett.
de Sousa, Ronald. (1987). *The Rationality of Emotion.* Cambridge: Massachusetts Institute of Technology Press.
Griffiths, Paul E. (1998). *What Emotions Really Are: The Problem of Psychological Categories.* Chicago: University of Chicago Press.
Heidegger, Martin. ([1927] 1996). *Being and Time,* tr. Joan Stambaugh. Albany: State University of New York Press.
Hume, David. ([1740] 1888). *A Treatise of Human Nature,* ed. Lewis Amherst Selby-Bigge. Oxford, Eng.: Clarendon Press.
James, William. ([1884] 1890). *What Is an Emotion?* New York: Dover.
Kaufmann, Walter, ed. (1954). *The Portable Nietzsche.* New York: Viking.
McKeon, Richard, ed. (1941). *The Basic Works of Aristotle.* New York: Random House.
Nehamas, Alexander, and Woodruff, Paul, eds. (1989). *Plato's Symposium.* Indianapolis, IN: Hackett.
Neu, Jerome. (1977). *Emotion, Thought and Therapy: A Study of Hume and Spinoza and the Relationship of Philosophical Theories of the Emotions to Psychological Theories of Therapy.* Berkeley: University of California Press.
Ryle, Gilbert. (1949). *The Concept of Mind.* London: Hutchinson's University Library.
Sartre, Jean-Paul. ([1939] 1948). *The Emotions: Outline of a Theory,* tr. Bernard Frechtman. New York: Philosophical Library.
Solomon, Robert C. (1993). *The Passions: Emotions and the Meaning of Life.* Indianapolis, IN: Hackett.
Solomon, Robert C. (1994). *About Love: Reinventing Romance for Our Times.* Lanham, MD: Rowman & Littlefield.
Spinoza, Baruch. ([1677] 1992). *The Ethics: Treatise on the Emendation of the Intellect,* 2nd ed., tr. Samuel Shirley, ed. Seymour Feldman. Indianapolis, IN: Hackett.

Robert C. Solomon

PHOBIAS

See Fear and Phobias

PLATO

b. Athens or Aegina, c. 429 B.C.E.; *d.* Athens, 347 B.C.E.; *philosophy, mind-body dichotomy.*

Most experts consider the ancient Greek philosopher Plato to be one of the leading philosophers of all time (if not *the* leading philosopher of all time), and many people consider his *Republic* to be the most important work in Western philosophy. Some individuals go so far as to suggest that much of the philosophy since Plato's time has been little more than commentary on or revisions to his ideas. While this may be an overstatement, there is no doubt that Plato was a central figure in establishing many of the basic elements of the Western worldview.

Although Plato's writing have survived and have been extensively studied by philosophers since the Middle Ages, little detail is known about his early life other than that he was born into an upper-class Athenian family, received an education, served in the military, and began his career as a poet. Plato met Socrates around 407 B.C.E., became one of his disciples, and then devoted most of the rest of his life to philosophy. It may be that philosophy was actually a second choice of interest for Plato since he tried unsuccessfully to become involved in Athenian government during the first few years of his philosophical studies and maintained a life-long interest in politics. Following the death of Socrates in 399 B.C.E., Plato and several other disciples fled to Megara. Plato then traveled throughout Italy, Sicily, and Greece for most of the next twelve

Plato is surrounded by a group of his students in this Pompeiian mosaic. (Corbis/Bettmann)

years. Upon returning to Athens, he founded his school near the tomb of the philosopher Academus, and it was from this location that Plato's Academy received its name.

Plato was a prolific writer, producing twenty-five to thirty major works that collectively are referred to as the dialogues. This title is derived from the structure of the works in which questions are posed and answers are given in dialogues between individuals, with Socrates being a primary participant in the dialogues. Experts believe that the dialogues can be divided into three periods and that they reflect the evolution of Plato's philosophy. As Plato never wrote a complete exposition of his ideas, scholars have had to rely on the dialogues and his letters to develop a full picture of his ideas. The earliest dialogues, such as *Apology, Euthydemus,* and *Gorgias,* rely heavily on Socrates. Dialogues from the second period, such as *Phaedo, Republic,* and *Meno,* continue to use Socrates as a major participant but reflect Plato's ideas. In the third period, dialogues such as *Philebus* and *Laws* afford Socrates a much reduced role or no role at all and present Plato's ideas in their most complete and complex form.

Among Plato's ideas that have come to shape Western civilization are the following: (1) the purpose of study is to seek wisdom, (2) education should focus on developing the entire person, (3) knowledge of the good leads to a better life while failing to know the good leads to evil, (4) a perfect society is one in which reason rules and controls the passions, (5) knowledge is the basis of democracy, (6) the soul is composed of reason, spirit, and desire, which should work together with reason being paramount. Plato's ideas have been influential in the understanding of emotions as well. First, by emphasizing the rule of knowledge and reason and the need to control the passions, Plato followed the teaching of Socrates that emotion is often a negative force that needs to be controlled. This view characterized general thinking about emotion for more than two thousand years. It was not until the twentieth century that emotions began to be the object of sustained study that viewed them as being more than something that needs to be controlled and channeled. Second, in Plato's teaching about the nature of the soul (in which the soul is seen as being separate from the body and surviving after death), he created the mind-body dichotomy, in which the mind and body are seen as separate entities that are subject to different forces. This idea has also survived into the twentieth century as a basic model for studying emotions, although research now shows that there is no clear mind-body dichotomy and that the two are closely integrated.

Plato's work had an enormous influence on later philosophers and theologians, including the Jewish philosopher Philo, the early Christian theologians Augustine and Origen, the Greek philosopher Cicero, and the Roman philosopher Plotinus (who founded the Neo-Platonic school of philosophy). Plato was also a gifted writer and is considered to be the most poetic and lyrical of Greek writers.

See also: AUGUSTINE; MIND-BODY DICHOTOMY; ORATORY; PHILOSOPHY

Bibliography
Barnes, Jonathan. (1992). *Founders of Thought: Plato, Aristotle, Socrates.* Oxford, Eng.: Oxford University Press.
Kraut, Richard, ed. (1992). *The Cambridge Companion to Plato.* Cambridge, Eng.: Cambridge University Press.
Plato. (1997). *Complete Works,* ed. John M. Cooper and D. S. Hutchinson. Hackett.

David Levinson
Ben Manning

PLEASURE

Pleasure is a subjective state that has commanded the attention of philosophers and psychologists for as long as they have studied the human mind. It has been a pivotal concept for many psychological theories of motivation and has played a central part in debates about ethics and the nature of the "good life." Despite this extensive scrutiny, however, the nature of pleasure remains strangely unsettled. Although in some respects it appears to be an emotion, it also seems to have sensory elements—like its supposed opposite, pain—and to be more intimately linked to bodily feelings and physiological drives than most emotions. Pleasure also seems to be the focus of a great deal of cultural ambivalence, a state of mind that is both sought after and mistrusted, prescribed and prohibited. Consequently, the investigation of pleasure offers many intriguing vantage points from which to examine mental life.

The Meaning of Pleasure

One way to begin to understand the meaning of pleasure is to examine people's intuitions about how it relates to other emotions. When people are asked to judge which emotions are similar, they judge pleasure to belong to a broad class of positive emotions that are not interpersonal in reference (unlike love and liking). Within this class are three subclasses, one involving relaxed passive moods (e.g., contentment), another involving personal esteem or superiority (e.g., pride), and a third involving active and relatively intense positive emotional states (e.g., happiness). Pleasure falls within this last subclass and exemplifies a group of emotions that occur in reaction to ongoing external events. This group also includes enjoyment, delight, and amusement. In sum, the general public understands pleasure to be a self-focused positive emotion based on people's active responses to their present circumstances. They distinguish it from related emotions that are purely passive responses (e.g., rapture, bliss), refer to past events (e.g., satisfaction), anticipate future events (e.g., hope), or are not related to any events at all (e.g., cheerfulness, joy).

Defining pleasure as a state of present-centered happiness that is reactive to external events represents a good first approximation, but this fails to provide the sort of fine-grained analysis that could distinguish pleasure from emotions such as enjoyment and delight. One way in which the concept of pleasure differs from these related emotion concepts is that pleasure has connotations of sensuality, bodily appetites, and illicit indulgence. These connotations are nicely captured by the title of Barbara Holland's 1996 book: *Endangered Pleasures: In Defense of Naps, Bacon, Martinis, Profanity, and Other Indulgences.* Whereas enjoyment and delight—as well as joy, elation, and rapture for that matter—have innocent or even transcendent connotations, pleasure is moralized, linked to concepts of sin, sensuousness, and danger. As Lord Byron wrote in *Don Juan* at the beginning of the nineteenth century, "pleasure's a sin, and sometimes sin's a pleasure." It is common for people to refer to "guilty pleasures" or "forbidden pleasures" but not to "guilty amusements" or "forbidden enjoyments." Dictionary definitions of pleasure touch on these connotations, frequently pointing to the frivolous, indulgent, sensual, or frankly sexual aspects.

In addition to having moral connotations, pleasure is also seen to be in some ways simpler or more primitive than its related emotions, a basis or stimulus for the other emotions rather than an equal alternative. It is therefore represented as a *source* of delight or joy, as if it were a sensory experience that could lead to further emotional elaboration. Compared to enjoyment or delight, pleasure is understood to be more closely linked to bodily states and drives, less a perception of general well-being than a sensation of "goodness" that is specific to a certain desire (e.g., to eat, drink, sleep, have sex). This belief that pleasure is largely sensory is encouraged by the common habit of contrasting pleasure and pain, whose sensory component is unmistakable. However, philosophers typically deny that pleasure is a sensory feeling, arguing that it is too intrinsically evaluative to be a mere sensation and too diverse in its subjective expressions to be a unitary feeling state.

Pleasure is clearly a distinctive subjective state, or class of related states. However, it remains questionable whether these states are best understood to be emotional. Although most writers agree that pleasure is not purely sensory and that it has the evaluative aspect common to all true emotions, many of them are unwilling to grant it full status as an emotion. Thomas Szasz (1988) groups it with pain as a "bodily feeling," while recognizing that it is less strictly such a feeling than is pain. David Perry (1967) argues that pleasure is neither sensation, perception, nor emotion but rather a particular variety of what he calls a "pro-attitude." By pro-attitude Perry means a favorable state of mind directed toward an object or experience for what it is in itself. For Perry then, to take pleasure in something is to apprehend it positively in a way that does not imply desiring or striving for it ("wanting") or attribute goodness or rightness to it ("liking"). Unlike a sensation, a pleasure involves the taking of an appraising attitude towards a specific object, and unlike an emotion, it need not be accompanied by any physiological arousal or disturbance. In short, pleasure has distinct affective, evaluative, and sensory aspects that make it difficult to encompass in a simple formulation.

If the status of pleasure as an emotion is in question, how else might it figure in the study of emotion? Rather than conceptualizing pleasure as a distinct emotion, some theorists prefer to understand it as a basic hedonic dimension, aspect, or quality of many emotions. In James Russell's "circumplex" model (1979), for instance, pleasure-displeasure is one of two primary dimensions that underlie all emotions. According to this model, emotions can be characterized by the combination of their valence (i.e., their positive [pleasurable] or negative [unpleasurable] quality) and their level of arousal (ranging from excitement to sleepiness). Joy and contentment exemplify positively valenced emotions that are high and low in arousal, respectively, while anger and sadness exemplify negatively valenced emotions that are high and low arousal, respectively. These two dimensions of pleasure and arousal are the aspects of emotions that people seem to consider most important in judging the similarities and differences among emotions, and therefore they seem to be quite fundamental. This conclusion implies that even if pleasure is not a distinct emotion—a question that is not fully resolved—it is certainly an affective component. All emotions are more or less pleasurable, a fact that many definitions of emotion recognize by acknowledging the centrality of hedonic (i.e., pleasure-related) valence or evaluation.

Sources of Pleasure

Little systematic research has been conducted on the sources of pleasure in people's lives. However, some sense of the variety of activities and experiences that give pleasure can be gleaned from an informal survey of the topics investigated by researchers who make reference to it. Although such a survey cannot hope to be exhaustive, the following sources attract the most empirical attention (in roughly descending order) from psychologists who study pleasure: sexuality, eating, addictive substances, exercise, hobbies, and recreational activities (e.g., sports, humor, play, reading, and art appreciation). Sexuality is the preeminent focus of the intellectual attention given to pleasure in the areas of psychology and the humanities, and often the word *pleasure* is used to stand exclusively for sexual pleasure. Academic scrutiny tends to fall on the more intense bodily and consummatory pleasures rather than the milder pleasures that may be more central to many people's daily lives. For instance, relatively little research has concentrated on the pleasures of conversation, child rearing, music, problem solving, and everyday pastimes. The de-emphasis of these pleasures in academic discourse mirrors the way in which the term *pleasure* carries connotations of sensuality and forbidden indulgence in everyday discourse.

The Neurobiology of Pleasure

Pleasure is a subjective state that is intimately connected to bodily feelings and drives, so it is not surprising that scientists have attempted to understand the biological mechanisms that underlie it. Much of their work has focused on the brain structures—

A young couple, embracing as they cruise the U.S. Virgin Islands on a yacht, experience pleasure both in terms of their close physical contact with each other and in terms of their shared recreational activity. (Corbis/Neil Rabinowitz)

known as "pleasure centers"—whose activation seems to accompany pleasurable experiences. Although the existence of pleasure circuits in the mammalian brain had been postulated or implied by many theories of motivation, it was not until 1954 that James Olds and Peter Milner located one. They found that when minuscule electrodes were implanted in specific sites deep within rats' brains, the rats would eagerly press a lever delivering brief "hits" of mild electrical stimulation to these sites. This "intracranial self-stimulation" appears to be extremely rewarding and is rivaled in power only by highly addicting drugs such as cocaine. Rats can perform, to the exclusion of all alternative activities and to the point of physical collapse, ten thousand lever-presses within a one-hour session. They will endure intense pain and forego water when thirsty, food when hungry, and sexual opportunities when they are made available. Several studies performed with humans have shown that the rewarding effects of intracranial stimulation are accompanied by intense subjective pleasure.

Anatomical mapping of the brain's pleasure centers reveals that many regions are involved. These regions occur in parts of the brain stem, the midbrain, and the forebrain, and they include the hypothalamus, the septum, the amygdala, and parts of the frontal cortex. This diverse collection of sites is unified by interconnections along the tracts of the "medial forebrain bundle," which appears to be dedicated to conducting pleasure-related neural signals using dopamine, a neurotransmitter that plays a crucial role in brain reward and pleasure.

Much of this work on the neurobiology of pleasure is particularly exciting because it offers some insight into the neural basis of drug addiction. Almost all addictive drugs—including cocaine, amphetamines, opiates, alcohol, and nicotine—produce pleasurable or euphoric effects upon consumption, and research indicates that they do so by acting on dopaminergic neurons within the brain reward centers located by intracranial self-stimulation studies. Different drugs appear to act on different parts of the medial forebrain bundle, but administration of each of them reduces the level of electrical self-stimulation, indicating that brain reward is already enhanced by the drugs. Consequently, any neurobiological account of addiction must give the brain's pleasure centers and the dopaminergic systems that operate within them central explanatory roles.

Although neurobiological research on pleasure has concentrated on dopaminergic systems operating in brain reward centers, attention has also been paid to another class of brain chemicals, the endorphins. These "endogenous opioids," which are structurally similar to opiates such as morphine and heroin, play a variety of physiological roles in such functions as pain and appetite control, sexual behavior, and temperature regulation. They are also released in increased quantities during or following a variety of pleasurable activities, suggesting that they are involved in subjective pleasure. For instance, endorphin release increases under sexual stimulation, alcohol consumption, exercise, and eating (perhaps especially fatty foods). Endorphins therefore seem to underpin pleasure and reward much as dopamine does. This strong possibility has led to the development of promising new opiate antagonist medications for the treatment of addiction. These medications, such as naltrexone, should block the rewarding effects of endorphin release, thereby dulling subjective pleasure and reducing the motivation for taking drugs.

Individual Differences in Pleasure

Do certain groups of people tend to experience more pleasure in their lives than others? This question can be examined in regard to demographic groups within the population and in regard to personality differences. Although only limited evidence exists, there do not appear to be systematic gender differences in overall levels of pleasure. Some research has been carried out on gender differences in sexual pleasure, and frequently women are found on average to derive less pleasure than men from sexual activity, especially outside of committed relationships, and to be more likely to receive diagnoses of sexual disorders involving diminished pleasure and inhibited sexual desire. Age differences in pleasure also appear to be small or nonexistent. Studies have not found age differences in reported levels of pleasure, although there is some evidence that younger people are apt to consider pleasure a more important component of their general well-being than older people and may be more likely to experience pleasures of an intense and interpersonal kind.

Do some people have personality characteristics that predispose them to experience pleasure? The answer to this question seems to be an unambiguous "yes." A variety of personality researchers have argued that extraverts—people who are highly sociable, outgoing, and impulsive—tend to report more pleasurable experiences and higher general well-being than introverts—people who tend to be reserved or shy. According to Hans Eysenck (1967), extraverts have relatively low resting levels of cortical arousal or activation. To compensate for their under-arousal, which leaves them prone to boredom, extraverts have a kind of "stimulus hunger" that motivates them to seek stimulation in the environment. They commonly do so through social activities that offer novelty, sensation, excitement, thrills, and risks. One obvious reason why extraverts tend to report higher levels of pleasure than introverts, therefore, is that they engage in more exciting and rewarding activities. Introverts, in contrast, are more self-sufficient; they need less stimulation to function optimally and therefore prefer more solitary and quiet activities that yield fewer and less intense opportunities for pleasure.

An alternative explanation of the association between extraversion and pleasure, proposed by Jeffrey Gray (1987), argues that extraverts are simply more sensitive to the reward value of behavioral alternatives than introverts. For extraverts, the rewarding possibilities of behaviors loom relatively large, motivating them to engage actively in a wider and more impulsive range of activities than introverts. Stated simply, the perceived benefits of behavior weigh more heavily in the extravert's decision making and are therefore more likely to overwhelm the perceived costs. According to this theory, extraversion is directly linked to pleasure (whereas Eysenck's account proposes an indirect link through the pursuit of stimulation); extraverts are simply people for whom pleasure is more salient, appealing, and vivid.

One partial but interesting exception to the link between pleasure and extraverted personality should be noted. Although extraverts tend to report more pleasure (as well as more positive emotions in general) than introverts, this tendency varies according to the situation or context. In leisure time, extraverts outpace introverts in pleasurable emotions, as expected. However, the pattern is reversed in work situations, with introverts reporting more positive emotions. One interpretation of this finding is that intraverts feel less restricted by the regularity, formality, and familiarity of the work environment than extraverts, who chafe under these restraints and prefer the freedom, excitement, and sociability that are available in leisure activities.

Rather than view pleasure as a correlate of basic personality dimensions such as extraversion-introversion, one theorist, Albert Mehrabian (1995), argues that the disposition to experience pleasure versus displeasure is itself a fundamental personality trait. "Trait pleasure," as he dubs it, is defined as the balance over time and across situations of positive emotional states over negative ones and resembles the dimension of "agreeableness" in the more widely known "five factor model" of personality (which proposes that there are five fundamental personality dimensions: extraversion, neuroticism, agreeableness, conscientiousness, and openness to experience). Mehrabian has carried out an extensive program of research that aims to characterize individual differences in many personality attributes in terms of trait pleasure, as well as its companion dimensions, trait arousal and trait dominance. He argues that these three dimensions are basic components of human temperament and can economically capture variation in more complex human dispositions.

Pleasure and Mental Disorder

Pleasure rarely figures in the description or conceptualization of mental disorders, where attention more commonly falls on the many varieties of misery (e.g., anxiety, fear, guilt, sadness, shame). However, this lack of attention is far from absolute, and pleasure is sometimes discussed in the context of mania, depression, and schizophrenia. The connection is clearest in the case of mania, which is one manifestation of the cycling emotional disturbance known as bipolar

disorder. People in a manic state often experience elevated or euphoric mood and an increased involvement in pleasurable activities, in addition to inflated self-esteem, distractibility, decreased need for sleep, and racing thoughts. Their frenetic seeking of pleasurable experiences often results in impulsive and self-destructive behavior, such as spending sprees, excessive gambling, reckless driving, sexual promiscuity, and illegal drug use. In mania, then, the unrestrained augmentation of pleasure frequently leads to consequences that the person regrets once the episode is over. However, people who experience mild forms of this mood disturbance, known as hypomania, sometimes fondly look back on their hypomanic episode as a time of self-confidence, sensuality, creativity, and efficiency. Indeed, many highly creative people, especially in the arts and literature, have been prone to manic or hypomanic episodes, as well as the recurrent depressions that usually accompany them.

Whereas mania and hypomania are often characterized by a surplus of pleasurable activities and experiences, depression is generally marked by a lack of them. Depressed people tend to be inactive and lack the motivation to seek out pleasurable involvements. However, something beyond this motivational deficit seems to underlie the pleasurelessness of the depressive. Not only do depressives fail to seek out or take an interest in pleasurable activities, but they also have a diminished capacity to take pleasure in these activities when engaged in them. This diminished capacity, known as anhedonia, is a primary symptom of depression and may in fact be partly responsible for the depressive's passivity and lack of drive. After all, if everyday activities are unrewarding, yielding little pleasure, then there is clearly little incentive for the depressive to engage in them. To the extent that behavior is motivated by the expectation of reward or reinforcement and depression involves a defective reward mechanism as some biomedical and behavioral theorists have argued, the depressive's motivational impairment is intimately connected with the capacity for pleasure, or "hedonic tone."

Anhedonia is an important aspect of depression not only because it may explain motivational symptoms but also because it may be more specific to depression than the negative emotional states with which most people identify depression. Although depression certainly involves an excess of unpleasant emotions such as sadness, dread, and guilt, these emotions are common to many other forms of psychological disturbance, particularly the anxiety disorders. Depression differs from these disorders in that it combines low levels of pleasure and positive emotions with these high levels of negative emotion. Anxious and depressed people all suffer mental pain, but only the depressed person also suffers the absence of pleasure.

Anhedonia is not limited to depressed people, however. It also occurs commonly in people suffering from schizophrenia and in people with personality traits that leave them vulnerable to developing the disorder. In schizophrenia, anhedonia is conceptualized as a "negative" symptom, one which represents a diminution of normal functioning, in contrast to positive symptoms—such as hallucinations and delusions—which represent an excess over normal functioning. The schizophrenic's diminished capacity for experiencing pleasure and other positive emotional states is usually accompanied by additional negative symptoms such as a general flattening of emotional responsiveness, reduced speech, and an inability to initiate or persist in purposeful activities. Among schizotypal personalities, who are at risk of developing schizophrenia under stressful conditions, anhedonia may be manifested in diminished interest in personal relationships and low sensitivity to physical or sensory pleasures.

Pleasure and Motivation

The concept of pleasure is unique among emotion-related concepts in the central role it plays in theories of motivation. Throughout the long history of philosophy, and the much briefer history of academic psychology, many thinkers have understood the pursuit of pleasure to be the fundamental impetus for behavior.

Utilitarianism and Decision Making

Classical philosophers were preoccupied with the role of pleasure in human affairs and varied in their recommendations about whether the good life was one in which pleasure was to be actively pursued (the Epicureans), distrusted and kept at arm's length (the Stoics), or accepted as an inseparable part of all activities (Aristotle). However, pleasure was first developed into a systematic prescriptive theory by the utilitarian philosophers Jeremy Bentham and John Stuart Mill. The utilitarians proposed that people should choose to act so as to achieve the greatest good for the greatest number and maintained that only pleasure was intrinsically good—or "the Good"—and only pain intrinsically bad. Consequently, they believed that moral decision making should be a form of "hedonic calculus" in which alternative courses of action are compared according to the summed quantities of pleasure and pain that would accrue to the people affected by them. Utilitarian thinking of this kind became a prominent form of moral philosophy, in addition to having a great social effect by leaving a deep impression on the evolving science of economics.

Psychoanalysis and the "Pleasure Principle"

Pleasure also plays a crucial role in the psychoanalytic account of motivation developed by Sigmund Freud. Freud (1920) argued that human instinctual life operates according to what he called the "pleasure principle," according to which drives seek immediate gratification regardless of the social and moral norms that might be violated in the process. In many of his writings, Freud identified unpleasure with states of instinctual tension and pleasure with the reduction or "discharge" of this tension, thereby basing the qualitative experience of pleasure on an underlying quantitative or "economic" dimension. However, at other times Freud expressed doubts about the precise connection between instinctual tension and pleasure and about the equation of pleasure with tension reduction, acknowledging that sometimes, as in sexual foreplay, the anticipation of a good meal, or the avid watching of horror movies, the build-up of tension is pleasurable. Nevertheless, Freud remained confident that pleasure was intimately related to the discharge of tension states derived from drives, the engines of human motivation. Even refined pleasures, such as those taken in the appreciation of music, art, and literature, ultimately derive from the satisfaction of basic drives that have been sublimated.

Although Freud proposed that much of human mental life operates according to the motivational economy of the pleasure principle, he also proposed an opposing force called the "reality principle." Whereas the pleasure principle urges immediate, oblivious action on the person's impulses, the reality principle takes the social, moral, and practical context into consideration and urges delay and postponement of impulses. The capacity to delay the gratification of impulses—to rein in the pursuit of immediate pleasures—is a capacity that increases over the course of the child's development and is the basis of the psychic agency that Freud dubbed the ego. However, the reality principle never completely dominates the pleasure principle, and the two opposed principles often leave the person in conflict between impulse, passion, and spontaneity on the one hand, and control, inhibition, and prudence on the other.

Behaviorism and Reinforcement

Although fundamentally different from psychoanalysis in most of their basic assumptions, behaviorist approaches in some respects share a view of motivation as the seeking or maximization of pleasure. This claim must be qualified, however, because most behaviorist theories do not make reference to pleasure or goal seeking, mentalistic and purposive concepts being disallowed on principle. Instead, behaviorist accounts of instrumental (voluntary) behavior propose that response tendencies are strengthened to the extent that they yield positive, or reinforcing, consequences. Reinforcement is not directly defined in terms of pleasurable states but in terms of the strengthening of the response tendency itself. An object or event is a reinforcer if presenting it to the organism increases the frequency with which the organism engages in the behavior it was performing when the reinforcer was presented. Even though reinforcement is therefore defined in purely objective terms, behaviorist theory implies that organisms engage in behavior to the extent that it is rewarding to them, and this reward mechanism is presumed to be mediated by the brain's pleasure centers and to have some sort of pleasurable subjective dimension. In short, the account of motivation implied by instrumental behaviorism is a disguised kind of hedonism.

Criticisms of Pleasure-Based Accounts of Motivation

Theories of motivation that are based on the pursuit or maximization of pleasure have not gone unchallenged. Moral philosophers and ethicists, who address the normative questions of how human action *ought* to be motivated, very rarely identify themselves as proponents of hedonism and have subjected hedonistic theories to many criticisms. Some of these criticisms hinge on the difficulty of measuring pleasure and comparing it between people, the question of whether some kinds of pleasure should be weighed more heavily than others, and the problems that arise when one person takes pleasure in ways that cause others to suffer. Even utilitarian philosophers, who draw their original inspiration from the hedonic theories of Bentham and Mill, no longer tend to conceptualize utility—the quantity to be maximized—in terms of pleasure, understanding it instead in terms of goal satisfaction or general well-being. These versions of utilitarianism therefore argue that behavior should aim to maximize the extent to which goals are met—whether or not these goals refer to pleasurable subjective states—or well-being is achieved.

Psychological writers tend to criticize hedonic theories of motivation on other grounds. Some argue that hedonic theories fail to acknowledge that human motivation also involves moral thinking and moral motives that cannot be reduced to pleasure seeking. People commonly subject themselves to plainly unpleasant activities out of a sense of moral obligation. Writers of a Darwinian bent similarly argue that people frequently act in pursuit of outcomes other than pleasure, such as reproductive (evolutionary) fitness. By this account, pleasure functions less as a motive in itself than as an evolved indicator of activities that carry adaptive advantages. Many contemporary psychoanalysts challenge Freud's drive theory's description of human motivation as pleasure seeking and propound a contrary view in which drives are relationship seeking. Some physiological psychologists question the view that pleasure is mediated by a unitary neural system, or they argue that the systems that underpin pleasure and "liking" are quite distinct from those that are involved in the more fundamental motivational processes of urges and "wanting."

In addition to criticizing hedonic theories of motivation for being incomplete, other writers argue that the pursuit of pleasure is destructive or self-defeating. Lionel Tiger (1992) maintains that because pleasure is a guide to what was adaptive in a distant evolutionary past rather than in the very different environment of modern society, pursuing it may lead to self-destructive consequences. Products of modern technology—such as many addictive drugs, processed sugar, and abundant fatty foods—that were unknown to distant ancestors may be intensely rewarding to people and generate damaging consumption patterns by fooling evolved pleasure mechanisms.

Other writers present variations on the theme that actively pursuing pleasures leads to the loss of their appeal. One version of this argument proposes that pleasure is best understood as a by-product of intrinsically motivated activities and that seeking the by-product rather than the activity diminishes it. Another version claims that it is in the nature of pleasures to diminish with repetition of the behavior that produced them. By this account, if impulses are not controlled and pleasures carefully rationed, the behaviors that produced pleasure will lose their power to deliver it or will escalate dangerously, as in addiction, in a vain effort to maintain it. A third version of this argument asserts that the pleasurableness of an experience is completely relative to the context of the person's other experiences, both real and imagined. Pleasure will be felt only to the degree that an experience falls toward the top of the person's normal hedonic range, so that someone who is dedicated to the pursuit of pleasure will require a more intense experience to yield a certain level of pleasure than will a more stolid person. This "hedonic relativism" implies that the active pursuit of pleasure simply raises the person's pleasure threshold, a problem that will be compounded if the pleasure-seeker is always imagining more vivid and intense experiences. In sum, a variety of psychological mechanisms appear to counteract the pursuit of pleasure and imply that hedonism is a problematic and possibly self-defeating doctrine.

Pleasure, Society, and Culture

Cultures seem to differ in their attitudes toward pleasure. Although much of the "evidence" for this

Isak Dinesen, in "Babette's Feast" (1953), portrays a French refugee who seeks safety in a small Scandinavian fishing village where life is as grim and pleasureless as the severe Lutheran sect expects it to be. But Babette, as a thank you to the town, prepares a sumptuous multi-course gourmet feast, which immerses everyone in splendid sensual tastes, aromas, and sights. The guests thoroughly enjoy the pleasures before growing severe again.

claim comes from ethnic stereotypes and inferences about "national character" that are no longer popular among anthropologists, cultures do appear to vary in their encouragement of passionate expressiveness versus restraint. Ruth Benedict (1934) attempted to capture this variation by drawing a contrast, first made by Friedrich Nietzsche, between "Apollonian" cultures (individualist, cerebral, reserved, and stoical), and "Dionysian" cultures (permissive, carnal, impulsive, and tolerant of excess). However, little systematic cross-cultural research into questions of this sort has been conducted. In one study, Taiwanese people differed from Western norms with respect to the sources of happiness, placing more emphasis on the evaluations of others and interpersonal satisfaction, but did not appear to differ on the perceived importance of pleasure to happiness. It may be that although cultures have different belief systems regarding pleasure and different norms and avenues for its expression, their members may not experience significantly different amounts of pleasure in their lives. In this connection it is important to learn the lesson of Margaret Mead's (1928) romanticized portrayal of Samoan society as an unconflicted paradise of pleasure seeking and pleasure-taking whose example Americans could emulate. Later work showed that the culture's apparent openness and devotion to pleasure concealed a more mixed and familiar picture.

Although apparent cultural differences in openness to pleasure may be more ideological than actual at the level of people's experiences, there is little question that the pursuit of pleasure is a source of social concern and restriction within all societies. The socialization of children always involves the teaching of control over impulses and delay of pleasurable gratification, as well as the learning of appropriate times, places, and objects for such gratification. People who violate norms for the appropriate regulation of pleasure and impulse are commonly ridiculed, shamed, reviled, and punished. Even if, as many social critics maintain, some Western cultures are overly puritanical and pleasure-denying, there is considerable

evidence that some forms of pleasure seeking have serious adverse social consequences. Substance abuse, which at least in its early stages is chiefly motivated by its pleasurable effects, carries huge human and economic costs. The sexual transmission of HIV infection is also in large measure a consequence of pleasure seeking, and one of the main obstacles to stopping the spread of infection is people's unwillingness to adopt preventive measures, such as condom use, that diminish their pleasure. Many serious accidents are caused by impulsive thrill seeking. The inadequately restrained pursuit of pleasure can also be held partly responsible for overeating, compulsive gambling, and their associated complications. Although it is far from clear that further cultural or societal restrictions on pleasure seeking would be appropriate responses to these situations, it is important to recognize that pleasure is a mixed blessing.

See also: ANXIETY DISORDERS; ARISTOTLE; BOREDOM; EYSENCK, HANS JURGEN; FREUD, SIGMUND; MOTIVATION; NEUROBIOLOGY OF EMOTIONS; NIETZSCHE, FRIEDRICH WILHELM; PERSONALITY; SEASONAL AFFECTIVE DISORDER; SENSATION SEEKING AND RISK TAKING

Bibliography

Ainslie, George. (1992). *Picoeconomics.* New York: Cambridge University Press.

Benedict, Ruth. ([1934] 1989). *Patterns of Culture.* Boston: Houghton Mifflin.

Berridge, Kent C., and Robinson, Terry E. (1995). "The Mind of an Addicted Brain: Neural Sensitization of Wanting versus Liking." *Current Directions in Psychological Science* 4:71–76.

Brandstatter, Hermann. (1994). "Pleasure of Leisure—Pleasure of Work: Personality Makes the Difference." *Personality and Individual Differences* 16:931–946.

Eysenck, Hans. (1967). *The Biological Basis of Personality.* Springfield, IL: C. C. Thomas.

Feldman, Fred. (1997). *Utilitarianism, Hedonism, and Desert: Essays in Moral Philosophy.* Cambridge, Eng.: Cambridge University Press.

Freud, Sigmund. ([1920] 1956). "Beyond the Pleasure Principle." *The Standard Edition of the Complete Psychological Works of Sigmund Freud, Vol. 18,* ed. James Strachey. London: Hogarth Press.

Gray, Jeffrey A. (1987). *The Psychology of Fear and Stress,* 2nd ed. New York: Cambridge University Press.

Hawkes, Charles. (1992). "Endorphins: The Basis of Pleasure?" *Journal of Neurology, Neurosurgery, and Psychiatry* 55:247–250.

Holland, Barbara. (1996). *Endangered Pleasures: In Defense of Naps, Bacon, Martinis, Profanity, and Other Indulgences.* Boston: Little, Brown.

Kagan, Jerome. (1996). "Three Pleasing Ideas." *American Psychologist* 51:901–908.

Mead, Margaret. (1928). *Coming of Age in Samoa.* New York: W. Morrow.

Mehrabian, Albert. (1995). "Relationships among Three General Approaches to Personality Description." *Journal of Psychology* 129:565–581.

Olds, James, and Milner, Peter M. (1954). "Positive Reinforcement Produced by Electrical Stimulation of Septal Area and Other Areas of Rat Brain." *Journal of Comparative and Physiological Psychology* 47:419–427.

Parducci, Allen. (1995). *Happiness, Pleasure, and Judgment: The Contextual Theory and its Applications.* Mahwah, NJ: Lawrence Erlbaum.

Perry, David L. (1967). *The Concept of Pleasure.* The Hague: Mouton.

Russell, James A. (1979). "A Circumplex Model of Affect." *Journal of Personality and Social Psychology* 39:1161–1178.

Storm, Christine, and Storm, Tom. (1987). "A Taxonomic Study of the Vocabulary of Emotions." *Journal of Personality and Social Psychology* 53:805–816.

Szasz, Thomas. (1988). *Pain and Pleasure: A Study of Bodily Feelings,* 2nd ed. Syracuse, NY: Syracuse University Press.

Tiger, Lionel. (1992). *The Pursuit of Pleasure.* Boston: Little, Brown.

Nick Haslam
Louis Rothschild

POETRY

"ONLY EMOTION ENDURES," declared Ezra Pound at the end of his seminal essay "A Retrospect" (1918). The figure most often associated with the transformations that American poetry underwent at the beginning of the twentieth century and a leader in the international literary movement generally known as modernism, Pound saw emotion as fundamental to poetic value, but at the same time, he was reluctant to specify the means through which emotion endures. Those verbal qualities that express the poet's emotion and that in turn move the reader of the poem are elusive and difficult to define; as Pound said in the same essay, "If we still feel the same emotions as those which launched the thousand ships, it is quite certain that we come on these feelings differently, through different nuances, by different intellectual gradations." Thus, changes in poetic style and the development of new techniques and devices are, in effect, intended to maintain poetry's emotional force. For Pound, nearly the only identifiable linguistic quality consistently found in poetry of great emotional effect was clarity: "One 'moves' the reader only by clarity. In depicting the motions of the 'human heart' the durability of the writing depends on the exactitude. It is the thing that is true and stays true that keeps fresh for the new reader" ("How to Read," 1929). Emotion in itself cannot make for good poetry, for emotion in itself, however sincerely felt by the individual, has yet to become a "thing that is true," that is, a verbal form or object. Poets, therefore, are not merely emotional individuals who set their feelings down in verse of whatever style. To quote Pound once again, "I suppose

that what, in the long run, makes the poet is a sort of persistence of the emotional nature, and joined with this, a peculiar sort of control" ("The Serious Artist," 1913). In composing poetry, the writer's emotional sensibility must in itself be controlled, and the language through which emotion is expressed must be controlled as well. The poet struggles to bring language to feelings and to charge language with feeling. Pound's criticism demonstrates that in considering the expression of emotion in poetry, and hence the role of emotion in poetic composition, romantic exuberance is always in conflict with classical restraint.

Self-Expression

To the popular mind, romantic exuberance takes precedence in this debate, for the popular conception of poetry is that it is fundamentally self-expression, an outpouring of feelings that may be decorated by metaphor and cast (though not necessarily) into meter and rhyme. Poetry is thus regarded as the art of the emotions par excellence, a notion that takes on definitive authority with the advent of Romanticism in the late eighteenth and early nineteenth centuries. But even as central a statement of the Romantic aesthetic as William Wordsworth's preface to his *Lyrical Ballads* (1800) indicates the degree of importance that the Romantic poets attached to matters of intellectual control and verbal precision. To be sure, for Wordsworth the emotional capacities of the poet are of the utmost significance. Yet in his most famous formulation of the relation of poetry to emotion, thought is just as important as feeling: "For all good poetry is the spontaneous overflow of powerful feelings: and though this be true, poems to which any value can be attached were never produced on any variety of subjects but by a man who, being possessed of more than usual organic sensibility, has also thought long and deeply." Throughout the Preface, Wordsworth associates poetry with pleasure; providing "immediate pleasure" is the one necessity of poetic composition, which he otherwise regards as an experience of the greatest freedom. (It is worth noting that the final section of Wallace Stevens's 1942 masterpiece, "Notes toward a Supreme Fiction," is likewise entitled "It Must Give Pleasure.") But the process of composition, through which pleasure is produced, is equally a matter of thought, a subtle interaction of heart and mind. Wordsworth's description of this process, however later poets have modified or argued against it, still provides the clearest understanding of emotion's role in poetry as both inspiration and content, and of the importance of conscious thought as well:

> [Poetry] takes its origin from emotion recollected in tranquillity: the emotion is contemplated till, by a species of

reaction, the tranquillity gradually disappears, and an emotion, kindred to that which was before the subject of contemplation, is gradually produced, and does itself actually exist in the mind. In this mood successful composition generally begins, and in a mood similar to this it is carried on; but the emotion, of whatever kind, and in whatever degree, from various causes, is qualified by various pleasures, so that in describing any passions whatsoever, which are voluntarily described, the mind will, upon the whole, be in a state of enjoyment.

Wordsworth's understanding of poetic form, especially meter, which prior to the advent of free verse was understood to distinguish poetry from prose, is directly related to his emphasis on pleasure, and on the excitement of the emotions that poetry produces. Because "[t]he end of poetry is to produce excitement in co-existence with an overbalance of pleasure," then "the co-presence of something regular, something to which the mind has been accustomed in various moods and in a less excited state, cannot but have great efficacy in tempering and restraining the passion by an intertexture of ordinary feeling, and of feeling not strictly and necessarily with the passion." Wordsworth's concern with the regularity of meter (which in this respect is analogous to Pound's emphasis on the poet's sense of "control") is yet another indication that even among poets for whom the expression of emotion is paramount, the deliberate artifice, the crafted poem, must make its "co-presence" felt by writer and reader.

The power of poetic form to universalize the individual's emotional life, making the experience of private or inner feeling accessible to poetry's general audience, has been a subject of frequent critical speculation. In "Tradition and the Individual Talent" (1919), the essay that may be said to inaugurate modern literary criticism, Pound's colleague T. S. Eliot argued strongly for what he calls the "impersonal theory of poetry." As an advocate of classical restraint and an explicit opponent of Wordsworth's position, Eliot regarded the origin of poetry as "neither emotion, nor recollection, nor without distortion of meaning, tranquility. It is a concentration, and a new thing resulting from the concentration, of a very great number of experiences which to the practical and active person would not seem to be experiences at all." Eliot stressed linguistic concentration rather than meditative emotion: When readers are moved by a particular passage in a poem, they are in contact with feelings that are not necessarily derived from the emotional life or private experience of the poet; rather, it is the concentrated power of language that moves individuals to an intensity and complexity of feeling that merely lived events usually cannot provide. This is why, in Eliot's view, "[h]onest criticism and sensitive appreciation is

directed not upon the poet but upon the poetry"; furthermore, "very few know when there is an expression of *significant* emotion, emotion which has its life in the poem and not in the history of the poet."

Eliot regarded the mind of the poet in the act of composition as a catalyst. The poet is possessed of a highly refined sensibility, but unlike Wordsworth, for whom the poet must be "a man pleased with his own passions and volitions, and who rejoices more than other men in the spirit of life that is in him," Eliot's poet has, "not a 'personality' to express, but a particular medium, which is only a medium and not a personality, in which impressions and experiences combine in peculiar and unexpected ways. Impressions and experiences which are important to the man may take no place in the poetry, and those which become important in the poetry may play quite a negligible part in the man, the personality." The individual poet's capacity for feeling is by no means irrelevant in Eliot's theory, but that individual's talent as a "medium" is developed less through lived experience than through exposure to the great works of literature which precede the new work. Emotion endures in and through tradition, what Eliot called "the main current" or (allowing for his limited cultural perspective) "the mind of Europe." This mind is "much more important than [the poet's] own private mind," for it is in the historical continuity of significant literary forms that the individual poet finds the means to universalize private experience. Personal feelings in themselves are therefore regarded with a good deal of suspicion. Hence Eliot's notorious declaration that poetry "is not a turning loose of emotion, but an escape from emotion; it is not the expression of personality, but an escape from personality. But, of course, only those who have personality and emotions know what it means to want to escape from these things."

Although many readers find Eliot's snobbery objectionable, the notion of the impersonal poet who serves as a catalyst or medium for the refinement of emotional experience is not uncommon and is held by writers of rather different temperament and ideological orientation. John Keats, Wordsworth's younger contemporary, argued in one of his letters (to Benjamin Bailey, November 22, 1817) that "Men of Genius are great as certain ethereal Chemicals operating on the Mass of neutral intellect—[but] they have not any individuality, any determined Character." Deeply influenced by Wordsworth's view that the poet is an individual attuned to the emotional nuances of life, Keats nevertheless departed from his mentor because Wordsworth privileged what Keats calls "the egotistical sublime." Keats readily acknowledged the importance of personal feeling to poetic composition, but rather than emphasize the gradual emotional growth of the autobiographical self (Wordsworth's major poem "The Prelude" is subtitled "Growth of a Poet's Mind"), he regarded the "poetical Character" as emotionally indeterminate, "every thing and nothing": "It has no character—it enjoys light and shade; it lives in gusto, be it foul or fair, high or low, rich or poor, mean or elevated" (letter to Richard Woodhouse, October 27, 1818). Keats's understanding of the poetic self was centered upon emotional exuberance or intensity rather than specific emotional content; he declared in the same letter that, as an individual, "[a] Poet is the most unpoetical of any thing in existence; because he has no Identity—he is continually in for—and filling some other Body."

At the same time, however, the poet must be continually conscious of the emotional tenor of shifting experience, of life as it is lived. "I am certain of nothing but of the holiness of the Heart's affections and the truth of the imagination" Keats declared in the letter to Bailey cited above. The instability of the poetic identity is directly related to the imagination, through which the poet's emotional responses to the world are tested and given form. Keats named such responsiveness "*Negative Capability,* that is when man is capable of being in uncertainties, Mysteries, doubts, without any irritable reaching after fact & reason" (letter to George and Thomas Keats, December 21, 1817), and naturally credited Shakespeare with a great measure of this power. Composed without preconception, a poem charged with emotion is the result of the poet's openness to experience. The feelings expressed in such a work, and the feelings elicited in the reader, are not those of private individuals but pertain to a universal state of being that the poem makes accessible. Keats called the world "The vale of Soul-making" (letter to George and Georgiana Keats, April 21, 1819), for the emotional experience that is latent in the world gradually forms and educates the human heart.

Poetry is, in effect, the record of that process; hence its importance for any theory of the emotions. Poets have been traditionally regarded as individuals who are particularly sensitive to the nuances of the emotional life. Yet they also possess the linguistic means to articulate these nuances and, even more important, to make them into beautiful forms. The appreciation of these images lead the readers to an empathetic state of mind, a state in which emotions are mostly deeply felt and understood. And yet a poem is a poem, a verbal pattern, and not the emotions it evokes. In his *Anatomy of Criticism* (1957), Northrop Frye argued that "Poetic images do not state or point to anything, but, by pointing to each other, they suggest or evoke the mood that informs the poem. That is, they express or articulate the mood. The emotion is not chaotic or

inarticulate: it merely would have remained so if it had not turned into a poem, and when it does so, it *is* the poem, not something else still behind it." Feelings are relatively ephemeral, and over the course of a lifetime, even the strongest currents of love and joy, anger and sorrow tend to fade after the intensity of the events that first produced them recede into the past. But if such feelings should inspire a poem, they will come to life again each time the poem is read.

The Lyric

The lyric is usually regarded as a relatively short poem in which the sensual and musical qualities of language are heightened in order to present a subjective, emotionally charged moment, an interior event with lasting resonance. Although the preceding discussion does not distinguish among particular genres of verse, it is assumed that the lyric (as opposed to epic or dramatic poetry) is that type of poem most closely associated with emotional experience, or the representation of emotion in personal or individual terms. Emotion, obviously, plays a great part in the development of narrative structure and characterization in epic and dramatic poetry, and any reader can recall scenes of overpowering pathos in the greatest works in these genres, such as the encounter with Paolo and Francesca in Dante's *Inferno* or the meeting of the blinded Gloucester and Edgar in William Shakespeare's *King Lear*. It is no accident that Keats invoked Shakespeare when presenting his idea of negative capability, and he was thinking of Shakespeare the dramatist, who entered more fully into the emotional being of invented personalities than any other writer before or since.

In "Everything and Nothing" (1960), his extraordinary parable of Shakespeare's life, the Argentine writer Jorge Luis Borges spoke of an uncanny emptiness in the poet that impels him to create the multitude of passionate personalities found in his plays. At the time of his death, the poet finds himself in the presence of God and cries, "I who have been so many men in vain want to be one and myself." God replies, "Neither am I anyone; I have dreamt the world as you dreamt your work, my Shakespeare, and among the forms in my dream are you, who like myself are many and no one." Borges's insight into the godlike quality of Shakespeare's negative capability proceeded to influence Harold Bloom's account of Shakespeare's canonical centrality. In *The Western Canon* (1994), Bloom asserted that one of Shakespeare's greatest contributions—not only to literature but to the human self-image—lies in the way his major characters "become free artists of themselves [the phrase is Georg Hegel's], which means they are free to write themselves, to will changes in the self. Overhearing their own speeches and pondering those expressions, they change and go on to contemplate an otherness in the self, or the possibility of such otherness." In other words, the volatile situations in which these characters find themselves produce emotional states which, through their poetic articulation, lead them to self-knowledge and to actions that further transform their inner lives. In Shakespeare's dramatic verse, emotions are not simply felt; they become the objects of self-reflection and thus powerful motivations in the shaping of an individual's destiny.

However permanently and powerfully the understanding—indeed, if what Bloom said is true, the very awareness—of emotions is transformed through Shakespeare's drama, it remains the case that since the Romantic period, the lyric is commonly regarded as the poetic form of emotional expression. Appropriately, Bloom (again in *The Western Canon*) credited Wordsworth with inventing the modern poem, in which the "subject is the subject herself or himself, whether manifested as a presence or as an absence." Just as poetry is popularly regarded as self-expression, the lyric is popularly regarded as the poetic form through which that subjectivity is expressed. The utterance with which the reader is confronted in a lyric presupposes a single speaker, and the use of the pronoun *I* in such a poem leads to the identification of the intensity of this utterance with the emotional condition of the poet, the individual who actually wrote the poem. The immediacy of this association is crucial to the artistic effect of the poem: When Emily Dickinson declares, "I felt a Funeral, in my Brain / And Mourners to and fro" (no. 280), the reader assumes that the deathly feelings of psychic weight and oppression reported in the text, if not strictly autobiographical, are nevertheless derived from the poet's intimate knowledge of these feelings. The reader enters

An engraving by the French printmaker Gustave Dore depicts the Spirits, Paolo, and Francesca in the second circle of Hell, a scene from Dante's Inferno. (Corbis/Chris Hellier)

into an unspoken contract with the poet, assuming that the emotions conveyed by the poem are real, are true. As Frye said in *Anatomy of Criticism,* "The radical of presentation in the lyric is the hypothetical form of what in religion is called the 'I-Thou' relationship, which is fundamentally a relationship of reciprocity and trust." Since the beginning of the twentieth century, the stability and unity of the subject have been radically interrogated by various trends in such disciplines as psychology and philosophy, as well as by literature itself. Yet lyric poetry remains a matter of language measured by emotional truth, even when the poet must, in all responsibility, register the most severe doubts about the process. "As soon as / I speak, I / speaks," declared Robert Creeley in "The Pattern" (from *Words,* 1967). The doubleness of the poet's personhood as expressed by the shift from first- to third-person may deliver an existential shock to the reader (perhaps no greater than Dickinson's funeral image), but although the self that feels is called into question, the truth of that feeling remains.

In his *Anatomy,* Frye called the lyric "preeminently the utterance that is overheard. The lyric poet normally pretends to be talking to himself or to someone else: a spirit of nature, a Muse (note the distinction from *epos,* where the Muse speaks *through* the poet), a personal friend, a lover, a god, a personified abstraction, or a natural object." The idea that the lyric is an overheard utterance, that the poet's back is turned to the reader, leads to the question of the relationship between lyric poetry and society. Are poets merely pretending to turn their backs, or is the gesture that initiates the lyric utterance a genuine rejection of the social in favor of the personal? How does the privacy, the intimacy implied by the emotional expressiveness of the lyric utterance move from the level of "I-Thou" relationship to that of a generalized "we"? Frye's answer was that each lyric poem expresses an archetypal pattern of recurrence, and the emotions it embodies are subordinated under the general force of desire, or "wish-thinking." For Frye, lyric expression is metonymic of the human process of civilization, "the process of making a total human form out of nature," and the emotional power of a poem was the power of desire, "the energy that leads human society to develop its own form. Desire in this sense is the social aspect of . . . emotion, an impulse toward expression which would have remained amorphous if the poem had not liberated it by providing the form of its expression." Frye, who began his career as an archetypal critic studying the visionary poetry of William Blake, was profoundly Romantic in this formulation. In the poem, what the individual feels is what human society feels. When the poem achieves the heights of emotional expression, the reader meets "a vision, not of the personal greatness of the poet, but of something impersonal and far greater: the vision of a decisive act of spiritual freedom, the vision of the recreation of man."

Other critics, however, find the relation between the apparently personal stance of the lyric poet and the social function of poetry to be more problematic. The passionate expressivity of a great lyric may represent Frye's "decisive act of spiritual freedom," but why should this freedom be anything more than a momentary instance of individual's rhetorical power? "At the lyrical moment," observed Georg Lukács, wrestling with the same issue in his *Theory of the Novel* (1916), "the purest interiority of the soul, set apart from duration without choice, lifted above the obscurely-determined multiplicity of things, solidifies into substance." For Lukács, the strength and the weakness of the lyric was in the momentary quality of its emotional intensity, for "only in lyric poetry do these direct, sudden flashes of the substance become like lost original manuscripts suddenly made legible; only in lyric poetry is the subject, the vehicle of such experiences, transformed into the sole carrier of meaning, the only true reality." The experience of pure interiority is hardly consistent: Sudden and individualized, an emotional state expressed in a lyric utterance impresses readers as "the only true reality" for a moment only, and cannot be sustained. Yet paradoxically, the momentary feeling of a lyric poem can resonate with a reader for a lifetime. How then does one account for what may be referred to as the poem's "social power"?

In "Lyric Poetry and Society" (1957), T. W. Adorno observed that "what we mean by lyric . . . has within it, in its 'purest' form, the quality of a break or rupture. The subjective being that makes itself heard in lyric poetry is one which defines and expresses itself as something opposed to the collective and the realm of objectivity." The intimate feeling-states of lyric poetry come into being on the far side of a divide between the individual poet and the social collective. According to Adorno's analysis, what bridges the gap is not the feelings expressed in the poem, however commonly felt they may be, but its language: "The most sublime lyric works, therefore, are those in which the subject, without a trace of his material being, intones in language until the voice of language itself is heard. The *subject's* forgetting himself, his abandoning himself to language as if devoting himself completely to an object—this and the direct intimacy and spontaneity of his *expression* are the same. Thus language begets and joins both poetry and society in their innermost natures." In Adorno's formulation, the poet's devotion to language causes the private self to dissolve into the greater social being, but with no loss of the "intimacy and spontaneity" ordinarily associated with the expressive power of the passionate individual.

Language, then, is always the determinant of the poem's emotional truth. The radical simplicity of the greatest lyric verse, and the overriding sense of inevitability the reader feels moving from line to line in such poetry, are the results of the poet's giving of the self to language, which enlarges the self and opens out its emotional condition. A linguistic community comes into being, as in the William Bronk's poem "The Tell" (1981):

> I want to tell my friends how beautiful
> the world is. Not but what they know
> it is terrible too—they know as well as I;
> but nevertheless, I want to tell my friends.
>
> Because they are. And this is what they are;
> and because it is and this is what it is.
> You are my friend. The world is beautiful.
> Dear friend, you are. I want to tell you so.

The poet's desire to "tell" of his feelings is so strong and pure that only the most direct and simple language can match the dignity—and urgency—of that desire. Against all that is terrible in the world, the poet offers his vision of friendship and beauty. This is how poetry sustains the emotional life.

See also: COMMUNICATION; CREATIVITY; DANCE; DRAMA AND THEATER; LITERATURE; MUSIC; ORATORY

Bibliography

Adorno, T. W. (1991). "Lyric Poetry and Society." In *Notes to Literature,* ed. Rolf Tiedemann, tr. Shierry Weber Nicholsen. New York: Columbia University Press.

Bloom, Harold. (1994). *The Western Canon: The Books and School of the Ages.* New York: Harcourt Brace.

Borges, Jorge Luis. (1960). *El Hacedor.* Buenos Aires: Emece.

Borges, Jorge Luis. (1964). *Labyrinths: Selected Stories & Other Writings,* augmented edition, ed. Donald A. Yates and James E. Irby. New York: New Directions.

Bronk, William. (1981). *Life Supports: New and Collected Poems.* San Francisco: North Point Press.

Creeley, Robert. (1982). *The Collected Poems of Robert Creeley: 1945–1975.* Berkeley: University of California Press.

Dickinson, Emily. (1960). *The Complete Poems of Emily Dickinson,* ed. Thomas H. Johnson. Boston: Little, Brown.

Eliot, T. S. (1975). *Selected Prose of T. S. Eliot,* ed. Frank Kermode. New York: Harcourt Brace Jovanovich.

Frye, Northrop. (1957). *Anatomy of Criticism: Four Essays.* Princeton, NJ: Princeton University Press.

Keats, John. (1958). *The Letters of John Keats,* ed. Hyder Edward Rollins. Cambridge, MA: Harvard University Press.

Lukács, Georg. (1971). *The Theory of the Novel,* tr. Anna Bostock. Cambridge, MA: MIT Press.

Pound, Ezra. (1935). *Literary Essays of Ezra Pound,* ed. T. S. Eliot. New York: New Directions.

Stevens, Wallace. (1982). *The Collected Poems of Wallace Stevens.* New York: Vintage Books.

Wordsworth, William. (1974). *The Prose Works of William Wordsworth,* ed. W. J. B. Owen and Jane Worthington Smyser. Oxford, Eng.: Clarendon Press.

Norman Finkelstein

POLITICS

See Advertising; Attitudes; Persuasion; Propaganda

POST-TRAUMATIC STRESS DISORDER

Post-traumatic stress disorder is a psychiatric diagnosis for people who have endured a highly stressful and frightening experience and are distressed by the memories of that event. It is as if a person is "possessed" by his or her memories of what happened and just cannot let go of them. Perhaps the traumatized person believes that there is something to learn from the experience and that by more fully understanding the experience they will be able to feel safer and more able to cope with the future.

Terminology

The term *post-traumatic stress disorder* (PTSD) first appeared in the American Psychiatric Association's *Diagnostic and Statistical Manual of Mental Disorder* in 1980. Because anxiety is the major sign of PTSD, it is classified as an anxiety disorder. Other anxiety disorders include, for example, phobias, panic disorders, and generalized anxiety.

The initial diagnosis of PTSD started an entire field: traumatology. Prior to 1980, psychiatrists and other mental health specialists attempted to describe the anxiety problems of rape victims with the term *rape trauma syndrome,* and they used the term *concentration camp syndrome* to describe the symptoms of Holocaust survivors. Today, these two syndromes—along with similar syndromes such as post-Vietnam syndrome, disaster victim disorder, battered woman syndrome, and many other syndromes that all involve very similar symptoms—are simply classified as PTSD mental-health problems. Despite the fact that the PTSD diagnosis and the field of traumatology have existed only since 1980, some scholars have traced the roots of the field and the concept to the very earliest medical writings in 1900 B.C.E., for example, ancient Egyptians recorded symptoms similar to PTSD and assumed that they were caused by movement of the womb. The Greeks first called this "hysteria." Throughout history various terms were used to describe what is now called PTSD. For example, the diagnosis of combat-related

PTSD has now replaced the previous diagnoses of shell shock, acute combat reaction, combat fatigue, and combat exhaustion.

To understand PTSD, it is important to understand the context within which a PTSD can emerge. This involves defining four basic concepts: trauma, traumatic event, tramatic stress reaction, and post-traumatic stress reaction. The original definition of trauma was derived from the psychoanalytic theory perspective. According to this theory, trauma is analogous to a foreign object, such as a wood splinter, that is lodged under the skin and causes all of the forces within the body to work to dislodge it. In this sense, trauma causes emotional tension until it is dislodged or discharged. Traditional psychotherapy theories suggest that only through an abreaction (i.e., a highly emotional reaction) that is either natural or clinically induced can the repressed emotions of the traumatic experience be relived and the tension discharged. Contemporary psychotherapy theories are more behaviorally based. They assert that trauma is simply an emotional state of discomfort and stress resulting from memories of an extraordinary, catastrophic experience that shattered the survivor's sense of invulnerability to harm. It is as if trauma, for various reasons, becomes something to worry about as a result of the experience that caused it. Traumatic events, the causes of PTSD, are defined as extraordinary events that are sudden, overwhelming, and often dangerous to individuals and their significant others. Therefore, exposure to any life-threatening event such as a car wreck, natural disaster, dangerous accident, war combat, being robbed at gunpoint, and a near drowning are examples of traumatic events. The definition includes significant others such as close friends, family members, and professionals helping those who survived these types of events because their empathy and compassion for the person in harm's way can cause them to be traumatized in the course of providing help. Thus, a traumatic event is a source or cause of stress that most people experience. The stress experienced during the traumatic event or catastrophe is traumatic stress. Traumatic stress reactions, then, are sets of con-

scious and unconscious actions and emotions associated with dealing with the stressors of a traumatic event and the period immediately afterwards. Similarly, the stress that is associated with the traumatic event and experienced well afterwards is post-traumatic stress. Post-traumatic stress reactions, then, are defined as sets of conscious and unconscious behaviors and emotions associates with dealing with the memories of the stressors of the catastrophe and immediately afterwards.

Diagnosis

Most people experience both traumatic and post-traumatic stress reactions when exposed to a traumatic event. However, only a small percentage of such people go on to develop PTSD, and this percentage varies by the degree of fright caused by the event. In a small number of cases, people simply pretend or convince themselves that they are traumatized and have PTSD because it serves their purposes (e.g., wanting attention, receiving free help, or payment). However, most people who do actually develop PTSD want to obtain treatment so they can get rid of the disorder. Therefore, it is important to be able to know who has PTSD and who does not.

There are many characteristic symptoms or signs that indicate that a person has in fact developed PTSD. Most authorities recognize five features: (a) confirmation that the person has been exposed to a traumatic event, (b) re-experiencing the trauma, (c) persistent avoidance of trauma reminders and numbing of responsiveness to the external world, (d) persistent arousal associated with the trauma, and (e) duration of the above symptoms is longer than one month.

To satisfy the "confirmation of surviving a traumatic event" criterion, there must be an affirmative response ("yes") to both of the following two questions. Did the person experience, witness, or confront a traumatic event? When he or she was exposed to the experience, was there a feeling of intense fear, helplessness, or horror (either at the time or immediately afterwards)?

To satisfy the "re-experiencing the trauma" criterion, there must be an affirmative response to at least one of the following five questions. Does the person experience recurrent and intrusive thoughts, feelings, images, and memories of the event? Does the person experience recurrent distressing and disturbing recollections of the event? Does the person experience a sense of actually reliving the experience (e.g., experiencing illusions, hallucinations, or dissociative flashback episodes)? Does the person have an immediate and intense psychological distress when exposed to reminders of the trauma? Does the person actually experience anxiety in various parts of the body (e.g.,

Virginia Woolf, in Mrs. Dalloway *(1925), creates the character Septimus, who comes back from World War I and is unable to deal with reality. He cannot taste things or feel things as he used to before the war. He feels guilty that he did not care when his buddy was killed. Fears and insomnia harass him; he hears voices. In spite of physicians' efforts to help him, Septimus finally commits suicide.*

pains in the chest, stomach, shoulders, head, or elsewhere)? If the person exposed to a traumatic event does not experience even one of these re-experiencing symptoms, they probably do not have PTSD. However, these and other symptoms often go undetected, either because of the traumatized person's reluctance or inability to relate the symptoms to a sufficiently knowledgeable clinician or researcher or because the person is misdiagnosed as psychotic.

To satisfy the "coping by avoidance or numbness" criterion, there must be an affirmative response to at least three of the following seven questions. Does the person go out of his or her way to avoid all thoughts, feelings, or conversations associated with the trauma? Does the person make the effort to avoid activities, places, or people that arouse recollections of the trauma? Even though the person may try, is he or she unable to remember important aspects of the trauma? Since the event, is there evidence that the person's interest and participation in activities once considered to be important have decreased significantly? Has the person become detached from his or her network of family and friends? Does the person seem to have gone through a personality change or become more depressed since the trauma? Has the person talked about not knowing if he or she would grow old or have much of a future?

The "increased arousal" criterion for establishing the PTSD diagnosis requires an affirmative response to at least two of the following four questions. Does the person have trouble falling asleep, staying asleep, or getting back to sleep? Is the person grouchy, losing his or her temper often? Does the person have difficulty concentrating? Does the person seem always on edge, jumpy? If the person is startled, does he or she overreact?

Although the "duration" criterion only requires that the other symptoms last longer than one month, there are, based on the actual duration, three classifications for PTSD: acute, delayed, and chronic. Acute PTSD occurs when the other symptoms last between one and three months after the trauma. Chronic PTSD occurs when the other symptoms last for at least three months following the trauma. Delayed PTSD occurs when the other symptoms do not show up until at least six months after the trauma.

Research has found that when PTSD is detected, other symptoms and characteristics are found as well, which is why PTSD is so often misdiagnosed. Among the major sets of symptoms are phobia and general anxiety (especially among former prisoners of war, hostages, and survivors of natural disasters), substance abuse, depression, psychosomatic complaints, an altered sense of time (especially among children), grief reactions and obsessions with death (especially among those who survived a trauma in which someone could easily have died), feelings of guilt, and increased interpersonal conflicts. These other features often disappear once the PTSD symptoms are eliminated through treatment.

Treatment Approaches

Treating PTSD is both an art and a science. Recent reviews of PTSD treatment studies reveal that both drugs and psychotherapy are helpful. The most effective treatment approaches could be classified as cognitive-behavioral because they focus both on how the traumatized person views the trauma and its consequences and what their resulting behavior is. Exposure therapy includes systematic desensitization (i.e., training to relax in the face of frightening reminders of the trauma) on the one hand and imaginable, techniques such as flooding or the process of putting the client back into the trauma psychologically.

Research has found that the most effective treatment for PTSD is cognitive-behavioral therapy, which includes a variety of anxiety management training strategies. Some of these include rational emotive therapy, relaxation training, stress inoculation training, cognitive restructuring, breathing retraining, biofeedback, social skills training, and distraction training. Innovative therapists are generally successful in combing various techniques to fit the trauma and the patient's unique requirements. An innovation that is becoming one of the most popular treatments among traumatologists is eye movement desensitization and reprocessing. This cognitive-behavioral approach uses eye movement or some other orienting response to enable the client to recall sufficient aspects of the traumatic event to both lower arousal (subjective units of disturbance) and change negative self-referencing statements to positive self-referencing statements. Clinical research trials show it to be equal or superior to other trauma treatment approaches.

Overall, however, most people agree with Judith Herman's (1992) three-phase approach that requires the practitioner working with PTSD patients to first establish safety, remembrance and mourning, and reconnection. Thus, the practitioner must establish the client's trust by establishing a sense of safety with the practitioner and with the traumatic material being considered and reconsidered. When this has been done, the practitioner gradually helps the client remember the trauma and reprocess the information, including mourning the losses. This also requires the need for helping the client with self-soothing techniques and ways to limit the distress during and between sessions. Finally, the practitioner helps the client disconnect from the trauma so that reminders do and avoidance symptoms, although fluoxetine, amitriptyline, and possibly valproate have shown effectiveness against avoidance symptoms.

Conclusion

There is considerable empirical proof for the diagnosis of PTSD in people traumatized by one or more highly stressful events. By focusing on the specific, measurable evidence of stress reactions, both during and after the traumatic event, social scientists have documented the remarkable and consistent patterns of emotional recovery from a wide variety of traumatizing events. This has lead to the development of a large number of treatment approaches. Some drugs are helpful, when used early in the program of treatment, in stabilizing the client and mobilizing him or her toward health. However, it is important that traumatized people feel safe from being re-traumatized, able to control their unwanted anxiety through self-soothing methods, able to recall and learn from their trauma experiences, and able to learn to live with and even thrive from what they have experienced. It is impossible to prevent traumatic events, but the field of traumatology exists to help understand the trauma recovery process and, thereby, promote quick recovery.

See also: ANXIETY DISORDERS; CULTURE-BOUND SYNDROMES; FEAR AND PHOBIAS; MOOD DISORDERS

Bibliography

American Psychiatric Association. (1994). *Diagnostic and Statistical Manual of Mental Disorders,* 4th ed. Washington, DC: American Psychiatric Association.

Figley, Charles R., ed. (1978). *Stress Disorders among Vietnam Veterans: Theory, Research, and Practice.* New York: Brunner/Mazel.

Figley, Charles R., ed. (1985). *Trauma and Its Wake: The Study and Treatment of PTSD.* New York: Brunner/Mazel.

Figley, Charles R. (1989). *Helping Traumatized Families.* San Francisco: Jossey-Bass.

Figley, Charles R.; Bride, Brian; and Mazza, Nicholas, eds. (1997). *Death and Trauma: The Traumatology of Grieving.* Philadelphia: Brunner/Mazel.

Friedman, Matthew J.; Charney, Dennis S.; and Deutch, Ariel Y., eds. (1995). *Neurobiological and Clinical Consequences of Stress: From Normal Adaptation to PTSD.* New York: Raven Press.

Herman, Judith L. (1992). *Trauma and Recovery.* New York: Basic Books.

Kulka, Richard A.; Schlenger, William E.; Fairbank, John A.; Hough, Richard L.; Jordan, Brenda K.; Marmar, Charles R.; and Weiss, Daniel S. (1990). *Trauma and the Vietnam War Generation.* New York: Brunner/Mazel.

Peterson, Kirtland C.; Prout, Maurice F.; and Schwarz, Robert A. (1991). *Post-Traumatic Stress Disorder: A Clinician's Guide.* New York: Plenum.

Shapiro, Francine. (1989). *Eye Movement Desensitization and Reprocessing.* New York: Guilford.

On May 17, 1994, a therapist tries to help a young boy overcome the trauma that he experienced during the 1994 Los Angeles earthquake. (Corbis/Roger Ressmeyer)

not arouse distress. This process is intended to help the client learn enough from the past so that there is no longer any need to think about the event. In doing so, the practitioner helps the client reconnect to life, now and in the future, without being haunted by the trauma. Sometimes this transition to life without the trauma is harder than expected.

Given the advances in the neurobiology of traumatology, drug treatment early on is a useful supplement to effective psychotherapy approaches for some clients. Drugs provide temporary symptom relief for general anxiety, depression, insomnia, and related problems. These drugs include imipramine, amitriptyline, phenelzine, fluoxetine, and propranolol. An analysis of all available drug studies with PTSD patients revealed that tricyclic antidepressants and monoamine oxidase inhibitors help control intrusion

Solomon, Susan D.; Gerrity, Ellen T.; and Muff, Ann M. (1992). "Efficacy of Treatments for Post-Traumatic Stress Disorder." *Journal of the American Medical Association* 268(5):633–638.

Trimble, Michael R. (1981). *Post-Traumatic Neuroses: From Railway Spine to the Whiplash.* Chichester, Eng.: Wiley.

Wilson, John P., and Raphael, Beverly, eds. (1993). *Wilson and the International Handbook of Traumatic Stress Syndromes.* New York: Plenum.

Charles R. Figley

PREJUDICE

Gordon Allport, in *The Nature of Prejudice* (1954, p. 9), crafted the basic definition of intergroup prejudice: "Ethnic prejudice is an antipathy based upon a faulty and inflexible generalization." It is of particular note that this influential view stresses both emotion (antipathy) and cognition (faulty generalization). For Allport, antipathy covered a wide range of negative emotions—from aggression, anger, and rage to hate, jealousy, and resentment.

Documenting antipathy with questionnaire measures of prejudice is difficult because many individuals resist revealing their dislike of minorities. Another difficulty involved in the measure of prejudice is the fact that people often withhold empathic feelings such as sympathy and admiration from outgroups (i.e., people not like themselves) and routinely accord these feelings to their ingroup (i.e., people "of their own kind"). Thus, antipathy itself is relative. At the least, prejudice entails restricted empathy for the minority outgroup, which lowers the threshold for aggression. At the most, prejudice involves such intense emotions that cognitive processing (i.e., logical thinking) is totally disrupted, which makes aggressive behavior against the outgroup even more likely.

In light of the fact that positive feelings toward outgroups do arise, some specialists question if negative feelings are a necessary ingredient of prejudice. However, stern conditions often provide the structure

Huckleberry Finn *(1885), by Mark Twain, reveals the prejudice against African Americans that pervaded the American South during the mid-nineteenth century, when slavery was still in effect. Huck, brought up in the culture of the South, is still an independent young teenager who has ethics of his own. Huck becomes good friends with Jim, a runaway slave, and his conscience tells him that this friendship is more true and decent than the white culture that enslaves people. He is willing to "go to hell" to protect Jim.*

within which such positive feelings can be observed and expressed. Slaveholders were sometimes emotionally attached to their house slaves, yet such positive feelings swiftly transformed into antipathy when the severe codes of the master-slave relation were violated. Similarly, antipathy felt by some men toward women may remain latent (i.e., hidden) until a woman crosses the boundaries that define females' traditional roles. A related view held by Irvin Katz and R. Glen Hass (1988) holds that emotional ambivalence, including both hostility and benevolence, is an underlying factor of prejudice. Indeed, complex combinations of positive and negative emotions characterize responses to many outgroups.

Social psychology neglected the emotional aspect of prejudice for a long time, choosing instead to focus almost exclusively on the cognitive component of prejudice (even though Allport's classic definition stressed both elements). This neglect of the emotional aspect led to a distorted view of prejudice. Armed with new theory, better measurement, and a greater understanding of cultural stereotypes (i.e., oversimplified images of groups), an overdue correction began in the late 1980s. Charles Stangor, Linda Sullivan, and Thomas Ford (1991) compared the value of emotional responses and preconceived stereotypes in predicting how individuals would relate to members of outgroups. The emotional response indicators, for a range of groups, proved to be stronger, more consistent predictors of both intergroup attitudes and social distance. Similarly, Victoria Esses and her colleagues (1993) had subjects report on the emotions they experienced when they saw, met, or thought about various minorities. These reports were related more strongly than stereotypes to their general favorability toward these outgroups.

Anton Dijker (1987), interviewing respondents in Amsterdam, found strong relationships between specific emotional states experienced during intergroup contact and attitudes toward minorities. He also noted that the conditions of the intergroup contact shape the emotional responses (e.g., strong emotional responses resulted when threat was involved).

Threat and Prejudice

Threat, both personal and societal, provokes strong emotion and prejudice. Walter and Cookie Stephan (1996) specify three types: realistic threat, symbolic threat, and intergroup anxiety. Realistic threats involve the perception of outgroup threats to the physical or material well-being of the ingroup and its members. Symbolic threats entail the perception of threats to an ingroup's cherished values, traditions, and worldviews. Intergroup anxiety is the feeling of threat experienced during direct interaction with the outgroup. Extensive evidence reveals that all three types of threat lead to heightened prejudice toward the outgroup involved. Esses and her coworkers (1998) found that perceived economic threat from immigrants (a threat that was reinforced by the mass media) had a strong negative effect on Canadian attitudes toward immigration.

Symbolic threat is the most studied of the three basic types of threat. One example of research related to this topic is the theory of "terror management" advanced by Jeff Greenberg and his colleagues (1997). They hold that a group's worldview serves as a buffer for the anxiety generated by the awareness of mortality. Anything that threatens this anxiety buffer—from ingroup deviants to outgroups with contrasting worldviews—will trigger hostility and prejudice.

Both realistic and symbolic threat increase the expression of authoritarianism—a major personality syndrome underlying prejudice. Experiments such as those conducted by Stephen Sales and Kenneth Friend (1973) show that threatening situations make authoritarian responses more likely. Societal threat also serves to heighten existing authoritarianism. During threatening times (e.g., when there are wars and poverty), there is an increase in many of the indicators of authoritarianism (e.g., religious conversions, longer sentences for convicted felons, registrations of "attack" dogs). During tranquil or prosperous times, there is generally a decline in these types of indicators.

Several processes explain these persistent findings. Threat produces authoritarianism. Threat sets the conditions for the arousal and acting out of existing authoritarianism in the population. Toleration for the beliefs and behavior of those with high authoritarianism expands during threatening times. People tend to swing sharply between authoritarian and equalitarian behavior and beliefs as a function of societal threat. These same processes probably describe the relationship between societal threat and prejudice as well.

Researchers have also paid considerable attention to the central role in prejudice of intergroup anxiety—the third form of threat.

Anxiety and Prejudice

A sharp distinction must be made between *trait* anxiety, which treats anxiety as an enduring personality trait, and *situational* anxiety. While the latter is clearly linked with prejudice, there is no consistent relationship between trait anxiety and prejudice. Situational anxiety is typically aroused for members of both groups during the initial phases of intergroup contact. Contact under optimal conditions, even vicarious contact, can dispel such anxiety.

Many factors trigger intergroup anxiety: prior conflict, stereotypes, differential group status, and intergroup competition. The Stephans (1985) note that there are behavioral, affective (i.e., emotional), and cognitive (i.e., mental) consequences of such anxiety. It can amplify behavior—enhancing the ingroup norm of either nondiscrimination or discrimination. It also can amplify affective reactions. Optimal positive contact leads to stronger positive affect, and problematic contact leads to stronger negative affect.

Cognitively, anxiety can cause simplification of informational processing by increasing the use of stereotypes. In this situation, attention is focused on stereotype-consistent information and away from stereotype-inconsistent information. David Wilder (1993) explains this phenomenon in terms of distraction: Anxiety causes a mental distraction, which limits cognitive functioning and results in the use of stereotypes as the simplest solution to dealing with the situation.

Mood and Prejudice

Moods, which are more general than emotions, also influence the stereotyping of outgroups. Good moods can lead to more favorable evaluations of an outgroup, and bad moods can lead to more negative evaluations. Positive moods allow people to view members of an outgroup as individuals, while negative moods tend to reinforce the perception of an outgroup as one homogeneous whole. When an outgroup is already disliked, negative moods induce harsh interpretations of existing stereotypes. Such effects are especially pronounced when an outgroup member is responsible for the mood in which the interaction occurs.

Positive and negative moods can both increase the use of stereotyping because they affect cognition by creating situations that involve "low-effort" and "high-effort" processing. For example, both happiness and anger encourage low-effort processing that triggers stereotyping as the simplest solution (similar to the result created by anxiety distraction). Other moods, such as sadness, can lead to high-effort processing that also can lead to stereotyping.

Joseph Forgas (1995) devised his affect infusion model to account for these mood findings and for the general influence affect has on judgment. According to this model, the features of the target (the outgroup), the subject (the ingroup), and the situation determine how judgments will be made. According to Forgas's model, the relevance of the outgroup influences the judgmental strategies of the ingroup. When the outgroup is of little relevance to the ingroup, positive moods lead to more detached processing and

Prejudice has been institutionalized in organizations such as the Ku Klux Klan, thirty members of which held an hour-long rally on the courthouse steps in Defiance, Ohio, on March 20, 1999, to recruit more members. (Corbis/AFP)

greater discrimination. When the outgroup is highly relevant to the ingroup, negative moods lead to slower, careful, motivated processing and, ultimately, discrimination.

Two caveats are needed for interpreting these mood phenomena. First, motivation and processing capacity may not be affected. Herbert Bless and his colleagues (1996) maintain that perceptions of the situation as safe or problematic, which correlate with happy and sad moods, are the critical elements. Second, conclusions should not be generalized across all positive and negative moods and emotions because specific moods and emotions often have specific effects. For example, happiness and anger can lead to more stereotyping than do gratitude and sadness.

New Approaches to Prejudice

The Stephans (1993) insist that affect and cognition usually are both involved and work together in shaping prejudice, although John Dovidio and Samuel Gaertner (1993) show that affective and cognitive influences on prejudice can sometimes act independently. Patricia Devine and Margo Monteith (1993) claim that cognition induces emotion that in turn shapes cognition. According to this theory, people have personal standards that proscribe the use of in-

tergroup stereotypes. When they violate these standards, they are upset with themselves, an affective response that in turn motivates them to be vigilant against making further stereotypic responses.

In this vein, Mark Zanna (1994) proposes a three-part model of prejudice consisting of stereotypes, symbolic beliefs, and emotions. These three components are only moderately connected, yet each is important in the prediction of global attitudes toward outgroups. Although they are the most studied, stereotypic beliefs about the outgroup's characteristics make up only part of the prejudice phenomenon. Symbolic beliefs about how the outgroup violates cherished ingroup values, traditions, and worldviews are more important than stereotypes—especially for individuals high in authoritarianism. Emotion is critical both for those individuals who are low in authoritarianism and for those who are high in authoritarianism. Indeed, Zanna's research showed that emotion (or affect measure) proved to be the most important correlate of prejudice against several target groups.

Eliot Smith (1993) goes further. He views prejudice as a social emotion toward outgroups, an emotion that is shaped by a person's social identity as an ingroup member. Smith's approach accounts for phenomena firmly established in intergroup research. Thus, the expression of prejudice often is specific to the intergroup situation in which particular emotions are elicited. Moreover, research often has shown the greater importance of a group focus over an individual focus in creating prejudice.

Combining Emotional and Cognitive Processes

People who perceive that an outgroup is gaining social position in relation to the social position of their ingroup reveal greater prejudice against the outgroup. This group-relative deprivation has both cognitive (perceiving the difference) and emotional (anger at the change) components, but most investigations of this situation focus only on the cognitive component. However, prejudice, the real problem in the situation (since perceiving the change in the outgroup's social position is not a problem in itself), results only when the emotional element is added. In other words, only if the ingroup becomes angry about the change does group-relative deprivation become a major predictor of intergroup prejudice.

Western European data test this "new look" further. A 1988 survey conducted by Thomas Pettigrew (1997) asked more than thirty-eight hundred respondents about a variety of immigrant groups. It measured two types of prejudice with different emotional bases. Blatant prejudice is the traditional form; it is hot, close, and direct. Subtle prejudice is the modern form; it is cool, distant, and indirect. Individuals who scored high on a key subscale related to empathic affect reported never having felt either sympathy or admiration for the outgroup. Respondents were also asked if they had any friends of a different culture, nationality, race, religion, or social class. This intergroup-friends measure related strongly and negatively with blatant and subtle prejudice and especially with the empathetic affect subscale (i.e., individuals who indicated a high number of intergroup friends tended to score low on the prejudice and empathic affect scales). Further analyses revealed that this is largely a result of intergroup friendships leading to less prejudice and not the reverse. Moreover, the power of intergroup friendships to reduce prejudice was generalized to other groups not involved in the initial contact. Such wide generalization of empathetic feelings flowing from intergroup friendships challenges theories of prejudice that are based exclusively on cognitive considerations.

Conclusion

Future advances in the understanding of intergroup prejudice will feature affect. These advances will employ emotion to explain better the situational specificity of prejudice, the relationship between prejudice and intergroup violence, and the dissociations typically found between stereotyping, discriminatory acts, and prejudice. Indeed, the study of prejudice affords an ideal realm in which to study the complex interrelations between emotion, cognition, and behavior.

See also: AGGRESSION; ANGER; ANXIETY; FEAR AND PHOBIAS; HATE; HATE CRIMES; XENOPHOBIA

Bibliography

Allport, Gordon W. (1954). *The Nature of Prejudice.* Reading, MA: Addison-Wesley.

Bless, Herbert; Schwarz, Norbert; and Kemmelmeier, Markus. (1996). "Mood and Stereotyping." *European Review of Social Psychology* 7:63–93.

Devine, Patricia G., and Monteith, Margo J. (1993). "The Role of Discrepancy-Associated Affect in Prejudice Reduction." In *Affect, Cognition, and Stereotyping: Interactive Processes in Group Perception,* ed. Diane M. Mackie and David L. Hamilton. San Diego, CA: Academic Press.

Dijker, Anton J. M. (1987). "Emotional Reactions to Ethnic Minorities." *European Journal of Social Psychology* 17:305–325.

Dovidio, John F., and Gaertner, Samuel L. (1993). "Stereotypes and Evaluative Intergroup Bias." In *Affect, Cognition, and Stereotyping: Interactive Processes in Group Perception,* ed. Diane M. Mackie and David L. Hamilton. San Diego, CA: Academic Press.

Esses, Victoria M.; Haddock, Geoffrey; and Zanna, Mark P. (1993). "Values, Stereotypes, and Emotions as Determinants of Intergroup Attitudes." In *Affect, Cognition, and Stereotyping: Interactive Processes in Group Perception,* ed. Diane M. Mackie and David L. Hamilton. San Diego, CA: Academic Press.

Esses, Victoria M.; Jackson, Lynne M.; Nolan, Jeffery M.; and Armstrong, Tamara L. (1998). "Economic Threat and Attitudes Toward Immigrants." In *Immigrant Canada: Demographic, Economic and Social Challenges,* ed. Shiva S. Halli and Leo Drieger. Toronto: University of Toronto Press.

Forgas, Joseph P. (1995). "Mood and Judgment: The Affect Infusion Model (AIM)." *Psychological Bulletin* 117:39–66.

Greenberg, Jeff; Solomon, Sheldon; and Pyszczynski, Tom. (1997). "Terror Management Theory of Self-Esteem and Cultural Worldviews: Empirical Assessments and Conceptual Refinements." In *Advances in Experimental Social Psychology,* ed. Mark P. Zanna. San Diego, CA: Academic Press.

Katz, Irvin, and Hass, R. Glen. (1988). "Racial Ambivalence and American Value Conflict: Correlational and Priming Studies of Dual Cognitive Structures." *Journal of Personality and Social Psychology* 55:893–905.

Pettigrew, Thomas F. (1997). "Generalized Intergroup Contact Effects on Prejudice." *Personality and Social Psychology Bulletin* 23:173–185.

Pettigrew, Thomas F., and Meertens, Roel W. (1995). "Subtle and Blatant Prejudice in Western Europe." *European Journal of Social Psychology* 57:57–75.

Sales, Stephen M., and Friend, Kenneth E. (1973). "Success and Failure as Determinants of Level of Authoritarianism." *Behavioral Science* 18:163–172.

Sears, David O. (1988). "Symbolic Racism." In *Eliminating Racism: Profiles in Controversy,* ed. Phyllis A. Katz and Dalmas A. Taylor. New York: Plenum.

Smith, Eliot R. (1993). "Social Identity and Social Emotions: Toward New Conceptions of Prejudice." In *Affect, Cognition, and*

Stereotyping: Interactive Processes in Group Perception, ed. Diane M. Mackie and David L. Hamilton. San Diego, CA: Academic Press.

Stangor, Charles; Sullivan, Linda A.; and Ford, Thomas E. (1991). "Affective and Cognitive Determinants of Prejudice." *Social Cognition* 9:359–380.

Stephan, Walter G., and Stephan, Cookie W. (1985). "Intergroup Anxiety." *Journal of Social Issues* 41:157–176.

Stephan, Walter G., and Stephan, Cookie W. (1993). "Cognition and Affect in Stereotyping: Parallel Interactive Networks." In *Affect, Cognition, and Stereotyping: Interactive Processes in Group Perception*, ed. Diane M. Mackie and David L. Hamilton. San Diego, CA: Academic Press.

Stephan, Walter G., and Stephan, Cookie W. (1996). "Predicting Prejudice." *International Journal of Intercultural Relations* 20: 409–426.

Wilder, David. (1993). "The Role of Anxiety in Facilitating Stereotypic Judgments in Group Perception." In *Affect, Cognition, and Stereotyping: Interactive Processes in Group Perception*, ed. Diane M. Mackie and David L. Hamilton. San Diego, CA: Academic Press.

Zanna, Mark P. (1994). "On the Nature of Prejudice." *Canadian Psychology* 35:11–23.

Thomas F. Pettigrew

PROPAGANDA

Every day, people are bombarded with one persuasive message after another. The average American will view more than seven million advertisements in her or his lifetime—advertisements that often play on social insecurities or desires for fame, fortune, sex, and belonging. The average American will watch more than 1,150 hours of television and listen to more than 1,160 hours of radio each year, including programs that scare people, compel them to laugh, make them feel superior or inferior, and arouse their hatred for their neighbors. More than 6.4 million sales agents in the United States will attempt to sell people things by arousing guilt, playing on the need for social recognition, or taking advantage of the desire to honor the norms of society. In everyday social relations, individuals may encounter the local gossip who tries to advance a cause by getting them to deprecate another or the friends and family members who use feelings of

> *Voltaire's* Candide *(1759) finds the gullible Candide subject to many kinds of propaganda, from Dr. Pangloss's insistence that, in spite of war and rape and misery, this is the best of all possible worlds, to the Inquisitors who blame all nonbelievers for every evil (including earthquakes) and who feel justified in punishing them by whipping or hanging.*

love to get the individuals to do something. Many of these messages can be classified as propaganda.

Propaganda is the use of short slogans, symbols, and messages that play on the target's emotions and prejudices. The goal of propaganda is to promote the adoption of a certain predefined position, belief, or behavior that is advocated by the propagandist. With their emotions aroused, individuals may not think clearly about that course of action and instead may adopt a position or execute a behavior merely to appease their passions.

Propaganda can be contrasted with other forms of persuasion such as debate, argument, discussion, or a well-crafted speech that presents the case for or against a given proposition. By presenting multiple sides of an issue, these forms of influence encourage deliberative persuasion or persuasion that invites thought, reflection, and analysis of the issues at hand. A democracy thrives on deliberative persuasion that allows the thoughtful citizen to discover the best course of action as opposed to emotional propaganda that locks the target into opinions and behaviors that he or she may not have ordinarily adopted.

How Are Emotions Used in Propaganda?

An effective emotional propaganda tactic follows this simple formula: arouse an emotion (e.g., fear or a threat to self-esteem) and then offer the target a way to respond to that emotion that just happens to be the course of action that is desired by the propagandist. Emotional appeals work because the target becomes preoccupied with dealing with the emotions that are aroused by the propaganda. Thought about the issue is truncated as the target devotes all of her or his energies to escaping a negative emotion or securing a positive one. The clever propagandist provides a course of action that allows the target a way of responding to these emotions—for example, eliminating fear by supporting a leader or gaining self-esteem by strengthening one's commitment to the group and cause.

Consider a trip by a husband and wife to buy some furniture. The prospective customers look over a variety of pieces and make a preliminary decision to purchase. However, since it is an expensive purchase, the couple decides to go home and think it over. As they are leaving the store, the sales clerk announces that they "better purchase today, because at the end of the month the manufacturer will be raising prices." The couple immediately feels a sense of urgency and panic and, not wishing to pay more for their furniture, makes the purchase. This simple exchange illustrates the formula for effective emotional propaganda. First, by threatening a price increase, the sales clerk arouses emotions of panic and urgency. Next, the couple is given a way to reduce these negative feelings—an immediate purchase. The emotion of panic overwhelms the ability of the couple to think about the purchase: Should they shop for a better price? Is the furniture well-made? Can they afford the price? Will the next store have something they like better? Instead, they have one thought: If we do not buy it now, then we will lose it.

Or consider another example of the use of emotional propaganda—the now infamous Willie Horton advertisement used by the George Bush campaign against Michael Dukakis in the 1988 U.S. presidential campaign. This advertisement tells the story of Horton, a black man who had been sent to prison for murder. During a time when Dukakis was governor, Horton was released on a prison furlough program where he escaped and raped a white woman after stabbing her companion. The advertisement plays on the voters' darkest fears—fear of crime and, in the case of white Americans, fear of African Americans. And there is a simple way to respond to these fears—disparage Dukakis as being weak on crime and vote for his opponent. The emotion of fear truncates further thought; the voter, for example, does not think about whether Dukakis was really to blame, whether similar incidents happened to other governors (or in the federal system under Bush and his predecessor Ronald Reagan), or whether there is value in the prison-release programs. The passions prevent the type of deliberative persuasion that is needed in a democracy.

Some Common Emotional Propaganda Tactics

The use of emotions to persuade goes back to the ancient Greeks (if not earlier). For example, Aristotle, in his book *On Rhetoric,* describes how to arouse emotions such as fear, shame, envy, kindness, and anger in an audience and how to use such emotions to accomplish the goals of the speaker. What emotions are typically used in today's propaganda? Although emotional propaganda can be as varied as human experience, some specific emotions and tactics are used extensively by the propagandist, including fear, guilt, granfalloon, the norm of reciprocity, and commitment.

Fear

Adolf Hitler warned his fellow Nazis of the impending threat to Germany from Jews and communists. Life insurance agents scare potential customers with tales of financial disaster for the loved-ones who are left behind. Purveyors of alternative medicines raise fears of the medical establishment and of the safety of the food supply. All of these examples make use of fear

to persuade. What makes for an effective fear appeal? Research has shown that not all fear appeals are effective, but the ones that are must meet the following three conditions: (a) raise high levels of fear, (b) offer a specific recommendation for overcoming the fear-arousing threat, and (c) make the target believe that he or she can perform the recommended action. For example, Howard Leventhal (1970) and his colleagues gave college students scary messages about the need to get a tetanus shot. However, only when he gave specific instructions about where and when the shots were available did the students actually obtain the tetanus shots. The successful fear appeal thus follows the general formula for effective emotional propaganda. First, raise a fear (of, for example, communists, financial ruin, or unsafe food). The target then is overwhelmed by the emotion to the extent that rational thought is terminated, at which point the target looks for a simple way to deal with the fear. If such a simple action is not available, the targets of the fear appeal may feel overpowered and "bury their heads in the sand." However, most propagandist provide such simple solutions

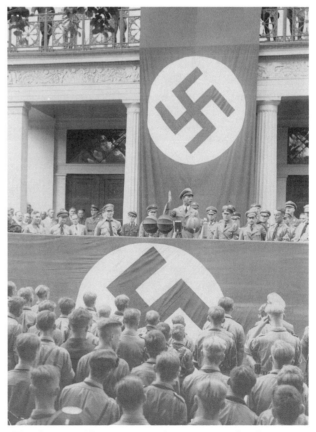

The German Nazi minister for propaganda, Joseph Goebbels, delivered a speech to foreign Hitler Youth members who had assembled in Berlin in August 1935. (Corbis/Hulton-Deutsch Collection)

for dealing with fear—such as voting Nazi, buying insurance, or purchasing alternative health care and different foods.

Guilt

The following is a sales pitch that was used by a fraudulent telemarketer to induce an elderly woman to invest in a phony financial scheme: "Suppose you could go to your grave knowing that you will not be a burden to anyone and that you can leave this earth knowing that those you love will have enough money to live a happy and prosperous life?" Such an appeal plays on guilt or the feeling of responsibility that people have for righting a wrongdoing or meeting an obligation. In this case, the fraudulent telemarketer played on the woman's guilt to keep her from thinking about the value of an investment—her thoughts were instead focused on her feelings of guilt about being a burden and not doing enough for her children. An experiment by J. Merrill Carlsmith and Alan Gross (1969) illustrates how guilt can lead to compliance. In this study, some subjects were led to believe that they had painfully shocked another person. (The other subjects merely noted that another person occasionally gave wrong answers in a learning situation.) At the end of the experiment, those subjects who believed that they had given unwarranted shocks (and thus felt guilty) were three times as likely to reply to a request to make phone calls for a committee to save redwood trees as the other subjects in the study. Subsequent research showed that guilt arouses a desire to make restitution for misdeeds and to repair a self-image that has been tarnished by a transgression.

Granfalloon

According to the novelist Kurt Vonnegut (1963), the granfalloon is a "proud and meaningless association of human beings," such as a Hoosier, a Buckeye, or a devotee of Paul Klee or Wassily Kandinsky. Sometimes the granfalloon can take on special meaning, such as Nazis, social psychologists, or the Fraternal Order of Police. Research by Henri Tajfel (1981) demonstrates that it is remarkably easy to place people in a granfalloon, often requiring no more than applying a simple label or group name to the individual and thus creating feelings of "we" versus "them." At the heart of the granfalloon tactic is the human tendency to want to associate with desired social identities. This allows the propagandist to use the granfalloon in at least two ways to secure compliance. First, the granfalloon provides a simple rule to tell the individual what to believe and do; in other words, "I am a _____ (fill in the blank with a social identity) and we do and believe _____ (fill in the blank with the appropriate identity-related behavior and belief)." Second,

since many social identities become important sources of self-esteem, propagandists can play on this emotion by focusing threats to this source of self-esteem and then providing a means, compatible with the propagandist's goals, for dealing with these threats. For example, a target can be told "If you are really one of us, you'll do this," or "Our enemies are attacking us; to defeat them you must do this."

Norm of Reciprocity

In human (and some animal) societies, there exists a norm of reciprocity—"if I do something for you, you should do something for me in return." Just the thought of breaking this norm (as with most norms) can produce a queasy feeling in the pit of one's stomach. Many people have had the experience of being invited to a terrible dinner and then being placed on the horns of a dilemma: Does one reciprocate and have another dreadful evening or does one live with that uneasy feeling of failing to reciprocate? In the 1960s, the Hare Krishnas, a religious cult, found a highly profitable way to make use of the norm of reciprocity. In airports and other public settings, a member of the Krishnas would approach a target and simply present a gift of a flower. The gift of a flower established a feeling of obligation and indebtedness that the Krishnas ensured could be repaid in only one way—by a contribution to their religion. Similarly, Dennis Regan (1971) showed in a simple experiment the power that the norm of reciprocity has to persuade. In his study, an accomplice of the experimenter left the room and returned either empty-handed or with two sodas (one for himself and one for the subject). At the end of the experiment, the accomplice sold twice as many raffle tickets when the subject received a gift of a soda (which invoked the norm of reciprocity) compared to when no soda was given.

Commitment

Consistency may or may not be the hobgoblin of little minds, but it is the basis of the propaganda tactic of commitment. As a personality trait, self-consistency implies that a person is honorable, logical, and true to her or his word, whereas inconsistency is considered to be undesirable. In general, people seek to live up to their commitments to avoid the feelings of disgrace that come with backing out on a promise. The desire to honor commitments is an important basis for the functioning of any society. (Imagine a world were no one could be trusted.) However, attempts to maintain self-consistency can be used as a propaganda device. This can be seen in an experiment that was conducted by Jonathan Freedman and Scott Fraser (1966) on the foot-in-the-door technique. In this study, a group of homeowners were asked to put up a huge, unattractive sign in their front yards that read "Drive Carefully." Only 17 percent complied. However, another group of homeowners were first asked to sign a petition that favored safe driving (which nearly everyone did). A few weeks later, the same homeowners were asked to put up the ugly sign. More than 55 percent of these residents, in an attempt to be consistent to their first commitment, put up the "Drive Carefully" sign in their front yards. Although this example is relatively benign, the commitment trap can often serve darker purposes. For example, former Secretary of Defense Robert McNamara saw the U.S. involvement in Vietnam during the 1960s as a series of failed commitments and attempts to make good on them. Cults often recruit new members in a series of ever-increasing commitments—attending weekly meetings, going to a weekend retreat, small and then larger donations, communal living, submission to authority, and then total obedience. From outside of the cult, it looks strange when members adopt unconventional lifestyles or even commit suicide; however, from inside, these "strange" behaviors appear to be merely the next small step in an attempt to act consistently with past commitments.

What Can Be Done About Emotional Propaganda?

On some occasions, emotions can be used to stimulate thought and deliberative persuasion. For example, Abraham Lincoln, in his Gettysburg Address, aroused the emotion of patriotism to induce Americans to think about the meaning of their country and creed. However, much of the use of emotions in persuasion can be classified as propaganda. How can people prevent this unwanted propaganda? Although the answer is complex, three simple steps are particularly useful.

First, people must monitor their emotions. If they notice that they are having an emotional response to a communication, they should ask "Why?" People should look for things that might induce emotions, such as a "free" gift that induces a feeling of obligation or a guilt-trip or a we-they distinction that elicits the granfalloon. The first step to taking actions is realizing that one is the target of an emotional appeal.

Second, if people feel their emotions are being played on, they should get out of the situation and then analyze what was going on. If they cannot physically remove themselves from the situation, they should redefine the situation mentally until they can escape. It is very difficult to fight propaganda when emotions are high and one is in a situation where more propaganda can be delivered to counter any attempt to dismiss it.

Finally, people must go on the offensive and identify common propaganda appeals and try to stop them at their source. This may include teaching others about propaganda, enacting legislation to prevent some of its more deceptive forms, and making the use of emotional propaganda a criteria in forming decisions and judgments. The politician, advertiser, or presumed friend who plays on emotions to get people to adopt a course of action should not be rewarded with consent. Instead people should consider anyone who would speak to them in this manner as being suspect and worthy of close scrutiny.

See also: ADVERTISING; ARISTOTLE; ATTITUDES; COMMITMENT; FEAR AND PHOBIAS; GIFT GIVING; GUILT; ORATORY; PERSUASION; PREJUDICE; SELF-ESTEEM

Bibliography

Aristotle. (1991). *On Rhetoric*, tr. George A. Kennedy. New York: Oxford University Press.

Carlsmith, J. Merrill, and Gross, Alan. (1969). "Some Effects of Guilt on Compliance." *Journal of Personality and Social Psychology* 11:232–239.

Cialdini, Robert B. (1984). *Influence*. New York: William Morrow.

Freedman, Jonathan, and Fraser, Scott. (1966). "Compliance without Pressure: The Foot-in-the-Door Technique." *Journal of Personality and Social Psychology* 4:195–202.

Leventhal, Howard. (1970). "Findings and Theory in the Study of Fear Communications." In *Advances in Experimental Social Psychology, Vol. 5*, ed. Leonard Berkowitz. New York: Academic Press.

Pratkanis, Anthony R. (1997). "The Social Psychology of Mass Communications: An American Perspective." In *States of Mind*, ed. Diane F. Halpern and Alexander E. Voiskounsky. New York: Oxford University Press.

Pratkanis, Anthony R., and Aronson, Elliot. (1992). *Age of Propaganda: The Everyday Use and Abuse of Persuasion*. New York: W. H. Freeman.

Pratkanis, Anthony R., and Turner, Marlene E. (1996). "Persuasion and Democracy: Strategies for Increasing Deliberative Participation and Enacting Social Change." *Journal of Social Issues* 52:187–205.

Regan, Dennis T. (1971). "Effects of a Favor and Liking on Compliance." *Journal of Experimental Social Psychology* 7:627–639.

Tajfel, Henri. (1981). *Human Groups and Social Categories.* Cambridge, Eng.: Cambridge University Press.

Vonnegut, Kurt. (1963). *Cat's Cradle.* New York: Dell.

de Waal, Frans. (1998). *Chimpanzee Politics.* Baltimore, MD: Johns Hopkins University Press.

Anthony R. Pratkanis

PSYCHOANALYTIC PERSPECTIVE

Sigmund Freud revolutionized the understanding of human emotions when in 1895 he collaborated with

Joseph Breuer in writing "Studies on Hysteria." Psychoanalysis, with its emphasis on unconscious emotional disturbances, evolved from their efforts to understand hysterics, patients who had unusual physical problems, such as paralysis or blindness, that could not be explained by medical findings. These patients appeared strangely at ease and demonstrated a lack of concern for their physical impairment; the expected emotional reactions of alarm or fear were absent. Freud discovered that by having these patients freely talk about whatever came to mind, regardless of its seeming irrelevance, a torrent of emotions could be unleashed, followed by a disappearance of the "physical" symptom. This catharsis or emotional release provided crucial insight into the role emotions played in causing psychopathology. Freud suspected that the physical symptoms were the by-product of a past traumatic experience during which emotions were not discharged. Although he later modified his emphasis on actual traumatic experiences, the notion of conscious and unconscious experience and the distinction between cognitive and emotional aspects of psychological functioning would continue to influence his concept of affect. Psychoanalysts use the term *affect* to describe the physiological, cognitive, and experiential qualities that constitute an *emotion*, a practice that will be used in this entry.

Psychoanalysis has never produced a comprehensive or unified theory of affect, despite the obvious importance of this concept. Freud himself struggled to integrate his hypotheses about affect with his thinking about innate drives related to sexuality (libido) and aggression. He abandoned his goal of an integrated biological and psychological theory early on yet continued to view affects as the representatives of biological drives, with the result that affect remained ubiquitous and ill defined within psychoanalysis. Since Freud's time, psychoanalytic theorists have expanded and revised his concepts with relatively little progress in clarifying the role of affect in relation to biology and cognition.

The Traditional Psychoanalytic Perspective on Affect

Freud's model of psychological functioning has been characterized as "drive theory." He suggested that two innate drives or instincts form the foundation of personality. These drives, libido and aggression, exist on a continuum between pleasure and unpleasure. Libido refers to pleasurable characteristics, including but not limited to physical and sexual gratification. Aggression has been alternately defined as a contrasting destructive impulse and an adaptive force that leads to differentiation and development of the self. Libido and aggression represent hypothetical forces that cannot be observed in their pure state. Once one is aware of a mental event, the drives have already been organized through associations to ideas and physical sensations.

Although his thoughts about affect were never fully articulated, Freud recognized that emotions and their disturbances were central to neuroses. He elaborated their development and role in psychic functioning in two 1915 metapsychological writings, "Repression" and "The Unconscious." An affect represents a feeling tone that accompanies an idea or mental representation, and both represent transformations of instinctual energy. Affects are characterized by sensations of pleasure or unpleasure that are accompanied by physiological reactions and arousal. By consensus, affects are defined in common terms such as joy, anger, and sadness even though each person experiences them differently. Ideas, the cognitive manifestation of instincts, involve thoughts and attributions, which are related to the affects and may be conscious or unconscious in nature. Since instincts are organized into both affective and ideational components, disparities can result as in the case of hysteria where the original idea has been repressed into the unconscious and the potential for affective experience has been blocked.

Most people would endorse the idea that affects could exist outside of consciousness, yet Freud was unable to reconcile the possibility of unconscious affect with his tenets related to the physiology and experience of affects. The physiological component of affect involves autonomic and voluntary aspects of the nervous system. The former involve such reactions as pulse and heart rate; the latter might include facial expressions and vocal tone. The experiential component involves its subjective classification in terms of pleasure and unpleasure. Finally, the cognitive component involves conscious and unconscious ideas, fantasies, and attributions that give meaning to the other components. According to Freud, only the ideational element of affect could exist in the unconscious, while affects, because of their physiological and experiential aspects, could not undergo a similar repression. In "The Unconscious," Freud put it simply and eloquently: "It is surely of the essence of an emotion that we should feel it, i.e. that it should enter consciousness. So for emotions, feelings, and affects to be unconscious would be quite out of the question." Only the idea originally associated with the affect has undergone repression and become unconscious. The experiential and physiological components of the affect are not realized but remain as potentials for certain kinds of experience. Successful repression will reduce the experience of unpleasure, specifically anxiety, whereas unsuccessful repression can result in signal anxiety and symptom formation.

Psychoanalytic Revisions to the Theory of Affect

Freud's final conception of affect is contained in "Inhibitions, Symptoms, and Anxiety" (1926), where he focused on anxiety as the prototypical signal of distress at the emergence of instinctual material into consciousness. The ego modified and controlled affects through repression and other defense mechanisms. Psychologists further integrated affect and cognition under the auspices of the ego, the agency of the mind that is charged with mediating between instinctual drives, external circumstances, and a developing sense of the self and others. With her book, *The Ego and the Mechanisms of Defense* (1936), Anna Freud became an early proponent of ego psychology by elaborating on various defense mechanisms and describing their role in adaptive and pathological conditions. Her focus on normal and pathological development highlighted the continuity between adaptive and maladaptive affect, both of which involve a mixture of experience and biology. For example, anger and aggressive actions can facilitate a child's sense of autonomy and his or her ability to tolerate separation from a caregiver, or they can reflect inadequate defenses against the aggressive drive. Her concept of "developmental lines" provided a means for describing normal and pathological development, as well as its inconsistencies, across a range of domains that are important to psychological development, including feeding, control of bodily functions, and play and language skills.

Other theorists expanded on the dual instinct theory by emphasizing an innate tendency or drive for relatedness. Adherents to a relational perspective supplement traditional psychoanalytic theory with an emphasis on the relationship between infant and caregiver as the foundation for personality development. Proponents of the object relations and attachment perspectives emphasize the development of schemata or representations of oneself and others that are organized along cognitive and affective dimensions and form templates for subsequent development, relationships, and psychopathology.

Otto Kernberg (1976) proposed a theory of object relations suggesting that biological drives derive from primary affects, rather than the reverse. From this perspective, primitive affects of pleasure and unpleasure form the basis for the emergence of positive and negative emotions, respectively. The nature of early experiences of pleasure and unpleasure in turn influence how sexual and aggressive drives are organized and directed. The roots of these changes to psychoanalytic theory are seen in Freud's later modifications with regard to affect, where he emphasized the role of the ego in mediating affective experience and the communicative aspects of affect in signaling intrapsychic danger.

John Bowlby (1969, 1973), a British psychoanalyst, extended Charles Darwin's (1872) observations of similarities in the affective expressions of humans and animals to emphasize the evolutionary advantage of a close relationship between caregiver and offspring. His attachment theory departed from traditional analytic theory, which viewed the parent-child relationship as being based on drive satisfaction through activities such as feeding and physical comfort, and it elevated the bond between parent and child to the status of a primary motivation for behavior. He identified three innate patterns of attachment, which form the emotional templates for subsequent relationships. A secure pattern of attachment arises out of consistent and responsive caregiving, while two forms of anxious attachment result from erratic or unresponsive caregiving and increase the likelihood of psychopathology. Children with anxious-ambivalent attachments may be prone to impulsivity, irritability, and low frustration tolerance; those children with an anxious-avoidant style are more likely to be characterized as hostile or antisocial in their behavior. Within attachment theory, psychopathology and emotional dysfunction represent maladaptive outcomes in the process of integrating affective, cognitive, relational, and biological aspects of the attachment system.

Some relational theorists reject drive theory altogether in favor of a position that asserts the primacy of affects in motivating behavior and defensive activity. They suggest that affective ties between child and caregiver provide the basis for internalization of representations or schemas about the self and others. Drives are seen as being superfluous, and affects are considered to derive their meaning from individuals' attributions about diffuse states of physiological arousal that arise in the context of early relationships. Affects are first experienced as diffuse states of arousal, which are subsequently organized through conscious or unconscious cognitive attributions of meaning.

The interaction of biological maturation and psychological development intertwines in child psychoanalytic theories of development. Infants first learn about affects through interactions with (predominantly) their mothers, who attribute emotional meaning to their actions. Satisfaction of physical needs, such as food and comfort, results in pleasure and diminished physical tension. Frustration of physical needs leads to a corresponding increase in physiological arousal along with unpleasure and frustration. The gradual accumulation of benign and frustrating experiences and their affective associations form mental representations of oneself and others that can eventually be drawn on as internal symbols of experience. Affects become less dependent upon immediate experience with another and can be experienced through memory and mental representation. Cognitive maturation, especially the ability to symbolize experience through play and language, propels overall development, including affective differentiation. The capacity to use defense mechanisms to modulate or disguise unacceptable affects allows still greater complexity, including the capacity to experience competing feelings simultaneously.

Affect in Psychoanalytic Treatment

People consult psychotherapists because of affective disturbances, interpersonal problems, or behaviors that result in personal distress or consequences. Freud reportedly commented, "Psychoanalysis deals with feelings. What else could it possibly be dealing with?" Psychoanalytic treatment elicits affective responses from patients with the assumption that awareness of disturbing affects and their subsequent integration with other aspects of psychological functioning results in therapeutic benefit.

Clinicians focus on patients' affective experiences or lack of appropriate affective expression. Kernberg (1976) suggested that the analyst should attempt to understand the affective content of a session in order to learn about enduring patterns of processing information about the self and others, and beginning therapists are often urged to focus on affective material as they attempt to understand their patients. Clinicians modulate patients' distress through defense analysis, highlighting strategies used to keep certain affects and affective experiences at bay. In contrast, cognitive behavioral treatments tend to focus on the acquisition of rational and logical cognition as a means for controlling or reducing negative affect.

Anxiety, Depression, Guilt, and Unconscious Affect

Throughout Freud's writings, anxiety serves as a signal for the failure of defensive activity and the emergence of forbidden, instinctual impulses. In "Inhibitions, Symptoms, and Anxiety" (1926), Freud elaborated his mature view of anxiety as a response to real or imagined danger. Psychic danger and anxiety become the focus for psychoanalysis, as they are viewed as real dangers by an immature ego that is incapable of distinguishing between psychological and objective danger. Freud tied his view of anxiety as the core of all neuroses to the structural model of personality, consisting of the id, ego, and superego. Psychoanalysis

began to emphasize the functions of the ego in terms of defensive activity and mediation of intrapsychic and external reality. The ego became the source of affective differentiation and defensive activity in response to the developmental achievement of signal anxiety as a response to insufficiently disguised instincts.

Charles Brenner (1982) questioned the stature of anxiety as a unique affect in the formation of psychological conflict. He maintained Freud's view that when drives become associated with unpleasure they result in conflict and defensive activity, but he also suggested that unpleasure can be divided into two primary affects, anxiety and depression. Anxiety represented unpleasure with the anticipation of danger occurring in the future. In contrast, depression consisted of unpleasure accompanied by the idea that the negative event has already occurred. Defenses can be mobilized to decrease either anxious or depressive affect, the nature of which is determined by its ideational content. While disputes continue with regard to Brenner's elevation of depression onto a par with anxiety, his approach exemplifies one manner in which psychoanalysts have expanded Freudian theory with its emphasis on anxiety as the precursor to psychopathology.

Guilt represents a complex affective state that may range from remorse to harsh self-recrimination for committing real or imagined actions of a reprehensible nature. Freud (1923) suggested that the third structural component of the mind, the superego, embodies an internalized sense of self-reproach and conscience that is originally based on parental prohibitions and expectations. Since parental standards are internalized during childhood through superego development, affects such as guilt and shame must also be viewed as unconscious. External experiences with caregivers become internal and unconsciously connected to aggressive and sexual drives. Freud spoke of an unconscious sense of guilt, which could motivate a range of psychopathology, including suicidal and delinquent activity. This apparent contradiction of earlier statements rejecting unconscious affect became problematic for Freud's theory as guilt became the leading edge in the debate about whether affects can be unconscious.

Many psychoanalysts have taken exception with Freud's rejection of unconscious affect, suggesting that in maintaining his basic tenets about drives he provided an unwieldy account of affect that failed to explain how people can be completely unaware of their emotions. Revisionist-minded analysts adopted two approaches to explain how affects can be unconscious. The first group, as exemplified by Brenner (1982), continued to view psychoanalysis from the perspective of drive theory while asserting that affects can become unconscious through defensive processes.

Drew Westen (1998) dispensed with drives altogether and argued that affects are the primary building blocks for internal representations and can remain as unconscious motivators of behavior and defensive activity. The conscious experience of an affect may differ markedly from its unconscious counterpart.

Biological and Developmental Influences

Ironically, neuroscience has provided renewed support for Freud's original goal of a neurologically based theory of mind. For example, Freud described two types of mental processing, primary and secondary. Primary process operated according to the pleasure principle as the mind sought gratification of sexual and aggressive drives without concern for reality or consequences. Secondary process was governed by the ego and its ability to use logic and defenses to mediate between reality, drives, and primitive affects that arise from the id. Neuroscientists have since described two types of emotional processing, one an innate, automatic product of evolutionary adaptation and the other based on individual experience and learning. The first type of emotional processing, according to Joseph LeDoux (1996), suggests that much emotional processing and experience remains unconscious.

The physiological substrates of affect have been localized to various areas within the brain, particularly the amygdala, the frontal cortex, and the limbic system. From the perspectives of psychoanalysis and neurobiology, affective differentiation is a developmental achievement that is inextricably linked to biological maturation. Certain experiences are not possible until sufficient neuronal maturation occurs during critical periods of childhood development. Andrew Schwartz (1991) suggested that affects originate in the limbic system and the amygdala and that they comprise the primary source of human motivation. Individuals experience pleasant and aversive sensations that serve as positive and negative reinforcers within the brain. These conditioned sensations of pleasure and unpleasure are elaborated and acquire the psychological attributes of emotions. Despite debate about the location of emotional encoding within the brain, psychoanalytic and biological approaches emerge on a shared ground and bring complementary data to this aspect of human experience.

Developmental psychopathology provides common ground for professionals from a range of biological and psychological perspectives through three basic assumptions: (1) normal and abnormal development exists on a continuum rather than as discrete categories of functioning, (2) researchers focus on the identification of adaptive and maladaptive developmental pathways that influence subsequent development, and

(3) developmental pathways can be altered by constitutional, psychological, and environmental factors that heighten risk or promote resiliency in relation to psychopathology. Within this realm, researchers who concentrate on infants, such as Margaret Mahler and her colleagues (1975) and Daniel Stern (1985), have elaborated on how a caregiver's affective responses govern an infant's emerging capacities for symbolizing affective experience, becoming aware of oneself, and recognizing distinctions between oneself and others.

Another significant attainment involves children's capacity for modulation or regulation of their emotions. Affect regulation involves automatic procedures that are used to reduce unpleasant affect states and sustain pleasant affect states. One strategy involves the use of defense mechanisms to detect and modify affects prior to their emergence into consciousness. Caregiving relationships, cognitive development (including play and language skills), and predictability in the external world facilitate affect regulatory capacities. The ability to contend effectively with feelings fosters a child's sense of internal stability and adaptation to external circumstances, while deficits in affect regulation can result in impulsivity and other serious behavior problems.

Criticisms of the Psychoanalytic Approach

Psychoanalytic approaches have been criticized as lacking scientific justification and failing to consider variations in normative psychological functioning that are attributable to gender and ethnic differences.

In an era of cost containment, where medications and brief cognitive-behavioral treatments are favored, the practice of psychoanalysis has declined. While few individuals opt for this intensive treatment of four or more sessions per week over a number of years, psychoanalysis remains active as a theoretical perspective for guiding therapeutic practice. Mary Target and Peter Fonagy (1994) of the Anna Freud Centre in London reviewed treatment effectiveness for more than three hundred children who received psychoanalysis or long-term, intensive psychotherapy. Most of the children benefited from treatment, but those who received psychoanalysis derived the greatest benefit. Target and Fonagy concluded that severe childhood psychopathology may require intensive and long-term methods of treatment.

Psychoanalytic clinicians have developed brief methods of treatment. Hans Strupp and his colleagues (1984) developed a short-term model of psychoanalytic therapy (of approximately six months duration) that focuses on a patient's prominent, maladaptive relational pattern. The therapist effects change by heightening awareness and exploring alternatives to this pattern as it is manifested in the treatment relationship and the patient's discussions of life events. Another brief treatment, interpersonal therapy for depression, targets disturbed patterns of relating that are evident in patients' everyday interactions and contribute to depressive feelings and symptoms. By changing these relational behaviors, patients develop more satisfying relationships and more positive feelings about themselves. Myrna Weissman and John Markowitz (1994) have found that interpersonal therapy appears to be as effective as antidepressant medication and relatively more effective than cognitive-behavioral therapy for the treatment of severe depression, while the three treatments seem comparable in treating moderate depression.

Psychoanalytic researchers have studied the relation of affective representations to psychopathology. Westen (1998) studied the emotional quality or "affect tone" of representations of people and relationships as they ranged from malevolent to benign. For patients who had borderline personality disorder, a history of maternal psychopathology was related to a malevolent view of relationships, along with decreased emotional investment and a tendency to experience relationships as disappointing and painful. Sidney Blatt and Richard Ford (1994) described two types of depression, anaclitic and introjective, which arise from the emotionally salient interactions between children and caregivers. Patients who have anaclitic depression struggle with issues that are related to loss, mistrust, and unsatisfied longings for intimacy. Those patients who have introjective depression struggle with aggressive impulses and an unstable sense of the self and are characterized by withdrawal, guilt, and self-punishment. Carl Gacono and J. Reid Meloy (1994) studied criminally involved adolescents and adults and found indicators of emotional detachment, indifference to relationships, and decreased tolerance or experience of anxiety, all of which heightened the potential for aggressive actions marked by a lack of remorse.

Psychoanalytic theories of emotional development have also been criticized for their emphasis on male experience as the standard for healthy development. The Oedipal Conflict, where boys substitute longings for their mother for an identification with their same-sex parent, has been particularly controversial for its relative neglect of female development. Although women, including Anna Freud and Melanie Klein, have been central to the development of psychoanalytic theory, feminist theorists have prompted important theoretical revisions. Jean Baker Miller (1976) retained the psychoanalytic emphasis on early experience and unconscious processing and shifted from traditional drive theory to an object relations approach that emphasizes the earliest caregiving relationships as the first template for personality and emotional development.

Similar charges have been leveled at psychoanalysis for neglecting racial, ethnic, and cultural differences by valuing insight and individuality as hallmarks of normal development. Once again, these criticisms provided a motivation for broadening the psychoanalytic scope to reflect cultural differences. For example, cultural variations influence the nature and affective tone of relational schemas, and J. Manuel Casas (1995) has asserted that many non-Western cultures maintain a standard of close intergenerational relationships that might be interpreted as a lack of independence from a traditional viewpoint.

See also: AGGRESSION; ATTACHMENT; BOWLBY, JOHN; COGNITIVE PERSPECTIVE; CONSCIOUSNESS; DEFENSE MECHANISMS; ERIKSON, ERIK HOMBURGER; FREUD, ANNA; FREUD, SIGMUND; HORNEY, KAREN; HUMAN DEVELOPMENT; MOOD DISORDERS; NEUROBIOLOGY OF EMOTIONS; PERSONALITY; PSYCHOLOGY OF EMOTIONS; PSYCHOPHYSIOLOGY OF EMOTIONS; PSYCHOTHERAPY; SULLIVAN, HARRY STACK

Bibliography

Blatt, Sidney J., and Ford, Richard Q. (1994). *Therapeutic Change: An Object Relations Perspective.* New York: Plenum.

Bowlby, John. (1969). *Attachment and Loss, Vol. 1: Attachment.* New York: Basic Books.

Bowlby, John. (1973). *Attachment and Loss, Vol. 2: Separation.* New York: Basic Books.

Brenner, Charles. (1982). *The Mind in Conflict.* Madison, CT: International Universities Press.

Breuer, Joseph, and Freud, Sigmund. ([1895] 1955). "Studies on Hysteria." In *The Standard Edition of the Complete Psychological Works of Sigmund Freud, Vol. 2,* ed. James Strachey. London: Hogarth Press.

Casas, J. Manuel. (1995). "Counseling and Psychotherapy with Racial/Ethnic Minority Groups in Theory and Practice." In *Comprehensive Textbook of Psychotherapy,* ed. Bruce Bongar and Larry E. Beutler. New York: Oxford University Press.

Cicchetti, Dante, and Cohen, Donald J. (1995). "Perspectives on Developmental Psychopathology." In *Developmental Psychopathology, Vol. 1: Theory and Methods,* ed. Dante Cicchetti and Donald J. Cohen. New York: Wiley.

Darwin, Charles. ([1872] 1998). *The Expression of the Emotions in Man and Animals.* New York: Oxford University Press.

Freud, Anna. (1936). *The Writings of Anna Freud, Vol. 2: The Ego and the Mechanisms of Defense.* New York: International Universities Press.

Freud, Sigmund. ([1915] 1957). "Repression." In *The Standard Edition of the Complete Psychological Works of Sigmund Freud, Vol. 14,* ed. James Strachey. London: Hogarth Press.

Freud, Sigmund. ([1915] 1957). "The Unconscious." In *The Standard Edition of the Complete Psychological Works of Sigmund Freud, Vol. 14,* ed. James Strachey. London: Hogarth Press.

Freud, Sigmund. ([1923] 1961). "The Ego and the Id." In *The Standard Edition of the Complete Psychological Works of Sigmund Freud, Vol. 19,* ed. James Strachey. London: Hogarth Press.

Freud, Sigmund. ([1926] 1959). "Inhibitions, Symptoms, and

Anxiety." In *The Standard Edition of the Complete Psychological Works of Sigmund Freud, Vol. 20,* ed. James Strachey. London: Hogarth Press.

Gacono, Carl B., and Meloy, J. Reid. (1994). *The Rorschach Assessment of Aggressive and Psychopathic Personalities.* Hillsdale, NJ: Lawrence Erlbaum.

Greenberg, Jay R., and Mitchell, Stephen A. (1983). *Object Relations in Psychoanalytic Theory.* Cambridge, MA: Harvard University Press.

Halgin, Richard P., and Murphy, Robert A. (1995). "Issues in the Training of Psychotherapists." In *Comprehensive Textbook of Psychotherapy: Theory and Practice,* ed. Bruce Bongar and Larry E. Beutler. New York: Oxford University Press.

Karon, Bertram P., and Widerner, Annmarie J. (1995). "Psychodynamic Therapies in Historical Perspective: 'Nothing Human Do I Consider Alien to Me.'" In *Comprehensive Textbook of Psychotherapy: Theory and Practice,* ed. Bruce Bongar and Larry E. Beutler. New York: Oxford University Press.

Kernberg, Otto. (1976). *Object Relations Theory and Clinical Psychoanalysis.* New York: Aronson.

LeDoux, Joseph E. (1996). *The Emotional Brain.* New York: Simon & Schuster.

Mahler, Margaret; Pine, Fred; and Bergman, Anni. (1975). *The Psychological Birth of the Human Infant.* New York: Basic Books.

Marans, Steven, and Cohen, Donald J. (1996). "Child Psychoanalytic Theories of Development." In *Child and Adolescent Psychiatry: A Comprehensive Textbook,* 2nd ed., ed. Melvin Lewis. Baltimore, MD: Williams & Wilkins.

Miller, Jean Baker. (1976). *Toward a New Psychology of Women.* Boston: Beacon Press.

Schwartz, Andrew. (1991). "Drives, Affects, Behavior—and Learning: Approaches to a Psychobiology of Emotion and to an Integration of Psychoanalytic and Neurobiologic Thought." In *Affect: Psychoanalytic Perspectives,* ed. Theodore Shapiro and Robert N. Emde. Madison, CT: International Universities Press.

Stern, Daniel N. (1985). *The Interpersonal World of the Infant: A View from Psychoanalysis and Developmental Psychology.* New York: Basic Books.

Strupp, Hans H., and Binder, Jeffrey L. (1984). *Psychotherapy in a New Key: A Guide to Time-Limited Dynamic Psychotherapy.* New York: Basic Books.

Target, Mary, and Fonagy, Peter. (1994). "Efficacy of Psychoanalysis for Children with Emotional Disorders." *Journal of the American Academy of Child and Adolescent Psychiatry* 33:361–371.

Weissman, Myrna M., and Markowitz, John C. (1994). "Interpersonal Psychotherapy: Current Status." *Archives of General Psychiatry* 51:599–606.

Westen, Drew. (1998). "Psychodynamic Theory and Technique in Relation to Research on Cognition and Emotion: Mutual Implications." In *Handbook of Cognition and Emotion,* ed. Tim Dalgleish and Mick Power. New York: Wiley.

Robert A. Murphy

PSYCHOLOGICAL ASSESSMENT

In order to test theories about emotion, researchers must accurately measure emotion. However, several conceptual and methodological issues are raised by the assessment of emotions in research with human subjects.

Consider the following scenario. A clinical researcher wants to assess whether a new technique developed for the treatment of small animal phobias (e.g., aversions to snakes and spiders) is effective. To conduct such a study, the researcher needs to decide how to assess fear or other emotions (e.g., disgust) that may be experienced by phobic individuals during an encounter with the phobic stimulus. Such assessments are necessary both to select participants for the treatment program (e.g., participants need to demonstrate a significant aversion in order to be included) and to evaluate how effective the treatment really is.

Consider the many alternatives that are available to the researcher for assessing the participants' emotional responses to phobic stimuli. He or she could ask subjects to report their responses on a series of rating scales. For example, the researcher might ask participants to indicate on a scale from 1 to 10 (with 1 being "not fearful at all" and 10 being "extremely fearful") how much fear they experience when they are exposed to the phobic object. This scale would be an example of what psychologists refer to as self-report measures. Such measures require subjects to give a verbal report that indicates the intensity of the target emotion.

Alternatively, the researcher could derive a measure of emotional expressivity by unobtrusively videotaping participants' facial expressions while they are exposed to the feared object. At a later point in time, trained raters could code the subjects' facial activity according to a system that links activity in particular muscle regions to facial expressions of emotion. Assessed in this manner, facial expressivity would be considered an observational measure of emotion. The researcher could also assess fear using behavioral methods. For example, he or she could conduct a behavioral approach test during which participants are asked to move as close to the feared object as they can tolerate. The researcher would then record the actual distance from the object ultimately achieved as an index of fear or avoidance.

There are yet other alternatives. For example, the researcher could assess the participants' psychophysiological responses to the feared object by recording (using electrodes that are placed on the surface of the skin) changes in heart rate, brain activity, or other physiological measures. Several neuro-imaging techniques (e.g., positron emission tomography, functional magnetic resonance imaging) have been developed that allow for a more fine-grained picture of brain activation.

As this example clearly indicates, emotions can be assessed using a variety of different methods (e.g., self-report, behavioral, and physiological). This is an important consideration because different methods for assessing emotions can yield different results and conclusions. In the case of phobias, it has been shown that self-report, behavioral, and physiological measures often do not agree. That is, an individual who reports extremely high levels of fear on a rating scale may demonstrate only small increases in heart rate. In addition, different types of emotion measures sometimes change at different rates over the course of treatment. Indeed, different classes of measures may actually reveal different primary emotions. For example, while people with small-animal phobias commonly report that fear is the predominant emotion being experienced, the primary emotion expressed on the face is disgust. Because of this lack of agreement among emotion measures, it should be remembered that different types of emotion measures are not interchangeable.

Theoretical Models of Emotion Should Guide the Assessment of Emotion

Because the primary goal of research studies on emotion is to test theories and hypotheses, researchers use theoretical models of emotion to guide the selection of emotion measures. Although there are a variety of perspectives on emotion, one structural model of emotion that can be used to guide the selection and interpretation of emotion measures is the circumplex model, which is shown in Figure 1. According to the circumplex model, emotion terms can be arranged in a circular structure. Some theorists believe that the primary dimensions of interest are the pleasant-unpleasant dimension (valence) and the high activation-low activation dimension (arousal). From this perspective, each emotion term represents a particular combination of valence and arousal. According to an alternative perspective, the primary dimensions of interest are those that are at 45 degree angles from the pleasant-unpleasant and arousal dimensions. These dimensions have been labeled "activated pleasant-unactivated unpleasant" and "activated unpleasant-unactivated pleasant" by Randy Larsen and Ed Diener (1992). Whatever sets of dimensions are considered primary, the circumplex model accommodates both sets.

As indicated by the emotion descriptors beside each of the eight octants in Figure 1, the circumplex structure is capable of representing a wide variety of emotion terms. One additional feature of the emotion circumplex model is that it precisely specifies the relations between different emotion measures. For example, points on the circle that are 180 degrees from each other (e.g., pleasant and unpleasant) are predicted to be strongly negatively correlated (i.e., high

scores on one should reliably predict low scores on the other), while points on the circle that are 90 degrees from each other are predicted to be essentially unrelated to one another. Another strength of the circumplex model is that it can accommodate research on short-term emotional responses to stimuli and individual differences in longer-term, stable patterns of emotion. Shorter-term responses are typically called "emotional states," while stable individual differences are typically called "emotional traits." Emotional traits can be represented in a circumplex structure in a manner that is similar to that depicted for emotional states in Figure 1. For example, the trait of neuroticism is located in the activated unpleasant affect region, while the trait of extroversion is located in the activated pleasant affect region.

Although optimal tests of the circumplex model may require specialized statistical procedures, it appears that this model provides an accurate representation of the actual relations among self-report measures of emotion. Moreover, this model is not simply relevant to the assessment of self-reported emotion. It is also applicable to other methods for assessing emotion, such as observational measures of facial expressivity. In addition, there is evidence for links between specific psychophysiological measures and specific dimensions of the circumplex model. Thus, the circumplex model is one structural model of emotion that can be used to integrate the assessment of emotion across both state and trait assessments and across several different types of emotion measures.

It should be noted that there are other perspectives on emotion. Some theorists emphasize the assessment of discrete emotions, such as anger, fear, and sadness, rather than more global dimensions, such as pleasant and unpleasant. Such theorists often argue that the circumplex model fails to differentiate clearly distinct emotions such as fear and anger. There is scientific support for both perspectives, which may in fact be more complementary than contradictory. The researcher's interests and hypotheses should guide the decision to use dimensional or discrete measures of emotion.

Whether researchers are interested in studying broad dimensions of emotion or specific discrete emotions, they need to ensure that the instruments that they plan on using have met several sets of measurement criteria. First, instruments used in research must yield consistent scores when administered under identical conditions (i.e., reliability). In addition, there should be prior evidence that the scores on a given emotion measure are in fact related or not related to measures of other constructs in a manner that would be expected on the basis of prior knowledge and the-

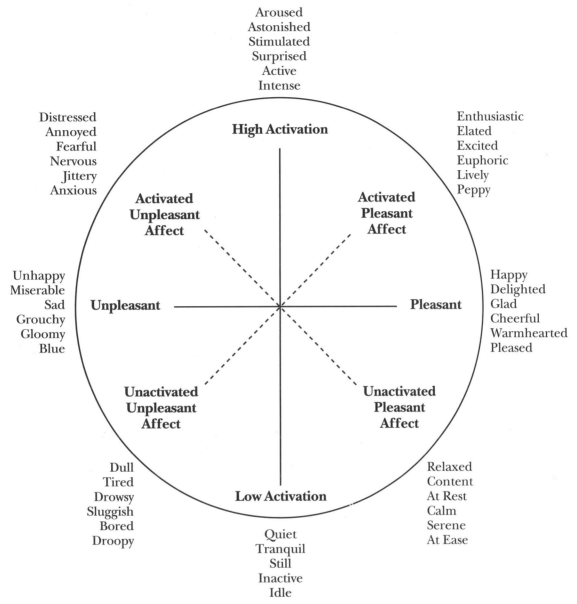

Aroused
Astonished
Stimulated
Surprised
Active
Intense

High Activation

Distressed
Annoyed
Fearful
Nervous
Jittery
Anxious

Enthusiastic
Elated
Excited
Euphoric
Lively
Peppy

Activated Unpleasant Affect

Activated Pleasant Affect

Unhappy
Miserable
Sad
Grouchy
Gloomy
Blue

Unpleasant

Pleasant

Happy
Delighted
Glad
Cheerful
Warmhearted
Pleased

Unactivated Unpleasant Affect

Unactivated Pleasant Affect

Dull
Tired
Drowsy
Sluggish
Bored
Droopy

Low Activation

Relaxed
Content
At Rest
Calm
Serene
At Ease

Quiet
Tranquil
Still
Inactive
Idle

FIGURE 1   *The circumplex model of emotions* (Larsen and Diener, 1992, p. 31; reprinted by permission of Sage Publications).

ory (i.e., validity). The criteria of reliability and validity are applicable to all types of emotion measures (e.g., self-report, facial expressive, psychophysiological).

Self-Report Measures

Self-report measures of emotion typically require experimental participants to respond to a set of items designed to assess specific discrete emotions (e.g., fear, disgust, happiness) or more global dimensions of emotion (e.g., positive affect, negative affect). Responses are typically indicated on rating scales, checklists, or other formats. Depending on the specific measure and the instructions used, respondents can indicate their moods at the present time, in the past week, in other time intervals, or "in general." As the time window broadens, self-reports are more likely to reflect stable individual differences in emotion—emotional traits. Measures that ask participants to indicate their moods at the present time assess emotional states. Thus, researchers can study individual differences in emotional traits, the effects of experimental manipulations on emotional states, or the interaction between the two. For example, one can assess whether the anticipation of public-speaking results in short-term increases in anxiety and whether individuals who are high in trait anxiety demonstrate the strongest emotional responses overall.

The Positive and Negative Affect Schedule (PANAS), developed by David Watson, Lee Anna Clark, and Auke Tellegen (1988), is an example of a self-report measure that is commonly used in contemporary emotion studies. Although this measure has been extended since its development, the original version is still commonly used. Participants are asked to respond to twenty words that describe different feelings and emotions. Using a scale from 1 to 5, where 1 means "very slightly or not at all" and 5 means "extremely," respondents indicate the degree to which they are experiencing or have experienced the target emotion. Ten of the PANAS items assess what Watson and his colleagues refer to as "positive affect" (i.e., a pleasant state of active engagement with the external environment) and the remaining ten items assess what they refer to as "negative affect." Positive affect does not involve happiness so much as a pleasant state of active engagement with the external environment. As such, it appears that PANAS actually assesses the activated pleasant affect octant of the circumplex model of emotion. Conversely, negative affect is a broad dimension of general distress and unpleasurable engagement with the environment that is aligned with the activated unpleasant octant of the circumplex model. Examples of PANAS items that are related to positive affect include "enthusiastic," "determined," and "interested." Examples of items that are related to negative affect include "distressed," "afraid," and "hostile."

The PANAS is easily administered (subjects typically can complete it within five minutes) and easily scored. Scores on positive affect scales and negative affect scales are computed by simply adding up the respondent's scores on the individual items that correspond to each scale (i.e., total scores can range from 10 to 50). The PANAS can also be completed with reference to a variety of time frames. Thus, researchers can assess feelings "right now," "today," "during the past few weeks," or "in general." The PANAS has been used in a number of studies to demonstrate, for example, that positive affect and negative affect as defined by Watson and his colleagues are not simply inversely related (with positive affect being linked to low negative affect and vise versa) but are separable dimensions of emotion with potentially unique relationships to other variables. In addition to the PANAS, there are a number of other measures that are available to researchers for assessing discrete emotions, emotional symptoms in clinical populations, the traits of positive and negative affect, related traits such as neuroticism and extroversion, and a variety of other emotional traits.

The PANAS and similar measures exemplify many of the advantages that are associated with self-report methods of assessing emotion. First, relative to other types of measures, self-report measures are typically considered to be a window on the conscious emotional experience of the individual. For some emotion researchers, and probably the clear majority of nonspecialists, it is precisely the *experience* of emotion that is the key component that should be scientifically studied.

Self-report measures of emotion also are associated with several significant methodological advantages—they are easy to administer and quantify. In several respects, they are also quite flexible—they are able to encompass several different time frames. A measure such as the PANAS can also be used to assess specific discrete emotions such as anger or fear as well as the broader dimensions of positive and negative affect that were originally intended. Indeed, there are a strikingly large number of terms that can be used to define emotional states, and each of these can at least potentially be assessed by self-report methods. Thus, self-report methods are ideally suited to reflect the breadth and complexity of the human emotional experience.

In addition, self-report measures can be used in both laboratory and naturalistic "real-world" contexts. The PANAS and other self-report emotion measures have been used in a number of studies in which experimental participants have completed daily mood diaries over several weeks or longer periods of time (e.g., four weeks). This is a significant development given that one potential weakness of laboratory studies of emotion is the failure to expose experimental participants to stimuli that elicit emotion of an intensity and duration that is comparable to that occurring in real-world contexts. The daily diary method is a potentially powerful tool for tracking emotional reactions to naturalistic elicitors. Research has shown that this approach is also an effective way to study emotion among clinical populations.

Self-report measures of emotion do, however, have some potential methodological disadvantages. First, some individuals cannot complete self-report measures. Such measures are impossible to use with infants, and it may be difficult to elicit valid self-reports from children. Another limitation of self-reports is that they may be biased by a number of factors, including response styles (e.g., individuals may consistently answer at one or the other extreme endpoints of a scale), intentional deception, self-presentational tendencies, or subjects' inability to introspect accurately about their feelings. Although researchers use a variety of methods to minimize such effects, these factors may still bias self-reports. For example, a number of studies have shown that subjects who report equivalent levels of negative affect on trait indices may display very different coping styles and very different physiological responses to stressors. These findings indicate that there may be substantial heterogeneity among individuals with equivalent scores on self-report indices of emotion.

It is also quite common in both basic and clinical studies for experimental participants to report retrospectively about their emotional states over an extended period of time. For example, individuals may report their levels of depression over the past few weeks. In these cases, another factor that can limit the validity of self-reports is inaccurate recall of emotional states. Participants in a study by David Thomas and Diener (1990) completed mood ratings daily for three weeks (Study 1) or six weeks (Study 2). After the daily rating phase was completed, subjects completed retrospective estimates of the intensity and frequencies of different types of emotional experiences over the course of the same period of time as that covered by the daily ratings. When Thomas and Diener compared these retrospective estimates to subjects' actual intensity and frequency measures derived from the daily diaries, they found that subjects tended to overestimate the intensity of both their positive and negative emotions. Thomas and Diener concluded that, "If any general statements can be made, it is that retrospective reports about one's emotional experiences over time tend not to be extremely accurate." (p. 295) Other researchers have found similar evidence of inaccurate or selective recall of emotional states. Retrospective biases may particularly confound assessments of the relation between personality traits and emotions, physical symptoms, or other variables.

There is a final limitation associated with self-report assessments of emotion that is attributable more to the habits of researchers than to intrinsic limitations of the method. This is the tendency (1) to use different labels for dimensions or measures that are so highly correlated as to be for all practical purposes indistinguishable and (2) to use the same label for dimensions or measures that are actually quite separable. Both tendencies can create substantial confusion for both students and researchers. As Watson and Clark (1984) pointed out, a variety of commonly used measures that are used to assess the traits of anxiety, negative emotionality, neuroticism, distress, and dysphoria all tend to be very highly correlated and to assess a general dimension that he referred to as "negative affectivity." Conversely, confusion sometime results from application of the same descriptor to different dimensions of emotion. There is an apparent disagreement between studies showing that positive and negative affect are clearly separable, perhaps independent, dimensions of emotion and studies showing that positive and negative affect are inversely related dimensions that fall at opposite ends of a single continuum. As Lisa Barrett and James Russell (1998) have pointed out, one reason for this discrepancy is that, across studies, measures with fundamentally different items have been given the same name. For example, some measures of positive affect have sampled predominantly from the pleasant octant of the circumplex model of emotion while other measures have sampled predominantly from the activated pleasant octant.

Psychophysiological Measures of Emotion

Psychophysiological researchers assess physiological processes in the autonomic nervous system, central nervous system, or skeletomotor system using electrodes placed on the surface of the body. The startle blink reflex is an example of a commonly used psychophysiological measure of emotion. The startle blink is a reflexive eyeblink that occurs in response to the sudden appearance of an intense or salient stimulus (e.g., a brief burst of white noise delivered through headphones). Such blinks can be recorded from electrodes placed on muscles underneath the eye region. The startle reflex can be affected by emotional factors. Research by Peter Lang and his associates (1990) has shown that when a white noise burst occurs while the individual is exposed to an unpleasant pictorial slide (e.g., one that elicits fear and disgust), the magnitude of the startle blink is increased relative to neutral conditions. Conversely, startle probes occurring during pleasant slides elicit a blink with diminished size relative to neutral conditions. Thus, the startle probe can be used to assess the individual's emotional state on a pleasant-unpleasant continuum.

The pattern of strengths and weaknesses for the startle blink and other psychophysiological measures is different from the pattern that is characteristic of self-report measures. One strength of psychophysiological measures is that they, unlike self-report measures, can often be used successfully in research studies with infants and small children. In addition, psychophysiological measures are often less susceptible to to the intentional deception, self-presentational tendencies, and related processes that produce biases in self-reports. Several psychophysiological studies have discriminated those individuals who report low anxiety and appeared to be "truly" low-anxious from those whose reports of low anxiety appear to reflect defensive denial, avoidance of anxiety, or other processes. Similarly, although this topic is a controversial one, psychophysiological measures are routinely used in studies of "lie detection."

More generally, psychophysiological measures can be used to assess unconscious processes (whereas self-report methods predominantly reflect those processes and experiences that gain access to consciousness). This is an important benefit for psychophysiological measures because many theories of emotion emphasize the importance of processes that are not accessible to consciousness. It is particularly difficult for individuals to discriminate processes that are relatively short in duration and that occur soon after exposure to a stimulus (e.g., within half a second). Assessing electrodermal activity (a measure of sweat responding recorded from the fingers), Arne Öhman and Joakim Soares (1994) showed that people who had a phobia of snakes demonstrated enhanced physiological responses to pictures of snakes even when such pictures were exposed so briefly that the experimental participants could not consciously recognize them.

Another advantage of psychophysiological measures is the ability to assess the ebb and flow of emotion processes over time. One major reason for this ability is that psychophysiological measures typically have excellent temporal resolution—they can resolve changes in physiological activity that occur within very small units of time (e.g., milliseconds or seconds). In addition, they can typically be measured in a relatively unobtrusive manner. A researcher can continuously record heart rate while experimental participants are viewing a film clip designed to induce emotion. Measures of variations in heart rate on a second-by-second basis can then be derived. Consider how difficult the assessment of second-by-second fluctuations would be for a researcher relying on self-report measures. He or she could attempt to obtain continuous self-reports from experimental participants during the film clip, but the rating task itself would certainly be distracting to subjects and thus weaken or alter their responses.

Because psychophysiological measures typically have excellent temporal resolution, they can be used to break down emotional responses into their specific components. An individual's reaction to an emotional stimulus (e.g., a pictorial slide that elicits happiness) is not a single, unitary entity. Rather, specific components of the reaction can be studied, such as the "peak intensity" (i.e., the most intense response during the slide interval), the "rise time to peak intensity" (i.e., the time required to reach peak intensity), and the average response during the whole slide interval. Moreover, one can focus on responses during exposure to the emotional stimulus, anticipatory responses before the stimulus, or the dampening of responses after the stimulus. Because of their temporal resolution, psychophysiological measures are ideally suited for assessing these different components of emotional responsivity. In this regard, they are typically superior to self-report measures.

Psychophysiological measures also have significant limitations in specific contexts. First, they have certain practical disadvantages relative to self-report measures. Psychophysiological assessments are typically more expensive and labor- and time-intensive that self-report assessments. At least basic technical knowledge in several different areas (e.g., electronics, computer programming) is often required to conduct methodologically sound assessments. In addition, unlike self-report measures that can be flexibly used in a variety of contexts, psychophysiological assessments of emotion are typically confined to a laboratory environment. Naturalistic assessments are typically unfeasible because of the reliance on equipment that is not easily portable and the need for a well-controlled environment. Thus, it is difficult for researchers to conduct psychophysiological assessments of responses to the types of stimuli that typically elicit emotion in the "real world." Clearly, this is a very significant limitation of the psychophysiological measures.

While self-report measures have the potential to assess the full breadth and complexity of human emotion, psychophysiological measures can only assess a more limited set of emotions. Such measures are typically used to assess broader dimensions of emotion or motivation (e.g., pleasure-displeasure, activation-deactivation, approach versus withdrawal) or, in some cases, a limited number of discrete emotions (e.g., fear, disgust).

An overriding goal of psychophysiological studies of emotion is to link psychophysiological measures to psychologically meaningful processes or the biological substrates of such processes. Unfortunately, another potential limitation of psychophysiological measures is that there sometimes is no immediately evident link between psychophysiological measures and emotion-related psychological processes. Even experienced researchers might well ask, "Precisely what psychological processes, if any, are indicated by changes in heart rate while experimental participants are viewing a film clip that induces happiness?" In other words, the meaning and implications of the results yielded by psychophysiological studies are sometimes less immediately evident than would be considered optimal.

Conclusion

Self-report and psychophysiological measures clearly have contrasting profiles of strengths and weaknesses that are important for both students and researchers to bear in mind. Awareness of these differing strengths and weaknesses can guide the selection of measures for specific studies and the evaluation of experimental write-ups. In addition, one clear implication of the preceding discussion is the wisdom of combining self-report, psychophysiological, and other (e.g., observational) measures of emotion. Indeed, an examination of contemporary programs of research in the area of emotion indicates that any comprehensive, long-term program must include multimodal assessments that include at least several different types of measures of emotion. Such an approach clearly has substantial methodological and theoretical advantages.

See also: EMOTION EXPERIENCE AND EXPRESSION; EMOTION SUPPRESSION; FACIAL EXPRESSION; PSYCHOLOGY OF EMOTIONS; PSYCHOPHYSIOLOGY OF EMOTIONS

Bibliography

Barrett, Lisa F., and Russell, James A. (1998). "Independence and Bipolarity in the Structure of Current Affect." *Journal of Personality and Social Psychology* 74:967–984.

Beck, Aaron T.; Rush, A. John; Shaw, Brian F.; and Emery, Gary. (1979). *Cognitive Therapy of Depression.* New York: Guilford.

Carver, Charles S., and White, Tara L. (1994). "Behavioral Inhibition, Behavioral Activation, and Affective Responses to Impending Reward and Punishment: The BIS/BAS Scales." *Journal of Personality and Social Psychology* 67:319–333.

Davidson, Richard J. (1998). "Affective Style and Affective Disorders: Perspectives from Affective Neuroscience." *Cognition and Emotion* 12:307–330.

Ekman, Paul, and Davidson, Richard J. (1994). *The Nature of Emotion: Fundamental Questions.* New York: Oxford University Press.

Eysenck, Hans J., and Eysenck, Sybil B. G. (1975). *Manual of the Eysenck Personality Questionnaire.* London: Hodder and Stoughton.

Frijda, Nico H. (1986). *The Emotions.* New York: Cambridge University Press.

Izard, Carroll E. (1977). *Human Emotions.* New York: Plenum.

Izard, Carroll E.; Kagan, Jerome; and Zajonc, Robert B., ed. (1984). *Emotions, Cognition, and Behavior.* New York: Cambridge University Press.

Kagan, Jerome; Reznick, Steven; and Snidman, Nancy. (1988). "Biological Bases of Childhood Shyness." *Science* 240:167–173.

Lang, Peter J.; Bradley, Margaret M.; and Cuthbert, Bruce N. (1990). "Emotion, Attention, and the Startle Reflex." *Psychological Review* 97:377–395.

Larsen, Randy J. (1987). "The Stability of Mood Variability: A Spectral Analytic Approach to Daily Mood Assessments." *Journal of Personality and Social Psychology* 52:1195–1204.

Larsen, Randy J., and Diener, Ed. (1992). "Promises and Problems with the Circumplex Model of Emotion." In *Review of Personality and Social Psychology, Vol. 13: Emotion,* ed. Margaret S. Clark. Newbury Park, CA: Sage Publications.

Öhman, Arne, and Soares, Joaquim J. F. (1994). "'Unconscious Anxiety': Phobic Responses to Masked Stimuli." *Journal of Abnormal Psychology* 103:231–240.

Ortony, Andrew; Clore, Gerald L.; and Foss, Mark A. (1987). "The Referential Structure of the Affective Lexicon." *Cognitive Science* 11:341–364.

Thomas, David L., and Diener, Ed. (1990). "Memory Accuracy in the Recall of Emotions." *Journal of Personality and Social Psychology* 59:291–297.

Tomarken, Andrew J. (1999). "Methodological Issues in Psychophysiological Research." In *Handbook of Research Methods in Clinical Psychology,* 2nd ed., ed. Philip C. Kendall, James N. Butcher, and Grayson N. Holmbeck. Oxford, Eng.: Wiley.

Watson, David. (1988). "Intraindividual and Interindividual Analyses of Positive and Negative Affect: Their Relation to Health Complaints, Perceived Stress, and Daily Activities." *Journal of Personality and Social Psychology* 54:1020–1030.

Watson, David, and Clark, Lee A. (1984). "Negative Affectivity: The Disposition to Experience Aversive Emotional States." *Psychological Bulletin* 96:465–490.

Watson, David; Clark, Lee A.; and Tellegen, Auke. (1988). "Development and Validation of Brief Measures of Positive and Negative Affect: The PANAS Scales." *Journal of Personality and Social Psychology* 54:1063–1070.

Watson, David, and Tellegen, Auke. (1985). "Toward a Consensual Structure of Mood." *Psychological Bulletin* 98:219–235.

Watson, David; Weber, Kris; Assenheimer, Jana S.; Clark, Lee A.; Strauss, Milton E.; and McCormick, Richard A. (1995). "Testing a Tripartite Model, I: Evaluating the Convergent and Discriminant Validity of Anxiety and Depression Symptom Scales." *Journal of Abnormal Psychology* 104:3–14.

Andrew J. Tomarken
Gabriel S. Dichter
J. Cara Pendergrass

PSYCHOLOGY OF EMOTIONS

"I was overcome with emotion." "We fell in love at first sight." "I was so angry, I didn't know what I was doing." As these phrases indicate, one quality of human emotion (or passion, as it used to be called) is the sense that it is somehow alien—that it can take control of people's actions and leave them as passive observers of actions "not their own." This nearly universal experience is even codified by the legal system, which recognizes that individuals have reduced responsibility for crimes of passion. Emotions are thus seen as something to be controlled or eliminated.

In contrast, people also experience emotions as the very core of their existence: it is feelings about things, people, or experiences that make them meaningful. When people are in a state without apparent emotion, they feel dull, bored, uninvolved, and hardly alive. It is the experience of emotion that gives color, purpose, direction, and liveliness to one's being and connects one to the environment. Rather than elimination, this view of the emotions suggests they should be embraced. That they seem both central to the self and alien to the self is only one of the many paradoxes and debates surrounding the experience of the emotions.

Discussion of the emotions first requires careful definition of terms that are frequently used interchangeably or with slightly different meanings. For example, the terms *affect, feelings,* and *emotions* are often treated as synonyms. However, it is useful to consider emotions as a subset of feelings, which also include other internally and externally located perceptions, such as hunger, fatigue, touch, warmth, pain, and pleasure. Conversely, affect refers to the positive and negative aspects of the emotions. The terms *emotion* and *motivation* are both derived from the Latin *movere,* to move. Again, the emotions are best viewed as a subset of motives, which include drives, such as sex or hunger, and socially based needs, such as achievement or respect.

Finally, it useful to distinguish emotion from mood, sentiment, temperament, and personality, which differ both in terms of time and specificity. While the emotions seldom last more than a few minutes or hours past the specific cues that elicited them, the other categories both last longer and are not tied so directly to the environment. Moods tend to last for days or weeks, even months, and while they may color people's emotional responses to the environment, external processes tend not to affect them immediately. Sentiments are more closely tied to the environment, but in a more lasting way. For example, people may have sentimental attachments to objects or activities. Love, itself, may be considered a sentiment. Temperament refers to innate or inherited predispositions to respond to experience with particular affects or moods and is only modified by significant or repeated experiences. Personality, finally, is used to refer to those resulting affective dispositions modified by experience.

Darwinian Perspectives

The scientific study of the emotions began in 1872 with Charles Darwin, who was interested in the evolution of emotional expression and noted the apparent continuity from animals to humans, such as the baring of teeth to express anger. Darwin noted the part-to-whole relationship between baring the teeth and biting and concluded that emotional expression has survival value because it communicates threat without subjecting the organism to the unnecessary risk of an actual fight. Other emotional expressions, such as the smile or relaxed posture that allows others (both of one's own and other species) to approach, also regulate social proximity. In addition, Darwin noted the self-regulatory aspects of expression. Thus, inhibiting expression appears to attenuate, while full expression amplifies the emotional experience. From Darwin's evolutionary perspective, three subsequent lines of research may be traced: emotion as adaptive functioning, facial expression, and the evolution of brain structures.

William James developed a theory in 1884 that focused on emotions as the body's preparation to respond adaptively to the environment. James's emphasis was upon awareness of the internal sensations of the body's preparations. The common sense view was that an individual sees a bear, becomes afraid, and then experiences the sensations of fear, such as a pounding heart and other visceral (i.e., internal organ) changes. In contrast, James suggested that individuals first have the bodily sensations and then know they are afraid. The James-Lange theory, which resulted from the combination of James's ideas with those of Carl Lange (1885), who independently developed similar ideas focusing on vasomotor changes such as flushing, has generated a debate that is yet to be resolved to every investigator's satisfaction.

Walter Cannon (1929) attacked the James-Lange or visceral specificity theory, noting that visceral changes are too slow, are relatively nonspecific, and occur both in very different emotional states and in nonemotional states. He also noted that when subjects were

Walter B. Cannon was a professor of physiology at Harvard University when he was elected president of the American Association for the Advancement of Science in 1939. (Corbis/Bettmann)

injected with adrenalin and experienced the visceral changes of a fight/flight response, they generally reported only feeling "as if" they were having a feeling. Cannon proposed that instead of the viscera, the central nervous system must be the source of the emotions, a position held by most contemporary cognitive theorists. Despite evidence gathered during the 1950s that induced anger and fear could actually be distinguished reliably with psychophysiological measures, Cannon's view of nonspecificity held sway until the 1970s.

John Cacioppo and his colleagues proposed in 1993 a possible answer to the James-Cannon debate. They note that stimuli initiating emotional responses can vary radically in potency and specificity and that the contextual cues can be either clear or ambiguous. Their model describes three stages of processing, each of which can vary in specificity: (1) somatovisceral (bodily and organ) responses can vary from undifferentiated to emotion-specific activation, (2) somatovisceral afferentiation (neural connections) to the cortex (subjective awareness) can vary from general arousal (Cannon) to unambiguous (James) visceral sensations, and (3) cognitive operations can vary from a need for evaluating and labeling the situation (Cannon) to an immediate pattern recognition (James). This model seems to account for most of the data and indicates that both are correct, but only within boundary conditions appropriate to the situation.

Robert Plutchik (1994) proposed that the emotions are adaptive predispositions to respond with one of eight prototypical behaviors present in all animals. These primary emotions may be organized into a "circumplex," with adjacent emotions such as anger (destruction) or anticipation (exploration) each being paired respectively with opposite emotions such as fear (protection) or surprise (orientation). Donald Fromme and Clayton O'Brien (1982) presented research supporting an alternative circular model, noting that their data, as well as that of Plutchik, showed fear and anger to be more similar than to be opposites. Fromme and O'Brien proposed that while visceral discriminations are difficult, it is not hard to distinguish arousal from relaxation or pain from pleasure. They suggest that arousal combined with pleasure elicits dominant emotions such as anger or elation, while relaxation combined with pain elicits submissive emotions such as grief or resignation.

Stanley Schachter and Jerome Singer conducted a landmark study in 1962 that supported a modified version of James's theory. Subjects were injected either with epinephrine or saline, given information, misinformation, or no information on epinephrine's effects, and then were asked to wait with a confederate who acted either angrily or euphorically. Schachter and Singer interpreted their results as indicative that emotion results only when arousal and cognitive appraisal of a situation occur together. Despite methodological problems and the difficulties that other researchers have had replicating these results, the "two factor" theory of emotion is still widely held. Not only was it an elegant resolution of the James-versus-Cannon controversy, but it reflected the cognitive revolution in psychology that was just beginning.

Following Darwin's observation that emotions could be amplified or inhibited (depending on whether their expression was encouraged or suppressed), theorists have proposed a "facial feedback hypothesis" to replace James's "visceral feedback hypothesis." They note that the face is highly sensitive, capable of quick reactions, and able to display a variety of feelings. If it is feedback from the face that informs one about emotions, then these processes must be "hard wired" by evolution. The adaptive significance of communicating threat or inviting approach provides a clear survival advantage and implies that those emotional expressions should be universal both within and across species. Paul Ekman (1972) showed photos of Americans expressing different emotions to New Guinea Highlanders and found that they had no difficulty interpreting expressions, nor did Americans have difficulty interpreting the expressions of the New Guinea Highlanders. Fritz Strack and his colleagues (1988) found interesting information on the hard wiring of facial expressions to emotion by asking subjects to hold a pen either with their lips (inducing a pout) or with their teeth (inducing a smile). Subjects induced to smile reported significantly more positive mood than did those who were induced to pout. Robert Levenson (1992) suggests that when voluntary facial expressions are made, the motor cortex also sends parallel signals to the autonomic nervous system (controlling the viscera), thus creating a circuit in which emotional processing may flow in either direction to create "action tendencies."

Paul MacLean (1972) pioneered the study of brain structures involved with the emotions. He emphasized the evolutionarily older "limbic structures" of the brain and their interactions with the prefrontal lobes of the neocortex. Joseph LeDoux (1995) has shown how one limbic structure, the amygdala, takes information relayed from the sensory thalamus and is able to initiate complete fight/flight responses to environmental stimuli without input from the neocortex. This seems to be a rapid, emergency response that, nevertheless, can ordinarily be influenced by parallel circuits going from the sensory thalamus to the cortex and back to the amygdala. The prefrontal cortex appears particularly important in "dampening" the amygdala's emotional response. Richard Davidson (1993) has demonstrated that asymmetrical activation of the left and right anterior prefrontal cortex is associated, respectively, with the arousal of social (generally positive) and selfish (generally negative) affects. He has also found that depressed patients, whether currently depressed or not, show less left frontal activation than do non-depressed patients.

Cognitive Perspectives

Cognitive psychologists, beginning with Magda Arnold in 1960, followed by Schachter and Singer (1962), Richard Lazarus (with Elizabeth Alfert, 1964), and George Mandler (1975), have stressed the importance of cognitive appraisal in emotional processing. Arnold felt James too easily glossed over "seeing the bear" as an emotion's starting point and noted that perceptions need to be appraised, however fleetingly, for threat or other significance. Lazarus referred to his approach as "motivational-relational," since in order to predict behavior one must know what an individual's expectations and goals are in a situation. Primary appraisal then assesses a situation for potential relevance, benefit, or harm, while secondary appraisals are about coping.

Robert Zajonc (1984) and Lazarus have stimulated significant debate about which comes first: emotion or cognitive appraisal. Zajonc equates emotion with "affective reaction," which would imply at least an assessment of positivity-negativity. Most observers see this debate as reflecting the depth of appraisal needed for an emotional response, rather than suggesting that no appraisal is needed. Mandler believes autonomic arousal to be undifferentiated but central to emotion and occasioned by events having survival implications. Most critical is the "interruption of ongoing plans and actions." Arousal has two functions: (1) to prepare appropriate physiological responses to the environment (action tendencies) and (2) to signal that attention is needed to seek relevant information and "troubleshoot" a means of responding. Mandler sees consciousness and the emotions inextricably involved in troubleshooting.

Keith Oatley and Philip Johnson-Laird revised their 1987 communicative theory of emotion in 1996, providing one of the broadest integrations of the literature. Emotional communication occurs not only with other individuals in the environment but also among components of the organism involved in emotional responding. These latter connections are rather loose and have evolved to prepare survival responses to four prototypic situations confronted by all organisms: happiness, sadness, anger, and fear. Oatley and Johnson-Laird note that these are the only emotions that do not seem to need an object and can be present as moods as well. They also propose additional emotions, such as love and contempt, that require objects and are associated with approaching or rejecting others.

Oatley and Johnson-Laird follow Mandler in asserting that emotion results from the interruption of goal-directed behavior (or its smooth functioning in the case of happiness) and is designed both to alert the organism and to begin a response to cope with the interruption. They propose two parallel assessments that accompany such interruption: (1) a rapid, nonverbal emotional signal (e.g., visceral or facial sensations) and (2) a propositional (verbal) analysis. Again, these analyses are only loosely associated, and it is possible for an individual to be aware of one process and not the other.

While Oatley and Johnson-Laird believe that emotion results from a discrepancy or the distance between what is observed and one's goals, Charles Carver, John Lawrence, and Michael Scheier (1996) proposed that emotion reflects continuous monitoring of the rate or velocity at which such distance is either increasing (negative affect) or decreasing (positive affect). Also, if there is an acceleration of that rate, then either exhilaration or "sinking feelings" (depression) result. The basis of their approach is taken from a general systems model of self-regulating systems and hierarchical organization proposed by William Powers (1973). In general systems theory, self-regulation occurs when there is a discrepancy between a measure or perception and some assigned value, reference point, or goal. This discrepancy is "fed back" to the system (e.g., thermostatic regulation), which acts either to reduce (negative feedback) or to increase (positive feedback) the observed discrepancy. Generally, self-regulation occurs when negative feedback reduces discrepancies from a desired goal; however, if the assigned value or reference is negatively valenced (e.g., something dangerous), then a positive feedback loop may be engaged to increase the discrepancy. In this latter case, positive feedback loops are typically governed by other, negative feedback loops; that is, a well-governed system moves both away from problems and toward solutions. The utility of systems models is that they account for what may seem to be very complex, purposeful behaviors in such simple systems as, for example, a car's speed control or feature detectors in an organism's perceptual motor systems.

Powers's hierarchic model suggests that individual sensory receptors may work together (around some threshold value given by evolution) in humans to serve as feature detectors. Similarly, feature detectors may work together to create a perception; perceptions join together to create awareness of relations; and relationships combine to constitute programs, which are organized into principles and finally into values. Superordinate levels set the reference values for lower levels, which in turn feed back environmental information to the higher levels to compare for discrepancies. The implication that Carver, Lawrence, and Scheier draw from this analysis is that conscious awareness is usually only involved in higher levels of this hierarchy, unless some problem at a lower level is not being handled "automatically" by either pre-programmed (nature) or learned (nurture) expectancies.

Carver, Lawrence, and Scheier draw a number of interesting conclusions, which seem well supported by research. Accelerations toward or away are signals to direct conscious attention toward what is happening. Negative affect is necessarily more motivating than positive affect because of its role in signaling that goals are not being met. Positive affect tends to disappear with repeated successes and as related expectancies are formed (preventing people from being caught in an endless behavioral loop, striving for achieving goals they know they can achieve and not developing new goals). People typically have multiple goals operating at any one time, with many not in present awareness and with their current activities frequently serving more than one goal; alternatively, people may reprioritize and shift to other goals when current goals are not being met. Since people may simultaneously have multiple goals, governed by differing programs or values, each requiring different levels of attention, it is possible that actions that move people toward one goal may move them away from another goal. Mixed feelings, shame, guilt, and confusion may be only some of the resulting emotions.

A radically different way of thinking about scientific knowledge, social constructivism, has begun to affect all of psychology, including emotion researchers, since the 1980s. Social constructivism suggests that all knowledge is a social construction, reflecting historical, economic, linguistic, and other contextual factors—people can never fully describe reality from an outside, objective position because their very categories for thinking about reality reflect societal and personal concerns. James Averill (1980, p. 3) believes that an emotion is nothing more than "a transitory social role that includes an individual's appraisal of the situation and that is interpreted as a passion rather than as an action."

The difficulty other theorists have agreeing upon what constitutes a "basic emotion" is non-problematic for Averill, who suggests that every culture develops as many emotions as are needed to regulate social situations deemed important in the culture. For example, anger is not just a response to any wrong or frustration; the wrong must be seen to have been committed voluntarily and unjustifiably to warrant anger—accidents are forgiven, retribution is understood. Averill discovered that subjects, although experiencing anger negatively, felt that expressing anger to a friend benefited their relationship in the long run. He suggests that anger and the threat of aggression serve the role of communicating to the recipient that a wrong is be-

ing committed (the norm of retribution) while allowing the angry person to disclaim responsibility for his or her "passion" (the norm of conciliation). Thus, emotions allow one to influence others according to social scripts while being protected from moral responsibility for personal actions.

Emotional Intelligence and Practical Applications

In the 1990s, psychologists such as Ross Buck (1997), Daniel Goleman (1995), and Peter Salovey and John Mayer (1990) developed the thesis that emotional regulation and communication are skills that underlie social competence or emotional intelligence. Buck describes three levels of emotional communication and regulation. Emotion 1 is the homeostatic regulation of the autonomic and immune system response to emotional cues. Emotion 2 is the expressive, ritualized behavior that has evolved to allow social regulation of the emotional response. Emotion 3 is the subjective experience, underlying self-regulation. When a child experiences Emotion 3, he or she will also express Emotion 2, which will often lead to a social response from parents and other adults. If parents generally accept the child's expressions, label the underlying feelings, and suggest constructive outlets for the emotions, then the child is likely to become socially competent. If expressions are met with punishment, then alexithymia (no words for emotion), emotional dysregulation, immune system suppression, and psychopathology are all possible consequences.

Salovey and Mayer define emotional intelligence with five skill domains: (1) knowing one's emotions, thus enabling monitoring and self-regulation, (2) managing emotions, self-soothing, or learning to cope adaptively with emotional situations, (3) motivating oneself and using the above skills to delay gratification and stifle impulses that would detract from achieving goals, (4) recognizing emotions in others and experiencing empathy, which is the fundamental "people skill," thus allowing one to understand and respond effectively to others, and (5) handling relationships or leadership skills, which builds upon all of the above.

Goleman marshals an impressive array of evidence to support his thesis that helping children develop these emotional skills is essential for addressing societal problems. He shows how lack of these skills contributes to marital discord, job stress, physical illness that is secondary to emotional suppression of the immune response, failure to develop cognitive potential, educational dropouts, antisocial behavior, and anxiety and depressive disorders. Goleman advocates that schools introduce social/emotional curricula, such as that introduced in inner city New Haven schools. This curriculum improved problem-solving skills, involvement with peers, impulse control, classroom behavior, interpersonal effectiveness, and coping with anxiety. It also led to fewer instances of delinquent behavior.

John Gottman and his colleagues (1997), starting with Davidson's findings on frontal lobe asymmetry, suggest that the left hemisphere of the brain is also responsible for most language and intentional behavior. Thus, talking about a negative emotion while experiencing it should not only bring the emotion under control but lead to self-soothing by blending positive social affect with the negative. They present evidence that children whose parents are able to coach such self-talk are indeed able to self-soothe and self-regulate. Parental warmth, by itself, is not particularly helpful; it must be accompanied by coaching based on the parent's awareness of personal feelings and the feelings of the child. Destructive behaviors include intruding the moment a child encounters difficulty or being critical and mocking of the child's feelings.

Conclusion

Research into the nature and function of human emotions developed exponentially during the twentieth century. Despite very few definitive conclusions, the field is bringing a number of challenging and illuminating perspectives to bear. The age-old question of whether emotions are alien or core to human existence seems answered—emotions are central to personal experience, and social convention allows one to express negative emotion with reduced responsibility so that one can sanction another's behavior without necessarily disrupting the relationship. The question of whether or not emotions should be suppressed also seems answered—many of the ills of society and the individual result from poorly regulated emotion. Because evolutionarily primitive brain circuits can short-circuit emotional responses, suppression of emotion backfires. Being aware of emotions, recognizing their sources, and having the ability to talk about them seems to give people the ability to regulate their emotions in ways that are productive both for themselves and for society.

See also: COGNITIVE PERSPECTIVE; DARWIN, CHARLES ROBERT; EMOTION EXPERIENCE AND EXPRESSION; EMOTION SUPPRESSION; JAMES, WILLIAM; NEUROBIOLOGY OF EMOTIONS; PERSONALITY; TEMPERAMENT

Bibliography

Arnold, Magda B. (1960). *Emotion and Personality, Vol. 1: Psychological Aspects.* New York: Columbia University Press.
Averill, James R. (1980). "A Constructivist View of Emotion." In *Emotion: Theory, Research, and Experience, Vol. 1,* ed. Robert Plutchik and Harold Kellerman. New York: Academic Press.

Buck, Ross. (1997). "From DNA to MTV: The Spontaneous Communication of Emotional Messages." In *Message Production: Advances in Communication Theory.* ed. John O. Greene. Mahwah, NJ: Lawrence Erlbaum.
Cacioppo, John T.; Klein, David J.; Berntson, Gary G.; and Hatfield, Elaine. (1993). "The Psychophysiology of Emotion." In *Handbook of Emotions,* ed. Michael Lewis and Jeannette M. Haviland. New York: Guilford.
Cannon, Walter B. (1929). *Bodily Changes in Pain, Hunger, Fear, and Rage: An Account of Recent Researches into the Function of Emotional Excitement.* New York: Appleton-Century-Crofts.
Carver, Charles S.; Lawrence, John W.; and Scheier, Michael F. (1996). "A Control-Process Perspective on the Origins of Affect." In *Striving and Feeling: Interactions among Goals, Affect, and Self-Regulation,* ed. Leonard L. Martin and Abraham Teaser. Mahwah, NJ: Lawrence Erlbaum.
Darwin, Charles R. ([1872] 1965). *The Expression of the Emotions in Man and Animals.* Chicago: University of Chicago Press.
Davidson, Richard J. (1993). "Parsing Affective Space: Perspectives from Neuropsychology and Psychophysiology." *Neuropsychology* 7:464–475.
Ekman, Paul. (1972). "Universals and Cultural Differences in Facial Expressions of Emotion." In *Nebraska Symposium on Motivation, Vol. 19,* ed. James K. Cole. Lincoln: University of Nebraska Press.
Fromme, Donald K., and O'Brien, Clayton S. (1982). "A Dimensional Approach to the Circular Ordering of the Emotions." *Motivation and Emotion* 6(4):337–363.
Goleman, Daniel. (1995). *Emotional Intelligence.* New York: Bantam Books.
Gottman, John M.; Katz, Lynn Fainsilber; and Hooven, Carole. (1997). *Meta-Emotion: How Families Communicate Emotionally.* Mahwah, NJ: Lawrence Erlbaum.
Izard, Carroll E. (1993). "Four Systems for Emotion Activation: Cognitive and Noncognitive Processes." *Psychological Review* 100(1):68–90.
James, William. ([1884] 1922). "What Is an Emotion?" In *The Emotions,* ed. Knight Dunlap. New York: Hafner.
Lange, Carl. ([1885] 1922). "The Emotions." In *The Emotions,* ed. Knight Dunlap. New York: Hafner.
Lazarus, Richard S., and Alfert, Elizabeth. (1964). "Short-Circuiting of Threat by Experimentally Altering Cognitive Appraisal." *Journal of Abnormal and Social Psychology* 89:195–205.
Lazarus, Richard S. (1991). *Emotion and Adaptation.* New York: Oxford University Press.
LeDoux, Joseph E. (1995). "In Search of an Emotional System in the Brain: Leaping from Fear to Emotion and Consciousness." In *The Cognitive Neurosciences,* ed. Michael S. Gazzaniga. Cambridge, MA: Massachusetts Institute of Technology Press.
Levenson, Robert W. (1992). "Autonomic Nervous System Differences among Emotions." *Psychological Science* 3:23–27.
MacLean, Paul D. (1972). "Cerebral Evolution and Emotional Processes." *Annals of the New York Academy of Sciences* 193:137–149.
Mandler, George. (1975). *Mind and Emotion.* New York: Wiley.
Oatley, Keith, and Johnson-Laird, Philip N. (1987). "Towards a Cognitive Theory of Emotions." *Cognition and Emotion* 1:29–50.
Oatley, Keith, and Johnson-Laird, Philip N. (1996). "The Communicative Theory of Emotions: Empirical Tests, Mental

Models, and Implications for Social Interaction." In *Striving and Feeling: Interactions among Goals, Affect, and Self-Regulation*, ed. Leonard L. Martin and Abraham Tesser. Mahwah, NJ: Lawrence Erlbaum.

Plutchik, Robert. (1994). *The Psychology and Biology of Emotion*. New York: HarperCollins.

Powers, William T. (1973). *Behavior*. Chicago: Aldine.

Salovey, Peter, and Mayer, John D. (1990). "Emotional Intelligence." *Imagination, Cognition, and Personality* 9:185–211.

Schachter, Stanley, and Singer, Jerome E. (1962). "Cognitive, Social, and Physiological Determinants of Emotional State." *Physiological Review* 69:379–399.

Strack, Fritz; Martin, Leonard L.; and Stepper, Sabine. (1988). "Inhibiting and Facilitating Conditions of the Human Smile: A Nonobtrusive Test of the Facial Feedback Hypothesis." *Journal of Personality and Social Psychology* 54:768–777.

Zajonc, Robert. (1984). "On the Primacy of Affect." *American Psychologist* 35:151–175.

Donald K. Fromme

PSYCHOPHYSIOLOGY OF EMOTIONS

Psychophysiology, as its name implies, is the study of the relationship between mental (psychological) and physical (physiological) processes. One hallmark of psychophysiology is the noninvasive measurement of physiological events, such as the use of electromyography to detect muscle movement. In addition, psychophysiologists take advantage of novel medical approaches, such as using pharmaceuticals to create temporary alterations in life functions (e.g., autonomic control of the heart). Scowls of disgust, a sinking feeling in the gut, and a racing heart are all indications that emotions are inherently physiological. For this reason, the understanding of human emotions has benefited greatly from psychophysiology's unique perspective.

Facial Expression and Muscle Activity

One question that has intrigued psychophysiologists is whether physiological responses (e.g., facial expressions) can be used to reveal the content of an individual's emotions. The study of facial expression as a marker of emotion can be traced back to Silvan S. Tomkins's (1962) proposition that facial movement and feedback play an important role in the experience of emotion. He suggested that high-speed filming could be used to perform microscopic analyses of facial expressions and emotion. These proposals led to important methodological advances by Carroll Izard (1971, 1977) and Paul Ekman and Wallace Friesen (1978) in the coding of facial expressions. Building on the foundation provided by these researchers, sub-

sequent investigators have provided provocative evidence that (1) at least a subset of discrete emotions are associated with distinct overt facial expressions, (2) induced states in which individuals report positive (e.g., happiness) and negative (e.g., fear, anger, sadness) emotions are associated with distinctive facial actions, and (3) displays similar to those of the adult can be found in newborns and the congenitally blind, suggesting that these displays are inherently linked to basic emotions.

Although it may be an intuitive conclusion that facial expressions reveal the nature of underlying emotions, many emotional and affect-laden information processes are not accompanied by visually perceptible facial actions. This fact has limited the usefulness of analyses of facial actions in understanding emotions. Furthermore, although James A. Russell (1994) has found that observers across cultures attribute the same emotional meaning to the expressions of happiness, sadness, fear, anger, surprise, and disgust, these attributions are not perfect. Complicating research in this area, the specific emotion that is evoked by a stimulus may vary across individuals and cultures. Finally, individuals can invoke display rules to mask or hide the emotions they are feeling, and observers can confuse the meaning of expressions (e.g., fear and surprise). For these reasons, the coding of overt facial expressions can be a less than perfect measure of affective state.

An important complement to visual inspection of facial expression has been the measurement of patterns of activity in facial muscles. This technique—facial electromyography (EMG)—has made it possible to index muscle activity even in the absence of observable facial expressions. This methodology involves placing electrodes on the surface of the face in order to measure electrical activity in the underlying muscles. As William E. Rinn (1984) noted, overt facial expressions are the result of varied and specific movements of the facial skin and connective tissue caused by the contraction of facial muscles. These movements create folds, lines, and wrinkles in the skin and the movement of facial landmarks, such as the brows and corners of the mouth. Although muscle activation must occur if these facial actions are to be achieved, it is possible for muscle action to occur even in the absence of any overt facial action, particularly if the muscle activation is weak. Thus, facial EMG measurements can be used to study emotions or emotional processes that are so weak that an observer would not be able to see them.

Facial EMG activity is useful for studying the effects of evoked emotions. Gary E. Schwartz and colleagues (1976) have demonstrated differences related to emotional imagery in EMG activity over the brow (*corru-*

gator supercilii, the frown muscle), cheek (*zygomaticus major,* the smile muscle), and perioral (*depressor anguli oris,* a muscle attached to the outer corners of the mouth that pulls the corner of the lips downward as in a frown) regions. Participants who were asked to imagine positive or negative events in their lives showed more EMG activity over the brow region and less over the cheek and perioral regions when they imagined sad as compared to happy events. John T. Cacioppo and Richard E. Petty (1979) found that measures of EMG activity over the cheek and brow muscle regions similarly distinguished individuals who were anticipating and who subsequently were exposed to communications that advocated a position that they either initially believed (proattitudinal) or initially disbelieved (counterattitudinal). The EMG activity differentiated these groups even though overt facial expressions were rare, did not differentiate these groups, and were excluded prior to analyses.

Subsequent research confirmed that EMG activity in some regions of the face is particularly good at differentiating positive from negative emotions. Specifically, Cacioppo and his colleagues (1988) have shown that EMG activity over the brow region is lower and EMG activity over the cheek and periocular regions is higher when emotions that are mildly positive, as opposed to mildly negative, are evoked. Furthermore, positive and negative affective stimuli tend to have opposing effects on facial EMG activity over the cheek and brow regions, with these opposing effects being more apparent at the group (nomothetic) level of analysis than at the individual (idiographic) level. It is important to note that because individual muscles alone are not good markers, it is *patterns* of facial muscle activity that best reveal the content of emotions. This is consistent with an important concept in psychophysiology: Patterns of multiple physiological markers often provide more sensitive information about psychological constructs than do individual physiological markers.

Research on the effects of discrete emotions on facial EMG activity also suggests that fundamental expressive actions only differentiate positive from negative states. In a comprehensive study, for example, Serena L. Brown and Schwartz (1980) had participants go through imagery conditions designed to elicit happiness, sadness, fear, and anger at three levels of intensity while EMG activity was recorded over the brow, cheek, forehead, and jaw regions. Results revealed that the negative emotions (fear, anger, and sadness) were associated with higher EMG activity over the brow muscle regions than was the positive emotion (happiness). EMG activity over the cheek region was highest during happy imagery, but it also was elevated at least somewhat during fear and anger imagery.

Whether these latter elevations reflect some participants engaging in miserable or distress smiling, crosstalk from other muscles of the middle and lower facial regions, or the purported genetic origin of smiling and laughter in primitive agonistic displays is unclear. EMG activity over the jaw and forehead muscle regions did not vary significantly. It is interesting to note that increased emotional intensity led to increased EMG activity, especially over the brow muscle regions during sadness, anger, and fear imagery, and over the cheek muscle region during happy imagery. Thus, facial EMG activity, particularly during low-intensity emotions, appears to be more closely associated with the activation of positive and negative emotional states (i.e., positivity and negativity) than with specific discrete emotions.

Facial EMG responses during conversations have also been found to be more predictive of positivity or negativity than of discrete emotional experiences. Cacioppo and his colleagues (1988) interviewed undergraduate women about themselves while facial EMG and audiovisual recordings were being made. Afterward, participants were asked to describe what they had been thinking during specific segments of the interview that were marked by distinctive EMG responses over the brow muscle region in the context of ongoing but stable levels of activity elsewhere in the face. Analyses of the videotapes indicated that observers could not differentiate the recorded segments associated with different emotions; the visible facial expressions did not differ as a function of self-reported emotion. Nevertheless, relatively low levels of EMG activity over the brow muscle region marked feelings of merriment and warm-heartedness, whereas relatively high levels of EMG activity over this region marked feelings of fear, sadness, disgust, tension, irritation, and contempt. That is, increased EMG activity over the brow muscle region was associated with lower reports of positive emotions and higher reports of negative emotions. Further differentiation based on facial EMG activity over this region was not reliable, suggesting again that facial EMG is more useful in marking positivity or negativity than in marking specific emotions.

Autonomic Activity

In addition to facial muscle activity, psychophysiological research of emotions has examined activity of the autonomic nervous system (ANS). The ANS is the system responsible for regulating homeostasis and providing energy for demands made by the body. Emotions often are associated with a need for action (e.g., fear and the need to flee or fight), and the ANS is responsible for ensuring that energy is available for action. Consequently, the links between emotions and the ANS have been a topic of interest for many researchers. Much of this research has been influenced by William James's (1884) proposal that peripheral physiological changes are antecedents rather than consequences of the perception of emotional experience. James's theorizing generated a great deal of interest in determining not only whether physical reactions precede emotional experience but also whether discrete emotions are associated with unique patterns of physiological activity. Because of the close links between emotions and ANS activity, many researchers have focused their search for emotion-specific patterning on the ANS.

Unfortunately, early research on autonomic activity and affective reactions was characterized by a lack of replicability and consistency. For example, heart rate responses have differentiated pleasant from unpleasant stimuli, but the direction of the effect has been inconsistent. Mark K. Greenwald and his colleagues (1989) reported significantly greater heart rate deceleration for participants who were exposed to pleasant as compared to unpleasant stimuli. In contrast, Scott R. Vrana and his colleagues (1989) reported that participants who were exposed to negative imagery experienced greater heart rate acceleration. Despite the lack of consistency in early findings, some researchers maintained that it should be possible to differentiate specific emotions using autonomic indices.

Ekman and his colleagues first presented evidence of differentiation of discrete emotions in an influential paper published in 1983. Heart rate, left- and right-hand finger temperature, skin resistance, and forearm flexor muscle tension were recorded during the manipulation of the emotional states of anger, fear, sadness, happiness, surprise, and disgust. One method for evoking emotions involved a directed facial action task in which a participant was induced to form a facial expression that was associated with a discrete emotion through muscle-by-muscle contraction instructions that omitted any reference to the emotional state. For example, a participant may be told to pull the eyebrows down and together, raise the upper eyelid, push the lower lip up, and press the lips together. These particular instructions correspond to the facial expression associated with anger. Using the directed facial action task, Ekman and his colleagues reported that (1) heart rate was higher in anger, fear, and sadness than in happiness, disgust, and surprise and (2) anger could be further differentiated from fear and sadness by its higher finger temperature.

Emotion was also evoked in this experiment with an imagery task in which participants were asked to relive a past emotional experience for thirty seconds. Physiological responses during a relived emotion period were compared to a non-imagery resting baseline,

revealing higher skin resistance during sadness than in fear, anger, or disgust. Together, the results from the two emotion induction techniques generated considerable enthusiasm for the idea of emotion-specific autonomic patterning, especially because emotions of the same valence (e.g., anger and fear) appeared distinguishable. Similar results were obtained by Robert W. Levenson, Ekman, and Friesen (1990) using the directed facial action task, leading these researchers to propose that each discrete emotion is associated with an inborn affect program whose role is to coordinate changes in the person's biological states. These changes are directed at supporting the behavioral adaptations and motor programs that are most likely associated with a particular emotion (e.g., fleeing in the case of fear) and can be recorded as emotion-specific changes in ANS activity.

There is now a large body of research that is relevant to this hypothesis, and several reviews have been performed that reveal that whereas some reliable autonomic differentiation has been obtained across studies, the results are far from definitive regarding emotion-specific autonomic patterning. For example, Cacioppo and his colleagues (1997) conducted a review of seventeen separate studies that provided data that were relevant to the question of whether emotion-specific autonomic patterning exists. Studies were included in the review only if they contrasted the effects of at least two discrete emotions on two or more autonomic measures. These criteria yielded nearly eight hundred separate effect sizes involving twenty measures.

Heart rate reliably differentiated several emotions in Cacioppo's review. In fact, heart rate provided the strongest evidence for emotion-specific differentiation. Greater heart rate acceleration was obtained to anger, fear, and sadness as compared to disgust, which was consistent with the findings of Ekman and his colleagues. There was also a tendency for happiness to be associated with greater heart rate acceleration than disgust. However, disgust was associated with the same heart rate response as control conditions; indeed disgust did not differ from control on any autonomic measure. Cacioppo's review also revealed heart rate responses to be larger in anger than in happiness, in fear than in happiness (which also differed on finger pulse volume), in fear than in sadness (which differed also on respiration rate), in anger than in surprise, in sadness than in surprise, and in happiness than in surprise. Emotion-specific differentiation for measures other than heart rate (e.g., measures of bodily tension, facial temperature, respiration amplitude, inspiration volume, or cardiac stroke volume) was less reliable.

Moreover, a study by Frans Boiten (1996) suggests that at least some of the heart rate differentiation of emotions may be a result of effort-related changes and respiration. Several reviews have also noted the failure of imagery to produce differentiation reliably, which is also problematic for the idea of emotion-specific patterning. The imagery data instead suggest that autonomic nervous activity is primarily responsive to the metabolic demands associated with or expected in response to an emotional challenge. Imagery would be expected to produce few such demands, which could explain the general lack of heart rate increases with this emotion-eliciting procedure.

The notion that ANS activity is mobilized in response to perceived or expected metabolic demands is consistent with a distinction made by Peter J. Lang and his colleagues (1990) between strategic and tactical aspects of emotions. Strategies are viewed as underlying organizations that direct actions in the pursuit of broad end goals. The dimensions of valence and intensity are viewed by Lang as being strategic aspects of emotion. Tactics, in comparison, are specific, context-bound patterns of action. Affective reactions can be organized into a finite set of discrete emotions, but tactical demands will vary among situations, making it possible for the same emotion to be associated with a range of behavior. For example, Lang and his colleagues note that the behaviors associated with fear can range from freezing to vigilance to flight. This tactical variability may account for the absence of reliable emotion-specific autonomic patterning. Taken together, the failure of imagery to produce autonomic differentiation, the lack of reliability of emotion-specific patterning on most measures of ANS activity, and the possibility that differences in effort are responsible for heart rate differentiation during the directed facial action task all suggest that autonomic activity may reflect strategic aspects of emotion rather than discrete emotions per se.

Conclusion

Several conclusions are suggested by this review of the research literature. First, facial EMG activity over the cheek and periocular muscle regions varies as a function of positivity whereas EMG activity over the brow muscle region varies as a function of negativity. Second, autonomic activation differs primarily as a function of the energetic (e.g., metabolic, action) components of affective states. Thus, research on facial EMG, which reflects response processes, suggests a tendency toward reciprocity between positivity and negativity. The ANS, in turn, serves to maintain homeostasis and to provide the metabolic support for approach and withdrawal. Accordingly, the ANS may be primarily responsive to the metabolic demands associated with an emotional challenge. Finally, research on facial EMG and on autonomic activity suggests that

while indices of these systems can differentiate positive and negative emotions, discrete emotions are not as easily distinguished.

Although facial muscle activity and ANS activity are two key areas of psychophysiological research, it should be noted that other measures are being used in this field. Some researchers are examining the evaluative processes using event-related brain potentials, while others are using electroencephalograms to investigate brain asymmetry and its relation to affective style. Study is also being conducted into the relation between attention and the startle reflex to emotion.

See also: BIOCHEMISTRY OF EMOTIONS; DEFENSE MECHANISMS; FACIAL EXPRESSION; JAMES, WILLIAM; MIND-BODY DICHOTOMY; NEUROBIOLOGY OF EMOTIONS; UNIVERSALITY OF EMOTIONAL EXPRESSION

Bibliography

Blascovich, Jim, and Tomaka, Joe. (1996). "The Biopsychosocial Model of Arousal Regulation." In *Advances in Experimental Social Psychology, Vol. 28*, ed. Mark P. Zanna. New York: Academic Press.

Boiten, Frans. (1996). "Autonomic Response Patterns during Voluntary Facial Action." *Psychophysiology* 33:123–131.

Brown, Serena L., and Schwartz, Gary E. (1980). "Relationships between Facial Electromyography and Subjective Experience during Affective Imagery." *Biological Psychology* 11:49–62.

Cacioppo, John T.; Berntson, Gary G.; Klein, David J.; and Poehlmann, Kirsten M. (1997). "Psychophysiology of Emotion across the Lifespan." In *Annual Review of Gerontology and Geriatrics, Vol. 17*, ed. K. Warner Schaie and M. Powell Lawton. New York: Springer.

Cacioppo, John T.; Martzke, Jeffrey S.; Petty, Richard E.; and Tassinary, Louis G. (1988). "Specific Forms of Facial EMG Response Index Emotions during an Interview: From Darwin to the Continuous Flow Hypothesis of Affect-Laden Information Processing." *Journal of Personality and Social Psychology* 54:592–604.

Cacioppo, John T., and Petty, Richard E. (1979). "Attitudes and Cognitive Response: An Electrophysiological Approach." *Journal of Personality and Social Psychology* 37:2181–2199.

Ekman, Paul, and Friesen, Wallace V. (1978). *The Facial Action Coding System: A Technique for the Measurement of Facial Movement.* Palo Alto, CA: Consulting Psychologists Press.

Ekman, Paul; Levenson, Robert W.; and Friesen, Wallace V. (1983). "Autonomic Nervous System Activity Distinguishes among Emotions." *Science* 221:1208–1210.

Greenwald, Mark K.; Cook, Edwin W., III; and Lang, Peter J. (1989). "Affective Judgment and Psychophysiological Response: Dimensional Covariation in the Evaluation of Pictorial Stimuli." *Journal of Psychophysiology* 3:51–64.

Izard, Carroll E. (1971). *The Face of Emotion.* New York: Appleton-Century-Crofts.

Izard, Carroll E. (1977). *Human Emotions.* New York: Academic Press.

James, William. (1884). "What Is an Emotion?" *Mind* 9:188–205.

Lang, Peter J.; Bradley, Margaret M.; and Cuthbert, Bruce N. (1990). "Emotion, Attention, and the Startle Reflex." *Psychological Review* 97:377–395.

Levenson, Robert W.; Ekman, Paul; and Friesen, Wallace V. (1990). "Voluntary Facial Action Generates Emotion-Specific

Autonomic Nervous System Activity." *Psychophysiology* 27:363–384.

Rinn, William E. (1984). "The Neuropsychology of Facial Expression: A Review of the Neurological and Psychological Mechanisms for Producing Facial Expressions." *Psychological Bulletin* 95:52–77.

Russell, James A. (1994). "Is There Universal Recognition of Emotion from Facial Expressions? A Review of the Cross-Cultural Studies." *Psychological Bulletin* 115:102–141.

Schwartz, Gary E.; Fair, Paul L.; Salt, Patricia; Mandel, Michel R.; and Klerman, Gerald L. (1976). "Facial Muscle Patterning to Affective Imagery in Depressed and Nondepressed Subjects." *Science* 192:489–491.

Tomkins, Silvan S. (1962). *Affect, Imagery, and Consciousness, Vol. 1: The Positive Affects.* New York: Springer.

Vrana, Scott R.; Cuthbert, Bruce N.; and Lang, Peter J. (1989). "Processing Fearful and Neutral Sentences: Memory and Heart Rate Change." *Cognition and Emotion* 3:179–195.

Kirsten M. Poehlmann
John M. Ernst
John T. Cacioppo

PSYCHOTHERAPY

Psychotherapy refers to a number of related approaches for treating mental and emotional disorders to promote psychological well-being. Psychotherapy may be used independently or in conjunction with medication. Sophisticated biological research in the 1990s has resulted in more differentiated psychiatric diagnoses and new drugs that target specific areas of the brain. Treatment, however, is usually conducted in the context of a psychotherapeutic relationship. The scope of psychotherapy has grown from the alleviation of symptoms in patients with severe mental disorders to the treatment or management of a wide variety of personality distresses (such as unhappiness, lack of emotional fulfillment, and social isolation). Therapy typically involves talking with a therapist, either individually or in a group, about one's experiences, feelings, and problems. However, there are also approaches that rely on nonverbal modes of communication such as dance/movement and art therapies. Some goals of psychotherapy are to change inappropriate or destructive behavior patterns, improve interpersonal relationships, improve self-esteem, and resolve conflicts or trauma.

Types of Therapy

Psychotherapists often modify the theories that guide their work in order to meet the needs of particular patients. This diversity has resulted in hundreds of different types of therapies, ranging from traditional psychoanalysis to eclectic approaches that integrate Eastern philosophies and meditation. Sigmund

Freud originated psychoanalysis in 1896 with a technique that used free thought association and the interpretation of dreams. He was the first to apply the theory of the unconscious, rooted in seventeenth century philosophy, to the treatment of psychiatric illness. Melanie Klein and Anna Freud adapted psychoanalysis for play therapy with children, which created two different concepts about child development.

Psychodynamic therapy, which is widely practiced, is derived from psychoanalytic theory and focuses on discovering unconscious conflicts that interfere with people's behavior and satisfaction. The interpersonal theory of Harry Stack Sullivan spawned an approach to therapy that focused on enhancing relationships and communication skills. The experiments of American psychologist John Watson, Russian physiologist Ivan Pavlov, and American psychologist B. F. Skinner paved the way for behavior therapy. Araon Beck's cognitive therapy aims at rearranging a person's maladaptive thoughts and actions. Other significant influences in the practice of psychotherapy include the client-centered therapy of Carl Rogers, the Gestalt therapy of Fritz Perls, the psychodrama of Jacob Moreno, and a broad array of existential and cognitive-behavioral approaches. However, according to the American Psychiatric Association, the most widely practiced and studied approaches are derived from one of two major theories of human behavior: psychoanalytic theory and learning theory.

Psychoanalytically oriented psychotherapy is based on the exploration of conscious and unconscious processes in the context of an ongoing therapeutic relationship. Treatment may be brief and focused on particular issues or longer with an emphasis on personal growth and self-understanding. Cognitive-behavior therapy actually refers to a group of therapies that include behavior therapy, behavior modification, and cognitive therapy in various combinations. These component therapies are all derived from learning theory but have fine distinctions in emphasis and techniques. A formal behavioral analysis of a patient's problem is often followed by the use of techniques intended to change behavior. Since cognitive approaches emphasize how thinking mediates feelings and behavior, and therapy consists of identifying maladaptive thought

Peter Shaffer's Equus *(1974) is set in a psychiatric hospital where a teenage boy is being treated after having blinded several horses with a hoof pick. The action of the play consists of the therapy sessions that gradually help the teenager reveal his obsessive belief in a horse god, Equus.*

patterns and teaching patients to change these, cognitive and behavioral techniques are often used together.

Emotion and Cognition

One common assumption among various models of psychotherapy is that the therapeutic process involves both emotional and cognitive components. Psychotherapy promotes understanding or insight that the patient can apply to future life experiences. However, many patients may exhibit behavioral change or improved functioning without corresponding insight or apparent cognitive awareness. Some people may generally feel better and perceive that they are functioning more effectively without a true understanding of the cause.

It is a generally accepted notion that purely intellectual awareness and insight produce little or no significant behavioral change. Rather, the experience and expression of feelings in psychotherapy fosters an increased tolerance of emotions, which in turn reduces the patient's defenses against them. For some, the goal of psychotherapy would be a less constricted, freer flow of emotional expression leading to a stronger sense of self.

Emotion is multidimensional, involving simultaneous cognitive (thought) and sensorimotor (movement) processes. The relationship between bodily feeling states and experienced emotion has been explored by psychotherapists and researchers of various disciplines. Philosophers such as Susanne Langer (1942) recognized that discursive language is not always adequate to express the content of an individual's inner life. Sigmund Freud illustrated how words may be diametrically opposed to the emotions being expressed through action or gesture. Peter J. Lang's (1994) three-system view of emotion is useful in examining the complexity of human emotional experience. His categories include (a) verbal reports (e.g., I feel sad), (b) actions (e.g., hug a child, run away from a feared object), and (c) physiological reactions (e.g., tears welling up in one's eyes, a lump in one's throat). All three categories provide information to the patient and therapist about the person's experience. Sometimes these systems are not in accord with one another, which produces a feeling of being out of synchronization with oneself. One goal for psychotherapy might be to help the patient achieve an integrated or more harmonious emotional life.

Psychotherapeutic techniques that use nonverbal tools such as movement or art may be helpful for people who tend to intellectualize their emotions or for those who are unable to express feelings verbally. Psychotherapists can also use an awareness of their own body feeling states in a session to provide valuable insight about a patient's experience. Sometimes the psychotherapist's instinctive sensations and responses can signal what a patient is feeling, even when the patient is, as yet, unaware of the feelings. Attention to bodily felt emotions in psychotherapy provides useful information for both patient and practitioner.

Emotion in the Therapeutic Relationship

Classic psychoanalysis advocated the notion of therapeutic neutrality (i.e., that the analyst should assume a neutral stance so the patient could project feelings onto this "blank screen" for the purpose of reflection and contemplation). Recognition of the potential for using the therapist's subjective experience in treatment led to a re-examination of the role. In the psychotherapeutic encounter there is a constant flow of messages about the emotions of both participants. Most practitioners agree that it is important for the therapist to be open and receptive to what the patient is communicating. The therapist's own expressive behavior greatly contributes to an awareness and empathic understanding of the patient's experience. The wide array coexisting psychotherapies place the therapist in varying roles, from coach to healer, parental figure to mentor. However, the value placed on the therapeutic relationship goes beyond theoretical and ideological differences.

Hans Strupp and Suzanne Hadley (1979), in their study of specific versus nonspecific factors in psychotherapy, looked at the experience of patients treated by trained psychotherapists and by an alternative group that consisted of college professors chosen for their ability to form understanding relationships. It was suggested that the positive changes reported by these patients were attributed to the healing effects of a benign and caring human bond. The intention was not to promote the practice of psychotherapy by untrained individuals but rather to offer evidence that supported the importance of an emotional connection in the therapeutic relationship.

How a therapist communicates interest and caring may take different forms and depends upon the practitioner's theoretical orientation and the specific needs of the patient. However, a positive outcome is more likely in the presence of cooperation and mutual respect.

Regulating Emotion

Emotion may be informative to the individual and play a constructive role in the shaping of one's experience, but people who feel overwhelmed or out of control often see themselves as being lost in a sea of

A counselor, in an attempt to strengthen her relationship with a hearing-impaired client, uses sign language to maintain one-on-one communication rather than using an interpreter. (Corbis/David H. Wells)

turbulent feelings. The smooth regulation of emotion is a goal in psychotherapy; deregulation, therefore, is a target behavior (i.e., one which becomes a focus for change).

While emotions are partly regulated by thought and action, emotions, in turn, have a regulatory effect on thought and action. The outcome may be successful or unsuccessful. The latter is evident when a person's emotional style is chaotic, rigid or otherwise maladaptive. Consider B., who was a fifty-seven-year-old woman with a long history of minimally successful psychiatric treatment. She had a diagnosis of borderline personality disorder, the essential feature of which is the inability to regulate emotions and interpersonal relationships. People with this disorder may report chronic feelings of boredom or emptiness, engage in recurrent suicidal or self-mutilating behavior, and exhibit poor impulse control. As a consequence of this illness, B. was frequently depressed, distressed, and overwhelmed. She often tried to control her emotions by threatening suicide or self-injury. At times she exhibited intense and inappropriate anger. Therapeutic approaches aimed at exploring and understanding her emotions did not reduce her distress, hospital admissions, or destructive behavior patterns. Her interpersonal relationships remained chaotic and unfulfilling. Ironically, insights gained about her experiences, feelings, and problems often resulted in exacerbation of her symptoms. It is little wonder that B. became frustrated and disillusioned with therapy. During another round of destructive behavior and a visit to the emergency room, a clinician suggested to B. that she try dialectical behavioral therapy (DBT). This therapeutic approach focuses on helping the patient develop self-acceptance while learning skills to change. Therapy sessions are conducted much like classes and are arranged in modules that include skill-building in mindfulness, interpersonal relations, effectiveness, emotion regulation, and distress tolerance. Patients identify and track target behaviors they want to change. B. reluctantly agreed to try DBT despite her skepticism about the usefulness of therapy. As she acquired new skills and gained self-confidence, she made observable progress. During the course of one year she had only one brief (overnight) admission to the psychiatric hospital, her suicidal thoughts were significantly reduced, and she did not engage in any self-injurious behavior. In this case, B.'s inability to regulate her emotions had been interfering with her treatment in that it often blocked the formation of a therapeutic alliance and prevented her from using therapy constructively. Change in B.'s case resulted from the combination of learning new skills and restructuring the patient-therapist relationship to facilitate accomplishing her goals.

Another characteristic of emotional pathology is an inability to interpret feedback correctly, such as misinterpreting one's own emotional cues and/or mes-

Regeneration, a 1991 novel by Pat Barker, describes the psychiatric hospital where soldiers with "battle fatigue" were sent during World War I. The doctor, William Rivers, has two major poets—Siegfried Sassoon and Wilfred Owen—under his care. In many ways, the madness of the war seems more insane than the poor men who are suffering from war traumas.

sages and the responses from others. Consider G., who was a thirty-two-year-old male diagnosed with Asperger's disorder, a pervasive developmental disorder which impairs social interactions and behavioral patterns. People with this disorder may also have difficulty interpreting social cues and nonverbal communication. Secondary to this disorder, G. frequently experienced depression, anxiety, and frustration as he tried to navigate his way through daily life. Attempts to facilitate increased understanding of his emotions often resulted in G. feeling overwhelmed and hopeless. Insight appeared to promote confusion and distress, which prevented behavioral change. He had difficulty regulating his emotions, could not accept his feelings, and was unable to enjoy being happy for long periods of time. In psychotherapy G. made limited gains by focusing not on his emotions but on his actions and the consequences of his behavior. This approach was particularly successful when G. could achieve a short-term, tangible goal. For example, G. was able to engage in appropriate social interaction with his peers when he knew that successful interaction would result in a trip to his favorite coffee shop at the end of the day. Instead of trying to understand the origin or cause of his emotions, he learned to look at the effect of his emotions on his behavior and the reactions of others to him. Despite his illness and deficits in processing information, G. made gains in the quality of his life and relationships. The therapist helped him learn from his setbacks, thereby supporting growth and instilling a sense of hope.

Although the interventions varied for B. and G., the therapeutic tasks for both were to change dysfunctional behavior and improve the quality of their lives. In each case, the therapeutic relationship provided an empathic framework within which this difficult work could be done.

Emotions in Group Psychotherapy

Among the therapeutic elements in group psychotherapy are the identification and sharing of emotions. The acknowledgment and validation of feelings among group members can bridge a person's sense of isolation and become a first step toward healing.

For example, a recently widowed, seventy-seven-year-old woman joined an outpatient psychotherapy group for older adults. When asked what brought her to treatment, R. talked about feeling lost and helpless after her husband of fifty years died suddenly two months earlier. She reported that her children were pressuring her to pull herself together and get on with her life. R., who was still grieving, did not feel ready to socialize. She told the group that her husband used to take care of her and she was missing him terribly. She admitted to feeling too depressed even to invite a neighbor in for a cup of coffee. H., also a widow, affirmed that she was feeling similarly, likening it to being in a twilight zone of unreality. An eighty-nine-year-old man looked across the circle at the two women and said, "You are not alone." His pronouncement dramatically increased the emotional intensity in the room. Most group members had suffered the loss of a spouse or sibling. A lively discussion followed, linking the participants' experiences and emotions about grief and loss. The therapist then focused on R.'s earlier statement about the pressure she was feeling from her children to be "normal." This facilitated a conversation about some families' lack of tolerance for their expressions of pain. Members identified the group as a safe place where they could share these feelings.

In group psychotherapy, the participants' contributions may have significant emotional effect on one another, particularly when there is resonance with their life experiences. The group structure provides support, validation, and feedback.

Music and movement are recognized as effective group therapy modalities for people with cognitive or expressive limitations. Therapists use rhythm, sound, and body action to establish emotional contact with patients. Sense memories often stimulate reminiscing and interaction, which can help maintain and even temporarily improve an individual's social relatedness. Even people with severe cognitive deficits are sensitive and responsive to the expression of emotions and to the prevailing emotional climate. Therefore, group therapy can provide social and emotional links for those who have limited verbal skills.

For example, in one group of seven women (all in their eighties with a diagnosis of dementia), the therapist identified that a feeling of disappointment was being expressed in sounds and movement. Although the participants were unable to attach verbally the emotion to a person or object, they all appeared to be experiencing it in their unison activity. The therapist herself felt a diffuse sense of mutuality with the group when they were moving together. Thus, the linking that occurs on a sensorimotor level can form a basis for relationships, even for people who cannot remember each other's names.

Conclusion

Psychotherapy involves the clarification and constructive use of emotions as modifiers of experience and sources of interpersonal attachments. The goal for some patients might be the increased awareness and expression of emotions, while others may aspire to emotional regulation and control. The full range of emotions cannot be captured in words alone because bodily felt sensations, actions, and cognition are all important elements. An emotional connection is crucial in the therapeutic relationship, regardless of psychotherapy theory or techniques, as it sets the stage for change and growth.

See also: COGNITIVE PERSPECTIVE; FREUD, ANNA; FREUD, SIGMUND; PERSONALITY; PSYCHOANALYTIC PERSPECTIVE; PSYCHOLOGICAL ASSESSMENT; PSYCHOLOGY OF EMOTIONS; ROGERS, CARL RANSOM; SULLIVAN, HARRY STACK

Bibliography

Buechler, Sandra. (1993). "Clinical Applications of an Interpersonal View of the Emotions." *Contemporary Psychoanalysis* 29(2):219–236.

Beck, Aaron. (1976). *Cognitive Therapy and the Emotional Disorders.* New York: International Universities Press.

Carek, Donald J. (1990). "Affect in Psychodynamic Psychotherapy." *American Journal of Psychotherapy* 44(2):274–282.

Colp, Ralph. (1995). "Psychiatry: Past and Future." In *Comprehensive Textbook of Psychiatry, Vol. 2,* ed. Harold Kaplan and Benjamin Sadock. Baltimore, MD: Williams and Wilkins.

Heesacker, Martin, and Bradley, Margaret M. (1997). "Beyond Feelings: Psychotherapy and Emotion." *Counseling Psychologist* 25(2):201–219.

Knapp, Peter H., ed. (1963). *Expressions of Emotions in Man.* New York: International Universities Press.

Moreno, Jacob. (1972). *Psychodrama, Vol. 1,* 4th ed. New York: Beacon House.

Lang, Peter J. (1994). "The Varieties of Emotional Experience: A Meditation on James-Lange Theory." *Psychology Review* 101:211–221.

Langer, Susanne. (1942). *Philosophy in a New Key.* New York: Mentor Books.

Linehan, Marsha M. (1993). *Cognitive-Behavioral Treatment of Borderline Personality Disorder.* New York: Guilford.

Pines, Malcolm. (1990). "Group Analysis and the Corrective Emotional Experience: Is It Relevant?" *Psychoanalytic Inquiry* 10(3):389–408.

Sandel, Susan. (1987). "Expressive Group Therapy with Severely Confused Patients." In *Waiting At the Gate: Creativity and Hope in the Nursing Home,* ed. Susan Sandel and David Johnson. New York: Haworth Press.

Scheflen, Albert. (1963). "Communication and Regulation in Psychotherapy." *Psychiatry* 26:128–136.

Scheidlinger, Saul. (1997). "Group Dynamics and Group Psychotherapy Revisted: Four Decades Later." *International Journal of Group Psychotherapy* 47(2):141–159.

Strupp, Hans, and Hadley, Suzanne W. (1979). "Specific vs. Nonspecific Factors in Psychotherapy." *Archives of General Psychiatry* 36:1125–1136.

Yalom, Irving D. (1994). *The Theory and Practice of Group Psychotherapy,* 4th ed. New York: Basic Books.

Susan L. Sandel
Joseph Forscher

QUANTIFICATION OF EMOTIONS

See Psychological Assessment

R

RAGE

See Anger

REJECTION

See Acceptance and Rejection

RELATIONSHIPS

In many respects, the existence of a close relationship is defined by the presence of emotional connections. Unlike social relationships that might form in a classroom or at work, close relationships are characterized by a wider range of emotions, greater duration of emotional response, and greater intensity of emotional feelings. Indeed, one of the paradoxes of close relationships is that they are the source of the most blissful and exhilarating sensations people feel as well as the source of the most hurtful and debilitating pain people feel. Poets, song writers, novelists, and advice columnists celebrate the joys of romantic love and try to make sense of its passing. Family and marriage counselors remind parents that the emotional fabric of their marriage is the cloth from which their children will cut their own emotional futures. In sum, those relationships that people call "close relationships" are likely to be those that have complex emotional connections.

What Is Meant by Emotion?

Although it would be possible to list the emotions that are associated with close relationships and define each separately, the purpose of this entry is to provide a broad discussion about emotion as a phenomenon in the context of relationships. Although several definitions of emotion can be found in the scholarly literature, this entry will follow the general notions set out by such scholars as James Averill (1980), Howard Leventhal (1984), Keith Oatley (1993), and Peter Stearns (1993) that emotions are acquired social constructions. Although human infants are born with the capacity to experience and express a small set of primary emotions, possibly useful at one time for evolutionary survival, socialization quickly takes over. Interactions with caregivers and family members provide labels for basic arousal patterns that are in turn shaped into increasingly differentiated and complex emotions. As children learn to function in their social environments, they learn what they "should" be feeling, how intensely they should be feeling it, and appropriate means of expressing these feelings. Situational cues and internal states become integrated into various emotional episodes, prototypes, or syndromes. Arousal becomes less informative about what emotion is being experienced and how it should be expressed than are situational cues—including who has performed what actions, in what context, with what real or attributed motives.

While there are a number of definitions of emotion and we recognize that some scholars make a convincing case for distinguishing primary from secondary

567

emotions and for distinguishing emotion from related concepts such as mood and affective disposition, this entry will define emotion broadly as a coherent set of responses to real, anticipated, or imagined situations. Further, the coherent set of responses is considered in this entry to be some combination of behavioral, cognitive, or physiological cues that lead a person to enact an emotion "script," which includes instructions for how to experience, manifest, and/or express the emotion being felt and how to respond to the actions of others who play a role in redefining, reducing or intensifying the emotion. The emotion scripts are shared by members of particular groups and cultures at a general level, but they are adapted and somewhat idiosyncratic within any particular relationship.

This perspective helps explain why it is the case that children who have rejecting parents often grow into adults who avoid emotional attachments with romantic partners and why children who have accepting parents grow into adults who form secure attachments with romantic partners. In the former case, the concepts of stability, trust, and sincerity simply do not get associated with the feeling that an individual labels as "love." In the latter case, they do. Because people often act in ways that express their emotional scripts, they cast others in certain roles. Thus, acting in ways that encourage others to reject them often leads to rejection and confirms expectations that lovers cannot be trusted. Conversely, acting in ways that encourage others to be trustworthy often leads to trust and confirms expectations that lovers can be trusted.

This perspective also explains how social emotions such as embarrassment, guilt, shame, and even jealousy may have their origin in the primary emotion of fear but take their own unique forms only after a child learns that he or she is connected to other persons, that behavior has social consequences, that loss of social approval or contact should cause negative arousal, and that specific labels apply to various types of circumstances. Thus, a sudden sound heard by an adult in a dark room might still elicit a startled sensation that is perceived (without any cognitive processing) as the basic emotion of fear. However, that same startled sensation in another context, perhaps realizing after an hour at a party that one has a large stain on the front of his or her clothing, might be experienced as embarrassment or shame, depending upon the formality of the occasion, the status of the other persons present, and cultural norms of propriety.

Relationship Schema and Emotion

Although it is true that people have general notions about various emotions and how they should be experienced and expressed, individuals adapt these emotion scripts in unique ways when they are in actual relationships. For example, when someone is insulted, he or she is likely to feel negative arousal. If the arousal is construed as anger, the individual may want to strike out against another person whereas if it is construed as hurt the person will probably want to close inward and withdraw from the person who caused the insult. However, as people learn more about each other, they adapt the general emotion scripts to the particularities of that relationship. Thus, they might realize that a given person is a "straight shooter" whose critical comments are intended merely to be honest feedback. They do not even feel anger or hurt over the critical comments because they do not hear the comments as insults—the interpretation that initiates a negative emotional response. Caryl Rusbult and her colleagues (1996) refer to this adaptation as "accommodation" or the tendency to respond to potentially destructive comments from a partner in a constructive manner. But how do people get to that point? There must be some kind of evaluation system in the human mind that tells how to distinguish one relationship from another, because if there is not a general sense about how relationships work, it is difficult to categorize, organize, and understand the uniqueness of the specific relationships in the social world.

Among the mental prototypes or schema that people develop for organizing information are relationship schema. These mental structures include expectations about persons, behaviors, obligations, rules, and outcomes when involved in certain types of relationships. These schema also include expectations about the types of emotion that should be experienced, how strongly an emotion should be felt, and how an emotion should be expressed. In a sense, relationship schema guide both individual production of behavior and the interpretation of the behavior of others. They inform people about when and how to enact (or avoid) certain types of emotion scripts and how to interpret and evaluate the emotions of others. Reciprocally, enacting certain emotion scripts or participating in the emotional enactment of others sometimes informs people about the nature of the relationship schema they associate with the other people. If the schema is unexpected, people tend to change the emotion script, modify some element of the relationship schema, or activate a search for an alternative schema that would be more consistent with the emotion scripts. But what is the link between relationship schema and emotion? Consider the following scenario:

A worker has been assigned to do a project with a colleague who seems friendly but is little more than a casual acquaintance. The worker is deeply involved in the project on Friday afternoon when the colleague asks about the worker's plans for that evening. The worker casually mentions plans for going to dinner and a movie with his or her partner. The colleague becomes visibly upset and says that he or she is jealous.

If the worker finds the colleague's reaction surprising in this context, he or she probably shares the view of most people in Western society that jealousy is an inappropriate emotion in relationships that do not include rules about sexual and/or emotional exclusivity. Stating this another way, the person who enacts a jealousy emotion script inappropriately casts himself or herself as a distraught lover and the other person as an unfaithful partner. These roles are far more expectable in a romantic relationship than in a social or task relationship. However, if the colleague responded to the answer about the Friday evening plans by saying that he or she was going to stay in the office to continue working on the project, the worker might be the one to react emotionally with a feeling of guilt stemming from the belief that he or she would not be carrying a fair share of the assigned responsibility, an important behavioral expectation in task relationships. In this case, the worker would probably feel it appropriate to move into the emotion script for guilt, expressing regret, apologizing, explaining that the plans had been made some time ago, and offering to come in early on Monday morning to compensate. The worker would probably expect that the colleague would graciously accept the expressions of guilt, provide exoneration, and close the episode in a friendly manner. If the project is especially important, some annoyance would even be a possible emotional reaction from the colleague. However, an extremely intense form of anger expression would not be expected because annoyance is a relatively mild form of negative emotion and anger is an intense form. For the colleague to experience and express an anger script would seem to be inappropriate. On the other hand, if the worker called the close friend to break the Friday evening date and he or she became jealous or angry, the worker would probably be far less surprised. In general, then, in most Western societies people expect a more narrow range of emotions (with less intense displays) to be present in casual relationships as compared to personal relationships.

What accounts for the greater range in type and intensity of emotional expression in personal relationships? In part, according to scholars such as Ellen Berscheid (1983), the complexity of emotion experiences in personal relationships stems from the interdependence of the relationship partners. As people become more interdependent in more numerous and varied aspects of their lives, the possibility that they will ex-

perience "interruptions" in their own plans and behavioral sequences increases and thereby increases the occurrence of arousal. More important, however, is the fact that the greater refinement and complexity in the relationship schema that individuals have developed for their personal relationships affects how they interpret and respond to (or not respond to) this arousal. Relationship schema guide people to make distinctions in how an emotion that might be found in several types of similar relationships (e.g., personal relationships such as marriage, family, dating, friendship) and in specific subsets of those relationships (e.g., casual, close, and best friend) should be experienced and expressed in appropriate ways.

The emotion of love offers a good illustration. If the differences in ways that love is experienced and expressed when felt toward a family member as compared to a romantic partner are considered, it is clear that there are some similarities and some defining differences in how the emotion scripts for love are enacted. This suggests that individuals have a sort of generic emotion script for love that might be associated with their personal relationships, as well as more specialized scripts based on the type of personal relationship. So an individual might have an emotion script for love called LoveFam (family) and an emotion script for love called LoveRom (romantic partner). Moreover, he or she might adapt the family script in different ways for certain members of the family, feeling free to hug the mother to show affection but not the father. For some people who feel that they love a friend, there might even be an emotion script for love called LoveFrd (friendship). In the generic version of this emotion script, Berscheid and Sarah Myers (1996) assert that most people would expect to say or hear the words "I love you" but would be surprised to say or hear the words "I am in love with you." But beyond that, because friendship relationships are quite varied, the nature of the love felt and expressed for different friends might, in some cases, "look" like a romantic love with a good deal of physical touching, expectations about exclusivity, and strong feelings of "specialness."

Before leaving this discussion of relationship schema and emotion, it is important that the association between these two constructs be clarified (or perhaps complicated) by remembering that their influence is reciprocal. Because relationship schema operate at low levels of consciousness most of the time and are connected to each by virtue of similarities in features of emotion scripts, changes in felt emotion can influence relationship schema as well as the other way around. In many ways what is called "growing up" for children is a subtle reconfiguring of the emotion scripts they associate with parental interactions in such

Weddings cause individuals to re-evaluate and redefine existing relationships with friends and family in terms of the new religious and legal bonds that are created through the ceremony. In addition, such events necessitate the creation of relationships that might not have existed before between the friends and family of the bride and the friends and family of the groom. (Corbis/Bob Rowan; Progressive Image)

a way that attributes associated with friendship begin to guide interactions. Parents are still, strictly speaking, parents; however, emotion scripts characteristic of dependent relationships become less salient for guiding interaction. For example, fear shifts to respect and resentment shifts to empathy as children learn to take the perspective of their parents. Even as adults, people find that the emergence of certain emotions can encourage them to alter the expectations of a relationship schema or shift one relationship schema in favor of an alternative schema. This can be seen, for example, when heterosexual cross-sex friends begin to realize that they are somewhat more aroused in the presence of each other than with other friends, or that they each feel a bit of jealousy when the other is on a date, or they begin to kiss more like "lovers" than like "friends." In some cases, the couple continues to define their relationship as a friendship but incorporates new parameters to encompass sexual involvement; in other cases, the couple decides that they are "in love," which for them means a shift to a new schema (LoveRom After LoveFrd). It is interesting to note that

for some people and some couples, a particular schema is, by its very nature, impervious to change. In the above example, if one member of the friendship is in a committed relationship (e.g., engaged or married), the very same sensations that could promote a change in the relationship schema for unattached friends might not be recognized, processed, or interpreted as romantic attraction. Another example of a relationship schema that for many couples is resistant to change is the relationship schema of "Ex-Partner." Some couples break up and, for whatever reasons, find the state of being ex-partners incompatible with any other relationship schema, even casual friends.

What this suggests is that relationship schema and emotion scripts are interconnected and dynamic. When two people come together to form a relationship, they bring their relationship schema with them. But over time, a unique relationship schema and idiosyncratic emotion scripts emerge for that particular relationship. Sometimes when people have very different notions about the nature of emotion and how emotion should be expressed in a relationship, they have to negotiate the workings of their relationship more actively by deciding what differences are important, what differences are unimportant, and where they will each compromise their individual schema and scripts. At other times, the individuals are so similar that the development of the mutually shared schema and scripts is almost effortless.

What is *not* suggested by this discussion is that the emergence of a mutually shared relationship schema and emotion scripts leads automatically to satisfaction in the relationship. The picture is far more complicated than that. Unavoidably, the unfolding of emotion scripts takes many twists and turns because individuals bring their past and present into each interaction. From the past, they bring expectations about how this person will probably act in certain circumstances; from the present, they bring the residue of the day, the good moods and bad moods, the need for comfort, the need for quiet time, or the need for affection. Moreover, during any particular interaction with their partners, people are juggling all that they feel and trying to respond to what they think their partners feel, while simultaneously trying to understand the content of the conversation. It is no surprise that at any given moment, a conversation can shift from one type of episode to another. An example of this is a playful and affectionate episode that turns into conflict when a teasing comment elicits hurt or anger rather than laughter. The couple may share the beliefs that they should not hurt each other and that play and teasing are appropriate ways to express affection, but the conversation takes an unexpected turn.

Emotion and Relationship Qualities

At any given moment, the assessments made about a relationship and a particular relational partner are colored by the mood of the individuals involved. When people feel good, they tend to make judgments that are more lenient and generous, whereas a negative mood produces harsher evaluations. So although individuals have a general or "average" satisfaction level with respect to any particular relationship, they naturally experience fluctuations in the sentiments about a partner and the relationship based upon their mood. If people chronically feel bad, then their relationship assessments will suffer accordingly.

Not surprisingly, in the context of close relationships, one of the most potent factors influencing a person's mood is the mood of his or her partner. The interactive nature of emotion scripts is demonstrated in the contagious nature of moods. When two people are communicating with each other, positive and negative mood states literally can be infectious. A partner who is happy, upbeat, and buoyant makes a person feel good, and he or she will mirror the positive feelings. The positivity can snowball as the person's own good mood stimulates positive perceptions of and behavior toward the partner whose good mood gets reinforced by the person's behavior. And by reinforcing the partner's good mood, the person elicits positive behavior from the partner, which reinforces the person's own good mood, and so on. The same dynamic occurs with negative emotions. Spending time with a person who is very sad, for example, can leave one feeling depressed.

The dynamic interplay of partner emotions is borne out in extensive research regarding marital interactions. One of the most robust research findings in the marital literature is that reciprocity of negative affect differentiates unstable and distressed marriages from stable and non-distressed marriages. Reciprocity occurs when the actions or sentiments of an individual increase the likelihood that similar reactions or sentiments will follow from the individual's partner. So when one person discloses something personal, the partner is more likely to do the same. When one person hurls an insult at another person, the chances increase that the other person will respond in kind (i.e., with another insult). John Gottman (1979, 1994) has found that in distressed marital relationships, partners tend to mindread with negative affect, show contempt for one another, emotionally withdraw, and become defensive. Although all relationships can exhibit negative behaviors from time to time, distressed relationships show more chronic, interconnected, and habitual patterns of negativity. In other words, the behavioral profile of each partner becomes rigidly connected to and reactive to the partner's profile. Moreover, the negative patterns become absorbing (i.e., more and more difficult to break out of once they begin). Thus, the pattern of behavior between the partners over time becomes one of attack–defend–attack–defend and complain–counter-complain. All of this occurs in an emotional climate of hurt, anger, and hostility. When reciprocity of negative affect becomes chronic and commonplace, relational dissatisfaction follows, and a host of interrelated dynamics are set in motion that indicate the unraveling of the relationship.

Each partner's experience of heightened negative feelings is accompanied by increased diffuse physiological arousal. According to Gottman's research, physiological reactivity emotionally conditions the individual to perceive threats and attacks in the relationship. At the same time, there is selective inattention to positive cues regarding the relationship. Gottman (1994) indicates that the heightened arousal "makes it unlikely that the couple will be able to process information very well, will have access to new learning, and more likely that they will rely on previously over-learned tactics for escaping from aversive bodily states" (p. 412).

Robert Levenson and Gottman (1983) demonstrate that absorbing negative states are associated with physiological *linkage* as well. In other words, the physiological responses of partners (as measured by heart rate, skin conductance, and the like) become highly interrelated. Thus, behavioral and somatic (i.e., bodily) states run a parallel course. In a marital couple, the wife's level of arousal is patterned after her husband's, and the husband's arousal level closely mirrors his wife's. This coupling of affect during conflict discussions is strongly and negatively associated with relational satisfaction. In another study, Levenson and Gottman (1985) found that greater physiological linkage during conflict discussions predicted lower marital satisfaction five years later.

When these negative states become chronic and absorbing, a person experiences flooding, which refers to feeling surprised, overwhelmed, and disorganized by a partner's expressions of negative emotions. Feeling flooded results in attributions about the partner that contribute further to the decline of the relationship. What was once seen as a partner's negative mood is now interpreted as a partner's negative trait. Conflicts that were attributed to situational circumstances are now blamed on the partner. Problems in the relationship that were once seen as specific and fleeting are now interpreted to be global, stable, unchangeable, and selfishly motivated.

Behaviors, perceptions, physical reactions, and emotional patterns interconnect and mutually influence one another over time. Thus, a negative emotional climate sets the stage for (and is exacerbated by) negative behavior, physiological reactivity, and unkind attributions. A positive emotional climate, on the other hand, diminishes the effect of negative behaviors and attributions, increases the likelihood of constructive behaviors and relationship enhancing attributions, and buffers against the adverse affect of arousal during episodes of conflict. Indeed, this latter pattern is characteristic of stable, non-distressed married couples.

The complex association of emotion scripts and relationship evolution is further illustrated by the fact that the effects of particular emotions on relational satisfaction are not always straightforward. Gottman and Lowell Krokoff (1989) studied married couples at two different time periods that were three years apart. Among other results, they found that a wife's expressions of contempt and anger were negatively associated with marital satisfaction at the beginning of the study but positively associated with her marital satisfaction three years later. Thus, some emotions that seem to be detrimental in the short term might have long-term benefits. Other related findings showed that the wife's sadness predicted declines in marital satisfaction for both the husband and the wife and that the wife's fear predicted subsequent declines in her satisfaction.

Culture and Emotion in Relationships

Although most people from Western cultures might respond to the intuitive logic of the examples given above, it must be recognized that persons from other cultures might not. In cultures where marriage is strongly influenced by parental choice (often resulting in "arranged" marriages between families), the script for romantic love and marital interaction would be different. Likewise, persons from urban communities might differ from persons in rural communities within the same culture.

One particularly salient feature of culture that figures prominently in the relationship between emotion and relationships is the set of sex-role expectations assigned to men and women. In America, for example, compared to men, women are expected to be (and generally are) more emotionally expressive in their relationships, to show more positive than negative emotions, and to refrain from showing strong emotions such as anger. Women are also better able than men to recognize affect displays in others. Leslie Brody and Judith Hall (1993) summarize sex differences in emotion scripts by linking them to cultural expectations. That is, women read and display emotions associated with affiliation and vulnerability (such as warmth, happiness, and guilt) because of their lower social status and caretaking roles, whereas men display emotions associated with competition and success (such as anger and pride) because of their higher social status and work roles.

Conclusion

It should be remembered that everything said in this entry about emotion, relationships, cultures, and sex-role expectations is subject to interpretation as "fact" only in accord with this particular place and time. In the modern world of rapid transportation, job mobility, global media dispersion (typically film and television originating in the West), and cross-global electronic communication systems, culture is a fluid concept. For example, Karen and Kenneth Dion (1996) have found that young people in Japan, Hong Kong, and Taiwan who attend college and encounter Western beliefs about individualism and self-gratification are becoming less similar to previous generations in their own culture and more similar to Western students in their marriage relationship schema, including the belief that love is a prerequisite for marriage.

Therefore, individual relationship schema, the emotion scripts they entail, and the association between emotion and relationship quality are not merely a product of one's personal experience. They are a product of one's personal experience as a member of a certain culture, society, community, family, and period in time—all of which are fluid and subject to change.

See also: ATTACHMENT; ATTRIBUTION; COMMITMENT; COMMUNICATION; CONFLICT; EMOTIONAL ABUSE; FRIENDSHIP; INTIMACY; JEALOUSY; LOVE; TRUST

Bibliography

Averill, James R. (1980). "A Constructivist View of Emotion." In *Emotion: Theory, Research, and Experience, Vol. 1,* ed. Robert Plutchik and Henry Kellerman. New York: Academic Press.

Berscheid, Ellen. (1983). "Emotion." In *Close Relationships,* ed. Harold H. Kelley, Ellen Berscheid, Andrew Christensen, John H. Harvey, Ted L. Huston, George Levinger, Evie McLintock, Letitia Anne Peplau, and Donald R. Peterson. New York: W. H. Freeman.

Berscheid, Ellen, and Myers, Sarah A. (1996). "A Social Categorical Approach to a Question About Love." *Personal Relationships* 3:19–43.

Brody, Leslie R., and Hall, Judith A. (1993). "Gender and Emotion." In *Handbook of Emotions,* ed. Michael Lewis and Jeannette M. Haviland. New York: Guilford.

Bush, Catherine Radecki; Bush, Joseph P.; and Jennings, Joyce. (1988). "Effects of Jealousy Threats on Relationship Perceptions and Emotions." *Journal of Social and Personal Relationships* 5:285–303.

Crawford, June; Kippax, Susan; Onyx, Jenny; Gault, Una; and Benton, Pam. (1992). *Emotion and Gender: Constructing Meaning From Memory.* London: Sage Publications.

Dion, Karen K., and Dion, Kenneth. (1996). "Cultural Perspectives on Romantic Love." *Personal Relationships* 3:5–17.

Fitness, Julie. (1996). "Emotion Knowledge Structures in Close Relationships." In *Knowledge Structures in Close Relationships: A Social Psychological Approach,* ed. Garth J. O. Fletcher and Julie Fitness. Mahwah, NJ: Lawrence Erlbaum.

Forgas, Joseph P.; Levinger, George; and Moylan, Stephanie J. (1994). "Feeling Good and Feeling Close: Affective Influences on the Perception of Intimate Relationships." *Personal Relationships* 1:165–184.

Gottman, John M. (1979). *Marital Interaction: Experimental Investigations.* New York: Academic Press.

Gottman, John M. (1994). *What Predicts Divorce? The Relationship between Marital Processes and Marital Outcomes.* Hillsdale, NJ: Lawrence Erlbaum.

Gottman, John M., and Krokoff, Lowell J. (1989). "Marital Interaction: A Longitudinal View." *Journal of Consulting and Clinical Psychology* 57:47–52.

Levenson, Robert W., and Gottman, John M. (1983). "Marital Interaction: Physiological Linkage and Affective Exchange." *Journal of Personality and Social Psychology* 45:587–597.

Levenson, Robert W., and Gottman, John M. (1985). "Physiological and Affective Predictors of Change in Relationship Satisfaction." *Journal of Personality and Social Psychology* 49: 85–94.

Leventhal, Howard. (1984). "A Perceptual-Motor Theory of Emotion." In *Approaches to Emotion,* ed. Klaus. R. Scherer and Paul Ekman. Hillsdale, NJ: Lawrence Erlbaum.

Metts, Sandra. (1998). "'But I Thought We Were More Than Error Variance': Application of the Social Relations Model to Personal Relationships." In *The Meaning of "Relationship" in Interpersonal Communication,* ed. Richard L. Conville and L. Edna Rogers. Westport, CT: Praeger.

Metts, Sandra, and Bowers, John W. (1994). "Emotion in Interpersonal Communication." In *Handbook of Interpersonal Communication,* 2nd ed., ed. Mark L. Knapp and Gerald R. Miller. Thousand Oaks, CA: Sage Publications.

Oatley, Keith. (1993). "Social Construction in Emotions." In *Handbook of Emotions,* ed. Michael Lewis and Jeannette M. Haviland. New York: Guilford.

Planalp, Sally, and Rivers, Mary. (1996). "Changes in Knowledge of Personal Relationships." In *Knowledge Structures in Close Relationships: A Social Psychological Approach,* ed. Garth J. O. Fletcher and Julie Fitness. Mahwah, NJ: Lawrence Erlbaum.

Rusbult, Caryl E.; Yovetich, Nancy A.; and Verette, Julie. (1996). "An Interdependence Analysis of Accommodation Processes." In *Knowledge Structures in Close Relationships: A Social Psychological Approach,* ed. Garth J. O. Fletcher and Julie Fitness. Mahwah, NJ: Lawrence Erlbaum.

Russell, James A. (1989). "Measures of Emotion." In *Emotion: Theory, Research, and Experience,* ed. Robert Plutchik and Henry Kellerman. New York: Academic Press.

Shaver, Phillip R.; Collins, Nancy; and Clark, Catherine L. (1996). "Attachment Styles and Internal Working Models of Self and Relationship Partners." In *Knowledge Structures in Close Relationships: A Social Psychological Approach,* ed. Garth J. O. Fletcher and Julie Fitness. Mahwah, NJ: Lawrence Erlbaum.

Sprecher, Susan, and Sedikides, Constantine. (1993). "Gender Differences in Perceptions of Emotionality: The Case of Close Heterosexual Relationships." *Sex Roles* 28:511–530.

Stearns, Peter N. (1993). "History of Emotions: The Issue of Change." In *Handbook of Emotions,* ed. Michael Lewis and Jeannette M. Haviland. New York: Guilford.

Sternberg, Robert J. (1996). "Love Stories." *Personal Relationships* 3:59–79.

Sandra Metts
William R. Cupach

RELIGION

See Dance; Mind-Body Dichotomy; Music; Philosophy; Sin

RESEARCH

See Anthropology of Emotions; Biochemistry of Emotions; Cognitive Perspective; Folk Theories of Emotion; Historical Study of Emotions; Neurobiology of Emotions; Psychoanalytic Perspective; Psychology of Emotions; Psychophysiology of Emotions; Sociology of Emotions

RESENTMENT

See Abandonment; Acceptance and Rejection; Anger; Conflict; Envy; Hate; Jealousy; Prejudice

RESPECT

See Acceptance and Rejection; Communication; Empathy; Friendship; Love; Sympathy

ROGERS, CARL RANSOM

b. Oak Park, Illinois, January 8, 1902; *d.* La Jolla, California, February 4, 1987; *psychology, psychotherapy.*

Carl Rogers was an American psychologist who developed what is called the client-centered, non-directed or person-centered theory and method of psychotherapy. After receiving his Ph.D. in psychology from Columbia University Teachers College in 1931, Rogers spent his entire career as a psychotherapist and held professorial appointments at the University of Chicago (1945–1957) and the University of Wisconsin (1957–1964). Rogers's early clinical experience working with children in upstate New York led him to begin questioning the prevailing thinking about psychotherapy, which rested heavily on Freudian and neo-Freudian psychoanalytic theory and methods. In 1964, Rogers relocated to La Jolla, California, where he later founded the Center for Studies of the Person.

Rogers found the psychoanalytic approach too rigid, too heavily reliant on the role and authority of the therapist, and not especially effective. In its place, he developed his client-centered treatment approach that avoided formal diagnosis and theorizing about causes and gave the patient a greater role in the treatment process. In his practice and those of his followers, patients had responsibility for defining their problem, bringing forth relevant information, setting treatment goals, and determining the length of the treatment. Equally important, Rogers redefined the role of the therapist from a distant, emotionally uninvolved expert to an open, empathetic individual who treats the patient as an equal and, through open communication, helps the patient develop insight into his or her problems and resolve them. Rogers was one of the first people to recognize what is now taken for granted in the treatment of emotional problems—that the personal characteristics of the therapist and how they match those of the patient is an important determinant of treatment success. During his career, Rogers set forth his radical—for the time—ideas in lectures, scholarly papers, articles in popular maga-

Carl Rogers served as the keynote speaker at the World Symposium on Humanity in 1979. (Corbis/Roger Ressmeyer)

zines, and a series of books: *The Clinical Treatment of Problem Children* (1939), *Counseling and Psychotherapy* (1942), and *Client-Centered Therapy* (1951), with this last publication containing the fullest statement of his theory and methods. Rogers also explained in the autobiographical chapter "This is Me" in *On Becoming a Person* (1961) how, as a student, his own personal development and movement from religious studies to psychology influenced his thinking.

Rogers's approach placed him in the forefront of humanistic psychology and led to his ideas being criticized by those who favored the more conventional medical or scientific approach to treating emotional problems. Among his critics were psychoanalysts, clinical psychologists who employed psychoanalytical-based psychotherapy, and behavioral psychologists who favored treatment approaches that paid less attention to emotional and interpersonal processes. Some of his critics went so far as to describe his ideas as being outside of clinical psychology and psychiatry, especially since he seemed to place little importance on the childhood causes of adult emotional problems. But Rogers also had his supporters and received numerous awards from psychology associations for his work in the field. He was also awarded honorary doctorates from several universities in the United States and Europe. Although labeled a humanist, Rogers was an innovator in the scientific study of the therapy process, primarily through videotaping sessions with his client's permission and then analyzing the tapes.

Throughout his career, Rogers continued to believe that the essence of the therapeutic relationship and the key to resolving emotional problems was the relationship between the patient and the therapist. As he put it in *On Becoming a Person,* "I have come to feel that the more fully the individual is understood and accepted, the more he tends to drop the false fronts with which he has been meeting life, and the more he tends to move in a direction that is forward."

See also: PERSONALITY; PSYCHOTHERAPY

Bibliography

Anderson, Rob, and Cissna, Kenneth N., eds. (1997). *The Martin Buber-Carl Rogers Dialogue: A New Transcript with Commentary.* Albany: State University of New York Press.

Farber, Barry A.; Brink, Debora C.; and Raskin, Patricia M. (1996). *The Psychotherapy of Carl Rogers: Cases and Commentary.* New York: Guilford.

Rogers, Carl R. (1939). *The Clinical Treatment of the Problem Child.* Boston: Houghton Mifflin.

Rogers, Carl R. (1942). *Counseling and Psychotherapy: Newer Concepts in Practice.* Boston: Houghton Mifflin.

Rogers, Carl R. (1951). *Client-Centered Therapy: Its Current Practice, Implications, and Theory.* Boston: Houghton Mifflin.

Rogers, Carl R. (1961). *On Becoming a Person: A Therapist's View of Psychotherapy.* Boston: Houghton.

Suhd, Melvin, ed. (1995). *Positive Regard: Carl Rogers and Other Notables He Inspired.* Palo Alto, CA: Science and Behavior Books.

David Levinson

S

SADNESS

When bad things happen, what determines a person's emotional response? According to cognitive theories of emotion, people experience emotions primarily when they appraise events (consciously or unconsciously) as either facilitating or obstructing their goals, necessitating a revision of their goals or the construction of new plans. The particular relationship that people discern between their goals and events determines the specific emotional response. In other words, interpretations of events, rather than events themselves, determine emotional responses. The same event could be expected to evoke sadness or a variety of other emotions, such as anger, shame, or fear, depending upon the aspects of the event to which people attend and the inferences they make about the event. Hence, a central question concerning sadness is, what kinds of interpretations evoke sadness as opposed to other emotions?

Antecedents of Sadness

Several researchers have taken up this question about what personal interpretations lead to sadness, and they have formulated models of the cognitive processes associated with particular emotions. According to most models, positive emotions, such as happiness, result from the attainment of a goal or desire, and negative emotions, such as sadness and anger, result from the failure to attain a goal or desire. Sadness is thus a response to viewing an event as *inconsistent* with one's goals. Although few researchers would disagree

with this basic conceptualization of sadness, it is fairly nonspecific and does not fully differentiate sadness from other negative emotions, in particular, anger. More specific claims about the types of appraisals that elicit sadness are controversial, however, and differ on two issues. The first issue concerns whether sadness is evoked by a simple assessment that an event is inconsistent with one's goals, or whether a more complex appraisal is necessary. For those researchers who hold that more elaborate appraisals are necessary for sadness to occur, a second issue arises: Do the further appraisals in question concern the agent responsible for goal failure or do they concern the possibility of reinstating the thwarted goal?

Some researchers hold that the interpretations of events that elicit sadness are quite simple. According to Bernard Weiner's (1985) attribution theory of emotion, events initially evoke a general positive or negative reaction—a "primitive" emotion—based on a simple appraisal of success or failure, with happiness being the response to success and sadness being the response to failure. Weiner holds that happiness and sadness are "attribution-independent" emotions that are determined solely by the attainment or nonattainment of a goal. Other emotions, such as pride, anger, pity, and guilt, are described as "attribution-dependent" emotions because they require further cognitive processing concerning the causes of goal attainment or failure. Thus, sadness is elicited by a simple, initial appraisal of goal inconsistency (e.g., "I wanted to go to the concert and I cannot go"), whereas anger requires not only this appraisal but also more complex, causal attributions concerning the agent responsible for the negative outcome and whether the agent could have prevented the outcome (e.g., "I wanted to go to the concert and I cannot go because you neglected to buy the tickets in time").

Other models hold that more complex cognitive appraisals play an influential role in causing sadness. According to Craig Smith and Phoebe Ellsworth (1985), in addition to an awareness that goal failure has occurred, sadness requires a belief that the unpleasant situation is controlled by impersonal circumstances rather than by another human. Similarly, Ira Roseman and his colleagues (1994) describe sadness as an emotion in which the cause of an event is disregarded, unspecified, or identified as circumstances beyond anyone's control. Appraisals concerning the agent responsible for failure are thought to differentiate sadness from other negative emotions, such as anger (in which the cause is identified as other people) and shame (in which the cause is identified as the self). In support of this claim, adults who are asked to describe events that made them sad typically include in their accounts a negative outcome that was caused by circumstances outside of their own or another person's control. In contrast, adults who are asked to describe events that made them angry typically include in their accounts a reference to another person's negligence or intention to do harm. Other studies have shown, however, that the conditions that evoke anger also generate a lot of sadness. Moreover, Nancy Stein and Linda Levine (1989) have found that although preschool children understand the meaning of both sadness and anger, they do not focus on the intentions of the person who caused failure when they describe events that evoked either emotion. Thus, while inferences about the agent who caused a negative outcome are important facets of emotional experience, they do not consistently distinguish sadness from anger.

Evidence suggests that people's beliefs about their ability to cope with a negative outcome influence whether or not they respond to negative events with sadness. Indeed, feelings of both sadness and anger

may depend less on people's beliefs concerning the agent responsible for goal failure than on their beliefs about whether they can do anything to reinstate the thwarted goal. Stein and Levine (1989) investigated the types of appraisals that evoke sadness as opposed to other emotions. Preschool children, first grade children, and adults were asked whether story protagonists would feel angry or sad, why they would feel that way, and what they would do. Stein and Levine found that attributions of agency and intent were important for the two older groups of participants. All age groups, however, attributed sadness to protagonists more often when they interpreted failure as being irrevocable; they attributed anger more often when they believed that something could be done to reinstate the goal. Other investigators, such as Smith and Richard Lazarus (1993), also have noted that sadness is associated with irrevocable loss and feelings of helplessness and powerlessness. In contrast to the claim that sadness is the simplest negative emotion, Stein and Levine also found that explanations given by children and adults for why people felt sad were just as complex as their explanations for feelings of anger. In particular, when explaining why people felt sad, participants did not limit their descriptions to the failure of a goal. They went on to describe the consequences of failure, exploring further losses likely to stem from the original irrevocable negative outcome. These findings suggest that sadness results not only from the appraisal that one has failed to attain something of value but also from the appraisal that one can do nothing to change the situation.

Whether people respond to negative events with sadness or with another negative emotion also depends upon the aspects of the situation to which they attend. Goal failure can take at least two forms: the absence of something desirable (loss) or the presence of something undesirable (aversive state). In many cases, the same negative event can be viewed either as a loss or as an aversive state. For example, a person who is ill can focus on the loss of health and its attendant privileges or on the presence of weakness, pain, and boredom. People tend to respond differently to events depending upon whether they construe them as losses or aversive states. Sadness is expressed more frequently in response to losses than in response to aversive states, whereas anger is expressed more frequently in response to aversive states than losses.

Consequences of Sadness

Once evoked, emotions motivate people to maintain positive situations, change negative ones, or revise their goals and expectations. Negative emotions signal the presence of a problem and the need for increased

---

Johann Wolfgang von Goethe, in 1774, published one of the most depressing and hopeless love stories, The Sorrows of Young Werther. *Young Werther falls passionately in love with a young woman who is already engaged to be married to Albert. Despite her engagement, Werther calls on the woman every day; he cannot overcome his need to be with her. Even after she marries Albert, Werther hovers in the area. However, he becomes more and more melancholy and depressed until he kills himself.*

A woman cries out of sadness as her husband returns to duty in Vietnam in December 1969. (Corbis/James L. Amos)

attention to specific features of the self and the environment. Expressions of emotion also function to communicate one's state to others. So what specific purposes does feeling sad serve? When is sadness an adaptive response to failure and when is it maladaptive?

One function of sadness appears to be the elicitation of empathy and assistance from others. Carroll Izard (1993) has demonstrated that, from early infancy onward, manifestations of sadness, such as crying and withdrawal, communicate helplessness and entice empathetic responses. When a person appraises a negative situation as being beyond his or her capacity to change and views the self as helpless, then other people may at least provide sympathy and comfort (and at most be instrumental in the alleviation of the negative situation and the resulting feelings of sadness).

Because sadness elicits empathic responses and aid from others, it has sometimes been characterized as a "passive" emotion marked by crying, withdrawal, and inaction. Although this view may adequately describe the behavioral manifestations of sadness, it is not representative of the mental activity that occurs when people feel sad. Because activity toward an unattainable goal must cease, sad people give the outward appearance of passivity when, in reality, they are engaging in a considerable amount of cognitive activity.

When people are sad, they tend to dwell on negative outcomes that cannot be changed and on the consequences of those outcomes. The types of wishes and plans expressed by sad people primarily consist of the desire to attain the goal that has been thwarted, followed by plans to forfeit the failed goal and substitute new goals. The sad individual thus exists in a state of tension where he or she still desires an outcome that is recognized as being unattainable. Sadness appears to motivate efforts to come to terms with irrevocable outcomes by revising beliefs and expectations that are inconsistent with those outcomes, by relinquishing goals that cannot be attained, and by turning attention to new goals that may be more realistic. Thus, when the sad person is withdrawn and apparently doing nothing, he or she may be engaged in the difficult mental work of understanding the implications of failure and substituting more attainable goals. When this process is complete, the feeling of sadness abates. This type of coping is important because it not only deters people from the endless pursuit of unobtainable goals but also increases the likelihood of achieving new, more realistic goals.

However, the strategies people employ to regulate sadness and to cope with changes in their goals are not always adaptive. Comparing sadness with clinical depression highlights the differences between adaptive and maladaptive responses to failure and loss. According to the standard diagnostic criteria set forth in the American Psychiatric Association's *Diagnostic and Statistical Manual of Mental Disorders* (DSM-IV, 1994), the essential feature of a major depressive episode is prolonged depressed mood or the loss of interest or pleasure in nearly all activities. The distress associated with clinical depression is experienced by individuals as qualitatively different from ordinary sadness such as that experienced during bereavement. Whereas the DSM-IV describes periods of sadness as inherent aspects of human experience, these feelings are not diagnosed as a major depressive episode unless specific criteria are met for severity, duration, and clinically significant distress or impairment. Ordinary sadness is also distinguished from depression by its adaptive, functional qualities. As Lee Anna Clark and David Watson (1994) note, few theories have convincingly demonstrated the function or adaptive significance of depression. Based on their study of bereaved caregivers of men with AIDS, Stein and her colleagues (1997) characterize the maladaptive goal processes associated with depression as not only the recognition that desired goals cannot be achieved but also the refusal to give up those goals or the failure to generate new goals that might lead to positive outcomes.

A related line of research examines how people's manner of coping with depression and sadness influences the severity and duration of these moods. Susan Nolen-Hoeksema (1991) has argued that people who ruminate in response to depressed moods often intensify and prolong their periods of sadness and depression whereas people who engage in distracting responses experience greater remediation of their negative moods. Nolen-Hoeksema defines ruminative responses as "behaviors and thoughts that focus one's attention on one's depressive symptoms and on the implications of these symptoms" and notes that these thoughts and behaviors are symptom-focused and contemplative (p. 569). Distracting responses, on the other hand, represent the "purposeful turning of one's attention away from one's symptoms of depression and its possible causes and consequences to pleasant or neutral activities" (p. 570). These response styles are contrasted in a brief exchange between Alice and the White Queen from Lewis Carroll's *Through the Looking Glass* (1872, pp. 250–251):

> "Only it is so *very* lonely here!" Alice said in a melancholy voice; and, at the thought of her loneliness, two large tears came rolling down her cheeks.
>
> "Oh, don't go on like that!" cried the poor Queen, wringing her hands in despair. "Consider what a great girl you are. Consider what a long way you've come to-day. Consider what o'clock it is. Consider anything, only don't cry!"
>
> Alice could not help laughing at this, even in the midst of her tears. "Can *you* keep from crying by considering things?" she asked.
>
> "That's the way it's done," the Queen said with great decision: "nobody can do two things at once, you know."

Ruminative responses to sadness and depression may be maladaptive not only because they repetitively focus attention on one's emotions and symptoms but also because they hinder problem-solving activities that might remedy the situation or alleviate the negative mood. Nolen-Hoeksema and her colleagues (1993) note that people engaging in ruminative responses spend much of their time thinking about how badly they feel and do not take action to change their situation. These findings may have been anticipated by George Bernard Shaw (1914), who wrote, "The secret of being miserable is to have leisure to bother about whether you are happy or not. The cure for it is occupation."

While attempts to understand the implications of failure are an adaptive feature of sadness, rumination on the causes of sadness and on the symptoms and experience of sadness appears to perpetuate the emotion. Further research is needed to clarify the features that differentiate the types of rumination that prolong and amplify sadness from the types of adaptive cognitive work necessary to recognize irrevocable changes in the status of goals, to restructure beliefs and expectations, and to substitute new goals.

The Expression of Sadness

Some research points to differences in the experience and expression of sadness between males and females and between individuals in different cultures. Gender differences in depression are well-established. Nolen-Hoeksema (1990) found that adolescent and adult females reported depressed mood almost twice as often as their male counterparts. Gender differences in the *experience* of ordinary sadness are less well-documented, but studies suggest differences in the ways that sadness is *expressed* by males and females. The early development of these differences has been examined in research on how parents talk about emotions with their sons and daughters. Susan Adams and her colleagues (1995) examined parents' and children's use of emotion language in the preschool years. They found that parents used more emotion words (and a greater variety of emotions words) when discussing emotions with their daughters than with their sons. Moreover, parents were more likely to mention sadness in conversations with daughters than with sons. From an early age, then, girls may be given greater encouragement than boys to attend to a variety of emotional states, especially sadness.

Gender differences in the expression of sadness also have been noted in older children and adults. Janice Zeman and Judy Garber (1996) asked first-, third-, and fifth-graders about the conditions in which they would express sadness, anger, and physical pain. Younger children reported expressing sadness more often than did older children, and girls reported expressing sadness more often than did boys. Richard Fabes and Carol Martin (1991) asked college students

> *The poet Theodore Roethke wrote "Elegy for Jane" in 1953 to honor one of his students who had been thrown from a horse. His own sadness at her death can find no consolation. He speaks of his anguish over her loss, which is very powerful though he was "neither father nor lover."*

to describe how often males and females of different ages feel and express sadness and other emotions. The students did not expect males and females to differ in their experience of sadness, but females were described as more likely to express sadness than males. A perceived effect of age was also found—prepubescent boys and girls were rated equally likely to express sadness whereas adolescent and adult males were expected to express sadness less often than their female counterparts.

Although sadness is found in almost every culture, the results of some research suggests the existence of cultural differences in the expression and experience of sadness, differences that may stem from emotion appraisals. For example, Roseman and his colleagues (1995) asked college students from the United States and India to recall an experience in which they felt a particular negative emotion (sadness, fear, or anger) and to describe their appraisals and emotional responses. Both Americans and Indians included appraisals of powerlessness in their accounts of sadness, but Indians reported feeling less intense sadness than did Americans. Consistent with the lower intensity of sadness expressed by Indians, negative outcomes were described by Indians as less discrepant from their actual goals. Hence, as Roseman and colleagues note, cultural differences in appraisals concerning goals might be responsible for differences in emotional responses.

According to Robert Levy (1982), large disparities exist in the extent to which specific emotions are emphasized in different cultures. He characterizes cultural approaches to specific emotions as either "hypercognized" or "hypocognized." An emotion is described as hypercognized if a society possesses an easily accessible cultural system for interpreting the emotion. An emotion is described as hypocognized if a society has little knowledge of the emotion (i.e., few references to the emotion are found in the lexicon, in everyday discourse, and in literature). Levy argues that sadness is a hypocognized emotion in Tahitian culture. Tahitians' experience of what would be described as sadness in many cultures appears to be manifested as physical symptoms of fatigue or disturbance. Differences in feeling may influence the ways in which emotions can be functional. For example, research indicates that the experience of sadness directs attention to the changes in the status of goals and initiates a sequence of cognitive restructuring. Levy (1973) describes how Tahitians might not share this experience. Observing a man who had separated from his wife and child, he interpreted the man's reaction as sadness caused by the separation. The man, however, described his own reaction in physical terms and did not attribute it to the same causes. These findings indicate that in some cultures (albeit a minority), the experience and expression of sadness may differ in important ways from the Western account.

Conclusion

Although gender and cross-cultural differences in the expression, and even the experience, of sadness cannot be denied, sadness in some form is an inevitable component of the human experience. As long as gaps exist between people's desires and their ability to attain their desires, sadness will be experienced. Because the emotional pain of sadness motivates people to relinquish beliefs and goals that are untenable and orient toward new goals, sadness plays an important role in people's adaptation to loss. The poet Rainer Maria Rilke (1904, p. 64) describes the value of sadness in his *Letters to a Young Poet:*

> Were it possible for us to see further than our knowledge reaches, . . . perhaps we would endure our sadnesses with greater confidence than our joys. For they are the moments when something new has entered into us, something unknown; our feelings grow mute in shy perplexity, everything in us withdraws, a stillness comes, and the new, which no one knows, stands in the midst of it and is silent.

See also: ANGER; ATTRIBUTION; CRYING; GRIEF; HELPLESSNESS; HOPELESSNESS; LONELINESS; PAIN; UNIVERSALITY OF EMOTIONAL EXPRESSION

Bibliography

Adams, Susan; Kuebli, Janet; Boyle, Patricia A.; and Fivush, Robyn. (1995). "Gender Differences in Parent-Child Conversations about Past Emotions: A Longitudinal Investigation." *Sex Roles* 33:309–323.

American Psychiatric Association. (1994). *Diagnostic and Statistical Manual of Mental Disorders,* 4th ed. Washington, DC: American Psychiatric Association.

Carroll, Lewis. ([1872] 1960). *The Annotated Alice: Alice's Adventures in Wonderland and Through the Looking Glass,* introduction and notes by Martin Gardner. New York: C. N. Potter.

Clark, Lee Anna, and Watson, David. (1994). "Distinguishing Functional from Dysfunctional Affective Responses." In *The Nature of Emotion: Fundamental Questions,* ed. Paul Ekman and Richard J. Davidson. New York: Oxford University Press.

Fabes, Richard A., and Martin, Carol Lynn. (1991). "Gender and Age Stereotypes of Emotionality." *Personality and Social Psychology Bulletin* 17:532–540.

Izard, Carroll E. (1993). "Organizational and Motivational Functions of Discrete Emotions." In *Handbook of Emotions,* ed. Michael Lewis and Jeannette M. Haviland. New York: Guilford.

Lazarus, Richard S. (1991). *Emotion and Adaptation.* New York: Oxford University Press.

Levine, Linda J. (1995). "Young Children's Understanding of the Causes of Anger and Sadness." *Child Development* 66:697–709.

Levine, Linda J. (1996). "The Anatomy of Disappointment: A Naturalistic Test of Appraisal Models of Sadness, Anger, and Hope." *Cognition and Emotion* 10:337–359.

Levy, Robert I. (1973). *Tahitians: Mind and Experience in the Society Islands.* Chicago: University of Chicago Press.

Levy, Robert I. (1982). "On the Nature and Functions of the Emotions." *Social Science Information* 21:511–528.

Nolen-Hoeksema, Susan. (1990). *Sex Differences in Depression.* Stanford, CA: Stanford University Press.

Nolen-Hoeksema, Susan. (1991). "Responses to Depression and Their Effects on the Duration of Depressive Episodes." *Journal of Abnormal Psychology* 100:569–582.

Nolen-Hoeksema, Susan; Morrow, Jannay; and Fredrickson, Barbara L. (1993). "Response Styles and the Duration of Episodes of Depressed Mood." *Journal of Abnormal Psychology* 102:20–28.

Oatley, Keith. (1992). *Best Laid Schemes: The Psychology of Emotions.* New York: Cambridge University Press.

Rilke, Rainer Maria. ([1904] 1993). *Letters to a Young Poet,* tr. M. D. Herter Norton. New York: W. W. Norton.

Roseman, Ira J.; Dhawan, Nisha; Rettek, S. Ilsa; Naidu, R. K.; and Thapa, Komilla. (1995). "Cultural Differences and Cross-Cultural Similarities in Appraisals and Emotional Responses." *Journal of Cross-Cultural Psychology* 26:23–48.

Roseman, Ira J.; Wiest, Cynthia; and Swartz, Tamara S. (1994). "Phenomenology, Behaviors, and Goals Differentiate Discrete Emotions." *Journal of Personality and Social Psychology* 67:206–221.

Shaw, George Bernard. (1914). *Misalliance, The Dark Lady of the Sonnets, and Fanny's First Play. With a Treatise on Parents and Children.* New York: Brentano's.

Smith, Craig A., and Ellsworth, Phoebe C. (1985). "Patterns of Cognitive Appraisal in Emotion." *Journal of Personality and Social Psychology* 48:813–838.

Smith, Craig A., and Lazarus, Richard S. (1993). "Appraisal Components, Core Relational Themes, and the Emotions." *Cognition and Emotion* 7:233–269.

Stein, Nancy L.; Folkman, Susan; Trabasso, Tom; and Richards, Anne T. (1997). "Appraisal and Goal Processes as Predictors of Psychological Well-Being in Bereaved Caregivers." *Journal of Personality and Social Psychology* 72:872–884.

Stein, Nancy L., and Levine, Linda J. (1989). "The Causal Organization of Emotional Knowledge: A Developmental Study." *Cognition and Emotion* 3:343–378.

Weiner, Bernard. (1985). "An Attributional Theory of Achievement Motivation and Emotion." *Psychological Review* 92:548–573.

Zeman, Janice, and Garber, Judy. (1996). "Display Rules for Anger, Sadness, and Pain." *Child Development* 67:957–973.

Tracy M. Laulhere
Linda J. Levine

SARTRE, JEAN-PAUL

b. Paris, France, June 21, 1905; *d.* Paris, France, April 15, 1980; *philosophy, literature, drama.*

Jean-Paul Sartre was a French philosopher, novelist, dramatist, critic, essayist, and social and political activ-ist. Within philosophy, he is considered to be the leading existentialist of the post-World War II era. In addition, he is the only person ever to have declined the Nobel Prize for Literature (1964) of his own free will. (Although he later wanted to obtain the money attached to the prize, it was not given.)

Sartre was the son of Jean-Baptiste Sartre, a naval officer, and Anne-Marie Sartre, a niece of Albert Schweitzer. His father died when Sartre was a young boy, so he was raised by his mother in the home of his maternal grandfather, Carl Schweitzer, a professor of German at the Sorbonne. Sartre was attracted to words and writing as a boy and attended the Lycée Henri IV in Paris and the prestigious École Normale Supérieure. There he met and became close with other intellectually gifted young men and women (including Simone Weil, Jean Hippolyte, and Claude Lévi-Strauss) and began a life-long relationship with the novelist and essayist Simone de Beauvoir, who also

Jean-Paul Sartre walks down a Paris street with Simone de Beauvoir in 1970. (Corbis/Hulton-Deutsch Collection)

shared his passionate concerns about the plight of the poor and the weak. Although they chose never to marry and agreed to take other partners, Sartre and de Beauvoir remained committed to one another until his death in 1980. She even supported him during the last decade of his life.

After graduating from school in 1929, Sartre taught in high schools in Le Havre, Laon, and Paris and traveled in Egypt, Greece, and Italy. He also studied for a year (1933–1934) in Germany, where he was influenced by the ideas of Edmund Husserl, Martin Heidegger, and Soren Kierkegaard. The phenomenological and existential ideas of these men influenced Sartre's own developing philosophy. Upon returning to France, Sartre continued to teach, but he also became part of an intellectual circle on the Left Bank and began writing and publishing essays, none of which brought him much attention. His first novel, *La Nausée*, was published in 1938 and a collection of short stories, *Le Mur* (*The Wall*), was published in 1939. Both were negative, stark psychological works that questioned the rationale for human existence.

Sartre also wrote a short and widely ignored work on emotion in 1939: *Esquisse d'une théorie des émotion*. This publication was not translated into English until 1948, when it was published under the title *The Emotions: Outline of a Theory*. Emotions were a lifelong concern for Sartre, and he is one of the few philosophers to have actually set forth a theory of emotion. This theory, which is best classified as phenomenological/existential, views emotion as a mechanism that is used by humans to interact with the world. Sartre asserted that emotional responses arise from consciousness and serve the purpose of enabling individuals to deal with worldly situations in non-rational ways. While this model has drawn some attention in humanistic psychology, it has not had much influence on the scientific study of emotion, nor on the clinical treatment of emotional disorder.

Having been called up for service in the French Army in 1939, Sartre was taken prisoner by the Germans in 1940. During this period of captivity, he took to writing plays, and after his release in 1941, he wrote *Les Mouches* (*The Flies*) and *Huis Clos* (*No Exit*), both of which were staged in Paris. Critics considered these plays, along with a dozen others produced over the next fifteen years, to be dark and pessimistic about the human experience. This reflected Sartre's desire to portray the human experience and human relationships in as much detail as possible. Unlike many other philosophers, he was as much concerned with how people felt and how they related to other people as with what they said and did. Sartre summarized his ideas and approach in *L'Etre et le neant* (1943; *Being* and *Nothingness*) and *L'existentialisme est un humanisme* (1946; *Existentialism and Humanism*).

After World War II, Sartre turned from studying the individual to studying society, and much of his attention was devoted to remedying social and political ills. Sartre, who was a Marxist but not a communist, spoke out and wrote against the Stalin government in the Soviet Union, supported freedom movements around the world, and condemned the involvement of the United States in Vietnam. From 1960 until his writing career was ended by the loss of his eyesight in the early 1970s, Sartre's major literary project was a detailed intellectual and psychological biography of the French novelist Gustave Flaubert—two volumes appeared in 1971, and another appeared in 1972. However, the work remained unfinished when Sartre died in 1980 of lung cancer. By that point, he had become a world figure, as a philosopher, novelist, dramatist, and social activist, and his funeral was attended by some fifty thousand mourners.

See also: CONSCIOUSNESS; PHILOSOPHY

Bibliography

Fourney, Jean-Francois, and Minahen, Charles D., eds. (1997). *Situating Sartre in Twentieth-Century Thought and Culture*. New York: St. Martin's Press.
Howells, Christina, ed. (1992). *The Cambridge Companion to Sartre*. Cambridge, Eng.: Cambridge University Press.
Schilpp, Paul A., ed. (1981). *Philosophy of John-Paul Sartre*. La Salle, IL: Open Court.
Wider, Kathleen V. (1997). *The Bodily Nature of Consciousness*. Ithaca, NY: Cornell University Press.

David Levinson

SATISFACTION

The term *satisfaction* is derived from Latin, *facere* (to do or make) and *satis* (enough). Thus, the experience of satisfaction is based on the perception of the situation and the judgment that enough has been done to meet expectations or standards of comparison, most likely as a part of some form of transaction. The role one's own mind may play in ascertaining personal satisfaction could be what led Abraham Lincoln to comment that "Most people are about as happy as they make up their mind to be." Over the years, the extent of applicable expectations or standards of comparison has grown among scientists who study satisfaction, particularly overall satisfaction with life.

Satisfaction As a Concept

Angus Campbell, Philip Converse, and Willard Rodgers (1976, p. 8) defined satisfaction to be "the perceived discrepancy between aspiration and achievement, ranging from the perception of fulfillment to that of deprivation." Social exchange theorists tended to focus on satisfaction as the emotional product of equity, the emotional response when an individual got what he or she thought was deserved. Frank Andrews and Aubrey McKennell (1980, p. 135) stated that "the concept of satisfaction requires some kind of comparison—either explicit or implicit—between a level of achievement and some standard (e.g., what one expects or aspires to)."

Campbell (1981, p. 22) cited three comparisons or standards when he stated that "satisfaction implies an act of judgment, a comparison of what people have to what they think they deserve, expect, or may reasonably aspire to." Alex Michalos (1985, 1986) used six types of comparisons, as part of a "gap theory," to explain satisfaction: what one wants compared to what one has, actual conditions compared to ideal conditions, actual conditions compared to expectations, actual conditions compared to best past conditions, what one has compared to what others have, and personal attribute compared to environmental attribute. In the context of satisfaction with one's standard of living, M. Joseph Sirgy (1998) discussed six expectations: one's ideal, what one deserves, what one minimally needs, what one thinks will happen, what one has had in the past, and what one's ability might obtain. However, Sirgy and his colleagues (1995) have further advanced the field conceptually and in terms of measurement by developing the life accomplishments satisfaction measure shown in Table 1.

It should be noted that Ruut Veenhoven (1995) has taken issue with both "folklore" and "social comparison" theory approaches to the effect of socioeconomic conditions on life satisfaction. Folklore theory suggests that the effects of objective socioeconomic conditions can be obscured because people never get over their perceptions of their status formed in early youth—they keep thinking they are better off, even if their standard of living declines or they keep thinking they are poorly off, even if their life improves. Social comparison theory raises several issues. First, as standard of living changes, people might get used to it, raising or lowering their expectations, with a net small change in overall satisfaction. Second, people might derive their satisfaction from a comparison of the past with the present (being better off leads to satisfaction even if still poor) or with other reference groups (being better off than others leads to satisfaction). In his analysis of data from many nations, Veenhoven found more support for his idea that objective standard of living predicts happiness, without a need for comparisons.

If the discrepancy approach is valid (remembering that Veenhoven questions it), there are many implications with regard to the definition of satisfaction as an emotional response to a cognitive process of evaluating the discrepancy between the current situation and a comparative standard or expectation. As Campbell (1981, p. 22) observed, "Satisfaction . . . may also be a satisfaction of resignation, when one comes to understand that what once seemed possible is no longer so and the best must be made of it." In other words, one can be disappointed and yet still (somewhat) satisfied.

More than a little research has demonstrated how objective conditions do not automatically translate into satisfaction. This is probably due to the fact that the comparative aspects of satisfaction make it a truly "relative" concept. The ancient tale of the Indian who felt bad that he had no shoes until he met a beggar who had no feet comes to mind. Poor people often report higher satisfaction than some rich people, while many rich people report lower satisfaction than some poor people, a situation referred to by Geraldine Olson and Brigitte Schober (1993) as the "satisfaction paradox." Learned helplessness among the poor may be one explanation for the satisfaction paradox. It may be more realistic for those with low incomes to revise their goals or expectations than to change their immediate objective circumstances. As Leo Tolstoy wrote in *Anna Karenina* (1875–1877, p. 823), "There are no conditions to which a man cannot become used, especially if he sees that all around him are living in the same way."

The satisfaction paradox affects those with higher incomes as well. Veenhoven (1991) cites the statistic that per capita real income doubled in the United States after World War II but overall personal satisfaction levels were stable—in other words, substantial objective improvements did not translate into higher satisfaction, perhaps because expectations about standard of living rose with per capita income. This implies that satisfaction with wealth is as much contingent upon one's standards or expectations as it is upon one's actual wealth.

However, the satisfaction paradox led Sally Lerner (1997) to recognize an important limitation of satisfaction as a policy variable. Because it is based on both the perception of a person's objective situation and a standard/expectation, it becomes possible for a society to manipulate information in a way that minimizes that society's focus on its difficult problems, such as racial inequity or poverty, through slogans such as "As long as the poor feel satisfied with their lot, who cares!" or "You may seem poor, but things are better now than they used to be and they will be better yet in the future!"

Table 1   Satisfaction with Life Accomplishments

Expectation/Standard	Item
One's life accomplishments compared to ideal outcomes	Compared to your lifetime goals, ideals, and what you had ideally hoped to become, how satisfied are you?
Deserved outcomes	Compared to what you feel you deserve to have happened to you considering all that you've worked for, how satisfied are you?
Versus relatives	Compared to the accomplishments of your relatives (parents, brother, sister, etc.), how satisfied are you?
Versus friends/associates	Compared to the accomplishments of your friends and associates, how satisfied are you?
Versus an average person in similar positions	Compared to the accomplishments of most people in your position, how satisfied are you?
Standard based on past experience	Compared to where you've been and how far you have come along (the progress you have made, the changes you have gone through, or the level of growth you have experienced), how satisfied are you?
Based on self-concept of one's own strengths and weaknesses (and resources)	Compared to what you have expected from yourself all along considering your resources, strengths, and weaknesses, how satisfied are you?
Based on predicted outcomes	Compared to what you may have predicted about yourself becoming, how satisfied are you?
Expected outcomes	Compared to what you feel you should have accomplished so far, how satisfied are you?
Minimum tolerable outcomes	Compared to what you feel is the minimum of what anyone in your position should have accomplished (and be able to accomplish), how satisfied are you?

Another implication of the comparative nature of satisfaction is that whether or not people describe themselves as being satisfied depends on the context in which they are asked to think about their level of satisfaction. Ed Diener (1994) summarizes previous research in which awareness of other's problems was associated with reports of greater personal life satisfaction while prior thoughts about one's own recent misfortunes were associated with lower satisfaction—prior thoughts about distant personal misfortunes led to higher personal satisfaction reports. Context can reverse expected outcomes. Fritz Muthny and his colleagues (1990) found that cancer patients facing imminent death were more likely (33%) to report very high satisfaction than were healthy subjects (13%).

Diener (1994) also notes that the order of the questions being posed also plays an important role in sat-isfaction assessments. If one is asked about satisfaction with marriage first and then family, the family satisfaction report may be lower if marital satisfaction is high; reversing the order might lead to an opposite result, even if the questions were worded exactly the same. The reason for this difference is that in the former case the family satisfaction question is interpreted as being family satisfaction without the marital component since a marital component question had already been asked. The net result is that the meaning of satisfaction will vary with the context, the expectations or standards of comparison being used, and how the information is being elicited.

Is it fair, however, to argue that satisfaction is *entirely* relative? In other words, do one's objective conditions matter or not? It might be that as one's income increases, one's standard of reference or expectations might increase just as much, so that any increase in satisfaction resulting from an increase in income will have a short life. Answering such questions has not been easy. For example, James Hagedorn (1996) was unable to clarify whether satisfaction resulted more from circumstances or from how people thought they had handled their circumstances (both of which factors were relevant). For example, Veenhoven (1996) found that most people who live in tolerable economic conditions report moderate to high levels of satisfaction with life, while people who live in economically advantaged nations are less satisfied. It appears that once an adequate economy is attained, further economic improvements may not improve average life satisfaction very much.

Although satisfaction is related to personality traits such as optimism, it nevertheless does vary, at the individual level, with the occurrence of objective life events (e.g., divorce), the lapse of long periods of time, and changes in living conditions (e.g., unemployment). Individuals who have professional jobs, better intimate relationships, internal control, and favorable life events are usually more satisfied with life. At the national level, average life satisfaction is greater in nations that have higher per capita incomes, that respect human rights and political freedom, and that have greater per capita education. Veenhoven (1996) has concluded that satisfaction, therefore, is not entirely relative; the correlation between objective conditions and life satisfaction is smaller than might be expected, but it is still substantial.

Satisfaction Compared to Related Concepts

Satisfaction is just one concept of affect amidst several related concepts, including pleasure, happiness, and joy. Compared to these other related concepts, satisfaction is perhaps the most straightforward—and perhaps the most amenable to scientific analysis.

Pleasure

L. W. Sumner (1996, p. 140) claims that "[classical] hedonism, the historically dominant subjective theory, reduces happiness to pleasure (and the absence of pain)." Pleasure is keyed to physiological, often tangible, influences. However, pleasure may have a short life, ending soon after the tangible influence ends or if the influence continues and is taken for granted. For example, lottery winners may be initially elated, but their euphoria soon wanes. James Averill and Thomas More (1993) developed the relationship between pleasure and happiness/satisfaction in more depth. They argued that momentary pleasures would probably only contribute to happiness or satisfaction in the long run if they were subsumed within broader

social or psychological systems that were informed by higher-order principles. They went so far as to argue that gaining pleasure for its own sake alone would be like eating junk food, which can satisfy the senses without providing real nourishment. Averill and More noted how drugs could be used to activate pleasure centers in the brain and produce pleasure extrinsically, but they also pointed out that the final result was a vague sense of dissatisfaction, regardless of how pleasurable the initial experience was. This led them to conclude that unless the pleasure had a purpose, it was no prescription for happiness. Sumner (1996) agreed and stated that having lots of pleasure will not guarantee happiness if a person wants deeper and more meaningful sources of satisfaction. Writers seem to concur as well with the transitory and unfulfilling nature of pleasure by itself. William Hazlett (1836, p. 382) commented, "So have I loitered my life away, reading books, looking at pictures, going to plays, hearing, thinking, writing on what pleased me best. I have wanted only one thing to make me happy, but wanting that have wanted everything."

Happiness

Correlations between satisfaction and happiness are substantial. In Lisa Feldman's (1995) circumplex model of emotions, satisfaction is located adjacent to happiness—both are positive moods, but satisfaction is related to a slightly lower level of arousal than is happiness. Veenhoven (1984) even goes so far as to argue that global satisfaction with life-as-a-whole and overall happiness with life are synonymous. Because happiness and satisfaction are so closely related, some scholars use the two concepts interchangeably.

Most scholars, however, recognize that satisfaction has a stronger cognitive as opposed to an affective component due to its evaluative aspects. For example, Campbell, Converse, and Rodgers (1976, p. 8) defined satisfaction to be the more cognitive component of well-being because "[s]atisfaction implies a judgmental or cognitive experience while happiness suggests an experience of feeling or affect." Lorne Tepperman and James Curtis (1995, p. 256) stated that "[t]hough in many studies, satisfaction and happiness are empirically correlated to varying degrees, they are nonetheless distinct. Happiness is an emotional state that appears to have physically measurable symptoms, while satisfaction is a cognitive or judgmental state without any obvious symptoms. While it may take the respondent some time to decide whether he or she is satisfied, no time is needed to decide whether he or she is happy." Diener and Suh (1997) have found that happy people smile more and have more left frontal brain activity. These people also think about, recall, and talk about more positive things. Although current mood does affect life satisfaction ratings, its effect is less than that associated with long-term mood; the reverse is probably true for happiness. John Stuart Mill (1873, p. 100) wrote, "Ask yourself whether you are happy, and you cease to be so." However, satisfaction, which is an assessment of a state of being, *requires* that people ask themselves about it. It might be possible not to rationalize happiness, but satisfaction depends on a rationalization process.

Compared to satisfaction, happiness may be influenced more by circumstances and situational factors that are pleasing or displeasing (circumstances that often are related to interpersonal relationships). According to David Myers and Diener (1995), happy people are less self-focused, less hostile and abusive, and less vulnerable to disease. They are more loving, forgiving, trusting, energetic, decisive, creative, helpful, and sociable. In addition, happy people are high in self-esteem, sense of personal control, optimism, and extraversion. Those individuals who are happily married are usually much happier in general than those who are unhappily married or not married at all. The idea that happiness might be related to good relationships is, of course, not new. Victor Hugo wrote in *Les Misérables* (1862, p. 145), "The greatest happiness of life is the conviction that we are loved, loved for ourselves, or rather, in spite of ourselves."

Research on happiness and satisfaction reveals that the same people may report high levels on one concept and low levels on the other; the concepts may have different correlations with common predictor variables and may change over the life course of individuals. James Horley and J. John Lavery (1995) found that, within a Canadian sample, life satisfaction increased from age thirty to age seventy-four, whereas happiness increased from age thirty to age forty-nine and then stayed level to age seventy-four. Another interesting example is Virgil Adams's (1997) research in which it was found that satisfaction increased among African Americans between 1980 and 1992 while their overall happiness declined. The stability over time of satisfaction usually marginally exceeds that of happiness measures.

One particularly interesting analysis of the differences between happiness and satisfaction was presented by Michalos (1980). He asserted that satisfaction might be achieved in two ways: through successful achievement (where aspirations match achievements through increases in achievements and the person is both happy and satisfied, making the person an "achiever") or through resignation (where aspirations match achievements through reductions in aspirations and the person is satisfied but unhappy, making the person "resigned"). Michalos also claimed that dissatisfaction can occur in two ways: through having much higher aspirations than achievements (where the person is happy about having such high aspirations, making the person an "aspirer") or through not meeting even low aspirations (where the person is unhappy about the lack of achievement, making the person "frustrated"). The key points here are that satisfaction can be elusive if one raises ones aspirations unrealistically and that people can be satisfied without being happy. Put another way, high satisfaction may not mean high happiness, but low satisfaction is likely to mean low happiness.

Joy

Joy is unique among the four concepts because it does not have an immediately obvious negative. Satisfaction has dissatisfaction, pleasure has displeasure, and happiness has unhappiness, but there is no such emotion as un-joy or dis-joy. Although some people consider sadness to be the opposite of joy, hopelessness or despair might be better opposites than mere sadness.

Some believe that joy is an aspect of positive affect that is influenced by transcendent experiences, often of a spiritual or religious nature. Along these lines of transcendence, Percy Shelley wrote the following lines about joy in Act IV of *Prometheus Unbound* (1820):

> To suffer woes which Hope thinks infinite;
> To forgive wrongs darker than death or night;
> To defy Power, which seems omnipotent;
> To love, and bear; to hope till Hope creates
> From its own wreck the things it contemplates;
> Neither to change, nor falter, nor repent;
> This, like thy glory, Titan, is to be
> Good, great and joyous, beautiful and free;
> This is alone Life, Joy, Empire and Victory.

One aspect of transcendence can occur with meaningful work, in which dedicated professionals gladly spend hours on their projects in an experience of intense joy or happiness that has been described by Mihaly Csikszentmihalyi (1997) as "flow." For many people, interesting work is more satisfying than mere recreational pleasure. It is also possible that concepts such as personal growth, self-actualization, and purpose in life may predict joy and be better indicators of psychological well-being than the traditional components of satisfaction and positive affect, even though there are strong correlations among such factors. Zipora Magen (1996) has reported finding, among adolescents in three different cultures, a relationship between commitment beyond self and joy.

Ian McGregor and Brian Little (1998) successfully differentiated happiness from meaning, the former being produced by effectively completing personal projects and the latter being produced by engaging in projects that allowed for self-expression with integrity. Joy is probably more likely to be produced as an affective response when integrity and meaningfulness are involved in the process, whereas merely reaching one's goals or encountering favorable circumstances may foster satisfaction or happiness. This analysis of joy differs considerably from that of Robert Plutchik (1991), in which he associates joy with sexuality and anger, considering joy to be a transient emotion. It is possible, however, that Plutchik has confused ecstasy or extreme, momentary pleasure with joy—even sexual orgasm, though it might entail ecstasy, might not involve true joy (depending upon the meaning or transcendental significance attached to the sexual encounter).

Figure 1 represents an attempt to diagram the relationship between pleasure, satisfaction, happiness, and joy in such a way that their overlap and their differences are highlighted. All four concepts have a common foundation in emotional affect. However, pleasure is keyed more to immediate, tangible influences while satisfaction is keyed to expectations and standards regarding (for the most part) transactions with one's environment. Happiness is keyed more to daily circumstances, particularly how one's interpersonal relationships with family and friends are going. Joy is keyed to more transcendent factors, such as religious or spiritual experiences and "flow" during the execution of one's professional work. In a very rough approximation, the emotional experiences toward the right side of the model in Figure 1 are more related to the Aristotelian concept of the "good life" than are

those toward the left side. How might these four emotions be evoked by the same setting? In practice, a nice backrub would give a person simple pleasure. A person would be satisfied if he or she thought the masseur's charge of thirty dollars an hour was worth the investment. A backrub given as part of a romantic evening would make a person happy. Joy might be experienced if a spouse had refused to give backrubs until some life-changing experience made him or her decide that a backrub would be a wonderful way of authentically expressing love. The joy would not result from the backrub itself but from the appreciation of the partner's transcendent change of heart.

Cross-Cultural Research on Satisfaction

Diener (1994) notes that similar levels of satisfaction are reported within cultures that feature different languages, suggesting that the effect of language differences and translation issues are relatively minimal. Veenhoven (1996) counters the argument that happiness and satisfaction are "Western" concepts by noting that only about 1 percent of respondents from a variety of nations around the world give "don't know" or "no answer" responses to such questions—if the concepts were less familiar, such societies should give much higher percentages of such indefinite responses. Veenhoven claims that all languages have words for satisfaction, thus making it a universal concept. It is interesting to note that survey data on life satisfaction for random samples of entire national populations are now available for many nations (with

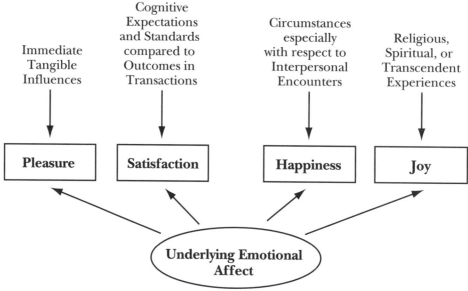

FIGURE 1 *Diagram of the relationship between pleasure, satisfaction, happiness, and joy.*

some of the data covering twenty to forty-five years). Much of this data is available on the internet, in addition to being listed in *Social Science Indicators.*

Robert Cummins (1998) has found individualism to be a reliable predictor of life satisfaction in a forty-five-nation study. Ed and Marissa Diener (1995) found in a thirty-one-nation analysis that in individualistic nations (those in which a normative goal is high self-esteem and high individual life satisfaction—e.g., the United States, Canada, New Zealand, the Netherlands) self-esteem and satisfaction with friends was more strongly correlated with life satisfaction than in collectivistic nations (those in which normative goals include fitting in with one's social groups—e.g., Bangladesh, Cameroon, Jordan, Kenya, Tanzania). Income was more strongly associated with life satisfaction in poorer nations. Suh and his colleagues (1998) found that affect and satisfaction were more strongly correlated in individualistic cultures than in collectivistic cultures. Ideal norms for life satisfaction predicted personal life satisfaction more in collectivist cultures than individualist cultures. Virginia Kwan and her colleagues (1997) found that self-esteem was a much stronger predictor of life satisfaction in U.S. samples than in Hong Kong samples and that relationship harmony played a more important role in predicting life satisfaction in Hong Kong than in the United States. Diener and his colleagues (1995) found few differences in satisfaction between college students in the United States and Korea or Japan, but they did find significant differences between students in China and the United States. The Chinese students thought less often about their satisfaction and thought overall subjective well-being was less important. Furthermore, feeling *or* expressing negative affect was considered more undesirable by Chinese students, compared to Korean or U.S. students. However, even those differences did not account for the considerably lower levels of satisfaction reported by Chinese students.

Thus, it appears that while the language of satisfaction is relatively universal, the importance attributed to thinking about one's own satisfaction or to an individual's being satisfied may vary cross-culturally. Usually, the same things predict satisfaction (e.g., self-esteem, income, friendships), but the importance of such items in predicting overall life satisfaction may vary across cultures.

Conclusion

Even though scholars are still assessing, with mixed results, whether overall life satisfaction causes satisfaction with the more specific areas of life or vice versa, it seems clear that success at love and work are most critical to overall life satisfaction. Still, they are no

guarantees. Abd-er-Rahman III, who ruled from 911 to 961 as the first caliph of the Umayyad Arab Muslim dynasty of Spain, was reported to have said,

> I have now reigned about fifty years in victory or peace, beloved by my subjects, dreaded by my enemies and respected by my allies. Riches and honors, power and pleasure, have waited on my call, nor does any earthly blessing appear to have been wanting to my felicity. In this situation I have diligently numbered the days of pure and genuine happiness which have fallen to my lot; they amount to fourteen [Prochnow and Prochnow, 1969, p. 154].

Does this mean that many ordinary people do better in the modern era than that ancient king did in his? Or was he just more honest or strict in his definitions?

See also: ACHIEVEMENT MOTIVATION; HAPPINESS; HOPE; MOTIVATION; PLEASURE

Bibliography

Adams, Virgil H., III. (1997). "A Paradox in African American Quality of Life." *Social Indicators Research* 42:205–219.

Andrews, Frank M., and McKennell, Aubrey C. (1980). "Measures of Self-Reported Well-Being: Their Affective, Cognitive, and Other Components." *Social Indicators Research* 8:127–155.

Averill, James R., and More, Thomas A. (1993). "Happiness." In *Handbook of Emotions,* ed. Michael Lewis and Jeannette M. Haviland. New York: Guilford.

Campbell, Angus. (1981). *The Sense of Well-Being in America: Recent Patterns and Trends.* New York: McGraw-Hill.

Campbell, Angus; Converse, Philip E.; and Rodgers, Willard L. (1976). *The Quality of American Life: Perceptions, Evaluations, and Satisfactions.* New York: Russell Sage Foundation.

Csikszentmihalyi, Mihaly. (1997). *Finding Flow: The Psychology of Engagement with Everyday Life.* New York: Basic Books.

Cummins, Robert A. (1996). "The Domains of Life Satisfaction: An Attempt to Order Chaos." *Social Indicators Research* 38: 303–328.

Cummins, Robert A. (1998). "The Second Approximation to an International Standard for Life Satisfaction." *Social Indicators Research* 43:307–334.

Diener, Ed. (1984). "Subjective Well-Being." *Psychological Bulletin* 95:542–575.

Diener, Ed. (1994). "Assessing Subjective Well-Being: Progress and Opportunities." *Social Indicators Research* 31:103–157.

Diener, Ed, and Diener, Marissa. (1995). "Cross-Cultural Correlates of Life Satisfaction and Self-Esteem." *Journal of Personality and Social Psychology* 68:653–663.

Diener, Ed, and Suh, Eunkook. (1997). "Measuring Quality of Life: Economic, Social, and Subjective Indicators." *Social Indicators Research* 40:189–216.

Diener, Ed; Suh, Eunkook; Smith, Heidi; and Shao, Liang. (1995). "National Differences in Reported Subjective Well-Being: Why Do They Occur?" *Social Indicators Research* 34: 7–32.

Feldman, Lisa A. (1995). "Variations in the Circumplex Structure of Mood." *Personality and Social Psychology Bulletin* 21:806–817.

Gotz, Ignacio L. (1995). *Conceptions of Happiness.* Lanham, MD: University Press of America.

Hagedorn, James W. (1996). "Happiness and Self-Deception: An Old Question Examined by a New Measure of Subjective Well-Being." *Social Indicators Research* 38:139–160.

Hazlitt, William. (1836). *Literary Remains of the Late William Hazlitt, Vol. 2.* London: Saunders and Otley.

Horley, James, and Lavery, J. John. (1995). "Subjective Well-Being and Age." *Social Indicators Research* 34:275–282.

Hugo, Victor. ([1862] 1952). *Les Misérables.* New York: Modern Library.

Kwan, Virginia S. Y.; Bond, Michael Harris; and Singelis, Theodore M. (1997). "Pancultural Explanations for Life Satisfaction: Adding Relationship Harmony to Self-Esteem." *Journal of Personality and Social Psychology* 73:1038–1051.

Lerner, Sally. (1997). "Indicators of Human Well-Being: Fine-Tuning Vs. Taking Action?" *Social Indicators Research* 40:217–220.

Magen, Zipora. (1996). "Commitment Beyond Self and Adolescence: The Issue of Happiness." *Social Indicators Research* 37:235–267.

McGregor, Ian, and Little, Brian R. (1998). "Personal Projects, Happiness, and Meaning: On Doing Well and Being Yourself." *Journal of Personality and Social Psychology* 74:494–512.

Michalos, Alex C. (1980). "Satisfaction and Happiness." *Social Indicators Research* 8:385–422.

Michalos, Alex C. (1985). "Multiple Discrepancies Theory (MDT)." *Social Indicators Research* 16:347–413.

Michalos, Alex C. (1986). "Job Satisfaction, Marital Satisfaction, and the Quality of Life." In *Research and the Quality of Life,* ed. Frank M. Andrews. Ann Arbor: Institute for Social Research, University of Michigan.

Mill, John Stuart. ([1873] 1924). *Autobiography of John Stuart Mill.* New York: Columbia University Press.

Muthny, Fritz A.; Koch, Uwe; and Stump, S. (1990). "Quality of Life in Oncology Patients." *Psychotherapy and Psychosomatics* 54:145–160.

Myers, David G., and Diener, Ed. (1995). "Who is Happy?" *Psychological Science* 6:10–19.

Olson, Geraldine, and Schober, Brigitte I. (1993). "The Satisfied Poor." *Social Indicators Research* 28:173–193.

Plutchik, Robert. (1991). *The Emotions: Facts, Theories, and a New Model,* rev. ed. Lanham, MD: University Press of America.

Prochnow, Herbert V., and Prochnow, Herbert V., Jr. (1969). *A Treasury of Humorous Quotations.* New York: Harper & Row.

Sirgy, M. Joseph. (1998). "Materialism and Quality of Life." *Social Indicators Research* 43:227–260.

Sirgy, M. Joseph; Cole, Dennis; Kosenko, Rustan; Meadow, H. Lee; Rahtz, Don; Cicic, Muris; Jin, Guang Xi; Yarsuvat, Duygun; Blenkhorn, David L.; and Nagpal, Natasha. (1995). "A Life Satisfaction Measure: Additional Validation Data for the Congruity Life Satisfaction Measure." *Social Indicators Research* 34:237–259.

Sternberg, Robert J., and Hojjat, Mahzad, eds. (1997). *Satisfaction in Close Relationships.* New York: Guilford.

Suh, Eunkook; Diener, Ed; Oishi, Shigehiro; and Triandis, Harry C. (1998). "The Shifting Basis of Life Satisfaction Judgments across Cultures: Emotions Versus Norms." *Journal of Personality and Social Psychology* 74:482–493.

Sumner, L. W. (1996). *Welfare, Happiness, and Ethics.* Oxford: Clarendon Press.

Tepperman, Lorne, and Curtis, James. (1995). "A Life Satisfaction Scale for Use with National Adult Samples from the USA, Canada, and Mexico." *Social Indicators Research* 35:255–270.

Tolstoy, Leo. ([1875–1877] 1950). *Anna Karenina.* New York: Modern Library.

Veenhoven, Ruut. (1984). *Conditions of Happiness.* Dordrecht, The Netherlands: Reidel Publishing.

Veenhoven, Ruut. (1991). "Is Happiness Relative?" *Social Indicators Research* 24:1–34.

Veenhoven, Ruut. (1995). "World Database on Happiness." *Social Indicators Research* 34:299–313.

Veenhoven, Ruut. (1996). "Developments in Satisfaction Research." *Social Indicators Research* 37:1–46.

Veenhoven, Ruut. (1998). "Two State-Trait Discussions on Happiness." *Social Indicators Research* 43:211–225.

Walter R. Schumm

SEASONAL AFFECTIVE DISORDER

Seasonal affective disorder is a recurrent type of affective (i.e., emotional) disturbance that occurs regularly at certain times of the year. Most individuals with seasonal affective disorder suffer from winter depression. During wintertime every year, these individuals often experience atypical depressive symptoms, such as increased appetite, increased duration of sleep, difficulty waking up in the morning, carbohydrate craving, and increased weight. Although these symptoms can be found in some non-seasonal types of depressive disorders, they are often the reverse of typical depressive disorders. Individuals with winter depression most commonly begin experiencing symptoms in early November, and the average duration of a winter episode is approximately five months.

Prevalence

Although the prevalence of seasonal affective disorder in clinical settings is not very clear at this point, various estimates have been made. Jacque Montplaisir (1989) found that 29 percent of the individuals attending clinics due to recurrent depression met the criteria for seasonal affective disorder. Michael J. Garvey, Robert Wesner, and Michael Godes (1988) found similar results in 38 percent of the individuals attending clinics due to recurrent depression. The prevalence of seasonal affective disorder in the general population is unclear. Researchers have estimated that about 6 percent of the general population in New York City display clinical levels of seasonal affective disorders. Other studies have found that about 5 percent of the general population experienced seasonal symptoms of clinical levels of depression in Montgomery County, Maryland, and 9.2 percent of the population in Fairbanks, Alaska, met diagnostic criteria for seasonal affective disorder. One interesting finding concerning the prevalence of winter depression is that episodes are longer and more severe at high latitudes in the Northern Hemisphere, but exactly the opposite phenomena occurs in the Southern Hemisphere.

Like most types of affective disorders, seasonal affective disorder seems to be more common among women than men. Researchers have reported that more women than men were found to have winter depression with women comprising 60 percent to 83 percent of the group. The *Diagnostic and Statistical Manual of Mental Disorders* (DSM-IV, 1994) of the American Psychiatric Association indicates that women comprise the majority (60%—90%) of persons with seasonal affective disorder. Thus the gender ratio for seasonal affective disorder seems to exceed slightly the 2-to-1 ratio of other affective disorders.

The severity of seasonal affective disorder is commonly perceived as a continuous variable since variations in the severity of seasonal mood changes have been observed in the general population. On the one end, there are individuals whose symptoms of depression are so severe that they require hospitalization. On the other end, many individuals appear to experience mild seasonal mood swings that slightly interfere with their productivity and well-being. In most cases, the individuals in the latter category neither meet the criteria for major affective disorder nor seek treatment.

Treatment Methods

A major cause of winter depression appears to be light deficiency. It has been found that individuals with winter depression respond well to light treatment or phototherapy. Norman Rosenthal (1988) conducted a preliminary review of studies on phototherapy and found that bright light is an effective and rapid treatment for winter depression. The effectiveness of phototherapy has been demonstrated in a wide variety of studies since then.

Since phototherapy has been found to be effective in treating individuals with winter depression, a variety of phototherapy techniques have been administered. The most common, and presently the most reliable, technique involves exposing the individual to light from a light box emitting a full spectrum white light of 2,500 lux or more with ultraviolet filters for a minimum of two hours a day throughout the season of risk.

Other techniques using light visors have also been administered in order to allow more mobility for the patients while they are in treatment. These light visors, placed on the patient's head, are designed to shine light into his or her eyes. Although useful and efficient, research on the use of light visors has not yet demonstrated adequate power to sustain positive results.

A third technique involves the simulation of dawn in the early morning by gradually increasing the intensity of light to a normal level (e.g., 250 lux). This technique provides a more natural environment for the patient and thus was hypothesized to be more effective than ordinary light treatment. Although research using dawn simulation techniques for phototherapy has revealed promising results, this method is still in its preliminary stages of development and more investigation is needed in order to arrive at any definite conclusions.

Based on research findings, phototherapy using a light box seems to be the most reliable form of treatment. Investigations concerning this type of treatment suggest the following general guidelines. The patient should be exposed to light that is sufficiently intense for a sufficiently long time (e.g., 2,500 lux for two hours). Treatment should generally be administered every day throughout the season of risk. According to most studies, relapse occurs equally rapidly if light treatment is discontinued and only about 10 percent of patients respond to light of lower intensity. Although some research has suggested that one week of treatment at the first signs of depression may be enough to prevent emerging full blown depression, more research is needed before it is recommended as a possible alternative. Morning treatments are preferable although evening treatments may be as effective. The patient should be informed of the possible side effects, such as becoming irritable, feeling eyestrain, experiencing insomnia, or having headaches, even though they are quite rare.

Although phototherapy is by far the most common form of treatment, various types of medication, such as selective serotonin reuptake inhibitors or monoamine oxidase inhibitors and beta-blockers, have also been used with mixed results for individuals with winter depression. Most of these types of medication are used in conjunction with light treatment, as the effectiveness of the medication by itself seems to be insufficient.

Summer Depression

Although most researchers imply winter depression when they use the term *seasonal affective disorder,* the category of seasonal affective disorders also includes summer depression and summer mania, even though they are extremely rare. Because of the rarity of these disorders, researchers know very little about summer depression and even less about summer mania. Summer depression usually begins around May and ends around September. Individuals with summer depres-

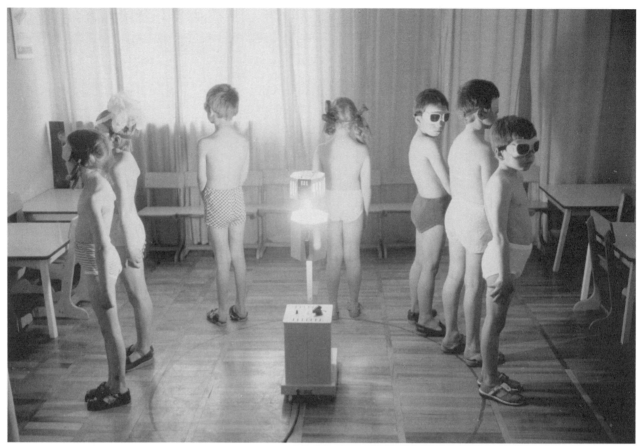

Children wearing protective glasses undergo light deprivation treatment at their school in Stavropol, Russia. Strong full-spectrum fluorescent light is used in these treatments, which are intended to lessen the effects of the long, dark Russian winter and prevent seasonal affective disorder. (Corbis/Wally McNamee)

sion are more likely to have coexisting anxiety disorders, and, in contrast, to individuals with winter depression, individuals with depressive episodes in the summer tend to experience typical symptoms of depression, such as insomnia, loss of appetite, and loss of weight.

Although the cause of summer depression is unclear, there have been reports suggesting that heat may be one cause. Researchers have reported that exposure to cold improved summer depression in some patients and the exposure to heat induced depressive symptoms. Various findings have suggested that summer depressions are longer and more severe at low latitudes in the Northern Hemisphere and the opposite phenomena occurs in the Southern Hemisphere.

Diagnostic Categorization

Seasonal patterns of affective illness have been examined throughout the history of medicine, but a revival in the interest of seasonal patterns of affective illness began in the early 1980s. Criteria for the diagnosis of seasonal affective disorder were developed in 1984, and in recognition of the significance of these disorders, the DSM-IV includes "seasonal pattern" as a description in the category of affective disorders.

See also: ANXIETY DISORDERS; HEALTH AND ILLNESS; MOOD DISORDERS; SADNESS

Bibliography

American Psychiatric Association. (1994). *Diagnostic and Statistical Manual of Mental Disorders,* 4th ed. Washington, DC: American Psychiatric Association.

Blehar, Mary C., and Rosenthal, Norman E. (1989a). "Seasonal Affective Disorder in the Southern Hemisphere." *American Journal of Psychiatry* 145:96–99.

Blehar, Mary C., and Rosenthal, Norman E. (1989b). "Seasonal Affective Disorders and Phototherapy: Report of a National Institute of Mental Health-Sponsored Workshop." *Archives of General Psychiatry* 46:469–474.

Booker, John M., and Hellekson, Carla J. (1992). "Prevalence of Seasonal Affective Disorder in Alaska." *American Journal of Psychiatry* 149:1176–1182.

Dalgleish, Tim; Rosen, Kate; and Marks, Melanie. (1996). "Rhythm and Blues: Theory and Treatment of Seasonal Affective Disorder." *British Journal of Clinical Psychology* 35:163–182.

Garvey, Michael J.; Wesner, Robert; and Godes, Michael. (1988). "Comparison of Seasonal and Non-Seasonal Affective Disorders." *American Journal of Psychiatry* 145:100–102.

Kasper, Siegfried, and Rosenthal, Norman E. (1989). "Anxiety and Depression in Seasonal Affective Disorders." In *Anxiety and Depression: Distinctive and Overlapping Features,* ed. Philip C. Kendall and David Watson. San Diego, CA: Academic Press.

Kasper, Siegfried; Wehr, Thomas A.; Bartko, John J.; Gaist, Paul A.; and Rosenthal, Norman E. (1989). "Epidemiological Findings of Seasonal Changes in Mood and Behavior." *Archives of General Psychiatry* 46:823–833.

Levitt, Anthony J.; Joffe, Russel T.; Moul, Douglas E.; Lam, Raymond W.; Teicher, Martin H.; Lebegue, Breck; Murray, Megan G.; Oren, Dan A.; Schwartz, Paul; Buchanan, Alan; Glod, Carol A.; and Brown, Joanne. (1993). "Side Effects of Light Therapy in Seasonal Affective Disorder." *American Journal of Psychiatry* 150:650–652.

Lingjaerde, Odd, and Haggag, Ahmed. (1992). "Moclobemide in Winter Depression: Some Preliminary Results from an Open Trial." *Nordic Journal of Psychiatry* 46:201–203.

Meesters, Ybe; Jansen, Jaap H. C.; Beersma, Domien G. M.; Bouhuys, Antoinette L.; and Van den Hoofdakker, Rutger H. (1993). "Early Light Treatment Can Prevent an Emerging Winter Depression from Developing into a Full-Blown Depression." *Journal of Affective Disorders* 29:41–47.

Montplaisir, Jacque. (1989). "Sleep in Depression, Schizophrenia, and Narcolepsy." In *The Bio-Clinical Interface: Sleep and Psychiatry,* ed. Jean-Paul Macher and Marc-Antoine Crocq. Basel, Switzerland: Aesopus.

Rosenthal, Norman E. (1988). "*Light Therapy and Treatment of Affective Disorders.*" Bethesda, MD: National Institute of Mental Health.

Rosenthal, Norman E.; Jacobsen, Frederick M.; Sack, David A.; Arendt, Josephine; James, Stephen P.; Parry, Barbara L.; and Wehr, Thomas A. (1988). "Atenolol in Seasonal Affective Disorder: A Test of the Melatonin Hypothesis." *American Journal of Psychiatry* 145:52–56.

Rosenthal, Norman E.; Sack, David A.; Gillin, J. Christian; Lewy, Alfred J.; Goodwin, Frederick K.; Davenport, Yolande; Mueller, Peter S.; Newsome, David A.; and Wehr, Thomas A. (1984). "Seasonal Affective Disorder: A Description of the Syndrome and Preliminary Findings with Light Therapy." *Archives of General Psychiatry* 41:72–80.

Sato, Toru. (1997). "Seasonal Affective Disorder and Phototherapy: A Critical Review." *Professional Psychology: Research and Practice* 28:164–169.

Schlager, David S. (1994). "Early Morning Administration of Short-Acting Beta Blockers for Treatment of Winter Depression." *American Journal of Psychiatry* 151:1383–1385.

Tam, Edwin T.; Lam, Raymond W.; and Levitt, Anthony J. (1995). "Treatment of Seasonal Affective Disorder: A Review." *Canadian Journal of Psychiatry* 40:457–466.

Terman, Michael. (1988). "On the Question of Mechanism in Phototherapy: Considerations of Clinical Efficacy and Epidemiology." *Journal of Biological Rhythms* 3:155–172.

Terman, Michael; Schlager, David; Fairhurst, Stephen; and Perlman, Bill. (1989). "Dawn and Dusk Simulation as a Therapeutic Intervention." *Biological Psychiatry* 25:966–970.

Wehr, Thomas A.; Giesen, Holly A.; Schulz, Patricia M.; Joseph-Vanderpool, Jean R.; Kasper, Siegfried; Kelly, Karen A.; and Rosenthal, Norman E. (1989). "Summer Depression: Description of the Syndrome and Comparison with Winter Depression." In *Seasonal Affective Disorders and Phototherapy,* ed. Norman E. Rosenthal and Mary Blehar. New York: Guilford.

Toru Sato

SELF-ESTEEM

Self-esteem is one of those frequently encountered psychological concepts that everyone seems to have ideas about. Parents and teachers want children and adolescents to have high self-esteem, so they devote considerable energy to fostering it in them. Adults often continue this quest for high self-esteem, selecting partners and activities that allow them to feel good about themselves. In fact, self-esteem has been implicated in such diverse areas of psychological functioning as delinquency and aggression, substance abuse, depression, satisfaction with one's life in general, satisfaction with and intimacy in one's relationships, and emotional reactions to failure. It then may come as a surprise that there is still considerable controversy surrounding the nature of self-esteem and its implications for psychological functioning.

What Is Self-Esteem?

As is the case with many issues relating to the self, William James (1890) provided the grist for a great deal of subsequent self-esteem research and theorizing. James actually offered two views on the nature of self-esteem. First, he suggested that self-esteem reflects the ratio of one's "successes" to one's "pretensions" or aspirations (i.e., what is important to the person). In other words, self-esteem is a summary evaluation that stems directly from the sum of these success/aspiration assessments (i.e., "How well am I doing in those domains that are important to me?"). Note that self-esteem is changeable according to this view; one can perform better or worse on different occasions, or take on new areas of importance or delete old ones. The second view held by James was that self-esteem reflects "a certain average tone of self-feeling which each one of us carries about with him, and which is independent of the objective reasons we may have for satisfaction and discontent" (p. 306). In other words, self-esteem reflects a general positive or negative orientation toward oneself that is not dependent upon specific successes or failures. Therefore, answers to the question "Do I like, value, and accept myself?" reflect one's self-esteem, whereas answers to such questions as "Am I good at making friends or at making money?" do not. Inherent in this view of self-esteem is that it reflects relatively stable global self-feelings that may be based on factors and processes of which the person is unaware.

These two views have both received considerable attention and some support over the years. In support of the assertion that self-esteem reflects the ratio of successes to aspirations, Marlene Moretti and Tory Higgins (1990) demonstrated that self-feelings are related to how different one's actual self (i.e., attributes currently possessed) is from one's ideal self (i.e., attributes ideally possessed), Brett Pelham (1995) reported that favorable self-feelings are associated with placing high importance on those self-aspects in which one shines and low importance on those self-aspects in which one fares poorly, and Michael Kernis and his colleagues (1993, study 2) found that day-to-day fluctuations in self-judgments about competence correspond to greater fluctuations in global feelings of self-worth, especially among people who highly value competence.

Findings such as these indicate that the importance and favorableness with which people evaluate themselves in specific domains do have implications for their self-esteem. However, this does not necessarily mean that self-esteem should be equated with the sum of specific self-evaluations (perhaps giving more weight to self-evaluations in domains of high importance). In fact, Jonathon Brown (1993) has argued convincingly that self-esteem should be conceptualized in terms of global feelings of self-worth, liking, and acceptance that are distinct from specific self-evaluations (in support of James's second view). Furthermore, Brown suggests that global self-esteem affects domain specific self-evaluations (a "top down" approach), not vice versa (a "bottom up" approach). That is, if people generally like themselves, they will tend to rate themselves positively across a wide variety of specific domains.

According to Susan Harter (1993), however, both directions of influence are likely to occur (global feelings affect specific evaluations, and specific evaluations affect global feelings), with the more powerful direction of influence varying from person to person and dimension to dimension. Regardless of the stance one takes on this issue, it is crucial to maintain the distinction between specific self-evaluations and global self-esteem (feelings of self-worth, liking, and acceptance). Some individuals dislike themselves despite being highly competent and proficient in a number of domains; others are satisfied and content with themselves despite not being "stars" at anything. Accordingly, it is inappropriate to assert that people can have low self-esteem in some domains (e.g., school achievement) but high self-esteem in others (e.g., appearance). Rather, they can have self-evaluations that are low in some domains but high in others.

Group Differences in Self-Esteem

Do men have higher self-esteem than women? Are blacks lower in self-esteem than whites? Are people in Western cultures higher or lower in self-esteem than people in Eastern cultures? Although some studies indicate higher self-esteem among men than among women, the vast majority of studies do not show such differences. It is interesting to note that men and women appear to differ in how much emphasis they place on specific evaluative domains as a basis for their self-esteem. Namely, Robert Josephs and his colleagues (1992) have found that whereas competence and its ramifications may be more important to the self-esteem of men than of women, interpersonal skills and relationships may be more important to the self-esteem of women than of men. These differences need not be limited to gender, as culture, ethnicity, and race surely contribute to how much certain self-evaluations affect (and are affected by) global feelings of self-worth.

A number of studies, as reviewed by Jennifer Crocker and Brenda Major (1989), indicate higher self-esteem among blacks than among whites, which contrasts sharply with the earlier conclusion that blacks suffered in their feelings of self-worth. This earlier conclusion was based primarily on studies that tended to focus on feelings about one's racial identity rather than personal worth. Research by Stephanie Rowley and her colleagues (1998) shows that blacks differ not only in the positivity of their racial identity but also in the extent to which their racial identity relates to their personal self-esteem. Crocker and her colleagues (1991) reported that one strategy that blacks use to protect their self-esteem is to attribute threatening information to the source's prejudice against their race rather than to any deficiency that they might possess.

Research examining cultural differences in self-esteem is rather limited. Jennifer Campbell and her colleagues (1996) reported that Japanese college students had lower self-esteem scores than did Canadian

---

Philip Roth's "The Conversion of the Jews" (1959) shows a young teenager, Ozzie, genuinely questioning the authority of parents, rabbis, and the established religion but finding himself being punished for his curiosity. Ozzie has enough self-esteem not to be cowed by their threats; he continues to ask his questions. Finally, Ozzie persuades everyone to promise that they would never hit anybody about God.

college students. Also, self-esteem and self-concept clarity (clear and confidently held self-beliefs) were more strongly related for Canadian than for Japanese participants. The extent to which these findings generalize across various Western and Eastern cultures is an important issue that needs to be addressed in future research.

Measuring Self-Esteem

Self-esteem usually is measured by asking people to respond to a series of potentially self-descriptive statements. The number and content of specific items, as well as what form responses are to take, vary considerably from measure to measure. As a general rule, though, respondents indicate the extent to which they agree or disagree with each statement or the extent to which each statement is true or characteristic of them. Two of the most widely known and used self-esteem measures are the Self-Perception Profile for Children and the Rosenberg Self-Esteem Scale.

The Self-Perception Profile for Children was designed by Harter (1985) to measure global self-esteem and specific self-evaluations (i.e., scholastic and athletic competence, social acceptance, physical appearance, and behavioral conduct). It is widely used in research involving elementary school children in grades three and higher. A valuable feature of this instrument (as well as versions created for adolescents and college students) is that it allows researchers to examine which self-evaluations relate most strongly to global self-esteem. Harter (1993) reports that, at all developmental levels (childhood through adulthood), self-evaluations of physical appearance relate most strongly to global self-esteem, followed by self-evaluations of social acceptance. Other theorists, including Edward Deci and Richard Ryan (1995) assert that a general sense of mastery (active and effective transactions with one's environment) also relates strongly to global self-esteem.

The Rosenberg Self-Esteem Scale, developed by Morris Rosenberg (1965), is the instrument most often used to assess self-esteem in adolescents and adults. Examining its items reveals both a considerable strength and a potential liability of the measure (a weakness that is shared by virtually all self-esteem measures). On the positive side, it is very brief, containing only ten items that clearly tap global feelings of self-worth and satisfaction. On the negative side, the obvious nature of the items may prompt people to give socially desirable responses (i.e., responses that suggest they are psychologically healthy) even if these responses are not accurate self-descriptions.

In fact, research has indicated that on a wide variety of self-esteem measures, very few people have scores that are below the scale's conceptual midpoint. For example, if scores on a ten-item scale could range from 10 to 50, few individuals will have scores lower than 30 (which would represent on average neither strong agreement nor strong disagreement with the statements). Some self-esteem researchers, including Roy Baumeister, Diane Tice, and Debra Hutton (1989), have taken this to mean that there may be very few people who truly loathe and hate themselves. Alternatively, given people's general reluctance to respond in a way that reflects poorly upon them, moderate responses on a self-esteem scale may reflect the existence of greater self-directed negativity than their literal meaning indicates.

High Self-Esteem

What does it mean to say that individuals have high self-esteem? One perspective is that people with high self-esteem feel very proud of themselves, superior to most other people, and very willing and able to defend against possible threats to their positive self-feelings. In other words, people with high self-esteem may engage in self-promoting activities to perpetuate their views that they are "above" most people. Furthermore, people with high self-esteem do not like to see weaknesses in themselves (or for other people to see them), so they work hard to undermine the legitimacy of threatening evaluative events or information. In short, one perspective is that people with high self-esteem are very caught up in the processes of protecting, maintaining, and enhancing their positive self-feelings.

Various research findings can be marshaled in support of this characterization of high self-esteem. For example, Howard Tennen and Sharon Herzberger (1987) demonstrated that people with high self-esteem are especially likely to explain their successes in ways that glorify themselves (e.g., "I am smart") but to explain away their failures by denying responsibility for them (e.g., "The test was unfair")—an explanatory pattern referred to as "self-serving." Similarly, Rick Gibbons and Susan McCoy (1991) reported that after performing poorly or being insulted, people with high self-esteem are especially likely to derogate or criticize others. Also, research conducted by Joanne Wood and her colleagues (1994) showed that being outperformed by another person heightens the desire of people with high self-esteem to engage in additional performance comparisons with that very same person, presumably to show that being outperformed was just a "fluke." These and other research findings portray people with high self-esteem as being insecure in their positive self-feelings and as taking great pains to bolster themselves against threats.

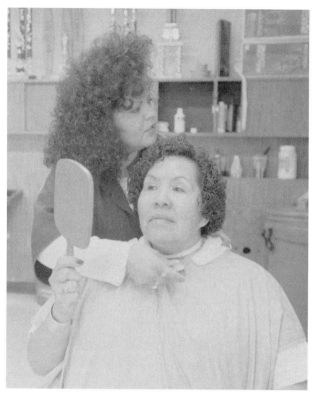

Satisfaction (or dissatisfaction) with one's personal appearance can greatly affect an individual's level of self-esteem. (Corbis/Kevin Fleming)

An alternative view, derived from a number of humanistically oriented theories, such as the one developed by Carl Rogers (1951), is that people with high self-esteem feel that they are worthwhile and valuable individuals, they like and are satisfied with themselves, and they are comfortable with and accepting of their weaknesses. To have high self-esteem, then, is to have positive feelings toward oneself that are built upon solid foundations that do not require continual validation or promotion. Moreover, one's feelings of self-worth will not be questioned or threatened with the inevitable adversities that life presents. One will be pleased with one's successes and disappointed with one's failures, but these reactions will not be excessively self-promoting (e.g., "I am better than you") or defensive (e.g., "Your stupid test is meaningless").

Which view of high self-esteem is correct? To cut to the chase, both appear correct, in that each characterizes at least some portion of the group of people with high self-esteem.

Low Self-Esteem

As was the case for high self-esteem, there are two viewpoints on what it means to have low self-esteem. One perspective, which has predominated for many years, holds that people with low self-esteem exhibit a wide variety of maladaptive cognitive, emotional, motivational, and behavioral patterns. In support of this characterization, research has shown that people with low self-esteem evaluate themselves quite negatively in many domains, readily accept the truthfulness of unfavorable feedback, experience a wide range of negative emotions (including anxiety and depression), and exhibit ineffective strategies in the face of adversity. Among adolescents, low self-esteem has been linked to such things as delinquency, drug abuse, and unsafe sexual practices, and, as reported by Harter (1993), it appears to be one of a number of factors that are associated with suicidal thoughts and behaviors.

Another more recent perspective characterizes people with low self-esteem as being cautious and uncertain (rather than highly maladjusted) individuals whose behavioral styles are geared toward minimizing exposure of their deficiencies. Proponents of this latter viewpoint, including Baumeister (1993), assert that the self-evaluations and self-concepts of people with low self-esteem are characterized more by uncertainty, confusion, and neutrality than by negativity, that people with low self-esteem do embrace their positive self-aspects, and that people with low self-esteem even engage in self-serving strategies when they feel safe to do so. This suggests that people with low self-esteem are not necessarily miserable people who loathe and despise themselves and inevitably engage in self-destructive behaviors.

Which of these two views best characterizes low self-esteem is a major point of contention among self-esteem researchers. It may be noteworthy that most of the research supporting the "cautious and uncertain" view of self-esteem involved college students, whereas most of the research that supports the "self-loathing and maladaptive" view of self-esteem involved children, adolescents, or "special" populations (e.g., substance abusers, juvenile delinquents). Perhaps by the time they reach college (or by virtue of being capable of reaching it), these people with low self-esteem take on qualities and use strategies that differentiate them from other people with low self-esteem. Alternatively, it may be the case that only a subset of people with very low self-esteem actually suffers from extreme self-loathing and maladaptive behavior patterns. More research on this issue is warranted.

Self-Esteem and Emotional Reactions to Failure

Setting aside the controversies for the moment, research consistently has shown that people with low self-esteem have more adverse emotional reactions to failure than do people with high self-esteem. In fact, when they fail, people with low self-esteem are more likely than people with high self-esteem to experience strong negative emotions and to feel ashamed, humiliated, and unmotivated to do better in the future. Why does this occur? Kernis, Joel Brockner, and Bruce Frankel (1989) found that people with low self-esteem are more prone than people with high self-esteem to believe that specific failures have negative global implications for whom they are as a person—that is, failure prompts people with low self-esteem to think that they are stupid, incompetent, and not capable of doing anything right. These thoughts only serve to intensify their negative feelings, leaving them demoralized and unmotivated.

Of course, some people with low self-esteem may not be very skilled at various tasks. Objectively, however, there is no hard evidence that people with low self-esteem are generally less skilled than their counterparts who have high self-esteem. This suggests that the tendency for people with low self-esteem to make global negative self-statements after a specific instance of failure (or even after several successive ones) is not justified. People with high self-esteem, on the other hand, tend to be better at compartmentalizing the negative implications of failure, which may alleviate some of their distress.

Beyond High Versus Low Self-Esteem

A growing number of researchers and theorists have focused their attention on a variety of components of self-esteem other than its level (high or low). Although much of this work is still in its infancy, many researchers believe that it holds the promise of reconciling divergent viewpoints on the role of self-esteem (particularly high self-esteem) in psychological functioning.

Defensive Versus Genuine High Self-Esteem

One distinction that has been made is between defensive and genuine high self-esteem. People with genuine high self-esteem are thought to truly have favorable feelings of self-worth that are not particularly threatened by specific failures. In contrast, people with defensive high self-esteem report favorable feelings of self-worth that are driven more by desires for social approval than by their actual feelings. In fact, they harbor negative self-feelings inside, but they are reluctant to admit to others that they have them. People with defensive high self-esteem are expected to have very strong reactions to failure and to work very hard to diminish any negative implications the failure may have in the eyes of others. Research by David Schneider and David Turkat (1975) supports these assertions.

Explicit and Implicit Self-Esteem

Some people with high self-esteem may report that they like themselves while simultaneously holding neg-

ative self-feelings of which they are unaware (and not just unwilling to report, as in defensive high self-esteem). Seymour Epstein and Beth Morling (1995) argue that people actually have two kinds of self-esteem: explicit and implicit. Explicit self-esteem refers to individuals' consciously held feelings of self-worth, which can be assessed by self-esteem measures such as those described above. Implicit self-esteem refers to feelings of self-worth that are nonconscious, but that nevertheless "seep through" to influence people's emotional and behavioral responses. Promising ways to measure implicit self-esteem currently are in development.

Epstein and Morling theorize that people with high explicit, but low implicit, self-esteem will be especially threatened by negative self-relevant information and that they will do what it takes (even if drastic) to maintain their consciously held positive self-esteem. In contrast, people whose conscious and nonconscious self-feelings are favorable would not be so easily threatened and would have less need to "defend" their self-esteem. Although very interesting, these speculations await confirmation in future research.

Contingent Versus True Self-Esteem

Deci and Ryan (1995) have made the distinction between contingent and true self-esteem. Contingent self-esteem is based on achieving specific outcomes, matching specific standards, or meeting specific expectations. As Deci and Ryan put it, contingent self-esteem "refers to feelings about oneself that result from—indeed are dependent on—matching some standard of excellence or living up to some interpersonal or intrapsychic expectations" (p. 32).

People who feel worthy only when they are achieving top grades in class, being asked out on dates, or invited to parties would have contingent self-esteem. If they are bright and get top grades in all of their classes, their self-esteem will be high, but it will not be secure. Rather, their contingent self-esteem requires continual validation through specific positive outcomes.

In contrast, true self-esteem is well-anchored and secure, flowing naturally from regulating one's behaviors with a sense of choicefulness and competence. People with true self-esteem are happy with their successes and disappointed with their failures, but they do not link their feelings of self-worth to these events. Methods to assess contingent self-esteem and to distinguish it from true self-esteem are now in development.

Self-Esteem (In)Stability

The aforementioned perspectives make distinctions relevant to people's chronic or typical feelings of self-worth (i.e., "How much do I generally or typically like myself?"). These chronic feelings may change, but this change usually occurs slowly, over and extended time period. Research by Patrick O'Malley and Jerala Bachman (1983) indicates that some children may experience a drop in self-esteem during the transition from elementary to middle school, which is then followed by a steady but gradual increase in self-esteem through the high school years. Also, people may use therapeutic settings to help facilitate positive changes in their chronic feelings of self-worth. While often successful, the process of changing these chronic feelings is likely to involve considerable effort.

Rosenberg (1986) observed that people also possess more immediate, temporary feelings of self-worth (i.e., "How much do I like myself at this moment?"). For some people, these immediate, contextually based feelings of self-worth are highly stable across time and context, whereas for other people, they are subject to considerable fluctuations on a daily—or even more frequent—basis. In fact, some people may move back and forth between very positive and very negative feelings of self-worth on a fairly regular basis.

Research, as reviewed by Kernis and Stefanie Waschull (1995), has shown that the tendency to exhibit short-term fluctuations in immediate feelings of self-worth is relatively distinct from whether a person's self-esteem level is high or low. That is, among groups of people who have high self-esteem and groups of people who have low self-esteem, there are some individuals who fluctuate substantially and others who fluctuate little if at all.

Unstable self-esteem (i.e., the tendency to exhibit substantial fluctuations in current self-esteem) reflects fragile and vulnerable feelings of self-worth that are influenced by evaluative information that is externally provided (e.g., being insulted by one's supervisor) or internally generated (e.g., thinking about one's progress toward important goals). In contrast, stable self-esteem (i.e., nonfluctuating current self-esteem) is more secure in the sense that it does not change from moment to moment as evaluative events are encountered or self-generated.

Kernis and his colleagues assert that one of the core characteristics of people with unstable, fragile self-esteem is that they react very strongly to events that they interpret as being self-esteem relevant—in fact,

---

The narrator of Sylvia Plath's "Face Lift" (1971) originally feels awful about her looks and calls herself "old sock-face." But after the face lift, she can tell herself, "I'm all right." Her face looks "pink and smooth as a baby," giving her a rejuvenated appearance and a recovered self-esteem.

---

they may see self-esteem relevance even where it does not exist. At one extreme, individuals with fragile self-esteem may respond by accepting and exaggerating an event's evaluative implications (e.g., feeling unworthy and dejected in response to a negative event). At the other extreme, they may respond by actively attempting to undermine the validity of the threatening information or the credibility of its source. As discussed above, specific evaluative events generally will have little effect on the immediate feelings of self-worth of people who have well-anchored or stable self-esteem, so their reactions to such events in general should not be extreme.

Several studies are particularly relevant to the assertion that unstable self-esteem reflects fragile and vulnerable feelings of self-worth. In one study, Kernis and his colleagues (1998) found that high levels of daily stressors were related to increases in depressive symptoms among college students with unstable, but not stable, self-esteem. In another study with college students, Keegan Greenier and his colleagues (1999) found that unstable self-esteem predicted greater reactivity to both positive and negative daily events. Also, among sixth-grade children, Waschull and Kernis (1996) found that unstable self-esteem related to greater tendencies to indicate becoming angry at one's peers (whose actions were depicted in hypothetical scenarios) because one's feelings of self-worth were being threatened. Other research has linked unstable self-esteem to phenomena such as anger and hostility proneness, excuse-making, and reactions to interpersonal evaluations.

Taking Stock of These Various Positions

A common theme that all of these perspectives of self-esteem share is that two people may report high (or low) self-esteem, but the nature of their self-esteem and how it relates to their psychological functioning may be quite different. For example, people who report high self-esteem may or may not be masking negative feelings that they are unwilling to admit (defensive high self-esteem) or that they are unaware of possessing (high explicit/low implicit self-esteem). In other instances, people may or may not be basing their self-esteem on the extent to which they are successful at achieving specific outcomes. If they are, their self-esteem is much more tenuous (contingent self-esteem) than if they are not (true self-esteem). Finally, people who report typically having high or low self-esteem may have immediate feelings of self-worth that fluctuate considerably (unstable self-esteem) or little, if at all (stable self-esteem).

These aspects or components of self-esteem are not mutually exclusive. In fact, it is probably rare for an individual to possess self-esteem that is totally devoid of aspects that are defensive, contingent, unstable, and so on. Put differently, although people may strive for high self-esteem that is true, genuine, and stable, it is not very likely that they will be completely and permanently successful. Recognizing this can help individuals to learn more about themselves and the ways that they deal with threatening information. For example, it can help them to understand that reacting to a perceived insult with an intense and anger-laden counterattack does not necessarily come from strength or satisfaction with oneself; instead, it may reflect "damage control" to protect fragile, defensive, or contingent self-esteem.

Research on these components of self-esteem is in its infancy, but they still provide considerable insight into the nature of self-esteem. Recall that two broad perspectives on what it means to possess high self-esteem were presented above. One perspective suggested that people with high self-esteem will go to great lengths to bolster and promote their positive self-feelings. The theory and research reviewed here suggests that engaging in self-aggrandizing and self-protective strategies (e.g., boasting and excuse-making, derogating others, getting angry easily) are associated with high self-esteem that is accompanied by defensive, contingent, or unstable components. A second perspective portrayed people with high self-esteem as feeling happy and content with themselves, as well as accepting of their weaknesses. The research and theoretical perspectives reviewed here indicate that this form of high self-esteem is secure and well-anchored, in that it does not include components reflecting hidden negativity, vulnerability, or fragility.

Conclusion

In an effort to gain a more complete understanding of self-esteem, researchers have begun to create conceptualizations that incorporate the basic dichotomy of high self-esteem versus low self-esteem but move beyond that dichotomy as well. In this way, they hope to provide substantial new insights into the nature of self-esteem and its role in everyday behaviors and psychological functioning. As the world takes on greater and greater complexity, it seems fitting that the conceptualizations of the people who live in it do so as well.

See also: ACHIEVEMENT MOTIVATION; ANXIETY; ATTACHMENT; EMBARRASSMENT; FEAR AND PHOBIAS; HAPPINESS; HUMAN DEVELOPMENT; JAMES, WILLIAM; MOTIVATION; PERSONALITY; ROGERS, CARL RANSOM; SHAME; SHYNESS; TEMPERAMENT

Bibliography

Baumeister, Roy F. (1993). "Understanding the Inner Nature of Low Self-Esteem: Uncertain, Fragile, Protective, and Conflicted." In *Self-Esteem: The Puzzle of Low Self-Regard,* ed. Roy F. Baumeister. New York: Plenum.

Baumeister, Roy F.; Tice, Diane M.; and Hutton, Debra G. (1989). "Self-Presentation Motivations and Personality Differences in Self-Esteem." *Journal of Personality* 57:547–579.

Blascovich, Jim, and Tomaka, Joe. (1991). "Measures of Self-Esteem." In *Measures of Personality and Social Psychological Attitudes, Vol. 1,* ed. John P. Robinson, Phillip R. Shaver, and Lawrence S. Wrightsman. New York: Academic Press.

Brown, Jonathon D. (1993). "Self-Esteem and Self-Evaluation: Feeling Is Believing." In *Psychological Perspectives on the Self, Vol. 4,* ed. Jerry M. Suls. Hillsdale, NJ: Lawrence Erlbaum.

Campbell, Jennifer D. (1990). "Self-Esteem and Clarity of the Self-Concept." *Journal of Personality and Social Psychology* 59:538–549.

Campbell, Jennifer D.; Trapnell, Paul D.; Heine, Steven J.; Katz, Ilana M.; Lavallee, Loraine F.; and Lehman, Darrin R. (1996). "Self-Concept Clarity: Measurement, Personality Correlates, and Cultural Boundaries." *Journal of Personality and Social Psychology* 70:141–156.

Crocker, Jennifer, and Major, Brenda. (1989). "Social Stigma and Self-Esteem: The Self-Protective Properties of Stigma." *Psychological Review* 96:608–630.

Crocker, Jennifer; Voelkl, Kristen; Testa, Maria; and Major, Brenda. (1991). "Social Stigma: The Affective Consequences of Attributional Ambiguity." *Journal of Personality and Social Psychology* 60:218–228.

Deci, Edward L., and Ryan, Richard M. (1995). "Human Agency: The Basis for True Self-Esteem." In *Efficacy, Agency, and Self-Esteem,* ed. Michael H. Kernis. New York: Plenum.

Epstein, Seymour, and Morling, Beth. (1995). "Is the Self Motivated to Do More Than Enhance and/or Verify Itself?" In *Efficacy, Agency, and Self-Esteem,* ed. Michael H. Kernis. New York: Plenum.

Gibbons, Rick, and McCoy, Susan B. (1991). "Self-Esteem, Similarity, and Reactions to Active Versus Passive Social Comparisons." *Journal of Personality and Social Psychology* 60:414–424.

Greenier, Keegan; Kernis, Michael H.; McNamarra, Connie W.; Waschull, Stefanie B.; Berry, Andrea J.; Herlocker, Caryn E.; and Abend, Teresa A. (1999). Individual Differences in Reactivity to Daily Events: Examining the Roles of Stability and Level of Self-Esteem." *Journal of Personality* 67:185–208.

Greenwald, Anthony G., and Banaji, Mahzarin R. (1995). "Implicit Social Cognition: Attitudes, Self-Esteem, and Stereotypes." *Psychological Review* 102:4–27.

Harter, Susan. (1985). *Manual for the Self-Perception Profile for Children.* Denver: University of Denver Press.

Harter, Susan. (1993). "Causes and Consequences of Low Self-Esteem in Children and Adolescents." In *Self-Esteem: The Puzzle of Low Self-Regard,* ed. Roy F. Baumeister. New York: Plenum.

James, William. ([1890] 1950). *The Principles of Psychology, Vol. 1.* New York: Dover.

Josephs, Robert A.; Markus, Hazel R.; and Tafarodi, Romin W. (1992). "Gender and Self-Esteem." *Journal of Personality and Social Psychology* 63:391–402.

Kernis, Michael H.; Brockner, Joel; and Frankel, Bruce S. (1989). "Self-Esteem and Reactions to Failure: The Mediating Role of Overgeneralization." *Journal of Personality and Social Psychology* 57:707–714.

Kernis, Michael H.; Cornell, David P.; Sun, Chien-Ru; Berry, Andrea J.; and Harlow, Thomas. (1993). "There's More to Self-Esteem Than Whether It Is High or Low: The Importance of Stability of Self-Esteem." *Journal of Personality and Social Psychology* 65:1190–1204.

Kernis, Michael H., and Waschull, Stefanie B. (1995). "The Interactive Roles of Stability and Level of Self-Esteem: Research and Theory." In *Advances in Experimental Social Psychology, Vol. 27,* ed. Mark P. Zanna. San Diego, CA: Academic Press.

Kernis, Michael H.; Whisenhunt, Connie R.; Waschull, Stefanie B.; Greenier, Keegan; Berry, Andrea J.; Herlocker, Caryn E.; and Anderson, Craig A. (1998). "Multiple Facets of Self-Esteem and Their Relations to Depressive Symptoms." *Personality and Social Psychology Bulletin* 24:657–658.

Leary, Mark R.; Tambor, Ellen S.; Terdal, Sonja K.; and Downs, Deborah L. (1995). "Self-Esteem As an Interpersonal Monitor: The Sociometer Hypothesis." *Journal of Personality and Social Psychology* 68:518–530.

Moretti, Marlene M., and Higgins, E. Tory. (1990). "Relating Self-Discrepancy to Self-Esteem: The Contribution of Discrepancy beyond Actual-Self Ratings." *Journal of Experimental Social Psychology* 26:108–123.

O'Malley, Patrick M., and Bachman, Jerala G. (1983). "Self-Esteem: Change and Stability between Ages 13 and 23." *Developmental Psychology* 19:256–268.

Pelham, Brett W. (1995). "Self-Investment and Self-Esteem: Evidence for a Jamesian Model of Self-Worth." *Journal of Personality and Social Psychology* 69:1141–1150.

Rogers, Carl R. (1951). *Client-Centered Therapy.* Boston: Houghton Mifflin.

Rosenberg, Morris. (1965). *Society and the Adolescent Self-Image.* Princeton, NJ: Princeton University Press.

Rosenberg, Morris. (1986). "Self-Concept from Middle Childhood through Adolescence." In *Psychological Perspectives on the Self, Vol. 3,* ed. Jerry M. Suls and Anthony G. Greenwald. Hillsdale, NJ: Lawrence Erlbaum.

Rowley, Stephanie J.; Sellers, Robert M.; Chavous, Tabbye M.; and Smith, Mia A. (1998). "The Relationship between Racial Identity and Self-Esteem in African-American College and High School Students." *Journal of Personality and Social Psychology* 74:715–724.

Schneider, David J., and Turkat, David. (1975). "Self-Presentation following Success or Failure: Defensive Self-Esteem Models." *Journal of Personality* 43:127–135.

Tennen, Howard, and Herzberger, Sharon. (1987). "Depression, Self-Esteem, and the Absence of Self-Protective Attributional Biases." *Journal of Personality and Social Psychology* 52:72–80.

Waschull, Stefanie B., and Kernis, Michael H. (1996). "Level and Stability of Self-Esteem As Predictors of Children's Intrinsic Motivation and Reasons for Anger." *Personality and Social Psychology Bulletin* 22:4–13.

Wood, Joanne V.; Giordano-Beech, Maria; Taylor, Kathryn L.; Michela, John L.; and Gaus, Valerie. (1994). "Strategies of Social Comparison among People with Low Self-Esteem: Self-Protection and Self-Enhancement." *Journal of Personality and Social Psychology* 67:713–731.

Michael H. Kernis
Brian N. Goldman

SENSATION SEEKING AND RISK TAKING

Individuals vary in the amount of sensory stimulation (input from the senses) that they experience as optimal. Too little stimulation and they feel bored or restless; too much stimulation and they feel overwhelmed. In an effort to avoid discomfort, a person adjusts the environment so that it provides the desired amount of stimulation. The degree of sensation seeking that is habitual to that individual—the amount required to meet these needs—places him or her somewhere on a continuum. Thus, it is possible to speak of high sensation seekers, low sensation seekers, or of someone falling between these two poles.

Sensory Stimulation

The early roots of research on sensation seeking can be attributed to studies of animal behavior. In a series of experiments beginning in the early 1950s, researchers demonstrated that laboratory animals would perform tasks with the sole aim of increasing the degree of stimulation in their environment. Monkeys, for example, would learn a task in order to receive the reward of having a window opened so they could look out into the laboratory, and rats would learn to press a bar in order to be allowed into a new compartment where they could sniff around. At times the animals persevered even when they became frustrated and fearful. In 1954, researchers Donald Hebb and W. R. Thompson concluded that an animal will always act in such a way as to produce an optimal level of stimulation and suggested that laboratory animals' efforts to increase the stimulation of their surroundings might provide insight into motivation for comparable activities in humans. In 1955, Clarence Leuba developed the concept of optimal stimulation, in which he proposed that there is a characteristic level of stimulation for each individual and that movement toward this level motivates the individual's manipulation of the environment, decreasing the amount of stimulation when there is too much and increasing it when there is too little. The theory was later supported by John Lilly's (1985) experimental work with sensory deprivation. Later research demonstrated that the experience of stimulation decreases as the individual becomes habituated to the stimulus. Thus, there is a continuous interplay between what the individual is feeling and the external environment, with attempts made to adjust the degree of available stimulation.

Sensation Seeking

It is a logical step from a theory of optimal stimulation to one of sensation seeking. When researchers say that an individual is experiencing less than an optimal level of stimulation and is manipulating the environment to relieve feelings of discomfort, they are in actuality saying that he or she is seeking sensation. Various researchers have developed theories of sensation seeking and designed sensation-seeking scales to measure it on a continuum. One of the most influential authors of sensation seeking scales is Marvin Zuckerman. The first of Zuckerman's scales was developed in the 1960s, but since then it has undergone a number of revisions, including the development of five subscales. Besides the general scale, which gives an overview, the various subscales measure thrill and adventure seeking, susceptibility to boredom, the desire to seek experiences through an unconventional lifestyle, and stimulation through social disinhibition such as drinking and partying. Sample items that constitute the scales include "I dislike people who do or say things just to shock or upset others"; "I get bored seeing the same old faces"; "I would never smoke marijuana"; "I would like to learn to fly an airplane"; and "I cannot stand watching a movie that I have seen before."

Zuckerman found that males scored significantly higher than did females on all of the measures (with the greatest difference being on the disinhibition scale), but he was not certain if this difference was due to conditions of biology, culture, or a combination of the two. Zuckerman also found that sensation seeking is apparently a more generalized trait for females than for males. While a female who scores high on one subscale is likely to score higher than average on all or almost all of the other subscales, a male is more likely to score high on only a specific subscale or cluster of subscales. Age differences in sensation seeking were also found, with peak scores occurring for subjects between the ages of eighteen and twenty.

Much of Zuckerman's work has involved the physiological factors related to sensation seeking. His findings, and that of other researchers, have suggested that inheritance plays a significant role in the individual's level of sensation seeking. Scores for identical twins were much closer than those for fraternal twins, which usually indicates that the genetic component is important. Zuckerman pointed out that the presence of behavior similar to sensation seeking among animals also demonstrated the importance of heritability. Furthermore, data from various studies with humans have suggested that the heritability of sensation seeking rests on the inheritance of specific biological phenomena that affect arousability of the central nervous system.

Although there is considerable agreement about the fact that there is a physiological basis for sensation seeking, there is disagreement about the exact physiological mechanisms involved. Perhaps the most basic disagreement, however, has to do with the relationship between optimal levels of stimulation and sensation seeking. Some researchers believe, as did the early scientists, that optimal stimulation levels vary among individuals, thus resulting in differences in sensation seeking. Others believe that the major difference lies not in the optimal stimulation level but in the individual's base level of arousal. That is, high sensation seekers are habitually underaroused and need a high degree of sensation to lift their arousal level. One of the most prominent researchers in the latter group is Frank Farley, who coined the term *Type T* (thrill seeking) personality to describe people whose base levels of arousal are so low that they continually seek stimulation and indulge in risk taking in an ongoing effort to keep their arousal levels at a comfortable level. The activities of these individuals can range from geographical exploration, risk taking in business, physical adventures, and high-risk sports to criminal activity and other antisocial behavior. Farley has pointed out the need to direct the thrill-seeking propensity of such individuals toward constructive rather than destructive ends.

Risk Taking

Risk taking is quite clearly a means of achieving stimulation. Zuckerman's sensation-seeking scale, for example, includes such items as: "I often wish I could be a mountain climber," "I sometimes like do to things that are a little frightening," and "I like to have new and exciting experiences and sensations even if they are a little frightening . . . or illegal." A number of studies have found correlations between physical risk taking and scores on Zuckerman's sensation-seeking scale in general and the thrill-and-adventure-seeking subscale in particular.

It could be said that in the psychological literature the motivation for risk taking is now generally thought to be sensation seeking. This theory has come to re-

The 1970 story "How I Contemplated the World from the Detroit House of Correction and Began My Life Over Again," by Joyce Carol Oates, is told in the voice of a fifteen-year-old girl from a wealthy family who starts shoplifting and then runs away from home. She gets picked up by a pimp and spends time as a prostitute in the slums of Detroit. The story is in the form of her notes on this experience, which she is trying to describe in an English class essay after she finally returns home.

A woman leaps from the bridge at the "Bungy Zone," a site located on the Nanaimo River in Canada and billed in September 1994 as the only legal bridge jump in North America. At that time, the owners of the jump operation claimed that up to 240 people a day were experiencing the thrill of bungee jumping off the bridge. (Corbis/Paul A. Souders)

place former, more pathological views of the motivation for such activities. In the first half of the twentieth century, when it was assumed that psychologically healthy individuals would choose to feel safe and secure, risk takers were thought to be motivated by such factors as a death wish, disguised feelings of inadequacy, or counterphobic reactions (whereby individuals expose themselves to situations that at a subconscious level provoke the greatest fear in order to reassure themselves that they are in control). There is agreement that such factors may be the motivation for risk taking some of the time; however, it is no longer thought that they are the most frequent motivator.

The theory that sensation seeking motivates risk taking does seem to have limitations. For one thing,

when questioned, many risk takers identify the desire for achievement and mastery as their chief motivation. Second, the theory of sensation seeking does not explain why people will take risks in one area of their lives and not in others. It would seem that if an individual was taking risks to satisfy some need for stimulation, the risk-taking behaviors would extend to all areas of his or her life. And finally, two studies of athletes who scored extremely high on risk-taking scales have produced mixed results regarding the role played in sports by sensation seeking. It is possible that limitations of Zuckerman's sensation-seeking scale, which was used in both of these studies, were responsible for the results. Perhaps the scale is not sensitive enough to distinguish extreme risk takers from more moderate risk takers. Or perhaps there are factors in addition to sensation seeking that are involved.

How then can one account for what allows an individual to overcome inhibitions against risk taking? If motivation explains why the individual takes the risk, what is it that allows the individual to overcome the fear, anxiety, and rational assessment of danger? A 1997 study by Elissa Slanger and Kjell Rudestam identified "perceived self-efficacy" (a concept named and defined by Albert Bandura) as that element. Perceived self-efficacy is the belief that one can do what is required, that a challenge is within one's ability. This self-assessment may or may not be accurate, because perception of effectiveness is partially independent from actual skill. A complete understanding of risk taking, then, is comprised of two considerations: motivation (be it sensation seeking or sensation seeking in concert with other factors) and whatever it is that allows the disinhibition necessary for a person to overcome the fear and take action.

See also: MOTIVATION; SPORTS

Bibliography

Bandura, Albert. (1986). *Social Foundations of Thought and Action: A Social Cognitive Theory.* Englewood Cliffs, NJ: Prentice-Hall.

Farley, Frank. (1986). "The Big T in Personality." *Psychology Today* 20(May):45–52.

Hebb, Donald O., and Thompson, W. R. (1954). "The Social Significance of Animal Studies." In *Handbook of Social Psychology,* ed. Gardner Lindzey. Cambridge, MA: Addison-Wesley.

Leuba, Clarence. (1955). "Toward Some Integration of Learning Theories: The Concept of Optimal Stimulation." *Psychological Reports* 1:27–33.

Lilly, John. (1985). *The Center of the Cyclone: An Autobiographical View of Inner Space.* New York: Julian Press.

Slanger, Elissa, and Rudestam, Kjell Erik. (1997). "Motivation and Disinhibition in High Risk Sports: Sensation Seeking and Self-Efficacy." *Journal of Research in Personality* 31:355–374.

Zuckerman, Marvin. (1974). "The Sensation Seeking Motive." In *Progress in Experimental Research, Vol. 7,* ed. Brendan Maher. New York: Academic Press.

Zuckerman, Marvin. (1985). "Biological Foundations of the Sensation Seeking Temperament." In *The Biological Bases of Personality and Behavior*, ed. Jan Strelau, Frank Farley, and Anthony Gale. Washington, DC: Hemisphere Publishing.

Zuckerman, Marvin. (1994). *Behavioral Expressions and Biosocial Bases of Sensation Seeking*. New York: Cambridge University Press.

Kjell Erik Rudestam
Elissa Slanger

SENTIMENTALITY

See Attachment; Attitudes; Hope; Intimacy; Love; Sympathy

SHAME

Shame has been discussed by philosophers and religious leaders for centuries. The relatively recent contributions of psychologists and other social scientists to this discussion have both confirmed and challenged longstanding assumptions about the nature and influence of this emotion.

The Basic Components of Shame

Shame is an emotion that is notoriously difficult to define. Day-to-day language often is vague when it comes to distinguishing shame from other "moral" emotions, such as guilt. Even social scientific discourse, which is presumably more precise than everyday speech, sometimes treats shame as a variant of guilt or embarrassment. One reason for the apparent confusion is that shame is difficult to observe. In contrast to emotions such as joy, sadness, and anger, shame does not involve particular facial expressions. Nor does it seem to be elicited consistently by specific situations. Getting caught in a lie may make some people feel shame while others may feel guilty or embarrassed.

In spite of the confusion sometimes associated with defining shame, researchers and theorists generally agree that shame can be described by several components. For example, shame involves a global, negative evaluation of the self. People who feel shame perceive that they have failed to meet certain standards of conduct. Their failure may be moral (e.g., lying or cheating) or it may center around their incompetence or faults (e.g., being too stupid or uncoordinated to pass an exam). Either way, the failure is seen as relatively uncontrollable.

Shame is also associated with a sense of being "exposed." When people feel shame, they are conscious of being critically observed. They perceive they are being scrutinized and evaluated—that others are all too aware of their flaws. In part as a consequence of having their defects unwittingly exposed to others, those who feel shame often want to hide or disappear. They may avert their gaze or bury their face in their hands. Erik Erikson (1950) provided an apt description of this desire to hide or shrink away from others when he noted the following: "Shame is early expressed in an impulse to bury one's face, or to sink, right then and there, into the ground" (pp. 252–253).

Perhaps because those who feel shame are unable to escape the sense that they are being scrutinized and often are unable to control their failures, they react in ways that reflect helplessness or extreme frustration. One common response to shame is passivity or dependence. If shameful flaws or failings are seen as unalterable, it may seem useless to try to change them. Individuals who feel shame also cope with their feelings by withdrawing from social interaction, as Karen Barrett (1995, p. 44) noted: "If one focuses on the self as a bad person who is evaluated as such by others, then the only recourse is to die, disappear, or at least withdraw from evaluating others. One cannot remake the self then and there." Another response to shame is to lash out at others in anger. When people react to shame with anger, they are defending themselves by externalizing their feelings of inadequacy. They are redirecting the rejection they feel from others. Helen Lewis (1987) further argues that many times individuals realize their rage is inappropriate and this realization, in turn, can make them feel more shame.

Distinctions between Shame and Other Emotions

Identifying some of the basic components of shame is just one way researchers and theorists define shame and explore what it means for individuals and their social relationships. Another way is to distinguish it from other, related emotions such as guilt and embarrassment.

Shame and Guilt

Although some theorists argue that shame and guilt are inextricably linked, most conceive of the two emotions as being quite different. According to scholars such as David Ausubel (1955), one theoretical distinction between shame and guilt involves the notion that shame is a "public" emotion, while guilt is a "private" one. People who feel shame believe they are being judged by others, whereas those who feel guilt are judging themselves based on a set of internalized standards. As noted by David Harder (1995), the source of self-evaluation for shame is external, and the source for guilt is internal.

John Merrick, the severely disfigured main character in Bernard Pomerance's Elephant Man (1979), cannot hide from his grotesque appearance. Even if he does not look in a mirror, he sees the reactions of others as they show shock, horror, and disgust. He wishes he could live in a home for the blind, where he would not have to feel ashamed every time someone looked at him.

Although this internal-external distinction has been adopted by many psychologists, it does not seem to be supported by empirical research. June Tangney (1995) examined children's and adults' autobiographical descriptions of shame and guilt experiences and found that both shame and guilt were most often felt in the presence of others. Individuals sometimes reported experiencing the two emotions when they were alone, but shame was just as likely as guilt to be felt when people were by themselves.

Other distinctions between shame and guilt have stood the test of empirical studies. The work of Lewis (1971) provided researchers with a clear, testable set of distinctions between the two emotions. Primary to this work is a differential emphasis on the self versus behavior. Lewis claimed that the focus of evaluation for shame is on the self as a person ("*I* did something bad"), whereas the focus for guilt is on a specific act ("I *did* something bad"). People who feel shame tend to denigrate and devalue themselves as human beings. They feel inadequate, worthless, and powerless. By contrast, those who feel guilt regret a particular behavior. They feel remorse, tension, and contrition. To test distinctions such as these, Paula Niedenthal and her colleagues (1994) conducted a study in which individuals described an instance when they experienced shame or guilt and then listed things that could have caused the experience to end differently. People's descriptions of shame were more often associated with counterfactual statements "undoing" the self ("If only I weren't . . ."), while guilt descriptions were more commonly linked to statements "undoing" behavior ("If only I hadn't . . .").

Given that shame is based on a global negative evaluation of the self and that, as a consequence, it can affect people's identity, Lewis (1971) also argued that it usually is more painful than guilt. In line with this thinking, Frank Wicker and his colleagues found that, compared to guilt, shame is a more intense, incapacitating emotion. The respondents in this study reported feeling weaker, more inferior, more helpless, more inhibited, and more submissive when they felt

shame. By contrast, people felt greater control and more active when they felt guilt. The researchers cautioned that their participants did not perceive shame as more "painful" than guilt, but other scholars, such as Janice Lindsay-Hartz (1984) and Tangney (1993) have found that, indeed, shame is the more painful of the two emotions.

In part because people who feel shame perceive that their inadequacies and failings are exposed to others, Lewis (1971) suggested that they have a desire to hide, cover themselves, or lash out. Their sense of powerlessness and their tendency to denigrate themselves leaves these shamed individuals extremely limited when it comes to making amends for their faults. Those who feel guilt, however, are in a very different situation. Because guilty feelings usually involve specific, controllable behaviors, individuals who feel guilt have a tendency to confess or to repair what they have done. They are able to make amends because their failing involves a particular behavior rather than their entire being. Indeed, when Tangney and her associates (1996) asked people to describe a shame experience and a guilt experience, they found that in cases where individuals felt shame, they were more likely to hide and less likely to admit their wrongdoing than when they felt guilt.

In a similar vein, Barrett and her colleagues (1993) conducted a study in which they differentiated a "shame-family pattern" from a "guilt-family pattern." They observed the behavior of two-year-old children who were allowed to play with an experimenter's toy that was rigged to break. After the toy broke, children who demonstrated a shame-family pattern of response tended to avert their gaze from the experimenter or physically avoid the experimenter after the toy broke. These children often hesitated to tell the experimenter about the broken toy and were less likely to try to repair the toy. In contrast, children who displayed a guilt-family pattern neither avoided the experimenter nor averted their gaze. They quickly told the experimenter about the broken toy and were more likely to try to repair the toy before the experimenter asked about it. Although it is difficult to discern whether the toddlers who participated in this study actually felt shame or guilt, the findings do indicate that, at a very early age, individuals show a tendency to behave in ways consistent with Lewis's distinctions between shame and guilt.

Shame and Embarrassment

If the line that separates shame and guilt is sometimes blurred, the one that distinguishes between shame and embarrassment is even more so. In fact, a number of scholars have argued that shame and embarrassment are quite similar. Carroll Izard (1977) conceived of embarrassment as a component of shame. Likewise, Gershen Kaufman (1989) claimed that shame and embarrassment actually reflect the same affect. Even Lewis (1971), who so carefully distinguished shame from guilt, did little to differentiate shame from embarrassment.

Those who do distinguish shame and embarrassment generally see shame as the more serious, more painful of the two emotions. This may be because the failures or defects associated with shame are characterized as more profound than are those linked to embarrassment. When people feel shame, the standards they have failed to meet, or the rules they have broken, typically are perceived as more important than are those associated with being embarrassed. Furthermore, some researchers suggest that shame-related flaws are more likely to be moral (e.g., stealing from a friend) than are flaws related to embarrassment (e.g., slipping and falling on stage). It is not surprising then that a number of scholars have argued that people's attributions about their shame-related behavior are more stable and global, whereas their attributions about behavior that stimulates embarrassment are more unstable and specific.

Studies have confirmed many of the conceptual distinctions between shame and embarrassment. For instance, Rowland Miller and Tangney (1994) found that shame was viewed as a more intense, long-lasting emotion than was embarrassment. People perceived that shame involved immoral behavior, while they felt embarrassment involved behavior that was awkward and sometimes humorous. Shame also was associated with relatively serious, foreseeable transgressions, while embarrassment was elicited by more trivial accidents. Tangney, Miller, and their colleagues (1996) extended this work by comparing shame, guilt, and embarrassment. They found that even when differences in the perceived intensity and morality of the emotions were controlled, people who felt shame or guilt felt more responsibility and regret than did those who were embarrassed. Embarrassment more often occurred suddenly and was more often associated with trivial, humorous events. Individuals who felt embarrassed reported more obvious physiological changes and were less likely to experience the emotion when they were alone. The findings of this study suggest that shame and embarrassment may have less in common than theorists initially thought.

Theoretical Approaches to Shame

One reason that shame has been difficult to define and distinguish from other emotions is that it has been studied from several very different theoretical perspectives. A cursory review of some of the more influ-

ential theoretical approaches to shame helps to explain current understandings of the emotion.

Psychodynamic Approaches

Psychodynamic theorists describe shame both as a response to perceived inadequacies and as a preventative defense mechanism. Conceived as a response to inadequacies or flaws, shame emerges from individuals' self-condemnation or their fears of rejection (sometimes, but not always, associated with children's failure to control bodily functions). Because shame, thus conceptualized, involves individuals' flaws being exposed, those who feel shame want to shrink away or hide to avoid being rejected by others. The tendency to hide or cover oneself also is apparent when shame is viewed as a defense mechanism. Sigmund Freud (1905) discussed shame as a response to people's visual or sexual drives. He argued that, as a defense mechanism, shame serves to control individuals' desire to exhibit themselves to others.

One of the most influential contributions of psychodynamic approaches to current understandings of shame is Freud's (1914) concept of the "ego ideal." According to Freud, the ego ideal is made up of ideal representations, grandiose fantasies, and parental representations. Shame occurs when people perceive they have failed to approximate their ego ideal. Karen Horney (1950) further specified that feelings of inadequacy and shame are associated with unrealistic ideals in a cyclical manner, such that greater feelings of inadequacy lead to more perfectionistic ideals, which, in turn, exacerbate feelings of inadequacy and shame.

While many psychodynamic theorists have suggested that shame is linked to early experiences of humiliation, Erikson (1950) placed the developmental aspects of shame at the forefront of his work. He argued that the tasks associated with identity development put children in a position where shame is easily elicited—that shame emerges from the unavoidable losses of self-control that occur as children work their way toward adulthood. Several scholars have elaborated on this developmental view, suggesting that children's individuation almost inevitably creates a sense of shame. As children try to separate from their par-

Monica Wood's "Disappearing" (1988) is told by an obese woman who is so powerfully ashamed of her appearance that she wants to disappear. Her husband asks her how she can stand herself. She goes on a diet and swims hours every day, losing so much weight that she becomes skeletal. By the end of the story, it is clear that she is trying to disappear altogether.

ents, they see that the separation creates parental pain. If they do not respond to their parents' pain, they feel shame because they have failed to meet their parents' needs. But they also feel shame if they do respond because by meeting their parents' needs, they acknowledge that their own wants and needs are unimportant.

Affect Theory

Affect theory is based on the notion that emotions are a product of evolutionary adaptations. Along with Charles Darwin (1872), adherents of affect theory argue that certain emotional expressions are universal and innate. These "fundamental emotions" emerge from physiological, neural processes. The neural processes create specific sets of muscular movements in the face and are associated with emotional feelings. The presumption is that people are hard-wired to display fundamental emotions under certain circumstances because the emotions serve important adaptive functions such as motivating behavior, communicating intent, and encouraging social interaction.

According to Silvan Tomkins (1963, 1987), shame is one of several "innate" affects. It is linked to a particularized set of muscular responses including decreased muscle tone in the face, hiding of the head, lowering of the eyelids, and blushing. Tomkins contends that shame occurs when an individual's interest or enjoyment has been interrupted. Shame, in other words, has the adaptive purpose of controlling other affects such as excitement or enjoyment. Although Tomkins's theoretical perspective has been criticized, the work of scholars such as Kaufman (1992) and Donald Nathanson (1992) demonstrates that it has also been very influential in explaining how shame affects individuals' well-being.

Cognitive Approaches

Appraisal theory and attribution theory are the two most well-known cognitive approaches to understanding shame. Both of these theories suggest that individuals' cognitive assessments are central to the experience of emotions. For instance, Richard Lazarus (1991), a strong proponent of appraisal theory, argues that the way people evaluate themselves and their social environment can elicit shame. Drawing from psychoanalytic approaches, he notes that shame involves the failure of individuals to meet their ego-ideal. When people feel shame, they "feel disgraced or humiliated, especially in the eyes of a parent or parent-substitute, who was the original source of the demanding ego-ideal" (p. 241). The components of an appraisal that evoke shame, according to Lazarus, thus, are twofold. First, people who feel shame must perceive they have failed to live up to a certain set of standards. Second, they must place blame for the failure on themselves.

Attribution theorists provide a different but related account of shame and other emotions. They argue that people's perceptions of the causes of behaviors or events are what evoke certain feelings. Traditionally, these causes are examined by researchers in terms of their locus or source (internal factors associated with the person versus external factors in the environment), stability (temporary versus enduring), globality (general versus specific), and controllability (the degree to which the individual can exert control over the event). Bernard Weiner (1986; 1995) suggests that shame and guilt occur when people make internal attributions about failure experiences. He distinguishes shame from guilt on the basis of controllability: Individuals feel guilt when they could have controlled their failure; they feel shame when the failure was uncontrollable. Jonathon Brown and Weiner (1984) have demonstrated that in achievement-oriented contexts, shame is associated with low ability, behavioral inhibition, and withdrawal from the situation. In contrast, guilt in failure situations is linked to a lack of effort and increased involvement in the task.

Michael Lewis (1993) takes a slightly different perspective on the attributions associated with shame. He argues that shame is elicited by internal and global attributions for negative events or behaviors. People feel shame, therefore, when they perceive that a failure was caused by a relatively general quality of the self ("*I* am bad"). More specific self-focused attributions ("I *did* something bad") elicit guilt or regret. This line of thinking is consistent with that of Helen Lewis (1971).

Phenomenological Approaches

The phenomenological description of shame provided by Lewis (1971) has been the impetus for a great deal of research. As previously noted, Lewis defined shame, in part, by distinguishing it from guilt. She noted that shame involves a perception of the self as flawed. The focus of evaluation is on the whole self, as opposed to a specific behavior. People experiencing shame see themselves as being worthless and weak. They feel exposed and, as a consequence, want to cover themselves, hide, or escape from their current situation.

Empirical studies largely support Lewis's conceptualization of shame. For example, in a series of in-depth interviews, Lindsay-Hartz (1984) found that when people experience shame they want to disappear or remove themselves from interpersonal interactions. She described the experiences relayed by her respondents by noting that when people feel shame, they are "stuck in the presentness of time, thinking about [their] small, helpless, worthless self and feeling that [their] true being is now exposed forever" (p. 694). Tamara Ferguson and her colleagues (1991) discovered that even children ranging from eight to twelve years of age linked shame with fear of embarrassment, blushing, ridicule from others, and a desire to escape. While these studies represent only two examples of the investigations that have been done to explore the phenomenological aspects of shame, they illustrate the contributions made by phenomenological approaches to the understanding of how people experience and respond to feeling shame.

Defining Characteristics of Shame

The characteristics of shame that theorists, researchers, and therapists choose to emphasize in their work affect the way they define the experience and expression of shame. Several potentially opposing characteristics are apparent in the literature. These include: individual versus interpersonal, enduring versus temporary, prosocial versus antisocial, egocentric versus sociocentric, and self-inflicted versus other-inflicted.

Individual Versus Interpersonal

Most researchers and theorists examine shame from the perspective of the individual who is experiencing the emotion. Psychodynamic approaches portray shame as being elicited by people's fears of their own inadequacies and their need to regulate their inner drives. Affect theorists view shame as individuals' adaptation to evolutionary forces. Those who advocate cognitive approaches see shame as being evoked by certain types of appraisals or attributions. Although these, and other, theoretical perspectives acknowledge that shame involves a real or imagined audience, they emphasize processes associated with individuals rather than those associated with interpersonal interaction or relationships. The interpersonal processes associated with shame have received relatively little attention from researchers and theorists. Yet, shame has a strong interpersonal element.

Lewis (1981) suggests that shame is a reaction to losing the approval or acceptance of a loved one. She claims that people feel shame when they are "helpless to restore a loved one's good feelings about the self" (p. 182). Ferguson and Hedy Stegge (1995) similarly note that shame in children is often associated with the absence of parents' positive response to the children's behavior. If, as V. I. Friesen (1979, p. 43) suggests, "the underlying dynamic of shame is fear of rejection," researchers and therapists need to understand the interpersonal processes that set up such a fear as well as those that may alleviate it.

Enduring Versus Temporary

The majority of research and theory treats shame as a relatively enduring quality or disposition—one that can cause problems for individuals and their social relationships. Enduring shame is associated with ongoing feelings of inadequacy or worthlessness. These feelings of inadequacy, in turn, affect how people function in their associations with others. Carolyn Zahn-Waxler and JoAnn Robinson (1995) elaborate on how self-focused, dispositional shame can foster psychological disorders: "If young children's actions are repeatedly linked to the distress of others, they come to feel they have brought harm to the others. Such beliefs about the role of the self in misfortunes befalling a loved one may become the basis for more enduring pathogenic beliefs and orientations" (p. 164).

Consistent with this line of thinking, theorists argue that shame plays a role in psychological disorders such as depression, and narcissism. Empirical studies confirm that feelings of shame are linked to eating disorders, alcohol addictions, narcissism and depression, childhood abuse, and neuroticism. The association between enduring shame and psychological adjustment has been shown by Ronald Johnson and his colleagues (1987) to hold up both in Asian and European-American cultures, in spite of data that suggest Asian cultures place a greater emphasis on shame.

Although the associations between ongoing feelings of shame and various psychological problems are compelling, it is important to note that shame also can be a relatively transitory state. People can feel inadequate or worthless for a time and then regain their sense of confidence. Temporary feelings of shame may be experienced, for example, after individuals perform badly (e.g., on an exam or in a sports event) or after they fail to live up to the specific expectations of a loved one (e.g., when they forget a special anniversary). Shame may be evoked when people enter certain psychosocial environments and may subside when the context changes. Furthermore, people may feel a passing sense of shame when they anticipate the possibility that they will be unable to meet certain standards. Such anticipatory shame may serve important regulatory functions—reminding people where to draw the line between appropriate and inappropriate behavior. Because the negative feelings associated with temporary shame are short-lived, the effects of this type of shame on individuals and on relationships are likely to be quite different from those of shame that is more enduring.

Prosocial Versus Antisocial

Although the feelings associated with shame are generally quite painful, shame itself is not necessarily "bad." The unpleasant feelings associated with shame can serve very powerful, prosocial functions. Shame —or the anticipation of it—can encourage people to behave in positive rather than negative ways. Leon Wurmser (1987) discussed shame as a "preventative attitude" and argued that feelings of shame can protect people from dangerous impulses. Carl Schneider (1987) further specified that "being ashamed" involves feelings of inadequacy and disgrace, whereas "the sense of shame" involves discretion or modesty. Shame can motivate individuals to uphold certain standards; it can support their ideals about who or what they want to be. Further, because shame highlights a discrepancy between people's actual behavior and what they perceive to be ideal behavior, it can motivate them to change for the better. Indeed, some scholars argue that a certain amount of shame is necessary for personal development.

Of course, the ability of shame to serve prosocial as opposed to antisocial functions depends in part on the frequency and the degree to which shame is experienced. Although shame can encourage positive behavior, people who are consistently besieged by feelings of inadequacy and worthlessness are at a greater risk of engaging in antisocial behavior. Because shame is associated with a desire to hide and withdraw from social interaction, these individuals tend to respond to social stimuli in one of two ways. First, people who are prone to shame may withdraw from interactions and relationships. This can create a sense of loss for others, which, in turn, can encourage further shame. For example, parents who are prone to shame may not provide their children with the nurturance and attention the children need. Because, as some argue, shame is engendered by a withdrawal of love, the abandoned children may respond to their parents' withdrawal with feelings of shame. Second, when people who are shame-prone cannot escape or withdraw from interpersonal situations, they may react with rage. Attacking the other person is one way for individuals who are prone to shame to defend themselves. Such attacks draw attention away from their inadequacies and can create an illusion of power or control.

Studies by Tangney and her colleagues (1992, 1996) confirmed that proneness to shame is associated with anger arousal, resentment, irritability, suspicion, a tendency to blame others for negative events, and indirect expressions of hostility. In both children and adults, shame-proneness was linked to destructive reactions to anger, including malevolent intentions, dis-

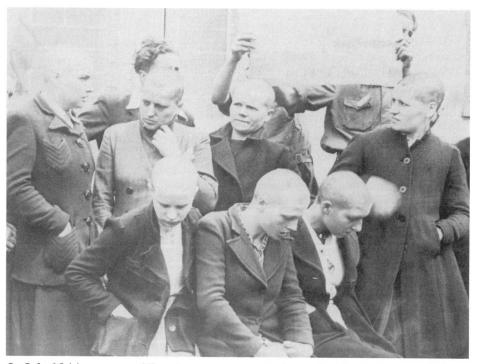

In July 1944, a group of French women who collaborated with the Nazis were shorn of their hair and shamed in public for violations of the rules of the French Resistance Party in regard to conduct with the Germans. The women were paraded through the streets of Cherbourg in disgrace. (Corbis/Bettmann)

placed aggression, and self-directed hostility. Proneness to shame also has been related to physical violence, verbal attacks, and emotional violence.

Egocentric Versus Sociocentric

Given that shame typically is associated with perceptions of one's own inadequacy and worthlessness, it is tempting to assume that the source of the perceived inadequacy lies within the self. And, indeed, many times this is the case—people often feel shame because they believe they, themselves, are fundamentally flawed. Their shame is egocentric. However, individuals can also feel shame because of their associations—real or imagined—with others. Friesen (1979) argues that any person, institution, or group an individual identifies with can elicit feelings of shame. This more sociocentric type of shame has been labeled "identification shame," "vicarious shame," or "empathetic shame."

Even when shame is sociocentric—when it is evoked by a source outside the self—it can be quite intense. The intensity of felt shame is likely to vary with the degree to which individuals empathize or identify with the relevant source. This identification may take several different forms. People may feel flawed because someone or something they see being as integral to their own lives is flawed. Children often feel shame when a family member commits an immoral act. Adults may feel shame when an organization they work for engages in unethical practices. Sociocentric shame can also occur, though, when the source is not all that relevant to the individual's life—when, for example, they observe strangers in shameful or embarrassing situations. In such cases, it is almost as if the act of watching another person's failure somehow implicates the observer. Finally, shame can be elicited by another person's shamelessness: Seeing another individual flagrantly violate an important social rule can make others feel shame. Taking on shame that someone else is unwilling to assume may serve as a way for people to acknowledge that a shameful act has been committed. When this situation occurs, those who feel shame may not be identifying so much with the perpetrator as they are with the rules and norms of the society or social group within which they live.

Self-Inflicted Versus Other-Inflicted

There are times when people, in effect, bring shame upon themselves—when, for example, they engage in behavior that they see as being morally reprehensible. Under such circumstances, individuals feel shame because they have failed to meet a certain set of standards. There are also times, however, when people feel worthless or inadequate because of something someone else did *to* them. Even though they did not engage in the shame-eliciting behavior and, in fact, even though they may have fought against it, they feel a deep sense of shame.

One very vivid example of shame that is elicited by the actions of another is rape. In spite of the fact that those who are raped are victims of another person's abhorrent behavior, they often consider themselves flawed or ruined. Indeed, some who are raped experience so much shame that they deem themselves unworthy to live. Similarly, children who are physically or sexually abused by their parents often come to see themselves as being flawed. Because they think in relatively concrete terms, these children may reason that if their parents—the people who are supposed to love and care for them—treat them as if they are worthless, they must deserve to be treated that way.

Feminists argue that women and children are particularly susceptible to being shamed by others because they are viewed as inferior to, and less powerful than, men. Although the reason for their greater sense of shame is debatable, women consistently report feeling more shame than do men.

Over time, shame that is undeservingly inflicted upon individuals by others may have very different sorts of effects, represented by two distinct models. One model suggests that people who are continually shamed become accustomed to shame-eliciting stimuli. Having shame repeatedly inflicted upon them makes them "numb" or relatively invulnerable to the elicitation of the emotion. If such a habituation model applies, those who have been repeatedly shamed should display muted responses to events that, for others, evoke shame. Alternatively, Zahn-Waxler and Grazyna Kochanska (1990) support a neurophysiological model of "kindling" that suggests people's responses to other-inflicted shame may become "kindled" or exaggerated over time. This model predicts that when organisms are repeatedly exposed to a noxious stimulus (e.g., electric shocks), they become sensitized so that, eventually, smaller doses of the stimulus are required to elicit a response (e.g., seizures). Eventually, the organisms may begin to display the response without being exposed to the stimulus. Applied to the elicitation of shame, this model suggests that repeated exposure to other-inflicted shame may make people "hypersensitive" to shame-relevant stimuli. Children who are emotionally abused, for example, may feel an exaggerated sense of shame when confronted with the slightest hint that they have done something wrong. Although the applicability of this model to the elicitation of shame has not yet been tested, anecdotal data from clinical psychologists suggest that the model may be quite useful.

Conclusion

The research literature is full of stimulating debates about the nature and influence of shame. In spite of many disagreements between scholars about issues such as the origins of shame and the various means by which it is elicited and maintained, one thing is relatively clear: Shame is a very powerful emotion. It profoundly affects individuals and their social relationships. Because shame is so closely tied to people's views of themselves, it can be a difficult emotion to study. When researchers, theorists, and clinicians examine shame, they peer into some of the most vulnerable areas of people's lives. Shame reveals where individuals feel they have failed, where they believe they are inadequate, and where they have been hurt by their own actions or the actions of others. Shame shows why some people strive so hard to be accepted and why others give up, believing they will never be loved. It can motivate great accomplishments, and it can crush the most lofty of dreams. Knowing what makes individuals feel shame means knowing something very intimate about their psyche and something very striking about the society in which they live.

See also: ANGER; ATTRIBUTION; DARWIN, CHARLES ROBERT; EMBARRASSMENT; EMOTIONAL ABUSE; ERIKSON, ERIK HOMBURGER; FREUD, SIGMUND; GUILT; HORNEY, KAREN

Bibliography

Ausubel, David P. (1955). "Relationships between Shame and Guilt in the Socializing Process." *Psychological Review* 62:378–390.

Barrett, Karen C. (1995). "A Functionalist Approach to Shame and Guilt." In *Self-conscious Emotions: Shame, Guilt, Embarrassment, and Pride,* ed. June P. Tangney and Kurt W. Fischer. New York: Guilford.

Barrett, Karen C.; Zahn-Waxler, Carolyn; and Cole, Pamela M. (1993). "Avoiders Versus Amenders: Implications for the Investigation of Guilt and Shame during Toddlerhood." *Cognition and Emotion* 7:481–505.

Brown, Jonathon, and Weiner, Bernard. (1984). "Affective Consequences of Ability Versus Effort Ascriptions: Controversies, Resolutions, and Quandaries." *Journal of Educational Psychology* 76:146–158.

Darwin, Charles. ([1872] 1965). *The Expression of the Emotions in Man and Animals.* Chicago: University of Chicago Press.

Erikson, Erik H. (1950). *Childhood and Society.* New York: W. W. Norton.

Ferguson, Tamara J., and Stegge, Hedy. (1995). "Emotional States and Traits in Children: The Case of Guilt and Shame." In *Self-conscious Emotions: Shame, Guilt, Embarrassment, and Pride,* ed. June P. Tangney and Kurt W. Fischer. New York: Guilford.

Ferguson, Tamara J.; Stegge, Hedy; and Damhuis, Ilse. (1991). "Children's Understanding of Guilt and Shame." *Child Development* 62:827–839.

Freud, Sigmund. ([1905] 1953). "Three Essays on the Theory of Sexuality." In *The Standard Edition of the Complete Psychological Works of Sigmund Freud, Vol. 7,* ed. James Strachey. London: Hogarth.

Freud, Sigmund. ([1914] 1957). "On Narcissism: An Introduction." In *The Standard Edition of the Complete Psychological Works of Sigmund Freud, Vol. 14,* ed. James Strachey. London: Hogarth.

Friesen, V. I. (1979). "On Shame and the Family." *Family Therapy* 6:39–58.

Harder, David W. (1995). "Shame and Guilt Assessment, and Relationships of Shame- and Guilt-Proneness to Psychopathology." In *Self-Conscious Emotions: Shame, Guilt, Embarrassment, and Pride,* ed. June P. Tangney and Kurt W. Fischer. New York: Guilford.

Horney, Karen. (1950). *Neurosis and Human Growth: The Struggle toward Self-Realization.* New York: W. W. Norton.

Izard, Carroll E. (1977). *Human Emotion.* New York: Plenum.

Johnson, Ronald C.; Danko, George P.; Huang, Yau-Huang.; Park, Jong Y.; Johnson, Steven B.; and Nagoshi, Craig T. (1987). "Guilt, Shame, and Adjustment in Three Cultures." *Personality and Individual Differences* 8:357–364.

Kaufman, Gershen. (1989). *The Psychology of Shame.* New York: Springer.

Kaufman, Gershen. (1992). *Shame: The Power of Caring,* 3rd ed. Rochester, NY: Schenkman Books.

Lazarus, Richard S. (1991). *Emotion and Adaptation.* New York: Oxford University Press.

Lewis, Helen B. (1971). *Shame and Guilt in Neurosis.* New York: International Universities Press.

Lewis, Helen B. (1981). *Freud and Modern Psychology, Vol. 1: The Emotional Basis of Mental Illness.* New York: Plenum.

Lewis, Helen B. (1987). "Shame and the Narcissistic Personality." In *The Many Faces of Shame,* ed. Donald L. Nathanson. New York: Guilford.

Lewis, Michael. (1993). "Self-Conscious Emotions: Embarrassment, Pride, Shame, and Guilt." In *Handbook of Emotions,* ed. Michael Lewis and Jeannette M. Haviland. New York: Guilford.

Lindsay-Hartz, Janice. (1984). "Contrasting Experiences of Shame and Guilt." *American Behavioral Scientist* 27:689–704.

Mason, Marilyn. (1991). "Women and Shame: Kin and Culture." *Journal of Feminist Family Therapy* 3:175–194.

Miller, Rowland S., and Tangney, June P. (1994). "Differentiating Embarrassment and Shame." *Journal of Social and Clinical Psychology* 13:273–287.

Nathanson, Donald L. (1992). *Shame and Pride: Affect, Sex, and the Birth of the Self.* New York: W. W. Norton.

Niedenthal, Paula M.; Tangney, June P.; and Gavanski, Igor. (1994). " 'If Only I Weren't' Versus 'If Only I Hadn't': Distinguishing Shame from Guilt in Counterfactual Thinking." *Journal of Personality and Social Psychology* 67:585–595.

Schneider, Carl D. (1987). "A Mature Sense of Shame." In *The Many Faces of Shame,* ed. Donald L. Nathanson. New York: Guilford.

Tangney, June P. (1993). "Shame and Guilt." In *Symptoms of Depression,* ed. Charles G. Costello. New York: Wiley.

Tangney, June P. (1995). "Recent Advances in the Empirical Study of Shame and Guilt." *American Behavioral Scientist* 38:1132–1145.

Tangney, June P.; Miller, Rowland S.; Flicker, Laura; and Barlow, Deborah Hill. (1996). "Are Shame, Guilt, and Embarrassment Distinct Emotions?" *Journal of Personality and Social Psychology* 70:1256–1269.

Tangney, June P.; Wagner, Patricia E.; Fletcher, Carey; and Gramzow, Richard. (1992). "Shamed into Anger? The Relation of Shame and Guilt to Anger and Self-Reported Aggression." *Journal of Personality and Social Psychology* 62:669–675.

Tomkins, Silvan S. (1963). *Affect, Imagery, Consciousness, Vol. 2: The Negative Affects.* New York: Springer-Verlag.

Tomkins, Silvan S. (1987). "Shame." In *The Many Faces of Shame,* ed. Donald L. Nathanson. New York: Guilford.

Weiner, Bernard. (1986). *An Attributional Theory of Motivation and Emotion.* New York: Springer-Verlag.

Weiner, Bernard. (1995). *Judgments of Responsibility.* New York: Guilford.

Wicker, Frank W.; Payne, Glen C.; and Morgan., Randall D. (1983). "Participant Descriptions of Guilt and Shame." *Motivation and Emotion* 7:25–39.

Wurmser, Leon. (1987). "Shame: The Veiled Companion of Narcissism." In *The Many of Shame,* ed. Donald L. Nathanson. New York: Guilford.

Zahn-Waxler, Carolyn, and Kochanska, Grazyna. (1990). "The Origins of Guilt." In *Nebraska Symposium on Motivation,* ed. Ross A. Thompson. Lincoln: University of Nebraska Press.

Zahn-Waxler, Carolyn, and Robinson, JoAnn. (1995). "Empathy and Guilt: Early Origins of Feelings of Responsibility." In *Self-Conscious Emotions: Shame, Guilt, Embarrassment, and Pride,* ed. June P. Tangney and Kurt W. Fischer. New York: Guilford.

Anita L. Vangelisti
Stacy L. Young

SHYNESS

Shyness is the ordinary language term most often used to label the emotional state of feeling anxious, awkward, and inhibited in social situations. Common synonyms include *bashfulness, timidity, reticence,* and *self-consciousness.* Because humans are social animals, it is assumed that all individuals have the capacity to experience at least some degree of shyness at some point in their lifetime. For example, even the most socially confident individuals make social blunders and presumably, for a short while afterward, feel somewhat awkward and tense in the social situation. Shyness also tends to be highly related to the reactive self-conscious emotions of shame, guilt, and embarrassment. However, shyness is typically assumed to be an anticipatory emotion because individuals who are prone to shyness often feel anxiety and tenseness before social events, typically as the result of worrying about, anticipating, or envisioning their own social awkwardness and negative evaluations from others.

The anticipatory anxiety that accompanies shyness can often be beneficial if it helps an individual to prepare successfully for a specific social situation such as a lecture, a meeting, or any potentially awkward social situation. Indeed, shyness, like shame and guilt, has been theorized to be an emotion that can serve to regulate inappropriate social behavior. In some cases, however, shyness can have serious negative consequences, interfering with satisfaction in work, love, and friendships.

Individuals who frequently experience shyness tend also to experience loneliness and depression. Shyness is not synonymous with low sociability (i.e., being tense and awkward in social situations does not mean that individuals do not want to be in the social situation). Individuals who are low in sociability prefer to be alone and do not desire social contact. These individuals may behave in ways that are similar to those of shy individuals (e.g., being withdrawn or reticent) even though the behaviors are due to different underlying motivations and mechanisms. When shyness is coupled with a desire for sociability, the individual experiences a heightened conflict between approach (sociability) and avoidance (inhibition and withdrawal).

Some individuals tend to feel shy across a wide variety of situations and social contexts. These individuals tend to be chronically or dispositionally shy. In other words, although shyness can be conceptualized as an emotional state, it can also be viewed as an enduring personality style or underlying trait. Shyness as a personality style tends to be considered a relatively non-situationally contingent social anxiety. For example, shy individuals tend to behave in an inhibited or withdrawn manner, feel tense or awkward, or experience social fears or worries fairly consistently across most social situations (although certain situations are more shyness eliciting than others, even for the shy individual). In addition, some individuals have a more debilitating form of shyness-related social anxiety that severely interferes with social behavior and contact. This cognitive-behavioral anxiety-based reaction is referred to as "social phobia," and it can be conceptualized as an extreme form of shyness that goes beyond the normal range of individual differences. This entry will focus mainly on shyness as a discrete emotion and its implications or consequences for personality in the normal range of individual differences.

Maggie, the scarred sister in Alice Walker's "Everyday Use" (1973), is so shy that her mother describes her as "chin on chest, eyes on ground, feet in shuffle." Maggie knows she is homely and not very smart, while her aggressive, attractive, and educated sister, Dee, steals all of the limelight. Maggie just hangs around in the background until her mother gives special quilts to her instead of to Dee.

Symptoms of Shyness

Symptoms of shyness fall into three main categories: feelings, thoughts, and behaviors. Although some shy individuals experience symptoms from all three of these categories, others experience shyness symptoms predominantly from only one or two of the categories. The symptoms that are elicited by shyness are closely related to a more primitive kind of fear response. Specifically, shyness tends to be experienced as a general feeling of tension or nervousness. In addition, shyness can be accompanied by bodily symptoms of emotional distress such as upset stomach, dry mouth, pounding heart, shaking, sweating, blushing, bladder pressure, or even dizziness. Individuals who experience shyness tend to have the additional worry that these emotional and physical feelings of distress are highly visible to others.

Shyness may also be accompanied by specific kinds of thoughts or worries. During social interactions, individuals who experience shyness may become excessively self-preoccupied with and painfully self-conscious about their every action. Research has demonstrated that individuals who experience shyness often have anxious meta-cognitions about their shyness symptoms. That is, shy individuals tend to have thoughts about their symptoms such as "Why can't I ever think of anything interesting to say?" or "I wish I didn't feel so awkward and tense." Ironically, these distracting thoughts tend to prevent the individual from paying attention to and engaging with others in the social environment. In addition, when individuals who experience shyness do think about other people, it is most often in the context of worrying about being evaluated negatively. In general, unlike those individuals who are not shy, dispositionally shy people tend to

1. perceive that a social interaction will be explicitly evaluative
2. expect that their behavior will be inadequate and that they will be evaluated negatively
3. hold "irrational beliefs" about how good their social performance should be and how much approval they should get from others
4. think about "Who does this situation want me to be?" rather than "How can I be me in this situation?"
5. adopt a strategy of trying to get along rather than trying to get ahead
6. become anxiously self-preoccupied and do not pay enough attention to others
7. judge themselves more negatively than others judge them
8. blame themselves for social failures and attribute successes to external factors
9. accept negative feedback and resist or reject positive feedback
10. remember negative self-relevant information and experiences.

The most overt and easily recognizable signs of shyness are the behavioral symptoms. Shyness tends to lead to reticence, social withdrawal, and social inhibition in some individuals. In addition, shyness can be related to the avoidance of expressing strong personal opinions as well as the adoption of a nonconfrontational style in order to avoid arguments. Shyness can also be related to awkward body language and behaviors such as gaze aversion, fidgeting, or playing with hands, hair, or clothing. Shyness can also lead to withdrawal or a desire to increase physical distance from other individuals, including keeping to the background or sidelines at social gatherings.

Physiological Aspects of Shyness

Physiological indicators of shyness often include symptoms of arousal of the sympathetic nervous system as the body prepares to either flee or fight an imminent predator, enemy, or harmful situation. In particular, arousal of the sympathetic nervous system entails diverting blood flow away from the peripheral blood vessels (such as in the hands and face) and the digestive system and redirecting blood flow toward the respiratory system, the heart, and other action muscles. Symptoms of activation of the fight-or-flight system include pale face, sweating, rapid heartbeat, heart palpitations, trembling, and nervous stomach. However, feelings of shyness can induce blushing. Most often, blushing is related to shyness in cases where embarrassment is also present. Blushing is related to the emotions that help to facilitate smooth social interactions and has been theorized to denote, nonverbally, social submission and an acknowledgment of the breach of social rules.

Exploration in the relationship between emotion and brain activity indicates that shyness tends to be related to heightened activity in the right anterior cerebral hemisphere. Activation in this hemisphere has been related to experiences of negative emotions, but it has also been, more theoretically, related to withdrawal tendencies such as reticence, solitude-seeking, and social withdrawal. In addition, shyness, in children as young as four years of age, has been found to be related to right frontal brain activity asymmetry (i.e., that the right frontal activity is greater than the left frontal activity). However, these studies have also revealed an interaction between shyness and motivation or preference for sociability such that sociability mediates the pattern of central nervous system physiological arousal that has been related to shyness. More surprising, however, is the related finding that shyness tends to be related to feelings of hostility. In general, patterns of brain activity show that anger, as an approach emotion, tends to be related to left frontal brain activity. Hostility, unlike anger, is not entirely an approach emotion. In fact, hostility is related to covert or verbally unexpressed anger. It is more likely that the experience of hostility in shyness is the combination of both anger (an approach emotion) and shyness (an avoidance emotion).

Research in behavior genetics indicates that shyness is the personality trait in the normal range of individual differences that has the largest genetic component. Jerome Kagan, in *Galen's Prophecy* (1994), has suggested that shyness, as it is rooted in temperamental reactivity to novel stimuli in childhood, is related to a lower threshold for arousal in sites in the amygdala, the fear center of the brain. This makes sense because the amygdala has been hypothesized to mitigate the fight-or-flight response that is related to a majority of the physiological symptoms of shyness.

Phenomenology of Shyness

Shyness tends to be experienced as a complex combination of both approach and avoidance tendencies, motivations, thoughts, and behaviors. For example, although shyness and sociability tend to be only modestly correlated, most shy individuals enjoy social contact, but they also fear it and tend to withdraw. In contrast, there are those individuals who are low in sociability so that no conflict exists between approach and avoidance. These individuals tend to prefer to spend time alone and do not feel a motivation to be sociable. It is possible that low sociability represents a form of social behavior that is less related to anxiety and more related to low cortical arousal as described by Hans J. Eysenck's theory of introversion presented in *The Biological Basis of Personality* (1967). These differences between shyness and low sociability may also be related to the distinction between temperamental shyness and self-conscious shyness.

Shyness-eliciting situations include those situations in which the individual perceives that the self is the focus of attention. In general, this explains why embarrassing or shaming moments tend to elicit shyness. In these moments, individuals perceive that they have become the (negative) center of attention. Shaming moments, in particular, tend to produce the feelings, thoughts, and behaviors that are most similar to shyness, such as the need to withdraw or hide. However, proud moments, such as receiving praise, compliments, or awards, can also elicit shyness in some individuals. Although here the individual has become

the center of attention in a positive sense, those individuals who tend to be chronically fearful of or anxious about being the focus of attention find even this focus on the self to be excessive and highly uncomfortable. In addition, any situation in which the self, literally, is the object of attention, such as when an individual must give a speech or presentation, can elicit shyness. It is not surprising, then, that stage fright closely resembles feelings of shyness, including the anxious self-preoccupation, worried meta-cognitions, and fear of negative evaluation. Stage fright, however, is much more common than shyness, with about 80 percent of Americans reporting a fear of public speaking versus about 40 percent who label themselves as being dispositionally shy people.

Other situations that tend to elicit shyness include those situations in which the individual needs to be assertive, needs assistance, or is in a large and unfamiliar group. Certain types of interpersonal interactions tend to elicit shyness. Interacting with authority figures and talking to possible romantic partners are two situations that tend to elicit feelings of shyness. In these instances, shyness and fear of negative evaluation seem to go hand in hand. In other words, the more an individual fears and expects negative evaluation from a social partner, the more likely it is that the individual will experience symptoms of shyness and anxiety, including reticence, performance worries, nervous stomach, racing heart, and sweating.

The experience of shyness is similar to and related to the experience of other self-conscious emotions such as shame or embarrassment. In particular, individuals who tend to be shy probably experience shame and embarrassment more easily and more frequently than do other individuals. In other words, individuals who are prone to social anxiety probably have a heightened sensitivity to experiencing shyness as well as shame, guilt, and embarrassment. It is interesting that some of these emotions share the phenomenological experience of wanting to hide and become smaller (e.g., shame). The phenomenological experience of shame seems to overlap with the motivation-like press of shyness (i.e., to become less visible). However, although these emotions are similar, shyness tends to be an anticipatory emotion; that is, shyness tends to be related to anticipating negative events or consequences. Shame, guilt, and embarrassment, on the other hand, tend to be reactive emotions or emotions that are elicited by specific events (e.g., making an awkward social mistake, hurting someone, or failing at an important task). In addition, shame and guilt tend to be reparative emotions (i.e., emotions that motivate an individual to make social repairs to relationships). In this sense, shame and guilt are seen as being

A shy boy clings to an adult during his first day of preschool, while the other children all participate in a group activity. (Corbis/Stephanie Maze)

emotions that regulate conformity to social rules, norms, or mores.

Shyness, however, tends to be much more related to social appeasement and submissiveness. In particular, shyness tends to be an emotion that regulates social dominance. Feelings of shyness tend to create a "go along to get along" mental set in individuals. In other words, feeling shy is related to agreeing with the plans and wishes of other individuals rather than being assertive about particular personal needs or wishes. Because of this, a moderate amount of shyness and social wariness tends to have an adaptive social benefit (e.g., negative behavior regulation and inhibition), but excessive shyness can be somewhat socially overpowering and debilitating. As mentioned above, feelings of shyness have been linked to feelings of hostility. This interesting relationship most likely represents the unresolved feelings of frustration that some individuals experience in situations that induce the conflict between approach and avoidance. It can be unpleasant for some individuals to experience fear and the resulting submissiveness, inhibition, and behavior regulation in social situations in which they would have ordinarily desired to be assertive, demanding, and, perhaps, dominant. In this case, feelings of shyness tend to produce reticence, withdrawal, and submission even if the individual is motivated to be sociable, assertive, and affiliative. In the United States, and some other countries as well, shyness is regarded as being a negative aspect of personality. It is possible that shyness elicits disdain or less sociability from those who are in the social network and that such feelings are easily or habitually noticed by individuals who are chronically shy. Thus, shyness is related to, but separate from, other emotions such as shame, guilt, and embarrassment. It is important to remember, however, that, phenomenologically, aspects of all of these complex self-conscious emotions are most likely experienced in tandem and thus are extremely hard to tease apart.

Shyness is often related to social anxiety and fears of social evaluation, disapproval, or awkwardness. In fact, although individuals who are chronically shy do tend to be less socially skilled, both verbally and nonverbally, they also tend to overestimate the visibility and effect of these deficiencies on those around them. Additionally, shyness is related to anxious self-preoccupation in which the individual is self-focused to the exclusion of the social environment. In this way, the shy individual focuses on his or her behavior and its effect on others rather than on the social characters or situation. It is ironic that this by-product of shyness can also feed back on other aspects of shyness, including social awkwardness and withdrawal. Shyness-induced self-preoccupation can also lead to reticence and aloofness. This somewhat egocentric aspect of shyness has generated some attention in both the clinical and nonclinical literature. Although some people have theorized that shyness is related to grandiosity, narcissism, or secretly desiring to be the center of attention, it is more probable that the anxious self-preoccupation can lead to an aloofness in social situations that is attributed by others to haughty disdain. In addition, the frustrated hostility that can be related to shyness also tends to be attributed to narcissistic tendencies in the shy individual. It is possible, however, that there exists a subtype of shyness in which anxious self-preoccupation is linked with narcissistic feelings of entitlement and manipulativeness (and hostility).

Development of Shyness

Researchers have found that shyness typically follows two developmental routes: early development and late development. Early-developing shyness, which typically emerges in the first year of life, has been described as being organic (biologically based), fearful, and temperamentally based. Later-developing shyness, on the other hand, seems to be related to self-consciousness and social anxiety and does not tend to emerge until around the time a child is four or five years of age. James Baldwin (1894) distinguished between early-developing ("organic") shyness and "true" (i.e., self-conscious) shyness, which emerges after the age of three. Later-developing shyness, then, like other self-conscious emotions, has been theorized to emerge only after a stable sense of the self is cognitively recognized by the individual. William McDougall (1963) extended Baldwin's dichotomy of shyness to include a third category: shyness that intensifies during puberty and the adolescent years due to the interaction between the hormonal changes and the self-conscious development of the adolescent. However, it is commonly assumed that it is the later-developing shyness that tends to peak during adolescence, between the ages of fourteen and seventeen, when social self-consciousness and cognitive self-preoccupation are heightened. It is this particular kind of shyness that is related to the most sex differences. In particular, later-developing shyness and social self-consciousness are higher in women than in men during the adolescent years (at least in the United States).

As would be expected, early-developing shyness tends to be characterized by biological symptoms of shyness, including anxiety, fear, and distress manifested in rapid heart rate, trembling, sweating, and nervous stomach. Infants who are shy and fearful when they encounter strangers often have unusually high heart rates when they confront any unfamiliar situation. This finding supports the hypothesis that the physiological component of early-developing shyness involves having a sensitive nervous system. Kagan (1994) has found that about 15 percent of infants exhibit this sensitivity to stress reactions, and his follow-up studies indicated that these same children are often described by their mothers as being shy children by the time they start kindergarten.

The later-developing shyness, in contrast, is more typically related to social anxiety—worries and thoughts that include anxious self-preoccupation and painful self-consciousness. The later-developing shyness is generally related to anxiety and worries about evaluation and fitting in to a social situation. It is not surprising, then, that this form of shyness is heightened during adolescence. Adolescents are maturing, both emotionally and physically, and these changes can make adolescents feel intensely self-conscious. In addition, adolescence is a developmental stage in which peer relationships and social groups tend to take on a sense of monumental importance, especially as adolescents shift their social reference and support group from family to friends.

It is interesting, however, that both prospective and retrospective accounts of shyness have shown that not all early-developing or later-developing shy individuals report or exhibit shyness later in life. In other words, despite the theoretical biological and genetic components of early-developing shyness, not all early-developing shyness continues into adulthood. Additionally, despite the theoretical links between later-developing shyness and cognitive appraisals, social anxiety, and self-concept disturbances, not all later-developing shyness continues into adulthood. However, retrospective reports of shyness have shown, according to Jonathan Cheek and Elena Krasnoperova (1999), that individuals who report early-developing shyness, as opposed to those who report later-developing shyness, are more likely to report continued symptoms and experiences of shyness in adulthood (75 percent versus 50 percent, respectively).

Culture and Shyness

Although shyness has been related to positive personality traits such as modesty, sensitivity, and warmth, it is often viewed as a negative and undesirable emotion and personality style in the United States. Because the United States is predominantly an individualistic or independent society (i.e., a society that values individual and autonomous expression and experience of the self) rather than an interdependent society (i.e., a society that values relational expression and experience of the self), a high value is placed on personality characteristics such as extroversion, uniqueness, and sociability—characteristics that can be construed as being the exact opposite of shyness. In the United States, at least, there is a fair amount of social pressure to be extroverted and sociable yet independent and autonomous. Thus, individuals who experience shyness in independent cultures may feel a heightened pressure to be sociable and to behave in an extroverted manner. This pressure may make the experience of shyness even more negative for the individual, who may experience the conflict between an internal pressure for avoidance and an external pressure for approach. In independent societies that encourage extroversion, shyness is not considered to be a social asset.

Countries that have lower rates of shyness than the United States, including Israel, the Philippines, and South Korea, have cultures that tend to encourage the expression of personal values and opinions. In addition, in cultures in which the child is reared among an extended family, such as in the Philippines, or in a collective environment, such as an Israeli kibbutz, oral communication, self-confidence, and assertive behaviors tend to be rewarded both because it is the cultural norm and because the non-shy children most likely receive more attention and resources.

Shyness rates tend to be higher in more interdependent societies, such as Japan. Interdependent countries tend to value more highly interpersonal harmony and balance (between family, friends, and members of the group), social conformity, emotional regulation, and behavioral inhibition—personality characteristics highly related to shyness. Indeed in Japan, talkative and assertive individuals are frequently not trusted. In these interdependent societies, it is the autonomous assertion of the self without regard for the group that is viewed negatively. In other words, shyness is a much more highly valued and beneficial emotion in interdependent societies than in independent societies.

Gender Differences in Shyness

In the United States, shyness tends to be considered a more feminine characteristic. Because of sex-role stereotypes and social expectations, it is more socially acceptable for girls to be shy than boys. During early

In The Glass Menagerie (1945), by Tennessee Williams, Laura Wingfield is so shy and self-conscious that she hides from reality and cannot deal with the terror that she feels in a classroom or in a social situation. She is as fragile as her collection of miniature glass animals.

childhood, for example, parents and teachers may invest time and effort in helping a boy become less timid or quiet because these traits are not considered to be masculine or appropriate for boys. Because parents and teachers may not be concerned with these traits in girls, they may be less likely to try to foster non-shy behaviors in girls.

Adolescent boys and girls are both put under tremendous socialization pressures from peers, parents, teachers, and the media. However, these socialization pressures may be, and frequently are, sex-role specific. The media tend to emphasize physical beauty and social skills in the socially construed image of the ideal woman. It is not surprising then that during the self-focused period of adolescence, girls tend to experience more symptoms of self-conscious shyness as they begin to worry about their attractiveness and how they will fit into social groups (i.e., how others will perceive them). The ideal man is often construed as being autonomous, assertive, and confident, and adolescent boys especially tend to struggle with the behavioral component of shyness (e.g., reticence, passivity, withdrawal). Although the social and socialization pressures placed on boys and girls tend to be different, Cheek and Lisa Melchior (1990) have found that equal amounts of both male and female adults (about 40 percent) consider themselves to be shy.

Evolutionary Perspectives on Shyness

The evolutionary perspective on human emotions, behaviors, and personality argues that those characteristics that confer the greatest adaptive benefits to the individual will survive and be passed on to future generations through the genes and/or through social learning or modeling. Shyness is a characteristic that is seen in both human and nonhuman animals, and it is an emotion that tends to regulate social interactions. In particular, shyness is mostly related to subordination and submissiveness in animals, and it is easily induced by the presence of a dominant or aggressive animal. In this way, shyness has an evolutionary benefit in allowing for peaceable relationships in a communal, hierarchical social living group. Shyness in humans has been shown to be related to fear of strangers or novel situations. This wariness can be extremely beneficial, especially when dealing with untrustworthy individuals or potentially life-threatening situations. In other words, although a shy person may never become a hero for protecting others from a violent attack, he may, nonetheless, survive the attack and live on to produce and raise children.

Shyness has also been recognized as an appeasement emotion in humans. Like nonhuman animals who become submissive in the presence of a dominant animal, humans also show the tendency to submit to others, social norms, or even to their fears of rejection, through appeasement emotions such as shyness. In humans, appeasement is shown by a host of processes, including submissive and affiliative processes. This submission allows an individual to reduce anticipated aggression, anger, or hostility of others while re-establishing or maintaining social relationships with individuals in the group. Because appeasement behavior conveys a sense of trustworthiness and a commitment to the group, it also tends to increase cooperative behaviors and reduce aggressive or punitive actions. It is easy to see how appeasement behaviors can be and have been beneficial to the individual and to the social group.

Consequences of Dispositional Shyness

Shyness tends to become less beneficial when an individual begins to exhibit shyness, timidity, or submission even in the absence of threats. This consistent non-situationally contingent shy behavior relates back to the earlier distinction between shyness as a discrete emotion and shyness as an enduring personality style or underlying trait.

Dispositional shyness can create a barrier to fulfilling one's potential at school or at work. Shy students avoid contributing to classroom discussions, do not seek help from teachers and advisors even when they are having trouble, and often develop a negative attitude toward school. Shy individuals may fear job interviews and may avoid well-paying careers that require oral communication. In addition, shy individuals tend to approach both school and work with the same type of attitude: Shy individuals do not play to win; they play not to lose. Their passive and conforming approach to educational and professional requirements may block the development and use of their creativity, and this may further contribute to a dissatisfaction with school and work.

Individuals who are dispositionally shy also tend to experience difficulties in their social and romantic relationships. In addition to their increased susceptibility to loneliness and depression, shy individuals tend to have a heightened fear of negative evaluation, and they tend to worry about other people's opinions of them. This social anxiety can have negative effects on the social relationships of shy individuals—friends may, at some point, become tired of constantly bolstering and reassuring a shy individual's social self-concept.

Because meeting potential mates and starting romantic relationships requires a great deal of assertive behavior, shy men in particular, because of sex-role norms, tend to have problems finding dating partners. However, shyness in men may actually confer some benefits once a romantic partner has been found—men who were shy as children tend to become more nurturing, warm, and caring fathers than non-shy men. Nevertheless, the difficulties that are associated with shyness for both men and women are sufficiently problematic that psychologists make the following recommendations for parents of shy children:

1. Do not overprotect or overindulge. Allow the shy child to experience moderate amounts of challenge, frustration, and stress rather than rushing to soothe away every sign of anxiety. With emotional support from parents, gradual exposure to new objects, people, and places will help the child learn to cope with his or her own special sensitivity to novelty. Gently and consistently nudge, but do not push, the child to continue gaining experience with new things.
2. Respect the shy temperament. Talk with the child about feeling nervous or afraid. Once the reality of these negative feelings has been acknowledged, encourage the child to talk about the positive things that can be gained from trying a new experience in spite of being afraid (an example from the parent's own childhood might be particularly helpful). Be aware that progress is usually slow and "one step at a time" because shy feelings may remain even after a particular shy behavior has been overcome. Sympathy, patience, and persistence are needed.
3. Do not let anyone tease the child about being shy. Shy children are highly sensitive to embarrassment and need extra comfort when they have been the victim of teasing. They also need more support and encouragement to develop positive self-esteem than do children who are not shy.
4. Help the child to build friendships. Inviting one or two playmates over to the house lets the child experience the security of being on familiar home territory. Sometimes a shy child will

do better when playing with children who are slightly younger.

5. Talk to teachers. The child's teacher can be an important ally, but teachers sometimes overlook the shy child or incorrectly assume that excessive quietness indicates lack of interest or lack of intelligence.

6. Prepare the child for new experiences. Take the child to visit a new school or classroom before school starts. Help the child rehearse by practicing for show-and-tell or for an oral book report. Role play in advance anticipated anxieties, such as what a party or the first day of summer camp will be like.

7. Find appropriate activities. Help the child get involved in a club or after-school activity that he or she really likes and that can help expand social contacts with others who share similar interests and enthusiasms. Be careful not to impose personal likes and wishes onto a child who has different likes and dislikes.

Conclusion

Certain individuals tend to experience some degree of shyness in all social situations. For these individuals, shyness becomes a chronically accessible and automatic cognitive appraisal of the majority of situations. In other words, when an individual constantly experiences shyness-related awkwardness, anxiety, reticence, and anxious self-preoccupation in social interactions, then it will be more likely that these behaviors and emotions will become linked with social situations. This link ensures a higher probability of the same or similar outcome (i.e., shyness-related behaviors, thoughts, and emotions) in all or most social situations.

Individuals who are dispositionally shy tend to experience a wide range of personal and interpersonal problems. Therefore it is not surprising that shyness is a frequent complaint for people who seek psychological counseling and that there are numerous self-help books related to overcoming shyness. Fortunately, research on the effectiveness of treatment programs for shyness has found that it is possible for shy people to increase their levels of both self-acceptance and social effectiveness.

See also: ACCEPTANCE AND REJECTION; AGGRESSION; ANGER; ANXIETY; ATTACHMENT; EMBARRASSMENT; EYSENCK, HANS JURGEN; FEAR AND PHOBIAS; GUILT; HUMAN DEVELOPMENT; INTIMACY; LONELINESS; NEUROBIOLOGY OF EMOTIONS; PERSONALITY; PSYCHOPHYSIOLOGY OF EMOTIONS; RELATIONSHIPS; SELF-ESTEEM; SHAME; TEMPERAMENT; TRUST

Bibliography

Aron, Elaine N. (1996). *The Highly Sensitive Person.* Secaucus, NJ: Carol Publishing.

Baldwin, James Mark. (1894). "Bashfulness in Children." *Educational Review* 8:434–441.

Beidel, Deborah C., and Turner, Samuel M. (1998). *Shy Children, Phobic Adults: Nature and Treatment of Social Phobia.* Washington, DC: American Psychological Association.

Bruch, Monroe A., and Cheek, Jonathan M. (1995). "Developmental Factors in Childhood and Adolescent Shyness." In *Social Phobia: Diagnosis, Assessment, and Treatment,* ed. Richard G. Heimberg, Michael R. Liebowitz, Debra A. Hope, and Franklin R. Schneier. New York: Guilford.

Buss, Arnold H. (1986). "A Theory of Shyness." In *Shyness: Perspectives on Research and Treatment,* ed. Warren H. Jones, Jonathan M. Cheek, and Stephen R. Briggs. New York: Plenum.

Cheek, Jonathan M., and Cheek, Bronwen. (1989). *Conquering Shyness.* New York: Putnam.

Cheek, Jonathan M., and Krasnoperova, Elena N. (1999). "Varieties of Shyness in Adolescence and Adulthood." In *Extreme Fear, Shyness, and Social Phobia,* ed. Louis A. Schmidt and Jay Schulkin. New York: Oxford University Press.

Cheek, Jonathan M., and Melchior, Lisa A. (1990). "Shyness, Self-Esteem, and Self-Consciousness." In *Handbook of Social and Evaluation Anxiety,* ed. Harold Leitenberg. New York: Plenum.

Eysenck, Hans J. (1967). *The Biological Basis of Personality.* Springfield, IL: Thomas.

Henderson, Lynne. (1992). "Shyness Groups." In *Focal Group Psychotherapy,* ed. Matthew McKay and Kim Paleg. Oakland, CA: New Harbinger Publications.

Kagan, Jerome. (1994). *Galen's Prophecy.* New York: Basic Books.

Keltner, Dachar; Young, Randall C.; and Buswell, Brenda N. (1997). "Appeasement in Human Emotion, Social Practice, and Personality." *Aggressive Behavior* 23:359–374.

McDougall, William. (1963). *An Introduction to Social Psychology,* 31st ed. London: Methuen.

Wilson, David S.; Clark, Anne B.; Coleman, Kristine; and Dearstyne, Ted. (1994). "Shyness and Boldness in Humans and Other Animals." *Trends in Ecology and Evolution* 9:442–446.

Holly M. Hendin
Jonathan M. Cheek

SIBLINGS AND EMOTIONAL ABUSE

See Emotional Abuse: Siblings

SIN

The human condition has concerned people throughout the centuries. The question that begs for an answer is "Why do people, intelligent and caring, manifest such capacity for self-centeredness and harm to themselves, to others, and to their environment?" A simple three-letter English word designates this condition: *sin.*

In *East of Eden,* a novel grappling with this question, American author John Steinbeck (1952, pp. 337–338) wrote:

> I believe that there is one story in the world, and only one, that has frightened and inspired us. . . . Humans are caught—in their lives, in their thoughts, in their hungers and ambitions, in their avarice and cruelty, and in their kindness and generosity too—in a net of good and evil. I think this is the only story we have and that it occurs on all levels of feeling and intelligence. . . . There is no other story. [At the end of life, each person] will have left only the hard, clean questions: Was it good or was it evil? Have I done well—or ill? . . . All novels, all poetry, are built on the never-ending contest in ourselves of good and evil.

In preparation for his 1973 book *Whatever Became of Sin?,* the pioneering psychiatrist Karl Menninger queried Lawrence S. Kubie, another mental health leader, about the idea of a book on sin from a mental health perspective. Kubie responded that he thought Menninger would be performing a great service if he could provide a critical analysis of the concept of sin—too often misused, but of value when properly used—in relation to errant behavior, thereby pointing the way toward wiser uses of the concept. Thus encouraged, Menninger set out to revive the word *sin,* not for its own sake but for use with the concepts of guilt and moral responsibility. Menninger said,

> Calling something a "sin" and dealing with it as such may be a useful salvage and coping device. It does little good to repent of a symptom, but it may do great harm not to repent of a sin. Vice versa, it does little good to merely psychoanalyze a sin, and sometimes a great harm to ignore a symptom. I contend that there is such a thing as moral concern and such a thing as personal responsibility [p. 48].

The interface of theology and psychology perhaps occurs no more fully than with the topic of sin: both theology *and* psychology function religiously—both are interpretive, and both are sciences of the human spirit in search of meaning. The following three dimensions of practical moral philosophy are manifested in modern psychology, especially the clinical psychologies: (1) visional or metaphorical—"What kind of world do humans live in and what is its most ultimate context?" (2) obligational—"What are humans obligated to do?" and (3) tendency-need—"What are the various fundamental needs and tendencies that should be morally and justly satisfied?"

Definition

The most prevalent, contemporary meaning of the word *sin* is a transgression of a religious or moral law, especially when deliberate. Other definitions include both vertical and horizontal dimensions—sin in relation to God and in relation to other human beings. *The Oxford Dictionary of Philosophy* (1994) defines sin as being a moral category that, by its implications of evil, disobedience, depravity, stain, and wickedness, goes beyond simple wrongdoing. Sin requires atonement, penitence, and self-abasement. As these ideas imply, redemption is an important element, which gives power to those who can provide it. However, these definitions neglect other important elements, such as social, cultural, corporate, political, and environmental wrongdoing, devastation, and abuse.

Colin Brown (1978), a religious scholar, points out that the many terms in the biblical record that are used to refer to sin run the gamut from the breaking of a single commandment to ruining one's entire existence. In the Middle Ages, according to A. E. McGrath (1995), the Roman Catholic Church came to categorize sin as follows:

- material sin: action that in itself is contrary to the will of God but is the yield of ignorance or coercion,
- formal sin: action that in itself is contrary to the will of God and is committed with the full knowledge that it is so,
- venial sin: sin that is considered to be of lesser importance and thus is not regarded as destroying the believer's relationship to God,
- mortal sin: a radical turning away from God to the idolization of the creation through one or more of "The Seven Deadly Sins" (the received prioritized list being pride, envy, anger, sloth, greed, gluttony, and lust), which threatens the believer's relationship to God and can be eliminated only by full confession and contrition.

In modern times, many actions that were formerly considered to be sins have become reclassified as crimes, monitored by the state rather than the church. In addition, the religious offences were translated into psychological situations that could be handled by psychological theories because calling them sins had no benefit. Menninger did allow, however, that sin did remain in the sense of alienating oneself from God. He maintained that this, for believers, was and would continue to be *the* sin. Anglican bishop and scholar William Temple (1963, p. 24) also holds that there is only one sin (which is characteristic of the entire world): "It is the self will which prefers 'my' way to God's—which puts 'me' in the center where only God [should be]."

Tradition distinguishes between sin as an underlying attitude or orientation and specific acts of sin. The

Satan, in the form of the serpent, tempts Adam and Eve to eat from the tree of knowledge of good and evil in a sixteenth-century engraving by Albrecht Dürer. (Corbis/Bettmann)

former is called "original sin"—the abiding condition of humanity that gives rise to specific instances of sin, whether of commission (performance of an act) or omission (a failure to act). Choice is an essential element in sins of both commission and omission.

It should be kept in mind that although an action may be legal or not proscribed by religious codes, it may still violate the humane standards of compassion, strength, faithfulness, freedom, forgiveness, and love. This drama between what is legal versus what is humane is acted out daily on both an individual and a group basis, whether in the home, the marketplace, or the political arena.

Experience and Expression of Sin

The award-winning movie *Amadeus* (1984) begins with the attempted suicide of official court composer Antonio Salieri, and then the scene shifts to an insane asylum where he is an inmate. The story is told through Salieri's eyes as he confesses his hatred and jealousy of fellow composer Wolfgang Amadeus Mozart. Salieri was bitterly angry with God for allowing a profane person like Mozart to be so musically gifted.

Indeed, Mozart was guilty of what would be considered numerous sins. In contrast, Salieri sought to live an exemplary life—by outward standards—but the reality was that he too was guilty of sin—jealousy, envy, and pride and, as a result, dedicated his life to Mozart's defeat and death. Salieri's external Christian dedication was merely a guise for envy and destructive actions. *Both* Mozart and Salieri were guilty of sin. In an effort to escape his feelings of overwhelming guilt following Mozart's death, Salieri attempted suicide.

Pastoral psychotherapist Michael Cavanaugh (1992) argues that it is helpful to have a contemporary understanding of sin. Toward this end, he has reworked the descriptions of four of the seven deadly sins: pride, gluttony, sloth, and cruelty (anger). The term *pride* traditionally has referred to boastfulness and feelings of superiority, which are to be distinguished from healthy self-esteem, wherein people properly value themselves. The term *gluttony*, from the Latin for "to swallow" or "to take in," originally referred only to overeating but is now recognized to have a much broader, more comprehensive meaning and application. The healthy pursuit of work, exercise, excitement, and success is not to be confused with gluttony, which, in its broader meaning, includes gluttony for work or for excitement. The term *sloth* traditionally meant laziness, failure to do one's share of the workload. However, considering its derivation—"a disinclination to action"—it has broader implications (not to be confused with proper rest, relaxation, and renewal). *Cruelty* is the more accurate term for what has traditionally been referred to by the term *anger*. The focus of cruelty is not anger per se but the destructive and/or abusive expression of anger, frustration, or resentment, as well as the harboring of a bitter, resentful attitude.

In "A Poison Tree," the eighteenth-century poet William Blake captures the outcome of anger when dealt with appropriately and inappropriately:

I was angry with my friend:
I told my wrath, my wrath did end.
I was angry with my foe:
I told it not, my wrath did grow.

I watered it in fears
Night and morning with my tears,
And I sunned it with smiles
And with soft deceitful wiles.

And it grew both day and night,
Till it bore an apple bright,
And my foe beheld it shine,
And he knew that it was mine—

And into my garden stole
When the night had veiled the pole;
In the morning, glad, I see
My foe outstretched beneath the tree.

"A Poison Tree," the Judeo-Christian scriptures, *Amadeus,* and modern psychology concur in their opinion that anger itself is not a sin; the key is what is done with the anger. When managed constructively, anger dissipates; when nurtured, it can become deadly. Other emotions that are typically connected with sin include shame, guilt, and embarrassment, as well as resentment, jealousy, loneliness, envy, discouragement, and sadness, to name a few.

Components and Theories

The biblical record, the basis of much of Western civilization's understanding of the origin and nature of sin, describes its origins as being the breaking of a covenantal relationship through willful disobedience. Parameters (specifying nature, privileges, and boundaries) are essential elements of any covenant. God initiated a positive, life-giving covenant with Adam and Eve, a covenant that the pair needed to confirm by their choosing to embrace and abide by its specifications. Instead of choosing to embrace life with its necessary parameters, they chose to break the covenant with God, thus setting themselves in God's place—to become egocentric (self-centered) rather than theocentric (God-centered). The result was alienation from each other and from God, producing a condition of pervasive "illness" that sabotaged their being, their relationships, their offspring, and the environment.

The personal/interpersonal covenant is the common theme throughout the variety of biblical terms for *sin.* Sin is *not* the result of people's creaturehood or any forces or factors beyond their control; it is the consequence of people having exercised freedom in an inappropriate way. Thus, acts of sin arise in the freedom of the human will. According to the Bible, there are two options for being: (1) an inauthentic existence in which people are alienated from their true being and destiny and (2) an authentic existence in which people are empowered to achieve their full potential. The first state corresponds with the idea of sin, while the second corresponds with the idea of salvation (which can take the form of liberation, forgiveness, personal affirmation, or wholeness with God, self, fellow humans, and the environment.

Seeking to understand what seems to be the dueling nature in people, Rosemary Radford Ruether (1995), a historical theologian, espouses the "two tendencies" concept (rooted in Jewish tradition). These tendencies—one toward good, one toward evil—confront individuals with a choice, compelling them to exercise their freedom to choose. When individuals choose to pursue the good, they are connected to their true nature, their authentic being, their "imago dei" (image of God). When individuals choose to pursue and embrace the evil, they are led to inauthentic existence—sin.

Effects of Sin

Sin is not simply an individual phenomenon; it is also a group phenomenon. Because people are creatures of community, embracing the evil yields inauthentic organizational and community patterns—structural evil. People and organizations compete rather than cooperate, victimize rather than empower. There is exploitation of people, other earth-creatures, and the environment for selfish advantage. The core dynamic is sin, the exploitative misuse of human freedom, producing a violation of the basic relations that sustain life physically, psychically, and spiritually. Thus, sin as a distorted relationship has three dimensions: personal-interpersonal, social-historical, and ideological-cultural. If sin is to be adequately addressed, it needs to be addressed in all of these arenas.

According to Ruether, evil systems are kept in place by appealing to the divine—to question or to seek to reform the system (which may be sexist, racist, classist, or exploitative) is going against divine provision and mandate. In such cases, the tendency toward evil has become the accepted norm and the good is purported to be the basis of the system, when in reality the system is opposed to the good. In spite of the pervasiveness of sin, humans are not left without a trace of the good, for there is still within them a capacity and a striving for healthy, life-giving relationality. In spite of the pervasiveness of alienation and "non-wellness," there are still models of good, life-giving relationships in family, friends, mentors in education, religion, work, and, sometimes, even politics. Thus, in all arenas, there is the struggle between the tendency be just and foster loving relations and the tendency to be hostile and negate or exploit the self and/or others.

The theme of Nathaniel Hawthorne's The Scarlet Letter *(1850) is the universality of sin. Hester Prynne, found guilty of adultery, is forced to wear a scarlet "A" for adultery on her breast. Her daughter, Pearl, is the evidence of her adultery. Pearl's father does not have the courage to reveal who he is. When Hester's husband arrives in town under an assumed name and embarks on a malicious quest to discover the culprit, Hester refuses to name the father of the child. The husband becomes devilish and persecutes the town minister, whom he suspects, correctly, to be the father. The minister keeps the secret until his guilt and hypocrisy wear out his life.*

Michael Brock, the main character in John Grisham's novel *The Street Lawyer* (1998), struggled with these two tendencies. Although he was only in his early thirties, Brock was in line to become a partner in the large, prestigious Washington, D.C., firm of Drake & Sweeney. Becoming a partner would mean his already lucrative salary of nearly $200,000 per year would jump into the millions. However, an encounter with homeless DeVon Hardy changed all that. Following the needless deaths of Hardy and of a homeless family, Brock extricated himself from the firm and became an attorney-advocate for the homeless. His transformation was the result of his formerly "blind" eyes now seeing the active, pervasive, insidious inhumanity of evil, in both himself and others (personal evil), in his firm (organizational evil), and in the government and its policies (structural evil). Until his eyes were "healed," Brock did not realize that he had chosen the evil tendency, interpreting its fruit as being divine blessing. After the revelation, he gave up all of the things that were cultural benchmarks of success because his life, though affluent, was hollow and meaningless—existentially unsuccessful. Others thought he was crazy; he knew that he had found his sanity. He turned from the evil and embraced the good. He became authentic through "transformative metanoia"— a comprehensive change of mind and attitude that results in redemptive action in all facets of one's life.

With Erik Erikson's eight stages of human development in mind, pastoral psychologist Donald Capps (1993) suggests the following correlation between the Seven Deadly Sins and the lifecycle:

infancy = gluttony
early childhood = anger
play age = greed
school age = envy
adolescence = pride
young adulthood = lust
adulthood = apathy
mature adulthood = melancholy.

Obviously, these sins can occur at any time in life, but Capps suggests that each tends to have special prominence in particular stages of life. In addition, adults, who have more sinful habits and traits at hand than do children, are able to combine the sins in such a way as to intensify the destructive effect. Further, if younger children, by habit or trait, already manifest sins that are assigned to later adult stages, the child is likely to experience greater emotional distress than is age-appropriate or acceptable.

To test gender differences with regard to sin, Capps conducted a study that involved 259 responses to a questionnaire. When asked to rank the deadly sins in order from "most deadly" to "least deadly," male and female opinions were similar. The results varied more in response to the question about which sins the individuals identified with personally. Men were most troubled by pride (24%), followed by envy and apathy (18% each). Women struggled most with envy (33%), followed by gluttony (24%) and pride (18%). It is significant to note that the sins with which both sexes struggle the most are the ones they consider to be the least deadly of the deadly sins.

Sin and Emotions

Little if any research has been conducted with regard to "sin and emotion," but efforts have been made to examine shame, guilt, and embarrassment. These studies were found to be rich in implications for future research on the topic of sin and emotions, not the least of which was that a sense of right and wrong plays a key role in experiencing these three particular emotions.

June Tangney and her colleagues (1996) sought to answer the question "Are shame, guilt, and embarrassment distinct emotions?" and concluded that they are related but distinct. Each emotion serves important interpersonal adaptive and coping functions. Because humans need to belong, they generally seek frequent, rewarding interactions with others within the context of close, lasting relationships. When relationships are threatened, these three emotions are triggered to alert people to the threat of exclusion and to motivate people toward remedial responses. Embarrassment is a response to one's awareness of having violated a social convention, while shame and guilt are responses to an awareness of personal failure in which one's actions have resulted in harm to others. All three of these emotions motivate interpersonally relevant behavior. Embarrassment tends to prompt actions intended to restore harmony, while guilt tends to promote behaviors intended to repair a relationship. Shame's adaptive functions are somewhat less clear. The findings of this study resonate with the concept

Flannery O'Connor's Wise Blood *(1952) is a grotesque story about Hazel Motes, a young man who wants to preach his own religion. His distorted faith leads him to murder a man who impersonated him, to take a fifteen-year-old mistress, and to torment his own body in an attempt to atone for his guilt. He blinds himself with lime and wraps barbed wire around his chest to punish himself for his sins.*

that sin, at the core, is a personal/interpersonal phenomenon.

Tamara Ferguson and her colleagues (1991) investigated the nature and function of guilt and shame. They concluded that each emotion plays a critical role in children's social development—guilt promotes prosocial and inhibits aggressive behaviors, while shame fosters conformity to group standards. In contrast to children, adults tend to associate guilt with feelings of agitation, worry, anxiety, and tension. They report a tendency to focus intensely on one's *own* opinion of self, plus a simultaneous desire to confess and escape (approach/avoidance conflict). Adults who feel shame tend to focus intensely on *others'* opinions of them. Shame is a dejection-based emotion that involves feelings of helplessness, depression, and sadness and a desire to hide or move out of the view of other people. Although they are physically full grown, adults who experience the emotion of shame report feeling physically small. They also report feeling very bad or incompetent and isolated from others. Shame can result from a wide variety of events that have the potential to elicit criticism, ridicule, or threats of love withdrawal from other people, while guilt tends to be more specifically linked to a failure to live up to internalized standards of conduct.

Whether they are children or adults, people engage in various efforts to deal with the emotions of shame, guilt, and embarrassment. Since shame mainly pertains to the fear of ridicule and rejection by others who have seen one's deeds, the primary tendency for one who feels shame is to withdraw and hide as a means of protecting oneself. With guilt, the person is focused more on the bad behavior and tends to cope through confession, reparation, self-criticism, and/or punishment. Although Ferguson and her colleagues did not examine the relationship of shame and guilt to sin, the results parallel the ancient biblical records—sin is interpersonally oriented and leads to guilt and shame.

One direction of research into the relationship between sin and human emotions that might prove fruitful would be to first study the relationship scientifically and then examine how the results do or do not correlate with depictions in various genres of literature, including the biblical records. James Russell (1991) examined the literature on culture and the categorization of emotions, asking the question "What in the categorization of the emotions is universal and what is culture bound?" rather than "What about emotions is pan-human [experienced by all people regardless of their culture or the point in time in which they live]?" The distinction between these two questions is essential to keep in mind because "peoples of different cultures could impose their own categorization on a universal emotional reality. Conversely, people could impose universal categories on a culture-bound reality" (p. 444). Research on sin and emotions would need to distinguish between what is and what is not pan-human, with regard to sin, emotions, and the relationship between the two. This would be no small enterprise, yet it would be a worthy one.

See also: ANGER; EMBARRASSMENT; ENVY; FORGIVENESS; GUILT; SHAME

Bibliography

Blake, William. (1967). "A Poison Tree." In *The Literature of England: An Anthology and a History,* revised single volume edition, ed. George K. Anderson and William E. Buckler. Glenview, IL: Scott, Foresman and Company.

Brown, Colin. (1978). "Sin." In *The New International Dictionary of New Testament Theology, Vol. 3,* ed. Colin Brown. Grand Rapids, MI: Zondervan.

Browning, Don S. (1987). *Religious Thought and the Modern Psychologies: A Critical Conversation in the Theology of Culture.* Philadelphia, PA: Fortress Press.

Capps, Donald. (1993). *The Depleted Self: Sin in a Narcissistic Age.* Minneapolis, MN: Fortress Press.

Cavanaugh, Michael E. (1992). "The Concept of Sin in Pastoral Counseling." *Pastoral Psychology* 41(2)81–87.

Dunning, H. Ray. (1988). *Grace, Faith, and Holiness: A Wesleyan Systematic Theology.* Kansas City, MO: Beacon Hill Press.

Ferguson, Tamara; Stegge, Hedy; and Damhuis, Ilse. (1991). "Children's Understanding of Guilt and Shame." *Child Development* 62:827–839.

Grisham, John. (1998). *The Street Lawyer.* New York: Doubleday.

Hiltner, Seward. (1966). "Christian Understanding of Sin in the Light of Medicine and Psychiatry." *Medical Arts and Sciences* 20:35–49.

Jewett, Robert. (1993). *Saint Paul at the Movies: The Apostle's Dialogue with American Culture.* Louisville, KY: Westminster/ John Knox Press.

McGrath, A. E. (1995). "Sin and Salvation." In *New Dictionary of Christian Ethics and Pastoral Theology,* ed. David J. Atkins and David H. Field. Downers Grove, IL: InterVarsity Press.

Menninger, Karl. (1973). *Whatever Became of Sin?* New York: Hawthorn Books.

Miller, J. Keith. (1987). *Sin: Overcoming the Ultimate Deadly Addiction.* San Francisco: Harper & Row.

Purkiser, W. T.; Taylor, Richard S.; Taylor, Willard H. (1977). *God, Man, and Salvation: A Biblical Theology.* Kansas City, MO: Beacon Hill Press.

Ruether, Rosemary Radford. (1995). "Feminist Metanoia and Soul-Making." *Women and Theology* 16(2/3):33–44.

Russell, James A. (1991). "Culture and the Categorization of Emotions." *Psychological Bulletin* 110:426–450.

Schimmel, Solomon. (1992). *The Seven Deadly Sins: Jewish, Christian, and Classical Reflections on Human Psychology.* New York: Oxford University Press.

Speake, Jennifer, ed. (1979). "Sin." In *A Dictionary of Philosophy,* rev. 2nd ed. New York: St. Martin's Press.

Steinbeck, John. (1952). *East of Eden.* New York: Viking.

Tangney, June Price; Miller, Rowland S.; Flicker, Laura; and Barlow, Deborah Hill. (1996). "Are Shame, Guilt, and Embarrassment Distinct Emotions?" *Journal of Personality and Social Psychology* 70:1256–1269.

Temple, William. (1963). *Readings in St. John's Gospel.* London: Macmillan.

Randy Michael

SMILING

The smile usually is associated with positive emotions such as happiness, joy, and pleasure. Moreover, classic cross-cultural studies by Paul Ekman and Wallace Friesen (1971) as well as by Carroll Izard (1971) demonstrated that adults in a wide variety of cultures judge the smile to be related to positive emotion. Although these cross-cultural studies have been criticized by some later researchers, they do suggest that people in a variety of cultures judge the smile to be related more to positive than to negative emotions.

Nevertheless, there also is abundant evidence that smiles do not always *communicate,* much less *express,* positive emotion. Research suggests that (1) there are many different types of smiles, which may have different meanings, (2) negative emotions may be accompanied by smiles, and (3) smiles are strongly affected by sociality, suggesting that they may serve social communicative functions (and suggesting to some researchers that they may have more to do with social communication than with emotion). Research also suggests that there are important gender differences in smiling.

Types of Smiles

Smile types have been differentiated from one another on the basis of many different factors, including anatomical or appearance differences (e.g., closed mouth smile versus horizontal bared tooth smile versus open bared tooth), differences in eliciting stimuli (e.g., endogenous versus exogenous smiles), veridicality (e.g., felt versus false versus miserable smiles), and purported emotion (e.g., embarrassment versus joy). Ekman (1985) actually distinguished eighteen different types of smiles on the basis of a number of anatomical/appearance differences (e.g., presence/absence of certain muscle movements, symmetry), timing differences, and smoothness of muscular action. These smiles were considered to be expressive of a variety of positive and negative emotions (e.g., pleasure, relief, amusement, smiles masking other emotions, and miserable smiles). However, of the many distinctions that Ekman made, clearly the most attention has been paid to a particular anatomical distinction that was first proposed by Guillaume-Benjamin Duchenne(1862), and which Ekman believes to distinguish "enjoyment" from "nonenjoyment" smiles.

The "Duchenne" smile involves movement of both the zygomatic major muscle (which pulls up the lip corners) and the obicularis occuli muscle (which crinkles the eyes and raises the cheeks); non-Duchenne smiles involve zygomatic major without orbicularis occuli. Ekman, Gowen Roper, and Joseph Hager (1980) claim that most people cannot voluntarily contract the outer portion of the orbicularis occuli; therefore, smiles involving this muscle comprise involuntary expressions of positive emotion. Moreover, Ekman, Friesen, and Maureen O'Sullivan (1988) found that subjects who truthfully described pleasant feelings were more likely to display Duchenne smiles than were those who (in order to follow the experimenter's instructions) claimed to feel pleasant while watching films of surgical procedures. Similarly, Robert Levenson (1989) found that Duchenne smiles were more associated with happy marriages; Ekman, Richard Davidson, and Friesen (1990) found that Duchenne smiles were more associated with pleasant films (versus non-Duchenne smiles' association with unpleasant ones); and Nathan Fox and Davidson (1988) found that when infants watched their mothers approach, they showed more Duchenne smiles, whereas, when they watched a stranger approach, they displayed non-Duchenne smiles. Moreover, according to research

French physician Guillaume Duchenne makes his patient smile by using an electrical device to stimulate the facial muscles. (Corbis/Hulton-Deutsch Collection)

conducted by Robert Soussignan and Benoist Schaal (1996), smiles that involve mouth opening and/or orbicularis occuli (as well as differences in timing and smoothness) were associated with pleasant more than unpleasant smells. In contrast, non-Duchenne smiles that were accompanied by a lip press, downward gaze, head movement to the left and down, and a face touch were systematically judged to be embarrassed smiles by adult judges, according to a study by Dacher Keltner and Brenda Buswell (1996). Moreover, the research by Fox and Davidson also indicated that the Duchenne smile was associated with the "approach" pattern of brain activation and the non-Duchenne smile was associated with the "avoidant" pattern of brain activation.

Nevertheless, it is also very clear that Duchenne smiles are not always associated with positive emotion; nor are non-Duchenne smiles always associated with negative emotion. The research of Alan Fogel and his colleagues (1997) indicates that Duchenne smiles typically are preceded and followed closely in time by non-Duchenne smiles, and the two patterns often seem to be distinguished more by intensity of social interaction than by veridicality or positivity. Even more damaging to the simple equation of Duchenne smiling with positive emotion and non-Duchenne smiling with negative emotion is the finding of Klaus Schneider and Ingrid Josephs (1991) that preschoolers were more likely to smile, smiled longer, and smiled more Duchenne smiles after they *failed* on a task than after they succeeded at the same task. Thus, it appears that there is not a single smile pattern that invariably expresses positive emotion, regardless of context.

In addition to research that distinguishes the Duchenne smile from other smiles, research has been conducted on the "play smile" (a smile with a jaw drop), which has been associated with high intensity and/or tactually stimulating interactions; the "endogenous" smile, which, according to Robert Emde, Theodore Gaensbauer, and Robert Harmon (1976), is associated with a rapid eye movement (REM) state in newborn infants; and the variety of smiles that were identified by Ekman and his colleagues.

Sociality and Smiling

Most people assume that smiles primarily indicate positive emotion, and, as mentioned earlier, people across a wide variety of cultures judge smiles to communicate positive emotion. Smiles are *displayed* by members of all cultures studied as well, and these facts together have been widely interpreted to mean that "joy" or "happiness" is a universal emotion. However, Alan Fridlund (1994) suggests that the primary function of smiles is to communicate with others—Duchenne smiles communicate readiness to play or affiliate, and non-Duchenne smiles communicate readiness to appease. He suggests that to the extent that facial displays are universal, with an evolutionary basis, it is much more sensible to construe them as signals of intentions to act rather than as "read-outs" of internal feeling states. Fridlund reasons that it would not be adaptive to display many of one's feeling states openly but that it would be adaptive to let others know what one intends to do (e.g., to attack them or not), so that they can react appropriately and avoid hurting one or being hurt themselves. He claims that the likelihood of smiling has more to do with the sociality of the situation than with what the person is feeling. As indicated above, many smiles are not necessarily "happy" ones; moreover, most adults smile as a greeting even when they feel unhappy.

Even if smiles often or typically do signal positive emotion, sociality may be a central influence on the likelihood that they are displayed. Karen Barrett and Joseph Campos (1987) propose that social communication is one of three crucial functions of emotions; thus, social communication and social context are crucial to study in connection with any emotional response. One's smiles obviously can not communicate anything—positive emotion or behavioral intentions—if a responsive recipient of those communications is not available.

A great number of studies support Fridlund's position that the sociality of the situation increases the likelihood that a person will smile. Fridlund himself has found that the sociality of the situation *in the person's perception* (an interactant need not actually be present) affects smiling. For example, using electromyography to enable detection of even small movements of the "smile muscle" (zygomatic major), Fridlund (1991) found that undergraduates smiled the least when they were alone (and not led to believe otherwise) and smiled increasingly when a friend (1) was believed to be nearby but occupied with an unrelated task, (2) was believed to be nearby and engaged in the same activity (viewing videotapes) as the subject, and (3) actually was nearby and viewing the same videotapes as the subject. Other researchers have found that having an attentive interactant increases smiling. For example, José-Miguel Fernandez-Dols and Maria-Angeles Ruiz-Belda (1995) found that Olympic gold medal winners did not smile during most of their awards ceremony—they smiled primarily when they were interacting with others.

Moreover, these effects are not limited to well-socialized adults. In the study by Schneider and Josephs (1991) of preschoolers in achievement situations, children smiled more when they were in face-to-face contact with the experimenter, even when they failed. Susan Scanlon Jones and her colleagues (1991, 1990) found that seventeen-month-old and even ten-month-old infants smiled more at their mothers (while playing with toys) when their mothers were attentive than when their mothers ignored them and read a magazine, even though the infants did not otherwise seem upset by the lack of attention toward them. Moreover, Sylvia Hains and Darwin Muir (1996) found that even infants who were between three and six months old smiled more at adults who made eye contact with them than with adults who interacted responsively with the infants by watching them on a monitor but did not make eye contact with them. Thus, sociality affects smiling beginning at a very young age.

Gender and Smiling

There is a general societal expectation that females will smile more than will males, and researchers have discovered that this expectation is well founded—female adults and children do smile more than their male counterparts. Moreover, Harry Reis and his colleagues (1990) found that smiling subjects are perceived to be more sociable but less independent and masculine. Similarly, Elizabeth Cashdan (1998) found that less masculine women smile more when they meet males; more feminine, popular, and caring females smile more when they are with friends; and more caring and popular women smile more when they are with strange males.

Many researchers have attributed gender differences in smiling to power/status differences between males and females. Consistent with this interpretation are findings by Francine Deutsch (1990) that both males and females who were assigned a more powerful role (interviewer) smiled less than did those who were assigned a less powerful role (job applicant). Moreover, James Dabbs (1997) found that men who have higher testosterone levels make smaller smiles and are judged to be more potent than men with low testosterone levels. However, as alluded to above, females who smile more have higher sociometric status (i.e., are rated by peers to be more popular), and in the same study, the more popular women and men were rated to be the better leaders.

Moreover, in most studies, women smile more when they are with other women than they do when they are with men, which is hard to interpret if power differentials are the primary reason why women smile more than men. Finally, a number of studies suggest that women who smile do not necessarily display other indicators of submissiveness. It seems likely that gender differences in smiling stem, at least in part, from the fact that smiling makes one appear more attractive, friendly, and caring (all of which are characteristics that females are socialized to have), as well as from the societal expectation that females will smile.

Functions of Smiles

Smiles serve a number of important functions in social interaction, many of which already have been mentioned (e.g., communicating with others, appearing more attractive, friendly, caring, and feminine). In general, smiles seem to foster the development and maintenance of relationships. In addition to findings already discussed, a study by Kathleen Zanolli and her colleagues (1997) indicated that toddlers who were in their first forty days of day care were more likely to be affectionate toward a teacher who smiled than toward one who expressed affectionate words or contact.

In addition to these important relationship-enhancement functions, smiles seem to increase the expressor's positive emotionality through facial feedback. Fritz Strack and his colleagues (1988) found that such feedback seems to occur even when subjects are made to "smile" by holding a pen in their mouths, making it unlikely that they are perceiving themselves to be smiling. Smiles also, according to Vivien Tartter and David Braun (1994), make the smiler's voice sound more positive to others, even when the others cannot see the smiler's face.

Conclusion

The smile is a complex form of communication that is not simply a "read-out" of positive emotion. There are many forms of smiles, which seem to differ in their likelihood of being associated with positive emotion; however, no particular smile (independent of context) invariably indicates a particular emotion. Smiles serve important functions, especially in terms of relationship enhancement, and are more likely to be displayed when an attentive recipient is present. Females in Western culture are more likely to smile than are males, and this gender difference does not seem to be reducible to male-female differences in power or status. Despite these complexities, the smile is judged to communicate positive emotion in every culture that has been studied, and it is the facial pattern that is judged most similarly across cultures. Clearly, it is an important facial pattern for those who are interested in emotion.

See also: CRYING; DEFENSE MECHANISMS; FACIAL EXPRESSION; GENDER AND EMOTIONS; HAPPINESS; PLEASURE; UNIVERSALITY OF EMOTIONAL EXPRESSION

Bibliography

Barrett, Karen Caplovitz, and Campos, Joseph J. (1987). "Perspectives on Emotional Development, II: A Functionalist Approach to Emotions." In *Handbook of Infant Development,* 2nd ed., ed. Joy Osofsky. New York: Wiley.

Briton, Nancy J., and Hall, Judith A. (1995). "Gender-Based Expectancies and Observer Judgments of Smiling." *Journal of Nonverbal Behavior* 19:49–65.

Cashdan, Elizabeth. (1998). "Smiles, Speech, and Body Posture: How Women and Men Display Sociometric Status and Power." *Journal of Nonverbal Behavior* 22:209–228.

Dabbs, James M. (1997). "Testosterone, Smiling, and Facial Appearance." *Journal of Nonverbal Behavior* 21:45–55.

Deutsch, Francine M. (1990). "Status, Sex, and Smiling: The Effect of Smiling in Men and Women." *Personality and Social Psychology Bulletin* 16:531–540.

Duchenne, Guillaume-Benjamin. ([1862] 1990). *The Mechanism of Human Facial Expression or an Electrophysiological Analysis of the Expression of the Emotions,* tr. R. Andrew Cuthbertson. New York: Cambridge University Press.

Ekman, Paul. (1985). *Telling Lies: Clues to Deceit in the Marketplace, Marriage, and Politics.* New York: W. W. Norton.

Ekman, Paul; Davidson, Richard J.; and Friesen, Wallace V. (1990). "The Duchenne Smile: Emotional Expression and Brain Physiology, II." *Journal of Personality and Social Psychology* 58:342–353.

Ekman, Paul, and Friesen, Wallace V. (1971). "Constants across Cultures in the Face and Emotion." *Journal of Personality and Social Psychology* 17:124–129.

Ekman, Paul; Friesen, Wallace V.; and O'Sullivan, Maureen. (1988). "Smiles when Lying." *Journal of Personality and Social Psychology* 54:414–420.

Ekman, Paul; Roper, Gowen; and Hager, Joseph C. (1980). "Deliberate Facial Movement." *Child Development* 51:886–891.

Emde, Robert N.; Gaensbauer, Theodore J.; and Harmon, Robert J. (1976). *Emotional Expression in Infancy: A Biobehavioral Study.* New York: International Universities Press.

Fernandez-Dols, José-Miguel, and Ruiz-Belda, Maria-Angeles. (1995). "Are Smiles a Sign of Happiness? Gold Medal Winners at the Olympic Games." *Journal of Personality and Social Psychology* 69:1113–1119.

Fogel, Alan; Dickson, K. Laurie; Hsu, Hui-Chin; Messinger, Daniel; Nelson-Goens, G. Christina; and Nwokah, Evangeline. (1997). "Communication of Smiling and Laughter in Mother-Infant Play: Research on Emotion from a Dynamic Systems Perspective." In *The Communication of Emotion: Current Research from Diverse Perspectives,* ed. Karen Caplovitz Barrett. San Francisco: Jossey-Bass.

Fox, Nathan A., and Davidson, Richard J. (1988). "Patterns of Brain Electrical Activity during Facial Signs of Emotion in 10-Month-Old Infants." *Developmental Psychology* 24:230–236.

Fridlund, Alan J. (1991). "Sociality of Solitary Smiling: Potentiation by an Implicit Audience." *Journal of Personality and Social Psychology* 60:229–240.

Fridlund, Alan J. (1994). *Human Facial Expression: An Evolutionary View.* New York: Academic Press.

Hains, Sylvia M. J., and Muir, Darwin W. (1996). "Infant Sensitivity to Adult Eye Direction." *Child Development* 67:1940–1951.

Izard, Carroll E. (1971). *The Face of Emotion.* New York: Appleton-Century-Crofts.

Jones, Susan S.; Collins, Kimberly; and Hong, Hye-Won. (1991). "An Audience Effect on Smile Production in 10-Month-Old Infants." *Psychological Science* 2:45–49.

Jones, Susan S.; Raag, Tarja; and Collins, Kimberly L. (1990). "Smiling in Older Infants: Form and Maternal Response." *Infant Behavior and Development* 13:147–165.

Keltner, Dacher, and Buswell, Brenda N. (1996). "Evidence for the Distinctness of Embarrassment, Shame, and Guilt: A Study of Recalled Antecedents and Facial Expressions of Emotion." *Cognition and Emotion* 10:155–171.

Levenson, Robert W. (1989). "Social Psychophysiology of Marriage." Paper presented at the April meeting of the Western Psychological Association, Reno, NV.

Reis, Harry T.; Wilson, Ilona M.; Monestere, Carla; Bernstein, Stuart; Clark, Kelly; Seidl, Edward; Franco, Michelle; Gioioso, Ezia; Freeman, Lori; and Radoane, Kimberly. (1990). "What Is Smiling Is Beautiful and Good." *European Journal of Social Psychology* 20:259–267.

Schneider, Klaus, and Josephs, Ingrid. (1991). "The Expressive and Communicative Functions of Preschool Children's Smiles in an Achievement Situation." *Journal of Nonverbal Behavior* 15:185–198.

Soussignan, Robert, and Schaal, Benoist. (1996). "Forms and Social Signal Value of Smiles Associated with Pleasant and Unpleasant Sensory Experience." *Ethology* 102:1020–1041.

Strack, Fritz; Martin, Leonard L; and Stepper, Sabine. (1988). "Inhibiting and Facilitating Conditions of the Human Smile: A Nonobtrusive Test of the Facial Feedback Hypothesis." *Journal of Personality and Social Psychology* 54:768–777.

Tartter, Vivien C., and Braun, David. (1994). "Hearing Smiles and Frowns in Normal and Whisper Registers." *Journal of the Acoustical Society of America* 96:2101–2107.

Zanolli, Kathleen M.; Saudargas, Richard A.; and Twardosz, Sandra. (1997). "The Development of Toddlers' Responses to Affectionate Teacher Behavior." *Early Childhood Research Quarterly* 12:99–116.

Karen Caplovitz Barrett

SOCIOLOGY OF EMOTIONS

Most of the strong emotions that individuals experience come from their contacts with other people. Sometimes these emotions motivate the individuals to conform to social norms. Other times, they make them respond in ways that seem unpredictable and irrational. Individuals use the emotional reactions of others to judge what kinds of people they are, and they try to control their own expressions to manage others' opinions of them. Exactly how do social situations affect emotions? What part does the social structure play in determining what individuals feel and how they express it to others? How do emotional reactions motivate social action? When do collective feelings reinforce the existing social order, and when do they spawn social changes?

Definitions

Sociologists define emotion as having several components: (1) appraisals of a situational stimulus, (2) changes in bodily sensations, (3) display of expressive gestures, and (4) a cultural meaning applied to the constellation of the first three elements. In the early 1980s, there was a lively debate among sociologists about whether emotion is a single undifferentiated physical response that is shaped into distinct emotions through cultural vocabularies or whether there is a larger set of physiologically distinct emotions. Theodore Kemper (1987) proposed a compromise. He argued that while some emotions are instinctive and physiologically distinct, others are differentiated from these basic emotions by cultural forces. The number and character of emotions that are experienced in a culture are determined by the social relationships that are central to that group's social fabric. This position was acceptable to most sociologists of emotion, so long as the question of how many emotions are basic was left open. The most culturally determinist position with regard to this problematic question argues for just one basic emotion (i.e., undifferentiated arousal), whereas Kemper argues for four basic, physiologically distinct emotions (i.e., anger, happiness, fear and sadness).

Classic Sociological Theory

Emotions occupied an important place in the works of Karl Marx, Max Weber, Emile Durkheim, and Georg Simmel, who all defined sociology as a discipline. These theorists used emotions during the late nineteenth century and early twentieth century to link social positions to individual experiences. Marx saw emotional life as being molded by social structures. Material economic arrangements led to alienation and disenchantment in the laboring classes; one's emotional experiences were heavily determined by one's class position. Conversely, Marx believed that religious fervor could work to support a repressive class structure.

Weber and Durkheim also focused on emotional responses to religion as powerful forces for the maintenance and change of social forms. Weber argued that capitalism arose partially because of the emotional responses of individuals to Protestant religious ideology. He also argued that, once capitalism was in place, rational bureaucracy required emotional management to isolate emotional response to private rather than formal institutional spheres. Weber analyzed charismatic leadership as an emotion-driven social force. Durkheim saw religious ecstasy as a social fact rather than a private experience. He analyzed emotional responses as societal constructions in which the moral sentiments of the group are reaffirmed. Such emotional experiences, in Durkheim's view, had a strong coercive element. Individuals were not free to resist such emotional forces since they were obligatory for true group membership.

Emile Durkheim, a French socialist philosopher and professor, was instrumental in establishing a methodology and theoretical framework for rigorous research in the social sciences. (Corbis/Bettmann)

Simmel emphasized the micro-structures of social interaction rather than the macro-structures of the economic and religious institutions. His discussion of the emotional instability of dyads created the basis for modern theories about how social interaction leads to emotion. Simmel discussed how emotional expression in interactions could be a bridge to knowledge of another person. This insight led to Erving Goffman's analyses of impression management in public encounters.

Goffman (1956, 1959) argued that embarrassment and shame resulted from inability to support one's desired self-presentation. Goffman greatly expanded the general understanding of the place of emotion in social control, viewing feelings as a force motivating the individual to conform to normative and situational pressures. In addition, Goffman introduced the idea of the emotional deviant, the actor who is unable or unwilling to maintain the appropriate affective orientation to the situation in which he is enmeshed. In his work, emotional responses of the actor are seen as a cue indicating his or her allegiance to the group; rules of social order prescribe feelings as well as actions.

These classic theorists showed how emotion is a social rather than individual phenomenon, but they fell far short of developing a coherent, systematic view of the place that emotions hold in social life. They usually studied emotions only as a facet of some other topic. In the 1970s, however, sociologists began to develop a more comprehensive treatment of emotion.

Emotion Culture

Arlie Hochschild (1983) built on the work of Goffman and Marx to develop the concept of feeling rules—cultural norms that specify the type of emotion, the extent of emotion, and the duration of feeling that are appropriate in a situation. For example, Western culture requires that a grieving spouse feel intense unhappiness immediately after the death and then "snap out of it" after a few months. When what individuals feel differs from the cultural expectation, Hochschild argued that they actively engage in emotion management to create a more appropriate response. Such management can take several forms. Surface acting adjusts the expression of emotion to normative patterns. By pretending an emotion that is not felt, individuals elicit reactions from others that bolster a performance and may eventually transform it into a genuine one. Flight attendants studied by Hochschild reported pretending to be cheery so that passengers would respond to them as if they were friendly. The passengers' responses then led to an authentic positive emotion. Deep acting involves a more basic manipulation of one's emotional state. Through physiological manipulation (deep breathing), shifting perceptual focus (concentrating on a positive aspect of a bad situation), or redefining the situation (thinking of a drunk passenger as a frightened childlike person), actors can change their feelings to conform to their ideas of appropriateness.

Sometimes, of course, emotions fail to match cultural expectations and management efforts are ineffective. Peggy Thoits (1985) argued that persistent emotional deviance is interpreted as evidence of mental illness. In particular, she noted that self-labeling is likely to occur when an individual frequently is confronted with unmanageable, counter normative feelings. For example, a person who is filled with rage at minor slights might interpret these responses as signs of a deeper mental problem.

Such emotional deviance could be created by inadequate socialization or by structurally induced stress. When children are not taught (through modeling and reward) appropriate emotional responses, they display behavior problems. But even competently socialized actors are likely to experience emotional deviance under some structural conditions when they (1) occupy inconsistent roles, (2) belong to subcultures, (3) undergo role transitions, especially if they are non-normative in timing or sequence, and (4) follow rigid rules associated with rituals or especially restrictive roles. For example, weddings are supposed to be times of joy, but the stresses of coordinating a complex social ritual often lead to negative emotion.

In many cases, occupations have well-developed feeling rules. When emotion management is done for a wage, Hochschild called it emotion work. She linked this type of labor to class position, arguing that middle-class service jobs often involve managing one's own feelings to make clients feel good. Alienation from authentic feelings may result when emotion management becomes a pervasive part of occupational life.

Emotion and Self-Identity

The groundbreaking work of Hochschild and Thoits emphasized the extent to which culture influenced how an actor experienced and managed emotional responses. The empirical work using this perspective has focused on the cultural norms that individuals use to interpret their experiences. Authentic emotion is there to be labeled, judged deviant, and managed. But what causes the emotional response in the first place? Symbolic interactionists have tried to answer this question by examining the relationship between emotion and identity.

In identity theory, Sheldon Stryker (1992) conceptualized the self as a hierarchically organized set of identities. The identities represented commitment to social roles such as wife, mother, lawyer, and athlete. Emotions serve as motivators in this identity system—role relationships that generate positive affect are enacted more frequently and move upward in the self hierarchy. Identity enactments that routinely cause dissatisfaction move downward in the hierarchy. Therefore, if an individual found a career path blocked at work, he or she might reorient personal priorities toward rewarding interactions with family and community organizations.

Emotions result from adequate or inadequate role performances. Emotions therefore serve a signal function, indicating how well interactions are supporting one's sense of oneself in the situation. If a professor feels elation after a classroom interaction with students, the emotion signals that the performance in that identity is above normal expectations for the role. Since adequate role performances require coordinated action with others, individuals can get angry at others as well as at themselves for failed role enactment.

A final insight from identity theory is the sense in which emotions signal the importance of relationships to the self. Stryker argued that the strength of emotional reaction to events can serve as a gauge to the centrality of an identity in the self structure. A mother's depression at leaving her child for a return to work signals the higher salience of the parental role compared to the worker role.

Affect control theory, as described by David Heise (1979) and Lynn Smith-Lovin (1990), uses a control system to specify which actions make up an adequate role performance. Its mathematical structure allows it to predict which emotional reactions will accompany adequate and inadequate performances. Affect control theory maps identities, actions, and emotions into three dimensions of cultural meaning: evaluation (good versus bad), potency (powerful versus powerless) and activity (lively versus quiet). The identity of *mother,* for example, is fundamentally nicer, more powerful, and more lively than the identity of *clerk.* In affect control theory, emotions are signals about the extent to which events confirm or discomfirm identity. When events are confirming, an actor's emotional response is determined by his or her identity and its cultural meaning. When things are going smoothly, mothers feel good, powerful, and lively because they occupy a positive identity. However, when events are disconfirming, the nature of the situation (and the deflection it causes) heavily determines the character of the emotional response. A mother who has hurt her child typically feels awful. In this case, emotions are powerful motivating forces that signal the need for social action to restore fundamental meanings.

Emotion and the Structure of Interaction

In contrast to the symbolic interactionist theories that focus on identities and their cultural meanings, Kemper (1978) proposed a theory of emotions based on social exchange principles. He argued that two dimensions of social relationships—status and power—are universal. Relative positions on these dimensions define the key aspects of a relationship and determine its emotional character. Kemper argued that the emotion caused by status and power changes depends on the perceived source of the change and, in some cases, on whether or not the other person in the interaction was liked or disliked. For example, he said that status loss would result in anger if the loss appeared to be remediable; such anger would be functional in that it motivated action to regain the lost status. If the loss was irredeemable, however, it would lead to sadness

and depression, saving energy and acclimating the individual to his or her new lowered state of resources. Status loss by another, if caused by oneself, led to guilt if the other was liked (facilitating group survival by preventing ingroup insult). If the other was not liked, his or her status loss would cause happiness.

Randall Collins (1981) joined Kemper in advocating status and power as the two fundamental dimensions of social interaction. Collins's goal was to account for macro-level structure through a compilation of low-level interactions among individuals. Following Weber's classic work, Collins developed the concept of emotional energy, which he argued is released by standardized sequences of interaction called interaction rituals. Actors who acquire large amounts of emotional energy from ritual encounters are able to claim property and authority. Therefore, individual-level interactions are combined to create societal forms.

Thomas Scheff (1979) developed another view of ritual that was rooted in the psychoanalytic tradition. He thought that distressing emotions (such as grief, fear, and anger) are universal because the social situations that produce them are universal. For example, attachment losses (e.g., from parental closeness) produce grief and fear. Scheff assumed that emotional discharge was necessary. Ritual, drama, contests, and other collective emotion management techniques allowed for the safe discharge of accumulated emotion. While Collins saw interaction ritual chains as generating solidarity and structure at the macro-level, Scheff saw the rituals as providing a safe outlet for the emotion built up from the common experience of distress. For Scheff, rituals are a functional solution to the problem of repressed emotions, a necessary element of human experience.

Survey Research about the Distribution of Emotions

All sociological theories (with the possible exception of Scheff's psychoanalytic approach) make the prediction that people occupying different social positions will experience different emotional climates. Survey research on self-reports of social distress, such as that reviewed by John Mirowsky and Catherine Ross (1989), shows clear patterns that support these predictions. Women report more distress than men. Unmarried people report more distress than married people. The uneducated poor report more distress than people who have more income and education. African Americans and other minorities show somewhat higher levels of distress, but the pattern gets more complicated if compensations are made for their generally lower socioeconomic status. Having children leads to distress; levels of marital satisfaction and well-being drop after a birth and do not return to their pre-child levels until after all the children leave home. People who experience undesirable life events (such as loss of a job, death of a spouse, sickness, or accidents) report more distress than those who do not. Those who have little religious faith are more distressed than those who have strong religious beliefs. Young individuals are more depressed and anxious than are middle-aged individuals. Anxiety declines steadily with age, while depression declines from youth to age fifty-five and then increases again in old age. In general, those who have few network contacts and few social roles are more distressed than those who are better integrated into society.

Clearly, disadvantaged persons have fewer resources at their disposal to help avoid negative events and respond to misfortunes. This powerlessness puts them at greater risk of stressful circumstances. Such victimization also leads to depression because of an implied lack of control—while some people may choose to be exploiters, few choose to be victims. In general, the survey results support the sociological view that social structural position strongly shapes one's emotional life.

Conclusion

The modern sociological theories of emotion offer comprehensive views of the place that emotions hold in social life. In particular, they articulate a model of the how the self feels, how the social world affects individuals, and how emotions motivate social action (and, cumulatively, support or change social structures). Experimental, ethnographic, and survey evidence supports the view of emotion as a social as well as an individual phenomenon.

See also: ANTHROPOLOGY OF EMOTIONS; COGNITIVE PERSPECTIVE; PSYCHOANALYTIC PERSPECTIVE; PSYCHOLOGY OF EMOTIONS

Bibliography

Collins, Randall. (1981). "On the Micro-Foundations of Macro-Sociology." *American Journal of Sociology* 86:984–1014.

Durkheim, Emile. (1912). *The Elementary Forms of the Religious Life.* London: Allen and Unwin.

Gerth, H. H., and Mills, C. Wright. (1946). "Part III: Religion." In *From Max Weber: Essays in Sociology,* ed. and tr. H. H. Gerth and C. Wright Mills. New York: Oxford University Press.

Goffman, Erving. (1956). "Embarrassment and Social Organization." *American Journal of Sociology* 62:264–271.

Goffman, Erving. (1959). *The Presentation of Self in Everyday Life.* New York: Doubleday.

Heise, David R. (1979). *Understanding Events.* New York: Cambridge University Press.

Hochschild, Arlie R. (1983). *The Managed Heart: Commercialization of Human Feeling.* Berkeley: University of California Press.

Kemper, Theodore D. (1978). *A Social Interactional Theory of Emotions.* New York: Wiley.

Kemper, Theodore D. (1987). "How Many Emotions Are There? Wedding the Social and the Autonomic Component." *American Journal of Sociology* 93:263–89.

Kemper, Theodore D., and Collins, Randall. (1990). "Dimensions of Microinteraction." *American Journal of Sociology* 96 (1):32–68.

Marx, Karl. (1983). *The Portable Karl Marx,* ed. and tr. Eugene Kamenka. New York: Penguin.

Mirowsky, John, and Ross, Catherine. (1989). *Social Causes of Psychological Distress.* New York: Aldine de Gruyter.

Scheff, Thomas J. (1979). *Catharsis in Healing, Ritual, and Drama.* Berkeley: University of California Press.

Scheff, Thomas J., and Retzinger, Susanne. (1992). *Shame, Violence, and Social Structure: Theory and Cases.* Lexington, MA: Lexington Books.

Simmel, Georg. (1950). *The Sociology of Georg Simmel,* ed. Kurt Wolff. New York: Free Press.

Smith-Lovin, Lynn. (1990). "Emotion As Confirmation and Disconfirmation of Identity: An Affect Control Model." In *Research Agendas in the Sociology of Emotions,* ed. Theodore D. Kemper. Albany: State University of New York Press.

Stryker, Sheldon. (1992). "Identity Theory." In *Encyclopedia of Sociology,* ed. Edgar F. Borgatta and Marie L. Borgatta. New York: Macmillan.

Thoits, Peggy A. (1985). "Self-Labeling Processes in Mental Illness: The Role of Emotional Deviance." *American Journal of Sociology* 92:221–49.

Thoits, Peggy A. (1986). "Multiple Identities: Examining Gender and Marital Status Differences in Distress." *American Sociological Review* 51:259–72.

Thoits, Peggy A. (1989). "The Sociology of Emotions." *Annual Review of Sociology* 15:317–42.

Lynn Smith-Lovin

SPINOZA, BARUCH

b. Amsterdam, The Netherlands, November 24, 1632; *d.* The Hague, The Netherlands, February 21, 1677; *philosophy.*

Spinoza, whose Hebrew name was Baruch and whose Latin name was Benedictus, was born into a Portuguese-Jewish family in Amsterdam. The family had fled to the Netherlands to escape persecution in Spain and Portugal. In Spain, the family had become nominal Catholics (*conversos*) to avoid persecution, but they had continued to practice Judaism in private. In the Netherlands, they returned to open affiliation with Judaism and became prominent members of the Dutch Jewish community. Spinoza received the typical education of a Jewish youth from a prominent family—under the guidance of esteemed rabbis, he studied the Talmud and the ideas of leading Jewish philosophers and theologians. In addition, his family's success allowed Spinoza to take advantage of a continental education, from which he learned the sciences, Latin,

Baruch Spinoza. (Corbis/Bettmann)

German, and probably some French as well. When Spinoza openly questioned various religious teachings, including those about the physical nature of God, angels, the soul, and even the identity of the author of the Bible, the leaders of the Jewish community were offended. They were also concerned that such ideas would bring criticism from Christians, which would lead to difficulties for the Jewish community. As a result, Spinoza was excommunicated from the Jewish religious community on July 27, 1656.

Following his excommunication, Spinoza moved outside of Amsterdam and continued his studies, primarily with Fanciscus van den Enden, a former Jesuit and a classical scholar. Spinoza supported himself as a lens grinder during this period, and he was considered a craftsman of some skill. In 1660, he moved to Rijnsburg, near Leiden, and became part of the Collegianten, a group of intellectuals and religious radicals who held unorthodox ideas about religion but were not seriously persecuted by either religious or civil authorities. In 1663, Spinoza moved to Voorburg, two miles outside of The Hague, and then in 1670, he moved to The Hague itself, where he lived until he died from tuberculosis in 1677.

During the final seventeen years of his life, Spinoza wrote several works that set forth his ideas about meta-

physics, ethics, politics, knowledge, religion, and the mind and body. His philosophy was in large part a reaction to the ideas of his contemporary, the French philosopher René Descartes. In fact, Spinoza's edition of Descartes's *Principia Philosophiae* was published in 1663 with a disclaimer that Spinoza did not share all of the ideas in the work. While he was a follower of Descartes in general, Spinoza questioned Descartes's ideas about several major matters, including the importance of God, the mind-body dichotomy, and the notion of free will as it applies to humans and God. The only other work by Spinoza to be published during his lifetime was his *Tractatus Theologico-Politicus,* which was published anonymously in 1670. Because he thought that his ideas were too controversial, Spinoza refrained from publishing his other works. Instead, he arranged for his friends to have his works published after his death. His wishes were carried out when a collection that included his *Tractatus Politicus, Tractatus de Intellectus Emendatione,* and *Ethica: Ordine Geometrico Demonstrata* appeared in Amsterdam before the end of 1677.

Spinoza was a rationalist with regard to the mind and the emotions; he viewed the emotions as a force that caused people to misinterpret the world and interfered with one's ability to obtain real knowledge. On the other hand, he recognized that certain emotions were pleasant and seemed to be beneficial to the human spirit. He therefore suggested, in anticipation of later cognitive theory, that clear thinking would lead to happiness. In this regard, he did not (as some earlier philosophers had done) reject the consideration of emotion in the human experience altogether. Spinoza offered no clear resolution to the problem of the mind-body dichotomy, but in suggesting that mind and body are parallel, dual aspects of the same essence, he anticipated the twentieth-century neurobiological research on the link between emotion and the body.

As Spinoza had anticipated, his ideas about religion were controversial, and his works were consequently banned by the Catholic Church. For more than one hundred years after his death, Spinoza was often criticized as an atheist or at least a supporter of atheism. In the late eighteenth century, however, his work came to the attention of several German and British philosophers and literary figures, and within several decades Spinoza's ideas had become a continuing subject of academic study.

See also: DESCARTES, RENÉ; MIND-BODY DICHOTOMY; PHILOSOPHY

Bibliography

Donagan, Alan. (1989). *Spinoza.* Chicago: University of Chicago Press.

Garrett, Don, ed. (1995). *The Cambridge Companion to Spinoza.* Cambridge, Eng.: Cambridge University Press.

Harris, Errol H. (1995). *The Substance of Spinoza.* New York: Prometheus Books.

Nadler, Steven M. (1999). *Spinoza: A Life.* New York: Cambridge University Press.

David Levinson
Ben Manning

SPORTS

Emotions play an integral role in human participation in sporting events. All athletes have experienced the joy of winning championships, the pride of physical accomplishment, and the intrinsic pleasure of simply playing the game. Conversely, athletes have also experienced the disappointment of falling short of goal achievement, the muscle-tightening anxiety that occurs under competitive pressure, the anger that results from frustration or physical threat, and the dreaded "choking" that occurs when emotions become unmanageable during an important competition. Thus, human beings participating in sports experience a spectrum of emotions that result from the inherent nature of sports as competitive and socially evaluative. This spectrum of emotions is illustrated in Figure 1. The positive emotions shown on the right side of the spectrum culminate in flow, which is the Zen-like feeling of total immersion and emotional connectedness of peak experiences. The negative emotions shown on the left side of the spectrum culminate in choking, which is a popular sport term that represents an unmanageable flood of negative emotion that disrupts performance control.

One basic premise in the study of emotions is that how people think influences how they feel. As shown in Figure 1, individual differences in athletes interact with the social processes involved in sports to influence the cognitive appraisal that typically gives rise to emotional responses. For example, an inexperienced young pitcher who lacks confidence might cognitively appraise a sell-out World Series crowd and an international television audience as extremely threatening and respond with negative emotions (fear and anxiety) that debilitate his performance. Conversely, a veteran pitcher with major league experience might appraise the same situation as the exciting and joyful pinnacle of his pitching career. Thus, cognitions (i.e., thoughts) give rise to distinct emotional feelings and therefore serve as important precursors for the diversity of emotions experienced by athletes.

A second basic premise is that emotions serve as the energizers of human behavior. The emotions that extend from thoughts are catalysts to behavior. An athlete who is impassioned about his or her sport, who enjoys the training and competition, and who gains great personal satisfaction and pride in achievement will behave very differently from another athlete who lacks the passion and emotional engagement.

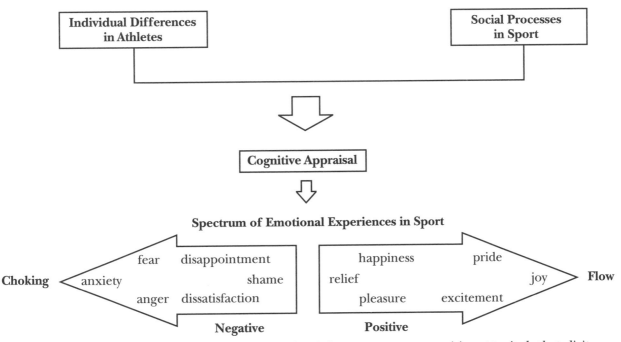

FIGURE 1 *Interaction of individual differences and social processes creates cognitive appraisals that elicit emotional responses in sport.*

Positive Emotions

Most people initially become involved in a sport to experience the positive emotions of enjoyment and pleasure. Research with children and adolescents in organized sports programs has repeatedly shown that the desire for enjoyment or fun is a major reason given for participation, while lack of enjoyment is an important reason for quitting. Research with elite adult athletes has indicated multiple sources of enjoyment, including social and life opportunities, perceived competence and mastery of the sport, social recognition of their competence, and opportunities for self-expression and creativity in performing.

The most positive extreme of feeling states in a sporting activity (as shown in Figure 1) is flow. Mihaly Csikszentmihalyi coined the term *flow* in 1975 to describe an optimal psychological state involving a holistic sensation of total absorption in a task. Athletes call this "being in the zone," and many people participate in sports because they are seeking the flow experience. Flow often leads to peak performance, which is an episode of superior functioning reflecting the upper limits of an individual's capability. Sports research indicates that athletes report the following characteristics of the positive emotional state known as flow: loss of fear of failure, no thinking about the performance, loss of ego or self-consciousness, a sense of control, feeling highly energized, optimal centering of attention, and enjoyment of the activity so that playing is the reward in and of itself (i.e., playing is autotelic). Sports possess qualities that increase the possibility of experiencing flow because they are challenging, creative, inherently fun, and absorbing of mind and body.

Satisfaction and pride are the two positive emotions that are most often studied among all of the emotions that are experienced as the result of a sporting experience. Research supports the idea that athletes who gain satisfaction and feelings of personal worthiness (pride) from their participation will continue to exert effort and persist in their sports. Satisfaction is a positive emotional state resulting from an athlete's cognitive appraisal of the outcomes associated with the athletic experience. Pride is an emotional state resulting from the internalization of an accomplishment that is highly valued and confirms or increases the athlete's sense of self-worth. The cognitive appraisal process in humans is very complex and unique for each individual, so satisfaction and pride result from a subjective personal assessment as to the extent to which experiences meet one's personal standards or expectations.

Negative Emotions

Because participation in sporting events can be a highly valued achievement area with stunning economic incentives and intense social pressure, it gives rise to many negative emotions. The most debilitating negative emotion experienced is anxiety, feelings of apprehension or nervousness that result from perceiving personal threat in competitive situations. Although this threat may be of bodily harm (in the case of high-risk sports such as football or boxing), the most common type of threat perceived by athletes is threat to their feelings of self-worth and perceptions of competence. Anxiety occurs when there is uncertainty about an athlete's perceived ability to meet the competitive demands and when the competitive outcome is important to the athlete. Thus, the greatest amount of anxiety for an athlete would occur when there is maximum uncertainty about his or her ability to be successful in an event that is the most important to that athlete. Often, anxiety is elicited by important competitions such as the Olympic Games or national championships, yet importance is relative to individuals and may be influenced by such factors as being watched by one's parents or competing against an arch rival.

The emotion of anxiety influences sporting performances in two ways. First, it may debilitate the physiological functioning of the muscles by creating unwanted tension and disrupting the smooth sequential pattern of muscle contractions necessary for skilled performance. Research has supported the notion that with higher levels of anxiety, agonist and antagonist muscle groups work against each other, as opposed to the smooth coordination that occurs when anxiety is absent. This type of anxiety is somatic anxiety, which is characterized by muscle tension, sweating, increased heart and respiration rate, and bodily jitters. The second way that anxiety disrupts sport performance is by interfering with attentional control. As anxiety increases, attention often narrows so that the athlete fails to process relevant cues from the environment. Another common occurrence with anxiety is that anxious athletes may tend to focus their attention inward toward thoughts of their possible inadequacies, as opposed to keeping attention fixed on the task demands and challenges. This type of anxiety is termed cognitive anxiety and is characterized by negative thoughts about possible bad outcomes.

Emerging research on anxiety has shown that elite athletes with more experience and success perceive anxiety to be more facilitative to performance as compared to less elite athletes who perceive anxiety to be more debilitative. Thus, although anxiety is a negative emotion comprised of physiological and attentional changes, some athletes have learned to manage it so it may be used in a facilitative manner. This is commonly known as "psyching up" for competition to a point of optimal physical and mental readiness to perform. However, if anxiety is not effectively managed, athletes may get "psyched out" which is simply a state of high anxiety that is uncomfortable and disruptive to performance. When athletes become psyched out, they move toward the extreme negative end of the emotional spectrum (see Figure 1) and risk "choking" (i.e., a complete debilitation of performance in stressful situations due to unmanageable cognitive and/or somatic anxiety). Choking is the opposite of flow or peak performance, and it occurs when attention is focused on the wrong things. This attentional problem gives rise to extreme negative emotion in the form of fear and dread. This negative emotional state makes it impossible for the athlete to relax and gain control of his or her thoughts and feelings to get the performance back on track.

Although not studied to the same degree as anxiety, anger is a negative emotion common in the context of sports for three reasons. First, sports are frustrating due to the very essence of competition in which the objective is to block the goal attainment of one's opponent. The frustration of goal blockage often gives rise to anger. Second, anger may stem from typical inequities that occur in sports such as poor judgments by officials or cheating by opponents. Third, anger often erupts because of the high levels of physical and mental activation that are required to perform sporting tasks. Research has supported the theory that higher levels of anger and aggression occur when individuals are at higher arousal states. Anger is also of interest to sports psychologists because it often leads to aggression, which is defined as the intent to do harm to another individual. Examples of anger leading to aggression include a baseball player charging the mound after a brushback pitch, a punch thrown in frustration due to extreme physical play in basketball, or a fight in ice hockey resulting from anger at being tripped or slashed by an opponent. However, anger as an emotion does not necessarily result in the behavior of aggression, and intervention with athletes focuses on managing the negative emotion of anger without resorting to the negative behavior of aggression.

Like the positive emotions of pride and satisfaction, shame and disappointment are consequence emotions that result from undesired outcomes. Shame typically involves a negative self-evaluation of ability that decreases perceptions and feelings of self-worth and perceived competence. Shame-related emotions include humiliation and embarrassment, and these emotions typically occur when outcomes are perceived as something the athlete could have controlled, yet did not. Disappointment is less personal as a negative emotion; it is more a consequence of uncontrollable negative outcomes. For example, an athlete may feel ashamed of losing because of inadequate preparation and effort, but he or she may feel more disappointed about losing in spite of an outstanding effort. Clearly, emotions are not experienced in isolation, and sporting outcomes can elicit a multitude of emotions simultaneously (e.g., disappointment in not winning, pride in effort and intensity, and satisfaction about achieving at a high level).

Individual Difference Factors

As shown in Figure 1, individual difference factors interact with social processes to influence athletes' cognitive appraisal of the world, or how they think. It is these perceptions that give rise to the various emotions experienced in sporting events. Several individual difference factors have been found to affect subsequent thoughts and emotions. These individual differences represent personality characteristics that make each athlete unique.

The motivational orientation of athletes refers to the internalized ways that individual athletes derive their energy (or motivation) to achieve in a sport. Athletes with intrinsic motivational orientations engage in a sport for the pleasure and satisfaction derived from doing the activity, for the fun and stimulation of competition, and/or to accomplish something important to their feelings of self-worth. Athletes with extrinsic motivational orientations are driven by the promise of some reward beyond the actual performance of the activity itself. Extrinsic motivators for participation in a sporting event typically include social status, college scholarships, professional contracts, parental approval, and trophies or prizes. The key difference between intrinsic and extrinsic motivational orientation is the degree of self-determination that individuals perceive based on the different types of motivation. It is this feeling of self-determination that influences the subsequent emotional responses of athletes. An intrinsic motivational orientation leads to the occurrence of positive emotions because of the important feelings of self-determination possessed by these athletes. Pride and satisfaction emanate when athletes feel that they are in control of their own behavior. Flow is enhanced by an intrinsic motivational orientation because the focus is on immersion in the task itself, as opposed to looking at the activity as only a means to some end. Extrinsic motivational orientations, however, lead to anxiety and choking, because athletes tend to focus on the outcome, which is always uncontrollable. Athletes who are extrinsically oriented also fail to experience the depth of pride and satisfaction in accomplishment because they lack the feelings of self-determination or control over their achievement.

Related to motivational orientation is attributional style, the typical reasons that athletes choose to explain why they succeed and fail on achievement tasks. Attributions directly affect emotional responses to competitive outcomes. For example, if an athlete is successful and attributes this success to ability and training, then pride, satisfaction, and joy in accomplishment is heightened. However, if this athlete is successful and attributes success to luck, then the positive emotional response to the experience is diminished. Attributional style is also related to the experience of negative emotions. If an athlete experiences failure and attributes this failure to stable and unchangeable factors ("I am unskilled" or "I'll never be able to get it"), then the negative emotions of shame and embarrassment are heightened. These negative emotions typically influence a subsequent lack of motivation to try as the athlete feels that he or she has no control over getting better. To buffer negative emotions after failure, athletes with a more productive attributional style focus on unstable and changeable attributions for failure ("I need to work harder on my skills" or "I know I can get better"). Thus, an attributional style that emphasizes personal control over success and failure is most conducive to positive emotional responses.

Self-esteem is perhaps one of the most influential personality characteristics that influence athletes' emotions. Self-esteem is the perception of personal worthiness, and most psychologists view it as the most central component of identity. Many emotional feelings (e.g., pride and shame) that humans experience are directly related to self-esteem. Research supports the idea that young athletes who possess healthy and strong self-esteem experience more positive emotions (pride, satisfaction), while athletes with low self-esteem are more susceptible to negative emotions (anxiety, shame, fear). Perceived competence, the perception by an athlete that he or she has the ability needed to be successful in a sport, is also related to self-esteem. A great amount of research in sports psychology has demonstrated that athletes who perceive they are competent and worthy respond with more positive emotions and are less debilitated by negative emotions.

Trait anxiety is an important individual difference that predicts emotional responses. As a personality disposition, trait anxiety is a tendency to perceive competitive situations as threatening and to respond to these situations with apprehension and tension. The threat perceived by trait-anxious athletes includes fear of failure, fear of evaluation, and fear of negative outcomes. Trait anxiety is predictive of negative emotions, and dampens positive emotions as high trait-anxious athletes enjoy sports less due to their perceptions of continuous threat. Another individual difference factor that affects athletes' cognitive appraisal process and leads to negative emotional responses is perfectionism. Perfectionism is defined as the setting of excessively high personal standards for performance that can become neurotic when the person uses inflexible evaluative criteria. Research shows that perfectionism can result in feelings of guilt, failure, shame, fear, anxiety, and depression. The negative emotions that result from perfectionism then influence motivation and behavior as evidenced by research that links perfectionism to burnout and dropout.

One of the oldest areas of research in sports psychology related to individual differences in emotions is the "iceberg profile." The iceberg profile is based on the premise that the presence of positive mood states or emotions in athletes is associated with higher performance levels as compared to the performance levels of athletes possessing less positive mood states or emotions. This pattern of emotions associated with better performance in sporting events is called the iceberg profile because it is characterized by scores above the population norm on vigor and below the population norm on tension, depression, anger, fatigue, and confusion. This profile has been supported using various athletic samples.

Social Processes

Although emotions in sporting activities are elicited by individual personality differences, they are also elicited by the powerful social processes operating within the sports subculture. Motivational climate is one such social influence that directly affects the emotional responses of millions of athletes. Basically, if a mastery motivational climate emphasizes improvement, a task orientation, and individual progress, then positive emotions such as enjoyment, satisfaction, and pride typically follow. However, an ego-oriented motivational climate that emphasizes a normative comparison with others and winning at the expense of individual development lends itself more to the negative emotions of anxiety, shame, and fear. This motivational climate is created by the individuals in the social environment—coaches, parents, teammates, and even administrators. Research has shown that coaching behaviors involving an autocratic style, an emphasis on outcomes versus improvement, and the use of punishment are related to anxiety and burnout in young athletes. Conversely, the coaching behaviors that involve democratic style, empathy, effective communication, and positive reinforcement are related to enjoyment, satisfaction, and motivation. Two of the top anxiety producers in children's sports are worrying about letting parents down and trying to live up to parents' expectations. Research has also shown that children are most satisfied with their sports experiences when their parents give them unconditional social support (acceptance and approval that is not contingent on performance) and help them set performance goals.

Often overlooked, particularly in children's sports, is the need to consider modifying the structure of the sport to enhance the emotional experiences for the athletes. Research in children's sports has demonstrated that simple modifications that increase activity levels, scale the activity to the smaller size of the children, and make qualitative rule changes to benefit participants serve to increase positive emotions such as enjoyment and satisfaction and decrease the anxiety and boredom that may accompany unmodified sporting events. An important determinant of the flow state of positive emotion is the fitting of the challenge to one's skill. Through all developmental levels, flow and other positive emotions may be enhanced when a sport is structured with this goal in mind. Flow is also enhanced when athletes are not continually disrupted with evaluative feedback and advice. Both parents and coaches should understand the need for athletes of all ages to "play the game" without continuous coaching that often disrupts the enjoyment and satisfaction inherent in participating in a sport.

Cohesion is defined as the team "chemistry," the tendency for a group to stick together and remain united in pursuing group goals. Groups perform better and group members are more satisfied when they are cohesive. Cohesion is facilitated by emphasizing uniqueness or a positive identity related to group membership. Cohesion is also facilitated when individual members of a team understand and accept their roles within the group.

The social processes involved in competition in Western society are often seen as precursors to negative emotions and aggression. Social learning theory views aggression as a learned behavior (usually accompanied by negative emotion) that develops as a result of modeling and reinforcement. Ice hockey players are glorified for angrily fighting with opponents, and baseball players are encouraged and even expected to charge the mound and fight with the opposing pitcher. It is popularly believed that competition reduces negative emotions and aggressive impulses in athletes by providing a release for emotion (called catharsis). However, research does not support this claim. On the contrary, research shows that anger and aggression increase after competing in vigorous physical activity or watching a competitive event. Observing competition has grown to fanatical proportions as sports fans experience the spectrum of emotions vicariously through watching athletes perform and identifying with favorite sports teams. Millions of people around the world enjoy the positive emotional experiences gained through watching sporting events. Examples of these positive emotions run from enjoyment and pleasure in watching the competition to the pride felt by an entire city when a hometown team wins a major championship. However, disappointment and depression have been reported in many sports fans whose teams lose or fall short of competitive goals. At extreme levels, this has turned to violence such as soccer riots or the destruction and looting in cities whose professional teams win championships. Thus, sporting events, as part of a fan's psyche, can create the same emotions in observers as it can in athletes.

Intervention for Emotional Management

Often called mental training or psychological skills training, intervention techniques are used in sports psychology to help athletes manage their emotions so they perform more effectively under competitive conditions. An important goal of intervention strategies is to help athletes maximize their chances of achieving the positive emotional state of flow or peak experience.

Goal setting is a basic technique used to focus on specific attainable behaviors presented as reachable yet difficult goals. Research indicates that goals are most effective if they are difficult and systematically monitored and evaluated. Other effective goal setting practices include the use of short-term goals as progressive steps toward reaching a long-term goal, with an emphasis on performance or controllable goals as opposed to outcome goals such as winning a race. Anxiety has been linked to a focus on outcome goals, as opposed to a task-performance focus, which is linked to personal satisfaction and enjoyment.

Another popular intervention technique is self-talk, personal statements that athletes make to themselves. As mentioned previously, thoughts precede emotions, so learning to manage one's self-talk is the first step in learning to manage one's emotions. The goal of effective self-talk is to engage in planned, intentional productive thinking that convinces the athlete's body that he or she is confident, motivated, and ready to perform. Athletes are taught to identify key situations or environmental stressors that cause them to choke and then create and mentally practice a plan that can be used to appropriately focus attention in that situation. Attentional control and focusing is perhaps the most important cognitive skill in competition, and human emotions typically distract athletes from their optimal focus. Self-talk strategies such as "centering" allow athletes to select relevant cues and design physiological (e.g., deep breath) and psychological (e.g., feeling

Canadian ice hockey player Geraldine Heaney kicks a U.S. player during a game at the 1998 Winter Olympics in Nagano, Japan. The U.S. women's team won their first gold medal after defeating the Canadians 3–1. (Corbis/Wally McNamee)

strong, quick, and confident) triggers to gain emotional control and focus attention effectively.

Imagery is a mental technique that involves using all of the senses to create or re-create an experience. Emotive imagery is commonly used by athletes to create, both mentally and physically, the appropriate emotion needed at a specific time. This may involve psyching up or using imagery to visualize intensity, body readiness, or explosive strength and quickness. Emotive imagery may also be used to calm down the body for sports that require fine motor control such as archery or shooting. Besides imagery, other physical relaxation techniques are used to help athletes manage their autonomic responses to typical competition-related emotions (e.g., nervousness, fear, tension). For example, athletes can learn how to regulate somatic anxiety by reducing their heart and breathing rates to induce a more relaxed state. Overall, intervention techniques help athletes to understand better their unique emotional triggers and responses, which helps them to manage their thoughts and emotions, which in turn allows them to enjoy the sport and perform better.

See also: AGGRESSION; ATTRIBUTION; MOTIVATION; SELF-ESTEEM; SENSATION SEEKING AND RISK TAKING

Bibliography

Csikszentmihalyi, Mihaly. (1990). *Flow: The Psychology of Optimal Experience.* New York: Harper & Row.

Fox, Kenneth R., ed. (1997). *The Physical Self: From Motivation to Well-Being.* Champaign, IL: Human Kinetics.

Hall, Howard K.; Kerr, Alistair W.; and Matthews, Julie. (1998). "Precompetitive Anxiety in Sport: The Contribution of Achievement Goals and Perfectionism." *Journal of Sport and Exercise Psychology* 20:194–217.

Jackson, Susan A. (1992). "Athletes in Flow: A Qualitative Investigation of Flow States in Elite Figure Skaters." *Journal of Applied Sport Psychology* 4:161–180.

Jackson, Susan A. (1995). "Factors Influencing the Occurrence of Flow States in Elite Athletes." *Journal of Applied Sport Psychology* 7:138–166.

Jones, Graham, and Swain, Austin. (1995). "Predispositions to Experience Debilitative and Facilitative Anxiety in Elite and Non-Elite Performers." *Sport Psychologist* 9:201–211.

Martens, Rainer; Vealey, Robin S.; and Burton, Damon. (1990). *Competitive Anxiety in Sport.* Champaign, IL: Human Kinetics.

Murphy, Shane M. (1995). *Sport Psychology Interventions.* Champaign, IL: Human Kinetics.

Orlick, Terry. (1990). *In Pursuit of Excellence.* Champaign, IL: Human Kinetics.

Orlick, Terry, and Partington, John. (1988). "Mental Links to Excellence." *Sport Psychologist* 2:105–130.

Riemer, Harold A., and Chelladurai, Packianathan. (1998). "Development of the Athlete Satisfaction Questionnaire (ASQ)." *Journal of Sport and Exercise Psychology* 20:127–156.

Rowley, Allan J.; Landers, Daniel M.; Kyllo, L. Blaine; and Etnier, Jennifer L. (1995). "Does the Iceberg Profile Discriminate between Successful and Less Successful Athletes? A Meta-Analysis." *Journal of Sport and Exercise Psychology* 17:185–199.

Scanlan, Tara K., and Simons, Jeffery P. (1992). "The Construct of Sport Enjoyment." In *Motivation in Sport and Exercise*, ed. Glynn C. Roberts. Champaign, IL: Human Kinetics.

Scanlan, Tara K.; Stein, Gary L.; and Ravizza, Ken. (1989). "An In-Depth Study of Former Elite Figure Skaters: II. Sources of Enjoyment." *Journal of Sport and Exercise Psychology* 11:65–82.

Terry, Peter. (1995). "The Efficacy of Mood State Profiling with Elite Performers: A Review and Synthesis." *Sport Psychologist* 9:309–324.

Williams, Jean M., and Krane, Vikki. (1998). "Psychological Characteristics of Peak Performance." In *Applied Sport Psychology: Personal Growth to Peak Performance*, ed. Jean M. Williams. Mountain View, CA: Mayfield.

Robin S. Vealey

STRESS

Stress and emotion are inherently intertwined. By definition, stress, especially psychosocial stress, involves a negative emotional response, such as anxiety, worry, and sadness, that can evolve into long-term problems such as depression. However, stress often involves positive emotions as well, depending in part upon the appraisal of the situation, the type of coping strategy used, and the outcomes of the coping effort. At first, a person may be worried and distressed when facing a problem but may feel elated once he or she resolves it, while another individual may relish the initial challenge of coping with particularly difficult problems and seek out challenges.

Indeed, it often is difficult to label emotions as being either purely "positive" or "negative" in a stressful context. Emotions serve both as social signals and as motivation sustainers. Negative emotions may serve positive functions, as when anxiety or anger evokes social support from others or stimulates positive coping efforts. Anxiety about an impending examination may prompt problem-focused coping efforts such as studying, and anger may increase the likelihood that an individual will confront others in problematic circumstances in order to get them to change their behavior. The difficulty arises when negative emotions are so strong that they overwhelm attempts to cope with stress. For this reason, there is growing interest in emotion regulation. While regulation is usually thought of as being an effort to contain negative emotions and their adverse consequences, it is important to note that emotion-focused coping efforts do not always serve to dampen emotions—sometimes the emotions are strengthened. Thus, emotions can be seen as a response to stress, something which can motivate and shape coping efforts, and as an outcome of the stress and coping process.

Definitions

Stress, according to John Mason (1975), can be viewed in three ways: as a response, as an event, and as a person-environment transaction.

Walter Cannon (1929) observed that there are strong physiological reactions to stress, which he called the "fight-flight" response. Stress activates the sympathetic nervous system, mediated by epinephrine and norepinephrine, and results in increased heart and respiratory rates, vascular constriction (increasing blood flow to the brain and striated muscles and elevating blood pressure), increased perspiration (dissipating excess heat generated by this arousal), and decreased parasympathetic activity, which is often experienced as "butterflies in the stomach" and a dry mouth. He argued that psychosocial stress could result in over-arousal of the sympathetic nervous system, which, if prolonged, could end in death through shock, even in the absence of a physiological stressor. Cannon called this phenomenon "voodoo death," as he first observed it when Australian aborigines died after being cursed by shamans. Hans Selye (1956) extended this stress response to include the adrenal glands, especially the adrenal cortex, which generates corticosteroids and is thought to mediate longer-term reactions to stress. His General Adaptation Syndrome model argued that stress is the body's generalized—or nonspecific—response to external demands, which occurs in three stages. In the first stage, stress activates the hypothalamic-pituitary-adrenal (HPA) axis, but in the second stage, the organism appears to recover from the stressor, allowing bodily systems to return to normal (homeostasis), even if the stressor still continues. However, if the stressor continues long enough, the organism may enter the third stage, exhaustion or death.

It is now known that stress also affects many aspects of the neuroendocrine and immune systems. Furthermore, there is evidence for "tailored" or specific physiological reactions to different types of stress, as well as more general responses. Emotional reactions may play a key role in this process, but there is little good evidence to link specific neuroendocrine responses to specific emotions.

Stress can also be defined as an event. Harold G. Wolff (1950), a physician, had his patients keep a diary, and discovered that illness episodes were often preceded by negative life events, such as job loss or a divorce. Thomas Holmes and Richard Rahe (1967) systematized this observation by developing scales to assess stressful life events and argued that any environmental demand, whether positive or negative, resulted in a deviation from homeostasis and thus constituted a stressor. Literally thousands of studies have shown that stressful life events are modestly related to a variety of illnesses and physiological outcomes. However, the situation is more complex than originally thought. Most studies have shown that it is primarily negative events rather than positive ones that have adverse psychological and physical consequences. Further, life events are often rare, and some researchers prefer to measure chronic role strain or daily stressors.

Richard Lazarus and Susan Folkman (1984) have argued that the appraisal or meaning of the stressor has more effect on well-being than the simple occurrence of an event. For a situation to be stressful, an individual must appraise it as involving threat, harm, loss, or challenge. These appraisals are influenced not only by environmental characteristics but also by the individual's values, goals, personality, and coping resources. Losing a job has a very different meaning for a teenager who did not want a summer job than it has for a fifty-year-old man who has a mortgage and two children in college. Appraisal is not static; it is an ongoing transactional process that involves continuous interplay between the person and the environment.

Role of Emotions

The role of emotions in the stress process varies in part by how stress is defined. Certainly, emotions are involved in the physiological responses to stress. But do they precede physiological responses or are they a consequence of them? In the 1880s, the James-Lange theory proposed that physiological responses preceded emotions and gave rise to them. In response, Cannon argued in the 1920s that emotional responses have a much quicker response time and thus must precede neuroendocrine responses. In this view, emotions form a key link between stress appraisals and physiological reactions.

Similarly, there are issues of causal directionality between emotions and stressful life events. While some researchers argue that stressful life events are "objective" and have adverse effects in and of themselves, others caution that characteristic emotional styles can evoke or precipitate negative events. Someone who is chronically angry may be more likely to be laid off, and someone who is depressed is more likely to receive negative reactions from others in his or her environment. Jan Strelau (1995) noted that temperament influences stress in three ways: by moderating the intensity characteristics of the stressful situation, by influencing the optimal level of arousal for the individual, and by eliciting features of the environment. In a longitudinal study, Carolyn Aldwin and her colleagues

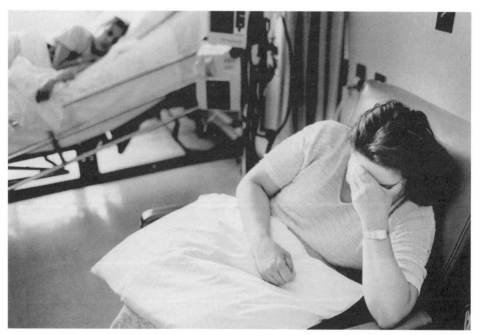

Coping with the extended illness of a loved one can be a source of great stress, as it was for this woman whose daughter was a patient at Valley Children's Hospital in Fresno, California, in 1988 because of recurring leukemia. (Corbis/David H. Wells)

(1989) showed that emotionality did predict the higher levels of reporting of both life events and daily stressors, but nonetheless, these stress measures had independent effects on mental health over and above emotionality.

There is also an ongoing debate about whether stress appraisals evoke emotions or whether negative emotions evoke stress appraisals. Robert Zajonc (1984) argued for the primacy of affect. He cited empirical evidence of the separate neuroanatomical structures for affect and cognition and argued that emotions are not necessarily responses to cognitive manipulation. There are subconscious reactions to verbal and nonverbal stimuli, and emotions can be induced by noncognitive methods (e.g., drugs and facial musculature manipulation). Lazarus's (1984) counter-argument emphasized cognitive activity as a precondition for emotional experience. He contended that emotion involves situational meaning as well as physiological structures and that there is no guarantee that efforts to induce emotions through noncognitive methods are free from cognitive activity. In later work, Lazarus (1991) suggested that there are two modes of appraisal, one rational and conscious, the other preconscious and largely automatic.

The human brain, as Michael Gazzaniga (1995) has indicated, is composed of modular systems with almost instantaneous intercommunication. Thus, it may be more useful to think of the cognitive and emotional systems as informing each other in a nearly continuous fashion. In most everyday situations, emotions and cognition are tightly intertwined, and it is important to note that emotions may play a role in many different parts of the stress process.

Short-Term Emotional Consequences

There are many different emotional reactions to stress, depending in part upon how individuals appraise the situation. The dominant short-term reactions to stress include anger, fright or anxiety, and sadness, but they may include a host of other reactions as well, such as disgust, guilt, shame, or simple annoyance. In general, anger and annoyance occur when goals are blocked, or when someone blames others; sadness results from loss appraisals; and anxiety results from concerns about future harm. However, most situations evoke multiple appraisals, and, in turn, people may experience multiple emotions in response to stress. While emotions may serve to galvanize action, as in the classic fight-or-flight response to stress, emotions may also encourage people to withdraw, heal, and recoup their losses. Thus, emotional reactions such as sadness may decrease activity.

A particularly intriguing short-term emotional response to stress is emotional numbing or dissociation. People who have experienced sudden trauma may report that they felt numb and that it seemed as if the event were not actually happening to them. However, this temporarily restricted range of affect may also be viewed as a coping mechanism whereby individuals disassociate themselves from the overwhelming emotional reality of a nightmarish situation.

Positive emotions, such as exhilaration or elation, may also occur as a function of stress. This is most likely to occur when an individual appraises a problem as being a challenge, which Joe Tomaka and his colleagues (1997) showed may result in greater physiological arousal than that produced by negative emotions. Some individuals, such as parachutists or rock climbers, may seek out stressful or dangerous situations precisely for this type of emotional "high." However, positive emotions may also occur after a stressor has passed. Anita DeLongis and her colleagues (1988) found that about one-third of the individuals they studied were more likely to report higher levels of positive affect after the occurrence of a daily stressor. Presumably people were pleased with an outcome, either because they resolved it successfully, they received social support from others, or perhaps they were just relieved that it was all over. However, most emotional reactions to stressors are relatively short in duration.

Long-Term Emotional Consequences of Stress

Although the effects of daily stressors typically dissipate within hours and the effects of stressful events tend to be gone within a year, there can be, under some circumstances, long-term emotional consequences of stress. In general, most people "bounce back" after exposure to one life event, but multiple problems or long-term chronic exposure to stress can result in major emotional disorders such as depression or post-traumatic stress disorder (PTSD). A classic study by George Brown and Tirril Harris (1978) showed that individuals who were most likely to be depressed were single mothers who were impoverished, socially isolated, and had two or more children under five years of age. Aldwin and Daniel Stokols (1988) hypothesized that problems that occur suddenly, affect multiple life domains, and are highly stressful are most likely to have long-term effects such as depression.

PTSD is a serious negative long-term consequence of traumas such as childhood physical abuse, natural disasters, or combat exposure and can last for decades. The emotional symptoms of PTSD include both hyperemotionality (i.e., fear, anxiety, intrusive thoughts, irritability, depression, and emotional lability) and hypoemotionality (i.e., emotional numbing). Andrew Baum and his colleagues (1993) hypothesized that long-term PTSD may be due to intrusive thoughts that maintain a state of arousal within the individual.

However, the long-term consequences of stress may also be positive. Richard Dienstbier (1989) showed that stressors occurring early in life may have positive long-term consequences on neuroendocrine functioning. Infant mice subjected to mild stressors showed faster maturation, more exploratory behavior in adulthood, and better neuroendocrine responses to stress, but only if there were sufficient respite time between stressful episodes. If there were no respite periods, the infant-handled mice tended to have poorer neuroendocrine responses to stress, resulting in greater and more prolonged emotional distress.

There have been numerous anecdotal reports of the positive aspects of stress for emotional well-being in adults. For example, after natural disasters, people interviewed on television routinely report how thankful they are that their lives were spared and how great it is that the community pulled together. These anecdotal findings were confirmed in a survey of more than one thousand adults. Aldwin, Karen Sutton, and Margie Lachman (1996) found that nearly 70 percent of adults who had recently experienced a major low point reported positive long-term effects of the stressor, such as increased mastery, greater self-understanding, and closer ties with loved ones, while only 20 percent reported exclusively negative effects. The ability to experience positive aspects of adversity may protect one against the development of PTSD.

Emotional Expression and Regulation

There is evidence that emotional expression and regulation begin very early in life, perhaps even before birth. Tiffany Field (1991) reports that fetuses respond to environmental noise and light, as well as movement, nutritional intake, and even the mother's stress hormone levels, by kicking, hiccuping, and waving their arms. They may also suck their thumbs, which in premature newborns has been shown to reduce physiological stress responses and decrease fussing and crying. While there is some debate about exactly which emotions emerge at which age, most researchers would agree that newborns show at least three emotions at birth: wariness-fear, rage-anger, and pleasure-joy. This conclusion is based on facial expressions, vocalizations, and the monitoring of heart rates. More complex emotions, such as shame, which require cognitive understanding of the environment (and a sense of identity) emerge in the second year of life. Certainly, infants and toddlers learn culturally-appropriate emotional expression by observing others and

modeling their behaviors, as well as by direct instruction by their parents. For example, even very young infants will mirror facial expressions, and parents will often exaggerate facial expressions and emotional reactions for their infants to copy.

According to L. Alan Sroufe (1996), infants rely almost exclusively on their parents or caregivers for emotional regulation. Infants express distress primarily by crying, and parents respond by soothing, rocking, feeding, and/or eliminating the source of the distress. However, Lois Murphy and Alice Moriarty (1976) argued that infants are not passive recipients of parental care—they quickly develop a number of strategies to regulate their environment. Infants can modulate their cries to indicate the type of distress they are experiencing, and they can regulate the amount of social stimulation by making eye contact or smiling when they are seeking to elicit interaction and by turning away, falling asleep, or crying when they are overstimulated.

By the end of the first year, emotion regulation is considered to be more dyadic—that is, babies and their caretakers work together to regulate emotions. Babies and toddlers are more able to elicit support from others by holding up their arms to be lifted up or by crawling or toddling to their primary caregivers for nurturance. Successful emotional regulation depends upon the ability of the caregivers to be sensitive to their babies' signals and to respond appropriately in a predictable fashion. Toddlers whose parents are unresponsive or inconsistent in their responses may develop problems in emotion regulation. Eventually, children become able to regulate their own emotions more independently, usually between two and three years of age.

Early attempts at emotion regulation tend to be behavioral—crying, rocking, sucking thumbs, and so on. Toddlers may invest in transitional objects, such as a favorite blanket or stuffed animal, which are sources of comfort when they are distressed. Preschoolers tend to have a larger coping repertoire that allows them to make more differentiated responses to emotional distress. Defense mechanisms such as repression, denial, and displacement can be observed in very young children. Between six and nine years of age, there is a dramatic increase in emotion-focused coping repertoires. By the time they reach middle school, children have become better at differentiating and verbalizing their feelings, and they are more able to use conscious cognitive strategies to calm themselves down (e.g., reassuring themselves that a nightmare was "only a dream").

In pre- or early adolescence, however, some children may fail to make the transition to successful cognitive-based strategies for emotional regulation, turning instead to substances such as tobacco, alcohol, or drugs to regulate their emotional distress. However, it would be a mistake to think of emotion regulation merely in terms of controlling emotions. Adolescents in particular may heighten emotional displays in order to elicit support from their parents or to try to control their environment. Emotional displays are social signals that can indicate that something is seriously wrong. Adolescents are the most likely of any age group to attempt to commit suicide (although luckily they are not often successful); certainly, displays of emotional distress or withdrawal need to be taken seriously by an adolescent's family.

There is some evidence that emotional expression and regulation increase in sophistication and complexity in adulthood. In a series of longitudinal studies, George Vaillant (1993) suggested that young adults are more likely to display "neurotic" or "immature" defense mechanisms, such as denial and projection, but middle-aged adults are more likely to rely upon "mature" defense mechanisms such as sublimation. In other words, young adults are more likely either to deny the existence of problems or to blame others for them, while mature adults are more likely to find socially-acceptable ways of dealing with their problems.

Fredda Blanchard-Fields and her colleagues (1995) found that older adults displayed a broader repertoire of emotion-focused coping strategies than did younger adults. They interpreted these results as supporting the idea that years of experience with stressful events allowed older adults to choose the most effective strategy for the situation. Further, adults may be more likely to report more complex emotional experiences and may be more sophisticated and effective in their use of coping strategies. Gisela Labouvie-Vief and her colleagues (1987) found that young and middle-aged adults are equally likely to use social support in coping with problems, but young adults tend to use social support as a means of self-validation, while middle-aged adults are more likely to try to get feedback on the appropriateness of their coping strategies.

In late life, there is some evidence that the nature of the appraisal process may change. Given dwindling resources, it may become more important to conserve energy. Although older adults are just as likely to experience major life events, daily stressors tend to decrease in frequency, perhaps due to the relinquishing of social roles such as work and parenting. They may be likely to appraise a situation as a problem, or appraise existing problems as less stressful than younger adults, perhaps because their long experience with stressors has given them perspective on the relative importance of various problems. Older adults who have no cognitive impairment may cope just as effec-

tively as middle-aged or younger adults, but they may expend less energy to solve their problems. Older adults do appear to make greater use of denial or minimization, often using positive comparisons to make light of their own problems—they can always point to someone they know with more severe problems. Older adults who have cognitive impairment, however, may experience greater difficulty in emotional regulation and, in later stages of dementia, may become much more emotionally unstable and aggressive.

Conclusion

Stress and emotions are intimately intertwined. There are marked individual differences in how people appraise situations and in their emotional responses. While stress is generally associated with negative emotions, people who appraise problems in terms of challenges may report positive emotions such as elation. Successful coping may also lead, in the long run, to positive emotions. Emotional expression and regulation increase in complexity throughout the life span. Indeed, it is likely that it is through the experience of coping with stressful events that emotional complexity and perhaps wisdom develop.

See also: ANGER; ANXIETY; DEFENSE MECHANISMS; FEAR AND PHOBIAS; HEALTH AND ILLNESS; HUMAN DEVELOPMENT; JAMES, WILLIAM; POST-TRAUMATIC STRESS DISORDER; SENSATION SEEKING AND RISK TAKING

Bibliography

Aldwin, Carolyn M. (1994). *Stress, Coping, and Development.* New York: Guilford.

Aldwin, Carolyn M.; Levenson, Michael R.; and Spiro, Avron, III. (1994). "Vulnerability and Resilience to Combat Exposure: Can Stress Have Lifelong Effects?" *Psychology and Aging* 9:34–44.

Aldwin, Carolyn M.; Levenson, Michael R.; Spiro, Avron, III; and Bosse, Raymond. (1989). "Does Emotionality Predict Stress? Findings from the Normative Aging Study." *Journal of Personality and Social Psychology* 56:618–624.

Aldwin, Carolyn M.; Sutton, Karen J.; Chiara, Gina; and Spiro, Avron, III. (1996). "Age Differences in Stress, Coping and Appraisal: Findings from the Normative Aging Study." *Journal of Gerontology, Series B: Psychological Sciences and Social Sciences* 51B:179–188.

Aldwin, Carolyn M., and Stokols, Daniel. (1988). "The Effects of Environmental Change on Individuals and Groups: Some Neglected Issues in Stress Research." *Journal of Environmental Psychology* 8:57–75.

Aldwin, Carolyn M.; Sutton, Karen; and Lachman, Margie. (1996). "The Development of Coping Resources in Adulthood. *Journal of Personality* 64:837–871.

Baum, Andrew; Cohen, Lorenzo; and Hall, Martica. (1993). "Control and Intrusive Memories As Possible Determinants of Chronic Stress." *Psychosomatic Medicine* 55:274–286.

Blanchard-Fields, Fredda; Jahnke, Heather Casper; and Camp, Cameron. (1995). "Age Differences in Problem-Solving Style:

The Role of Emotional Salience." *Psychology and Aging* 10: 173–180.

Brown, George W., and Harris, Tirril W. (1978). *Social Origins of Depression: A Study of Psychiatric Disorder in Women.* New York: Free Press.

Cannon, Walter B. (1929). *Bodily Changes in Pain, Hunger, Fear, and Rage: An Account of Recent Researches into the Function of Emotional Excitement,* 2nd ed. New York: Appleton.

Compas, Bruce E.; Worsham, Nancy L.; and Ey, Sydney. (1992). "Conceptual and Developmental Issues in Children's Coping with Stress." In *Stress and Coping in Child Health,* ed. Annette M. La Greca, Lawrence J. Siegel, Jan L. Wallander, and C. Eugene Walker. New York: Guilford.

Delongis, Anita; Folkman, Susan; and Lazarus, Richard S. (1988). "The Impact of Daily Stress on Health and Mood: Psychology and Social Resources As Mediators." *Journal of Personality and Social Psychology* 54:486–495.

Dienstbier, Richard A. (1989). "Arousal and Physiological Toughness: Implications for Mental and Physical Health." *Psychological Bulletin* 96:84–100.

Epstein, Seymour. (1982). "Conflict and Stress." In *Handbook of Stress: Theoretical and Clinical Aspects,* ed. Leo Goldberger and Shlomo Breznitz. New York: Free Press.

Field, Tiffany. (1991). "Stress and Coping from Pregnancy through the Postnatal Period." In *Life-Span Developmental Psychology: Perspectives on Stress and Coping,* ed. E. Mark Cummings, Anita L. Greene, and Katherine H. Karraker. Hillsdale, NJ: Lawrence Erlbaum.

Gazzaniga, Michael S. (1995). "Consciousness and the Cerebral Hemispheres." In *The Cognitive Neurosciences,* ed. Michael S. Gazzaniga. Cambridge, MA: Bradford.

Holmes, Thomas, and Rahe, Richard. (1967). "The Social Readjustment Rating Scale." *Journal of Psychosomatic Research* 11:213–218.

Labouvie-Vief, Gisela; Hakim-Larson, Julie; and Hobart, Cathy. (1987). "Age, Ego Level, and the Life-Span Development of Coping and Defense Processes." *Psychology of Aging* 2:286–293.

Lazarus, Richard S. (1984). "On the Primacy of Cognition." *American Psychologist* 39:124–129.

Lazarus, Richard S. (1991). *Emotion and Adaptation.* New York: Oxford University Press.

Lazarus, Richard S., and Folkman, Susan. (1984). *Stress, Appraisal, and Coping.* New York: Springer.

Mason, John. (1975). "A Historical View of the Stress Field." *Journal of Human Stress* 1:6–27.

Murphy, Lois Barclay, and Moriarty, Alice E. (1976). *Vulnerability, Coping and Growth from Infancy to Adolescence.* New Haven, CT: Yale University Press.

Selye, Hans. (1956). *The Stress of Life.* New York: McGraw-Hill.

Sroufe, L. Alan. (1996). *Emotional Development: The Organization of Emotional Life in the Early Years.* New York: Cambridge University Press.

Strelau, Jan. (1995). "Temperament and Stress: Temperament As a Moderator of Stressors, Emotional States, Coping, and Costs." In *Stress and Emotion: Anxiety, Anger, and Curiosity, Vol. 15,* ed. Charles D. Speilberger, Irwin G. Sarason, John M. Brebner, Esther Greenglass, Pittu Laugani, and Ann M. O'Roark. Washington, DC: Taylor & Francis.

Tomaka, Joe; Blascovich, Jim; Kibber, Jeffrey; and Ernst, John M. (1997). "Cognitive and Physiological Antecedents of Threat and Challenge Appraisal." *Journal of Personality and Social Psychology* 73:63–72.

Vaillant, George E. (1993). *The Wisdom of the Ego.* Cambridge, MA: Harvard University Press.

Wallerstein, Judith S., and Kelly, Joan Berlin. (1980). *Surviving the Breakup: How Children and Parents Cope with Divorce.* New York: Basic Books.

Wolff, Harold G. (1950). "Life Stress and Cardiovascular Disorders." *Circulation* 1:187–203.

Zajonc, Robert B. (1984). "On the Primacy of Affect." *American Psychologist* 39:117–123.

Carolyn M. Aldwin
Loriena A. Yancura

SULLIVAN, HARRY STACK

b. Norwich, New York, February 22, 1892; d. Paris, France, January 14, 1949; *psychiatry, psychoanalysis.*

Harry Stack Sullivan was an American psychiatrist and psychoanalyst who made important contributions to psychiatry and the social sciences as a therapist, theorist, and teacher. Sullivan grew up on a farm in upstate New York. Because of the isolation of farm life and his family being Irish Catholic in a Protestant region, Sullivan experienced frequent periods of loneliness. This loneliness was alleviated by a friendship with one other boy, Clarence Bellinger, who like Sullivan also later specialized in psychiatry. Sullivan's later professional interest in hard-to-treat emotional disorders, as well as his interest in interpersonal relationships, have been traced by commentators to this early experience of loneliness. Sullivan, who never married, graduated from Cornell University and attended the medical school at the University of Chicago. Although Sullivan did have a degree on parchment dated 1917, it is unclear if he actually graduated, if the degree was forged, or if it was issued illegally by a college official—records indicate that he dropped out in 1915. It is this and other mysteries concerning his personal life, in addition to his well-deserved reputation for being a warm, caring, sincere, and thoughtful man, that contributed to the interest in Sullivan both during his career and after his death.

After medical school, Sullivan entered the psychiatry field in Maryland, under the stewardship of leading American psychiatrist William Alanson White. Sullivan worked with schizophrenics and was perhaps the first psychiatrist to demonstrate that psychotherapy could be effective with this difficult disorder. In the 1930s, Sullivan moved to New York City, where he established a private practice, entered psychoanalysis himself, and helped to found the William Alanson White Psychiatric Foundation and the Washington School of Psychiatry, a psychoanalytic training institute. Upon moving to New York, Sullivan initially specialized in treating obsession disorders, another problem many therapists choose to ignore. In 1939, Sullivan moved to Washington, D.C., where he spent much of the remainder of his life in consulting with the government and then the United Nations on mental health issues, in accord with his wish to alleviate suffering and injustice around the world. He died in Paris in 1949 while returning from a meeting of the World Federation for Mental Health.

Beyond being a successful therapist and teacher, Sullivan was an active, creative thinker and developed what later came to be known as the interpersonal theory of psychiatry. Sullivan rejected the idea of "individual personality" and argued instead that a unique feature of being human, and therefore the key to understanding human behavior and to treating emotional problems, was the continual interaction that took place between people. When these interactions go awry, and especially when people react to one another in inappropriate emotional ways, problems result, and psychiatry can be useful. Interpersonal theory was developed both through work with patients and collaboration with sociologists and anthropologists, the most important of whom were the anthropological linguist Edward Sapir and the political scientist Harold Laswell.

Sullivan's ideas strongly influenced later generations of social scientists who followed his lead in moving the study of personality from the individual to the interpersonal situation. Although he was co-editor of the journal *Psychiatry* from 1938 to 1946, Sullivan wrote relatively little, and only *Conceptions of Modern Psychiatry* (1947) was published before his death. After his death, his former students and colleagues organized his lectures and notes into a series of books that set forth his ideas about psychiatry, therapy, social science, and his interpersonal theory.

See also: PSYCHOANALYTIC PERSPECTIVE

Bibliography

Perry, Helen S. (1982). *Psychiatrist of America: The Life of Harry Stack Sullivan.* New York: W. W. Norton.

Sullivan, Harry Stack. (1947). *Conceptions of Modern Psychiatry.* New York: W. W. Norton.

Sullivan, Harry Stack. (1953). *The Interpersonal Theory of Psychiatry.* New York: W. W. Norton.

Sullivan, Harry Stack. (1954). *The Psychiatric Interview.* New York: W. W. Norton.

Sullivan, Harry Stack. (1964). *The Fusion of Psychiatry and Social Science.* New York: W. W. Norton.

David Levinson

Harry Stack Sullivan. (Corbis/Bettmann)

SURPRISE

It is generally assumed that surprise is a basic or fundamental emotion. It has a distinctive facial expression and behavior, and it is associated with underlying physiological change and subjective experience. The defining feature of surprise is that it involves the violation of an individual's expectations. This violation serves a clear function. It interrupts ongoing thought processes, and this interruption results in an involuntary focus of attention toward the surprising event. This process of selective attention leads to an evaluation of the event in terms of its implications for an individual's goals or well-being. A number of people argue that parts of the same emotion are stored or represented as an organized whole. Surprise, like most emotions, has, however, typically been studied in a piecemeal fashion. In this entry, the different features of surprise are considered with a view toward understanding this emotion in its entirety.

Toward a Common Understanding

Philosophy and psychology both provide conceptual frameworks with which to understand and approach the study of emotion. Philosophers working within the natural language tradition have, for example, presented clear definitions and examples concerning the way in which individuals use the word *surprise* to relate their own experiences of this emotion and to understand the experiences of others. Similarly, psychologists have characterized the defining features of surprise in terms of, for example, its eliciting conditions and expression. Psychological research has provided a significant amount of empirical evidence that shows how different aspects of surprise develop and vary across cultures.

Views from Philosophy

Philosophers in the tradition of natural language proposed that emotion terms are used only to highlight the logically necessary connections with other mental states. In other words, with emotion, people do not describe some internal state—they express different ways of being aware of the world. Anthony Kenny (1963), for example, argued that when people talk about emotions, a common understanding of the cause and outcome is assumed. To make the statement "I feel surprised" involves a shared understanding of the context surrounding this event. In this way, emotions are defined as intentional states; they are about or relate to events in the world. Surprise is defined as a response to an unexpected event. Robert Gordon (1987) argued, in this sense, that surprise is "backward looking" (p. 25) because it refers to situations that are occurring now or have occurred in the past. In relation to surprise, Gordon said, "A person is surprised that P [occurs] only if he *knows* or *believes* that P [should not occur]" (p. 36). He gives the example that "John is surprised (about the fact) that the plane arrived on time. This is only so if the plane's punctuality was at the time he learned of it contrary to his expectations" (p. 54). Therefore, in these philosophical analyses of what it means to use the word *surprise*, it is assumed that surprise results from an event that contradicts an individual's expectations or beliefs.

Gordon also raised the issue of specific beliefs versus general expectations about the world. In relation to the above example, Gordon discussed the possibility of John feeling surprised if he sees a meteorite fall in the road on his way to the airport. This event may be surprising, but John does not have a specific belief to the contrary regarding the occurrence of this event. Gordon therefore narrowed his definition of surprise to include only individuals' reactions to events when the individuals have a specific belief that something is true about the event and that belief is later discovered to be false. Other authors have addressed this issue. William Charlesworth (1969) compared surprise to novelty. He proposed that surprise involves precise expectations, while novel events are not preceded by any expectancies. Charlesworth argued that "the important point is that what makes an event surprising is that the individual mis-expects it, rather than does not expect it (as in the case of novelty) and that this expectation presupposes previous experience" (p. 275).

Consistent with these views, Donald Davidson (1982) recognized that surprise requires an awareness of a contrast between a current and revised belief. Davidson did, however, concede that some surprise "is a necessary and sufficient condition of thought in general" (p. 325). Individuals will feel surprised in situations where the specific beliefs they hold are violated. For example, a person might feel surprise if he or she thought a bag had been left on a specific chair but found out that it was not there. It also seems reasonable to expect a surprised reaction in situations that contradict common expectations. Such situations could involve violations of everyday events, such as an individual arriving at work to find that his or her office has been redecorated. Although the individual may not have any specific beliefs about this event, he or she can still feel surprise when it happens. Surprised reactions can also result from events that violate expectations about the ways of the world, including violations of physical laws, such as magical events.

These commonsense ideas about the context in which emotion words are used and understood have been viewed as intuitive or folk theories. Involving the ascription of beliefs and desires to explain the actions and reactions of others, these ideas are something that people develop as they get older.

Views from Psychology

Consistent with philosophical discussions of surprise as a reaction to an unexpected event, psychologists in the 1920s started to investigate surprise as a reaction to novel or unexpected stimuli. A number of psychologists, such as George Mandler (1984) and Richard Lazarus (1991), include cognitive appraisal as an important element in emotion. They argue that the way in which individuals appraise events determines the resulting emotion and provides meaning to physiological arousal and subjective experience. The ap-

---

William Faulkner's "A Rose for Emily" (1930) is narrated by an unnamed member of the community who, from a respectful distance, watches over an old lady, Miss Emily Grierson. The town knew that although she had once had a lover and planned to get married, the man had disappeared. When Miss Emily dies, after having stayed in her house with no visitors for more than fifty years, the whole town goes to her funeral. After the funeral, when the townspeople go through her house, they are surprised to find the man's decayed body lying in a double bed, with the indentation of another person's body still on the pillow next to him, along with a gray hair.

praisal process can be affected by many factors, including whether the event is expected or unexpected, whether the event is desirable or undesirable, and whether the event has implications for an individual's well-being and ability to cope. Other authors, such as Magda Arnold (1968), have emphasized the role of appraisal as part of a motivating system that prepares the individual for specific responses

Some psychologists have presented conceptual frameworks to structure emotion in terms of the underlying cognitive dimensions. Ira Roseman (1984) proposed a structural model of emotion that had six cognitive dimensions, one of which he referred to as "unexpectedness and bad tastes and smells" (p. 29). This dimension underpins surprise and disgust, where surprise results from an unexpected event. Similarly, Nancy Stein and Janet Jewett (1986) defined surprise as resulting from an unexpected or novel event. Klaus Scherer (1984) viewed emotion as resulting from "stimulus evaluation checks" (p. 306). The first of these checks, he proposed, relates to the novelty or unexpectedness of an event and predicts emotions such as boredom or surprise. The second check relates to whether the stimulus is pleasant or unpleasant. Scherer noted that it is possible to feel joyful at an unexpected event. He stated, however, that "it would be difficult to argue that the source of the joy is the unexpectedness rather than the conduciveness of the event to an affiliation need" (p. 57). In other words, joy stems from an evaluation of something being pleasant or unpleasant, not from something being expected or unexpected.

Some psychological studies have asked adults to describe what makes them feel happy, sad, surprised, and so on. Descriptions of surprise are consistent with both the philosophical and psychological conceptualizations presented above. In general, people consider surprise (in comparison to other emotions) to be more related to uncertainty, and they often describe surprising events as being unexpected. Wulf-Uwe Meyer and his colleagues (1991) took a more experimental approach in their study of surprise. They defined surprise as an emotion that is elicited by an event that deviates from a schema. Exploring schema-discrepant events experimentally, they showed that these events led to participants reporting more subjective experiences of surprise.

With regard to differences in the intensity of surprise, Stephen Peck (1987) discussed inconsequential and feigned surprise. He suggested that if an event is unusual, but has no real significance for an individual, any outward expression of surprise may be minimal (a simple raise of the eyebrows). Feigned surprise involves the raising of one eyebrow to communicate, for example, a message of reservation. At the other extreme, comparisons have been made between surprise and startle. Robert Plutchik (1980) argued that the level of intensity differentiates surprise and startle. Others have, however, argued that startle is more like a reflex than an emotion. Peck (1987) described startle as a reflex pattern where the eyes blink and the mouth is drawn apart into a wide grin. Paul Ekman (1984) also recognized that startle has a distinctive facial expression. He argued that unlike other emotional expressions, startle is difficult to stimulate. Consistent with the idea of startle as a reflex-like phenomenon, Ekman noted that it is difficult to inhibit startle. A further difference between surprise and startle stems from the eliciting conditions and subsequent actions. Charlesworth (1969) suggested that startle and surprise are primary reactions to sudden events, but the eliciting events for the two are quite different. Surprise is cognitive (resulting from something unexpected) and startle is sensory (resulting from a sudden and intense stimuli). In addition, Charlesworth argued that only surprise has a secondary reaction that directs the individual toward the eliciting event, with a view to further investigation. It is these processes of secondary attention that authors have highlighted as the function of surprise.

Psychologists have emphasized the role of surprise in updating beliefs. Michael Niepel and his colleagues (1994), for example, proposed that the function of surprise is to signal discrepancy to an individual, leading to an update of knowledge. He argued that individuals, by updating knowledge, are in a better position to predict and control their environment. Silvan Tomkins (1962) described surprise as a "general interrupter of ongoing activity" (p. 948). This interruption allows individuals to focus their attention on unexpected events, with a view to analyzing and evaluating these events. Similarly, Joachim Steinsmeier-Pelster and his colleagues (1995) suggested that the function of surprise is to prepare and motivate individuals to explore the surprise-eliciting event. They characterized this motivation as an action tendency that reflects cognitive curiosity. Whatever action individuals take, they suggest, will depend on the evaluation of the situation and its significance. Niepel and his colleagues proposed that the experiential, physiological, and behavioral components of surprise play some role in this function. Surprise has, therefore, been characterized as a transient reaction to an unexpected event, where this reaction is quickly replaced by emotions that reflect subsequent evaluations of the event.

Ekman and his colleagues (1983) commented on the transience of surprise. The initial surprise reaction to an unexpected event, they argued, will be quickly replaced by a negative or positive evaluation of this event. Therefore, the significance of the event to an individual's goals, rather than its unexpectedness, will determine the emotional outcome. (Ekman and his colleagues do note that surprise may be transient, but then most emotions only last between one-half and four seconds.) The notion that reactions to events are negative or positive depending on an individual's evaluation has led a group of researchers to question the status of surprise as an emotion. Andrew Ortony and his colleagues (1988) defined emotion as a valenced (i.e., positive or negative) reaction to some event. Since surprise is neither positive nor negative, they argue that is not an emotion. In their conceptualization of emotion, unexpectedness is referred to as a variable that affects the intensity of emotion. Surprise, they argue, is pure unexpectedness and could not, for example, be separated from a desired event (leading to happiness) or an undesirable event (leading to sadness). The example they give is a child who returns home from school to discover a new bike. Rather than feeling surprised (because the bike was unexpected) and then happy (because the evaluation of the situation is desirable and congruent with the child's goals), they suggested that the child will feel joyful and his joy will be increased because the event was unexpected. This desirable reaction, Ortony and his colleagues argued, can be more accurately characterized as a "pleasant surprise" and, its undesirable counterpart can be characterized as "shock."

Expressing Surprise

For those researchers who emphasize emotion as part of an adaptation process, expression plays a significant role. It is an important signal of internal state or subjective emotional experience, allowing people to communicate their own emotions and to understand the emotions of others.

Facial Expression

The distinctive facial emotion that is associated with surprise has led researchers to argue for surprise as a basic emotion. In 1872, Charles Darwin published his influential book *The Expression of the Emotions in Man and Animals*. In this publication, Darwin proposed that the facial expression of surprise allows individuals to see and to respond to novel events. Darwin's description of the facial expression of surprise is typical of the descriptions that are found in more recent literature: "Dr. Duchenne was given a photograph of an old man with his eyebrows well elevated and arched by the galvanisation of the frontal muscle; and with his mouth voluntarily open" (pp. 293–294). The rounded position of the mouth opens itself naturally with surprise, Darwin suggests, to allow the verbal expression of "oh"

A young boy looks surprised by what he sees on the screen as he and his father watch a movie together in a theater in Minneapolis, Minnesota. (Corbis/Layne Kennedy)

or "phew." Similarly, Peck (1987) asserts that the open mouth reflects the need to fill the lungs with air in response to an unexpected event. William James (1884) linked the characteristic raising of the eyebrows in surprise to its functional role of increased attention, allowing better vision, thereby reflecting the need for further investigation. It is the open eyes that sometimes leads to confusion with the facial expression of fear. Ekman's (1984) work has shown that adults are, however, generally competent at recognizing static facial expressions of surprise and discriminating these from other expressions. He has also found that movement can facilitate this recognition process.

The study of atypical populations has allowed researchers to investigate the potential neural substrates that underlie different emotions. Andrew Calder and his colleagues (1996), for example, described two patients who had bilateral amygdala damage. (The amygdala is believed to have a role in emotional recognition.) They showed impairment in the patients' recognition of fearful expressions, while the recognition of other emotions, including surprise, remained intact. On the basis of this result, Calder and his colleagues proposed that basic emotions have separate neural substrates. Simon Baron-Cohen and his colleagues (1993) investigated surprise in a different clinical group. They explored whether children with autism could recognize the facial expression surprise.

Children with autism have difficulty understanding belief. Since surprise is a belief-based emotion, the research question was whether this belief basis would have any negative effect on surprise recognition in children with autism. Relative to control groups, children with autism showed difficulties in matching one surprised expression to another. Such difficulties were not evident for happy and sad facial expressions. The finding of a specific deficit supports the results found by Calder and his colleagues, indicating that there are distinct neural substrates for different basic emotions.

Gestures

In addition to facial expression, emotions are typically associated with other characteristic behavioral responses. Darwin (1872) described bodily gestures that are linked with the emotion surprise: "a surprised person often raises his opened hands high above his head or by bending his arms only to the level of his face. The flat palms are directed towards the person who causes this feeling, and the straightened fingers are separated" (p. 302). Darwin's description of the surprise gesture is one that rings true. Studies that look at competence in recognizing and discriminating emotions on the basis of gesture are, however, scarce. In one study that compared visual and auditory cues for surprise and happiness and the visual and auditory cures for sadness and anger, Harald Wallbott and Scherer (1986) found that adults recognized gestures for some emotions better than for others. In this case, surprise was identified less accurately than were the other three emotions.

Cross-Cultural Perspectives

In describing the specific gesture of surprise, Darwin (1872) identified other gestures that were closely related to the expression of surprise in European cultures. These related gestures included whistling in surprise and placing the hand over the mouth in surprise. He also described related gestures that were peculiar to different cultures. Australian bushmen, for example, put their hands to their necks and bent their heads backward in surprise. One native Australian was said to have "protruded his lips, making a noise with his mouth as if blowing out a match" (p. 301). It is the diversity of behaviors across cultures that led Darwin to suggest that these gestures have specific cultural origins.

Ekman and his colleagues (1987), based on their cross-cultural investigations, have argued that "the evidence now for universality [of facial expression] is overwhelming and the evidence for cultural differences is sparse" (p. 717). Evidence for cross-cultural similarities in emotional meaning, however, is less well established. For example, in an early study, Ekman and Wallace Friesen (1971) asked New Guinean adults to match facial expressions to stories, and the participants failed to discriminate fear from surprise. Ekman and Friesen argued that fearful faces might not have been discriminated from surprise faces because fearful events in that particular culture were always surprising.

The Development of Surprise

Jean Piaget (1952) proposed that surprise plays a significant role in cognitive development. He argued that when infants experience novel events, the experiences are compared to stored schema, and through a process of accommodation, infants adapt their ways of thinking to these new experiences. Sensitivity to environmental stimulation that deviates from common expectations is reflected in increased "looking" in preverbal infants. In a series of studies, René Baillargeon (1994) showed that infants as young as three and four months of age will focus for longer periods on unusual events, in this case events that violate physical laws. It is likely that a surprise reaction preceded this increased looking, and this reaction led infants to focus their attention on these unexpected events in order to try to understand them.

Facial Expression

Adults have identified discrete facial expressions of surprise in the first three to six months of life. Carroll Izard and his colleagues (1980) use this evidence to support their argument for surprise as one of a set of basic hardwired emotions (the other emotions being anger, contempt, disgust, distress, fear, guilt, interest, joy, and shame). By the time they are six months of age, infants show clear surprise responses (brow flashes) to unexpected events. This pattern of development also serves to highlight further differences between surprise and startle. Surprise facial expressions are not seen until some weeks after birth. In comparison, startle responses can be elicited in the first days of life. Infants show an early ability to discriminate surprise facial expressions from happy expressions. In addition, adults are able to predict the facial expression that the infants are looking at from the infants' simultaneously expressive displays. For example, infants who are younger than one month show increased mouth opening when looking at surprise versus happy faces. It has been suggested, however, that infants at this age fixate more on the mouth region and it may not be until the second half of the first year that they discriminate emotions based on whole face configurations.

Infants' abilities to produce and discriminate facial expressions of emotion provide few clue as to what

Shirley Jackson, in "The Lottery" (1948), manages to include the reader in the community gathering, so that by the time the reader figures out something sinister is going on, the reader is already compromised. The story, thus, surprises not only the character who "wins" the lottery but also the reader who realizes he or she is participating in a scapegoat ritual that will cost the "winning" woman her life.

infants' experience when they themselves show facial expressions or how they interpret expressions of others. In the second half of the first year, studies have demonstrated, through a process of social referencing, that infants use caregivers' facial expressions to guide their own actions. With age and the development of language, studies have shown that children, when given the verbal label surprise, can match this label to the facial expression surprise. This recognition develops at around three to four years of age (a relatively late development compared with the recognition of happy and sad faces when they are two years of age). It is not until much later that children show competence in producing a label for surprise expressions. Michael Lewis (1989) found, for example, that few five-year-old children could produce a label for this expression. Pamelyn MacDonald, Sue Kirkpatrick, and Laurie Sullivan (1996) asked children to construct emotional expressions from face parts. They found that more than half of the children who were between three and five years of age chose a smiling mouth for surprised expressions, and one child even described their surprised construction as a "happy surprised face" (p. 77). Conceptual confusion between happiness and surprise is a common and recurring theme in the development of surprise.

During the second and third years of life, children begin to talk about their own emotional world and the emotional worlds of others. Inge Bretherton and Marjorie Beeghly (1982) examined, using maternal report, the level of understanding that children have when they discuss emotional states. At around 2.5 years of age, one-tenth of the children were reported to use the word *surprise* (compared to six-tenths who used the word *happy*). During the preschool years, children's talk about the emotions that are experienced by themselves and by others increases, as do references to causes and consequences of emotions.

Situational Knowledge

Martin Conway and Deborah Bekerian (1987) pointed out that, relative to cognitive appraisal, situational knowledge of emotion has received little attention. They proposed that some emotional experiences could be predicted on the basis of situational knowledge. For example, people feel sad at funerals, happy when they receive a gift, surprised when they see a magic trick, and so on. Conway and Bekerian argued that if events can be clearly linked to emotions, then individuals' knowledge of these situations is an important component of their emotional life. In relation to surprise, the focus of interest in developmental psychology has been to study children's emerging ability to link surprised faces to relevant situations. Often, situations of surprise contain violations of general expectations about the world. For example, surprise situations have been depicted as a mother with pink hair, monkeys inside an ice-box, and a tower rebuilding itself. Children from around four to five years of age match these situations competently with the relevant surprised facial expression.

False Beliefs and Surprise Judgments

Conceptual frameworks in philosophy and psychology proposed that surprise results from a misrepresentation of reality. In order to feel surprise, individuals must hold a belief that is false. If children are to understand surprise, then they must develop an understanding that people can misrepresent reality. Research has shown that children understand false belief when they are three to four years of age. However, even when children understand belief, they do not use this understanding to either predict or to understand surprise. Rick MacLaren and David Olson (1993) found that children who were four to five years of age conceptualized surprise as something desirable, rather than as a reaction to something unexpected. Understanding surprise as a reaction to belief violation emerges at around five to six years of age. Henry Wellman (1992) suggested that children's early understanding of surprise as being something that is desirable reflects their early experience of this emotion. Children are more likely to experience unexpected events within a pleasant context. Even though surprise can be pleasant or unpleasant, Wellman found that surprise references in parents' speech tended to refer to positive experiences (e.g., "I have a surprise for you," before giving a child a present). The prevalence of references to surprise as being pleasant may stem from children's own emotional experiences or parents' early socialization of this emotion.

See also: BODY MOVEMENT, GESTURE, AND DISPLAY; CROSS-CULTURAL PATTERNS; DARWIN, CHARLES ROBERT; DISGUST; FACIAL EXPRESSION; FOLK THEORIES OF EMOTION; HAPPINESS; HUMAN DEVELOPMENT; JAMES, WILLIAM; SOCIOLOGY OF EMOTIONS

Bibliography

Arnold, Magda B., ed. (1968). *The Nature of Emotion*. New York: Penguin.

Baillargeon, René. (1994). "Physical Reasoning in Young Infants: Seeking Explanations for Impossible Events." *British Journal of Developmental Psychology* 12:9–34.

Baron-Cohen, Simon; Spitz, Amy; and Cross, Pippa. (1993). "Do Children with Autism Recognise Surprise?" *Cognition and Emotion* 7:507–516.

Bretherton, Inge, and Beeghly, M. (1982). "Talking about Internal States: The Acquisition of an Explicit Theory of Mind." *Developmental Psychology* 18:906–921.

Calder, Andrew J.; Young, Andrew; Rowland, Duncan; Perrett, David; Hodges, John R.; and Etcoff, Nancy L. (1996). "Facial Emotion Recognition after Bilateral Amygdala Damage: Differentially Severe Impairment of Fear." *Cognitive Neuropsychology* 13:699–745.

Charlesworth, William R. (1969). "The Role of Surprise in Cognitive Development." In *Studies in Cognitive Development: Essays in Honor of Jean Piaget*, ed. David Elkind and John H. Flavell. New York: Oxford University Press.

Conway, Martin A., and Bekerian, Deborah A. (1987). "Situational Knowledge and Emotion." *Cognition and Emotion* 1:145–191.

Darwin, Charles. (1872). *The Expression of the Emotions in Man and Animals*. London: John Murray.

Davidson, Donald. (1982). "Rational Animals." *Dialectica* 36: 318–327.

Ekman, Paul. (1984). "Expression and the Nature of Emotion." In *Approaches to Emotion*, ed. Klaus Scherer and Paul Ekman. Hillsdale, NJ: Lawrence Erlbaum.

Ekman, Paul, and Friesen, Wallace V. (1971). "Constants across Cultures in the Face and Emotion." *Journal of Personality and Social Psychology* 17:124–129.

Ekman, Paul; Friesen, Wallace V.; O'Sullivan, Maureen; Chan, Anthony; Diacoyanni-Tarlatzis, Irene; Heider, Karl; Krause, Rainer; LeCompte, William Ayhan; Pitcairn, Tom; Ricci-Bitti, Pio E.; Scherer, Klaus; Tomita, Masatoshi; and Tzavaras, Anthanase. (1987). "Universals and Cultural Differences in the Judgements of Facial Expressions of Emotion." *Journal of Personality and Social Psychology* 53:712–717.

Ekman, Paul; Levenson, Robert W.; Friesen, Wallace V. (1983). "Autonomic Nervous System Activity Distinguishes among Emotions." *Science* 221:1208–1210.

Gordon, Robert M. (1987). *The Structure of Emotions: Investigations in Cognitive Philosophy*. Cambridge, Eng.: Cambridge University Press.

Izard, Carroll E.; Huebner, Robin R.; Risser, Daniele; McGinnes, G. C.; and Dougherty, Linda M. (1980). "The Young Infant's Ability to Produce Discrete Facial Expressions." *Developmental Psychology* 16:132–140.

James, William. (1884). "What Is an Emotion?" *Mind* 9:188–205.

Kenny, Anthony. (1963). *Action, Emotion, and Will*. London: Routledge and Kegan Paul.

Lazarus, Richard S. (1991). *Emotion and Adaptation*. New York: Oxford University Press.

Lewis, Michael. (1989). "Cultural Differences in Children's Understanding of Knowledge Scripts." In *Children's Understanding of Emotion*, ed. Carolyn Saarni and Paul L. Harris. Cambridge, Eng.: Cambridge University Press.

MacDonald, Pamelyn M.; Kirkpatrick, Sue W.; and Sullivan, Laurie Ann. (1996). "Schematic Drawings of Facial Expressions for Emotion Recognition and Interpretation by Pre-School-Aged Children." *Genetic, Social, and General Psychology Monographs* 122:375–388.

MacLaren, Rick, and Olson, David. (1993). "Trick or Treat: Children's Understanding of Surprise." *Cognitive Development* 8:27–46.

Mandler, George. (1984). *Mind and Body: Psychology of Emotion and Stress*. New York: W. W. Norton.

Meyer, Wulf-Uwe; Niepel, Michael; Rudolph, Udo; and Schutzwohl, Achim. (1991). "An Experimental Analysis of Surprise." *Cognition and Emotion* 5:295–311.

Niepel, Michael; Rudolph, Udo; Schutzwohl, Achim; and Meyer, Wulf-Uwe. (1994). "Temporal Characteristics of the Surprise Reaction Induced by Schema-Discrepant Visual and Auditory Events." *Cognition and Emotion* 8:433–452.

Ortony, Andrew; Clore, Gerald L.; and Collins, Allan. (1988). *The Cognitive Structure of Emotions*. Cambridge, Eng.: Cambridge University press.

Peck, Stephen R. (1987). *Atlas of Facial Expression*. Oxford, Eng.: Oxford University press.

Piaget, Jean. (1952). *The Origin of Intelligence in Children*. New York: Harcourt Brace.

Plutchik, Robert. (1980). *Emotion: A Psychoevolutionary Synthesis*. New York: Harper & Row.

Roseman, Ira J. (1984). "Cognitive Determinants of Emotion: A Structural Theory." In *Review of Personality and Social Psychology, Vol. 5: Emotions, Relationships, and Health*, ed. Phillip Shaver. Beverly Hills, CA: Sage Publications.

Scherer, Klaus R. (1984). "On the Nature and Function of Emotion: A Component Process Approach." In *Approaches to Emotion*, ed. Klaus R. Scherer and Paul Ekman. Hillsdale, NJ: Lawrence Erlbaum.

Stein, Nancy L., and Jewett, Janet L. (1986). "A Conceptual Analysis of the Meaning of Negative Emotions." In *Measuring Emotions in Infants and Children, Vol. 2*, ed. Carroll E. Izard and Peter B. Read. Cambridge, Eng.: Cambridge University Press.

Steinsmeier-Pelster, Joachim; Martini, Alice; and Reisenzein, Rainer. (1995). "The Role of Surprise in the Attribution Process." *Cognition and Emotion* 9:5–31.

Tomkins, Silvan S. (1962). *Affect, Imagery, Consciousness, Vol. 1: The Positive Affects*. New York: Springer.

Wallbott, Harald G., and Scherer, Klaus R. (1986). "Cues and Channels in Emotion Recognition." *Journal of Personality and Social Psychology* 4:690–699.

Wellman, Henry M. (1992). *The Child's Theory of Mind*. Cambridge: Massachusetts Institute of Technology Press.

Julie A. Hadwin

SYMPATHY

In 1739, philosopher David Hume wrote the following in *A Treatise of Human Nature:*

> No quality of human nature is more remarkable, both in itself and in its consequences, than that propensity we have to sympathize with others, and to receive by communication their inclinations and sentiments, however different from, or even contrary to our own.

Hume recognized that sympathy—that often-experienced surge of concern or compassion for others' troubles—is an extraordinary, and an extraordinarily social, emotion. It takes two: *one* to feel for *another's* plight. It requires people to make imaginative leaps into what others are thinking and feeling and to care about their pain and problems. Humans have a greater capacity for making these imaginative leaps than any other species. Furthermore, sympathy has enormous potential for motivating people to help each other, thereby cementing social ties and helping to make society possible.

To Hume, sympathy seemed to be a natural, reflexive reaction. Yet research shows that people are not born knowing when, for whom, and in what circumstances sympathy is appropriate. Rather, they learn elaborate, highly specific cultural rules—different rules for men than for women—that guide when to feel or display sympathy, when to claim it, and how to accept it. As people follow these rules—referred to by Arlie Hochschild (1979) as "feeling rules"—for how to give and receive sympathy, they create webs of interaction that can bind them together. In this way, sympathy give-and-take contributes to the cohesion of relationships, communities, and society as a whole. The rules guiding sympathy give-and-take in Western society today are not the same as they were in the past, and they are not the same as in other societies. To understand sympathy processes in contemporary society, one must first understand the power that cultural rules and beliefs have to shape and guide sympathy.

Culture and Sympathy

Anthropologist Colin Turnbull's (1972) study of the Ik, a small society in central Africa, uncovered sympathy rules that contrast markedly with Western rules. Turnbull lived with the Ik after they had been relocated from their familiar farmlands to hilly territory where it proved impossible to find enough food for the group. As the Ik moved closer to starvation, they developed an unsympathetic approach to life: feel sorry for no one. They were once a kindhearted and gentle people, but laughter came to be their automatic reaction to others' troubles. In Turnbull's words, "misfortune of others was their greatest joy" (p. 260). They sent their children away to forage for themselves at about age three, and they joked about those who were hungry or hurt. They laughed at the elderly and the infirm who fell or injured themselves. Turnbull, a highly educated person trained to study cultures without accepting their way of life, eventually found himself adopting the Ik's unsympathetic approach to others' troubles. When he realized that he himself had started laughing when he saw an elderly or blind person who was injured or ill, he felt personally the phenomenal power of cultural rules to shape human emotions.

Another example of variation in the cultural rules governing sympathy comes from anthropologist Nancy Scheper-Hughes. In her book *Death without Weeping* (1992), Scheper-Hughes describes an emotional culture among the impoverished inhabitants of the Alto do Cruzeiro region in northwest Brazil. Alto women, themselves suffering from malnutrition, bore as many as ten or more babies. Fewer than half of the children survived. When an infant was sick, mothers and other family members did not feel sympathy for them or try to help them get well. Instead, they distributed the family's meager supplies of food and clothing to older, healthier children who had a better chance of survival. As Scheper-Hughes explained, "In a world of great uncertainty about life and death it makes no sense at all to put any *one* person—not a parent, not a husband or lover, and certainly not a sickly toddler or fragile infant—at the center of anything" (p. 403). When an infant died, no one cried at the burial. Their cultural view held that tears would slow a dead infant's journey to heaven. Nothing could be further from the typical American reaction to a child's illness or death.

Lest value judgments about Alto or Ik culture be made, one should also realize that throughout the twentieth century both Europeans and Americans engaged in a great deal of brutality and heartlessness, often fueled by ethnic animosities. And as Philippe Ariès (1962) and John Boswell (1988) have reported, until the late 1800s, adult-centered Western European families abandoned about a third of their children to almost certain death working in factories or wandering the streets. In the child-centered family that evolved during the twentieth century, many parental practices that formerly would have been routine and not given a second thought (e.g., corporal punishment and shaming) came to be labeled negatively as abusiveness. Yet even though it is now viewed negatively, "child abuse" is quite common. Thus, Westerners are sometimes cruel and unsympathetic too.

The Ik and the Alto do Cruzeiro mothers show that sympathetic reactions to others' troubles are not dictated by "nature" but rather are heavily influenced by culture. Understanding how sympathy flows among people in Western society requires paying attention to feeling rules. Candace Clark (1997) has studied these rules using surveys that elicit responses to stories of unexpected troubles, interviews, observations in settings such as hospitals and funeral parlors, and analyses of novels, greeting cards, charity appeals, blues lyrics, the Bible, and media reports. These studies have shown that historically, the grounds for sympathy in Western societies were limited to extreme poverty, severe illness, bereavement, natural disasters, and other serious life-altering and life-threatening events. However, a host of new grounds for sympathy has become accepted during the twentieth century. Many of these grounds have been set forth by newly emerging professions, such as medicine, psychology, sociology, economics, and social work. For example, most societal members once held to a belief in social Darwinism, viewing poverty as the result of poor people's laziness or incompetence. Today, many societal members view the poor as victims of an economic system that creates a "blocked opportunity structure." Once, disobedient or disruptive school children were viewed as bad or even evil; nowadays they are called hyperactive, victims of troubled families, or psychologically troubled. In other words, the cultural ways of looking at many plights have allowed an increasingly sympathetic "spin." Charity organizers, the greeting card industry, etiquette-book writers, spokespeople for twelve-step programs, and many others have taken up these new constructions of people's plights and instruct the public about what are the acceptable grounds for sympathy. For example, in the "Neediest Cases" charity drive, which has been sponsored by the *New York Times* since 1912, problems such as drug addiction, drinking, or divorce were never mentioned in case histories printed in the early years of the twentieth century. Beginning in the 1960s and 1970s, however, the *Times* featured people with these problems and others, including abusing their children and gambling, presenting them as sympathy-worthy cases. Also, greeting card manufacturers used to market cards primarily for illness and the loss of family members. Of late, they have added lines of cards for the death of pets, being the child of divorced parents, growing old (anything over thirty years of age), "having a bad day," having a demanding boss, and feeling "blue."

Thus, although humans have an extraordinary capacity for sympathy, cultural prescriptions determine the kinds of plights and people that actually elicit that sympathy. In modern society, with its increased standard of living, even minor problems are viewed as important, and the accepted grounds for giving and getting sympathy have escalated.

The Sympathy Process

Social science researchers do not all agree about what constitutes sympathy, how and why it arises, or how it functions in human society. They sometimes use different words to refer to what is being discussed in this entry as sympathy (e.g., compassion, empathy, synesic role-taking, and pity). However, most psycho-logical researchers do agree that sympathy can encompass a combination of cognitive, affective, and physiological factors. Sociological researchers emphasize, in addition, behaviors that overtly express or display to others a person's inner orientations. All of these elements are shaped and guided by cultural feeling rules that vary from one society to another and from one historical period to another.

Rather than get tangled up in definitions, the term *sympathy* is used here in the way that most Americans use it in everyday conversation. In common usage, sympathy encompasses a group of negative feelings (e.g., concern, sadness, indignation, fear, or worry) and actions (e.g., somber facial expressions, soothing gestures, and gingerly treatment) that one person may direct toward another who is experiencing trouble, suffering, or some sort of bad luck. Americans rarely use the English word *sympathy* to refer to positive emotions one person feels for another's joy, success, or good fortune, although words for sympathy in other languages include such positive emotions.

The sympathizing process begins with empathy, or role-taking—putting oneself in another's situation. It is humans' ability to empathize—to imagine what another person is feeling—that makes sympathy possible. However, empathy does not necessarily lead to sympathy—or to any emotions. A person can, like the Alto do Cruzeiro mothers or many modern day citizens passing homeless people on city streets, look on impassively at another's suffering. Or, as with the Ik, empathy can lead to such feelings as *schadenfreude* (i.e., glee at another's misfortune). A torturer empathizes with a victim's pain but enjoys it. Sometimes, though, empathy leads to sympathy sentiment, feelings that to some extent mirror the negative emotions an unfortunate person is undergoing.

When people do not feel sympathy for the plights of others, they may be engaging in an alternative mental set that social psychologist Melvin Lerner (1980) has called "belief in a just world." Lerner described this mental set as a tendency to blame victims or to discredit and devalue people who experience misfortune. He concluded that when two cognitions (thoughts) are incongruous or "dissonant," people who "believe in a just world" alter one cognition—a neutral or positive opinion of a person—to fit the other cognition—that the person finds him- or herself in a negative situation. Lerner's research has shown that people are more likely to alter their opinions of unfortunate people than to experience the sometimes painful feelings that make up sympathy.

When empathy does lead to sympathy, people may experience sympathy sentiment in many ways. Sympathy sentiment may be acute (for a sudden problem) or chronic (for persistent feelings about another per-

An outpouring of sympathy following the death of Diana, Princess of Wales, in September 1997 was manifested in a sea of floral tributes that continued to be amassed outside of the gates of Kensington Palace, her London home, from soon after the news of her death broke until after her funeral. (Corbis/Christopher Cormack)

son's long-term plight). One may feel one's "heart going out" to a bereaved person. An angry, indignant feeling may result from learning of a case of unjust treatment. Or, one may feel a gut-wrenching shock of horror or dread at hearing of another person's illness or accident. Sometimes, of course, sympathy is experienced as a mere twinge of discomfort quickly extinguished.

Furthermore, at times sympathy is not experienced emotionally or physiologically at all. In these cases, a person merely experiences a cognitive understanding that someone is having a problem. A man who worked in New York City as an executive for an international textile-manufacturing corporation gave this illustration to Clark (1997, p. 36):

> I'm walking over to the bus terminal one night and there's a guy, basically a derelict, lying on the sidewalk with his head bleeding and two policemen within ten feet of the guy. I go over to the policemen and I say, "Hey, you've got a guy lying over here and he could be bleeding to death. Aren't you going to do something?" I didn't go

over there and lean down and try to dress his wounds. I did something, but not a real positive something, for him. Did I think about him five minutes later? Probably not.

The executive sympathized, but he did not connect with the derelict's pains or fears. Instead he viewed his plight from a mental distance.

Beyond empathizing and feeling sympathy sentiment, the *display* of sympathy is an important step in the sympathizing process. Western culture includes rules for displaying sympathy in certain situations, rules that people may follow even when they *do not feel* sorry for another. People believe sympathy to be an emotional gift, but they also believe they owe this gift to others in times of trouble. One sends a greeting card, flowers, or candy to a hospitalized friend or neighbor. One puts on a concerned facial expression when listening to a family member's troubles. One tut-tuts when a coworker describes a run-in with the boss. All of these displays can occur without the sympathizer feeling anything.

Some people might say that this kind of surface sympathy is not sympathy at all. Yet surface sympathy is a meaningful recognition of the hurt or worry of the person experiencing a problem. It symbolizes connection and closeness, a social bond. In this way surface sympathy can serve to forge a new relationship or keep an existing relationship going. Sometimes it can even lead the sympathizer to genuine sentiment. Etiquette expert Judith Martin provided a case in point in *Miss Manners' Guide to Rearing Perfect Children* (1984). In response to a letter from the parents of a seven-year-old boy who refused to let him visit an injured friend because he wanted to gawk, she wrote,

> Miss Manners disagrees with your decision not to allow your child to visit his friend because his motives were not noble. Send him off with strict instructions to pretend to be sympathetic with the illness, but apparently not unduly curious. (Some interest in the nature of the illness is usually agreeable to patients.) Perhaps his sympathies will truly be aroused. . . . He still will have done better by his friend than he would have by ignoring the friend. Form comes first, . . . and while one hopes that feeling will follow, going through the form well without it is more acceptable . . . than eschewing the form because the feeling is not there [p. 322].

Western cultural feeling rules call on women to handle much of the display work in the family, the community, and the workplace. For instance, women send the majority of sympathy cards and flowers to hospital patients. Observations at funerals show that men often linger at the back of the room, while women actively engage the bereaved in sympathetic conversation. For men, then, sympathy is often more of an interior process of empathy and sentiment. For women, the display aspect of sympathy is important.

Thus, sympathy can consist of empathy plus sentiment and display, empathy plus sentiment (interior sympathy), or empathy plus display (surface sympathy). Empathizing, feeling sympathy sentiment, and

Richard Selzer, in "Toenails" (1982), tells of a physician who takes his Wednesday afternoons off at the local library, where several elderly citizens also spend their time. The doctor notices that one of the old men is limping badly and discovers that the man's toenails, which he can no longer reach, have grown around under his foot and are cutting into his skin. The doctor takes the old man to the restroom, where he spends more than an hour trimming and filing until the man can walk normally. He then does the same sympathetic treatment for all of the other older people who frequent the library reading room.

displaying sympathy all cost time, emotional energy, and sometimes money. It is for these reasons that people consider their sympathy an emotional gift. And they often expect returns for their gifts. Recipients cannot count on others' unlimited gifts of sympathy. A concept that helps make sense of the limits to sympathy give-and-take is sympathy margin, or an account of sympathy credits that one person makes available for another.

Sympathy Margin and Sympathy Etiquette

In everyday life, people do not give their gifts of sympathy constantly or indiscriminately. Each person holds in reserve a limited number of "sympathy credits" to give to another in cases of misfortune. A person who has a sympathy "account" with another can "collect" some sympathy in appropriate circumstances. Although a sympathy margin "belongs" to one individual, it exists only because someone else has created it. The number of credits a person can count on depends on his or her social value and history of dealing with sympathy in the past. However, no matter how many credits a person has on account—how large the sympathy margins that family and friends hold—he or she can exhaust them much as one can exceed a credit limit or overdraw an account at the bank. When one person gives another sympathy for a problem, the recipient has fewer sympathy credits available in case of later misfortunes. Once a person cashes in all the sympathy credits another person has been holding on account, the other may react to future predicaments with indifference.

Claiming, receiving, owing, and giving sympathy are subject to an intricate etiquette. Following Western culture's sympathy etiquette allows people to maintain and rebuild their sympathy margins. This sympathy etiquette has four main rules:

1. Do not make false claims to sympathy. Like the boy in Aesop's fable who "cried wolf" when no wolves were threatening him, people who manufacture problems merely to get sympathy soon exceed their sympathy margins. Others become reluctant to offer sympathy when legitimate plights occur.
2. (a) Do not claim sympathy too long or too often. Even when one's plights are legitimate, claiming sympathy too long for a particular plight or for too many problems can diminish margins.
   (b) Do not accept sympathy too readily. One should not ask for sympathy openly, but instead should appear to face life's problems bravely and not "wallow in pity."

3. Claim some sympathy to keep accounts open. People who never allow others to give them sympathy may appear too lofty or too fortunate to get sympathy when they need it and want it. They may find that others have not opened sympathy margins for them.

4. Reciprocate to others for their gifts of sympathy with deference, gratitude, or sympathy. Because giving emotional gifts such as sympathy costs people time, energy, and money, repaying these gifts—even if only with an expression of thanks—acknowledges the sympathizer's efforts and balances sympathy margins. When a person reciprocates with sympathy, he or she not only expresses concern and caring for another, but also accrues sympathy credits.

Of course, these rules for potential recipients of sympathy imply a basic rule for potential sympathizers: Do not "waste pity" on those who are undeserving or do not appreciate gifts.

The gift relationship is inherently unequal and especially so when the gift is sympathy. The person who gives a gift is in a "superior" position because the recipient is put in a position of owing gratitude or future gifts. In the case of sympathy, the recipient also has more problems than the donor—or sympathy would not have been appropriate in the first place. Over time, if people pay and repay gifts of sympathy, they are tied together in webs of reciprocity. However, sympathy has a darker and less obvious side. People can use it to gain power over others in everyday encounters. In these cases, sympathy recipients may feel belittled and hurt. When it points out people's problems or their inability to handle those problems and puts people in a position of owing a return, a show of sympathy can humiliate or diminish the recipient.

See also: EMOTIONAL ABUSE; EMPATHY; FRIENDSHIP; GIFT GIVING; GRIEF; HUME, DAVID; INTIMACY

Bibliography

Ariès, Philippe. (1962). *Centuries of Childhood: A Social History of Family Life,* tr. Robert Baldock. New York: Knopf.

Boswell, John. (1988). *The Kindness of Strangers: The Abandonment of Children in Western Europe from Late Antiquity to the Renaissance.* New York: Pantheon.

Clark, Candace. (1997). *Misery and Company: Sympathy in Everyday Life.* Chicago: University of Chicago Press.

Hochschild, Arlie Russell. (1979). "Emotion Work, Feeling Rules, and Social Structure." *American Journal of Sociology* 85: 551–575.

Hochschild, Arlie Russell. (1983). *The Managed Heart: Commercialization of Human Feeling.* Berkeley: University of California Press.

Hoffman, Martin L. (1978). "Psychological and Biological Perspectives on Altruism." *International Journal of Behavioral Development* 1:323–339.

Lauer, Robert H., and Warren H. Handel. (1983). *Social Psychology: The Theory and Application of Symbolic Interactionism,* 2nd ed. Englewood Cliffs, NJ: Prentice-Hall.

Lazarus, Richard. (1994). "Universal Antecedents of the Emotions." In *The Nature of Emotion,* ed. by Paul Ekman and Richard J. Davidson. New York: Oxford University Press.

Lerner, Melvin J. (1980). *The Belief in a Just World: A Fundamental Delusion.* New York: Plenum.

Martin, Judith. (1984). *Miss Manners' Guide to Rearing Perfect Children.* New York: Atheneum.

Scheper-Hughes, Nancy. (1992). *Death without Weeping.* Berkeley: University of California Press.

Turnbull, Colin M. (1972). *The Mountain People.* New York: Simon & Schuster.

Candace Clark

T

TEACHING

See Education and Teaching

TEMPERAMENT

Temperament refers to one's disposition toward experiencing and expressing emotions, as well as one's general level of activity and attentional control of emotions and actions. Although there is a rich history of temperament research, the specific characteristics listed for temperament have not been consistent across different studies. Still, there is considerable agreement about the genetic origin, stability, and early evidence for a set of these characteristics. In addition, research is increasingly moving toward agreement on a short list of temperament dimensions, including individual differences in positive emotions (e.g., smiling, laughter), approach/extraversion (e.g., rapid responses, preference for novelty, and ease in new social situations), fear/behavioral inhibition (e.g., delayed/slow responses, negative emotions associated with novelty), irritability or frustration (e.g., negative emotions associated with blocked goals, interruptions of activities), and two aspects of attention, reactive (orienting) and regulatory (effortful or executive control). Orienting attention involves direction of attentional focus, whereas effortful control refers to voluntary/willful regulation of attention and behavior.

Research and Classification

Research addressing genetic influences on the development of temperament has generated considerable evidence of heritability (i.e., genetic contributions). Greater temperamental similarity has been found for identical twins than for fraternal twins on many aspects of temperament, which suggests that there is a significant genetic influence on temperamental characteristics. Because considerable similarity between twins who have been separated from birth would also suggest a significant genetic contribution to temperament, some researchers have also evaluated samples of twins reared together and twins reared apart. An influential report by Auke Tellegen and his colleagues (1988) found more similarity for identical than for fraternal twins on negative emotionality (neuroticism) and constraint (fear and effortful control). Considerable heritability was reported for positive emotionality as well (although environmental effects were also significant for this dimension of temperament). These differences were found both when twins had been reared together from an early age and when twins had been separated and reared in different families. Behavioral genetics research by H. Hill Goldsmith, Kristin Buss, and Kathryn Lemery (1997) also has shown substantial similarity between identical twins on a variety of temperamental characteristics, with lower similarity for fraternal twins.

Psychobiological research on temperament also includes studies of the neural differences in activation of the two hemispheres of the human brain (associated with approach versus withdrawal behavior) and studies of the physiological changes that are associated with temperament reactions and self-regulatory activities. In addition, studies addressing behavioral marker tasks for neural activity, such as conflict tasks used to evaluate flexibility of responding, have also been conducted. Nathan Fox and Richard Davidson (1984) proposed that the brain's left hemisphere is associated with approach and positive affect and that the right hemisphere is associated with negative affect and avoidance processes. They further suggested that toward the end of the first year of life the inhibition of the right hemisphere by the left hemisphere becomes possible and leads to a decrease in the level of negative affect. A number of studies have confirmed the association between right hemisphere activation and negative affect.

Other lines of research have used behavioral indicators to identify and classify dimensions of temperament. Alexander Thomas and Stella Chess (1977), through parent interviews, identified the following nine interrelated dimensions of temperament with the New York Longitudinal Study (NYLS): activity level, approach/withdrawal, adaptability, mood, threshold, intensity, distractibility, rhythmicity, and attention span/persistence.

The interdependence of the nine dimensions of temperament proposed by Thomas and Chess led to some difficulties in constructing scales to measure these characteristics. Generally, when constructing scales (i.e., subsets of questions or items) to measure different characteristics, the goal is to produce scales that are relatively independent of each other. That is, how a parent rates his or her child on activity should be independent of how he or she responds to questions that address intensity. However, when the scales measure overlapping constructs, this differentiation of scales cannot be achieved. As a result, other researchers have constructed scales that can effectively measure a shorter list of six temperament dimensions: positive emotions, approach/extraversion, fear/behavioral inhibition, irritability or frustration, reactive attention, and regulatory attention.

Personality and Temperament

Research addressing the dimensions of temperament in childhood also suggests possible links with studies of adult personality. Investigations of children's temperament frequently reveal broad factors consistent with the so-called Big Five factors reported in research with adults: extraversion, agreeableness, conscientiousness, neuroticism, and intellect/imagination. Extraversion, which is related to approach tendencies, involves positive emotion, high levels of talk-ativeness and assertiveness, and low levels of passivity and hesitation. Agreeableness is related to high levels of trust and warmth and low levels of hostility and selfishness. Conscientiousness is associated with high levels of organization and thoroughness and low levels of carelessness and negligence. Neuroticism is associated with more frequent episodes of moodiness and nervousness and less frequent episodes of calmness and stability. The intellect/imagination factor involves high levels of creativity and curiosity and low levels of shallowness and disinterest. John Digman and Alexander Shmelyov (1996) linked child temperament attributes of Russian children between eight and ten years of age to four of the Big Five personality factors: extraversion, agreeableness, conscientiousness, and neuroticism. Mary Rothbart and John Bates (1998) described a negative affectivity factor reported in studies of children as being similar to the neuroticism factor demonstrated in adult research. Positive affect/approach in children was described as being similar to extroversion. Factors of persistence, self-regulation, and effortful control reported for children may be related to the adult dimension of conscientiousness.

There are important differences, however, between concepts of temperament and personality. First, temperament traits emerge in infancy and early childhood, while personality characteristics emerge later in development. Second, the personality domain includes many more characteristics (e.g., self-concept, attitudes, expectations, and preferred coping strategies) than does temperament. Infant's and young children's temperamental attributes form building blocks for personality, but additional personality characteristics will develop with maturation and experience. For example, individual differences in positive emotion (smiling and laughter) that are discernible at six months of age are related to differences in approach tendencies, sensation seeking, activity level, and lack of shyness later in childhood. Preschool children who exhibit strong approach tendencies often become adolescents who tend to be impulsive and effective in social contexts. Measures of fear and frustration tend to be positively related to each other and stable during the early part of the first year of life. These behavioral tendencies become differentiated toward the end of the first year, with the emergence of fearful behavioral inhibition. Jerome Kagan (1994, 1998) has studied extensively the children who show the highest levels of inhibition of their approach behavior at this point in their development. These individuals tend to continue to exhibit fearful and shy behavior later in childhood, although not all children who are described as being inhibited as infants continue to demonstrate the inhibited approach as they grow older. The anger/frustration dimension appears to be related to the approach systems, being activated by blocked reward, and is linked with aggressive behaviors. Evaluations of temperament are informative of individual differences in emotional processing and evaluation of experience, given that a particular stimulus provides different emotional experiences for children who vary in temperament. Thus, temperamental dispositions can affect the nature of social learning and the development of attitudes and expectations, thereby contributing to the development of personality.

Difficult Temperament

Thomas and Chess (1977) introduced the term *difficult temperament* to serve as a label for irregularity of biological functions, withdrawal from new/unfamiliar stimuli, slow adaptability, intensity of mood, and frequent negative mood. This combination of temperamental attributes was seen to make child rearing more difficult for most parents. In later work by temperament researchers, the classification of difficult temperament was expanded to include any child who poses considerable challenges to parents because of any number of characteristics. Children included in this category have been shown to be at risk for the development of behavior problems in a number of investigations. One problem with the classification is that the term *difficult* represents a value judgment imposed on a particular behavior by the observer—behavior that is perceived to be difficult in one situation may not be perceived to be difficult in another. For example, a child's ability to maintain an attentional focus is generally construed to be a positive characteristic. If a parent is attempting to get the child's attention, however, and the child is not responsive because he or she is concentrating on a particular activity, difficulty may ensue for the parent. Thomas and Chess also argue that a temperamental characteristic seen as being positive at one age (e.g., the distractible and easily soothed infant) may be seen as being difficult at another (e.g., the school-age child who is unable to focus on assigned tasks). Different conceptualizations and measures of difficult temperament have thus emerged in the literature. Although these conceptualizations generally overlap to some extent, they are not identical, so caution should be used in making comparisons across studies.

Social Interaction and Temperament

Kagan (1998) has adapted temperamental characteristics of fear and approach into a temperamental classification, assigning children to inhibited and uninhibited categories and demonstrating differences between these groups. Inhibited children can also be described as shy, cautious, and fearful. Uninhibited children tend to be social and outgoing (extraverted) in new situations, and they do not show as much motor restraint as inhibited children. Kagan and his colleagues have reported a number of physiological differences between inhibited and uninhibited children (e.g., higher, more stable heart rates and higher levels of cortisol for inhibited children), and they see this classification system as reflecting underlying biological differences. However, this classification scheme creates a number of unresolved issues that include stability of classification, variability within the two groups, and patterns of physiological responses. In addition, questions have been raised about the appropriateness of temperament classification systems that rely on types (i.e., assigning children to groups based on temperamental characteristics) rather than on evaluations along a continuum of performance/functioning ability.

Temperamental attributes contribute directly to social-emotional and personality development, and they interact with parenting, family, and other environmental variables that in turn affect the development of children. Sandra Scarr and Kathleen McCartney (1983) have used the term *niche picking* to describe the individual differences in temperament that contribute to the selection of environments. For example, children who are prone to shyness have been shown to exhibit stress in adapting to a preschool setting only late in the year of their introduction to school. Nonshy children initially show effects of stress associated with the adjustment to a new setting, but these reactions decrease over time. Shy children do not show these effects of stress initially, presumably because their shyness leads them to avoid potentially stressful interactions (e.g., initiating with unfamiliar children). However, over time, the children who are more shy begin to interact and then show effects of stress.

Interactions between temperament and attachment have important implications for social-emotional development. Attachment refers to thoughts, feelings, and behaviors that are exhibited by a child in close relation to others, most often the primary caregiver. Attachment security, generally assessed by observing a child in a stressful "strange" situation, is associated with feelings of safety and the ability to depend on the caregiver for sensitivity and responsiveness. The effect of child temperament on attachment security has been described as being twofold. First, individual differences in temperamental characteristics, such as fear or approach, can influence the attachment classification—a child who is low in fear is likely to appear to be less securely attached because he or she may not react to the stressful situation. Second, infant temperament during the first year of life can influence the

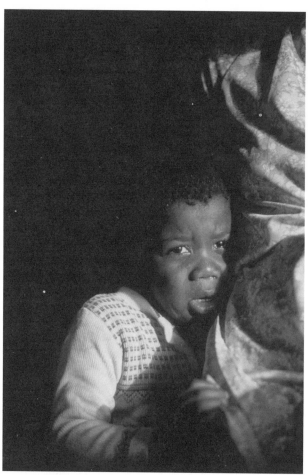

An inhibited, shy child in Beulah, Mississippi, cries and clings to his mother in the presence of a stranger. (Corbis/Nathan Benn)

relationship with the primary caregiver, thus contributing to the development of attachment security.

Although studies have not been consistent, there are numerous reports of significant relationships between temperament and attachment measures. Children who are higher in negative reactivity and distress have been described as exhibiting lower levels of attachment security. Irritable newborns have also been found, by Dymphna van den Boom (1989), to be more likely to be insecurely attached than nonirritable newborns. One interpretation of this finding is that infant irritability serves to prevent mothers from acting in a sensitive/responsive manner, so that the mothers of irritable infants may not employ effective soothing techniques. A larger sample of irritable infants and their mothers then took part in an intervention study that emphasized parenting skills, such as sensitivity to the infant's cues, prompt soothing, and positive interaction when the infant is not exhibiting distress. This intervention resulted in greater mater-

nal responsiveness; infant sociability, self-soothing, and higher levels of exploratory behavior, as well as a greater likelihood of a secure attachment classification.

Another important interaction between child temperament and socialization involves mutual influences of temperamental characteristics and the quality of parenting on the child's adjustment. Children with certain temperamental attributes (e.g., intensity, frequent negative mood) appear to be more likely to have experienced ineffective parenting practices (e.g., harsh and inconsistent discipline). The quality of parenting may in turn be related to children's development of behavior problems. Child temperament has an effect on the development of coercive family processes in that the child's aggressive tendencies and refusal to follow parental rules/requests may contribute to poor discipline practices (e.g., harsh punishment, inconsistent enforcement of rules), which in turn often lead to significant behavior problems.

Children who have challenging temperamental characteristics may also be at risk for insufficient and/or ineffective guidance and instruction from their parents. For example, Mary Gauvain and Beverly Fagot (1995) found that children who were described as being "difficult" received more cognitive assistance and disapproval from their mothers during a problem-solving task, and these mothers showed greater involvement in more challenging aspects of the task. These behaviors are not ideal in terms of guiding children through a problem-solving task. Optimal strategies involve providing the child with structure (e.g., reminding the child of the rules, providing suggestions regarding possible approaches to the problem) but allowing him or her to discover strategies independently and take on greater responsibility in the activity as he or she gains more skill.

Effortful control may influence the way in which negative emotionality, approach, and aggression are related to each other. Children with effective effortful control can be expected to show little aggression, even when they are experiencing high levels of approach and negative emotionality. That is, effective effortful control can be expected to prevent the expression of excessive levels of approach and negative emotionality associated with aggressive behavior. Relationships between fearful behavioral inhibition and approach tendencies have been described by Douglas Derryberry and Rothbart (1997). A relatively fearless child with strong approach tendencies may respond impulsively and is likely to focus on the rewarding, rather than the punishing, aspects of the experience. Alternatively, children who are strong in approach but also have strong fear tendencies are more likely to inhibit impulsive behaviors and to appreciate rewards and punishments in a given situation more equally. Thus, fear motivation may play an adaptive role in regulating approach behaviors and may lead to lower levels of aggression.

Temperament and Psychopathology

Temperamental characteristics and aspects of socialization, as well as their interactions, have been found to be related to adjustment in childhood, adolescence, and adult years. Temperamental attributes can be linked to personality characteristics, as well as difficulties in social-emotional adjustment (psychopathology) in adulthood. Indicators of difficult temperament in childhood have been linked with difficulties in adulthood, including psychopathology, criminality, and lower occupational attainment. For example, negative emotionality, evident early in childhood and often described as neuroticism in adulthood, may be seen in symptoms that are associated with depression, anxiety, and/or health-related complaints (e.g., stomachache, backache). Very high levels of approach may be related to hyperactivity.

The mechanism underlying the relationship between temperament and/or personality and psychopathology can be understood in different ways. First, extreme levels of temperamental and/or personality attributes may appear very dissimilar to the generally accepted picture of normal functioning. Thus, individuals who exhibit such extreme levels may be seen as different and therefore categorized as having a disorder. Second, psychopathology may represent extremes in the effects of interactions of different temperamental characteristics. For example, problems with aggressive/violent behavior may be a result of a high level of approach coupled with low levels of fearful inhibition and effortful control. A person who is often aggressive toward other people is unlikely to exhibit characteristics that are associated with fearful behavioral inhibition, such as concern with punishment or effortful control.

Conclusion

Considerable progress has been made in the study of temperament. Nevertheless, continuing research into the biological underpinnings of temperament, the relationships between different temperamental attributes and aspects of the parenting/family experience, and the complex ways in which temperament and personality develop is needed.

See also: AGGRESSION; ATTACHMENT; ATTITUDES; GENETICS; HUMAN DEVELOPMENT; PERSONALITY; PSYCHOPHYSIOLOGY OF EMOTIONS

Bibliography

Clark, Lee A.; Watson, David; Mineka, Susan. (1994). "Temperament, Personality, and the Mood and Anxiety Disorders." *Journal of Abnormal Psychology* 103:103–116.

Derryberry, Douglas, and Reed, Marjorie A. (1994). "Temperament and the Self-Organization of Personality." *Development and Psychopathology* 6:653–676.

Derryberry, Douglas, and Rothbart, Mary Klevjord. (1997). "Reactive and Effortful Processes in the Organization of Temperament." *Development and Psychopathology* 9:633–652.

Digman, John, and Shmelyov, Alexander G. (1996). "The Structure of Temperament and Personality in Russian Children." *Journal of Personality and Social Psychology* 71:341–351.

Fox, Nathan A., and Davidson, Richard J. (1986). "Taste-Elicited Changes in Facial Signs of Emotion and the Asymmetry of Brain Electrical Activity in Human Newborns." *Neuropsychologica* 24:417–422.

Gauvain, Mary, and Fagot, Beverly. (1995). "Child Temperament As a Mediator of Mother-Toddler Problem Solving." *Social Development* 4:257–276.

Goldsmith, H. Hill; Buss, Kristin A.; and Lemery, Kathryn S. (1997). "Toddler and Childhood Temperament: Expanded Content, Stronger Genetic Evidence, New Evidence for the Importance of Environment." *Developmental Psychology* 33:891–905.

Gunnar, Megan R. (1994). "Psychoendocrine Studies of Temperament and Stress in Early Childhood: Expanding Current Models." In *Temperament: Individual Differences at the Interface of Biology and Behavior,* ed. John E. Bates and Theordore D. Wachs. Washington DC: American Psychological Association.

Kagan, Jerome. (1994). *Galen's Prophecy: Temperament in Human Nature.* New York: Basic Books.

Kagan, Jerome. (1998). "Biology and the Child." In *Handbook of Child Psychology, Vol. 3: Social, Emotional, and Personality Development,* 5th ed., ed. William Damon and Nancy Eisenberg. New York: Wiley.

Reid, John B., and Patterson, Gerry R. (1989). "The Development of Antisocial Behavior Patterns in Childhood and Adolescence." *European Journal of Personality* 3:107–119.

Rothbart, Mary Klevjord. (1981). "Measurement of Temperament in Infancy." *Child Development* 52:569–578.

Rothbart, Mary Klevjord, and Ahadi, Stephan A. (1994). "Temperament and the Development of Personality." *Journal of Abnormal Psychology* 103:55–66.

Rothbart, Mary Klevjord, and Bates, John E. (1998). "Temperament." In *Handbook of Child Psychology, Vol. 3: Social, Emotional, and Personality Development,* 5th ed., ed. William Damon and Nancy Eisenberg. New York: Wiley.

Rothbart, Mary Klevjord, and Sanson, Ann. (1995). "Child Temperament and Parenting." In *Handbook of Parenting, Vol. 4,* ed. Marc H. Bornstein. Mahwah, NJ: Lawrence Erlbaum.

Scarr, Sandra, and McCartney, Kathleen. (1983). "How People Make Their Own Environments: A Theory of Genotype-Environment Effects." *Child Development* 54:424–435.

Tellegen, Auke; Lykken, David T.; Bouchard, Thomas J.; Wilcox, Kimerly J.; Segal, Nancy L.; and Rich, Stephen. (1988). "Personality Similarity in Twins Reared Apart and Together." *Journal of Personality and Social Psychology* 54:1031–1039.

Thomas, Alexander, and Chess, Stella. (1977). *Temperament and Development.* New York: Brunner/Mazel.

van den Boom, Dymphna C. (1989). "Neonatal Irritability and the Development of Attachment." In *Temperament in Child-*

hood, ed. Geldolph A. Kohnstamm, John E. Bates, and Mary Klevjord Rothbart. Chichester, Eng.: Wiley.

Vygotsky, Lev S. (1978). *Mind in Society.* Cambridge, MA: Harvard University Press.

Maria Amy Gartstein
Mary Klevjord Rothbart

TESTING

See Psychological Assessment

THEATER

See Drama and Theater

THEORIES OF EMOTION

See Anthropology of Emotions; Biochemistry of Emotions; Cognitive Perspective; Folk Theories of Emotion; Historical Study of Emotions; Neurobiology of Emotions; Psychoanalytic Perspective; Psychology of Emotions; Psychophysiology of Emotions; Sociology of Emotions

TRUST

Trust in another person is an experience that is essential not only for daily interaction within society but also for the formation and establishment of other important interpersonal relationships. In fact, perhaps its greatest effect lies in the fact that one's beliefs about trust are at the heart of all social cognition, and thus various thoughts and beliefs are greatly influenced by what one believes to be the character of humankind.

Trust can be defined as an individual's set of expectations that a relational partner will behave in positive and accepting ways toward the individual or that he or she can be relied on not to harm the individual. It is believed that trusting feelings arise from experiences with specific partners and then are translated into experiences with others. However, one may begin to trust different partners to provide distinct resources and forms of security; that is, the expectations may vary based on the type of relationship. For example, the trust that one feels for a romantic partner may not be perceived in the same way that trust for a parent or sibling is perceived because the emotions, information, and experiences that one shares in the different relationships may vary. Similarly, the trust one feels in these close relationships can be subjectively distinguished from that felt during interactions with strangers (or others with whom the individual is not close) because the experiences he or she has had with the strangers are vastly different.

Theorists such as John Rempel, John Holmes, and Mark Zanna (1985) have argued that trust is not unlike a feeling of optimism about the future of a relationship, where the optimism is based on past experiences with the partner or others similar to him or her. If one gains knowledge that a partner's responses are dependably and predictably positive, an individual may begin to develop faith that the partner will continue to behave in these ways. This emotional bond between relationship partners then allows an individual to go beyond the uncertainty of the future, enabling participation in the relationship as if certain possible negative futures will not occur.

The Need for Trust

Believing others to be trustworthy (i.e., having trust in them) is considered by many important theorists, such as Julian Rotter (1967) and Lawrence Wrightsman (1974), to be essential to positive social behavior and functioning and a critical aspect of human life. Ostensibly, the widespread assumption of mutual trust in a society allows for increasingly complex social systems and interactions. For example, various factors clearly contribute to one's acceptance by peers, an element of human interaction that arguably promotes survival. The ability to "get along" with others has been a key feature in allowing the evolution of humans because trust facilitates banding together, forming and living in groups, and developing cultural solutions to common problems. Because individuals in human evolutionary history experienced many hardships, including struggling for resources, shelter, and protection against other forces in nature (e.g., predators), they may not have survived without living in groups to help them deal with these problems. Trust was necessary to live in these groups, so in this way, it promoted survival. Therefore, it is reasonable to speculate that the capacity to trust was selected through the process of evolution as promoting individual and societal survival through the mechanisms of group acceptance and popularity. In fact, it has been argued that trust is so essential to social systems that there is no need or occasion to worry about trust except in personal interactions with others.

To illustrate further the point that trust is crucial to human interaction, one need only consider the critical nature of trust in close relationships. Self-disclosure is viewed by many who study relationships to be a defining characteristic in the development of intimacy. However, it does carry such risks as rejection, ridicule, and/or lessened security of information. Research such as that conducted by John Wilson and James Carroll (1991) supports the necessity of trust in forming intimate bonds. Without a high degree of trust during such a risky interaction, an individual is less willing to reveal personal information to the partner, and without self-disclosure, the relationship is not likely to develop or progress toward intimacy.

The Development of Trust

Understanding the critical nature of trust, several scholars have attempted to describe how an individual comes to have trust. Erik Erikson (1950), John Bowlby (1973), and Rotter (1967) all suggested that trust develops through one's experiences with others. However, while Erikson and Bowlby argued that the relationship an infant has with the primary caregivers (e.g., parents) is responsible for basic trust, Rotter contended that all relationships with others contribute to the development of trust.

Erickson believed that one must pass through developmental stages or crises, the first of which is labeled "basic trust versus basic mistrust." Basic trust is defined as a general sense of the correspondence between one's needs and one's world, whereas basic mistrust is defined as an expectation of danger or an anticipation of discomfort that results from discrepancies between one's needs and one's world. Trust is hypothesized to develop from the attachment bond formed between an infant and his or her primary caregivers, which results from interactions during the first year of life. In this conceptualization, two basic manifestations of trust are emphasized: (a) trust of specific other persons, such as caregivers, and (b) a trustworthy social environment from which a sense of the meaning of life emerges. In order for basic trust to evolve, the infant must come to rely on the dependability of his or her caregivers. Furthermore, if this first crisis in life is resolved in a positive manner, the infant

will develop a "favorable ratio" of basic trust over basic mistrust. According to Erikson, this ratio endures throughout life although it is (to some extent) subject to the effects of subsequent experiences.

Bowlby referred to the relationship between an infant and discriminated persons (caregivers) by suggesting that trust is believed to serve a biological function—trust serves to protect the attached individual from physical and psychological harm. Bowlby believed that, in order to avoid such harm, the biological drive to become attached is one of the infant's strongest motivations. At birth, human infants show evidence of behaviors that bring them into closer proximity and interaction with a caregiver (i.e., attachment). The information gained about the caregiver during these interactions (e.g., whether the caregiver can be trusted to be responsive) is translated into the child's view of the responsiveness of this and other potential relational partners—in other words, a sense of trust. According to Bowlby, anticipated availability and responsiveness (as well as anticipated unavailability and unresponsiveness) on the part of the primary caregiver will have a permanent effect on the child's development of a mental representation of the world and significant persons within it. For example, if interactions suggest the caregiver will be unavailable and unresponsive in a time of crisis, the child will be more highly motivated to monitor the caregiver's whereabouts (i.e., low trust) than if responsiveness is certain (i.e., high trust). However, these representations that develop as a result of the attachment between the child and caregiver must be continually updated over time with the new information provided by subsequent interactions. Because the new information is assimilated into the existing model, representations tend to be resistant to dramatic changes. Therefore, the child's worldview tends to remain moderately stable across time. In this way, trust develops into a stable personal characteristic.

From a somewhat different perspective, Rotter (1967) agreed that trust evolves through interactions with others, but he also argued that *any* social agent may influence an individual's level of trust. Rotter's social learning account holds that behaviors or judgments depend, in part, on an individual's expectancy that a given behavior will lead to a particular outcome or reinforcement in that situation. Accordingly, trust is seen to develop through observation during experiences of positive and negative outcomes with social agents, such as parents, peers, teachers, and other sources of interpersonal interaction. These experiences presumably generalize from one social agent or situation to another so that a "generalized expectancy" emerges in which the individual assumes that the words or promises of others can be relied upon (or

---

Raymond Carver's "Cathedral" (1981) describes an interesting triangle: a cynical and skeptical husband who drinks and smokes pot to "take the edge off," his outgoing wife who carries on a long-term friendship with a blind man for whom she once worked, and the blind man himself who comes to visit. The husband distrusts him, but gradually the blind man wins him over, until at the end, the husband teaches the blind man what a cathedral looks like by guiding his hand as both of them draw a cathedral together. The husband comes to trust enough to do this with his eyes closed.

not) to varying degrees. Rotter also claimed that one may learn differential trust expectancies without direct personal experience because important others can model trusting behaviors or attitudes.

Research has supported the idea that trust develops early in life and continues to be translated into trust in subsequent relationships. For example, to address Bowlby's conceptualization of the process of trust development, Mary Ainsworth, Mary Blehar, Everett Waters, and Sally Wall (1978) developed the "strange situation" paradigm in which infants and their caregivers were placed in an unfamiliar playroom where they were given the opportunity to explore toys and interact with an unfamiliar adult in the presence or absence of the mother. The researchers found that children with a warm and positive history of parental interaction were securely attached and acted with a high degree of trust, approaching the mother and seeking physical contact with her if they had been overtly distressed. Infants who had a negative history of interaction with little indication that the parent would be responsive were avoidantly attached and developed low trust. These infants snubbed and avoided the mother on her return. Finally, infants who had an inconsistent history of interactions with a caregiver (i.e., sometimes the parent had been responsive and sometimes not) became anxiously/ambivalently attached and developed low to moderate levels of trust. These children showed angry resistant behavior interspersed with attachment behavior in the study.

In addition, research evidence has supported the idea that the concept of trust continues to develop and become more complex as children get older. It is clear that children as young as the first and second grades can verbalize determinations about their trust of peers, even though trust may not function in the same way as it does during adolescence or adulthood. Cary Buzzelli (1988) reports that younger children base their trust on a peer's overt behaviors, whereas older children place emphasis on the reliability of other's promises and the degree of understanding and empathy that they provide in the friendship. He also found that children in the fourth through sixth grades report trust to be important in friendships and that adolescents use trust to decide different levels of intimacy and amounts of shared activity. By the time an individual reaches adolescence, good friends are considered to be primarily accepting and noncritical listeners that preserve confidences and offer advice about others' perceptions of them. The extent to which each of these expectations is fulfilled is believed to affect the adolescent's satisfaction with the friendship and the trust placed in the friend.

Several general conclusions summarize the convergent ideas of Bowlby, Erikson, and Rotter. First, trust is seen as a precursor of adequate functioning in a social world. Second, trust is considered from a developmental perspective in which experience with other important people at one point in life contributes to the capacity to trust at a subsequent point of development. Third, once acquired, trust is described as evolving into fairly complex and stable global or generalized dimensions of personality. Due to the different experiences that individuals may have with their relational partners earlier in development, they may develop very different perspectives on the world and/ or patterns of interacting with others.

Individual Differences in Trust

The idea of individual differences in trust has long been important in the theoretical literature, as well as in studies of personal development and relational success. This work, along with speculation about the importance of trust for functioning and cognition surrounding social interactions, suggests that individuals who have differing experiences with trust in key relationships may also experience life differently. For example, individuals high in trust are seen to have more satisfying relationships than individuals low in trust, whereas individuals low in trust may experience lower levels of self-esteem and use less constructive problem-solving techniques than individuals high in trust.

Individuals' levels of trust have been found to vary in relation to demographic variables as well. For example, age, gender, and ethnicity have all been shown to influence one's trusting orientation. Non-traditional (i.e., older) college students have been found to score higher on measures of global trust than traditionally aged students. Women and girls have been found to be more trusting in general than men and boys. Indeed, a study by Lawrence Kurdek (1988) found that long-term lesbian couples reported more trust than did couples consisting of gay men. In addition, Caucasians score consistently higher on trust and lower on measures of suspicion than do other ethnic groups such as African Americans and Asian Americans.

Research has begun since the 1970s to examine the link between relevant personality traits and trust and has demonstrated the importance of trust in everyday social functioning and well-being. For example, high levels of trust have been found to be related to general adjustment and a sense of control over one's life, happiness, and need for approval. Individuals who score higher on measures of trust tend to out-perform their more suspicious counterparts on several social tasks, and they report less anger and physical distress. Lower levels of trust are associated with increased competitiveness, loneliness, jealousy, shyness, and suspicion.

A trust exercise in which a black student was paired with a white student—one being blindfolded and the other leading the way—was carried out by these students in 1972 in an attempt to facilitate school integration. (Corbis/Jack Moebes)

Individuals who are high in trust may also be perceived differently by others. For example, those individuals who are high in trust are perceived to be more attractive and have greater common sense. Persons high in trust are also more likely to be sought by others as friends and tend to exhibit trust behaviorally (e.g., closing one's eyes and falling backward into another's arms with the expectation of being caught). Perhaps with good reason, individuals with high levels of trust in others are also perceived by others as being trustworthy. Individuals high in trust are less likely (compared to individuals low in trust) to lie, cheat, steal, betray others, or conceal their attitudes from others. In addition, findings from studies of friendship indicate that a child's trustworthiness (as viewed by others) is correlated with his or her standing in the peer group and may have much to do with the process of trust development in early social encounters. Children who are perceived as less trustworthy by teachers and other children are less likely to be selected by their same-sex classmates to be play partners or work partners. Conversely, children who are perceived as more trust-

worthy are more popular than the less trustworthy children. These perceptions are important because if children are not selected they may also lack relational experiences that, in turn, allow them to develop trust.

As suggested above, not only does trust seem to arise out of experiences with important others, but it also has been found to be strongly related to the development and maintenance of intimate relationships. Because of the vulnerability experienced by most people in intimate relationships, it is here that trust is perhaps most salient. Indeed, independent areas of research have reinforced the idea that trust plays an important role in intimate relationships. For example, the value of friendship is often directly related to the level of trust an individual experiences within the relationship. In fact, trust may actually serve as a means of distinguishing between types of friends, where "best" friends experience the most trust. Parent-child relationships are also found to be satisfying to the degree that each participant trusts the other. Similarly, what is known as the companionate love experience (i.e., a close love relationship often present after a couple has spent many years together) is thought to be best defined by its trusting nature. In addition, trust has been viewed by Nena and George O'Neill (1972) as a prerequisite for romantic/marital stability, happiness, and the realization of romantic/marital potential. Thus, in most types of relationships, trust appears to be an essential psychological feature, and relationships are generally considered to be functional to the degree that partners trust one another.

Further investigations of this idea have revealed that trust is meaningfully related to interpersonal adjustment, satisfying relationships, communication, and cooperation. Attributions of honesty are found to be related to higher trust in one's relational partner and to predict positive behavioral outcomes such as constructive behavior in marital communication. For example, communication satisfaction, partner competence, and the exclusion of distributive tactics during the conflict resolution process (i.e., competition and primacy of personal over relational goals) have been found by Daniel Canary and William Cupach (1988) to be associated with increased trust. In addition, love in romantic relationships is linked to higher levels of trust in one's romantic partner, and trust is reliably associated with passionate and selfless love styles. Individuals high in trust also tend to be more willing to disclose information to a close relational partner than do individuals who are low in trust.

Trust has also been found to vary with the length of the romantic relationship, as well as with level of commitment, as the developmental theories would suggest. Specifically, Robert Lazelere and Ted Huston (1980) found that as the level of commitment to and/or intimacy in a relationship increased, so did feelings of trust for the partner. Self-disclosure also increased and individuals' trust for one another was higher and more strongly reciprocated in married couples than in dating or divorced couples. Finally, Charles Hill, Zick Rubin, and Letitia Peplau (1976) reported that when a romantic relationship is terminated, not surprisingly, trust decreases. Obviously, at this point in the relationship, commitment to the partner is no longer an issue. However, Stephen Banks, Dayle Altendorf, John Greene, and Michael Cody (1987) make the less obvious suggestion that those individuals with low trust during breakups feel more anger toward the ex-partner, whereas those with high trust report feelings of freedom.

Conclusion

Generalizations regarding trust have been largely confirmed by empirical research. Trust is assumed to arise out of experiences with important others and

then develop into complex patterns of cognition and behavior that persist through the life of a relationship (or perhaps for the life of the individual). In addition, these feelings are believed to greatly influence one's social interactions (especially in close relationship situations), as well as one's subjective experience of life. More specifically, trust is related in predictable ways to relevant personality, demographic, behavioral variables (e.g., cheating and stealing, jealousy, locus of control, suspicion) and important outcome variables such as health, adjustment, and the social judgments of others. Because trust is so crucial in intimate relationships, it may dramatically affect the experiences that one has with family, friends, and romantic partners.

See also: ATTACHMENT; ATTRIBUTION; BOWLBY, JOHN; COMMITMENT; COMMUNICATION; CONFLICT; ERIKSON, ERIK HOMBURGER; FRIENDSHIP; INTIMACY; JEALOUSY; LOVE; PERSONALITY; RELATIONSHIPS; SELF-ESTEEM

Bibliography

Ainsworth, Mary D. S.; Blehar, Mary C.; Waters, Everett; and Wall, Sally. (1978). *Patterns of Attachment: A Psychological Study of the Strange Situation.* Hillsdale, NJ: Lawrence Erlbaum.

Banks, Stephen P.; Altendorf, Dayle M.; Greene, John O.; and Cody, Michael J. (1987). "An Examination of Relationship Disengagement: Perceptions, Breakup Strategies, and Outcomes." *Western Journal of Speech Communication* 51:19–41.

Berry, Diane S., and McArthur, Leslie Z. (1986). "Perceiving Character in Faces: The Impact of Age-Related Craniofacial Changes on Social Perception." *Psychological Bulletin* 100:3–18.

Bowlby, John. (1973). *Attachment and Loss, Vol. 2: Separation.* New York: Basic Books.

Brehm, Sharon S. (1992). *Intimate Relationships.* New York: McGraw-Hill.

Butler, John K. (1986). "Reciprocity of Dyadic Trust in Close Male-Female Relationships." *Journal of Social Psychology* 126: 579–591.

Buzzelli, Cary A. (1988). "The Development of Trust in Children's Relations with Peers." *Child Study Journal* 18:33–46.

Canary, Daniel J., and Cupach, William R. (1988). "Relational and Episodic Characteristics Associated with Conflict Tactics." *Journal of Social and Personal Relationships* 5:305–325.

Cash, Thomas F.; Stack, James J.; and Luna, Gloria C. (1975). "Convergent and Discriminant Behavioral Aspects of Interpersonal Trust." *Psychological Reports* 37:983–986.

Couch, Laurie L. (1994). "The Development of the Trust Inventory." M.A. thesis, University of Tennessee, Knoxville.

Couch, Laurie L.; Adams, Jeffrey M.; and Jones, Warren H. (1996). "The Assessment of Trust Orientation." *Journal of Personality Assessment* 67:305–322.

Doherty, William J., and Ryder, Robert G. (1979). "Locus of Control, Interpersonal Trust, and Assertive Behavior among Newlyweds." *Journal of Personality and Social Psychology* 37: 2212–2220.

Erikson, Erik H. (1950). *Childhood and Society.* New York: W. W. Norton.

Golembiewski, Robert T., and McConkie, Michael. (1975). "The Centrality of Interpersonal Trust in Group Processes." In *Theories of Group Process,* ed. C. L. Cooper. London: Wiley.

Heretick, Donna M. (1984). "Trust-Suspicion and Gender Differences in Interpersonal Functioning." *Journal of Research in Personality* 18:27–40.

Hill, Charles T.; Rubin, Zick; and Peplau, Letitia A. (1976). "Breakups before Marriage: The End of 103 Affairs." *Journal of Social Issues* 32:147–168.

Jones, Warren H.; Couch, Laurie L.; and Scott, Susan. (1997). "Trust and Betrayal: The Psychology of Trust Violation." In *Handbook of Personality,* ed. Stephen Briggs, Robert Hogan, and John Johnson. New York: Academic Press.

Jourard, Sidney M. (1971). *The Transparent Self.* New York: D. Van Nostrand.

Komarovsky, Mirra. (1974). "Patterns of Self-Disclosure of Male Undergraduates." *Journal of Marriage and the Family* 36:677–686.

Kurdek, Lawrence A. (1988). "Relationship Quality of Gay and Lesbian Cohabitating Couples." *Journal of Homosexuality* 15: 93–118.

Lazelere, Robert E., and Huston, Ted L. (1980). "The Dyadic Trust Scale: Toward Understanding Interpersonal Trust in Close Relationships." *Journal of Marriage and the Family* 42: 595–604.

Mellinger, George D. (1956). "Interpersonal Trust As a Factor in Communication." *Journal of Abnormal Social Psychology* 52: 304–309.

O'Neill, Nena, and O'Neill, George. (1972). *Open Marriage.* New York: Avon.

Rawlins, William K., and Holl, Melissa. (1987). "The Communicative Achievement of Friendship during Adolescence: Predicaments of Trust and Violation." *Western Journal of Speech Communication* 51:345–363.

Rempel, John K.; Holmes, John G.; and Zanna, Mark P. (1985). "Trust in Close Relationships." *Journal of Personality and Social Psychology* 49:95–112.

Rotenberg, Kenneth J. (1984). "Sex Differences in Children's Trust in Peers." *Sex Roles* 11:953–957.

Rotenberg, Kenneth J. (1991). *Children's Interpersonal Trust: Sensitivity to Lying, Deception, and Promise Violations.* New York: Springer-Verlag.

Rotter, Julian B. (1967). "A New Scale for the Measurement of Interpersonal Trust." *Journal of Personality* 35:651–665.

Rotter, Julian B. (1980). "Interpersonal Trust, Trustworthiness, and Gullibility." *American Psychologist* 35:1–7.

Schill, Thomas; Toves, Carmen; and Ramanaiah, Nerella. (1980). "Interpersonal Trust and Coping with Stress." *Psychological Reports* 47:1192.

Steele, Jennifer L. (1991). "Interpersonal Correlates of Trust and Self-Disclosure." *Psychological Reports* 68:1319–1320.

Terrell, Francis, and Barrett, Ronald K. (1979). "Interpersonal Trust among College Students As a Function of Race, Sex, and Socioeconomic Class." *Perceptual and Motor Skills* 48:1194.

Wilson, John M., and Carroll, James L. (1991). "Children's Trustworthiness: Judgement by Teachers, Parents and Peers." In *Children's Interpersonal Trust: Sensitivity to Lying, Deception, and Promise Violations,* ed. Kenneth J. Rotenberg. New York: Springer-Verlag.

Wrightsman, Lawrence S. (1974). *Assumptions about Human Nature: A Social-Psychological Approach.* Monterrey, CA: Brooks Cole.

Laurie L. Couch

U

UNIVERSALITY OF EMOTIONAL EXPRESSION

Are the expressions of emotion universal, pancultural patterns of motor behavior, or are they culture-specific signals? This issue has been hotly debated ever since, at the turn of the twentieth century, the emotions became a serious object of study for the biological, behavioral, and social sciences. Evidence for either universality or cultural specificity of emotional expression is expected to determine whether emotion is to be treated as a psychobiological form of behavioral adaptation or as a communicative act deriving its meaning from cultural and interactional contexts. However, as is often the case in "either/or" debates, upon closer inspection the phenomenon exhibits a mixture of elements from both of these extreme positions.

Historical Roots of the Debate

Neither the philosophers who have analyzed the human emotions during two thousand years of investigating human nature nor the pioneers of the study of emotional expression seem to have doubted the universality of the expressions they were describing. The explicit formulation of a "universality of emotional expression" hypothesis, however, must be credited to Charles Darwin. In extending his theory on the evolution of species and the descent of man to the realm of behavior, Darwin postulated in *The Expression of the Emotions in Man and Animals* (1872, pp. 130–131) that "the different races of man express their emotions and sensations with remarkable uniformity through-

out the world." He set out to confirm this claim empirically by writing to numerous correspondents in exotic places to inquire about the similarity of the emotional expressions found there to those commonly observed in Western countries. Following Darwin, many early emotion psychologists assumed—explicitly or implicitly—that emotional expressions were largely universally shared.

The opposite approach, concentrating on differences rather than similarities in human behavior, was adopted by early anthropologists and ethnologists who, at the beginning of the twentieth century, started to explore systematically the differences in thought, language, and customs between Western societies and cultures in Africa, Asia, and the Pacific islands.

Whereas the efforts of biologists and psychologists are generally directed toward finding similarities in the mechanisms that underlie human behavior, anthropologists and ethnologists tend to be concerned with the discovery of cultural differences. This fundamental difference in approaches led to the first major clash in the universality debate in the late 1960s when Paul Ekman and Carroll Izard, two psychologists strongly influenced by the neo-Darwinian theory of Silvan Tomkins, reported the first truly empirical evidence suggesting that emotional expressions observed in one culture could reliably be recognized in others. The anthropologist Margaret Mead (1975) and the linguist Ray Birdwhistell (1970) were among the most vociferous critics of this type of research, arguing instead for viewing emotional expression as language-like sign structures expressing meaning in a culturally specific manner.

669

Yet, in a period of almost thirty years (between 1960 and 1990) universalist theories of expression and the empirical evidence generated by this tradition enjoyed widespread acceptance and dominated textbook coverage of emotion in many disciplines. In the late 1990s, however, the approach has met with renewed criticism.

Theoretical Arguments

One of the most detailed theoretical justifications for the assumption of universal emotional expressions has been formulated on the basis of the pioneering work on animal behavior (i.e., ethology) done by Konrad Lorenz and Niko Tinbergen (who shared the 1973 Nobel Prize in Physiology or Medicine for "their discoveries concerning organization and elicitation of individual and social behavior patterns"). The comparative human ethologist Irenäus Eibl-Eibesfeldt (1989) has postulated that a large number of emotional expressions are universal because of genetically inherited "fixed actions patterns," a construct widely used in animal ethology. This translation of the original German term (*Erbkoordination,* better rendered as "innate coordinated movement") falsely implies a rigid unfolding and a stereotypical form of movement in response to typical releasing stimuli. Eibl-Eibesfeldt likens universal expression patterns to the activity of automatically triggered movement programs that do not have the same form—with respect to the combination of body parts and the change over time—in each case. Furthermore, the triggering of the coordinated movement in emotional expression is seen to depend on individual and contextual factors.

A similar theoretical notion, although less developed in detail, was suggested by Tomkins (1984), who strongly influenced work in this area. He assumed a limited number of basic emotions for which he postulated neuromotor expression programs. Ekman (1992), influenced by the thinking of Tomkins, also postulates such neuromotor programs to account for the observed universality in emotional expression. A similar approach is taken by neuropsychologists, such as Jaak Panksepp (1982), who postulate the existence of specific neural circuits for individual emotions.

Most of the theorists mentioned so far have based their theoretical propositions on Darwin. However, Darwin himself did not postulate unique neuromotor patterns for basic emotions. Rather, he suggested three fundamental principles to explain specific motor activities resulting in observed expressions: (1) expressive movements, or parts thereof, are functional for the organism's response or are rudiments of formerly adaptive movements, (2) general arousal can produce unspecific expressive movements, and (3) some expressions are the opposites—or antitheses—of specific functional expressions. In highlighting the functionality of specific expressive movements, Darwin was influenced by the mid-eighteenth century French scholars Duchenne de Boulogne and Pierre Gratiolet, who, rather than assuming coherent, emotion-specific programs of muscle movements, suggested that particular motor movements have clearly circumscribed adaptive functions.

In the 1980s, a number of emotion theorists within the tradition of appraisal theory independently adopted Darwin's original proposal concerning the functional role of particular movements by linking their occurrence to appraisal processes and action tendencies (or behavior intentions) rather than to discrete neuromotor emotion programs. These psychologists suggest that expressive patterns are adaptive movements that follow specific situational appraisals (e.g., eyebrow raising in the case of novel unexpected events, teeth grinding in the case of preparation for biting). In consequence, emotion-specific expression can be seen as an accumulation of appraisal-based adaptive movements. This account assumes that the links between the appraisal of an event and the adaptational consequences in the form of motor expressive movements are at least partly genetically determined and, therefore, universal.

Alternatively, rather than assuming that adaptational responses are genetically encoded, one can argue that emotional expression is partly universal because of microgenetic adaptive pressure. In this view, individuals have learned to react consistently in similar ways all over the world because of the immediate advantage particular motor movements (such as raising the eyebrows in order to improve visual acuity) provide in similar situations.

In contrast, universality of emotional expression is generally de-emphasized by theorists such as Catherine Lutz and Geoffrey White (1986) and Richard Shweder (1993) who highlight the communicative function of expression and the role that sociocultural factors play in shaping the respective expression to the established communicative patterns in a society. The central claim in this tradition is that most emotional expressions are based on culturally shared values and meanings, particularly in specific interactional contexts. This tradition of work also emphasizes the creative and performative nature of expression in a cultural context rather than just its functionality or adaptiveness.

A number of theorists leaning towards sociobiological explanations have suggested that the *expression* of internal states of the organism is much less important than the message intentions that are expected to be of a predominantly tactical and/or deceptive nature. In this view, as described by Richard Dawkins and J. R. Krebs (1978), the expression is determined by the desired *im*pression of the respective motor movement patterns on a real or imagined audience. Theorists who hold this view would admit universality to the extent that similar patterns of strategic signaling can be demonstrated for individuals in different cultures.

Evidence from Cross-Cultural Research

To examine the extent to which patterns of emotional expression are indeed universal and to evaluate the different theoretical claims, one would want to examine systematic observations of many different emotional expressions as they are actually occurring in comparable situational contexts in many different cultures. Unfortunately, the only observational data of this nature is a library of film documents established by comparative human ethologists. Over many years, Eibl-Eibesfeldt and his collaborators have routinely filmed, in an unobtrusive fashion, sequences of emotional behavior in a number of non-Western societies that had relatively little contact with Western culture. This film material, while fairly unsystematic with respect to emotions and contexts, provides important illustrations for similarities in emotional expressions in standard social situations and is a unique resource for research in this area. Ekman and his collaborators have also filmed facial emotion expressions in an isolated society in New Guinea. There are, however, quite a few ethnographic studies that use informant reports about different kinds of emotional expression.

Apart from these pioneering efforts at audiovisual documentation and analysis by human ethologists, there have been few attempts to demonstrate empirically that similar events would produce similar expressions in members of different cultures. The vast majority of research in psychology focuses on investigating whether members of one culture can reliably recognize expressions produced by members of an-

other culture. In contrast, anthropologists and ethnologists generally concentrate on the use of expression in social interaction.

The most extensive work by far has been done in the area of facial expression. Following pioneering work by Tomkins, Ekman (1972, 1992), Izard (1971, 1992), and their collaborators—as well as other investigators—have conducted studies using a standardized series of photographs of theoretically defined expressions of discrete emotions. Generally, these photographs are shown to respondents who are asked to indicate which emotion, to be selected from a preestablished list, is being portrayed. The results, as summarized in Table 1, show that these expressions are in fact accurately recognized by members of many different cultures. While judges from non-Western cultures have a somewhat lower accuracy than Western cultures, they are still able to recognize the expressions at a rate that is higher than would be expected if responses were based solely on chance or guessing conditions. Results of this type have consistently been interpreted as evidence for the universality of emotional expression in psychology textbooks.

While both Darwin and Tomkins saw vocal expression as being parallel to facial expression and expected similar universal patterns, there has been little research done on vocal expression. The exception is a small number of studies that have compared the ability of judges from one culture to recognize the vocally expressed emotions demonstrated by members of another culture. This lack of research is due to the procedural difficulties posed by the dynamic nature of the vocal stimuli (as compared to static photographs) and the dependence on linguistic content (as compared to context-free photographs). Yet, using mostly standard content or nonsense utterances, all of the studies in this area have found better-than-chance accuracy in the recognition of emotion from vocally portrayed stimuli. A large-scale intercultural study by Scherer and his colleagues has found evidence, as summarized in Table 1, for the ability of judges to recognize vocally

Table 1   Accuracy of Emotion Recognition in Intercultural Studies (reported in percentages)

	Neutral	Anger	Fear	Joy	Sadness	Disgust	Surprise	Mean
Facial								
Western (20)	*	78	77	95	79	80	88	78
Non-Western (11)	*	59	62	88	74	67	77	65
Vocal								
Western (11)	74	77	61	57	71	31	*	*
Non-Western (1)	70	64	38	28	58	*	*	*

Numbers in parentheses indicate the number of countries studied.
Asterisks indicate that the respective emotions have not been studied in these regions.

portrayed emotions consistently across many different cultures, including one non-Western culture. An important finding is that the patterns of errors or confusions are very similar across cultures, suggesting that the use of specific vocal cues to infer the portrayed emotions is highly comparable. The results also suggest that it will be profitable to study the effect of language differences between encoders (portraying emotions) and decoders (inferring emotions).

While it has been suggested that there are characteristic postures (i.e., bodily expressions) for particular emotions, there has been virtually no research in this area. Since the postural reactions for particular emotions such as sadness or depression may be due to physiological effects such as lax muscular tension, these types of patterns are likely to be universal. On the other hand, Desmond Morris (1977) has provided some illustrative evidence on cultural differences with respect to posture. In addition, based on his rich film records from various non-Western cultures, Eibl-Eibesfeldt (1989) reports that there are both universal and culturally specific body gestures. For example, foot stamping as a sign of anger seems to be universal, whereas presentation and squeezing of the breast as a signal of fear is found in only a few of the societies studied.

Extensive cultural differences have been demonstrated for emotionally toned hand gestures in social interactions, particularly on iconic or emblematic gestures (i.e., gestures that have a clear meaning). However, most of these gestural expressions cannot be treated as authentic emotional expressions in the same sense as facial or vocal expressions. Emblematic gestures must be considered to be gestural speech acts (i.e., elements of intentional communication) rather than spontaneous expressions of an underlying emotional state. In many cases, especially in the case of emblems, the underlying message intention can be easily described by words. While part of the message intention underlying the use of emblematic gestures may be emotionally based, these movements generally do not resemble the spontaneous expression of emotional reactions. Hand movements that accompany speech, however, are very often determined by speech planning as well as by individual habits. While their general form may be affected by emotion, this has mostly been studied in terms of individual differences; cross-cultural comparisons are not available.

In many cases emotional arousal gives rise to a verbalization in order to communicate the emotional reaction to others. While cultures vary greatly with respect to the type of languages spoken, aspects of both the content and form of such verbalizations may be very similar. Unfortunately, except for some attempts by Anna Wierzbicka (1994) to show the existence of universal semantic features relevant to emotion communication across different languages, there has been very little work done in this area.

Anthropologists have shown remarkable differences in the labeling of emotional states in different cultures. These differences seem to reflect culture-specific ways of focusing on or evaluating the meaning of the respective emotions. In this sense, one can in fact reasonably speak of a sociocultural construction of verbally mediated emotion expressions.

Research Considerations

As shown above, the majority of the work that demonstrates the existence of universal emotional expressions is based on decoding studies showing that members of one culture can recognize emotional expressions portrayed by members of another culture. One debate over this research concerns the possibility that the accuracy percentages reported may be inflated due to issues such as the nature of the subjects used, the presentation of the stimuli, the order of presentation, the posing of the expressions, the response format, and so on. However, the exact size of the accuracy percentages found, or shortcomings of specific studies, seem to be of little importance in comparison to the uniform demonstration of a firmly established core of findings that emotional expression is recognized with better-than-chance accuracy across cultures.

The interpretation of this evidence is even more controversial than the manner in which it was gathered. Except for the studies conducted by Ekman with isolated tribes in New Guinea, researchers in this area used portrayals from Western countries and judges who had been exposed to Western mass media and other cultural contacts. Critics claim that these judges have become familiar with the meaning of certain Western expressions, allowing them to categorize the portrayals correctly. While such claims are difficult to verify, explanations invoking cultural contact and learning are not very economical since they require a large number of assumptions, in particular that all judges have been exposed with similar frequencies to comparable media stimuli. This is quite improbable, especially with respect to vocal expression (given that most films or television shows are dubbed into local languages, presumably using local paralinguistic features for emotion encoding).

Obviously, relying on results from decoding or recognition studies as exclusive evidence for the universality of expression is problematic because this work is limited to only one aspect of emotional communication: impression. While these findings provide important indirect evidence, it would be far more conclusive to have direct evidence (i.e., to show that people in different cultures actually produce the same expressions in comparable emotional states). Apart from the expressions filmed by Eibl-Eibesfeldt, there is little material available. To obtain strong evidence on pancultural expression production, experimentation with similar methods of emotion induction or audiovisual recording of standard emotional situations (e.g., burials, celebrations, fights) in many cultures would be necessary. Ekman (1972) and his collaborators conducted an experimental study in which they had American and Japanese subjects watch emotion-inducing films both alone and in the presence of an interviewer. Fine-grained analyses of the facial expressions of the subjects in the two conditions were interpreted as systematic differences in display rules, with Japanese subjects showing much less negative affect in the presence of a stranger. Of course, learning due to culture contact can also be invoked for the production of emotional expression, but it seems even less plausible than in the case of emotion recognition.

One should not forget that important information on the universality issue can be obtained by looking at the development of children and by comparing human and animal behavior. If organized patterns of expression can be shown to be present at a very early age, as predicted by theorists arguing for innate expression coordination, some of the theoretical assumptions of a psychobiological basis for universality described above would receive strong support. In particular, if a high degree of universality of expression in response to specific emotional stimuli can be demonstrated for young infants, the argument for learning via cultural contact would be much weakened.

To examine the possibility of phylogenetic continuity of emotional expression, as proposed by adherents of an evolutionary approach to the study of expression, it is necessary to investigate the role of analogy in comparative research. There is some evidence, as reviewed by Scherer (1985), that similarities in the acoustic structure of emotional vocalizations—such as high voice pitch in fear, low pitch and rough voice in anger—of different species of mammals, particularly primates (including man), may actually represent analogous evolution. For facial expression, these issues are more difficult to explore, given the large differences in facial anatomy between different species.

Conclusion

None of the theorists arguing for the universality of emotional expression would claim that all expressions are similar across cultures in all instances. Most universalist theorists acknowledge very explicitly that culture exerts a considerable influence on the nature of expression. One of the earliest statements to this effect

was Wilhelm Wundt's (1900) observation that cultural norms severely limit the ways in which emotions are shown in social situations. Most of the scholars who argue that emotional expressions are—to a greater or lesser extent—universal also assume the operation of culture-specific expectations or norms that lead people to suppress, modify, or amplify spontaneously produced emotional expressions or even to feel a culturally or contextually proscribed emotion. Thus, accepting universality does not mean rejecting the possibility of strong cultural influences on the production of emotional expressions. Nor does it mean accepting the claim of a limited number of basic or fundamental emotions that are supposedly universal. Rather, it means entertaining the notion of a universal core of expression that assists in the production of certain types of motor expressions as adaptive reactions to an event.

The term *push effects* denotes these core features of an expression that are pushed to the surface by the operation of physiological changes in the service of adaptation. Conversely, the effects of culture and social context are described by the term *pull effects*. These specify the ideal form the expression should take given the particular social context and control needs, including the person's strategic intentions. To demonstrate the nature of the interaction between push and pull effects that account for particular patterns of expressions, research has to be specific in identifying cultural expectations or norms, as well as individual intentions. Both of these factors are involved at all times, so it is exceedingly difficult to find cases in which only one of the two factors dominates (except, possibly, in the case of a purely tactical use of emotional expression). For this reason, it is difficult to establish the relative importance of push factors.

As the influence of Western civilization spreads, it will be increasingly difficult to study the issue of universality by comparing independent cultures (although there has always been cultural contact and there are no "hermetically sealed" cultures). Therefore, it is important to underline the utility of comparative research in general to understand the role of the biological building blocks that are assembled under cultural control when emotion expression occurs. In this respect, evidence from animal biology and ethology concerning motivational or/and emotional expressions in different species is of considerable importance. This kind of indirect comparative evidence suggesting the existence of psychobiological links between the appraisal of particular situations and the resulting expressive motor movements need to be taken into account in explaining the phenomenon of emotional expression. Similarly, cross-cultural studies on the development of expression in infants and children hold high promise.

Unfortunately, these issues cannot be settled by armchair theorizing or by illustrative accounts from individual anthropologists' fieldwork. Any effort to separate push effects (which are likely to be mostly universal) from pull effects (which are likely to show important cultural differences as well as similarities) will require studies in which all of the cognitive, physiological, control, and social context variables are measured along with the motor expression variables. To obtain the necessary evidence from such large-scale, cross-cultural research, major efforts toward interdisciplinary and intercultural cooperation will be required.

See also: BODY MOVEMENT, GESTURE, AND DISPLAY; CROSS-CULTURAL PATTERNS; CULTURE; CULTURE-BOUND SYNDROMES; DARWIN, CHARLES ROBERT; EMOTION EXPERIENCE AND EXPRESSION; FACIAL EXPRESSION; HISTORICAL STUDY OF EMOTIONS; HUMAN DEVELOPMENT; NEUROBIOLOGY OF EMOTIONS; PHILOSOPHY; PSYCHOPHYSIOLOGY OF EMOTIONS

Bibliography

Birdwhistell, Ray. (1970). *Kinesics and Context*. Philadelphia: University of Pennsylvania Press.

Brakel, Jaap van. (1994). "Emotions: A Cross-Cultural Perspective on Forms of Life." In *Social Perspectives on Emotion, Vol. 2*, ed. William M. Wentworth and John Ryan. Greenwich, CT: JAI Press.

Darwin, Charles. ([1872] 1998). *The Expression of the Emotions in Man and Animals*, 3rd ed., ed. Paul Ekman. London: HarperCollins.

Dawkins, Richard, and Krebs, J. R. (1978). "Animal Signals: Information or Manipulation?" In *Behavioural Ecology*, ed. N. B. Davies and J. R. Krebs. Oxford, Eng.: Blackwell.

Eibl-Eibesfeldt, Irenäus. (1989). *Human Ethology*. Hawthorne, NY: Aldine De Gruyter.

Ekman, Paul. (1972). "Universals and Cultural Differences in Facial Expression of Emotion." In *Nebraska Symposium on Motivation, Vol. 19*, ed. James K. Cole. Lincoln: University of Nebraska Press.

Ekman, Paul. (1992). "An Argument for Basic Emotions." *Cognition and Emotion* 6(3–4):169–200.

Harré, Rom M., ed. (1986). *The Social Construction of Emotions*. Oxford, Eng.: Blackwell.

Izard, Carroll E. (1971). *The Face of Emotion*. New York: Appleton-Century-Crofts.

Izard, Carroll E. (1992). "Basic Emotions, Relations among Emotions, and Emotion-Cognition Relations." *Psychological Review* 99(3):561–565.

Lutz, Catherine, and White, Geoffrey M. (1986). "The Anthropology of Emotions." *Annual Review of Anthropology* 15:405–436.

Mead, Margaret. (1975). "Review of Darwin and Facial Expression." *Journal of Communication* 25:209–213.

Morris, Desmond. (1977). *Manwatching*. London: Jonathan Cape.

Panksepp, Jaak. (1982). "Towards a General Psychobiological Theory of the Emotions." *Behavioral and Brain Sciences* 5:407–467.

Redican, William K. (1982). "Facial Displays of Emotion by Monkeys and Apes: An Evolutionary Perspective on Human Facial Displays." In *Emotion in the Human Face*, 2nd ed., ed. Paul Ekman. Cambridge, Eng.: Cambridge University Press.

Rimé, Bernard, and Schiaratura, Lisa. (1991). "Gesture and Speech." In *Fundamentals of Nonverbal Behavior*, ed. Bernard Rimé and Robert S. Feldman. Cambridge, Eng.: Cambridge University Press.

Russell, James A., and Fernandez-Dols, José-Miguel, eds. (1997). *The Psychology of Facial Expression*. Cambridge, Eng.: Cambridge University Press.

Scherer, Klaus R. (1985). "Vocal Affect Signaling: A Comparative Approach." In *Advances in the Study of Behavior, Vol. 15*, ed. Jay S. Rosenblatt, Colin Beer, Marie-Claire Busnel, and Peter J. B. Slater. New York: Academic Press.

Scherer, Klaus R. (1992). "What Does Facial Expression Express?" In *International Review of Studies on Emotion, Vol. 2*, ed. Kenneth T. Strongman. Chichester, Eng.: Wiley.

Segerstrale, Ullica, and Molnar, Peter, eds. (1997). *Nonverbal Communication: Where Nature Meets Culture*. Mahwah, NJ: Lawrence Erlbaum.

Shweder, Richard A. (1993). "The Cultural Psychology of the Emotions." In *Handbook of Emotions*, ed. Michael Lewis and Jeannette M. Haviland. New York: Guilford.

Tomkins, Silvan S. (1984). "Affect Theory." In *Approaches to Emotion*, ed. Klaus R. Scherer and Paul Ekman. Hillsdale, NJ: Lawrence Erlbaum.

Wierzbicka, Anna. (1994). "Emotion, Language, and Cultural Scripts." In *Emotion and Culture: Empirical Studies of Mutual Influence*, ed. Shinobu Kitayama and Hazel R. Markus. Washington, DC: American Psychological Association.

Wundt, Wilhelm. (1900). *Anthropological Psychology*. Leipzig, Germany: Kroener.

Klaus R. Scherer

V-W

VALUES

See Philosophy; Sin

VISUAL ARTS

Visual art, as one form of cultural production, has often been concerned with the display of human emotion, both conceptually and therapeutically. Visual art is probably the most sacred form of cultural production. Unlike musicians, dancers, stage performers, filmmakers, and even writers, visual artists are the furthest away from a system of commerce that plays into the expected norms of mass consumption. This reality allows these individuals to pursue their goals and expectations as a select though growing few who see the visual artist as a generous and honest interpreter of human emotion.

Perceptions of the Artist

Although humans have continuously used art as a form of emotive expression since the beginning of time, the contemporarily popular depiction of emotion in visual art has most often taken the form of psychologically charged and often negatively driven biographies of artists, where the emotion in their artistic output is often subordinated to the emotion in their personal lives. This phenomenon can be seen especially in commercial feature films based on the lives of artists such as Paul Gauguin, Vincent van Gogh, and Jean-Michel Basquiat. This filmic depiction

of visual artists is relevant here because, more than any other art form, film seems to present a global point of reference for the viewer of contemporary cultural production, albeit as interpreted through Hollywood, though often Bollywood (the Asian Indian film industry), as well. Who is not familiar with the Italian Americans of Francis Ford Coppola and Martin Scorsese, the African Americans of Spike Lee, the Asian Indians of Mira Nair, the British of Mike Leigh, and the future world of Ridley Scott?

While Leonardo da Vinci and Pablo Picasso are widely admired as great visual artists (surveys and museum attendance records regularly cite Picasso as being the most popular visual artist worldwide), filmic material (i.e., widely accessible material) devoted to their works is often hard to find. Yet, there is a tremendous supply of films that feed a popular image of the artist as one who is not at all in control of his or her own emotions. While Picasso's womanizing is well documented and da Vinci's eccentricities are noted, they were men in control.

Gauguin left "civilization" to live among the natives of Tahiti and made them the central focus of his paintings. In fact, Gauguin, whose life spanned the last fifty years of the nineteenth century (including the Industrial Revolution), can be seen as a symbol for the emotions of Western civilized men of that time. While colonialist tendencies were the general norm for the governmental policies of most Western nations, illustrated poignantly in Joseph Conrad's *Heart of Darkness* (1902), Gauguin represented the artists who were unsatisfied with the world around them. Gauguin sought to live among the natives of the regions that his coun-

675

trymen were so busy exploiting, but he nonetheless exhibited colonialist tendencies of his own, just as did Conrad's protagonist. The side effects of colonialism can be most easily discerned in the use of "primitive" signs in the works of Gauguin—and later in those of Picasso and a host of others in the first decade of the twentieth century. For visual artists, the work of "primitives" in Africa, Asia, and Oceania often represented something closer to human emotion. This is no surprise when one considers the fact that much of the works that were created in Africa at this time were to be functional and utilitarian with a religious designation or purpose. It is perhaps ironic that, as Robert Farris Thompson (1983) has documented, the objects of nineteenth- and early twentieth-century Africa, particularly in the western region of Yorubaland, were created with an aesthetic of the cool in mind. Much of the cultural expression there was a means of preserving what Ernest Hemingway later discussed as "grace under pressure" and maintaining one's composure in times of difficulty or stress—in short, suppressing any outward display of human emotion.

Yet, Gauguin's emotional livelihood was predicated upon his humanitarian experience and his understanding for those people who were not considered to be a part of the "civilized" world, those people who were closer to a more spiritual point of view for humanity. In 1899, he stated,

> Standing before one of my pictures of Tahiti, the idol is there not as a literary symbol but as a statue, yet perhaps less of a statue than the animal figures, less animal also, combining my dream before my cabin with all nature, dominating our primitive soul, the unearthly consolation of our sufferings to the extent that they are vague and incomprehensible before the mystery of our origin and of our future.

Simultaneously, van Gogh, who was perhaps less emotionally stable, perpetuated an idea of art as therapy that could possibly be discerned as an idea of art as a necessary evil. It was Van Gogh's feeling that people could not understand him or his art (sales of his work during his lifetime were almost nonexistent) that led him to prize also the importance of a sort of heroic alienation. Taking a place in the countryside of France, he created hundreds of paintings in swirling expressionist primary colors that speak volumes of his own emotional state, perhaps reflected in the fact that he cut off his own ear. Or at least this is the way that he has been perceived as a result of the 1956 film *Lust for Life*, which starred Kirk Douglas.

Basquiat was an American artist who was born in Brooklyn, New York, to a Puerto Rican mother and a

In 1955, Kirk Douglas posed beside a self-portrait of Vincent Van Gogh (painted by the artist in 1886–1887) to show his remarkable resemblance to the painter, who he was portraying in the movie Lust for Life. *(Corbis/Bettmann)*

Haitian father. Emotional alienation in the largely white sphere of contemporary art certainly played a part in Basquiat's art and subsequently in his drug abuse in much the same way that race affected American jazz icons Charlie "Bird" Parker and Billie Holiday (two heroes of the young artist). Being an artist in the 1980s, a period defined by its heightened sense of commodity critique, Basquiat (who died when he was only twenty-seven years of age) played with such ideas as the artist as idiot savant, although he always remained two steps ahead with his incredible talent. The titles of his works included such deprecating misnomers as "Portrait of the Artist as a Young Derelict" and "Self-Portrait as a Heel."

What Basquiat, Gauguin, and Van Gogh share is their historical edification as emotional outsiders who were devoid of the strength to function in the daily world. It is this vision of the visual artist that all subsequent artists have had to grapple with in their lives. What these three artists also share is a depth of vision that went far beyond what their contemporaries were willing to see.

Expressionism

Historically, there are movements or genres that register as being more akin to a certain form of emotional release on behalf of the artist. The primary example of this connection is the earliest cave drawings of prehistoric man. There is a valid argument that such original creations (as with other forms of cultural production) were a means of understanding and documenting instances of human emotion. To reflect themselves, early humans took to mark-making, the description of which has changed only slightly over the years in relation to paintings, be they on canvas or made directly to a preexisting wall. One such movement in the modernist vein is expressionism.

The discussion of expressionism fits squarely into the broad framework of history. While the era of World War I saw much new experimental art in an avant-gardist theorem, these creations could be seen as a reaction to the war in many ways. Artists such as Hugo Ball and Marcel Duchamp amplified the "noise" of visual art with dadaism. Although they were acting in the sphere of visual art, Ball and Duchamp both sought to present the performance aspects of art by emphasizing a collective production aesthetic that granted equal weight to visual art, dance, theatre, poetry, and so on. As Ball stated in 1916,

> [The dadaist] loves the extraordinary, the absurd even. He knows that life asserts itself in contradictions, and that his age, more than any preceding it, aims at the destruction of all generous impulses. Every kind of mask is therefore welcome to him, every play at hide and seek in which there is an inherent power of deception. The direct and the primitive appear to him in the midst of this huge antinature, as being the supernatural itself.

For the dadaists, the canvas or the static sculpture was no longer enough to express the spirit within, a spirit of humanity characterized by the rejection of the nationalist impulses characterized by the global polarities of war. In this respect, the visual movement was akin to Albert Camus's existentialist feelings in regard to the war in his birth country, Algeria, so poignantly summed up in *The Stranger* (1942).

These feelings of alienation with regard to war and human emotion found a great release in the work of many German artists in the World War II era. Max Beckmann, George Grosz, and others used the canvas as a wall to portray the suffering and lack of humanism of war and Adolf Hitler's fascist prophecies. While it is ironic that Hitler's own application to art school had been rejected, some people would say that his personality was reflective of the human emotions of many good artists—strong willed, somewhat egotistical, and successfully charismatic. Artists such as Beckmann and Grosz sought to use paint as a means of expressing human emotion through a thick brushstroke with heavily impastoed oil paint. Their paintings owed a debt to the fauvism of artists such as Edvard Munch, whose 1907 painting *The Scream* is impossible to ignore in a discussion of human emotion and visual art—the bulbous head leers sideways on a draped dark body with its round mouth opened in a primal scream.

American abstract expressionism sought to apply human emotion on a plane that could not be figuratively expressed. Emotion represented an abstract idea that was too cerebral to be represented by a recognizable sign or depiction. Artists such as Jackson Pollock, Franz Kline, Arshile Gorky, and Mark Rothko all used color and abstract form to express emotion without a didactic or demarcated name. Their work closely parallels the inventions of their contemporary musicians, the jazz artists who perfected the idea of improvisation and bebop, which adhered to tenets of impulse and reaction that were similar to the call and response espoused by the African-American church (a repository

The Scream by Edvard Munch. (National Gallery of Art, Washington, D.C.)

of human emotion that provided the backbone for cool resistance in the face of incredible adversity).

Like the many cycles in the small history of modern visual art, the ensuing reaction to the abstract expressionist movement was one of opposition. Just as dadaism was closely followed by constructivism and non-objective art, pop art and minimalism following on the heels of abstract expressionism favored the cold hardness of mechanical reproduction and the absence of the emotional hand of the artist. These movements subsequently led to the formulation of conceptualism and the thoroughly objective forms of art that were expressed across a range of media similar to that of the dadaists, with crucial attention to the aesthetic union of form and content. Human emotion became closely related again to the politics of the day, something that continues to influence contemporary art.

Conclusion

Human emotion is often represented as the existentialist and humane province of the mind of the artist. The artist, in an individual effort, is fed by the desire to comment on society at large from the vantage point of the African griot—that is, a person who is external to the community but who is held accountable for expressing the community even though he or she is often an outsider looking in.

See also: CREATIVITY

Bibliography

Ball, Hugo. ([1916] 1992). "Dada Fragments." In *Art in Theory, 1900–1990: An Anthology of Changing Ideas,* ed. Charles Harrison and Paul Wood. Cambridge, MA: Blackwell.

Baudelaire, Charles. ([1860] 1986). *The Painter of Modern Life and Other Essays,* tr. and ed. Jonathan Mayne. New York: Da Capo.

Chipp, Herschel B., comp. (1968). *Theories of Modern Art: A Source Book by Artists and Critics.* Berkeley: University of California Press.

Gauguin, Paul. ([1899] 1992). "Letter to Fontainas." In *Art in Theory, 1900–1990: An Anthology of Changing Ideas,* ed. Charles Harrison and Paul Wood. Cambridge, MA: Blackwell.

Marshall, Richard, comp. (1992). *Jean-Michel Basquiat.* New York: Whitney Museum of American.

Nelson, Robert S., and Shiff, Richard, eds. (1996). *Critical Terms for Art History.* Chicago: University of Chicago Press.

Thompson, Robert Farris. (1983). *Flash of the Spirit: African and Afro-American Art and Philosophy.* New York: Random House.

Franklin Sirmans

WIDOWHOOD

See Grief; Human Development: Old Age

WOMEN AND EMOTIONAL ABUSE

See Emotional Abuse: Women

X-Z

XENOPHOBIA

Xenophobia is a complex psychological and social attitude whose primary emotional elements are based on (1) negative affect (antipathy) toward those perceived as outsiders or as "foreign" and (2) a sense of threat emanating from the outgroups (often manifesting itself as fear of harm to the privilege, status, or culture of the ingroup). Two additional elements are often present in the form of (3) a political ideology that designates certain outgroups as threatening, dangerous, or harmful to the ingroup and (4) a potential for direct aggression or punitive public policy aimed at the restriction or exclusion of the outgroups. It is not always necessary for the threat to be objectively present, though there is usually at least some plausible element of competition or conflict. The most critical element is that the outgroup be targeted (named and blamed) as being harmful. There is some debate about the relative importance of real (objective) threat versus the symbolic threat, but obviously both are important—subjectively perceived threat has at least some objective basis, and objective threat generally has a symbolic component.

Xenophobia As General Antipathy

Where a single outgroup serves as the primary target, it serves as the specific "designee" for the accumulation of negative affect that provides a complex motivation of aversion, fear, anger, hate, and potential aggression. In this case, it is common to refer to a specific "prejudice" (against people of color, Jews,

Catholics, etc.). Xenophobia, on the other hand, is not a specific prejudice of this sort but rather the generalization of antipathy to a wide variety of outgroups.

A specifically designated outgroup is a real or symbolic reference group that serves as a target; it represents competition or threat. The outgroup serves an important psychological function by anchoring the identity of ingroup members—it provides the negative reference point, the antithesis of the virtues that are attributed to the ingroup, and serves as what Vamik Volkan (1988) calls "suitable targets for aggression." The most common prejudices, or specific antipathies, have their own names, such as anti-Semitism or homophobia. But xenophobia refers to a more generalized antipathy directed against a wide range of outgroups because they are perceived to be strange, foreign, or simply different (i.e., unlike oneself or significantly different from the group with which one identifies).

Reference groups may be characterized by certain characteristics, or "markers," that differentiate the ingroup with which one identifies and the outgroups one rejects. Markers may be physical/morphological (e.g., skin color, sex-related, physiognomic), or they may be symbolic (e.g., religious, cultural). Some markers seem more tangible and "real" than others, particularly if they refer to physical characteristics such as skin color. But all such markers are ultimately symbolic because they acquire their meaning through a process of learning and attribution that is primarily social. Race, ethnicity, gender, sexual orientation, religion and political belief all can serve as markers for ingroup-outgroup demarcation, depending on the circumstances. Each such marker can serve to define a specific antipathy, but the xenophobe is likely to have a generalized antipathy against many or all of these markers whose common element is only that they represent the "otherness" of the target groups.

Individual and Social Processes in Xenophobia

At one level, xenophobia can be seen as an individual trait resulting from the psychological development of the specific person. The trait does not exist in isolation but is often associated with other personality traits such as authoritarianism and ethnocentrism. There is disagreement as to whether the acquisition of such traits is best described in terms of psychoanalytic theory or social learning theory, but both approaches generally describe a process by which the individual develops an emotional response to the markers that signify ingroups and outgroups. This acquisition process reflects both the direct experience and the broader process of social learning (socialization) that the person undergoes. In this case, the individual is the "carrier" of the trait, even though its development will no doubt reflect elements of the social environment in which the individual has been socialized. This means that xenophobia is also a social phenomenon, with social groups as "carriers" of the trait.

Social collectivities may develop and maintain a collective antipathy toward one or more outgroups. In this process, the specific characteristics (or markers) of the outgroup are identified, evaluated, and made salient by a process of social definition and reinforcement—group-level xenophobia is collectively maintained and expressed. Individuals are expected to share in this collective process and in so doing are motivated by a combination of individual and social factors. Regardless of whether the individual member of the group shares the collective antipathy fully, the group exerts pressure for conformity and solidarity. In this way, xenophobia can exist at the collective level even when many individuals in the group do not share in the general antipathy and perception of threat.

There is an interaction between individual and collective forces. Where the individual and the group an-

tipathy coincide there is minimum conflict. Where the individual is more xenophobic than the group, the person may appear to other members of the collectivity to be "prejudiced" or even paranoid. Where the group (or broader cultural environment) is more xenophobic than the individual, the person may appear to the group as deviant or even treacherous for not sharing the ingroup ethos. The individual may resolve the conflict by complying with the collective ethos in order to show solidarity with the group.

Is Xenophobia Universal?

Since xenophobia exists at both the individual and collective levels, does this mean that it is a fundamental and unavoidable aspect of human behavior? Is it part of the basic (phylogenetic) nature of the humans as a species? The widespread historical and cultural presence of outsider anxiety and rejection has produced a substantial discussion as to whether xenophobia is deeply anchored in the emotional composition of human beings.

The belief that human beings have an innate tendency to be fearful and rejective of "strangeness" takes a variety of forms, but in general these forms fall into two broad categories. The first is the argument that intergroup conflict is widespread throughout human history and that it therefore must be "natural." The second is that humans show strong emotional reactions to certain categories of others ("strangers") and that this indicates a physiological and emotional basis for stranger anxiety. The first argument, which is supported in a very general way by the finding that all cultures are ethnocentric (i.e., they value their own way of life more than other ways of life), is not to be taken lightly, but to evaluate it would require a review of virtually all of the social sciences (particularly anthropology, international relations, political science, psychology, and sociology). Since this entry is primarily concerned with the emotional basis for xenophobia, it will concentrate on two forms of the argument—the implicit assumption that xenophobia is literally a "phobia" in the clinical sense and the scientific evidence that there may be an innate stranger anxiety in humans.

The term *xenophobia* is problematic in both parts of the term (*xeno*, meaning foreign, and *phobia*, meaning fear). The second component, *phobia*, conveys the medical/psychological meaning of an irrational and uncontrollable fear. Common examples are intense emotional reactions to closed spaces (claustrophobia), to heights (acrophobia), and to certain animals such as spiders (arachnophobia). Panic reactions in the presence of such stimuli can be extremely intense and virtually automatic; in the case of a true phobia, the aversive response can only be dealt with through long

---

Flannery O'Connor's "The Displaced Person" (1955) opens with a Catholic priest persuading a Southern farm owner to hire a displaced person and his family during World War II. Both the African Americans and the poor whites who work on the farm fear these foreigners who threaten to take over their jobs. These people ultimately let an accident happen that kills the interloper and restores the old order.

and intensive therapy. This is clearly not the case with xenophobia—one may have a strong aversion to certain categories of individuals, but this is scarcely of the clinical or medical significance of, say, a true fear of heights or spiders. The first component of the term —*xeno*—is at least as troublesome. The term *foreign* is indistinct and may refer to any number of objects that appear strange to the individual. Foreignness is not a naturally given property of objects but is defined by the experience of the individual and learned in a social context. What comes to be understood as familiar or unfamiliar, as bringing comfort or threat, as representing danger or safety is not given in nature but acquires these meanings over the life of the individual. While intergroup conflict is indeed universal, xenophobia itself is not an automatic or uncontrollable emotional reaction (contrary to the implications of the etymology of the word). What the bewildering diversity of human conflict does indicate is that humans (both as individuals and in collectivities) possess or develop mechanisms for recognizing familiarity and unfamiliarity in their social environment, and that they invest this distinction with strong emotional reactions such as antipathy and fear. This brings the discussion back to the second argument, which was that stranger anxiety exhibited by infants indicates a phylogenetic basis for this human tendency.

Developmental studies have shown that infants show anxiety and fear when they are confronted by strangers. This phenomenon, well known to most parents, has often been cited as evidence that humans have a reaction to strangers that appears at a preconscious, or at least preverbal, level. Such arguments have sometimes been used by racial conservatives to argue that stranger anxiety (and stranger rejection) is tied to specific racial markers such as skin color. If so, this might indicate humans had some innate aversion to racial differences, but there is no evidence for this conclusion.

What is strange or anxiety provoking to a particular infant is defined in the experience of that individual; it is not based on any specific racial, gender, or ethnic marker. Infants do have the ability to recognize what is familiar and unfamiliar, and they associate certain emotions with those categories. The specific marker that indicates unfamiliarity (e.g., gender, age, quality of voice, facial hair) can be quite variable from one infant to another, and there is no reason to believe that an infant of one ethnic group has an innate reaction against other ethnic groups. Furthermore, there is no long-term evidence that the markers that trigger anxiety in infancy retain their potency in the adult life of the individual. Thus, even if a racial marker were associated with anxiety in infancy, there is no evidence that it would retain its strength into adulthood—unless it were supported by the socialization of the individual and the norms of the collective. If the latter is the case, then it is not an innate aversion to a specific ingroup-outgroup marker but a socially defined and reinforced characteristic.

In summary, there does seem to be something universal about xenophobia, but there is no evidence that there is a naturally occurring aversion to a specific racial or ethnic marker (whether it manifests itself as stranger anxiety among infants, or as a phobia among adults). Instead, it appears (1) that humans have a complex set of abilities, needs, and emotions that predispose them to distinguish familiarity and unfamiliarity in their social environment, (2) that this predisposition is useful to the individual and the social group, and (3) that some form of this response is observable as early as infancy. It also appears (4) that the targets of stranger recognition (and of stranger anxiety) are not given in nature but acquired through the socialization and experience of the individual. Perhaps even more important, (5) the markers separating ingroup from outgroup are given content and meaning by the society and culture within which the individual matures, and (6) recognition and adherence to those markers are supported and reinforced by the need of individuals to achieve solidarity with and conformity to a social group.

Xenophobia and the Foreigner

When xenophobia is broadly distributed in the society, it can have wide-ranging social and political consequences. The collective ingroup feels that its privileges, status, and benefits are threatened by the presence and behavior of the outgroup. When the target of xenophobia is the foreigner, there are likely to be political demands for public policy that will discriminate against, restrict, punish, and exclude immigrants (or newly arrived non-citizens). When this happens, xenophobic movements or political parties may emerge. In Europe, where the traditions of parliamentary government (and proportional representation) favor the establishment and continuation of smaller political parties, xenophobic parties have achieved some measure of success. In the United States, there were "nativist" political parties and movements in the late nineteenth and early twentieth centuries, but the American two-party tradition has generally forced xenophobic movements to agitate within the two major parties. In either case, this form of xenophobia is virtually synonymous with "anti-immigrant."

Formal citizenship is important in defining the rights and obligations of residents in a politically defined territory; citizenship also has a strong symbolic component, defining the ingroup (the citizens and those who arrived earlier) and differentiating them from the outgroup (the immigrants, the foreigners,

An 1882 political cartoon, "The Anti-Chinese Wall," points out many of the various ways, both legal and symbolic, in which xenophobic movements were trying to prevent or at least limit immigration to the United States. (Corbis/Bettmann)

those who arrived later). The two demarcations—the legal and the symbolic—tend to coincide in most modern societies, but the symbolic element may have a life of its own. Individuals who have achieved citizenship status do not automatically lose their symbolic status as foreigners. They may achieve citizenship but still be perceived by the dominant culture (or even by themselves) as "second-class citizens"; they may even be subject to official limitations on their right to participate in the military, education, public service, or other conventional activities of the dominant class of citizens. In that case, outgroup members are legal members of the community, but subject to restrictions. A few prominent examples include the facts that African Americans in the United States were subject to legal restrictions on their political rights and access to public accommodations for more than one hundred years after the Civil War, Israeli citizens of Arab ethnicity are restricted in their access to military service and some forms of public employment, and special legislation was required to reduce discrimination against Japanese citizens of Korean ethnicity.

These borderline situations represent the efforts of a political community to constrain the nature of legal citizenship among elements of the population that are

still, to some extent, considered to be foreign. This is a special case of the situation where an element of the population is perceived to be in some way alien or threatening to the dominant normative community. Thus, political xenophobia can manifest itself in political debates over restricting immigrants' access to citizenship, in fact that citizenship itself can become a political battleground. It also points out that acquisition of legal citizenship rights does not automatically guarantee ingroup status and that the dominant culture may still be xenophobic, excluding them from full acceptance in the normative community. Thus, xenophobia can refer to anti-immigrant sentiments and policies of a group (a political xenophobia) as well to the more informal antipathy and fear that the ingroup attaches to the outgroup (a social xenophobia).

These last examples provide a useful lesson in the difficulty of defining xenophobia at the level of the political system. In each of these situations, the respective governments and large segments of their populations could cite compelling reasons of national security and public order for their policies. Critics of those policies—both inside and outside those systems—might see restrictive policies as unwarranted discrimination or the result of an unresolved xeno-phobia in the society. But these are complex political debates about the nature of threat, righteousness, and citizenship rights; much more is involved than simple xenophobia. Such discussions often revolve around the conditions under which a system is threatened and the extent to which the system and its citizens should be tolerant of political difference. Therefore, it is often not very helpful, and it is certainly not very precise analytically, to use the term *xenophobia* to describe an alleged trait of entire cultures or political systems. The term is, however, useful for designating two primary features at the individual or collective level: a general antipathy toward outgroups and a perception of threat emanating from those groups. Closely related to this are the likelihood of a political ideology that targets outgroups and intensifies the emotional response and a predisposition toward direct aggression or punitive public policy against those groups.

See also: CROSS-CULTURAL PATTERNS; CULTURE-BOUND SYNDROMES; FEAR AND PHOBIAS; HATE; HATE CRIMES; UNIVERSALITY OF EMOTIONAL EXPRESSION

Bibliography

Altemeyer, Bob. (1996). *The Authoritarian Specter.* Cambridge, MA: Harvard University Press.

Bennett, David H. (1995). *The Party of Fear: The American Far Right from Nativism to the Militia Movement.* New York: Vintage.

Bobo, Lawrence, and Kluegel, James R. (1993). "Opposition to Race-Targeting: Self-Interest, Stratification Ideology, or Racial Attitudes?" *American Sociological Review* 58:443–464.

Flohr, Heiner. (1987). "Biological Bases of Social Prejudices." In *The Sociobiology of Ethnocentrism,* ed. Vernon Reynolds, Vincent Falger, and Ian Vine. London: Croom Helm.

Kitschelt, Herbert. (1995). *The Radical Right in Western Europe: A Comparative Analysis.* Ann Arbor: University of Michigan Press.

Levinson, David. (1996). "Ethnocentrism." In *Encyclopedia of Cultural Anthropology,* ed. David Levinson and Melvin Ember. New York: Henry Holt.

Marcus, George E.; Sullivan, John L.; Theiss-Morse, Elizabeth; and Wood, Sandra L. (1995). *With Malice Toward Some.* New York: Cambridge University Press.

Sears, David O. (1988). "Symbolic Racism." In *Eliminating Racism: Profiles in Controversy,* ed. Phyllis A. Katz and Dalmas A. Taylor. New York: Plenum.

Sroufe, L. Alan. (1977). "Wariness of Strangers and the Study of Infant Development." *Child Development* 48:731–746.

Stone, William F.; Lederer, Gerda; and Christie, Richard. (1993). *Strength and Weakness: The Authoritarian Personality Today.* New York: Springer-Verlag.

Volkan, Vamik D. (1988). *The Need to Have Enemies and Allies: From Clinical Practice to International Relationships.* Northvale, NJ: Jason Aronson.

Watts, Meredith W. (1997). *Xenophobia in United Germany: Generations, Modernization, and Ideology.* New York: St. Martin's Press.

Watts, Meredith W., ed. (1998). *Cross-Cultural Perspectives on Youth and Violence.* New York: JAI Press.

Meredith W. Watts

YOUTH

See Human Development: Adolescence

ZEAL

See Desire

BIBLIOGRAPHY INDEX

James, William T., 112
Jamison, Kay Redfield, 462
Janes, Carolyn, 49
Jansen, Jaap H. C., 593
Jefferson, James W., 462
Jemelka, R., 362
Jenike, Michael A., 144
Jenkins, C. David, 357
Jenness, Valerie, 331
Jennings, Joyce, 573
Jennings, Sue, 200
Jenny, Carole, 227
Jewett, Janet L., 651
Jewett, Robert, 623
Jezl, David R., 219
Jin, Guang Xi, 590
Jinks, John L., 298
Joffe, Russel T., 593
John, Oliver, 241, 293
John, Richard S, 50
Johnson, Allen, 123
Johnson, Colleen L. 394
Johnson, D. Paul, 429
Johnson, David W., 208
Johnson, Jeffrey L., 430
Johnson, Jennifer S., 237
Johnson, Michael P., 130, 131
Johnson, Orna, 123
Johnson, Robert E., 136
Johnson, Roger, 208
Johnson, Ronald C., 610
Johnson, Steven B., 610
Johnson, Susan M., 140
Johnson, Virginia E., 188
Johnson-Laird, Philip N., 121,
    324, 556, 556
Johnston, Deirdre, 368
Jonas, Ruth, 241
Jones, Anthony K. P., 499
Jones, Bill T., 177
Jones, Edward E., 98
Jones, Ernest, 280
Jones, Graham, 638
Jones, Morris T., 499
Jones, Stanley E., 112
Jones, Susan S., 627
Jones, Warren H., 66, 130, 429,
    430, 666, 667
Jordan, Brenda K., 531
Jorgensen, Peter F., 509
Josephs, Ingrid, 627

Josephs, Robert A., 599
Joseph-Vanderpool, Jean R., 593
Jourard, Sidney M., 667

K
Kagan, Jerome, 14, 71, 105, 165,
    315, 376, 522, 551, 618, 661
Kahneman, Daniel, 98
Kaiser, Marvin A., 285
Kamin, Leon J., 252
Kane, Martha T., 71
Kant, Immanuel, 357, 420
Kanter, Melissa E., 343
Kapferer, Bruce, 177
Kaplan, George A., 362
Kaplan, Harold I., 462
Kaplan, Helen Singer, 188, 441
Kaplan, Nancy, 79
Kapp, Bruce S., 485
Karen, Robert, 79
Karl, Gregory, 473
Karl, Jonathan, 331, 336
Karno, Marvin, 462
Karon, Bertram P., 545
Karp, Ivan, 169
Karp, Lynn, 454
Karsten, Rafael, 307
Kashima, Yoshihisa, 166
Kasmer, Jeff A., 86
Kasper, Siegfried, 593
Kass, Leon, 273
Kassinove, Howard, 55
Kastenbaum, Robert J., 5
Kaszniak, Alfred W., 143
Katz, Ilana M., 599
Katz, Irvin, 535
Katz, Lynn Fainsilber, 556
Kaufman, Gershen, 610
Kaufmann, Walter, 487, 514
Kavanagh, David H., 17
Kawakami, Kiyobumi, 165
Kayson, Wesley, 429
Kearsley, Richard, 165
Keating, David, 386
Keats, John, 528
Kelley, Harold H., 92, 98, 131,
    140
Kelly, David J., 246
Kelly, George A., 504
Kelly, Joan Berlin, 644
Kelly, Karen A., 593

Kelly, Kelly, 362
Kelman, Harold, 364
Keltner, Dachar, 618, 627
Kemeny, Margaret E., 343
Kemmelmeier, Markus, 535
Kempe, C. Henry, 225
Kemper, Theodore D., 32, 98,
    631
Kendall, Laurel, 177
Kendall, Philip C., 71
Kendler, Kenneth S., 298
Kennedy, William A., 485
Kenny, Anthony, 184, 651
Kenny, Michael G., 169
Keough, William, 331
Kerckhoff, Alan C., 403
Kernberg, Otto, 545
Kernis, Michael H., 92, 599, 600
Kerr, Alistair W., 638
Kerr, John H., 17
Kerszberg, Pierre, 420
Kestenbaum, Roberta, 246
Kibber, Jeffrey, 644
Kidd, Robert F., 98
Kihlstrom, John F., 231
Kim, Min-Sun, 237
Kim, Ray S., 71
Kim, Sung Hee, 249
Kimerling, Rachel, 219
King, Gillian, 98
King, Laura A., 42
Kinney, Terry, 430
Kinsey, Alfred C., 188
Kippax, Susan, 573
Kirkpatrick, Brian, 478
Kirkpatrick, Lee A., 418
Kirkpatrick, Sue W., 651
Kirkson, Donald, 50
Kirsch, Irving, 397
Kirson, Donald, 136, 269, 324,
    409
Kirwan, Christopher, 100
Kitayama, Shinobu, 155, 237, 241
Kitschelt, Herbert, 683
Kivett, Vira R., 429
Klapp, Orin E., 115
Klass, Dennis, 307
Kleban, Morton H., 370, 394
Klein, Daniel N., 462
Klein, David J., 454, 556, 560
Klein, Melanie, 32, 437

SUBJECT INDEX

Page numbers in **boldface** indicate article titles.
Page numbers in *italics* indicate tables and illustrations.

A

Aaker, David, 20, 23
Abandonment, **1–6**
    defense mechanisms, 181
    fear of, 1, 2–3, 4, 80, 405, 408
Abbey, Antonia, 263
Abd-er-Rahman III, 589
Abrahams, Matthew, 262
Abramson, Lyn, 207, 345, 356
Abstract expressionism, 677–678
Abu-Lughod, Lila, 57, 148
Abuse
    emotions preceding, 137–38
    horror response, 365
    See also Child abuse;
        Emotional abuse; Violence
Academus, 515
Acceptance and rejection, **6–14**
    abandonment feelings and,
        1–5
    body movements expressing,
        110
    emotional scripts and, 568
    intimacy and, 404–405, 408
    ParTheory of, 8–13
    prejudice and, 532–535
    shame and, 605, 607
    as symbolic, 7
    trust and, 663
    See also Abandonment;
        Attachment; Attribution;
        Emotional abuse
"Accident prone," 180
Accidents
    aggression and, 25

embarrassment from, 210
Accurate empathy, 241
Achievement motivation, **14–17**
    acquired drives and, 466, 552
    attributions and, 96–97
    happiness and, 320
    risk taking and, 602
    satisfaction and, 584, 587
    school performance and,
        204–205
    sex differences and, 466, 467
    sports performance and,
        635–636
    See also Motivation
Achievement Motives Scale, 14–15
Achiever vs. aspirer, 587
Acquired drives, 465–466, 552
ACTH. *See* Adrenocorticotropic
    hormone
Action
    anger vs. annoyance, 52
    as emotional expression, 562
    hopelessness as barrier to,
        358
Actor-observer bias, 94
Actors, emotional state of, 195–
    196, 197
Actualization. *See* Achievement
    motivation; Motivation; Self-
    esteem
Acute stress disorder
    horror and, 365, 366
    See also Post-traumatic stress
        disorder
Adam and Eve, *620*, 621

Adams, Jeffrey, 125, 126
Adams, Susan, 580
Adams, Virgil, 587
Adaptation syndrome, 101–102
Adaptive responses
    affect and, 541
    appraisal-based movements,
        670
    facial and body emotion
        expression as, 108, 293,
        552, 553, 554, 606, 670,
        673
    fear as, 62
    fight-or-flight, 62, 66, 337
    happiness as, 317–318, 321
    learned helplessness as, 344–
        345, 347
    sadness as, 579
    shyness as, 616–617
    smiling as, 625
Addictions. *See* Substance abuse
ADHD (attention deficit
    hyperactivity disorder), 477
Adler, Alfred, 486
Adler, Georg, 497
Adler, Shelley R., 169
Adolescents and emotions, 369–
    370, 381–386
    anxiety disorders, 68
    bipolar disorder, 458
    cultural anthropological
        theory, 56
    defense mechanisms, 181,
        182
    defensive independence, 10

707